RELIGIOUS DISCRIMINATION AND CULTURAL CONTEXT

Generations of festering culture wars, compounded by actual wars in predominantly Muslim countries, the terrorism of ISIS and the ongoing migrant crisis, have all combined to make religious discrimination the most pressing challenge now facing many governments. For the leading common law nations, with their shared Christian cultural heritage balanced by a growing secularism, the threat presented by this toxic mix has the potential to destabilise civil society. This book suggests that the instances of religious discrimination, as currently legally defined, are constrained by that cultural context, exacerbated by a policy of multiculturalism and in practice conflated with racial, ethnic and other forms of discrimination. Kerry O'Halloran argues that many culture war issues – such as those that surround the pro-choice/pro-life debate and the rights of the LGBT community – can be viewed as rooted in the same Christian morality that underpins the law relating to religious discrimination.

KERRY O'HALLORAN is a professionally qualified lawyer and social worker, and Adjunct Professor at the Australian Centre for Philanthropy and Non-profit Studies at The Queensland University of Technology, Brisbane. He is the author of *Religion, Charity and Human Rights* (Cambridge, 2014).

Issues of religious discrimination – whether real or imaginary – have become ever more important in a world that is increasingly polarised between secularism and religious fundamentalism. This book is an important contribution to the debate on the "culture wars" as viewed through the lens of some of the major multi-cultural common law jurisdictions.

Frank Cranmer
Centre for Law and Religion, Cardiff University, UK

Religious Discrimination and Cultural Context tackles some of the most perplexing social issues that are facing liberal democracies today as Christianity wanes and the ISIS challenge to social cohesion grows. The laws of England and Wales, Ireland, the USA, Canada, Australia and New Zealand and their cultural context are examined in relation to the main areas of religious discrimination. The book tracks how infractions are processed through regulatory or judicial systems and considers the significance of any jurisdictional similarities or differences in the way issues are resolved. This poses questions such as: will governments be moved from a position of State neutrality to assert a positive policing role, regulating for the public benefit, in respect of religious matters? It is a thought-provoking contribution for our times.

Myles McGregor-Lowndes
Australian Centre for Philanthropy and Nonprofit Studies, QUT, Australia

This book is an intriguing and challenging assessment of the ability of the law to address the problem of religious discrimination in an increasingly multicultural society. In particular, O'Halloran explores the manner in which religion and culture are frequently intertwined in ways that often result in religious discrimination becoming a means of expressing cultural animus. The so-called "culture wars" provide the backdrop for a study of the ways in which the moral arguments advanced by its various participants often merely serve as proxies for religious or cultural discrimination. The book contains an exhaustive survey of legal prohibitions against religious discrimination across the common law world that will prove invaluable to researchers in religion, human rights and comparative law. More importantly, O'Halloran shows that the common law has not yet developed the tools to address claims of discrimination where culture and religion are intertwined. *Religious Discrimination and Cultural Context* is an important contribution to a debate that is sure to intensify as our society becomes ever more globalised in the years to come.

Matthew P. Harrington
Law Faculty, University of Montreal, Canada

RELIGIOUS DISCRIMINATION AND CULTURAL CONTEXT

A Common Law Perspective

KERRY O'HALLORAN

Queensland University of Technology

CAMBRIDGE
UNIVERSITY PRESS

CAMBRIDGE
UNIVERSITY PRESS

University Printing House, Cambridge CB2 8BS, United Kingdom

One Liberty Plaza, 20th Floor, New York, NY 10006, USA

477 Williamstown Road, Port Melbourne, VIC 3207, Australia

4843/24, 2nd Floor, Ansari Road, Daryaganj, Delhi – 110002, India

79 Anson Road, #06–04/06, Singapore 079906

Cambridge University Press is part of the University of Cambridge.

It furthers the University's mission by disseminating knowledge in the pursuit
of education, learning, and research at the highest international levels of excellence.

www.cambridge.org
Information on this title: www.cambridge.org/9781108423052
DOI: 10.1017/9781108394871

First published 2018

Printed in the United Kingdom by Clays, St Ives plc

A catalogue record for this publication is available from the British Library.

ISBN 978-1-108-42305-2 Hardback

CONTENTS

ACKNOWLEDGEMENTS

A sincere debt of gratitude is owed to Professor Myles McGregor-Lowndes[1] for his support and friendship and to the Australian Centre for Philanthropy and Nonprofit Studies, my academic base as Adjunct Professor for the past thirteen years. This book has built on foundations laid in *Religion, Charity and Human Rights*,[2] as supplemented by other earlier publications, and I am mindful of the very many who advised and contributed along the way.

Particular thanks are due to those who offered comment on draft chapters: Neil Foster,[3] Beth Gaze[4] and Myles (Australia); Bill Atkins[5] (New Zealand); Frank Cranmer[6] and Maleiha Malik[7] (England and Wales); Gerard Whyte[8] and Eoin Daly[9] (Ireland); Fred Gedicks[10] and David Smolin[11] (USA); and Matthew Harrington[12] (Canada).

Your thoughtful contributions and encouragement have meant a lot and this book, and its author would have suffered without them.

I am very thankful to Cambridge University Press for commissioning the book and for the editorial diligence that has seen it through to completion. Responsibility for any mistakes, inconsistencies or other faults, and for all views expressed, must rest exclusively with me.

[1] Founder Director, the Australian Centre of Philanthropy and Nonprofit Studies, Queensland University of Technology, Brisbane, Australia.
[2] Cambridge University Press 2014.
[3] Associate Professor, Newcastle Law School, the University of Newcastle, Australia.
[4] Professor, Law School, University of Melbourne, Victoria, Australia.
[5] Professor of Law, Victoria University of Wellington, New Zealand.
[6] Research Fellow at the Centre for Law & Religion, Cardiff and Director, Central Lobby Consultants, Wales.
[7] Professor of Law, King's College London, England.
[8] Professor of Law, Trinity College Dublin, Ireland.
[9] Lecturer, the National University of Ireland, Galway, Ireland.
[10] Professor of Law, J. Reuben Clark Law School, Brigham Young University, USA.
[11] Professor of Law, Director, Center for Biotechnology, Law, and Ethics, Samford University, USA.
[12] Professeur, Faculté de droit, Université de Montréal, Canada.

As always, Elizabeth, I am hugely grateful to you for your endless patience, tolerance and good humour, when you had so many other worries and preoccupations – and thanks also to Maddy for your impromptu but always uplifting violin concertos.

~

Introduction

The eruption of ISIS[1] onto the international stage registered the issue of culturally based religious discrimination as one of the most important challenges facing civilisation in the early decades of the twenty-first century. The putative caliphate may have been inspired by an ambition to achieve religious/cultural coherence, within redrawn geo-political borders in the Middle East, but its efforts to do so have impacted on such coherence much further afield. Within its present boundaries, religious/cultural communities non-aligned with ISIS values have suffered, and continue to suffer, not just religious discrimination but mediaeval barbarism and possible annhiliation. Outside those boundaries, ISIS atrocities in Western cities and the scale of armed response – including aerial bombing of Islamic cities – from the developed and mainly Christian nations, are threatening to both reopen East/West religious divisions and rupture the religious harmony and carefully cultivated multi-culturalism that, in general, have grown to become the hallmark of Western civilisation in the post-cold war period.

While the ISIS challenge and the response of the Western nations demand attention, the resulting jolt to social cohesion in those nations also calls for close examination – and has been a motivating impulse for this book. The fact that the ISIS cause attracted volunteers from all over the world, adherents prepared to kill and die for it, is in itself significant: they came not only from eastern Islamic countries, as might be anticipated, but also from the traditionally Christian countries of Europe, the USA, Canada, Australia and elsewhere; from nations, communities and families where values of tolerance, equality and non-discrimination have been long and deeply embedded. Thousands of citizens of democracies chose to uproot themselves from the cultural context that had nurtured them for an opportunity to launch murderous attacks, in the name of religion, against that culture, its values and people. Moreover, a reverse flow,

---

[1] Also known as Daesh, Islamic State or ISIL, but referred to as ISIS in this book.

1

comprising many hundreds of thousands of migrants seeking refuge in the West, is now flooding into those still largely Christian countries, where the mainly Muslim migrants are experiencing some difficulty in accepting, and being accepted within, democratic lifestyles. The international and multi-cultural dimension of this religiously driven, ideological phenomenon is inescapable. How did it get to this? What are the implications for Western society?

This book sets out to explore such matters. Being primarily a law book, however, it doesn't presume to address geo-political issues, except insofar as seems appropriate to draw attention to the causes and effects of not dealing with discriminatory activity when it first surfaces. Instead, it confines itself, primarily, to examining the flow of religious discrimination cases through the courts in order to better understand the main types of issues that are currently deemed to meet that definition and the reasoning behind the judicial response. It proceeds on the basis that religious discrimination cannot be satisfactorily addressed without considering the cultural context in which it has been formed and now functions. It therefore takes a checklist of the main areas of such discrimination as statutorily identified, tracks how they are processed through regulatory or judicial systems and considers the significance of any jurisdictional similarities or differences in the way issues are resolved.

In the main, the book concentrates on this age-old scourge of civilisation as defined in statute and manifested in everyday settings such as family life, employment and education. The focus is largely on a comparative analysis of judicial judgments on the same agenda of issues – accommodating religious practices in the workplace, religious beliefs in education, wearing religion-specific clothing and so on. It is an exercise restricted to six common law nations chosen because they share the same legal system, have been engaged in prolonged warfare in the same Muslim countries and are now struggling to adapt their domestic multi-culturalism policies to cope with the influx of refugees and migrants from those countries. Of necessity, that policy context also arises for consideration as it forms a largely shared jurisdictional backdrop for discriminatory activity, and its role – whether as part of the problem or part of the solution – deserves attention.

In addition to religious discrimination as statutorily defined, the book also considers the phenomenon known as "the culture wars". It links the two. It argues that the same morality may be seen at work in both phenomena: that, in effect, the latter often serves as a proxy extension of the former; that many if not most of those resisting legalised abortion, same-sex marriage and other such contemporary moral imperatives are doing so in defence of traditional religious values and beliefs (although not always; e.g. it is not necessary to have religious values to oppose gay marriage). It suggests that the morality platform of the culture wars is often little more than a collapsed version of its legal counterpart – religious discrimination. Only by taking into account the associated culture-war issues is it possible to give a full picture of the jurisdictional experience of religious discrimination in a cultural context. This important theme is developed throughout the book.

Parts I and II of this book examine the causes, nature and consequences of religious discrimination. The four chapters therein deal with themes of "identity" and "alienation", with what in contemporary society is meant by "culture" and what now constitutes "religion" and how we understand, in the light of those constructs, what is meant by "religious discrimination". Part III, the heart of the book, contains six chapters, each focusing on a developed, multi-cultural, common law democracy – England and Wales, Ireland, the USA, Canada, Australia and New Zealand – in which the institutions, laws and legislatures take care to respect and differentiate between the many cultures they now accommodate. In these modern societies, a reassuring principle – that to differentiate is not to discriminate – is often trotted out as the rationale for a multi-cultural policy. Cultures, we are assured, are categorically distinct and must be treated in ways that acknowledge and maintain their particular characteristics. Identity – whether for individual, group or culture – is wholly dependent upon difference, and difference must be respected. All very well, but even if the delineation of difference is pursued for the most laudable of motives, it will still result in social divisions where pride in distinctiveness can lead to disparagement of others, and from there perhaps to discrimination.

While each chapter in Part III focuses on jurisdiction-specific judicial rulings, arranged in accordance with a schematic of legally defined religious discrimination issues, they also draw attention to associated "culture-war" disputes. The previously mentioned premise – that culture-war issues often operate as religious discrimination by proxy – forms a unifying theme for Part IV. This concluding section ties the findings in Part III to themes examined in Parts I and II. It identifies and considers areas of jurisdictional commonality and difference in the judicial treatment of religious discrimination and then reflects on the bearing these might have on the themes explored earlier.

It is hoped that *Religious Discrimination and Cultural Context* will lend a little weight to a recommendation in a recent British report, with relevance for all the jurisdictions surveyed, that the time has come for government to "review the anomalies in how the legal definitions of race, ethnicity and religion interact in practice".[2]

---

[2] See Commission on Religion and Belief in British Public Life, *Living with Difference: Community, Diversity and the Common Good*, Cambridge, The Woolf Institute, 2015, at p. 8.

PART I

Background

1

Identity, Alienation and the Law
The Twentieth-Century Legacy

Introduction

This chapter begins by tracing the roots of discrimination back to "identity" and "alienation". While the very considerable body of academic work on these concepts – largely drawn from psychology,[1] philosophy,[2] anthropology[3] and sociology[4] – is by no means the focus of this chapter, inevitably it is informed by some material from such sources. A narrower and more legal approach is adopted, which is framed to explore the following: how an entity acquires an identity; the effect of that status; the boundaries that include and exclude; and the scope for change. Most importantly, for present purposes, it examines the nature and consequences of identity violation: of rejection, alienation and the process of ultimately acquiring recognition and affirmation.

The closing section of the chapter considers some of the more brutal late twentieth-century examples of what can happen when a group becomes caught up in a cycle that starts with social differentiation, continues with religious discrimination and alienation and ends with violent confrontation, where its members are usually the victims. The Holocaust atrocity provides the most obvious example of this dynamic, but the persecution of a religious minority is also graphically illustrated by the war in Bosnia. Finally, recognising the history of civil unrest in Northern Ireland as the sole and relatively recent example of sustained community violence grounded on religious discrimination in a common law jurisdiction, the

---

[1] See Erikson, E., *Identity and the Life Cycle: Selected Papers*, New York, International Universities Press, 1959 and *Identity: Youth and Crisis*, London, Faber, 1968.

[2] See Heidegger, M., *Being and Time* (trans. by Macquarrie, J. and Robinson, E.), London, SCM Press, 1962.

[3] See Brubaker, R. and Cooper, F., "Beyond 'Identity'", *Theory and Society*, 2000, vol. 29, pp. 1–47 and Calhoun, C. (ed.), *Social Theory and Identity Politics*, Oxford, Blackwell, 1994.

[4] See Weinreich, P. and Saunderson, W. (eds.), *Analysing Identity: Cross-Cultural, Societal and Clinical Contexts*, London, Routledge, 2003.

chapter concludes with a consideration of the role it played before, during and after the period known as "the troubles".

Identity

Prescribed characteristics (imposed genetically or otherwise), experiences, culture and other contextural influences all contribute to the formation and continuity of identity; their summation can be seen in the singular attributes of an individual and in the shared distinctive profile of a group, community or nation. Identity development is generally an ongoing process. It is never fully and finally formed – although aspects can be – being no more than a label that captures salient characteristics at a particular point in time, as entities are constantly adjusting in response to changes in their environment.

The Significance of Identity

The need for identity, and the drive to assert or protect it, has probably always been a primary social force – for every society and for all entities within it. Whether inherent or ascribed, identity is clearly a prerequisite for all forms of discrimination. Historically, it has mobilised communities and nations in wars to conquer or resist being conquered, thereafter being commemorated in monuments and ceremonies as reminders of the events that shaped them. Currently, it can be seen in the unique blend of language, culture, artefacts and customs that combine to express a sense of patriotism. The governments, legislators and judiciary of such nations are now being increasingly challenged by the need to balance the identity rights of citizens and society: allowing more elasticity for citizenship, facilitating filtered immigration, while also preserving a traditional sense of national identity.

Fixed

Ostensibly, religion provides the classic model of a fixed "identity": the effect of subscribing to a set of doctrines and tenets, believing in a specific theistic being or other central feature and performing ordained rituals of worship is intended to be that the integrity of the entity remains inviolable; a sealed time capsule, future-proofed against possible internal or external change. To some extent, this is so – mostly as regards Muslims, orthodox Jews and the "closed" monastic orders of Christianity. In many cultures, it is fixed at birth, being determined – partly, largely or even entirely – by the family and community into which a person is born, and by how they are perceived and treated by others. In such circumstances, having little or nothing to do with personal choice, it may be reinforced by markers and badges of religious identity, which can include, for example, the person's given first name and surname.

Arguably, it is not so much the "fixed" nature of religion as the effect of some religions on the identity of adherents that is particularly revealing. While all religions lay down guidelines for leading a good life compliant with doctrinal beliefs, some do so to a greater extent than others. Islam, for example, with over a billion followers making it the second largest religion in the world, is rigorously prescriptive and, at its most extreme, has a defining influence on the identity of Muslim women. Islam, meaning "submission to Allah",[5] requires women to demonstrate their subjection to both Allah and to their husbands; in the absence of the latter, a woman must be seen to be under the guardianship of, or to belong to, a male member of their family. While there is some cultural flexibility in how female submission is interpreted, this can stretch to an expectation that they: be accompanied by their husband or male family member when outside their home; be fully covered with the abaya or otherwise hide their femininity when in public; and refrain from engaging in any activities that might indicate independence. Female identity is in effect publicly nullified and the personal identity of a woman is subsumed within that of her husband. This is neither stereotypical of all contemporary Islamic cultures nor of all female Muslims, but it is true of many, and pockets of such culture subsist throughout the social fabric of the developed common law nations.

Despite the resort to fundamentalism by some Muslims, and its persistence in some Christian churches, a prominent theme of this book is that religion and religious entities cannot hope to be wholly insulated from contemporary social trends and, in fact, do adapt to pressures from their cultural context, and that this causes religious discrimination to adjust accordingly.

Contingent

It may be that an identity is contingent, negotiated or has been manufactured for a purpose. The national identity of member states of the

---

[5] Islam's primary sacred text is the *Qur'an*, which is regarded as dictated by Allah and thus not open to interpretation (*taqlid*). Of secondary importance are the *Sunnah* and the *Hadith*, which continue to be interpreted (*itihad*). At the core of Islam is the *Shahadah*, a declaration that "There is no god but God", to which was later added "and Muhammad is his messenger".

European Union, for example, is contingent upon the extent to which their governments and laws are subservient to the authority exercised from Brussels and by their shared commitment to furthering a composite European identity: the more compromised their sovereignty, the less autonomous their identity; while social class is contingent upon personal socio-economic variables, which may change over time. Sexual orientation can be contingent upon environmental factors: heterosexuality may give way to homosexuality in male prisons, and a contrary outcome may result from laws constraining gay relationships. Occupation, on the other hand, is a negotiated identity – allowing many to change the type or terms of employment during the course of their working lives – as are all identities that depend upon contractual relationships.

Manufactured identities – driven by internal or external pressures – result in an entity being moulded to represent some idealised construct. The State of Israel can be seen as the positive outcome of such a process, while for all but a few Muslims the putative ISIS caliphate is its negative counterpart: an unjustifiable interpretation of the Muslim identity. Some States, such as the former Yugoslavia or Northern Ireland, are manufactured to fit prevailing political circumstances, but the artificiality of the acquired identity is so apparent to citizens and neighbours that it remains inherently compromised. Following manufacture, any such entity then serves as a rallying point requiring others to conform with the image it presents. Most often, this process manifests itself in brand marketing. It can also, however, be seen as an empowering tool, for example in the context of feminism.

Many other identities are similarly constructed: "asylum seekers" identifies a class of migrants politically designated as particularly deserving assistance; "the poor", "neglected child", "disabled", "the elderly" and many other such elastic labels are also politically or sociologically contrived identities, some of which overlap. To complicate matters further, the opportunities for multiple identities and for identity fraud provided by globalisation, as expedited by the Internet, have so diluted and attenuated this concept that queries as to whether an entity is authentically defined by its declared identity now often require corrorborating evidence.

Changing

Changes in identity can result from entity choice made in response to benign or malign influences and from imposed intervention. In the former case, positive contextual developments may present such an irresistible attraction that an entity wholly conforms to fit with them and share their benefits or, alternatively, is so repelled that it makes adjustments to signify disassociation and set it on a different path. In the latter, the impact of external random events or purposeful force, as in the case of Henry VIII in relation to the Catholic Church and its monastries in England, can violate and override an entity's aspiration for self-determination, destroy its public identity and dictate real change. This has been demonstrated more recently by Islamic extremists in their destruction of communities perceived as heretical and the attempted eradication of monuments and artefacts that have stood for millennia as identifying icons for other cultures. Such acts of culture stripping are ruthlessly determined efforts to delete an identity by erasing its memory trail and removing all physical evidence of its history.

The latitude granted to those who "self-identify" – thereby dismissing any need for contextural corroboration or independent validation – has become a particularly complicating factor in modern life with regard to matters such as sexual orientation, beliefs and political allegiance. The accompanying aura of transience creates uncertainty in the relationships between those affected and others. Mostly, however, an identity simply develops in a contiguous fashion: remaining true to itself but shedding and acquiring peripheral characteristics as circumstances dictate.

The threat of imminent danger may trigger the forming of an identity: many amorphous, dispersed or mutually antagonistic entities have found themselves welded into a new aggregated identity in response to aggressive threats; while actual violence or the extinguishing of resources can, of course, strip away or destroy identities, as in circumstances of extreme poverty or of incarceration in concentration camps, and in the political dismemberment of Yugoslavia. More prosaically, the passage of time, large-scale migration and the impact of globalisation can do much to erode national identity and have led, perhaps, to Europe becoming what Modood and Werbner describe as "a novel experiment in multiple, tiered and mediated multiculturalism, a supernational community of cultures, subcultures and transcultures inserted differentially into radically different political and cultural traditions".[6]

Personal Identity

In the developed common law jurisdictions presently being considered, personal identity is largely something that is chosen and purposefully

---

[6] Modood, T. and Werbner, P. (eds.), *The Politics of Multiculturalism in the New Europe*, London, Zed Books, 1997, p. vii.

cultivated. The choices made in relation to higher education, career, religious affiliation, marriage and family, country of residence, sport, hobbies and investments all provide opportunities to build a composite persona. They are, however, exposed to internal and externally generated influences which may dictate unforeseen change. In contrast, some identities are imposed from the outset and remain impervious to change: ethnicity, race and gender provide relatively firm anchor points.

Sexuality

While sexual identity usually corresponds to gender as determined at birth (cisgender), for some it does not, and this can lead to profound feelings of alienation; homosexuals, lesbians and bisexuals may well suffer somewhat similar alienation, but because of social rejection rather than a self-perceived disconnect between gender and sexuality. For transsexual or transgender people, the route to re-alignment of sexuality and gender is more likely to involve traumatic self-doubt, require medical intervention and ultimately need social affirmation and acceptance of that person's new identity. The extent to which societies now accept varying interpretations of sexual identity has become a factor in religious discrimination and in the make-up and spread of the "culture wars", as illustrated by the current sad contention over transgender bathrooms.

Gender, Race and Ethnicity

To be born into an identity, by virtue of one or more of these determining characteristics, is to be assigned a basic template with a significant capacity to define and differentiate; although, in the case of gender, allocation this is now less fixed and permanent than formerly. Other identity-defining characteristics – such as disability and sexual orientation – may be acquired at birth or at any stage in life and may be affected by personal health and wealth. For present purposes, the primary significance of racial and ethnicity classification lies in the fact that some groups are associated with a specific religion, set of customs and cultural practices which can make them "particularly vulnerable to racism, xenophobia, anti-Semitism, and intolerance".[7] This would seem to be borne out, for example, by the victim experiences of black Americans and Spanish Americans in the USA and Asians in the UK (see further Chapter 2).

---

[7] As stated by the European Commission Against Racism and Intolerance, 1998, at www.coe .int/t/dghl/monitoring/ecri/activities/gpr/en/recommendation_n4/Rec04en.pdf.

Morality, Beliefs and Values

A large part of that which distinguishes persons, groups and communities is to be found in their particular profile of values, beliefs and related aspirations. Unlike fixed characteristics, these are commonly viewed as elective – governed by freedom of choice, they can theoretically be selected and changed at will. In practice, however, as already mentioned, it is often the case that they are pre-set and continuous, with individuals being born into and absorbing the values of their parents just as the latter assumed those of their extended family and immediate community. When it comes in the form of a religion, the moral code – reinforced by collective ceremonies and rituals – most often confers a specific and powerful sense of identity upon the entity concerned, requiring both a private commitment to doctrines and a principled way of life, together with a public expression of that commitment by way of participation in worship and in some cases adherence to a theologically ordained but highly visible manner of personal appearance and diet. Where that public manifestation of religious belief takes symbolic form – such as a crucifix in a classroom – it can assume immense significance: an iconic representation not just of religious belief but also of an accompanying weight of cultural heritage.

Ironically, the public manifestation of religion can also be fatuous – a superficial gesture signaling a wish to be seen as associated with a particular religion or culture – performed by those who may have no understanding of or even sympathy with the doctrines and values so represented. The identity acquired by brandishing a label indicating a particular religious affiliation, like wearing a football club scarf, can amount to little more than a public claim of solidarity with, and recognition for, everything that religion currently signifies, at minimum personal cost; default tokenism towards an affected social identity unaccompanied by any commitment to the beliefs necessary to substantiate it.

To be committed to a particular set of values, especially when packaged as a religion, is to reject alternatives. With that adherence comes a sense of belonging and exclusiveness, an absence of concessions to outsiders and their moral code: Quakers, for example, perceive their value set as superior to that of Muslims and vice versa. Morality, as has been said, can bind a group together – but it may also blind.[8] The values of others are readily regarded as mere prejudices, and differences are highlighted in order to

---

[8] Haidt, J., *The Righteous Mind; Why Good People are Divided by Politics and Religion*, New York, Pantheon Books, 2012.

strengthen the cohesion of adherents and increase the distance between "us" and "them".

Cultural Identity

"Culture" has been defined as "people's values, languages, religions, ideals, artistic expressions, patterns of social and interpersonal relationships and ways of perceiving, behaving and thinking".[9] Such characteristics are commonly taken into account when distinguishing the identities of nations, communities or groups. Cultural identity was once readily ascertained in accordance with the stage of development of a nation state (the "age of Enlightenment", "the Renaissance", etc.), as expressed by its leading writers and artists and embodied in the innovatory ideas and artefacts representative of that period. The social homogeneity, conducive to the phased evolution of a nation, has now largely given way to globalised trends determined by the changing patterns of consumer demand in conjunction with widespread government reliance upon a policy of multi-culturalism (see further Chapter 2).

Closed

"Culture", a ubiquitous term, is now commonly used in relation to any relatively "closed" group. It can be ascribed to a profession or trade – including banking, second-hand car dealership, media celebrity and academia – in which the participants are perceived as sharing similar values. It may be described as a way of doing something, as in a "culture of secrecy", "cynicism" or "exploitation". It subsumes an individual into governing group norms, requiring conformity in all respects and moulding the individual into a representative of everything the group stands for. It can be specific to a particular sub-group at a certain point in time: a culture of entitlement, for example, was notoriously held to characterise some bankers and other financial dealers in the early twenty-first century, mainly in the USA and the UK. The individuals need not know one another, nor be located in the same area; they need not speak the same language or have anything in common other than an assumed shared approach.

Increasingly, the modern developed societies are generating a patchwork of "cultures" which reflect lifestyle choices and a nuanced sense of group membership: some based within the immediate community, some

---

[9] Manning, M. L. and Baruth, L. G., *Multicultural Education of Children and Adolescents*, 5th edn, UK, Allyn & Bacon, 2009, p. 24.

pursued internationally; some interchangeable, with multiple and over-lapping membership not uncommon. These are often short-term serial commitments, where membership is viewed less as publicly acquiring an exclusive group identity and more as a private opportunity to address personal needs to be accessorised by other arrangements or discontinued as circumstances change. Belonging to a group can now be satisfied anonymously via the Internet without any racial, ethnic or religious complications. The contemporary social role of religion and beliefs can only be fully understood against this backdrop.

Religion

Cultural identity most often has a pronounced and self-perpetuating religious dimension. Adherents, being born into an ethnic or national religion, will usually automatically assume and propagate its beliefs as an inherent part of their cultural heritage. Even when they don't subscribe to relevant beliefs and doctrines, and indeed might be atheists – as members of that community, they may well be imprinted with the accompanying values, appreciative of the artistic and architectural outworkings of that religion – they will nonetheless share and represent that cultural identity. This is not without significance for an understanding of what constitutes religious discrimination: sectarianism or anti-Semitism can be directed as much against a culture as against a religion; non-believers may still be its victims. The symbiosis of identity and discrimination has always fuelled religious discrimination, ensuring that probably all religious organisations suffer and/or inflict discrimination. It is a relationship that lies at the heart of this book.

Globalisation

Although the cultural homogeneity that once characterised each European nation, as transferred by conquest to other continents, has long since been dissipated, a post-colonial residue of national affiliation allows some groups of countries to retain a degree of shared cultural identity. This is most extensive in the relationship between the UK and the jurisdictions that once made up the British Empire (see further Chapter 2); it is also evident, for example, in the Canada/France relationship. Possibly the British experience of colonialism, coupled with the wartime support received from its colonies and ex-colonies, has given the UK a greater familiarity with ethnic and racial differences than has been experienced elsewhere. It may be that cultural bonds and a sense of shared commonwealth identity have facilitated its integration of minority groups.

Undoubtedly, however, the promotion of international consumer brands, together with the growth in tourism, television programming and social media and a general tendency towards "Americanisation", have combined to superimpose a standardised veneer upon all culture-specific entities. In particular, the brands of leading products are now so carefully constructed and marketed that globalisation can usually place a uniform product identity within any cultural context at any time. Similarly, international health and safety concerns – including terrorism, AIDS, avian flu and the Zika virus – reveal the vulnerability of national boundaries.

The Common Law and Identity

The common law jurisdictions, by definition, share the same legal foundations and consequently are similarly constrained when their legal systems face complex social problems. Arguably, some of these constraints significantly impact their capacity to address matters of cultural identity and associated religious discrimination.

Common Law and Its Constraints

Prevailing in England since the twelfth century, and later exported to its colonies, the common law was grounded on the rights and duties of the individual.[10] Unlike civil law, it was derived not from the prescribed directives of statute but from tradition, custom and judicial precedent, as embodied in rules and interpreted and applied by the judiciary, adopting an inquisitorial approach on a case-by-case basis. Often referred to as "judge-made law", it was heavily reliant on case precedents. There was no sense of collective legal interests, no provision for class or community actions; the common law consisted merely of categories of causes actionable by or against individuals, leaving the latter to fit their complaints to an established cause. This approach – listing subjects available for legal redress and permitting subsequent empirical extension by analogy – proved to be problematic. Its grindingly logical approach led to the law being constrained by the rigidity of the specified, coralled by established case precedents, where any development to meet emerging needs could only be achieved by painstakingly distinguishing the facts of new cases from those of the old. The result was a reliance on endless lists and categorisation, producing a patchwork effect rather than a coherent body of law.

[10] See Blackstone, Sir William, *Commentaries on the Laws of England*, Oxford, Clarendon Press, (1765–69).

The common law would also seem to have been instrumental in maintaining the status quo in society: most particularly, it embodied a respect for contemporary social institutions and sources of authority, giving recognition to the governing power, the place of religion, and to the roles of Church and judiciary. It was concerned less with matters of public policy and contemporary politics than with maintaining an almost feudal respect for king and country and for the institutions of the land.

From Common Law to Legal Rights and Social Justice

While the foundations for the evolving legal systems of all jurisdictions that formerly constituted the British Empire remained similarly grounded on the bedrock of common law, the changes introduced by the gradual spread of legislation, together with the concepts of legal rights and justice, shifted the dynamic from the personal to the public domain, but still left the law anchored on specified causes of action or "entitlements". This approach – statutorily encoding legal rights and corresponding legal duties, enforced by legal powers – formed the basis for national legal systems; often complemented, in due course, by constitutions enshrining principles of collective justice. It was not until the introduction of international conventions, protocols and so on that such principles acquired a transcending effect; in particular, those embodied in the European Convention for the Protection of Human Rights and Fundamental Freedoms 1950. Over recent decades, an international safety net of provisions has grown which requires standards of equity, equality and non-discrimination to be entrenched in the legislation of signatory nations (see further Chapter 4).

Definitional Complications

The common law categorisation approach, with its focus on specific causes of action, on the particular rather than the collective, has obstructed the capacity of the related legal systems to address issues of cultural identity: most obviously, where that identity is in reality a conflation of racial/ethnic/religious components. The law then tends to dis-aggregate, to focus on the primary element and proceed on a specific-issue basis. This approach may well have difficulty in processing complex issues arising from intangible and often subjectively perceived matters of identity – as associated, for example, with a particular belief system that repudiates homosexuality or requires animal sacrifice. In particular, it may well seriously disadvantage citizens subscribing to a wholly different culture, viz. the Indigenous People who constitute a sizeable proportion of the populations and disproportionately impact the legal and welfare systems of many common law jurisdictions. Being predicated upon shared Christian values and culture, with a presumption of citizen fealty to related social institutions, the common law is not equipped to cope with cultural differences – a deficit which arguably extends to difficulties in recognising and responding to discriminatory conduct based on beliefs outside its cultural frame of reference.

Legal Status and Identity

Also by definition, once an entity acquires its status as such, it becomes differentiated from all others: its raison d'être, resources, field of operations and objectives are recognisably distinct; its boundaries delineate those who belong from those who do not; and the grounds for possible future discrimination by or against that entity are thereby established.

Legal Personality

The concept of "legal personality" is an artificial construct which holds that an entity is considered capable of exercising legal rights and obligations. It provides the means for creating a legal identity or "juridical personality". This enables an entity to be named and distinguished and to take action in accordance with its particular profile of rights, protections, privileges, responsibilities and liabilities.

In law, certain entities are deemed to have such capacity. These include individual persons, associations, companies and sovereign nations. All are vested with specific rights and duties attached to their defining characteristics or attributes, and each has the ability to contract, prosecute or defend its interests. Where the entity is the holder of a "post" – such as the priest of a diocese or an archbishop – then the person presently in the post will be deemed to be the legal representative of that office, and as such vested with its duties and liabilities. Where the entity is an aggregate of individuals and assets – such as a religious organisation – the concept allows for "a piercing of the corporate veil" and for holding the culpable individual to account; indeed, both the individual and the organisation may be separably liable for the same offence (e.g. for child abuse).

There are parameters to the recognition of entities within the law: traditionally, a lack of intellectual capacity – due, for example, to childhood or insanity – has been held sufficient to withhold legal accountability and indicate the need for the subject's interests to be professionally represented. In the context of religion and religious discrimination, the extent of such recognition gives rise to heated controversy. This is very evident in relation to matters such as the legal standing of a foetus, access to abortion, genetic patenting, the use of human embryos for research purposes and the status of newly emerging faith and spiritualist groups.

Associations

An association exists when any group of people comes together by agreement to form an organisation in pursuit of a common purpose. It may be unincorporated or incorporated; the former will not necessarily have separate legal personality, nor will its members usually enjoy limited liability; the latter will have those legal attributes and will most probably be subject to mandatory registration and monitoring by a designated regulatory body. This, the lowest form of social organisation known to the law, has been in existence since the earliest stages of civilisation. The right to freely form an association, and to hold meetings to pursue a common purpose, is a well established fundamental human right.[11]

For present purposes, its significance lies in the fact that while beliefs are a personal matter and thus not amenable to legal processes, an "association" provides a legal vehicle for religion, religious organisations and the common enterprises of religious adherents. As explained in *Shergill* v. *Khaira*:[12]

> The law treats unincorporated religious communities as voluntary associations. It views the constitution of a voluntary religious association as a civil contract as it does the contract of association of a secular body: the contract by which members agree to be bound on joining an association sets out the rights and duties of both the members and its governing organs. The courts will not adjudicate on the decisions of an association's governing bodies unless there is a question of infringement of a civil right or interest.

Not until it acquires such status is an entity such as a minority religious or ethnic group recognised in law, able to sue or be sued or considered to have the legal capacity to determine its own future development (see also Chapter 12).

Vicarious Liability

The common law principle of "agency", or *qui facit per alium, facit per se* (the one who acts through another, acts in his or her own interests), has been interpreted as the relationship between a principal and an agent

---

[11] See e.g. the Universal Declaration of Human Rights (UDHR), Article 20 and the ECHR, Article 11.

[12] [2014] UKSC 33, at para. 46.

whereby the principal, expressly or impliedly, authorizes the agent to work under his control and on his behalf".[13] Whether an agency relationship exists turns on the facts in each case: not all delegated authority necessarily constitutes agency; the span of control exercised is crucial. When a relationship can be demonstrated to exist, as it will most clearly do if an employee is acting on behalf of their employer and within the scope of their terms of employment, then the principal will be held vicariously liable for the agent's acts and omissions, and their consequences.

This doctrine is of some considerable significance in relation to the many historical cases of alleged child abuse by clergy. It is also not without relevance in the broader context of religious beliefs and doctrines: a committed adherent may well be driven by the conviction that their acts and lifestyle must conform to religious doctrine; a particular manifestation of belief (e.g. polygamy, type of clothing, ritual slaughter of animals for food) may be viewed as ordained by god; they have no option but to act in accordance with received religious instruction. This, at its most extreme, can currently be seen in the brutal actions of ISIS against those they perceive to be "infidels" or "apostates".

The Law and Cultural Identity

While the Convention on the Rights of the Child (Articles 7 and 8) is the only international convention that explicitly refers to identity as a fundamental human right, others do so at least implicitly.[14] In recent years, rulings of the European Court of Human Rights (ECtHR) have drawn attention to the need to ensure and respect the right to personal and cultural identity.

The State has to ensure that the practices of minority cultural groups – even if very sizeable and established for some generations – conform to the values embedded in national civil law. This cannot be guaranteed, as illustrated by the persistence in developed Western nations of practices such as arranged marriages, child marriages, honour beatings and female genital mutilation (FGM). Some of these nations seek to accommodate culture specific laws – such as the Islamic Shari'a[15] and the Jewish

---

[13] See e.g. Markesinis, B. S. and Munday, R. J. C., *An Outline of the Law of Agency*, 4th edn, London, LexisNexis, 1998.

[14] Including the UDHR, Article 19 and the ECHR, Articles 8, 9 and 10.

[15] Shari'a is a body of rules, norms and laws according to which Muslims (are supposed to) live their lives. It is found in, and derived from, two main sources: the Qur'an and the hadith. Shari'a was formulated between the eighth and the fourteenth centuries AD.

Halakhah – alongside the domestic legal system. This can provide important affirmation for cultural minorities, but gives rise to jurisdictional issues when citizens are induced to resolve matters within their faith-based legal processes instead of seeking relief through the secular national courts. It is probable that a high proportion of "hidden" civil disputes fail to find redress in the national courts because religious leaders divert them towards in-house processes where culture reinforcing outcomes may be prompted by a degree of intimidation. It is in the public manifestation of religious beliefs – through practices that impinge upon the rights of others (e.g. wearing the full-face veil) – that the law, particularly equality law, generates most litigation (see further Chapter 2). The criminal law is clearly also relevant when disputes between adherents of different sects – such as between Shia, Sunni and Ahmadi Muslims – result in murder or other breaches of domestic criminal legislation.

Alienation

The study of "alienation" (from the Latin *alienus*, meaning "of another – place or person") has a long history, with major contributions from such disciplines as politics,[16] philosophy,[17] psychiatry,[18] anthropology[19] and sociology.[20]

The Significance of Difference

Xenophobia, or fear of the other, is a powerful psychological response to difference that probably precedes the forming of groups, communities or any concept of society. It implies a vulnerability, a fear that the perceived difference may represent a threat to an established identity. It suggests that an "in-group" should distrust others, places it in a position to "name" the other, to "objectify" them, and has been responsible for many forms of discrimination throughout history.

---

[16] See e.g. Marx, K., *Economic and Philosophic Manuscripts of 1844*, New York, International Publishers, 1990 and Engels, F., *Dialectics of Nature* [1883], Moscow, Progress Publishers, 1976.

[17] See e.g. Kierkegaard, S., *Either/Or* [1843], Princeton, NJ, Princeton University Press, 1988 and Sartre, J.-P., *Being and Nothingness* [1943], London, Allen and Unwin, 1956.

[18] See e.g. Freud, S., *The Ego and the Id*, USA, Createspace, 2010 [1923].

[19] See e.g. Veblen, T., *The Theory of the Leisure Class*, New York, Macmillan, 1914.

[20] See e.g. Durkheim, E., *The Elementary Forms of Religious Life*, Mineola, NY, Dover Publications, 2008 and Habermass, J., *Legitimation Crisis*, London, Heinemann, 1976.

Catering for difference has now become a significant challenge for all institutions in Western society. The range of ethnic, racial, religious and other types of groups and communities seeking recognition for separate and distinct identities has multiplied exponentially in recent years, and with this has come legislation requiring that all be respected, accommodated and treated equally. While, as has been pointed out, "many minority populations have attempted to avoid, in various ways, assimilation becoming erasure",[21] this would seem to have been replaced in recent years by a competitive striving to assert a unique identity. The change is accompanied by international acknowledgement of the human right to do so[22] – which has perhaps licensed an upsurge in short-term identities as new groups emerge, fragment and reform – to the detriment of the collective.

Difference

To be different is to have acquired a singular "other" identity. It suggests a degree of predictability and, in terms of a group or culture, it is representative: to an outsider, there is a presumption that to know one is to know all; particular values and proclivities can be ascribed; a homogenised sense of identity labels an entity.

Difference is crucial to identity. Inviting or asserting recognition for a degree of independent autonomy is probably as old as society itself. It produces the diversity that can enrich society and stimulate creativity. The integrity and longevity of cultural groups such as the Amish of Pennsylvania in the USA and the indigenous communities of Australia, New Zealand and North America speaks to the capacity of society to at least tolerate difference. Unfortunately, the phenomenon has also been responsible for the dynamics of inclusion and exclusion that provoke confrontation. Difference may be extreme but is often infinitesimal. Tweaking a profile sufficiently to disassociate from others can be enough. Sigmund Freud saw this as "the narcissism of the small difference... It is precisely the minor differences in people who are otherwise alike that form the basis of feelings of hostility between them".[23] Shades of difference can represent

---

[21] See Herman, D., *An Unfortunate Coincidence: Jews, Jewishness and English Law*, Oxford, Oxford University Press, 2011, p. 51.

[22] See Mende, J., *The Human Right to Culture and Identity*, London, Rowman & Littlefield International, 2016.

[23] See Freud, S., *Civilization, Society and Religion*, London, Penguin, 1991, pp. 131 and 305. See also Hitchens, C., "The Narcissism of the Small Difference: In Ethno-National Conflicts, It Really Is the Little Things that Tick People Off", at www.slate.com/articles/news_and_politics/fighting_words/2010/06/the_narcissism_of_the_small_difference.html.

very significant identity characteristics, with attendant loyalties, that some are prepared to aggressively assert or bitterly defend. To be different is to run the risk of being defined by others: having your identity defined by what you're not.

Ideology

A composite set of ideals, together with a related socio-economic policy and the leadership to give effect to them, form an ideology and thereby constitute what is probably the most radical, coherent and structured means for imposing social differentiation. It has been responsible for some of the most important paradigm shifts that have shaped modern civilised society, but also for some of the major threats to its existence. It can conflate politics and religion: arguably, the Christian Crusades of the eleventh to fifteenth centuries, as much as the twenty-first century ISIS efforts to build a caliphate, were ideologically driven; representatives of fundamentalist religious views are often ideologists. Difference grounded in ideology has been responsible for civilisation's most lethal confrontations. In doing so, it has demonstrated the dangers involved in labelling, provided clear examples of the causes and effects of alienation and starkly revealed the worst consequences of religious discrimination (see later). The harm caused by the chosen methods of implementation often far outweigh any benefits that an ideology, if realised, could have brought to society.

When the fall of the Berlin Wall on 9 November 1989 brought the "cold war" to an end, it seemed that ideology as an international polarising and dividing force had been consigned to history: Western democracy no longer had a credible ideological opponent; and the "Arab Spring",[24] with its challenge to theocracy, offered comforting testimony to the relative superiority of democratic structures. The promise of a new political era instilled greater confidence in all Western democratic governments. Internationally, this was evidenced by the rise of neo-conservatism in the USA, and to some degree in the UK and Australia, and a spreading engagement in war with autocratic rulers, often coupled with a "regime change" agenda, which aimed to at least encourage a transition to democracy. On the domestic front, the political potency of socialism was correspondingly weakened, and with it the "welfare state" approach to public benefit service provision: government cutbacks on unemployment and disability benefits

---

[24] A term used to describe the phenomenon of civil unrest and uprisings that affected a sequence of Middle East Arab countries (Libya, Tunisia, Yemen, Syria) starting in the spring of 2010.

became the norm; campaigns to drive down taxes became increasingly common; trade unions decreased in number and negotiating power; and for-profit companies competed for a greater share of public benefit service provision, especially in the fields of health, education and social care. In short, the collapse of communism, and with it the general diminution of socialism, inaugurated a new post-ideological era in which liberal democracy was, seemingly, left as the only sustainable political model – at least in the "Western" world. The resulting surge in political self-confidence may have given permission for the excesses that triggered the 2008 financial crisis, causing a prolonged global economic recession from which the newly affirmed political model emerged tarnished by evidence of exacerbated and growing social inequality: the consequent systemic alienation of increasing numbers of the poor has since been attested to by many leading Western academics.[25]

The Alienated

The sociologist Seeman[26] recognised five prominent features of alienation: powerlessness, meaninglessness, normlessness, isolation and self-estrangement, to which he later – and revealingly – added cultural estrangement. These features can be readily recognised as characterising the position of those excluded by others, because of their perceived inferiority or their threat to the status quo. Most obviously, they accompany those defined as "outside the tent" by ideological, cultural or religious frames of reference.

Alienation has featured in the many struggles – on a spectrum from the absolutionist movement in the late eighteenth century to the "glass ceiling" that currently obstructs female career advancement – that have sought to combat inequality in Western society. Along the way, successive bastions of exclusivity eventually tumbled, including: racial segregation in the USA and South Africa; patriarchical control (submitting to universal suffrage and the achievements of the feminist movement); the legal status of "illegitimate" children; various classifications of "disability"; and, most recently, the heterosexual monopoly on legal sexual relationships (making room for LGBT relations). Each struggle brought with it much the same

[25] See e.g. Stiglitz, J., *The Price of Inequality*, London, Penguin, 2013; Picketty, T., *Capital in the Twenty-First Century*, Cambridge, MA, Harvard University Press, 2014; and Watson, W., *The Inequality Trap: Fighting Capitalism Instead of Poverty*, Toronto, ON, University of Toronoto Press, 2016.

[26] See e.g. Seeman, M., *On the Meaning of Alienation* [1959], New York, Irvington Publishers, 1993.

polarisation between an in-group, assured of its righteousness, firmly resolute and inclined to be at best patronising towards those regarded as unfit to share, and an out-group that conformed to the Seeman typology.

At present, the struggle ebbs and flows between adherents of different religions, and between them and secularists, with confrontations between mutually alienated groups encamped on associated sets of values. This is illustrated most clearly by the stand-off between the pro-choice and pro-life divisions on the intractable abortion debate. All of this forms part of the "culture wars" that have festered and divided the USA in recent generations, before being exported to similar effect in the UK and elsewhere; this phenomenon represents the deep divides, on a narrowly construed but ever-expanding agenda of moral imperatives, that may now present a serious challenge to the consolidation of civil society in the developed common law nations.

Religious Fundamentalism

Although the transition from the twentieth to the twenty-first century was indeed marked by momentous political change,[27] it also witnessed a revival of fundamentalism (see further Chapter 12). The previously noted mutual estrangement that characterises the relationship of parties now intransigently engaged on religion-related issues, both domestically and internationally, is not untypical of that which has been symptomatic of ideological polarisation. Just when it appeared that ideology had been left behind with the collapse of communism, it now looks likely that this will be replaced by a new era of confrontation, again featuring fundamentalism but, despite appearances, not necessarily grounded in religion.

Domestically, it may seem that the culture wars are rooted in religion, are guaranteed to spawn ever more standoffs as new proxy religious issues emerge and are thus set to cause a long-term fracturing of Western society. That outcome is unlikely. The culture wars have to be seen against the background of a more prominent social trend – the steady rise in the proportion of secularists in all developed nations – and, paradoxically, the fact that social cohesion is to a growing extent facilitated by the Internet: virtual communities offer endless opportunities to compensate for the deficiencies of their "live" counterparts; to patch, fill-in and accessorise. Moreover, "religion" is no longer a coherent entity as traditionally defined. It now often shades into philosophical or spiritualist beliefs,

---

[27] See e.g. Judt, T., *Ill Fares the Land: A Treatise on Our Present Discontents*, London, Allen Lane, 2010.

some ephemeral and convertible, with no need for a "god", and requiring little more than compliance with a moral code or outlook. Lifestyle choices, sometimes expediently dressed in a religious guise (where religious practice is essentially socially conditioned and church attendance is confined to ceremonies marking birth, marriage and death), are as likely as religious belief to determine the way of life of contemporary citizens. The freedom to make such choices has for many in the developed nations become emblematic of modern liberal democracy – a means of exercising their right to acquire and shape a unique identity; to indulge, flaunt and change their attachments – and is seen, perhaps all too often, as a sufficient end in itself. It's a freedom that does not sit comfortably with the commitment to humility, good works and consistency of devotion required by religion. For those trying to integrate within the prevailing national culture, it forces a choice in allegiances – between fitting in or aligning themselves with those purporting to represent their traditional religious beliefs.

Internationally, Taylor asserts, "religious intolerance continues to fuel a high proportion of the situations of armed conflict around the world".[28] While not obviously wrong, it is difficult to know just how right he is. The wars promulgated by the Western powers in the late twentieth century were neither religiously inspired nor conducted with any reference to religion, but it is impossible to avoid recognising a distinctly religious dimension: they were launched by the traditionally Christian Western powers; fought almost exclusively in Muslim countries;[29] devastated the social infrastructure of only those countries; and cost the lives of multiple Muslims (mainly civilian) for every Western member of the armed forces (mainly Christian). The outcome, perhaps inevitably, has been both a surge in Muslim migrants fleeing their devastated countries and a violent Muslim backlash. The latter, launched with ideological if not religious fervour by ISIS, directs destructive hostility towards all non-Muslims, but particularly towards the Western powers and everything they are held to represent. It remains an open question, though, whether the atrocities perpetrated in the name of Islam by ISIS in the Middle East, Boko Haram in Nigeria, Al-Shabaab in Somalia, the Taliban in Afghanistan and al Qaeda in Libya can meet any definition of "religious intolerance", given their barbarity, the concern for territorial gain, the proportion of victims that are

---

[28] Taylor, P. M., *Freedom of Religion: UN and European Rights, Law and Practice*, Cambridge, Cambridge University Press, 2005, p. ix.

[29] Including invasions in Iraq in 1991 and 2003, Sierra Leone in 2000, Afghanistan in 2001 and Libya in 2011 and continuing aerial warfare in Syria.

fellow Muslims and the fact that they are repudiated as non-Islamic by the majority of Muslim religious leaders.

In short, from the standpoint of the developed nations, alienation as a social phenomenon has relatively recently acquired a more salient profile both domestically and internationally. While the reasons for this are generally associated with religion, the inference that the latter is a causal factor is at least questionable.

The Twentieth-Century Legacy

The vision of how a society might differ in future from how it is now presents challenges. It can lead to a clinical classification of social components: a drawing of lines, a labelling of identities, discrimination and the alienation of those who do not or will not conform to the designated formula. It may include a eugenic component: an assertion that some human types are intrinsically better than others, providing justification for furthering social goals at the expense of those at the lower end of such a supposed hierarchy. Perhaps most importantly, it shows that however disguised, ideological stereotyping must be confronted; it cannot, or should not, co-exist with democratic liberalism; and such confrontation may justify illiberal modes of intervention.

There have been a number of instances in the twentieth century when ideological vision, accompanied by stereotyping and autocratic leadership, has led to discrimination and to great harm being inflicted upon an alienated group by their fellow citizens. These include, but are not limited to, the suffering experienced by the Armenians in Turkey, the Jews in Nazi Germany, the Muslims in the former Yugoslavia and both Catholics and Protestants during the period referred to as "the troubles" in Northern Ireland. Before going on to focus on the contemporary experience of religious discrimination, it is important to pause and take account of such lessons as may be learned from these twentieth-century reminders of the damage it can cause.

Religious Discrimination: Ideology and Culture

As manifested in the twentieth century, ideology most usually entailed a dismissal of religion:[30] the communism of Marx and Stalin, Hitler's

---

[30] But not always, as demonstrated, for example, by the genocidal purges of Armenians in Turkey in 1915 and the Tutsi in Rwanda in 1994.

fascism, the more agrarian movement led by Pol Pot and Mao's cultural revolution all sought to crush religion and its institutional organisations, but only as an incidental part of a wider agenda; the fascism of Mussolini, Franco and the South American dictatorships merely sought to harness it as an expedient means of reinforcing their autocratic rule. When religion was deliberately targeted – as in Germany with Hitler and the Jews, or in the former Yugoslavia with Milosevic, Karadzic and the Muslims – it was conflated with racism and constituted what has come to be termed "ethnic cleansing".

Genocide

The methods chosen for implementing an ideology have sometimes culminated in genocide. As defined by the United Nations in 1948, this means intending to destroy, in whole or in part, a national, ethnic, racial or religious group.[31]

Although it has involved religious persecution, in many instances neither the perpetrators nor the victims of genocide have had any particular association with religion. This was the case, for example, in Stalin's oppression of the Kulaks (1932–33), Pol Pot's purge of the intelligentsia in Cambodia (1975–79) and the systematic killing of some 800 000 Tutsis by Hutus in Rwanda (1994). When, as in the following examples, the oppression inflicted by one group upon another in the same society did involve religious discrimination, it also incorporated many aspects of the UN definition.

Nazi Persecution of the Jews

Any consideration of religious discrimination cannot begin without reference, however inadequate, to the Nazi persecution of the Jews during World War II.

Identity Stripping

Nazi persecution targeted the Jews not just because of their religion but also because of their race and culture. Adopting a Darwinist racial perspective, the Jews were viewed as an inferior race; neither they nor their culture belonged in Germany. Jews were denied citizenship rights: their property, land and businesses were confiscated; they were prevented from

---

[31] See further the Genocide Convention on the Prevention and Punishment of the Crime of Genocide, 1948.

praying or attending places of worship; they were labelled, given star badges and separated out from their German neighbours; often, they were forced into labour camps and required to perform street-cleaning duties. The fact that some had lived for many generations in Germany, had inter-married with Christian families, had contributed to national commer-cial progress and were thoroughly integrated into German society was ignored. While Jewish specific cultural artefacts were destroyed – par-ticularly synagogues – other mainstream artistic works, including paint-ings, sculptures and notable architectural buildings, were seized and redis-tributed among non-Jewish citizens. This approach also involved the enforced removal of many infants with Aryan characteristics from Jew-ish birth parents. In Poland alone, an estimated 200 000 such children were forcibly transferred from Jewish and other families and given to Ger-man and Austrian couples. Such practices highlighted a dimension of cul-tural discrimination: Germany and Aryanism were to be purged of the perceived taint of Jewishness (and of other sources of dilution, such as communism).

The Holocaust

The crime against humanity known as "the Holocaust" entailed the sys-tematic mass murder of some 6 million Jews between 1941 and 1945. It included eugenic experimentation. Nazis viewed themselves as the custo-dians of Aryanism, and as such were required to "save" it from others; this was not just a rejection of the "other" – the Jews, their religion and eth-nicity – but also a sanitation device, to protect the integrity of the Aryan race and culture from being tarnished by any contact with that other. Nazi ideology, together with the mass executions, constituted a comprehensive State assault upon a specific religion, its adherents and culture, with the sole purpose of extinguishing them. Neither before nor since has any form of discrimination come close to reaching the extremes inflicted upon the Jews by Hitler's "final solution".

Liquidation of the Jews became a State priority, but whether this truly meets the definition of religious discrimination is open to doubt. While the long history of pogroms against Jews in Europe was undoubtedly initially founded upon religious dogma – essentially that the Jews were responsible for the death of Jesus Christ – by the time they were sin-gled out for genocide by Hitler and the Third Reich, ethnic labelling had arguably come to displace religion as the primary trigger for perse-cution. That is to say, religion was clearly an identifying factor, but the resulting discrimination was not confined by that label; the religious beliefs of neither Jews nor their persecutors were particularly relevant.

Contemporary Alienation of Jews

The ancient monotheistic religion of Judaism, with the Torah as its foundational text, has spread over many continents and engaged with a range of different ethnic groups and cultures over its 3000-year history. Consequently, it has attracted the comment that "Jewishness disrupts the very categories of identity, because it is not national, not genealogical, not religious, but all of these, in dialectical tension".[32]

Anti-Semitism is presently interpreted as meaning prejudicial ideas, attitudes or actions against a Jew or Jews, whether on ethnic, racial or religious grounds. Although rooted in the Judeo-Christian conflict, anti-Semitism in modern times has transcended its religious origins and come to be understood as signifying a blend of connotations that also include political, cultural, racist and economic elements. By a process of aggregating various crude derogatory caricatures – as betrayers of Christianity, moneylenders, dealers in gold and art, nomads with no national loyalties, global Machiavellian political manipulators, treacherous and stingy, a racially inferior species and so on – what had started out as religious discrimination became transformed into a composite and more culturally defined form of abuse. A Jew, or Jewishness, came to attract discrimination despite the absence of any link with that religion: the assimilated Jew was still a Jew even after baptism; identity had been distorted; the power wielded by an in-group had ascribed an alienated identity to an out-group.

This reinterpretation of religious discrimination applies also to the State of Israel. Again, the subject was inflated beyond its initial religious definition and anti-Semitism extended to include derogatory attitudes or actions directed against the State. The Zionist[33] claim that the State was established for the resettlement of the Jews in their "ancestral homeland" would seem to have licensed a broader equating of religion and country, despite the fact that much of the State institutions, administrative machinery and domestic and foreign policy functions in the same secular

---

[32] See Boyarin, D., *A Radical Jew: Paul and the Politics of Identity*, Berkeley, CA, University of California Press, 1994, at http://publishing.cdlib.org/ucpressebooks/view?docId= ft7w10086w&chunk.id=ch9&toc.id=ch9&brand=ucpress.

[33] Zionism emerged in the late nineteenth century as a political movement dedicated to establishing a homeland for Jews in their biblical birthplace of Israel/Palestine. It represents a cultural stand for the assertion of a separate Jewish identity against the assimiliationist approach that had resulted in a Jewish diaspora over the preceding millennia.

manner as that of other countries, and despite the fact that many non-Jews and atheists are numbered among its citizens. The consequences are apparent in the political anti-Semitism directed at the State by rulers in Iran and elsewhere in the Middle East.

Serb Persecution of Muslims

Instability in the Balkans has a very long history. The State of Yugoslavia was beset with identity problems from its inauguration, although none could have foreseen the Bosnian war of 1992–95, the armed conflict in Kosovo that lasted from 28 February 1998 until 11 June 1999, the hundred thousand deaths or the subsequent convictions for crimes against humanity that confirmed the extent of Serbian wartime brutality towards Muslim fellow citizens.[34]

When initially created, under Anglo-French auspices in 1918, Yugoslavia was a kingdom uniting the quite different ethnic groups of Serbs, Croats and Slovaks. Its inherent instability was exacerbated following reconstitution as a federation in 1945, when it consisted of six republics (Serbia, Croatia, Slovenia, Bosnia, Macedonia and Montenegro), two provinces (Kosovo and Vojvodina), incorporating five nations, four languages, three religions and two alphabets. The Socialist Republic of Yugoslavia was thus a manufactured entity containing deep divisions, most acutely represented by the enmity between those who had aligned with either the fascist or the communist forces during World War II. Until the closing decade of the twentieth century, the country was held together by the grudging consent of the constituent parties, by fear of the mutual destruction that could accompany any breaking of ranks and by strong political leadership.

Bosnia

By the time of President Tito's death in 1980, Bosnia was an ethnically mixed republic of Serbs, Croats and Muslims, in which the latter constituted some 44 per cent of the total, but the Serbs had largely gained control of administration and the armed forces. It was the most integrated of the republics, and its capital Sarajevo was a not untypical multi-cultural, cosmopolitan European city. The period of political instability, growing

---

[34] See e.g. *Prosecutor v. Kupreskic and Others* (IT-95–16-T, judgment of 14 January 2000, s.751), *Prosecutor v. Krstic* (IT-98–33-T, judgment of 2 August 2001, ss.577–580) and *Jorgic v. Germany* (Application no. 74613/01).

economic crisis and nationalist unrest that followed Tito's death allowed Slobodan Milošević to gain power as president of Serbia in 1987 and thereafter to invoke and manipulate Serbian nationalism. In due course, this led first to ethnic confrontations between Muslims and Serbs in the Serbian city of Kosovo, then to independence being declared by Slovenia, Croatia and finally, in 1992, Bosnia. The latter event was followed immediately by a Serbian declaration of a "Republika Srpska", which was to include a large part of Bosnia, and by a Serbian assault on non-Serbian-dominated areas of Bosnia, including Sarajevo. The resulting mayhem involved carnage committed and suffered by Serbs, Croats and Muslims as each sought to carve out or defend territory, but between 1992 and 1995 the latter endured the most systematic discriminatory brutality. The forces of Karadžić, President of Republika Srpska, aided by the likes of Ratko Mladić and Željko Ražnatović (or Arkan), with the complicit support of Slobodan Milošević, were only prevented from destroying or expelling the Muslim population by international armed intervention in 1999 following Serbian ethnic cleansing and atrocities in Srebrenica, Sarajevo and Kosovo.

Alienation of Muslims

The Muslims of Bosnia, known as Bosniaks, had populated that region since the fifteenth and sixteenth centuries. Their religion (mainly Sunni Muslim), language and culture – including dress, music and lifestyle – had long given them a distinct identity, but not until 1961 were they recognised as an ethnic group.

During the war, the Muslims suffered not just military violence against defended positions but intimately targeted intimidation and degradation. Within cities, towns, villages and hamlets, the Serb forces – including paramilitaries and Serb vigilantes – destroyed mosques, ransacked or burnt down Muslim homes and murdered their occupants: the Serb perpetrators were frequently former neighbours of their Muslim victims. By 1995, some 100 000 had died in Bosnia and several times that number had been displaced, of whom by far the majority were Muslims,[35] in what was the worst act of genocide and the largest displacement of people in Europe since the Nazi era.[36]

---

[35] See further Human Rights Watch/Helsinki, *War Crimes in Bosnia-Hercegovina*, Vol. I, New York, Human Rights Watch, August 1992, pp. 1–2.

[36] In 2001, Serbian General Radislav Krstic, who played a major role in the Srebrenica massacre, was convicted of genocide and sentenced to forty-six years in prison.

Contemporary Affirmation of Muslim Identity

Serbian persecution of Muslims led directly to a firming up, if not a radicalisation, of the latter's ethnic identity. The political self-assertion of
Bosnian independence on 3 March 1992 received formal acknowledgment when, on 7 April 1992, the USA and the EEC jointly recognised
Bosnia/Herzegovina as an independent State, as did the UN a month
later. Defending that independence gave rise to the Kosovo Liberation
Army (KLA), which imported weaponry and volunteers from Albania,
other Islamic countries and the ethnic diaspora, to protect Muslims and
their cultural identity. This was reinforced from 1995 by increased NATO
armed intervention against Serb forces, which served to further validate
the rights of Bosnian Muslims. Ultimately, international acknowledgment
of Bosnian Muslim identity was assured by the terms of the Dayton Accord
in 1995, which provided constitutional protection for Bosniaks supported
by ongoing NATO monitoring.

Despite the casualties and the widespread diaspora, the 4 million population of Bosnia currently comprises some 48.4 per cent Muslims, 32.7
per cent Serbs and 14.6 per cent Croats, or roughly what it was at the outbreak of war, but for Muslims that experience had destroyed the assimi-
lationist ethos of the late twentieth century. The post-war years revealed
not only extensive physical destruction and severe socio-economic damage, but also a new high visibility for Muslim cultural identity: minarets
and mosques have been rebuilt; alcohol is less widely available; religion-
specific marriages are much more likely; Shari'a law is the norm; fewer
women are in employment and many more now adopt Islamic attire.

Northern Ireland: Catholics and Protestants

Over the course of three decades in the latter half of the twentieth century,
some 3600 persons died, many thousands more were injured and considerable population displacement occurred in Northern Ireland during the
course of "the troubles", which, ostensibly, was a conflict rooted in religious differences. Although religious discrimination and its consequences
in this jurisdiction are clearly of a different order to those considered so
far, this conflict merits attention both because the jurisdiction provided
a setting for the only recent and lethal religious confrontation within the
common law framework of nations presently being studied and because it
illustrates the potency of identity and alienation issues that can arise when
communities divided by religion and culture are confined within artificial
but tight geographical and political parameters.

Duality of Cultural Identity

Constitutionally part of the UK and geographically part of the island of Ireland, Northern Ireland had been a compromised entity for at least the fifty-year period that preceded the outbreak of violence.[37] During that time, the Protestant majority, mostly "unionists", with their strong allegiance to the British government, and particularly to the Queen as Head of State, controlled the key administrative institutions and remained resolutely determined to maintain the political union with the rest of the UK; while the Catholic minority, some of whom were "nationalists", sought at least civil rights and equality of opportunity. Both held very strong religious views, reflected in their respective approaches to associated matters such as abortion, and they had perhaps the highest rate of church attendance in Europe.

The religious and cultural differences had survived relatively intact for the previous four or more centuries, during which the communities had seen to it that their members were for the most part born, christened, married, lived and eventually buried within their respective religious boundaries. Protestant and Catholic communities were not just theologically separated but for generations had found ways to reinforce the schisms of Christianity through institutional arrangements in education, housing, socialising and burial, which coalesced to constitute and maintain the "integrity of their quarrel".[38] Each community looked over its shoulder for cultural affinity with the adjacent jurisdictions of England and Ireland, respectively, taking their cultural cues from those sources while resolutely declining to share in those of actual neighbours of a different faith, and publicly flaunting the symbols, flags and icons that exacerbated their separateness.[39] Like other religious/ethnic confrontations, this one had prominent firebrand religious leaders who conflated religion and politics, revelled in historic victories and grievances, and appealed to their respective ethnic centres outside the jurisdiction for support.

Catholics, a minority within the jurisdiction but part of the religious majority on the island, largely identified with the Republic of

---

[37] Northern Ireland, an artificial political entity, was established under the Government of Ireland Act 1920 by shearing off the three largely nationalist counties of the province of Ulster to create a shrunken jurisdiction of six counties in which Protestants, with their natural fealty to England, would be assured of an overall and continuing electoral majority.

[38] See Churchill, W., address to Parliament, Westminster, 1920.

[39] See e.g. Mitchell, C., *Religion, Identity and Politics in Northern Ireland: Boundaries of Belonging and Belief*, London, Routledge, 2005.

Ireland,[40] its religion, the Irish language, sport, dance and music, and with extended clan and family networks across the island that had survived for many generations. For Protestants, the position was reversed, and for centuries this minority on the island had identified with England, its politics, values and cultural attributes, and had nurtured links with English family members. Both adhered to their respective competing religious traditions and continued to generate a mutual cultural antipathy. By the late 1960s, the poor socio-economic climate, which adversely affected Catholics and had long necessitated a disproportionate rate of emigration, combined with a change in the UK funding of university places that allowed admission to a sizeable cohort of students from poorer families (mainly Catholic in Northern Ireland), against a background of media attention given to the civil rights movement in the USA, increased Catholic frustration to the point where it tipped the balance in the strained tension between communities in Northern Ireland.

Alienation of Catholics

From the time of the English colonisation of the province of Ulster by Protestant settlers in the seventeenth century, the Catholic population in Northern Ireland had remained politically, socially and economically subjugated. By the 1960s, the 60/40 population imbalance that had long favoured Protestants was slowly slipping towards 55/45 but the subordinate socio-economic position of Catholics remained stubbornly unchanged. Protestant hegemony continued to be exercised through: the political system, with its gerrymandered electoral wards and a rule that restricted voting in local elections to ratepayers, which disenfranchised many Catholics; the police force, which was armed and was almost exclusively Protestant; the education system, which ensured that State-controlled schools were exclusively Protestant; the allocation of social housing, which was blatantly biased against Catholic families; and denial of Catholic access to employment in the main shipbuilding, engineering and manufacturing plants. The annual triumphalist marches of the Orange Order – established centuries ago to promote Protestant ideals and to oppose the ascendancy of Roman Catholicism – in Catholic residential areas reinforced the Catholic sense of oppression.

The discrimination was religious, in that it was directed by one religious community against another, but it was politically motivated and structural

---

[40] This affinity was politically strengthened by claims in Articles 2 and 3 of the Irish Constitution to sovereignty over the entire island of Ireland.

in its social effect. This was a sectarian context that imprinted two quite separate sets of identity, each a product of religiously determined social conditioning, but one oppressing the other. Although the relative socio-economic disadvantages were in the main borne by the poorer Catholic families – many Catholics and Protestants continued to live in religiously homogenous communities, and numerous middle-class neighborhoods were religiously mixed – they constituted a sizeable proportion of the total population, and by the late 1960s they had begun to see parallels between their situation and the apartheid system in South Africa and to identify with those such as Martin Luther King who were successfully campaigning for civil rights in the USA.

By 1968, the alienation of Catholics and their Church from Protestants and the latter's control of social institutions gave rise to increased Catholic protest, initially in demand of civil rights but, in the face of harsh measures by police and para-military forces, eventually calling for Irish nationalism, as a minority of Catholics resorted to violence against the State. The IRA,[41] with financial aid from a sympathetic Irish diaspora, together with volunteers and weapons from across the Irish border, embarked upon a 30-year guerilla war against the police force, their para-military supporters and the British army, which theoretically had been brought in to restore order but in practice engaged directly and almost exclusively with Irish nationalists. The intervention of that army was initially welcomed by Catholics as evidence of British willingness to ensure their protection, but as it assumed a more partisan role it became viewed by many, who were otherwise opposed to the IRA, as facilitating a return to colonial rule. The ensuing long period of civil unrest saw atrocities committed by many different factions – not just in Northern Ireland but also in England, the Republic of Ireland and elsewhere in Europe – as the confrontation narrowed to focus on the nationalist aspirations of a minority of Catholics in Northern Ireland.

Contemporary Affirmation of Identity

The Northern Ireland peace process was a protracted affair, lurching from one crisis to another. It included important milestones such as the Anglo-Irish Agreement in 1985 and the Downing Street Declaration in 1993,

---

[41] A para-military organisation dedicated to ending English rule in Ireland and re-unifying the island as an independent republic, the Irish Republican Army (IRA) in its various factions (mainly "Officials", "Provisionals" and "INLA") led a prolonged armed insurrection in Northern Ireland from 1970 to approximately 1994.

before politically concluding with the Belfast "Good Friday" Agreement in 1998. That settlement was signed by the main political parties involved and then approved in referendums by a majority of both communities in Northern Ireland and by citizens of the Republic of Ireland. In practice, peace was not assured until the IRA stood down and de-commissioned its weapons in 2005, followed in 2007 by full implementation of the Assembly, which provided a power-sharing administration of devolved government for the Catholic and Protestant communities.

Strategically, by locking in all interested parties, crucially including the UK and Irish governments, the settlement gave a comprehensive assurance that the separate religious/cultural identities of both Northern Ireland communities would be given long-term recognition and protection. It was an assurance that gained considerably from the active involvement and scrutiny of the US president and from international monitoring more generally. Removing the power to determine matters from the combatants and imposing instead wider terms of reference that provided guarantees in return for co-operative partnership, subject to external vetting, prepared the ground for the regional administration provided by the Assembly.[42]

While securing the political framework was vital, the application of equality and non-discrimination legislation has also been very significant in terms of identity affirmation. Although religious discrimination in employment has been illegal since 1976,[43] discrimination in provision of goods and services only became so in 1998; in keeping with all other equality legislation, it is now supervised by the Equality Commission for Northern Ireland, which functions alongside the Northern Ireland Human Rights Commission (NIHRC) as it addresses allegations of discrimination. Illustrations of the difficulties, but also of the assiduousness with which issues of equality and non-discrimination are now pursued, accompanied by caution in relation to the religious/cultural sensitivities of both communities, can be seen in court cases such as *In the Matter of an Application for Judicial Review by the NI Human Rights Commission*[44] and *Lee v. Ashers Baking Co Ltd and Ors.*[45] The first dealt with the right to

---

[42] See further Brewer, J. D., *Religion, Civil Society and Peace in Northern Ireland*, Oxford, Oxford University Press, 2011.

[43] The anti-discrimination legislation included: the Prevention of Incitement to Hatred Act (Northern Ireland) 1970, creating the offence of provoking hatred on grounds that included religious belief; the Fair Employment (Northern Ireland) Act 1976, prohibiting direct discrimination on religious grounds; and the Fair Employment (Northern Ireland) Act 1989, which extended the prohibition to indirect discrimination.

[44] [2015] NIQB 96.   [45] [2015] NICty 2.

abortion as governed by the Abortion Act 1967 and the Offences Against the Person Act 1861, the practical effects of which meant that medical staff carrying out abortions could be jailed unless the life of the woman concerned was directly under threat or there would be lasting, long-term negative effects on her mental or physical health from continuing with her pregnancy. The second concerned Christian defendants, owners of a bakery, who were alleged to have directly discriminated against their would-be customers by refusing to bake a cake which had printed on it a picture of Bert and Ernie from Sesame Street and the slogan "Support Gay Marriage". The cases triggered the religious beliefs of both communities, generated public controversy and attracted much media attention, but were judicially resolved by referencing the protagonists to the secular requirements of national and international law. The government's response to such evidence of an abiding social rift along religious/cultural lines was to introduce the Northern Ireland Freedom of Conscience Amendment Bill 2015, intended to provide widespread opt outs from equality legislation for religious entities. This has been resisted by the Equality Commission, which argues that the introduction of the proposed amendments would significantly weaken legal protection against discrimination for those accessing goods, facilities and services – particularly for members of the LGBT community – while also being inconsistent with equality law across the rest of the UK. Essentially, while the parties in the centuries-long religious/cultural standoff are to be guaranteed the right to maintain and manifest their respective beliefs, any issues between them will in future be exposed to and resolved in accordance with secular benchmarks as embedded in national and international law.

Implications for Religious Discrimination and Cultural Context

Religious discrimination provided a trigger for the instances of persecution described in this section, but other factors, including ethnicity, territory, politics and power, also played their part. Cultural context was particularly significant. Indeed, in each case, without taking that dimension into account, it would be impossible to fully appreciate the why, what and when of the experience or to grasp its impact and weigh the nature and extent of its consequences. Issues of cultural identity, abuse of power, alienation and, ultimately, of cultural affirmation as recognised and protected by an authority outside the protagonists' struggle but respected by them, were of central importance. In each instance, the variant of religious discrimination provided a setting for widening the definition of that term and has illuminated particular aspects of it.

Anti-Semitism

The Holocaust transformed the meaning of what could constitute "anti-Semitism". In doing so, it also reinterpreted "religious discrimination".

This transformation was reinforced inexorably by the establishment of the State of Israel. The perpetrator/victim dynamic that underpinned religious discrimination against the Jews for many centuries – grounding, perhaps, studies on the "psychology of victimhood" – was thereby radically readjusted. Rooting the Jewish cultural heritage within geographical boundaries, protected by one of the world's most modern and powerful armed forces, and one with nuclear capacity, has served to tangibly conflate religious/cultural/ethnic identities, allowed Jews an opportunity to escape the forced nomadic/assimilationist choice of their history and given them an insurance policy in the event of any repetition of discrimination's worst effects. As an inevitable corollary, the iconic significance of the State of Israel presents a target that can attract regional and international religious/cultural discrimination. Moreover, the price for State foreign policy may be paid by Jews resident within and outside Israel who are victimised in proxy retribution for its incursions into Palestine and for its strategic alliance with Western powers, particularly the USA.

Fulfilling the Zionist vision has also literally brought home, poignantly and ironically, an in-built quandary for the Jewish identity: the unity of its many cultural and religious parts. The State now provides a common homeland for individuals, families and communities that hitherto had been embedded in very different cultural settings across the world, some for many generations. It has been a considerable and ongoing challenge to build a nation and collective sense of shared civic engagement from refugees fleeing conflict in Sudan, Eritrea, Syria and elsewhere, voluntary immigrants from Russia, the USA and other developed nations and second and third generations of rich and poor Israelites. Judaism has also been exposed to considerable pressure for reform and reinterpretation. To the many problems of language and multi-culturalism have been added the complexities of hard-held distinctions between the orthodox, conservative, reform and other branches of Judaism. These divisions can provoke a form of internal religious discrimination, echoed by that to be found at times between the citizens of Israel and the Jewish diaspora. The differences and tensions between Judaism's traditional or conservative branches and those which have become more liberal are now very real and are reflected in Jewish law.

Religious discrimination in a cultural context has been altered by the emergence of the State of Israel. Fifty years on, an argument can be heard that Jews are sometimes tempted to engage in reverse discrimination: that many Jews – whether or not they are citizens of Israel – interpret any criticism of the State as anti-Semitic; and that the authority of the State is used to deny citizenship rights to non-Jews resident within its jurisdiction or sphere of control. This argument points to the continued enlargement of the "settlements", the erasure of Palestine villages and the daily humiliation of Palestinian "guest workers" by Israeli armed forces as evidence of State-sponsored religious discrimination. It can be further argued that the risk of being labeled anti-Semitic has prevented any Western power from challenging Israel's domestic and foreign policies and forestalled effective international intervention in what has been allowed to become the intractable Israel/Palestine conflict.[46] Again, arguably, this in turn has permitted the continuation of regional instability, leaving space for Hamas and Hezbollah to acquire legitimacy and for Iran to obtain a pivotal position which possibly they would not otherwise have, and has probably provoked the growth and spread of Wahhabi fundamentalism from its roots in Saudi Arabia (see further Chapter 2). The possible links between Western acquiescence to a militant Jewish nation and Middle East support for the rise of militant Islam may have broad and worrying long-term implications for religious discrimination, but this is too complex a topic for this book.

Islamophobia

Defined at the end of the twentieth century as "an outlook or world-view involving an unfounded dread and dislike of Muslims, which results in practices of exclusion and discrimination",[47] Islamophobia has since been redefined by the atrocities of ISIS in a manner that is certain to taint relationships between Muslims and all others for most of the twenty-first.[48]

As the European Commission against Racism and Intolerance (ECRI) has pointed out, whether it takes the shape of daily forms of racism and discrimination or of more violent forms, Islamophobia is a violation of human rights and a threat to social cohesion.[49] The European

---

[46] See e.g. Shafir, G., *A Half Century of Occupation: Israel, Palestine, and the World's Most Intractable Conflict*, Berkeley, CA, University of California Press, 2017.

[47] See the Commission on British Muslims and Islamophobia, *Islamophobia: A Challenge for Us All*, London, The Runnymede Trust, 1996.

[48] Islamic militancy, of course, precedes the current ISIS crisis; efforts to establish a caliphate in the north Caucasus have seen Russian troops engaged in conflict with Islamic fundamentalists since the early years of this century.

[49] See the European Commission Against Racism and Intolerance at http://lib.ohchr.org/ HRBodies/UPR/Documents/session12/IS/CoE-ECRI-EuropeanCommissionAgainst-RacismIntolerance-eng.pdf.

Monitoring Centre on Racism and Xenophobia (EUMC) adds that "policy responses need to acknowledge that Muslim communities in general have experienced long-standing discrimination, whether direct or indirect, which has impacted on employment opportunities, education standards and social marginalisation. Policy responses need to react to the diversity of Muslim communities . . . "[50] While this is unquestionably true, such policy responses are now set to be more international and strategic in nature, and thus to influence if not govern domestic social interaction with Muslim communities.

In retrospect, for all developed nations, the Bosnian war and its aftermath provided the first visceral intimation of what Islamophobia in the heart of contemporary Western society might entail. Having endured the worst genocidal persecution in Europe since the Nazi era, a resurgent Islam has since been consolidating its ethno/religious identity within the protected geographic and political boundaries of Bosnia. One reaction to being pushed to the edge by sustained violent religious discrimination has been a retreat into a more trenchant and often aggressive assertion of Muslim identity. This was graphically demonstrated in the 9/11 atrocity, which brought Islamic fundamentalism onto the global stage,[51] was subsequently fuelled by successive wars in Muslim countries such as Afghanistan[52] and Iraq,[53] and became evident in the willingness of some Bosnians to accommodate ties with ISIS.[54] It is now unmistakably manifested in the jihad challenge presented by the latter to the rest of the world, not least to the identity of Islam.

Unlike Judaism and Christianity, Islam has not undergone any comparable process of reform or reinterpretation.[55] While by far the majority of Muslims choose to lead a peaceful life in co-operation with their non-Islamic neighbours, all nonetheless wholly and unquestioningly respect the doctrines set out in the Qur'an, as elaborated upon in the hadith and

---

[50] See the European Monitoring Centre on Racism and Xenophobia, *Muslims in the European Union – Discrimination and Islamophobia*, Vienna, EUMC, 2006 at p. 4.

[51] The attack on the twin towers in New York on 11 September 2001, in which some 3000 people died, was planned and executed by Islamic militants who were mostly linked to Saudi Arabia.

[52] From initial attacks by the USA and UK in 2001 until 2014.

[53] From initial US invasion in 2003 until 2011.

[54] See e.g. Mayer, W., "Sharia Villages: Bosnia's Islamic State Problem", *Der Spiegel*, 2016, at www.spiegel.de/international/europe/islamic-state-presence-in-bosnia-cause-for-concern-a-1085326.html#.

[55] See e.g. Ali, A. H., *Heretic: Why Islam Needs a Reformation Now*, New York, HarperCollins, 2015.

regulated by Shari'a law. This body of prescriptive injunctions shapes Muslim relationships and lifestyles in ways that not only inhibit integration within any liberal democratic society, but serve to alienate Muslims, and in so doing generates a predisposition to Islamophobia. Partly, this is to do with the power imbalance in Islamic family relationships, which seems inequitable and at variance with Western values: the patriarchical status of males; the separation of males and females and relative subordination of the latter; the pressure on females to hide their femininity, dress largely in black and appear humbled and subservient when in public; the recourse to practices such as arranged marriages, child brides and FGM; and the misogynist stress on family honour that results in the beatings and deaths of many girls and women. Partly, it results from the interaction of Muslim and other communities: the sexual harassment and abuse of young females in Western cities (Rotherham, Cologne, etc.) by predatory Muslim males; the high visibility and intrusiveness of Islamic religious practices within increasingly secular societies; and the apparent reluctance of many Muslims to make the concessions necessary to share in the civic life of their host communities. It can also be evident in the at times murderous relationships between the main schools or sects within Islam – Shia, Sunni and Ahmadiyya – which have given rise to bitter internal religious discrimination, resulting in wholesale massacres in the Middle East and many brutal murders in Western countries. The negative consequences of such interactions cause further alienation, prompting Muslims to look more inward towards an Islamic identity rather than to identify with their host nation and local community.

This identity issue is illustrated by the numbers of Muslim volunteers travelling to Iraq and Syria to join ISIS – not just from Muslim countries but also from all European countries, the USA, Canada, Australia and elsewhere – in order to become jihadists and die fighting against the forces of the same Western nations that, in many cases, have provided them and their families with homes and nationality. The determination to prioritise religious identity over nationality for the sole purpose of inflicting harm upon those of a different religion constitutes a lethal form of religious discrimination that strongly resonates with that of the late twentieth century.

Until the prescriptive rules of the Qur'an are moderated to take account of changes in cultural context, and Islam follows the route taken by Christianity to free itself from the mediaeval values and fears that shaped its foundational doctrines and instead become more relevant to evolving contemporary circumstances, it is difficult to see how Islamophobia can be defused.

The view that presently prevails in many developed Western nations is one of Islam as a political ideology rather than simply a religion. In that vein, a comparison is sometimes drawn between the current efforts of some Muslims to establish a caliphate and the past successful construction of the State of Israel in the Jewish historical homeland; however, arguably, while the latter was initiated as a safe haven for Jews escaping persecution, the former more closely resembles triumphalist empire-building. Any grounds for assuming similarity would seem to be negated by the manner and purpose of the ISIS onslaught: it has sought to ruthlessly purge all other religions and ethnic groups within its territorial boundaries; a harsh form of Shari'a law has been imposed upon all Muslims, without consultation and to the exclusion of any parallel independent political process; and it has exported its jihad extremism to inflict terror and destruction upon Western cities. The recent spate of brutal attacks in Europe and the USA by jihadists has greatly extended the Western/Islamic interface and leaves little doubt that Islamophobia will become a growing international phenomenon.

Christian Schism

The "troubles" in Northern Ireland demonstrated that religious discrimination within Christianity retains its mediaeval potential to ignite murderous violence. While it is generally accepted that this confrontation was at least compounded by ethnic, political and civil rights issues, it would be a mistake to underestimate the religious dimension.[56]

Any temptation to downplay the role of religion would have to account for the sustained leadership role of the Rev. Ian Paisley.[57] This Presbyterian minister, with his Old Testament biblical exhortations and vehement rejection of the Pope as "the Anti-Christ", was the most prominent politician of his time in Northern Ireland. As a founder member and elected party leader of the Democratic Unionist Party, he stood firmly for retaining the union between Northern Ireland and England and wholly renounced any suggestion of Irish nationalism. His brand of religious and

---

[56] See e.g. the Northern Ireland Society of Labour Lawyers, "Discrimination – Pride for Prejudice", August 1969, at http://cain.ulst.ac.uk/issues/discrimination/nisll.htm.

[57] The Rev. Ian Paisley (1926–2014) founded and led the fundamentalist Free Presbyterian Church of Ulster until 2008. He had a long political career, beginning in 1970 when he became MP for North Antrim. In 1971, he founded the Democratic Unionist Party, which he led for almost forty years. In 1979, he became Ulster's first elected Member of the European Parliament. Finally, in 2010, he was made a life peer, before retiring from politics in 2011.

political leadership was such that at one point his electoral mandate in Northern Ireland was greater than that of any other Member of Parliament in the House of Commons; that is, his staunch Protestant religious beliefs and his anti-Catholicism found such broad support that he was able to build the strongest constituency of any UK politician. This sectarian blending of religious and political beliefs enabled him to lead the Protestant community and galvanise followers into flagrantly discriminatory attacks upon Catholics and Irish nationalists. It also led him to champion political causes that aligned with his religious views. So, for example, he launched the "Save Ulster from Sodomy" campaign in 1977 in opposition to the government policy to introduce homosexual law reform and he opposed the use of contraceptives and abortion. He was consistently virulently anti-Catholic. Such theocratic leadership was more typical of the preferred model in the Middle East than in Europe in the late twentieth century.

However, the Rev. Ian Paisley was first and foremost a fundamentalist evangelical Christian; a powerful demagogue. It was his brand of Protestantism, and the rousing rhetoric with which he proclaimed its beliefs and denounced those of Catholics, which gave him political leadership. That leadership was primarily religious, if verging towards ideology: at various times he scorned English politicians, with whom he purported to be aligned, as papal sympathisers; his agenda deliberately blurred the Church/State boundary but was pursued only insofar as it served to strengthen his religious identity. The Free Presbyterian Church, which he founded in 1951, subsequently grew to have over 100 churches and extensions in Northern Ireland, England, Scotland, Wales, the Irish Republic, Australia, Canada, the USA, Germany, Jamaica and Spain, with missionaries in many other places; in recent years, sister Presbyteries have been founded in North America and Nepal. Among other basic tenets, an in-built element of religious discrimination is evident in the requirement that its members maintain a strict separation from "any church which has departed from the fundamental doctrines of the Word of God".[58]

The spread of this church, with its traditional Puritan approach to morality and lifestyle issues, can only serve to harden the battle lines in the culture wars that have proved so divisive in the USA and are now becoming a feature of society in most developed Western nations. In keeping with other, more strident religions, it is somewhat inward looking, encouraging members to demonstrate their allegiance to its values and community

----

[58] See further www.freepresbyterian.org.

rather than contribute to the interests of a wider society. The inevitable clash of religious values generated by this church, which constituted no small part of the "troubles" in Northern Ireland, should serve as a health and safety warning for civil society in the jurisdictions currently being considered.

Conclusion

Religious identity, involving a synthesis of religion and culture, is proving to be of increasing importance within and between nations. This can be particularly fraught where there are conflicts of interest between nations, communities or groups – for example, to do with territory or a difference in social status – leading to alienation and a consequent drive for recognition and equality on the part of a disadvantaged party. Where issues of religious identity are represented by proxy areas of social contention, such as abortion or homosexuality rights, there is a risk that this sublimation may be elevated to become a matter of acute contention as those involved seek to sharpen the differences between "us" and "them", prompting the alienated to seek a means for self-affirmation which may include resorting to violence or political extremism.

2

Religion, Culture and Religious Discrimination

Introduction

Religion is always culturally contextualised. The same religion may differ in its practices and values, if not its core beliefs, from country to country and within the same country over time, according to prevailing cultural norms. Probably also, it is the conflation of religion and culture that almost always is the target for religious discrimination. Beyond such broad generalisations, however, the inter-relationship of these three subjects becomes quite complicated. Some of the complexities are only too graphically illustrated in Edmund de Waal's study of his family's history:[1] Jews from the poorest shtetls of Eastern Europe were as cruelly discriminated against as their bank-owner co-religionists in Paris and Vienna; a non-gentile identity was sufficient to attract the most invidious and stringently undifferentiating form of religious persecution across a wide range of very different cultural contexts; and this led to, among other things, the fulfillment of Zionist aspirations in the fusion of culture and religion represented by the State of Israel. These and other aspects of the religion/culture relationship, together with the impact upon it of religious discrimination in its various forms, are explored in the following pages.

The chapter begins with an overview of the book's central subject: religion. It considers what, in the contemporary developed common law nations, now constitutes religion or religious-type beliefs, and how this is defined in law. It then examines culture, the variation in its interpretation, and its capacity to shape the social role of religion. It considers the significance of race, ethnicity, the religion/culture conflation and the interaction of equality and culture. Finally, it broadly explains the principles, definitions and grounds relating to religious discrimination, outlines the different forms this discrimination can take and describes how the law

---

[1] De Waal, E., *The Hare with Amber Eyes*, London, Chatto & Windus, 2011. See also Mendelsohn, D., *The Lost*, New York, Harper Perennial, 2008.

is applied. Attention is drawn to the tendency for such discrimination to be either refracted through a lengthening range of activities – including abortion, genetic editing and LGBT issues – which often serve as a proxy magnet for religious dissidents, or to be distilled into the concentrated vitriol of sectarianism. Some discussion focuses on the accurate targeting of discrimination, particularly as regards the blurred boundaries between ethnicity and religion. The chapter concludes with a brief consideration of the effects of religious discrimination, a matter pursued in greater depth in Chapter 3.

Religion

The question as to whether the set of beliefs adhered to by a person or group constitutes a "religion" has recently become an open one. Historically, there was little difficulty: each of the main institutional religions had for centuries been only too emphatic in proclaiming the doctrines, tenets and modes of worship that required the devotional attention of its respective body of adherents; imposing secular punishments on any "heretics" found to be in breach of same; outlawing atheism;[2] and, not infrequently, declaring war on those of other faiths, or none. Discrimination was traditionally promoted as a religious duty: each religion was equally certain that only its body of beliefs and values represented "the will of god", and as such must prevail over others. The traditional religions continue to be readily recognisable – although over the past century or so they have generated many subsidiaries and sects – but the rapid expansion of modern and post-modern quasi-religious entities has greatly compounded the theological landscape.

Religious fragmentation has been accompanied by a steady growth in secularism.[3] From at least the mid-nineteenth century, this has had a marginal if growing social profile, but to some it has evolved to become more "militant". All developed common law jurisdictions now have complex religious environments in which previously dominant institutional religions are losing ground to secularism; the traditional social role of religion is being eroded and fragmented by an ever-growing proliferation of new quasi-religions and belief systems; and fundamentalism, particularly from within Islam, is a growing threat.

[2] Atheism continues to be illegal in some countries, e.g. Indonesia.
[3] The term "secularism" was first coined by George Jacob Holyoake (1817–1906).

Religion, Beliefs and Sin

The range of religious groupings is lengthy, varied and probably inde-terminate. In some countries, the traditional religions are experiencing a modest revival due to the modernising efforts of a minority of adher-ents, while the growth of Islam relative to all other religions continues steadily. In many religions, there is a continuing process of fragmentation: the major ones are experiencing a number of subdivisions, with extrem-ists from Islamic and evangelical Christian backgrounds gaining adher-ents and prominence but causing more moderate adherents to abandon a religious belief capable of generating such exclusiveness. The Wahhabi branch of Sunni Islam,[4] for example, espouses a particularly virulent and fundamentalist interpretation of Islam (despising Jews and Shia Muslims, among others) which is expanding rapidly in many parts of the world. The concept of "sin", and its correlatives "heresy" and "apostasy", also play an interesting role in this context, as do the concepts of "pre-destination" and the "afterlife". However, it is the multiplying and mutating array of para-religious groups, each driven by a commitment to a singular social agenda or set of principles, that is most striking. This phenomenon con-stantly gives rise to issues in determining which groups may or may not fall within the legal definition of "religion".

Institutional Religions

Christianity, Judaism and Islam are among the oldest of the extant reli-gions; each is monotheistic, and has accompanying doctrines and ritu-als of worship. Other prominent religions with well-established histories include Buddhism, Hinduism and Sikhism; these tend to be non- or mul-titheistic, and rituals are of central importance. In addition, there are a large and fluctuating number of organisations with a varying quotient of religious characteristics, of which Mormonism, Scientology, Druze and Zoroastrianism are perhaps the most notable. Then, there are religious-type groupings that derive from and represent a particular ethnic culture, such as may be found among the Indigenous People of Australia, Canada and elsewhere. Many of these are of ancient origin, preceding Christianity, and merge theism with nature. They include distinctive and more modern entities, such as the Rastafarians.

---

[4] Wahhabism was founded by Muhammad ibn Abd al-Wahhab (1703–1792), a preacher and scholar whose protection by the House of Saud ensured that Wahhabism continued and continues to be rooted in Saudi Arabia.

The Concept of "Sin"

Adherents may occasionally suffer from the external pressures of religious discrimination, but that pressure exerted internally by their religion's strictures requiring compliance with its beliefs and practices is constant. The concept of "sin" is religion's most basic enforcing mechanism, backed up by a range of conduct designated as "profane" and "heinous", being both criminal and sinful, including apostasy,[5] heresy[6] and blasphemy.[7] These have traditionally played a central role in Christianity, Judaism and Islam, among other religions. Their interpretation and associated modes of punishment are prone to variation between religions and, usually, within the same religion over time. Arguably, the disputes that now make up the culture wars can also be seen as rooted in "sin" – refracted through contemporary morality issues.

In general, conduct regarded as sinful is not confined by any religion to transgression of its beliefs: it extends to most behaviour that would be construed as breaching secular laws or which, in ethical or morality terms, could be viewed as "bad"; and it is held to encompass related thoughts and preparations. In theocratic societies – and in those pockets of modern democracies where theocratic social groups are accommodated – there is a synergy between the concepts of "sin" and "crime". Islam is singular in that its basic beliefs and corresponding sins, as declared in the Qur'an in the seventh century and regarded by Muslims as initially stated, largely continue to shape the cultural norms of Muslim communities – whether in Asia and the Middle East or in the hearts of Western cities. While Christianity and the developed nations have long since moderated their approach to profanity, for example, Islam continues to regard it as a sin. Much of the conduct traditionally designated as sinful in the Qur'an – such as adultery and homosexuality – is so regarded today. The latter attracts such opprobrium that for many Muslims – and for some evangelical Christians – sin and crime are so conflated as to result in homophobia, which is wholly irreconcilable with the requirements of human rights and equality that now govern the social norms of modern democracies.

In the developed Western nations, the growth of democracy and secularism has mostly broken the traditional theocratic ties that ensured State

---

[5] Apostasy occurs when someone who has been religious explicitly renounces their adherence to their religion and denies its validity.

[6] Heresy occurs when someone pronounces beliefs or principles that are at variance with those of the prevailing religion.

[7] Blasphemy occurs when someone insults or shows contempt or lack of reverence for a religion or for any of its beliefs or practices.

punishment for religion's sins:[8] conduct deemed purely sinful is now a matter to be addressed within the relevant religion. However, for some Muslims in such nations, and for many in Islamic countries, it is accepted that the sinful conduct of those deemed to be infidels, heretics, apostates or blasphemers continues to merit the harshest punishment. This virtually mandates religious discrimination by such believers towards all those of other faiths, or of none, and even towards those who share the same faith but are judged to have inadequately demonstrated their commitment to supposedly shared core religious beliefs – as illustrated by the summer 2016 ISIS bombs in Baghdad, Istanbul and the sacred Islamic city of Medina. It also maintains a discriminatory regime of role allocation within the family and seriously obstructs harmonious multi-cultural relationships.

Pre-Destination and the Afterlife

The theological doctrine that God ordains everything and that no one has the free will necessary to change the course of events in this life, or to alter their trajectory towards heaven or hell in the next, is one that varies between religions. It is most commonly associated with a Calvinist strain of Protestantism, but is rooted in Roman Catholicism, subject to the caveat that "salvation" remains possible for the individual who amends for sins through contrition, sacrifice and dedicated belief.

The fact that religions differ as regards whether or not sinners can atone for their transgressions and consequently be assured of eternal salvation has important implications for religious discrimination and cultural context. Is it the sin or the sinner that must be rejected? If the former, then atonement is possible. Christianity generally favours atonement: Catholics, by way of prayer and sacraments; Protestants, by making amends, for example by proselytising others and facilitating their conversion. In contrast, the atonement prospects for Muslims are few: little short of martyrdom in defence of Islam will guarantee the forgiveness of sins. This belief probably incentivises those who attack – physically or by means of religious discrimination – adherents of other religions deemed to be infidels and thus an insult to Islam, and may well contribute to the rigour with which the Muslim community polices the conduct of its members.

New Religions, Beliefs and Philosophies

The modern spin-offs from core religions are innumerable: all accommodate an ever-growing number of splinter groups and sects. Christianity, initially fractured into its Roman Catholic, Orthodox and Protestant

---

[8] Blasphemy being an exception, as it is still retained on some statute books.

branches, has since embraced many distinct bodies, including Methodists, Baptists, Plymouth Brethren, Lutherans, Quakers, Latter Day Saints, Jehovaha's Witnesses and the Christian Reformed Church. Protestantism alone comprises some 33 000 different denominations.[9] Hinduism includes Vaishnavism, Shaivism and Shaktism, while the mutual estrangement between Sunni and Shia in Iraq is rapidly making this Islamic schism a threat to world peace. Some groups, such as evangelical Christian churches and strains of Islam, have so refined their beliefs or reduced them to fundamentalist precepts that they face rejection by their parent religion; in others, adherents have developed individual interpretations of their religion's basic beliefs.

In addition to theistic religions, there is a swathe of those such as the Baha'i, Krishna Conciousness and Falun Gong with a spiritualist dimension, and many others, including the Freemasons, that espouse philosophical principles. These differ from religion by not having a theistic component and by being less reliant upon the supernatural. They share with religion the fact that the belief of adherents rests on conviction and commitment to a set of principles that informs their world view. The range of organisations acquiring legal status as a "religion" through registration with a statutory regulatory body has now extended beyond such groups as Scientology to include those with a spiritualist or faith-healing focus, such as Druids. There are also various forms of paganism, and a variety of cults which have little in common with religion other than commitment to a central belief.

The Law and Religion/Beliefs

While the law avoids being drawn into an assessment of the merits or otherwise of any particular religion or belief, it looks for substantive corroborating evidence of what it is that a putative religion's adherents collectively believe and the form and manner in which they express their beliefs. To qualify as a religion or system of beliefs, the law requires evidence of views that are "more than mere opinions or deeply held feelings" but involve "a holding of spiritual or philosophical convictions which have an identifiable formal content" and which have "a certain level of cogency, seriousness, cohesion and importance".[10] The existence of a body of

[9] Barrett, D. B., Kurian, G. T. and Johnson, T. M., *World Christian Encyclopedia: A Comparative Survey of Churches and Religions in the Modern World*, 2nd edn, New York, Oxford University Press, 2001.

[10] See Article 13 of the European Directive on Race (2000) and Resolution 16/18 (March 2011), which calls for UN Member States to combat "intolerance, negative stereotyping and

doctrines or principles upon which an organisation was founded can provide an important evidential source, as it would for any association. Attention may then turn to whether or not an adherent does in fact understand and wholly subscribe to those beliefs, is genuinely committed to pursuing them and is doing so through activities that are designed for and are likely to progress the organisation's particular doctrines or principles. In recent decades, this has become considerably more complicated. Religious belief, traditionally viewed as simply a derivative of religion, can no longer be seen in that light. In Protestantism, for example, the doctrine of *sola scriptura* (by scripture alone) declared the Bible to be the sole authority for Christian faith and practice, as was the Qur'an for Muslims. Once the "religion" was established, the prescriptive nature of the associated "beliefs" could be safely assumed and ascribed to an avowed adherent. In law, this assumption has become more than questionable.

Religious adherents now have the legal (if not the theological) right to interpret their religion as they see fit: the new faiths and forms of belief provide limitless opportunities for individuals to find their own religion, construe the associated beliefs and change these as their understanding develops or diminishes, provided that any such interpretation relates to a significant and substantive belief, is cogent, is authentically held and is not inappropriate in a democratic society.

Theism

The basic indices traditionally employed by the judiciary to differentiate a religious entity from all others have been a belief in a "Supreme Being" and a shared commitment to faith and worship; the House of Lords ruling that the first was of paramount importance has been followed in other common law jurisdictions.[11] Gradually, religion became redefined to include multi-theism and, ultimately, to transcend the need for theistic beliefs. As has been said, "the atheist, the agnostic, and the sceptic are as much entitled to freedom to hold and manifest their beliefs as the theist".[12]

Doctrines, Tenets, etc.

A body of core doctrines, creeds or tenets forms the essence of a religion: they serve to affirm the beliefs that commit and bind the members as

---

stigmatization of, religion or belief". See also *Leela Förderkreis e.V. and Others* v. *Germany*, no. 58911/00, s.80 (6 November 2008).

[11] *Bowman* v. *Secular Society* [1917] AC 406.

[12] *R (Williamson)* v. *Secretary of State for Education and Employment* [2005] 2 AC 246, per Nicholls LJ.

adherents of a particular religion and to differentiate that religion from all others. However, while Lord Halsbury's observation that "speaking generally, one would say that the identity of a religious community described as a Church must consist in the unity of its doctrines"[13] remains accurate in relation to the more traditional religions, it is less so as regards the many new bodies adhering to philosophical or other belief systems.

The doctrines of a religion exist not just as an inert public document – a record of how and why it was established – but also as a continuing source of inspiration, guidance and direction for its members, to be manifested in normal, everyday life (in employment, education, service provision, etc.).[14] They also, of course, are intended to impose constraints upon an individual's freedom of choice: consideration of differing moral and ethical permutations is not available to an adherent; the route to be taken is prescribed. This conviction that, for "believers", all conduct must conform to their beliefs is a very potent force, which, as has been argued, not unreasonably, by Jurgen Habermas and others, is capable of divisive social and political consequences.[15]

Collective and Subjective Worship

The "two essential attributes of religion are faith and worship: faith in a god and worship of that god".[16] Worship has been held to have at least some of the following characteristics: submission to the object worshipped, veneration of that object, praise, thanksgiving, prayer or intercession, and the collective assembly of adherents in a church, or other building designated for that purpose, in order to participate in prayerful rituals. However, the broadening spectrum of religions, sects and belief systems has diluted the previous legal requirement for the beliefs of such a body to be corroborated by a body of doctrines, while the manifestation of one's religion or belief is simply required to take the form of worship, teaching, practice and observance.[17] A designated place of worship may no longer be necessary.

---

[13] *Free Church of Scotland* v. *Overtoun* [1904] AC 515, HL (Sc), per Lord Halsbury LC at pp. 612–613.

[14] Wolterstorff, N., "The Role of Religion in Decision and Discussion of Political Issues" in Audi, R. and Wolterstorff, N., *Religion in the Public Square: The Place of Religious Convictions in Political Debate*, New York, Rowman & Littlefield, 1997.

[15] Habermas, J., "Religion in the Public Sphere", *European Journal of Philosophy*, 2006, vol. 14:1, pp. 1–25.

[16] *Re South Place Ethical Society, Barralet* v. *Attorney General* [1980] 1 WLR 1565, (1980) 124 SJ 774, [1980] 3 All ER 918, per Dillon J at p. 924.

[17] See *Cha'are Shalom Ve Tsedek* v. *France* [GC], no. 27417/95, s.73, ECHR 2000-VII.

Moreover, whereas belonging to a recognised religion – whether by birth, marriage or conversion – and attendance at the appropriate place of worship was traditionally quite enough to substantiate a claim of religious adherence, this may no longer be sufficient in law and, indeed, may not reflect reality. Courts and regulators have steadily moved their focus from the collective to the individual experience: away from examining institutional structures, modes of worship, and doctrines and tenets as indicators for defining an "organised religion", and towards looking at the authenticity of an individual's subjective interpretation and experience of that religion.[18] This may well correspond with the contemporary religious experience of many adherents, who have seemingly retreated from the need to express their faith in solidarity with family and community by joining with them in a commitment to traditional doctrine and public worship, and instead find private prayerful activity to be sufficient. As will become clear, in all relevant common law jurisdictions, the onus now rests on the entity concerned, whether an organisation or an individual, to demonstrate that their convictions are sincerely held and constitute a religion or equivalent belief system, as opposed to membership of just another association or special interest group or little more than a personal hobby or form of therapy.

Religious Adherence

Traditionally, and still most usually, religious adherence is demonstrated by private prayer or participation in collective worship. It is also customarily expressed in the form of charitable work on behalf of the sick, elderly or infirm, and extends to include religious/cultural practices – such as the Islamic *mahr* agreement ("bride price" or dowry, payable to the wife on divorce).

It can be difficult to judge from the nature of some conduct whether it is necessarily causally and substantively related to, and adequately reflective of, something that falls within a definition of "religion" or "belief". Instead, it may be a facile posture, a hollow pretence or an induced response. It may be only too obvious that an expression of religious adherence, such as many of the punishments meted out by ISIS – purportedly in furtherance of Shari'a law – is simply criminal, and some may indeed constitute a crime against humanity. Such conduct could also: be related but unintended or peripheral; emanate from something else entirely, such as the idiosyncratic

---

[18] See Edge, P. W., "Determining Religion in English Courts", *Oxford Journal of Law and Religion*, Jan 2012.

convictions of an individual or minority group; or be fervently held but random, opportunistic or fleetingly transient in nature.

Adherents often view proselytism – or spreading the word and encouraging others to commit/convert to a particular religion – as an aspect of their religious duty. Questions can be raised as to why an activity that promotes competitiveness between religious organisations and contributes to social divisiveness should be condoned. Nonetheless, where authentic and compliant with the law of the land, an adherent's conduct in giving effect to their religious beliefs in this way is assured of protection in law. It becomes more complicated when the practice is only tenuously related to the religion or belief, intrudes into the rights of others, and/or is at variance with neutral laws of general application. In such circumstances, an adherent's rights are subject to legal limitations.

Culture

Religion has traditionally been the defining characteristic of a culture: probably even more so than language or stage of economic development. From the Aztecs to the Amish to the Arab Emirates, it has demonstrated a capacity to differentiate cultural groups, dominate the life of adherents, weld solidarity among the like-minded and require deference from others.

Culture in the Common Law Nations

The imperial blueprint that transferred with the British armed forces to all jurisdictions presently being considered is most usually thought of in terms of administrative structure. This comprised a fairly uniform system of parliamentary government, of common law and judiciary, of institutional machinery, language and customs that is still a recognisable feature of the bonds that unify this most developed group within the commonwealth of nations.[19] A conspicuous aspect of that shared cultural infrastructure has been the mosaic of churches, mainly Catholic and Protestant, that have spread much the same web of parishes, ministers/priests and parishioners across many lands. These continue to be highly visible reminders of the shared Christianity that forms the underpinning foundations of the common law cultural legacy.

Architecture, however, is only the tip of a religious iceberg. What remains largely unseen but represents the bulk of that Christian heritage

---

[19] Ireland, in fact, is not among the fifty-two countries that now constitute the commonwealth.

is: the body of values, ethics and principles, strained from the gospels and scriptures, ingrained and passed on from one generation to the next, that has shaped a communal sense of right and wrong; a felt duty to demonstrate Christianity not just in ritual acts of worship, but also through public good works; the law of charity,[20] which defined altruism and governed charitable action on behalf of neighbours and community; perhaps also attitudes of acceptance towards the status quo; and the freedom to privately pray and to make personal commitments of faith and atonement. This common morality imprinted on the nations concerned, over the centuries, a shared understanding of what constitutes a family, of actions that are sinful or virtuous.[21] As Lord Finlay LC commented in *Bowman* v. *Secular Society Ltd*, when reflecting on previous centuries of caselaw:[22]

> It has been repeatedly laid down by the Courts that Christianity is part of the law of the land, and it is the fact that our civil polity is to a large extent based upon the Christian religion. This is notably so with regard to the law of marriage and the law affecting the family.[23]

This has been particularly evident with regard to Christian dogma and its core moral imperatives associated with the "Nazarene family"[24] model, which included: monogamous, heterosexual marriage for life; the sanctity of marriage to the exclusion of non-marital sex, any children thereof, and unmarried partnerships; the prohibition of abortion; and the rejection of a Darwinian approach to the meaning of "life". It has also, more mundanely, provided an inter-generational profanity vernacular. Christian morality permeates archives of legislation, particularly family law; is infused throughout institutions, schools, workplaces and health and social care systems; and deeply affects all citizens – whether or not they are religious adherents.[25] It is clearly evident in centuries of cultural output – in

---

[20] The Statute of Charitable Uses 1601 (43 Eliz. 1, c.4) provided four centuries of shared charity law jurisprudence throughout the common law jurisdictions.

[21] A long catalogue of cases beginning with *De Costa* v. *De Paz* (1754) 2 Swans 487, Chancery, including *Lawrence* v. *Smith, Murray* v. *Benbow* (1822) The Times 2 Feb. 1822, *Briggs* v. *Hartley* (1850) 19 L. J. (Ch.) 416, and finally *Pare* v. *Clegg* (1861) 29 Beav 589, 54 ER 756 established that "the Courts will not help in the promotion of objects contrary to the Christian religion".

[22] Op. cit.

[23] Ibid., citing *Briggs* v. *Hartley* (1850) 19 L. J. (Ch.) 416, *Cowan* v. *Milbourn* (1867) L. R. 2 Ex. 230, *De Costa* v. *De Paz* (1754) 2 Swanst, 487, and *In re Bedford Charity* (1819) 2 Swanst. 470, 527.

[24] A reference to the original Christian family unit in Nazareth, consisting of married parents and the child "of their marriage".

[25] Laws LJ acknowledged as much in *McFarlane* v. *Relate Avon Ltd* [2010] IRLR 872, 29 BHRC 249 when he observed that "the Judaeo-Christian tradition, stretching over many centuries,

literature, music, paintings and sculptures – and it provides the shared cultural umbrella under which the common law jurisdictions presently being considered must deal with contemporary forms of religious discrimination.

Ethnic Groups

Fraser LJ, in *Mandla* v. *Dowell Lee*, listed the following factors which he considered constituted an ethnic group identity:[26]

> it must, in my opinion, regard itself and be regarded by others, as a distinct community by virtue of certain characteristics... The conditions which appear to be essential are these: (1) a long shared history of which the group is conscious as distinguishing it from other groups, and the memory of which it keeps alive (2) a cultural tradition of its own, including family and social customs and manners, often but not necessarily associated with religious observance. In addition to these two essential characteristics the following characteristics are, in my opinion, relevant: (3) either a common geographical origin, or descent from a small number of common ancestors; (4) a common language, not necessarily peculiar to the group; (5) a common literature peculiar to the group; (6) a common religion different from that of neighbouring groups or from the general community surrounding it; (7) being a minority or being an oppressed or a dominant group within a larger community, for example a conquered people

Rastafarians, Jews and Sikhs could be fairly viewed as exemplars of the many that conform to such a depiction. While the majority of its members will have been born into an ethnic group and have had its distinguishing characteristics duly ascribed to them, a few will have married into it or otherwise volunteered their membership. Ethnic group identity has usually been specific to a race and location, and, whether hereditary or voluntarily assumed, membership most often mandated adherence to the group's religion.

Cults

As the name suggests, the "cult" is a narrower and blunter version of "culture". Contemporary social life would seem conducive to the forming of closed insular associations with a restricted membership and charismatic leadership dedicated to a fixed set of ideals. Cults are characterised

---

has no doubt exerted a profound influence upon the judgment of lawmakers as to the objective merits of this or that social policy" at para. 23.

[26] *Mandla (Sewa Singh) and another* v. *Dowell Lee and others* [1983] 2 AC 548 at para. 562D–H.

by a membership that chooses to "opt in", by collective adherence to a system of quasi-religious beliefs, and by the psychological pressures that constrain members from "opting out". Their beliefs, together with members' goals and lifestyles, may constitute a valid form of culture, but cults tend to be in opposition to mainstream social norms, often have a pronounced political dimension and consequently detract from the consensus necessary for civil society. The Branch Davidians, for example, many of whose members died in an armed confrontation with State authorities in Waco, Texas in 1993, was a self-proclaimed but socially isolated religious organisation. The line to be drawn between cults and other small special interest groups with religious or philosophical leanings has become uncertain.

Religion and Culture

Traditionally, differences in "culture" have often been associated with corresponding distinctions of a racial (e.g. white Caucasian or Asian) or ethnic (e.g. the Punjabi in India or the Māori in New Zealand) nature. There may have been a time when a specific religion or belief system, being an aspect of culture, could be neatly correlated with such distinctions (e.g. Catholicism with the Irish, Shintoism with the Japanese, etc.), but that time has largely passed. Religion, as the defining hallmark of a nation's culture, would seem to have little future, at least in modern democratic States.

The unifying role of religion and religious organisations, which traditionally played such a crucial part in bringing coherence to nation states, has become greatly diluted. To some extent, this has been due to the fading authority of the family, extended family and clan: the implicit power of the group, to perpetuate the inter-generational beliefs and loyalties of those born within it, dissolved as families became more nuclear and drifted in search of employment and other opportunities. Perhaps also, the increasing role of the professional has played a part: problem solving is no longer a group responsibility, but has largely been franchised out to the safe anonymity of the detached professional; although, for some communities – notably Jews and Muslims – the continuing authority of their legal system mitigates the tendency to seek secular solutions to problems traditionally defined as religious. Globalisation has also clearly played its part. While some self-perpetuating ethnic groups continue as distinct entities, with characteristics that may to some degree include a shared religion or belief system, they all now also make room for those of other religions/beliefs and those of none: atheism, in itself, not constituting a denial of ethnic group identity.

Conflating Religion and Ethnicity

The modern complex entanglement of religion, ethnicity and culture can often give rise to a confused sense of identity for communities, groups and individuals. There is a tendency to conflate religion and ethnicity: ethnic groups such as Rastafarians come to mind. In that context, a person's ethno-religious identity is then determined not by a system of religious beliefs or practices, to which they may or may not adhere, but by who their parents and family are and how they are perceived, approached and treated by others, regardless of their own wishes and preferences. Weller has recognised this in his reference to "belonging without believing".[27] In fact, however, while some religions, such as Sikhism and Hinduism, continue to be deeply rooted in certain ethnic groups, others are less bounded: Islam and Buddhism are inherently multi-ethnic; many Christian Churches have racially mixed or predominately black congregations; some forms of Christianity are specifically associated with African or African Caribbean cultures; and today's Islamists can be yesterday's white Christians. In addition, the developed common law nations all contain examples of ethnic groups – Sikhs, Muslims, Jews and Hindus – that have generated religiously fundamentalist sub-groups, contain atheists or lapsed adherents, and accommodate those who have converted and/or "married out". Any simplistic stereotyping of religion and ethnicity runs the risk of being inaccurate and misguided.

Religion, Sexuality and Culture

Religion and sexuality have an uneasy relationship. In some important respects, this is culturally conditioned, which means that in those respects, religious discrimination is similarly culturally tailored. Sexual orientation, a crucial and very personal aspect of identity, is subject to religious and cultural validation, which would traditionally have restricted approval to heterosexuality. For some religions more than others, sexuality is held to correspond to gender at birth and will thereafter govern identity, family and social roles, career opportunities, etc. In particular, for Muslims, whose gender defines their family and social roles, issues of sexuality are powerful cultural determinants of identity.

Same-Sex Relationships

Homosexuality and same-sex marriages are, in some Islamic countries, regarded as breaching qur'anic principles and therefore attract religious

---

[27] See Weller, P., *Time for a Change: Reconfiguring Religion, State and Society*, London, T&T Clark, at p. 9.

discrimination, which can lead to State-sanctioned lethal persecution. Most Muslim-majority countries, and the Organisation of Islamic Cooperation, have opposed moves to advance LGBT rights, and in 2013 the Pew Research Center found a widespread rejection of homosexuality in many such countries.[28] Other religions, too, have become polarised on issues of homosexuality: secular Jews are more than twice as accepting as their traditional or ultra-Orthodox counterparts; evangelicals are similarly more rejecting than other Christians. The strong correlation between a country's religiosity and its laws relating to homosexuality and gay marriage is naturally reflected in the cultural context of religious discrimination.

Transgender Matters

Again, there is a marked religious/cultural difference in the approach to transsexual and transgender issues. In the common law countries presently being considered, the advances in medicine that in recent years have eased the physical aspects of transition have been accompanied by a weight of psychosocial research on the personal questioning and trauma associated with it. In Islamic culture, while uncertainty in matters of gender identity is regarded sympathetically, homosexuality is generally not: the Qur'an explicitly condemns it. Medical intervention to re-align sexuality and gender is accordingly welcomed and widely sanctioned mainly as a "cure" for homosexuality, but also as a means of enabling and ensuring that the person concerned is returned to the gender-role conformity required by family and society. This accounts for the fact that the highest rate of transgender operations is carried out in Iran, where State-sponsored medical treatment is widely available. Ironically, perhaps, the sympathetic Islamic approach to transgender matters is a positive outcome of culture-based religious discrimination.

State, Religion and Culture

Where Church and State maintain a joint relationship – as with Protestantism in England, and to some extent with Catholicism in Ireland – the political nexus thus created provides a distinctive centre of gravity and a cultural ethos for that society which may well be perceived as alienating by those of other religious beliefs and those of none. Where they do not – most obviously in the USA – this separation facilitates and safeguards the

---

[28] See Pew Research Centre, *The Global Divide on Homosexuality*, at www.pewglobal.org/2013/06/04/the-global-divide-on-homosexuality/.

self-determined evolution of culturally diverse communities (see further Chapter 3).

Theocracy

When the authority of religion merges with that of the State to establish a theocracy – as most recently and aggressively demonstrated in the case of ISIS – culture is then religiously defined and firmly stamped with a distinctive set of beliefs, values and prescribed standards for social conduct. This was the case in England following the Reformation, to a considerable degree in Ireland with the establishment of the Republic and is currently true of countries such as Iran, Pakistan and Saudi Arabia. It is also evident in some ex-colonial African countries, which assimilated and continue to apply the religious precepts of the culture imposed by their colonial power.

However, as previously mentioned, the ever-lengthening litany of cultural issues facing modern democracies is also, often, a manifestation of religion by proxy. Moreover, the authority of religion can be imported as an alternative to civic norms. Ultra-Orthodox Jews, Muslims and evangelical Christians are among those who turn to fundamental religious principles and to their own religious tribunals rather than to statutory legal proceedings as their preferred way of addressing issues such as family planning or marriage breakdown.

Democracy, Religion and Culture

Historically, governments in the democratic nations of the common law world have sought to support and sustain national culture. Layers of statutes, accreted over the centuries, are saturated with assumptions specific to a nation's culture and religious heritage, invariably of a Christian nature. This was reinforced by legislating to: assert and protect emblems, icons, language and traditions; endorse related values and principles and develop relevant social policy; police boundaries; and safeguard national culture from being swamped or eroded by unplanned immigration. Governments have often also used their authority to grant aid and otherwise support organisations dedicated to cultural preservation. As these nations become rapidly more multi-cultural, government intervention that preferences the nation's cultural heritage has become more contentious: most particularly, when it aligns with that most emblematic aspect of culture – the traditional primary religion. Governments are, accordingly, being steadily pushed by national equality legislation and international human rights to adopt a more neutral stance: to treat all religions and beliefs equally. This inevitably has implications for religion generally, more so for primary religions, with consequent adverse effects on national cultural identity. As Trigg puts it: "do the requirements of equality and the demands of freedom, involve giving up the traditions that have made a people what they are?"[29]

If a nation's cultural identity is to be preserved then some government intervention must be directed towards salvaging its traditional primary religion and its ancillary social attributes, but this immediately runs into the problems presented by the principles of democracy, equality and multi-culturalism, which are further compounded when the spectrum of associated religious outreach facilities, such as faith schools, is brought into the equation. However, times may be changing. In the aftermath of the European 2015/16 migrant crisis, there would seem to be a readiness to question the merits of continuing a government policy of neutrality towards national cultural identity. Mendelsohn alludes to the same dilemma in *Waiting for the Barbarians*, in which he points out that in Cavafy's poem under that title not only were there no barbarians but "the poem may well be a parable about artistic growth – the unexpectedly complex and even, potentially, fruitful interaction between old cultures and new... there rarely are any real 'barbarians'. What others might see as decline and falls look, when seen from the bird's eye vantage point of history, more like shifts, adaptations, reorganisations."[30] The dilemma, or just the "waiting", does, however, concentrate the mind (see also Chapter 12). For present purposes, the parable forces a reflection on what exactly may be at risk. What are the cultural assets, so valued that their protection must be prioritised? What does religious discrimination threaten, whether in the form of the very real ISIS barbarians or of a more insidious domestic variety? An answer of sorts is revealed in the types of issues now being brought before the courts requiring adjudication as to whether or not respondents have done or not done something that can be construed as so threatening that State intervention is required to restore the integrity of religious/cultural identity.

Religious/Cultural Practices

Culture-specific practices that have religious connotations are many and varied. Food is a sensitive area: for Jews and Muslims, it must be kosher and halal compliant, respectively; while vegetarianism is mandatory for

---

[29] Trigg, R., *Equality, Freedom and Religion*, Oxford, Oxford University Press, 2012 at p. 125.
[30] See Mendelsohn, D., *Waiting for the Barbarians*, New York, New York Review of Books, 2012 at pp. x–xi.

most Buddhists. Clothing, most obviously, is religiously regulated for Muslim women, the wearing of jilbab, hijab and abayas being variously prescribed. The grooming of hair is a particular issue for Sikh males, as is the carrying of a kirpan. Medical treatment is frequently problematic: for Jehovah's Witnesses, the religious prohibition on the use of blood transfusions and other forms of blood-based medication frequently leads to court cases; for Jews and Muslims, issues connected with circumcision of male children can give rise to problems; while for many Christians, there are difficulties around elective abortion, genetic editing, etc. These and various other cultural/religiously determined practices can become a source of social tension and possible discrimination in settings such as hospitals, classrooms, school dining halls and mixed-gender public swimming pools.

Within the Christian nations, practices that may be acceptable for one generation can be rejected by those that follow: over a period of centuries, there was nothing incompatible between Christianity and, for example, slavery, colonialism, restricted suffrage, patriarchy, the criminal responsibility of children, the absence of "civil rights" or the death penalty – including hanging of children. Also, the religious/cultural practices of one social group can become an issue for another – even if they were formerly upheld by the latter, as in the traditional Christian approach to women.[31] So, the somewhat misogynistic values of some immigrants from Eastern religions/cultures now often clash with the recognition given to women's rights in host countries, such as when marriages are arranged or divorce proceedings instigated; FGM, a traditional African practice (in countries such as Ethiopia, Sudan and Mali),[32] is now increasingly common in the developed West, where it is generally both legally prohibited and largely overlooked; even the presence of a mosque or synagogue, or an Imam's public call to prayer, can be contentious in many common law jurisdictions.

The cultural dissonance experienced by immigrants from tribal and most often Muslim countries as they settle in the very differently structured societies of the developed common law nations, still coloured by

---

[31] See 1 Corinthians 14:33–34, 37: "As in all churches of the saints, the women should keep silence in the churches. For they are not permitted to speak, but should be subordinate, even as the law says ... what I am writing to you is a command of the Lord" (omission in original) and 1 Timothy 2:11–12: "Let a women learn in silence with all submissiveness. I permit no woman to teach or to have authority over men; she is to keep silent."

[32] For a first-hand account, see Ali, A. H., *Infidel*, London, Simon & Schuster, 2008, at pp. 32–33.

their pronounced Christian heritage, is naturally conducive to their coa-lescing in communities of their own kind. Consequently, as ghettoes of culture-specific but very different communities – such as Jews from East-ern Europe, Muslims from Somalia, Packistan and Kosovo, and Rastafari-ans from Jamaica – assert their independent identities within a developed Western society, which is itself undergoing change in response to the chal-lenge of secularism and proliferating new belief systems, so cultural disso-nance becomes endemic. It may be only a short step from cultural alien-ation within a host country to choosing to identify with the culture and politics of one's country of origin. There can be no doubt, after the suc-cession of atrocities by Islamic militants, that a particularly lethal form of religious discrimination has grown from the cultural dissonance that now characterises Western societies.

Conflating Culture and Religion

A conflation of religion and culture is most readily recognised in those countries where settled communities have lived within the same frame-work of borders and allegiances for many generations. It is also evident in circumstances where geographical boundaries are less relevant but elec-tive social mores are mutually binding, as, for example, when sexual ori-entation or sexual practices function as a proxy for religious belief (e.g., in the eyes of those who adhere to a more traditional strand of Christianity – but also often Islam, Judaism, Mormonism and other religious perspec-tives – in relation to matters such as abortion or LGBT issues). Mostly, its effects are positive, providing a basis for reciprocal trust and shared values that contribute to a building and sustaining a cohesive society.

Coherence and Dissonance

Some countries have been stamped with a particular religious ethos for so long and so pervasively – permeating customs, art, architecture and often language, dress and family names – that their cultural identity has become immersed in and emblematic of that religion. Italy, Ireland, Spain and the former Spanish colonies of South America are thus associated with Catholicism, and, similarly, England, Scotland and the Scandina-vian countries with Protestantism. In such countries, a single dominant religion has long been such a defining influence on culture that national identity and social cohesion would be severely impaired by a stripping out (if that were possible) of the religious component. It may be argued that in circumstances where the cultural identity of a nation has become indivisible from its association with a particular religion, there is justification for the State to permit its public institutions to reflect that mutuality and for it to preference the interests of related religious organisations against all others. Any such justification would be conditional upon appropriate measures being taken to safeguard the interests of minority religions, prevent their alienation and facilitate their sharing in the national identity.

By extension, this argument also holds good for those geographic regions within a country where the religious cultural identity of a particular group has long been dominant – such as the Amish in the counties of Lancaster and Chester in Pennsylvania or the Hutterites in western Canada. There is clearly a case to be made for protecting the cultural/religious identity of an entity which is authentic and self-supporting, gives security and nurture to successive generations and offers respect to its neighbours; Zionism and the State of Israel owe their existence to just such advocacy. The case is less readily made for hybrid jurisdictions, where territory and culture/religion are not in alignment. Centuries of war, conquest and colonialism have resulted in redrawn borders enclosing communities that live in an uneasy mutual relationship and with conflicting allegiances. Northern Ireland is one such culturally compromised entity.

Sectarianism

Religious discrimination has, in the past – the very recent past, in the case of Northern Ireland – led to sectarian violence.[33] This particular conflation of culture and religion is one with decidedly negative outcomes, as bigoted individuals or polarised communities become locked in mutual antagonism. Being more amenable to analysis on political terms, sectarianism is not examined in this book, except insofar as it serves as a reminder of how religious discrimination can deteriorate into serious social instability if left unchecked.

Culture Wars

Religious discrimination in contemporary Western society is still visible – often, overtly so – but in the main is now less likely to take the form of explicit denigration of others on religious grounds, and is instead manifested in more subtle ways. This tendency has been evident in recent

---

[33] See also the sectarian conflict in the Lebanon between Muslims, Druze and Catholics, among other factions – roughly coterminous with the Northern Ireland conflict – which resulted in the deaths of some 250 000.

decades in the developed common law nations as the social cohesion pro-vided by their Christian heritage has given way to clusters of membership-based groups pursuing their separate sets of interests. At best, these group-ings co-exist with little reason to interact. At worst, relationships are tense and can become confrontational – as in the current competition between the religious and the secularists, between fundamentalists and mainstream adherents, between the traditional organised religions, and between these religions and a proliferating and mutating range of new forms of belief – which undoubtedly contributes to an overall splinter-ing of society. This reductionist tendency, responsible for proliferating "islands of exclusivity",[34] is now commonly referred to as "the culture wars".

In its current phase, the phenomenon probably originated in the USA, where it evolved from a number of morality-laden issues, including the death penalty as a legitimate form of State punishment, female combatants in national armed forces, gun laws, abortion, homosexuality and prosti-tution. These were often linked to "life" and/or sexuality.[35] The related moralising proved to be deeply divisive in the USA – when manifested in settings such as education, employment, medicine, etc. – and subsequently has become so in Europe, the Antipodes and elsewhere. These are matters crucial to identity – an individual's social role is shaped by their educa-tion and employment for most of their adult life, while sexual orienta-tion can be the most defining aspect of their identity – and also, therefore, crucial to alienation. The attendant morality is infused with religious pre-cepts – God creates all life, man is created in God's image, etc. – resulting in the neat elision of religious belief and identity, which leads to the deeply divisive social consequences that religious discrimination has always been able to generate. Abortion, gay marriage, transsexualism, assisted suicide, genetic engineering, DNA patenting, cloning and stem cell research are now among the host of morally charged, contentious and socially disrup-tive issues that have grown to constitute the heartland of the culture wars. This spread of issues and settings is where the struggle between old and new cultures, as pictured in the Cavafy parable, would now seem to be taking place.

While there is little prospect of any retreat from these front-line issues, and every likelihood of new fronts opening up, the indications in Europe

---

[34] See Esau, A. J., "'Islands of Exclusivity': Religious Organisations and Employment Discrim-ination", *University of British Columbia Law Review*, 2000, vol. 33, p. 719.
[35] See e.g. Sands, K. M. (ed.), *God Forbid: Religion and Sex in American Public Life*, New York, Oxford University Press, 2000.

and the USA are of an interest in rebuilding a firmer sense of national cultural identity and protecting national boundaries: the filtering of immigrants and the introduction of citizenship tests being examples, coupled with a requirement that a level of competence be achieved in literacy and language skills shortly after immigration. The equality legislation entrenched in all developed nations, requiring the State to be neutral in its relationship with religion (subject to statutory exemption privileges favouring religion, religious organisations and adherents) and to ensure that religion-specific practices (e.g. polygamy) are subject to uniformly applicable social rules, is also serving to reduce social differences. Such measures, together with an investment of the resources needed to assist recent and settled immigrants to appreciate and share the values and heritage of their adopted culture, may serve as a stimulus for closer social integration.

However, there is, of course, a difficult balance to be struck here: between reviving the notion of the "nation state", complete with a closed-borders approach to cultures and issues that are deemed incongruent with national concerns, and developing a "cultural synthesis" approach, which, while recognising and protecting a nation's cultural identity, also proactively seeks to give recognition and space to other cultures within national borders and promotes the building of bridges with minority cultural groups. The political willingness to introduce measures that both protect the cultural integrity of the host nation and prevent the erasure of that of immigrants is becoming an interesting stress test of "citizenship" for contemporary democracy in the developed Western nations (see further Chapters 3 and 12).

Culture Wars and Religious Discrimination: The Links

Religion is layered into culture and often provides the trigger that turns cultural dissonance into dissension (which can be anything from the sectarian aspects of religious discrimination to the lesser skirmishes of the culture wars). Religious discrimination has been with us for millennia, causing death and destruction on a scale only barely touched upon in the previous chapter, but is now statutorily defined, confined and comprehensively prohibited in a range of national and international laws. Culture war, on the other hand, is an ill-defined modern social phenomenon that manifests itself in response to a fluctuating agenda of moral imperative issues, in generally permissive activities that are subject mainly to the laws governing freedom of expression. The unmistakable overlap between the two – mostly on issues where there is a fusion of sexuality and religion – means that one cannot be satisfactorily examined without taking into account the relevance of the other.

Arguably, religion in the jurisdictions being considered is becoming steadily more culturally sublimated, its differentiating characteristics nuanced and diffused throughout the various public activities and forums of society, rather than represented in institutional places of worship. Its latent divisiveness tends to emerge tangentially, as when a person brings a symbol of their private religious belief – of their not belonging to the prevailing culture – into a public space such as their place of employment, education, health care, etc. The sublimation may, then, be little more than an expedient artifice: religious discrimination, generated in fact by religion or belief, may be passed off as an objection to sexual orientation (e.g. the refusal of bakers with strong religious views to bake a celebratory cake for a gay couple) or a concern for animal welfare (e.g. an objection to the non-stunning of animals slaughtered for food). To a large extent, such "domestication" of a traditionally polarising source of social unrest has served to defuse its potency, with culture war sophistication gradually displacing overt religious discrimination and dispelling any excuse for sectarianism. Meanwhile, the crude barbarity of ISIS stands as a chastening reminder of the latter.

Culture, Religion and Citizenship

It is possible that the migrant crisis will be seen, in time, to have had a significant impact upon the conflation of religion and culture and the general preoccupation with identity politics. This phenomenon – depicted as the greatest trans-border movement of people since World War II – has seen waves of uprooted and homeless families, mostly Islamic, arrive in various northwestern European countries and in those of North America. The sudden influx of such a volume of dependent foreigners has sharply accentuated the usual culture clashes and triggered an acute awareness in the host countries of domestic cultural norms and values usually taken for granted. Consequently, government uncertainty regarding the balance to be struck between intervention in support of national culture, including traditional religious affiliation, or in support of multi-culturalism, would seem to be tipping towards a resurgent "nation state" ethos. A revival of interest in asserting and protecting national cultural identity is now emerging as a legitimate government goal. While this is an understandable response to the scale of current migratory activity and the totalitarian challenge of ISIS, it carries with it implications for how, in the future, we will construe citizenship and religious discrimination.

Religious Discrimination

The freedom of religion or belief, which entails an entitlement to be free of religious discrimination, is now a universal human right enshrined in the Universal Declaration of Human Rights (UDHR), the International Covenant on Civil and Political Rights (ICCPR) and the constitutions and/or legislation of all the common law nations currently being considered. In those countries, religion has largely lost its former power to label and alienate persons and divide communities in mutual enmity. There are exceptions, Northern Ireland being recently the most notable, and there are also many major cities with socially alienated ghettoes of religion-specific groups that survive in a relationship of tension and mutual suspicion with one another and with the wider community. Their significance, among other things, is to serve as a reminder that religious discrimination is seldom simply about "religion" but lies more in an antipathy towards everything seen as represented by that label. Moreover, as always, it is newcomers who tend to attract discrimination, and there is good reason to believe that minority religions and the newly emerging faith or belief groups are particularly vulnerable.[36] For some of the latter, paradoxically, it is the refusal of the regulatory processes to recognise their belief system as a religion that is perceived to be religious discrimination.

Differentiation is clearly not the same as discrimination: while both draw attention to indices of difference, the former does so on a neutral basis, the latter with an added value judgment – one entity is to be regarded as inferior to an other. It is this latter dimension that can be threatening to civil order: within a religion, as between Shia and Sunni Muslims or between evangelising Christians and all others; between religions, as in the Hindu and Muslim relationship; and between those of religious belief and those of none. Until exposed to the naked aggression of Islamic militancy – with its selective use of the Qur'an to justify jihad and the infliction of Shari'a punishments – the developed common law nations had little recent experience of unadorned, large-scale, concentrated religious discrimination.

Definitional Issues

As has been pointed out, "while discrimination law in countries such as Canada, New Zealand and Australia often has a historical and often

---

[36] See further Ridge, P., "Religious Charitable Status and Public Benefit in Australia", *Melbourne University Law Review*, 2011, vol. 35, pp. 1071–1098.

continuing caselaw connection with English law, the operative legal definitions of discrimination can and do differ".[37]

The expression "intolerance and discrimination based on religion or belief" means any distinction, exclusion, restriction or preference based on religion or belief and having as its purpose or as its effect the nullification or impairment of the recognition, enjoyment or exercise of human rights and fundamental freedoms on an equal basis.[38] The problem is that, in practice, religious discrimination can also be present in different guises: most usually, for example, in conduct that overtly denigrates ethnicity or sexual orientation. In addition to the issues already explored regarding what exactly qualifies as a "religion" in contemporary society and the bearing of cultural context on that definition, religious discrimination can itself be complex: the perception of those being discriminated against may or may not be shared by those who discriminate against them.

Discrimination on Grounds of Religion/Ethnicity

Whether discriminatory conduct against another is in fact based upon religion or instead on caste, race or ethnicity is often uncertain: sometimes, it will be purely racial or ethnic, as in the case of the Roma, or gypsies, who have suffered systematic discrimination in many European countries for generations; sometimes, as with anti-Semitism, its origins may lie more in religious differences; at other times, it may be a blend. As noted by Hewitt, "courts around the world have determined that some religious groups are also ethnic groups (such as Jews and Sikhs), while others (such as Muslims and Christians) are not".[39]

Religions which coincide with ethnicity, such as Islam, Sikhism and Hinduism, experience the most discrimination, including a degree of overlap between religious and racial discrimination. The ethnic, cultural and religious aspects of individuals' identities are often closely related and visibly apparent. The response to this visible difference may lead to an intensification of unfair treatment. Where religious identities, beliefs and practices are closely linked to an individual's cultural, ethnic and national

---

[37] See Weller, P., Purdam, K., Ghanea, N. and Cheruvallil-Contractor, S., *Religion or Belief, Discrimination and Equality*, London, Bloomsbury Academic, 2013, at p. 10.

[38] See Article 2 of the UN Declaration on the Elimination of All Forms of Intolerance and of Discrimination Based on Religion or Belief. Adopted by the 36th session of the UN General Assembly on 25 November 1981.

[39] Hewitt, A., "It's Not Because You Wear Hijab, It's Because You're Muslim: Inconsistencies in South Australia's Discrimination Laws", *Queensland University of Technology Law and Justice Journal*, vol. 7:1, pp. 57–69, at p. 69.

background, negative responses and unfair treatment based upon their identities and traditions may also represent expressions of racism and xenophobia. This is especially so in the case of those who self-identify as belonging to a "foreign religion" – such as female Muslims and male Sikhs – regardless of their actual ethnicity.

For many Muslims, Hindus, Sikhs and, quite often, Jews, such distinctions have little if any relevance: their self-perceived identity is an amalgam of religion and ethnicity, and any discrimination directed at them on the grounds of the former may well be felt as offending the latter. This is particularly true for first-generation immigrants; later generations will tend to have a more nuanced or compromised sense of identity. Some Christian and other religious communities – for example, in Africa, Iran and Iraq – may be indistinguishable on ethnic grounds, and any discrimination is then clearly targeted at their religious identity. On the other hand, a single religion, such as Christianity, has the capacity to absorb many differences of race and ethnicity and often attracts discrimination purely on its own terms, all other factors being disregarded. Where the visual presentation of the religious entity is confusing – as, perhaps, with black Christians or white Muslims – the discrimination may be targeted at a perceived betrayal of ethnic identity but be felt as religiously motivated. Ignorance or indifference will not in itself constitute discrimination.

Discrimination by Religious Entities

When committed by a religious organisation or person against those not sharing their faith, it is reasonably clear that discrimination is almost always religiously based – advancing or protecting their interests as such – although much depends on the extent to which the action taken is necessary to give effect to or protect religious beliefs. Most obviously, as has been repeatedly demonstrated by ISIS in its ruthless application of Shari'a law, this can simply be an abuse of power when used to punish the unfaithful, encourage compliance of adherents and intimidate all others. Added complications arise when the discrimination is religion by proxy: as when a religious entity discriminates against women's rights,[40] the feminism movement,[41] sexual orientation, abortion, gay marriage, genetic engineering, etc. – the activity, then, is seen and treated as an attenuated indicator of irreligious values.

---

[40] See Daly, M., *The Church and the Second Sex*, New York, Harper and Row, 1968.
[41] See Friedan, B., *The Feminine Mystique*, New York, Norton, 1963.

Discrimination within Religious Entities

Many religious communities, groups and organisations have a record of internal schisms leading to discriminatory treatment of those that have chosen to establish a separate church or sect. The tensions between Orthodox and Progressive Jewish communities or between the new evangelical Christian churches and their traditional counterparts are among the many examples of such relationships. In recent years, there have been increasing instances of schisms within Protestant churches – mainly in the USA, but also in the UK and Australia – with theological divisions triggering divisions in ministry, congregation and property, which have at times been accompanied by allegations of discriminatory conduct.

Discrimination by Secularists

Intervention by secularists, including government bodies, in the affairs of religious entities can constitute religious discrimination even if intended to be in the latter's best interests: grant-aiding the maintenance of Church of England cathedrals but not that of the places of worship of other religions could be so construed. The secularist argument against faith-based schools – indeed, that schools should be free from any religious influence – is a familiar point of contention in all modern developed nations. Similarly, continuing the tax-exempt status of traditional religions and their affiliated organisations while denying parity of status to new minority religious/belief groups may well amount to religious discrimination.

Conduct can prove to be religiously discriminatory even though it is not intended as such. Legislation can have this effect, as when laws are introduced permitting Sunday shopping or prohibiting the slaughter of poultry without stunning. Conversely, it can be intended, as when laws prohibit polygamy, child marriages or FGM.

Harassment and Similar Conduct

Religious discrimination can shade into other offences. For example, the offence of harassment related to religion or belief occurs where a person engages in unwanted conduct which has the purpose or effect of violating another person's dignity, or where they create an intimidating, hostile, degrading, humiliating or offensive environment for another person. Unfair treatment can constitute discrimination, although the dividing line between the two is not readily drawn. The latter may be accidental, or may occur even if the subject is unaware of it. Black-led Christian organisations are quite likely to be the subject of unfair treatment, as are religions with large numbers of visible minorities, such as Sikhism, Hinduism and Islam. Incitement to religious hatred and victimisation may also be cited in this context.

Types of Religious Discrimination

On the face of it, in the context of religion or belief, the distinction between direct and indirect discrimination is reasonably clear: the first occurs where the less favourable treatment is due to religion or belief; the second arises because of the use of neutral criteria which have an unequal impact causing disadvantage to a minority for reasons related to religion or belief. In practice, the difference is not always clear-cut. For example, some have queried whether rules such as a ban on face coverings, which applies almost exclusively to one religious group (Muslim women), ought to be treated as direct rather than indirect discrimination. Further distinctions arise in circumstances where an organisation: fails to provide an appropriate and professional service to people because of their religion; fails to make the kind of "reasonable accommodation" that would enable someone from a religious minority to take up a job or make use of a service; or engages in "affirmative action" by selecting certain religious entities for preferential treatment (for direct and indirect discrimination, see further Chapter 4).

Discrimination: Affirmative Action

As the UN Human Rights Committee has noted:[42]

> The principle of equality sometimes requires States to take affirmative action in order to diminish or eliminate conditions which cause or help to perpetuate discrimination prohibited by the Covenant. For example, in a State where the general conditions of a certain part of the population prevent or impair their enjoyment of human rights, the State should take specific action to correct those conditions.

This gives credence to action which might otherwise be interpreted as "positive discrimination", and therefore prohibited. However, an alternative argument is that where quotas are introduced – for example, as regards the proportion of women, those who are disabled or are Muslim in a certain area of employment or educational facility – as an affirmative action strategy, there is the possibility of the beneficiaries being stigmatized, or

---

[42] See UN Human Rights Committee, "General Comment Relating to Discrimination under the ICCPR", 1989, no. 18, at para. 10.

of perceiving themselves to be so. Moreover, such a strategy could prove counterproductive in an employment situation, as an employer might consider that by adopting it they would be attracting undue attention to the preferenced person(s), which could make them more difficult to dismiss should this become necessary. The additional risk might actually dissuade an employer from offering such employment in the first place, resulting, perversely, in a form of hidden discrimination.

Discrimination: Faith and Equality

The distinction between discrimination and equality laws as they relate to religion/belief is one that attracts debate. The legislative intent governing the first is straightforward, its premises clearly understood and its insistence on impartial objective application generally welcomed. The second is controversial, because it is viewed as having a levelling effect. This has led some to challenge what they perceive to be the reductionist approach of equality law: one that treats religion in secular terms, to be regarded in law as equivalent to other characteristics – such as disability and sexual orientation – that differentiate the status of citizens and indicate a common need for protection (see also Chapter 3).

State Neutrality

The principle that the State must adopt a neutral approach to religion and religious matters suggests that in law, the State should both be "religion blind", by treating religion as it would anything else, and make no distinction between religions, treating them all, as well as secularism, with equal impartiality. The difficulties for the State in implementing such neutrality have been well expressed by Moon:[43]

> If secularism or agnosticism constitutes a position, worldview, or cultural identity equivalent to religious adherence, then its proponents may feel excluded or marginalized when the State supports even the most ecumenical religious practices. But by the same token, the complete removal of religion from the public sphere may be experienced by religious adherents as the exclusion of their worldview and the affirmation of a non-religious or secular perspective . . .
>
> Ironically, then, as the exclusion of religion from public life, in the name of religious freedom and equality, has become more complete, the secular

---

[43] Moon, R. (ed.), *Law and Religious Pluralism in Canada*, Vancouver, BC, UBC Press, 2008, at p. 231.

has begun to appear less neutral and more partisan. With the growth of agnosticism and atheism, religious neutrality in the public sphere may have become impossible. What for some is the neutral ground on which freedom of religion and conscience depends is for others a partisan anti-spiritual perspective.

Moreover, as pointed out by Ahdar and Leigh,[44] the "religion blind" approach is problematic in that "equality of form can be accompanied by inequality of effect".[45] An undue burden can, unintentionally, be placed upon a particular religious minority. For example, the legal requirement that safety helmets be worn by all motorcyclists, even though it cannot be fitted over the turban worn by a Sikh, causes the latter to be relatively disadvantaged due to their religion. It is an approach that requires religious values and principles to be treated in law the same as those of any secular organisation. This results in the protest from religious organisations that to do so is to entirely miss the point: their values are transcendent. Not only are they intended to be different from those that inform secular matters, but, by definition, adherents have no option but to adhere to them; to be a religious person is to accept and give effect, throughout the course of one's daily life, to values that transcend secular concerns. It is argued that by insisting on parity, the State is diluting or dismissing the values that our civilisation has been founded upon.

Another significant problem with the principle that the State should treat all religions equally is, as already mentioned, that many States – particularly in Europe, and more obviously in the theocratic regimes of the Middle East – have dense and deep ties with a particular religion. This conflation of culture and religion, often over centuries, has shaped the identity of many States. Some, such as England, continue to have formal constitutional arrangements with a designated "established" church in which one specific religion is clearly preferenced above all others. In the developed common law nations, most noticeably the USA, where new religious groups are constantly forming and reforming, the application of this principle requires traditional religions and those of newly emerging minority groups to be legally levelled, which seemingly implies a corresponding overall dilution in the status of religious values. There is an argument that this imposes a disadvantage upon the primary traditional

---

[44] Ahdar, R. and Leigh, I., *Religious Freedom in the Liberal State*, 2nd edn, Oxford, Oxford University Press, 2013, at pp. 113–114.
[45] Ibid., citing Barry, B., *Culture and Equality: An Egalitarian Critique of Multiculturalism*, Cambridge, Polity Press, 2001, at pp. 18 and 258.

religion that is so disproportionate – because of the collateral damage to cultural integrity – that it in itself constitutes religious discrimination.

Effects of Religious Discrimination

Denying some the opportunities and equality of rights enjoyed by all others on the grounds of differences in religion or belief is a dynamic as old as society itself. It has taken many forms, from passive restrictions on access to community facilities to insults, persecution and genocide; it has been perpetrated on a one-to-one basis, by institutions and by the full power of conquering armies. For the modern sophisticated societies of the common law jurisdictions, religious discrimination now most often takes the form of unjust and unequal treatment in the course of everyday life, such as in the workplace or in the provision of services. Nevertheless, it is always experienced as nothing less than a humiliating rejection, a reminder of not belonging.

Marginalisation

The effect of religious discrimination is both to marginalise the targeted minority group(s) and to strengthen their sense of solidarity and identity; it reinforces differences. The prejudice and stereotyping serves to ascribe social stigma and alienate the marginalised, while reminding society as a whole, as well as the victims, that assimilation is not permissible. If not addressed, discriminatory action lowers the threshold for tolerance and paves the way for further and worse discrimination, generating a sense of superiority in the discriminating and grievance in those discriminated against.

Sectarianism

As a next step, the assertive repudiation of some specific groups by others on religious grounds makes sectarianism a particularly pernicious social phenomenon, and one with a proven incendiary capacity. In recent years, particularly in the Arab world – Egypt, Libya, Syria, Iraq, Tunisia, Yemen, etc. – it has been the driving force for a form of regional identity politics, demonstrating a powerful capacity to divide communities and nations. As in Northern Ireland and Kosovo, sectarianism can be a precursor to serious civil disorder (see further Chapter 1).

Implications for Democracy

Religious discrimination is plainly incompatible with democracy. Its existence is a standing affront to the moral order of a political system that purports to represent and balance the interests of all citizens within the jurisdiction and to offer support and refuge to those without who flee the persecution or collapse of other regimes; yet it persists in all democratic nations.

The challenge to democracy is systemic. As a fundamental human right, recognised as such in a barrage of national legislation and international conventions, non-discrimination is required to be treated as equally inviolable. Other fundamental rights – such as the freedom of expression – are breached if exercised in a manner that constitutes religious discrimination. The characteristics of such discrimination – rejection, prejudice, violation of identity, subordination – accompany those discriminated against and may be applied to disempower them in any or all social settings, sometimes on an inter-generational basis. The integrity of the web of civil rights is flawed by the enduring accommodation of discriminatory conduct. The network of civic institutions and communities necessary to consolidate a democratic society cannot be sustained in the face of endemic discrimination against the beliefs of minority groups – but nor can it hope to withstand an accommodation that preferences a certain religion/cultural nexus (e.g. Christian) or is blind to the practices of others (e.g. Muslim) that breach the equality principle, the hallmark of such a society.

The right not to be discriminated against on the grounds of religion or belief constitutes a fixed benchmark for a value system that differentiates a democratic State from all others. As a reference point for democracy, it serves to reassure citizens that the principle of equality will be upheld and that a legally sanctioned threshold of community tolerance will protect them from religious prejudice. The fact that such safeguards are in place offers a model, or sometimes a place of refuge, for the citizens of non-democratic States. It is a model that promises the State will recognise and balance the interests of different cultures, as represented in its democratic institutions and processes, to form a cohesive pluralistic society free from religious discrimination, whether exercised by State or citizen (see further Chapter 3).

Conclusion

Identity issues would seem to be central to the cultural context of religious discrimination, providing a basis for social division and exclusion. While appearing in many forms – often overlapping – the main areas of identity-related contention include: the core traditional religions, their contemporary social role in the countries whose cultures they once dominated and the relationships between them and their fundamentalist offshoots;

the proliferating belief systems and the individualised interpretations of established faiths now gaining legal recognition as religions; the ethnicities of the many different migrant groups from underdeveloped, often Islamic, countries, and the adjustments they must make to fit in with the structures and institutions of their host countries; and the secularists who, with increasing assertiveness, are claiming recognition for a new and growing religion-free zone in society. The former, reasonably coherent, national cultural identities of the common law jurisdictions presently being considered have in recent decades given way to fluid uncertainty, exacerbated by the globalisation of media, products and services, the ease and frequency of international travel and Internet access to an infinitely varied choice of culturally based associations. There are now many ways to be different.

The resulting struggle to accommodate and balance such differences – differentiating, but not discriminating – while facilitating sufficient integration to consolidate civil society is currently exercising the governments of all jurisdictions examined in Part III. Religious belief, conflated with ethnic diversity, is playing an increasingly potent role, partially due to hostilities in the Middle East and the menacing shadow of ISIS. Other relevant factors include the fragmentation of Christianity on gay marriage, euthanasia, LGBT issues, etc. and the volume, demographic profile and high visibility of recent migrants, which have challenged the assimilation capacity of host nations. Multi-culturalism, as the generally favoured policy for managing these tensions, has been stress-tested by the European 2015/16 migrant crisis and found wanting. Instead, there are indications of a right-wing drift towards a return to the traditional defensive nation state ethos, with political protection for national boundaries, resources and cultural heritage.

PART II

Balancing Public and Private Interests

3

Religion

The Public and the Private

Introduction

Religion and associated values permeate everyday life:[1]

> If I wish to discipline my children, refrain from taking advantage of life preserving medicine, construct a place of worship, hire only workers who share my faith, decline to rent my bed and breakfast accommodation to unmarried couples (heterosexual or homosexual), the State will have something to say about it. The domain of the "public" and "private" are becoming increasingly blurred in the wake of a much more "omnipresent" State.

There can be no doubt that equality legislation, and fundamental rights awareness more broadly, has prised open the door of private morality and exposed to the scrutiny of public law many matters hitherto considered as secluded in the domain of religious belief. Personal morality, whether or not shaped by religious belief, can no longer necessarily be regarded as private if its manifestation impacts upon others.

This chapter considers the public/private balance in the law relating to discriminatory conduct triggered by religion, belief or secularism. Beginning with the realm of personal religious belief, it examines the balance to be struck between private piety and public conduct. It then turns to reflect on the background political context – the social democratic framework that provides a common mode of governance for the nations presently being considered – giving particular attention to the nature of the relationship between Church and State. This is followed by a review of public policy as a determinant of what constitutes religious discrimination and how it is to be treated. It introduces key themes that will be tracked through Parts III and IV. Particular attention is therefore given to the growing importance of secularism, to the role of the State in regulating matters of religion and discrimination, and to the impact of human rights,

---

[1] Ahdar and Leigh, *Religious Freedom in the Liberal State*, at p. 15.

81

equality and non-discrimination legislation. The relevance and application of pluralism and multi-culturalism policies are considered, and their relative merits briefly outlined. Religion and religious discrimination – their contribution to social capital and civil society – are discussed. The chapter concludes with a brief review of the threat posed by religious fundamentalism.

Private Piety and Public Conduct

Religious belief, experienced by an individual, is clearly an entirely personal matter: the interests served by prayer and worship are crucial to private piety but are of no relevance to the general public, save to the extent that any effect they have on that individual may serve to influence others. Experienced collectively, however, through the bonding experience of shared values and through participation in the activities of a religious organisation, such belief can make a significant contribution to social well being. Moreover, religious buildings and associated artefacts, ritual and ceremonial practices, preaching, evangelism, proselytism and, of course, religiously motivated violence, may well impact upon public life and have the power to play a central role in developing and perpetuating a culture. Not until an individual or organisation chooses to manifest their piety, however, by engaging in activities intended to give effect to it, does religious belief become a matter of public interest.

Private Piety

For the religious individual, as for religious organisations, private piety and public conduct should be synonymous: both strive to ensure that conduct conforms with religious belief; their views and actions are necessarily often dogmatic because religious dogma leaves them unable to compromise. This has become less true for Christianity, as, on the whole, beliefs have become moderated over time by changes in cultural context, but more so for Muslims, who consider themselves bound by the precepts of the Qur'an and hadith, and to an extreme extent for the more radical elements within Islam who adhere to the prescriptive directives of Shari'a law and the sanctions of jihad as laid down in the early Middle Ages. The distinction is one that is rapidly growing to become a faultline for our times: how to reconcile the moral propositions derived from traditional religious beliefs with modern equality and non-discrimination law to ensure that religiously inspired conduct conforms to the norms required to sustain contemporary civil society. Are the pious – be they evangelical Christians, Muslims or others – to be treated as archaic bigots and tolerated only if they conform to social norms or encouraged to retreat to "gated" religious communities? Or should there be an "islands of exclusivity" policy,[2] facilitating their participation in civil society but granting them a free pass from particularly onerous constraints of equality and non-discrimination law? Is a "regime change" approach permissible to support religious leadership initiatives that might prompt the pious to reinterpret the fundamentalist precepts of ancient cultures so that they accord with contemporary cultural developments?

Public Conduct

The State requires private action to conform to basic social norms. Habermass, however, notes that religious dogma imposes a particular burden on religious individuals and organisations, as they are not free to take any action or advance any views which may compromise their beliefs. To that extent, law may well disproportionately burden such religious individuals and organisations, and may do so more onerously to some than to others (e.g. Sikhs and helmets in the context of general safety regulations for riding motorbikes). He suggests that "the liberal State must not transform the requisite institutional separation of religion and politics into an undue mental and psychological burden for those of its citizens who follow a faith".[3] An answer, initially suggested by Essau and later supported by Rivers, is for "the State to recognise 'islands of exclusivity' at any rate in the core dimension of collective religious activity".[4] However, if there is to be such an exemption for religious entities on matters of equality that are binding on the rest of society, its exercise must somehow be conditional upon this being demonstrably compliant with the best interests of that society. The challenge is to find a way of engaging with those of religious belief to ensure: that their interests find proportionate representation in the institutions and public policy of the common law nations; that any privileges – e.g. tax and equality exemptions – are balanced by verifiable public benefit; and that the body politic does not allow itself to become hostage to a possible religious veto.

Problems tend to arise when it comes to agreeing where, in a democratic society, the thresholds should be fixed for permitting private

[2] See Esau, "Islands of Exclusivity" (19930 33 UB Col LR 719).
[3] Habermas, "Religion in the Public Sphere", at p. 9.
[4] Rivers, J., The Law of Organised Religions, Oxford, Oxford University Press, 2010, at p. 135.

manifestations of religious belief in public places, or for balancing the tensions between religious adherents and others as regards accessing public services such as divorce and birth control or determining eligibility for opportunities in employment, etc. In the former instance, the veto can take the form of an insistence that a manifestation of private belief – such as wearing a burqa when teaching or a crucifix on a necklace when nursing – is a contra-indicator of suitability to perform a public task. In relation to accessing public services, such as registering a gay marriage, a veto may be asserted on religious grounds by a registrar seeking to deny others their right to that service. As regards employment opportunities, a religious organisation may impose such a veto restricting applicants to fellow religious adherents. In such cases, a threshold of intolerance can then trigger religious discrimination. As Trigg says, "the problem is where to draw the line between religious practices we may not share but must tolerate, and those that cannot be allowed in a democratic society".[5]

This problem is one that evolves in keeping with developments in such a society and is conditional upon the acceptance of that line by all cultures within it. For example, before the feminist movement, democratic societies accepted gender disparity and tolerated no-go areas for women in certain occupational and social roles. Subsequently, tolerance has faded for continuing practices such as the non-appointment of female clergy to certain posts in the Protestant Church, the constraints upon divorce for Jewish women and the general submission to patriarchical control required of all Muslim females – but seemingly not to the point where there is full social consensus that they breach a line and can no longer be allowed.

Political Context

Christianity and its canon law precepts have provided a unifying thread, guiding the development of the common law nations, giving them a shared cultural identity and preparing the ground for the subsequent similar evolution of associated bodies of law. Shared basic principles, having gained common law currency, continued to produce an almost identical jurisprudence schematic – particularly as regards family law and related moral matters – well into the twentieth century. Such law still remains recognisably similar between States, although there are evolving cultural differences, including: a drift towards secularism, resulting in the civil law

---

[5] Trigg, Equality, Freedom and Religion, at p. 110.

of some jurisdictions remaining closer to their canon law heritage (e.g. Ireland) while that of others moves further away (e.g. the USA); a distinct Islamic cultural nexus with some characteristics at variance with those of host jurisdictions; and an emerging patchwork of competing morality-based sub-cultures. The challenge of accommodating and managing these different cultures within a morality coherent legislative framework is becoming steadily more real for all common law nations.

Church and State

The separation of Church and State provides the best possible guarantee that government and the courts will ensure that public life is neutral and remains free from the undue influence of either religion or secularism. However, not all nations make such provision, and the traditional role of religious organisations, as authoritative social institutions, continues to exert a political presence in many.

Government and Religion

Although the symbiotic Church/State relationship is usually considered to be associated with mediaeval kingdoms, Barro and McCleary, in their survey of 188 countries, established that in 2000 some 40 per cent, or 75 countries, could be classified as having a State religion.[6] This, they explain, enables a government "to favor the majority religion by subsidizing its practices and by restricting religious expression of minorities".[7] In 2011, Bielefeldt, a Special UN Rapporteur, echoed their assessment when he cautioned against the use of "official" religion for purposes of national identity politics and commented that "it seems difficult, if not impossible, to conceive of an official 'State religion' that in practice does not have adverse effects on religious minorities, thus discriminating against their members".[8]

Religion's span of population permeation and the ability of its organisations to accumulate wealth, together with its inherent capacity to inculcate values, maintain order and thereby contribute to social cohesion, have always assured it of special attention from government. While the modern

---

[6] See Barro, R. J. and McCleary, R. M., "Which Countries Have State Religions?", *The Quarterly Journal of Economics*, November 2005, pp. 1331–1370.

[7] Ibid. at p. 13.

[8] See Bielefeldt, H., "Report of the Special Rapporteur on Freedom of Religion or Belief", presented to the UN General Assembly, Human Rights Council Nineteenth session, 22 December 2011.

Western democracies have outgrown their theocratic context, the legacy of having once been so conditioned is very apparent in the caution with which their governments now deal with religion, religious organisations and religious discrimination. In some common law countries, most obviously the USA, where Church and State are constitutionally separated, domestic politics are overshadowed by the need to constantly demonstrate both an immunity from religious influence and a disinterest in preferencing any one religion, or the interests of religion per se, over secularism. In others, most notably Ireland, the "hidden hand" of religion continues to influence law and policy despite robust denials from the government of the day.

Public Service Provision and Religion

Throughout the common law world, much of the initial infrastructure for hospitals, social care services, schools and colleges was founded by religious organisations. Faith-based provision – most obviously in education, but also in health and elderly care – has more recently become the preferred government option, leading to a noticeable scaling up in the level of schools and residential care facilities provided on a religion-specific basis in the UK and the USA. This stepped-up faith-based contribution to public service provision has been accompanied by steadily louder protests from secularists, who challenge the use of public benefit service provision as a platform for showcasing religion, for religious evangelising and for discriminatory practice. There are several different aspects to this challenge, including: that government should not be in the business of strengthening the social role of religion,[9] let alone any particular religion; that public benefit service providers should deliver on a religion-free basis; that recipients should have a choice not to be dependent upon making concessions to a particular religion, or to any, in order to access such services; and that when acting as government service delivery agents, religious organisations should be required to act in a non-discriminatory fashion, not just as regards service access, but also in relation to the nature of the services delivered and in the hiring of staff to be employed in the delivery of such services. These matters have been particularly contentious in the USA, where they trigger constitutional issues regarding the separation of Church and State.

---

[9] A policy most contentious in the USA: see e.g. *Dodge v. Salvation Army* 1989, WL 53857 (S.D. Miss).

Religion, Beliefs and Democracy

For almost all of the two millennia that have so far measured the progress of Christianity, and indeed from much earlier, as Lucretius,[10] among others, has observed, there have been religious disputes. These have tended to be rooted in perceptions of a "true" or "false" God and the righteousness or otherwise of his adherents. The modern permutation of such disputes has now broadened beyond Christianity to include participants of no belief (neither in God nor in religion) and those who do believe, but without any need for a God (e.g. in a philosophy or way of life). The latter is a relatively recent development, the treatment meted out in the past to those deemed to be "heathens", "pagans" or "witches" being a considerable deterrent to non-believers. This evolving process contrasts sharply with Islamic culture, which, over much the same period, has ensured that Muslims in the main continue to be governed by the prescriptive injunctions of Shari'a law and its resolute intolerance of "heretics" and "apostates".

Religion, Democracy and Discrimination

The white, Christian and largely Protestant cultural context which provided the framework for building the democratic institutions that now govern contemporary society in the common law countries has had some difficulty accommodating religious diversity. Discrimination was present from the outset: within Christianity, between Catholics and Protestants and against minority groups such as Quakers; without, in opposing other religions such as Hindus and Muslims and in the persecution or conversion of the "heathens" who constituted the indigenous populations of many of these countries.

Nonetheless, the fact that the same Christian principles infused the formulation of constitutions, legislation, legal processes and judicial decisions did much to build a degree of cultural homogeneity among these nations, and, arguably, laid an institutional foundation for a shared policy that discriminated against all other religions. As mentioned in the previous chapter, this consensus was particularly apparent in the principles informing the law relating to the family, which continue to provide the grounds for those of traditional religious beliefs to challenge the changes being driven by equality and human rights legislation. Now, as then, it remains impermissible in a democracy for the courts to undermine

---

[10] The Roman poet, Lucretius (96–55 BC). See further the 1911 *Encyclopedia Brittanica* at www.studylight.org/enc/bri/view.cgi?n=20770&search=span.

Parliament by grasping opportunities to change such crucial incidences of Christianity. As Lord Bingham observed in R *(Countryside Alliance)* v. *Attorney-General*,[11] "the democratic process is liable to be subverted if, on a question of moral and political judgment, opponents of the Act achieve through the courts what they could not achieve in Parliament".

While there has been a shift from judicial discrimination favouring Christianity to one favouring religion per se, the assurance that religion and religious organisations will continue to be afforded special legal protection nonetheless constitutes discrimination against secularists.

Religion, the Culture Wars and Democracy

The Christian ethos – largely Protestant-based – that characterised the British colonial administration, informing the civic morality of its settlements, inevitably laid the foundations for the divisive disputes that are now such a feature of democratic society: mainly in the USA, but also, to a varying degree, in all the common law jurisdictions. The morality and values represented in the clashes over issues such as gay marriage derive from that ethos and provide the raw materials for waging the ever-extending culture wars. These disputes, often proxy sublimations of fundamental differences rooted in religious belief, can be construed as a form of culturally based religious discrimination; an interpretation pursued throughout this book. As new discoveries push back the boundaries of science and medicine, while legal rights/human rights further shrink the space left to religion and secularists and emerging belief systems continue to undermine the once pervasive Christian morality, the range of such issues, the accompanying discrimination and the degree of acrimonious contention can only increase.

In some ways, these "culture wars" can be seen as a further stage in a post-independence process of working out an authentic sense of identity for societies that have for so long been constricted by the architecture of an English, Christian and very ordered, transposed culture. At its most extreme, this struggle is highlighted by the difficulties facing the Indigenous People as they strive to free themselves from centuries of colonial policies which, alternating between assimilation and disregard, have left them fighting to retrieve the basic elements of cultural identity: language, customs, territory and religious beliefs. It is also evident more generally in the relative under-representation of non-Christian religious values. If democracy in the developed common law nations is to be representational

---

[11] [2008] AC 719 at para. 45.

and effective then a place must be found in the culture wars to address issues specific to the currently marginalised communities. It has been said that in democratic societies, the role of the State is not to remove causes of tension between religious organisations, or within them, which might constrain the flowering of pluralism, but to ensure that they tolerate one another.[12] However, this presupposes that such organisations and their interests are effectively represented, in all relevant institutions and processes, in the first place.

Public Policy

Historically, public policy and religion have had a fraught relationship. Many of the most significant public policy issues – including the abolition of slavery, temperance laws to curb alcoholism, universal suffrage and apartheid – were the focus of heated debate, bitterly dividing society on religious grounds, and yet were ultimately resolved largely through appeals to religious beliefs. The same pattern can currently be seen playing out in relation to issues such as abortion, gay marriage and genetic engineering – but against a background dominated by an international confrontation with the religious zealotry of ISIS, in a cruel mimicry of the religious discrimination and persecution pursued centuries ago by the Christians in the Crusades and Inquisition. In the aftermath of atrocities in Paris and elsewhere, the need to rigorously safeguard religious minorities such as Jews from murderous attacks by religious extremists such as ISIS has become a pressing public policy concern. All developed common law (and other) countries are now recalibrating domestic religious discrimination policies and reframing them to integrate with national and international security strategies.

Religion and Public Policy

Arguably, religion itself does not have a social utility function and therefore does not require a public policy: the effects of intercessory prayer are not measurable – it is directed towards the salvation of the soul or souls in the next life and thus is not readily amenable to a quality audit in this one. As has been said, "the purpose of the Church is to evangelise

---

[12] See *Hasan and Chaush v. Bulgaria* [GC], Application No. 30985/96, ECHR 2000-XI; *Metropolitan Church of Bessarabia and Others v. Moldova*, Application No. 45701/99, ECHR 2001-XII; and *Serif v. Greece*, Application No. 38178/97, ECHR 1999-IX.

not civilise".[13] However, religion, religious organisations and their adherents, with few exceptions, have always impacted upon society, and managing the positive and negative aspects of that impact is a public policy matter.

The Public Interest: Benefits

The benefits of religion and other forms of belief can be most clearly seen in their direct effect on adherents – in the peace and equanimity instilled by the prospect of eternal salvation or other forms of redemption – and on communities of the like-minded – through being part of a collective bound by a shared set of values and modes of worship. For the general public, the benefits are more indirect: in the main, they result from exposure to the modelling of responsible civic conduct and the dissemination of related virtuous teachings; by leading a good life and doing good works, the spiritual welfare of the believer – and the more secular welfare of the beneficiary and the wider community – may be furthered. They also emanate from the outreach work of religious organisations. The faith-based contribution to society has always been considerable: religious believers largely built and staffed the education, health and social care infrastructure throughout the common law world.

There are other benefits that may be seen as intrinsic to religion and which enhance the community and public life more generally. These would include: its physical presence in the form of churches and other places of worship, which represent pastoral care and signify a source of solace, a refuge or somewhere to turn for those in need; the moral leadership practised by the clergy; the body of acquired theological and legal knowledge; and churches, cathedrals, ceremonies, music, literature, sculpture and other artefacts, which are culturally enriching. Religious principles of good and evil, justice and mercy, continue to inform and set boundaries for acceptable social relationships, and the heritage of values centred on generosity, altruism, philanthropy and care for the poor and needy – generated by religious doctrines, teachings and practice – has done much to counterbalance other social pressures.

As a "pillar of society", religion (together with other forms of faith and belief) has continued to uphold and represent virtuous and decent behaviour and to remind citizens that "good works" are needed if society is to be a better place. However, the accumulated weight of architectural

---

[13] See Fiorenza, F. S., "The Church's Religious Identity and its Social and Political Mission", *Theological Studies*, vol. 43:2, pp. 197–225, at p. 198.

and general cultural heritage, values and network of outreach facilities just listed can also be perceived as overbearing and intimidating for minority religions and newly emerging faith-based groups. In its own way, it can constitute a form of religious discrimination.

The Public Interest: Negatives

Religion's innate capacity for generating and maintaining social cohesion has a dark side. It tends to be perceived by others as excluding and marginalising them, which can lead to polarisation and mutual antipathy within and between communities. Arguably, religion is fundamentally discriminatory. Throughout the centuries, most recently in the latter half of the twentieth (see further Chapter 1), it has demonstrated an ability to cause social divisions and provide grounds for violent confrontations. Where religion or other forms of belief shade off towards the closed-group thinking typical of cults, the sense of separateness is exacerbated, which can be destructive for both the group and the wider community. Religion may also incline its adherents towards attitudes of acceptance of the status quo and deference to higher authority, and thereby act as a conservative force in politics: possibly explaining why it has traditionally earned its reputation as "a pillar of society".

Secularism and Public Policy

Among the crucial differences between the traditional and the contemporary approach to formulating and applying public policy is that secularists in general and the decidedly more secular institutions of the State, together with an array of equality and non-discrimination legislation, now play prominent roles in resolving issues that polarise society on religious grounds. This in itself has done much to shunt religion-related policy into the public arena, making it more transparent and amenable to electoral challenge. In the developed Western world, as religion and its adherents diminish relative to secularists, there is a growing confidence in the secular challenge now being levelled at the privileges traditionally enjoyed by religious entities.

Secularism

Secularism,[14] as a social construct, is not without its complications. It broadly suggests that matters of government should be wholly insulated

---

[14] The term "secularism" was first coined by George Jacob Holyoake (1817–1906).

from any religious influence. As Habermas puts it: "every citizen must know and accept that only secular reasons count beyond the institutional threshold that divides the informal public sphere from parliament, courts, ministries and administrations".[15]

For secularism to be maintained, government must preserve individual freedom of religion, religious harmony and mutual tolerance and accommodation between those with and without religious belief. As they grow in number and assertiveness, secularists bring a harder edge to the customary quiet standoff between religious adherents and all others as to the grounds on which the law should preference religion and related organisations in a modern democracy. The contention is partially to do with the propriety of any form of government support for or engagement with religion, particularly in relation to any specific religion, and of its links to bodies associated with a religion.

There are serious issues for all governments regarding how they should be positioned in relation to religion and associated matters: the distinction between the State as a neutral impartial broker and a secularist actor can have significant consequences. As McConnell points out:[16]

> When the State is the dominant influence in the culture, the "secular State" becomes the equivalent of a secular culture... This makes achievement of religious freedom far more difficult... As the domain of government increases in scope, some government involvement in religious activity becomes necessary if religious exercise is to be possible at all.

Secularism and Democracy

A strong secularist lobby is now demanding to know what it is about religious beliefs that attracts an entitlement to exemption from human rights principles. Secularists have become very alert to the vulnerability of public institutions, such as schools, to penetration by covert prosleytism, both in the classroom (through the use of teachers, teaching materials and fixtures that suggest particular, or any, religious belief) and in pastoral care (through the role of a chaplain, etc.).[17] This debate is far from

[15] Habermass, J., "Religion in the Public Sphere", in *European Journal of Philosophy*, 2006, vol. 14:1, at p. 10.

[16] McConnell, M., "Why is Religious Liberty the 'First Freedom'", *Cardozo Law Review*, 2000, vol. 21, at p. 1261.

[17] This wariness is not confined to instances where the Christian religion intrudes on public institutions. The founding of the Islamic Shari'a Council in 1982, with its remit to address issues such as marriage breakdown, has also caused controversy. The eighty-five Shari'a "courts" in Britain have since processed many thousands of cases, and there is concern

being merely academic: courts have ordered religious hospitals and personnel to offer services that breach their religious beliefs; regulators have forced the closure of religious facilities due to their inability to meet legislative non-discrimination requirements; and legislation has been introduced specifically to override the capacity of medical personnel to exercise a religious veto regarding the availability of abortion. Secularists protest that there is no good reason why taxpayers should be left to subsidise the discriminatory practices (religious, sexual and gender) of religious organisations.

Secularism can be interpreted as licensing the State to assume responsibility for all decisions, facilities, administrative systems and processes associated with matters in the public interest, without having to make any concessions to a religion or religions or accept any input from religious organisations. It may also be interpreted as affording religion protection from government interference in all circumstances where there is no evidence of criminality. This might be understood, in the developed Western nations, as starting with constitutional arrangements that clearly separate State and religion. As Neuhaus once explained, it is an affront to democracy when those who make political points do so on the basis of private truths: "public decisions must be made by arguments that are public in character".[18] Statute law should declare that government: has neither the interest nor the power to impose any form of restriction on religious belief and practice; will not interfere in the self-governance of religious bodies; will allow such bodies to determine internal arrangements for recruiting staff and for teaching and training adherents; will stand aside from any donation of funds, time or other resources freely made to religious bodies; and will permit missionary work or proselytism to be undertaken by such bodies or on their behalf within or outside the jurisdiction.

For the developed common law nations, secularism has presented something of a dichotomy: the public arena is either an open market in which all religions are equally free to proclaim and manifest their beliefs, compete for adherents and be assured of equal respect and engagement from State authorities, or it is one in which all religions are equally prohibited from exercising any presence, that space being reserved entirely for secular entities and their activities, with all religions assured that they will be equally ignored by State authorities. In recent years, there is evidence

that they may exercise an intimidating influence on Islamic communities: see the BBC's Panorama programme at www.familylawweek.co.uk/site.aspx?i=ed112864.
[18] See Neuhaus, R. J., *The Naked Public Square*, Grand Rapids, MI, Erdmans, 1984, at p. 36.

of government experimentation in new models that move away from such polarising aridity and allow for different balances to be struck between the interests of the religious and the secular.

Public Policy and Religious Discrimination: State Regulation and Support

In all Western democracies, State intervention in religious matters – whether as regulator or supporter – is controversial. Some consider it to be a given that State support is owed to religion and its organisations and that it is verging on the heretical that the judiciary or regulators should be empowered or required to question the bona fides of institutions that have survived and flourished for centuries in a particular society, stabilising it, enriching its culture and being venerated by its adherents. Others, especially the growing number of secularists, consider that religion, its associated organisations and its adherents are as capable of crime, civil offences and anti-social conduct as any other entity – pointing to the well-documented and multi-national record of child abuse by clergy – and must be made subject to the same standards of transparency and accountability as those other entities, and that they are no more deserving of State support than any other. Given the emergence of so many new forms of religion and the current prevalence of religion-inspired violence, there is good reason to consider the merits of introducing State regulatory agencies with a specific brief for Churches and their ancillary organisations – if only to ensure that demagogues neither inflame the discriminatory conduct of adherents nor attract that of others.

State Regulation

The fact that religious organisations – like citizens – are deemed to be legal entities, vests them with legal responsibilities and in theory has the effect of requiring transparency and introducing processes of accountability into operations that were traditionally regarded as the private internal business of the Church. In practice, however, churches and their associated religious organisations are not amenable to any specific State regulatory body, but are very largely left to maintain their traditional mechanisms for self-regulation. The organisational management of parishes, dioceses, etc. complies with the usual requirements of corporate structures, but it is a system in which internal affairs are monitored, inspected and determined by boards of directors dominated by clergy and church hierarchical officials. Other than when their service-provision programmes – schools, child care, family planning, etc. – interface with government agencies and are then subject to standardised public regulatory processes, Churches are very much left to their own devices. Even though they have charitable tax-exemption status, religious organisations encounter at most only very light intrusion from charity and/or tax authorities. The introduction of an independent State regulatory regime that intruded in the affairs of a Church and its emanations only to the extent necessary to monitor matters such as ensuring compliance with criminal law, checking that beliefs and their mode of dissemination were compliant with human rights and equality legislation and that appropriate procedures were complied with in appointing and assigning the rights and duties of all Church officials (accompanied by clear arbitration mechanisms and related sanctions) and ensuring general adherence to transparency and accountability principles would do much to generate confidence among religious adherents and secularists in their local community Churches.

State Support

It is perhaps axiomatic that organisations and activities deemed to be conducive to promoting the public good are on those grounds entitled to State support.

Arguably, however, the contribution of religion to society rests simply on the assurance it instils in individuals that their beliefs and good works in this life will be rewarded in the next; the inducement to better citizenship is essentially self-serving rather than altruistic. Any tangible social utility is merely incidental, so there are no good grounds for State support. Religion and its ancillary organisations must take their place in the open market alongside such other social forces as for-profit concerns, philosophy, philanthropy, etc., compete for their own niche and be subject to the same regulatory constraints.

Alternatively, it might be argued that a distinction should be drawn between "religion" as an institution, with its churches, ministers, forms of worship, etc., and any secular role that a religious organisation may have in the community. The former could be entitled to State support on the grounds that, notwithstanding its purpose in preparing those of faith for a supernatural existence, its beliefs embody mankind's higher aspirations, its values as modelled by adherents contribute to making contemporary society a better place and, anyway, for some millennia, civilisation has accorded it a special status. The latter might also warrant State support to the extent that the outworkings of religious organisations make a contribution to overall public-benefit service provision.

Where provided, support is most usually by way of subsidising the running costs of religious organisations. It may also take the form of representation at central or local government level in offices established to focus policy development. Where funding is provided, this is necessarily discriminatory: the more marginal the religious group, the greater the level of funding it will need if parity with the social standing of others is to be achieved. However, a side effect of subsidies is to reinforce differences: targeted grants induce prospective recipient groups to emphasise their distinctive identity in order to gain government recognition, thereby triggering a cycle which becomes self-fulfilling.

Tax Exemption and the State

The tax privileges generally awarded to religious organisations – such as churches, other places of worship and faith-based hospitals, schools, colleges and universities, as well as their buildings, lands and running costs – but denied to their secular counterparts are seen by some as a long-standing form of State religious discrimination. This is a strategy which, as history teaches, may be self-defeating – as became apparent to the feudal British monarchy when it witnessed the taxes needed to raise armies being drained by clergy privileges. A consequence of extending the definition of "religion" to ethical, moral and other such belief systems is that they and their ancillary properties will qualify for similar tax exemption. Such positive discrimination may also occur in relation to discretionary and differentiated State grants to particular religious organisations that comply with government policy regarding same-sex marriages or are facilities belonging to an "established" church.

Tax preferencing can give rise to a conflict of interests on the religion and human rights interface. The right of religious parents, for example, to expect that their contribution as taxpayers will result in their child accessing education within a school that promotes their particular religious beliefs may well conflict with the equal right of non-religious taxpaying parents to expect a secular education for their child. Similarly, perhaps, taxpayers who fund public services have a right to expect that children in care will be placed by agencies for adoption in accordance with the needs of the child regardless of the adopters' gender; that mosques and Christian churches will not preach that homosexuality is wrong when it is a right permitted by civil law; and that teachers in faith schools will not teach that abortion is wrong (it may be challenged as unethical or immoral, perhaps, but "wrong" is to deny prevailing civil law). Taxpayers might wish to question the government subvention of religion through national lotteries and the discrete political massaging of VAT, GST and donor incentive schemes – such as Gift Aid, PBI, etc. – that tend to favour religious organisations. Then there is the more vexed issue of direct government channelling of tax revenues through religious organisations to pay for religiously flavoured public benefit services, including those provided in the USA to fund faith-based penitentiary rehabilitation schemes, not to mention the Charitable Choice programme.

These practices raise the question: What exactly is it that is intrinsic to the identity of such entities that justifies State positive discrimination? Why do religions and related entities warrant such a double take on the tax revenue base: privileged by exemptions and preferential donor incentive schemes, etc., while also receiving targeted government funding? The permissive parameters of piety, accommodating religious institutions that warrant tax exemption privileges denied to their secular counterparts, are likely to be increasingly contentious.

Security and Public Policy

While public policy has always justified State intervention into matters otherwise regarded as governed by private rights, the ongoing domestic and international engagement with militant Islamists is licensing greater inroads than usual. It is clearly a policy with a discriminatory bias.

International Terrorism and Domestic Security

The degree and extent of security-related government powers now being applied in all Western jurisdictions are extensive and routinely intrude upon the rights of citizens to protection from "stop and search" and arbitrary arrest, from discriminatory treatment and from harassment by police forces. There is much evidence to indicate that these powers are being applied with a particular emphasis on monitoring the movements of young Muslim men. Armed troops on patrol in cities, intrusive surveillance by drones, the covert accessing of communications data, the use of CCTV technology and the international exchange of information between government security forces have now become an accepted part of daily life. Also of concern has been the use of extradition and rendition, almost exclusively in relation to ethnic minorities, which again has been perceived as negatively discriminating against Muslims.

Human Rights, Equality and Civil Liberties: An Introduction

In all jurisdictions presently being considered, public policy now places a high priority upon embedding human rights – including promoting the freedom of religion and the prohibition of religious discrimination – while also pursuing an equality agenda. By introducing statutory provisions, particularly those requiring sexual and gender equality and non-discrimination, the beliefs and practices of traditional religions have been fundamentally challenged.

Human Rights

The right to freedom of religion first received international recognition with the introduction of the UDHR in 1948. The boundaries of that right are now very uncertain, and some would argue that it is in danger.[19] There are a number of fundamental definitional issues. Of particular importance has been the judicial weighting given recently in some jurisdictions to the subjective understanding of the individual as the key determinant of religious belief.[20] This has brought to an end the traditional assumption that religious belief is simply a derivative of religion: once the identity of the "religion" was established, the prescriptive nature of the associated "beliefs" could be safely assumed. As mentioned in the preceding chapter, adherents would now seem to be legally entitled to interpret their religion as they see fit – a development accompanied by a corresponding proliferation in the forms of association and modes of communication necessary to give effect to the new belief systems.

The inescapable corollary of such a widespread deconstruction of what constitutes "religion" in contemporary developed Western societies is that "religious discrimination" must now also be re-defined. It has to encompass not just the bigotry and sectarianism to which we have become accustomed, but also any prejudicial treatment of or by groups such as the Wiccas, faith-healers and, in some countries, the Jedi.[21] In addition, it has to accommodate the proxy religious confrontations on issues such as abortion and gay marriage. It must also, of course, make room for the regression to mediaeval barbaric persecution perpetrated by Islamic militants.

---

[19] See further www.religious-freedom-report.org.
[20] See e.g. *Ex parte Williamson* [2005] UKHL 15, [2005] 2 AC 246 (HL).
[21] The 2001 census in New Zealand recorded 53 000 citizens affirming adherence to the Jedi in response to the question on religious affiliation.

Equality

Public policy in relation to religious freedom has been shaped by a wealth of related international jurisprudence, accumulated over the past six to seven decades, since the introduction of the UDHR. This has firmly entrenched the right to such freedom, with little wriggle room remaining for equality rights to operate in parallel and without conflict.

This was clearly the case when issues arose in the context of testamentary dispositions subject to a religious condition or, indeed, when subject to a condition that breached parental rights. So, for example, in *Re Lysaght*, a testamentary gift was made to the Royal College of Surgeons for the purpose of providing a scholarship to a medical student but its terms discriminated against Roman Catholic and Jewish students;[22] Buckley J said that it would be "going much too far" to say that such a trust was contrary to public policy.[23] Again, in *Blathwayt v. Baron Cawley*,[24] a testamentary disposition that discriminated against Roman Catholics was upheld. In upholding the disposition, members of the House of Lords acknowledged that equality norms informed public policy but thought that, on the facts of the case, any such equality norms were clearly outweighed by the testator's freedom of disposition.[25] For Lord Wilberforce, "neither by express provision nor by implication has private selection yet become a matter of public policy".[26] However, equality norms as given effect by legislative provisions have in recent years made inroads into long-established principles such as those that protect the rights of testators and parents. Public policy has evolved to accommodate these norms, and this has compromised many religions, their associated organisations and their adherents. Some of the most fundamental beliefs and practices of Christians, Muslims and others are now inescapably in conflict with equality legislation.

There is also an argument that equality is all very well, but when religion conflates with culture to give a nation or region a coherent identity – and all that goes with it in terms of a secure sense of belonging for successive generations (generating its distinctive art, artefacts and other cultural characteristics) – then it is not feasible to regard religion as separable from culture. In terms of achieving equality, this may mean that it would be unreasonable to expect any religiously–culturally coherent jurisdiction to jettison such customs and practice: it would, in fact, be treating that

---

[22] [1966] Ch 191.   [23] Ibid., 206.   [24] [1976] AC 397.
[25] [1976] AC 397, 425–426 (Lord Wilberforce), 429 (Lord Cross), 441 (Lord Edmund-Davies).
[26] Ibid., 426.

jurisdiction unequally relative to other, more pluralist societies, by requiring a devaluation of the role traditionally played by religion in order that parity be achieved. To do so could be construed as a form of religious discrimination, where the standard application of regulatory requirements has a particularly onerous effect on an entity precisely because of its religious characteristics. That the corollary favouring secularism also holds true was alluded to by the Advocate General in the recent case of *Samira Achbita & Anor* v. *G4S Secure Solutions NV*[27] when he drew attention to the need to have regard to the national identities of Member States and pointed out that in France, for example, where secularism has constitutional status and therefore plays an instrumental role in social cohesion, the wearing of visible religious symbols may legitimately be subject to stricter restrictions than in other Member States.

Civil Liberties and Public Policy

The areas of public policy that provide the main settings for domestic religious contention in the twenty-first century are much the same as in the twentieth: family, education, employment and health, housing and social service provision. Equality and non-discrimination legislation has already demonstrated its ability to impact these areas. Religious organisations providing outreach facilities and services in areas – such as faith-based schools, adoption, marriage and family counselling, youth clubs and children's camps – where religious principles conflict with statutory equality requirements have found their service provision being terminated. Religious adherents employed in public service agencies such as child care, wedding registry offices and family planning programmes are experiencing a similar conflict, and some have felt obliged to resign. Religious colleges and universities providing student accommodation are encountering the same issues when faced with applications from married same-sex couples. Religious employers are finding themselves compromised when staff enter into same-sex relationships. Government grants and contracts to religious universities and charity social service providers are being discontinued where recipients are unable or unwilling to accept the limitations imposed by equality legislation and related public policy, which will similarly cause the very many religious institutions with charitable tax-exempt status to lose that privilege, particularly if they maintain a conscientious objection to same-sex marriage. The range of possible disruptions

---

[27] [2016] EUECJ C-157/15 (31 May 2016) at para. 125.

to civil life as a consequence of the conflict between religious principles and equality/non-discrimination legislation are endless.

More attention is now paid to policies conducive to building a diverse but equitable civil society, which entails a special focus on matters such as immigration, faith schools and the needs of particularly disadvantaged groups. The importance of a nuanced approach, recognising that inequities require intervention and adjustment in some areas more than in others, has led to a conclusion that a one-size-fits-all strategy for addressing social inequality is inadequate and that policies such as "affirmative action" (favouring the more marginalised) and "islands of exclusivity" (exempting entities that are liable to be be unduly burdened) may therefore be justified. There is mounting pressure to make some such adjustments in order to meet the challenge that, in effect, public policy is now disadvantaging religion; that its adherents, organisations and those of emerging belief systems are effectively downgraded as they must compete, on terms contrary to their raison d'être, with other social priorities for equal status. However, the growing proportion of secularists relative to believers in the populations of most developed nations would make any such recalibration of public policy in favour of religion contentious. It could be construed as a culturally driven but inverted form of religious discrimination. Moreover, it may not even be effective. There is an argument against affirmative action, such as the imposition of quotas favouring those of a particular religion in an attempt to redress disadvantage, on the basis that competitive markets with free entry could offer better and more certain protection against invidious discrimination.[28]

Pluralism and Multi-Culturalism

Cultural dissonance has become a serious threat to social stability. Whether within families and communities, between Indigenous People and others, between settled communities and immigrant groups or between such groups, or indeed between nations, a lack of mutual understanding and willingness to respect and value cultural difference is causing destructive tensions. There can be no doubt, after the succession of atrocities by Islamic militants, that a particularly lethal form of religious discrimination has now become a key component of such dissonance.

---

[28] Epstein, R., *Forbidden Grounds: The Case Against Employment Discrimination Laws*, Cambridge, MA, Harvard University Press, 1992.

Pluralism: An Introduction

The policy of pluralism places considerable importance upon protecting the cultural identity and equality of minority groups. However, while it encourages their recognition, promotes their interaction, and welcomes their enriching contribution to the texture of life, it also resolutely requires that all such groups should function under the umbrella of the national cultural heritage, the primacy of which attracts State support. It is a policy well represented by the settled approach of successive US governments towards immigrants. The premium placed upon interactive diversity promotes the "melting pot" cultural exchange that results in the foods, lifestyles, values and cultural practices of migrant communities being absorbed into mainstream society. Pluralism requires the identity of a cultural minority to be respected by providing opportunities for its members to express their distinctive identity through related practices – provided they remain within the law (see further Chapter 12). This promotion of cultural diversity does, however, also give rise to uncertainty as to areas of consensus: What constitutes the common good? Which set of religious beliefs should inform and govern society? Are the values/beliefs of particular religions incompatible with democratic social norms? What should be the role of secularism? Beyond the rhetoric, there are also questions as to whether pluralism actually works, given the evidence of continuing deep racial divisions in US society.

Multi-Culturalism: An Introduction

This necessitates holding in equitable balance the interests of the national culture and those of an increasing range of other cultures, religions and belief systems which, together with secularists, co-exist alongside it. Following the introduction of equality and non-discrimination legislation, multi-culturalism requires that all minority groups and the traditional national culture be accorded equal respect, equal rights and equal opportunities. It places considerable importance upon protecting the cultural identity of minorities against being overshadowed by the inherited national cultural identity, which is largely left to fend for itself. This entails supporting minority cultures and ensuring both that their distinctive cultural identities are maintained and that they are encouraged to participate in community life and are represented in decision-making forums on an equal basis with representatives of the traditional national culture. It requires host countries to accommodate, simultaneously, variations in the primary national religion, together with other traditional institutional faiths, alongside a mutating range of belief systems, some of which are philosophical or socio-political and often quite transient in nature. Such societies must make room available both structurally and psychologically, providing a level playing field and evidence of welcome and engineering a reduction in the permeating influence and high visibility of traditional religions relative to all other religious and belief entities. Unfortunately, however, multi-culturalism has also tended to generate a narrow, rights-driven approach towards complex problems, which has a fragmentary effect on social cohesion (see further Chapter 12).

Pluralism, Multi-Culturalism and Religion

Immigrant ethnic groups naturally rely on religion as a form of short hand to represent their identity and to discriminate against others, and as a means of asserting the cultural values, language, and traditions which provide them with a comforting sense of commonality in an unfamiliar environment. In Europe, where each country has had many centuries of nurturing its own distinctive cultural identity, religious and secular values are often at variance with those of immigrants. Although some such countries, notably the UK, have confidently proclaimed their commitment to multi-culturalism, the dominance of a particular religious culture is a reality which must be perceived as intimidating by immigrants. Moreover, while policy-makers may debate the respective merits of pluralism and multi-culturalism, the reality for religious adherents is that the distinction is beside the point: their first loyalty is to the religious community.

Religion, Social Capital and Civil Society

Religion, with its explicit doctrines, its shared values, beliefs and places of worship, its built-in commitment to doing good, its collective public ceremonies for birth, marriage and death, its institutions and its outreach facilities, brings with it a unique potential for creating social cohesion. For all its emphasis on the private salvation of souls, it has always done much to mediate and order the public space between citizen and State and, as Schnabel[29] and others have pointed out, to contribute to building civil society. However, discrimination – by and of religion, its organisations and

[29] See Schnabel, P. and Giesen, P. (eds), *What Everyone Should Know About the Humanities*, Amsterdam, 2011, pp. 198–202.

its adherents – with its proven track record for inciting social polarisation, has a capacity for achieving precisely the opposite.

Law, Religion and Social Capital

For the World Bank, "social capital" refers to "the institutions, relationships, and norms that shape the quality and quantity of a society's social interactions".[30] It argues that "increasing evidence shows that social cohesion is critical for societies to prosper economically and for development to be sustainable". The operational effect of the concept is evidenced by a range of formal and informal networks and the willing engagement of a significant proportion of a community in civic activity of a reciprocal and mutually beneficial nature, which, together with a shared ethos of trust, values and responsible behaviour, produces positive outcomes within that community. Undoubtedly, this interpretation captures, in part, the role played by religion, religious organisations and their adherents over the past two millennia or so in building social capital; a role enabled by a secure and responsive legal framework.

Law

The law supports and sustains social cohesion by: asserting and protecting a nation's culture and its associated emblems, icons, language and traditions; reinforcing its values and principles; policing its boundaries; and setting the terms for negotiation with other societies. By legitimising the particular institutions, bodies, officials and processes that bind together the constituent elements of a society, it enables that society to function as a coherent entity. It affords recognition and protection for the interests of minority groups through equality and non-discrimination legislation and the use of human rights provisions to accommodate diversity and achieve a balance in circumstances of competing rights.

The law also facilitates cohesion by virtue of its integrative effect. Whether as cause or effect, the bonds that draw a society together are represented by its civil and criminal laws and managed through the balancing of various sets of legal rights, the rights and reciprocal duties of each of the parties being statutorily delineated, moderated through related administrative bodies and enforced by the courts. To some degree, the integrative effect of legal rights is counterbalanced by a tendency for a

---

[30] See World Bank, *What is Social Capital?*, 2000, at www.worldbank.org/poverty.

rights-conscious approach towards complex problems to have a fragmentary effect on social cohesion (see further Chapter 12).

Religion

The contribution of religion to generating social capital can take many forms, including: reinforcing respect for common values and institutions; raising awareness as regards social needs; setting standards and improving coping capacity; and putting in place processes for positive social interaction. In the years between World War II and the late 1960s, religion maintained its centuries-old investment in politics, at least in those European countries that had not succumbed to Communism. This was particularly true in Catholic States, where the Church retained its powerful influence in reinforcing conservative domestic policies while encouraging the compliant conduct of adherents and guiding their voting choices. Not until a new era was introduced by contraceptives, more generous welfare benefits and greater social mobility did the ability of religion to influence domestic politics begin to fade.[31] Thereafter, the increased secularisation of matters central to the traditional role of the Church in the community – marriage, education, child care, etc. – inexorably weakened its role. However, there was always a distinction to be drawn between the contribution of religion to "bridging" and "bonding" forms of social capital.

Social Capital: "Bridging" and "Bonding"

For four centuries, and in all common law nations, religious organisations established and maintained the institutional facilities that formed the foundations of present educational, health and social care services. Their churches, schools, universities, and hospital complexes provided essential social functions, together with a unifying Christian ethos and architecture. Indeed, the distinctive pastoral landscape of a Church of England parish became the familiar, comforting, socially consolidating context for communities throughout the British Empire. In modern times, however, they may well have the opposite effect: the vast range of religious buildings, artefacts, activities, services, etc. raises questions as to how such an array of material that advertises the separateness, exclusiveness and competitiveness of religious organisations and their respective adherents can be conducive to promoting a collective sense of public good. Because of

---

[31] See Judt, T., *Postwar: A History of Europe Since 1945*, New York, Vintage, 2010, at pp. 374–377.

its capacity to emphasise difference – including through the socially divisive activity of proselytism – religion has proven to be challenging in the
context of social capital. Lord Scott of Foscote's warning, in *Gallagher* v.
Church of Jesus Christ of Latter-Day Saints, has a relevance for all jurisdictions presently being considered:[32]

> [S]tates may ... recognise that, although religion may be beneficial both
> to individuals and to the community, it is capable also of being divisive
> and, sometimes, of becoming dangerously so. No one who lives in a coun-
> try such as ours, with a community of diverse ethnic and racial origins
> and of diverse cultures and religions, can be unaware of this. Religion can
> bind communities together; but it can also emphasise their differences. In
> these circumstances secrecy in religious practices provides the soil in which
> suspicions and unfounded prejudices can take root and grow; openness in
> religious practices, on the other hand, can dispel suspicions and contradict
> prejudices.

Being essentially a member-benefit activity, religion is constrained by the
exclusiveness of its adherents' commitments and their consequent rejection of those adhering to all other religious beliefs, or to none. Experiences
in many parts of the world, from Sarajevo to Belfast to Baghdad, provide
evidence of religion's capacity to further the "bonding" form of social capital at the price of the "bridging".[33] Clearly, religion can serve to emphasise
differences, accentuate the marginalisation of minority groups and exacerbate any tendencies towards polarisation. In so doing, it provides the basis
for discriminating against others and for being discriminated against.

Religion and Civil Society

Across many Western and Westernised nations, there has been a growing demand for governments to put in place (and encourage others to
do so) the institutions and infrastructures necessary to establish or consolidate "civil society", which has been defined as the aggregate of non-
governmental organisations and institutions that manifest the interests
and will of citizens, or as the individuals and organisations in a society
who are independent of the government.[34] Religion has always played a

---

[32] *Gallagher* v. *Church of Jesus Christ of Latter-Day Saints* [2008] 1 WLR 1852, 1867 [51].

[33] See Puttnam, R., *Bowling Alone*, New York, Simon and Schuster, 2000. See also Çelik, G.,
"Breakpoint or Binder: Religious Engagement in Dutch Civil Society", *Journal of Civil Society*, 2013, vol. 9:3, pp. 248–267.

[34] See Dictionary.com's 21st Century Lexicon at www.coursehero.com/file/p37k6sn/
2-Dictionarycoms-21st-Century-Lexicon-defines-civil-society-as-1-the-aggregate/.

role in this middle ground between State and citizen. In particular, the framework of liberal democracy has provided a political setting conducive to the flourishing of religion, its institutions and its adherents, together with the vast range of associated public-benefit activity. As modern common law jurisdictions wind down their public service provision, they are increasingly looking towards religious institutions and their related infrastructure to supplement, or substitute for, government efforts. They seek to harness the selflessness, goodwill, manpower and resources of religious organisations and adherents, not just to achieve tangible public benefit outcomes, but also to strengthen civil society by generating direct political engagement with the electorate and prompting a sense of civic responsibility.

Civil Society

While there is some uncertainty as to how this concept should be defined,[35] most definitions require the free association of people in the pursuit of aims that complement the public-benefit efforts of the State and result in a more coherent and engaged body politic. Most also concur that religion is of central importance: scholars such as Schnabel[36] are strongly of the view that "believers" have traditionally formed the cornerstone of civil society, while Çelik[37] argues that "whereas the traditional Christian civil society is becoming smaller, there is a significant role for new religious groups in which religion often has a stronger role in members everyday life".

In his magesterial *Postwar*, Judt refers to "the need to construct a morally aware civil society to fill the anomic space between the individual and the State".[38] The UN adopts the same perspective when it states that civil society is the "third sector" of society, along with government and business.[39] The distinction being made by both is one that rests on a line drawn between the interests and terms of reference of government and those of all others, including religious organisations. However, in recent years, this line has become decidedly blurred. First, there is the ascendant trajectory of secularism, which, in the eyes of some, is bringing with it a "totalitarian liberalism" – implying that institutions such as the

---

[35] See Bothwell, J., "Indicators of a Healthy Civil Society", in Burbridge, J. (ed.), *Beyond Prince and Merchant*, Brussels, Institute of Cultural Affairs International, 1997.
[36] See Schnabel and Giesen, *What Everyone Should Know*.
[37] Çelik, "Breakpoint or Binder", at p. 261.   [38] See Judt, *Postwar*, at p. 695.
[39] See www.un.org/en/sections/resources/civil-society/index.html.

Church exist only with the permission of the State – which suggests that religion, its organisations and its adherents must abide by the social norms determined by the State.[40] Advocates of this view point to the intent of equality and non-discrimination legislation and to the resulting levelling effect of provisions which ignore the unique selling point of religion – its core transcendant element – and reduce it to just another socially differentiating characteristic. While it seems fanciful to suggest that secularism has made such progress as to establish a symbiotic relationship with the State that rivals the latter's previous theocratic relationship with the Church, there can be little doubt that it has developed to the extent of creating meaningful cross-sector links which now bind government and non-government organisations in terms of policies and standards to be applied when addressing social issues. Second, as already mentioned, there is the ever-growing input of third-sector organisations – led by religious bodies – to the government's traditional public benefit service provision programme.[41] The tactic of franchising out service delivery to non-government bodies – thereby reducing costs due to the subsidies of volunteer involvement and public donations, while also fudging accountability – is placing governments and such bodies in the positions of principal and agent, respectively. Very many of the service delivery agencies are religious organisations, or are affiliated to them. This arrangement may well result in the growing contractual dependency of religious organisations, the diluted independence of the third sector and a hollowing out of civil society.

Society and Religious Discrimination

For society to withstand the challenge of religious discrimination, it needs: laws that allow it to prosecute those who discriminate on the basis of religion in everyday contractual or transactional exchanges, or who abuse or commit violence on that basis; a regulatory framework that provides for the monitoring of discriminatory conduct and intimidatory manifestations of belief, as well as for the investigation and prosecution of alleged offences; and, most of all, willing support from across the broad base of society, with organisations and citizens prepared to demonstrate

---

[40] See Tartaglia, P., "At the Door of the Temple: Religious Freedom and the New Orthodoxy", *Public Discourse*, 27 June 2012, at www.thepublicdiscourse.com/2012/06/5751/.

[41] See e.g. the experience in the Netherlands following the introduction of the Social Support Act 2007, as outlined by Malda-Douma, W., "Religious Organisations in Civil Society", in Moksnes, M. and Melin, M., *Faith in Civil Society: Religious Actors as Drivers of Change*, Uppsala, Uppsala Centre for Sustainable Development, Uppsala University, 2013, p. 144.

leadership by vigorously defending the rights of individuals to practice their religion, reasonably manifest their beliefs and exercise their related freedom of expression.

Human Rights, Discrimination and Society

For religion, its organisations and its adherents, there has been no greater challenge in recent years than the spreading ambit of human rights, equality and non-discrimination law and the consequent legitimation of activities such as the aforementioned. There is now a growing slippage between Church and State on an agenda of contemporary social issues, and also, in many cases, between Church pronouncements and the practice of religious adherents. Gay marriage, in particular, is exacerbating the tension between the right to religious freedom and equality principles, religious discrimination being central to that tension. Euthanasia, or the right of an individual to choose to end their life and be assisted to do so, is set to be another road block for those of religious belief. The right to free speech is licensing media criticism of organisations that discriminate, on the basis of sexual orientation, gender, or such like, thereby undermining the moral high ground traditionally claimed by all religious organisations. The latter and their members are faced with a double bind: either stand by their beliefs, rely on their religious exemption rights and be placed in moral opposition to principles now sanctioned by law as of central importance to civil society; or become more flexible and accommodating in their beliefs, but risk losing their religious rights, their adherents and their traditional role in society – either way, the prospects would seem to entail considerable loss.

For Church and State, it has become increasingly difficult to avoid clashes of principle and belief on issues such as divorce, birth control, homosexuality and gay marriage. However, where any religion imposes public negative constraints upon the practices of its adherents – e.g. on the role of women, on non-heterosexual relationships, or on those of alternative beliefs or of none – then, to some, even if exemption can in law be justified, the Church is patently in breach of the State's basic equality precepts.

Conclusion

Religious discrimination can take many forms. Most often, it refers to denigrating conduct directed against adherents of a particular religion, because of their religion, but this has now been legally extended to include references in similar terms to a wide range of beliefs and to secularists. It can also signify actions taken by religious organisations or their adherents against others in order to assert or protect the perceived exclusiveness of their religion. In either instance, it may, confusingly, be misdirected more towards culture than towards religion, but the intent and effect of the conduct is the same – an attempt to tarnish, subordinate or negate one identity relative to others. It is frequently associated with the role of the State in providing preferential or unfair treatment of a religion or religions, whether through legislation, tax privileges, grants or other forms of intervention.

The mode of such discrimination is also varied. Hate, bigotry and sectarianism are readily recognised and addressed by the law, but other forms can be culturally elided: the agenda of proxy manifestations – e.g. abortion, homosexuality, gay marriage and euthanasia – arguably presents religious issues in sublimated secular guise; while the misogyny evident in the Islamic treatment of women (honour killings, subjugation, constraints on dress and social roles, etc.) may be viewed as religiously inspired discrimination. Secularism itself is attracting criticism, as it is accused of displacing religion and providing a policy platform that invites an approach to religious organisations and their adherents which requires them to be audited for their social utility and thus discriminates against their innate transcendental nature. By far the most extreme form of religious discrimination currently being deployed is, of course, that being used by ISIS in relation to all other religions as it imposes its interpretation of Islam upon those it has conquered.

Addressing religious discrimination within the civil society framework of modern democratic nations necessitates making a distinction between those aspects of religion and any associated discriminatory attitudes which remain matters of private piety and those which are manifested through conduct which impacts upon public life. The complexity of the policies and laws which are now in place to deal with the latter bears testimony to the difficulties involved.

4

The International Framework and Themes of Religious Discrimination

Introduction

This chapter builds upon its predecessors, particularly Chapter 3, to construct a frame of reference for examining the law relating to religious discrimination. For the purpose of setting out from a consistent baseline, which can serve as an anchor point for comparative analysis when conducting the jurisdiction-specific survey in Part III, it does so from a perspective that is European but capable of a general common law application. By drawing from the mosaic of cultures that constitute the EC, sifting the caselaw generated in the main by the European Court of Human Rights (ECtHR) and correlating cases with the pattern of key issues identified in previous chapters, it determines the metrics that may be applied to compare and contrast the law in all six jurisdictions studied in Part III.

Beginning with an exploration of public policy as it relates to religion and religious discrimination, the chapter considers the increasing significance of secularism and the tensions in contemporary democratic societies that are making a multi-culturalist policy unworkable. It outlines the relevant EC legal framework of courts, treaties, conventions and protocols, before examining the definitions of "religion", "belief", "religious discrimination" and various types of discrimination. The chapter then turns to focus on the caselaw and to organise it thematically so as to facilitate the jurisdiction-specific analysis that follows in Part III. This starts with the Church/State relationship and moves on to consider, in turn, the main categories attracting litigation: religious icons, apparel, etc.; the family; issues relating to "life"; employment; medicine; and service provision.

Public Policy Background

Religion's leverage in shaping public policy has greatly changed over the past century or so. Cultural changes driven by science, technology, economy and demography necessarily impact upon traditional religious doctrines and beliefs, while human rights and equality legislation are inevitably having a levelling effect upon areas previously privileged. As secularism increases, so the social role of the traditional religions weakens. As a myriad of new religions, sects and beliefs compete for public recognition, so the domestic interpretation of what constitutes "religion", "religious discrimination" and an appropriate public policy response has had to adjust. Since 2015, however, the impact of militant Islam on international public policy has greatly raised the salience of domestic public policy relating to religious discrimination, particularly as regards relationships between Muslims and other religious communities.

Contemporary Democratic Society

In the post-war period, the common law nations, together with many others, developed much the same policies of social liberalism. Central to this approach was an acceptance that no one culture could or should be regarded as superior: all must be regarded as deserving of respect; multiculturalism was the goal. As expressed by the ECtHR:[1]

> The court takes the view that the force of the collective beliefs of a community that is well-defined culturally cannot be ignored . . . there may be said to be an emerging international consensus amongst the Contracting States of the Council of Europe recognising the special needs of minorities and an obligation to protect their security, identity and lifestyle . . . not only for the purpose of safeguarding the interests of the minorities themselves but to preserve a cultural diversity of value to the whole community

The centrality of religion within this evolving democratic context was acknowledged by Justice Pettiti in *Kokkinakis*.[2]

Democracy

In *Moscow Branch of the Salvation Army* v. *Russia*,[3] the ECtHR asserted that "the freedom of thought, conscience and religion is one of the foundations of a 'democratic society' within the meaning of the Convention" and noted that this freedom is not restricted to those of religious belief but is also available to "atheists, agnostics, sceptics and the unconcerned".[4]

---

[1] See *Chapman* v. *the United Kingdom*, Application No. 27238/95 (ECHR 2001-I) at paras 59 and 93.
[2] *Kokkinakis* v. *Greece* (Ser. A) No. 260-A (1993) ECtHR.
[3] Application No. 72881/01, 5 October 2006.   [4] Ibid., at para. 57.

This sentiment was enlarged upon in *Bayatyan* v. *Armenia*[5] when it was declared that:

> This freedom is, in its religious dimension, one of the most vital elements that go to make up the identity of believers and their conception of life, but it is also a precious asset for atheists, agnostics, sceptics and the unconcerned. The pluralism indissociable from a democratic society, which has been dearly won over the centuries, depends on it. That freedom entails, inter alia, freedom to hold or not to hold religious beliefs and to practise or not to practise a religion.

The desire to manifest religious belief was acknowledged in *Eweida and others* v. *the United Kingdom* to be a fundamental right, because "a healthy democratic society needs to tolerate and sustain pluralism and diversity; but also because of the value to an individual who has made religion a central tenet of his or her life to be able to communicate that belief to others".[6]

Imposing such limitations upon the right to freedom of religion may be "necessary in a democratic society... for the protection of the rights and freedoms of others" (see later). This may have a disproportionate impact upon certain religions, however: Islam, for example, as family law in that culture imposes restrictions upon women – although, as emphasised in *Refah Partisi* v. *Turkey*, the corollary is that Islam itself is suspect in terms of compliance with Convention values, "particularly with regard to its criminal law and criminal procedure, its rules on the status of women and the way it intervenes in all spheres of private and public life in accordance with religious precepts... Shari'a is incompatible with the fundamental principles of democracy".[7] This ruling, obviously hugely significant for religion in a multi-cultural context, stands as a challenging benchmark for the judiciary – and others – in all the jurisdictions presently being studied.

Secularism

The fact that for many "believers" all conduct must conform to their beliefs has the effect of transferring private convictions into the public arena. That "bearing witness in words and deeds" is an integral part of religious freedom for those with religious convictions[8] has been recognised by the

---

[5] (2012) 54 EHRR 15, 494.
[6] [2013] ECHR 285, 36516/10, 51671/10, at para. 94.
[7] Application Nos. 41340/98, 41342/98, 41343/98, at paras 39–49.
[8] See *Kokkinakis* v. *Greece*, Application No. 14307/88 and *Otto-Preminger-Institut* v. *Austria*, Application No. 13470/87.

ECtHR but is perceived as threatening by secularists, who constitute an increasing proportion of the population in all modern common law countries, with divisive social and political consequences.

Pluralism and Multi-Culturalism

The autonomous existence of religious communities is held to be indispensable for pluralism in a democratic society, and therefore, as in *Sindicatul "Păstorul cel Bun"* v. *Romania*,[9] such communities should be allowed to function free from arbitrary State intervention.[10]

In *Folgero and Others* v. *Norway*,[11] the Grand Chamber ECtHR ruled, by a narrow majority, that the State had an "obligation to safeguard pluralism in State schools which are open to everyone".[12] Pluralism required equal treatment of all beliefs, although the court did add that "democracy does not simply mean that the views of a majority must always prevail: a balance must be achieved which ensures the fair and proper treatment of minorities and avoids any abuse of a dominant position".[13] This sentiment was reinforced by the court's observation in *Akdaş* v. *Turkey* that it is frequently necessary "to take into consideration the existence, within a single State, of various cultural, religious, civil or philosophical communities". More recently, in *Mansur Yalçın & Ors* v. *Turkey*,[14] the court reiterated that:

> in the exercise of its regulatory power in this area and its relationship with various religions, faiths and beliefs, the State, as the ultimate guarantor of pluralism in a democratic society, including religious pluralism, must be neutral and impartial.

By way of contrast, in *Lautsi* v. *Italy*,[15] a case which focused on the perceived religious discrimination represented by a crucifix in a classroom, the court questioned how "the display of a symbol which is reasonable to associate with Catholicism could uphold the pluralism in education which is essential for the preservation of a democratic society".[16] Ultimately, the court ruled, by a fifteen to two majority, that displaying a crucifix in a classroom is permissible, as "a European court should not be called upon

---

[9] 2013, Application No. 2330/09.
[10] See *Hasan and Chaush* v. *Bulgaria* [GC], op. cit.; *Metropolitan Church of Bessarabia and Others*, op. cit.; and *Holy Synod of the Bulgarian Orthodox Church (Metropolitan Inokentiy) and Others* v. *Bulgaria*, Nos. 412/03 and 35677/04, s.103 (22 January 2009).
[11] Application No. 15472/02 (29 June 2007).
[12] Ibid., at para. 101.   [13] Ibid., at para. 85(f).
[14] *Mansur Yalçın & Ors* v. *Turkey* [2014] ECHR 938, at para. 68.
[15] Application No. 30814/06 (18 March 2011).   [16] Ibid., at para. 56.

to bankrupt centuries of European tradition . . . this court ought to be ever cautious in taking liberties with other people's liberties, including the liberty of cherishing their own cultural imprinting".[17] This ruling can be seen as representing a shift in the ECtHR away from its earlier position that the State should treat all cultural groups equally, including its own signature religion, to one of acknowledging a State right to give precedence to the latter.

International Legal Framework

As yet, there is no such thing as a fixed international framework of law governing religion and religious discrimination, to which all six nations currently under study are subject and against which the performance of each could be audited. There is, however, a growing body of international treaties, conventions and protocols variously addressing such matters, some of which are commonly binding on all of these nations and all of which are binding on a few, together with a body of related jurisprudence which binds some but provides a common point of reference for all.

Human rights provisions are now increasingly supplemented, and sometimes stretched, by equality legislation. When determining questions concerning the relationship between State and religion the role of the national court, tribunal or regulator is of special importance.[18]

Conventions

The Universal Declaration of Human Rights (UDHR) This Declaration provided the foundation for all international human rights instruments and is equally applicable to each of the six nations studied in Part III. Article 18 initially declared the right to freedom of thought, conscience and religion. This included the freedom: to change religion or belief; to exercise religion or belief publicly or privately, alone or with others; and to exercise religion or belief in worship, teaching, practice and observance. It also provided for the right to have no religion and to have non-religious beliefs protected.

The European Convention on Human Rights (ECHR) The UDHR was enlarged by the European Convention on Human Rights (ECHR).

---

[17] Ibid., per Bonello J., at para. 1.2.
[18] See *Leyla Şahin v. Turkey* [GC], Application No. 44774/98, ECHR 2005-XI.

Article 9(1) of the latter, replicating Article 18, together with the conditional Article 14, now constitutes the key element of this legal framework[19] throughout Europe, and therefore is directly binding upon the UK and Ireland.[20] Other ECHR provisions also have a bearing upon religion, its manifestation and discrimination in respect of it.

Article 8 has a particularly wide reach. The protection it extends to "private and family life" could conceivably encompass personal religious activity. The limitations exercisable by the State as set out in Article 8(2)[21] – necessary in a democratic society in the interests of national security, public safety and the economic well being of the country, for the prevention of disorder or crime, for the protection of health or morals and for the protection of the rights and freedoms of others – may similarly impose boundaries upon personal religious activity.

Article 2 of Protocol 1[22] has a bearing on religious discrimination, as it provides for the parental right to determine a child's religious education:

> No person shall be denied the right to education. In the exercise of any functions which it assumes in relation to education and to teaching, the State shall respect the right of parents to ensure such education and teaching in conformity with their own religious and philosophical convictions.

The International Covenant on Civil and Political Rights (ICCPR)
This is of particular relevance because of its wide international application and accompanying monitoring process. Article 18 guarantees everyone the right to freedom of belief and religion, which includes the freedom to have or to adopt a religion or belief of choice and the freedom, either individually or in community with others, and either in public or in private, to manifest religion or belief in worship, observance, practice and teaching. Article 18(3) provides that the freedom to manifest one's religion or beliefs may be subject only to such limitations as are prescribed by law and are necessary to protect public safety, order, health and morals, and the

---

[19] Specifically, Article 9(1), Article 14 and Article 2 of Protocol 1.
[20] Although it is not enforceable; see e.g. *Hirst* v. *the United Kingdom* (No. 2), Application No. 74025/01 (2004), the case of *Ms C in A, B and C* v. *Ireland*, Application No. 26499/02 (2006) and *Northern Ireland Human Rights Commission, Re Judicial Review* [2015] NIQB 96.
[21] See also Article 29 of the UDHR.
[22] This Protocol was established on 20 March 1952. The leading case on Protocol 1 Article 2 is Belgian Linguistic (1968) 1 EHRR 252. See also *Folgerø and Others* v. *Norway*, Application No. 15472/02 (2007), *Hasan and Eylem Zengin* v. *Turkey*, Application No.1448/04 (2007) and *Appel-Irrgang and Others* v. *Germany*, Application No. 45216/07 (2009).

fundamental rights and freedoms of others. Moreover, under the terms of Article 4(2) (derogation in time of public emergency), rights under Article 18 are non-derogable.[23]

The UN Human Rights Committee, in General Comment 22, emphasises that protection extends to theistic, non-theistic and atheistic beliefs, as well as the right not to profess any religion or belief. This includes "not only ceremonial acts but also such customs as the observance of dietary regulations, the wearing of distinctive clothing or headcoverings, participation in rituals associated with certain stages of life, and the use of a particular language customarily spoken by a group". It also notes that "the concept of worship extends to ritual and ceremonial acts giving direct expression to belief, as well as various practices integral to such acts, including the building of places of worship, the use of ritual formulae and objects, the display of symbols, and the observance of holidays and days of rest".[24]

The general freedom of expression is enshrined in Article 19(2), but, under Article 19(3), this is subject to "the interests of other persons or to those of the community as a whole", which permits restrictions when they are (i) "provided by law" and (ii) "necessary" for (iii) "respect of the rights or reputations of others" or for "the protection of national security or of public order or of public health or morals". Article 20(2) states that any "advocacy of national, racial or religious hatred that constitutes incitement to discrimination, hostility or violence shall be prohibited by law". Article 26 declares that everyone is entitled to equality before the law and equal protection by the law, without discrimination on the ground of religion, among other grounds, while Article 27 gives an assurance that minority groups are entitled to profess and practice their own religion.

The International Covenant on Economic, Social and Cultural Rights
Adopted by the UN General Assembly in 1966, with effect from 1976, the Covenant guarantees the right to freedom of religion, and specifically requires State parties to ensure that enumerated rights – e.g. to work, to training, to equal pay, to join trade unions – can be enjoyed without discrimination of any kind, specifically including religious discrimination.

---

[23] The author acknowledges advice from Frank Cranmer on this matter (note to author, 8 April 2017).

[24] See the UN Human Rights Committee, General Comment No. 22: Article 18 (Freedom of Thought, Conscience and Religion) (1993), at para. 4.

The Declaration on the Elimination of All Forms of Intolerance and of Discrimination Based on Religion or Belief   Proclaimed by the UN General Assembly in 1981, this Declaration prohibits unintentional and intentional acts of discrimination. Article 2 defines religious discrimination as:

> Any distinction, exclusion, restriction or preference based on religion or belief and having as its purpose or as its effect nullification or impairment of the recognition, enjoyment or exercise of human rights and fundamental freedoms on an equal basis.

Article 6 states that a religious community's joint or shared expression of beliefs is protected equally with the individual's right. It protects manifestation of religion or belief including, but not limited to: worshipping and assembling, and maintaining places for this purpose; establishing and maintaining charitable or humanitarian institutions; practising religious rites and customs; writing and disseminating religious publications; teaching religion and belief; soliciting voluntary financial support; the training and appointment of religions leaders in accordance with the requirements and standards of the religion or belief; observing religious holidays and ceremonies; and communicating with individuals and communities on matters of religion and belief.

Other   Also relevant are: the ILOC; the ICERD, which guarantees the freedom of religion principle in Article 5; the International Convention on the Rights of the Child, which clearly enshrines the same principle in Articles 2, 14 and 30; the FCNM, a monitoring body of the Council of Europe; the UN Convention on the Elimination of all forms of Discrimination Against Women (CEDAW), together with its Optional Protocol; and the Resolution on the Elimination of All Forms of Religious Intolerance, which designates related responsibilities to a Special Rapporteur.

Protocol 12 to the ECHR came into force for those States that ratified it on 1 April 2005 and provides for a free-standing right to non-discrimination, irrespective of whether the difference in treatment engages another Convention right. It therefore provides for protection equivalent to non-discrimination guarantees in ICERD and the ICCPR.

A series of Directives, binding upon the UK and Ireland, have an influence on religion and related matters (see later). Of particular importance is Council Directive 2000/78/EC of 27 November 2000, establishing a general framework for equal treatment in employment and occupation, which gives direct protection against discrimination based on religion or belief in employment (see later). Also important are: the Race Equality Directive 2000/43/EC; the Recast Gender Directive 2006/54/EC on equal treatment in employment; and the Gender Directive 2004/113/EC dealing with sex equality in goods and services. In July 2008, the European Commission published a proposal for an anti-discrimination directive covering goods and services in the four remaining grounds – age, sexual orientation, religion or belief and disability – which is as yet not finalised.

The UN took an early stand against discrimination that conflates religious and racial prejudices with its 1978 Declaration on Race and Racial Prejudice,[25] which recognised that "religious intolerance motivated by racist considerations" was a form of racism. Of wider application is Resolution 16/18, initially introduced in March 2011 at the UN Human Rights Council by the Organisation of Islamic Co-operation, which calls upon UN Member States to combat "intolerance, negative stereotyping and stigmatization of, and discrimination, incitement to violence and violence against, persons based on religion or belief". By way of counterpoint, it should be noted that when ratifying international human rights instruments that support gender equality, many Muslim countries have entered reservations on the grounds that they consider some provisions to "contain values and pronouncements contrary to Shari'a on the status of women", which would seem to constitute a frank acknowledgment that Islamic religion/culture is at variance with human rights – at least as regards gender equality.[26]

Courts

The European Court of Justice (CJEU) Officially the Court of Justice of the European Union (CJEU), but normally referred to as the ECJ, the court has two constituents: the European Court of Justice (ECJ) and the General Court, which hears complaints against the institutions of the EU from individuals and Member States. This is the highest court in the European Union in matters of EU law. Established in 1952, its role is to ensure that EU law is interpreted and applied fully and consistently throughout the EU. It adjudicates on legal disputes arising between national governments and EU institutions, enforces decisions taken and settles compensation

---

[25] Followed in 2001 by the Council of Europe's First Additional Protocol to the Cybercrime Convention, which defines "racist and xenophobic material" as including "religion if used as a pretext" for racial/ethnic discrimination.

[26] Ali, S. S., *Gender and Human Rights in Islam and International Law: Equal Before Allah, Unequal Before Man?*, The Hague, Kluwer Law International, 2000, at p. 2.

for any entity that has had its interests harmed as a result of the action or inaction of the EU.

The European Court of Human Rights (ECtHR) The ECtHR was established in 1959 and functioned alongside the European Commission of Human Rights until 1998, when ECHR Protocol 11 created a single, full-time, permanent Court and abolished the Commission. The ECtHR rules on issues arising from the domestic litigation of forty-seven Member States, including the UK and Ireland, concerning alleged violations of rights enshrined in the Convention and its protocols. In making its determinations, the ECtHR is guided by principles such as "proportionality", "compatibility with democracy" and "a margin of appreciation". The first requires a fair balance to be struck between the demands of the general interests of the community and the requirements of the protection of the individual's fundamental rights.[27] The ECtHR looks at the interference complained of in the light of the case as a whole to determine whether the alleged interference is "prescribed by law" and was: (i) for a legitimate aim which is important enough to justify interfering with a fundamental right, (ii) rationally connected to achieving that aim, (iii) no more than reasonably necessary to achieve it and (iv) in the light of this, striking a fair balance between the rights of the individual and the interests of the community.[28] The second principle imports a liberal measure of balance and tolerance.[29] Frequently, the ECtHR can be seen applying the following test: Is this form of State intervention necessary in a democratic society?[30] The third principle permits States a degree of latitude in their interpretation of human rights obligations.[31] Each State enjoys a margin of appreciation when assessing what constitutes "discrimination" and the extent

---

[27] See *Olson v. Sweden* (No. 1) (1988) 11 EHRR 299; *Sporrong v. Sweden* [1982] 5 EHRR 35, at para. 69; *Tsirlis and Kouloumpas v. Greece* (1997) 25 EHRR 198, at para. 116; *Razgar v. Secretary of State for Home Department* [2004] UKHL 27, at para. 20; and *Kozac v. Poland* [2010] ECHR 280 (2010) 51 EHRR 16.

[28] See *Huang v. Secretary of State for the Home Department* [2007] 2 AC 167, at para. 19; *R (Quila) v. Secretary of State for the Home Department* [2012] 1 AC 621, at para. 45; and *Bank Mellat v. HM Treasury* (No. 2) [2013] UKSC 39, [2013] 3 WLR 179, 222, at para. 20.

[29] See *Refah Partisi v. Turkey* (2003) 37 EHRR 1, [2003] ECHR 87.

[30] See *Olson v. Sweden* (No. 1), op. cit., where it is explained that to be justifiable, such interference must be "relevant and sufficient; it must meet a pressing social need; and it must be proportionate to the need".

[31] See e.g. *Lithgow v. United Kingdom* (1986) 8 EHRR 329; *Fredin v. Sweden* (1991) 13 EHRR 784; *Abdulaziz, Cabales and Balkandali v. United Kingdom* (1985) 7 EHRR 471.

to which differences in otherwise similar situations may justify a corresponding difference in treatment.

The Venice Commission   This organ of the Council of Europe was established in 1990 and has a membership of sixty States (the forty-seven Members of the Council of Europe plus thirteen others). Its primary task is to assist and advise individual countries in constitutional matters in order to improve the functioning of democratic institutions and the protection of human rights. It does so by appointing a working group of rapporteurs to advise national authorities on relevant issues.

The Human Rights Committee (HRC)   Composed of a body of independent experts, the HRC is established under Article 28 of the ICCPR, and provides an independent and impartial monitoring function which reports on implementation of the Covenant by State parties. The latter are required to submit progress reports, usually at 4-year intervals. For present purposes, the operative provision is Article 18(2), which declares that "no one shall be subject to coercion which would impair his freedom to have or to adopt a religion or belief of his choice".

The Human Rights Council   This body assigns responsibility for identifying existing and emerging obstacles to the enjoyment of the right to freedom of religion or belief to a Special Rapporteur on the Freedom of Religion and Belief. The Rapporteur reports to the Council and presents recommendations on ways and means to overcome such obstacles.

The Committee on the Elimination of Discrimination Against Women (CEDAW)   CEDAW was established under the UN Convention on the Elimination of all forms of Discrimination Against Women with its Optional Protocol; this international treaty was adopted in 1979 by the UN General Assembly. The Committee reviews and makes recommendations on national reports submitted by the State parties within one year of ratification or accession, and thereafter every four years.

Human Rights Commissions   It has been customary for human rights issues, including religious discrimination, to be regulated by a designated national or regional Human Rights Commission, with a right of appeal to the appropriate court. As equality and non-discrimination legislation has grown, it has become not uncommon for all matters of inequity, inequality and discrimination to be assigned to the same administrative body.

Other   The Committee for the Elimination of Racial Discrimination monitors compliance with the UN's International Convention on the Elimination of All Forms of Racial Discrimination (ICERD). In its General Recommendation XXIX, the Committee strongly reaffirmed that discrimination based on descent in Article 1 of ICERD includes discrimination "against members of communities based on forms of social stratification such as caste and analogous systems which nullify or impair their equal enjoyment of human rights". Also relevant is the Advisory Committee on the Framework Convention for the Protection of National Minorities (FCNM), a monitoring body of the Council of Europe.

International Reports

In 2006, the UN General Assembly introduced the Universal Periodic Review procedure,[32] which is truly international, with a remit to review human rights, including those relating to the freedom of religion and belief, in respect of all 193 UN Member States. This procedure has a uniform application to all nations presently being considered. It provides an opportunity for each State to make a periodic declaration to the Human Rights Council regarding the actions taken to improve human rights in its country (including protection against religious discrimination), to receive comment from its peer signatory States and to agree goals for the next review. This process operates in conjunction with the Principles relating to the Status of National Institutions (the Paris Principles), adopted by the UN General Assembly in 1993,[33] which set out the minimum standards required from national human rights institutions if they are to operate effectively and to be considered credible. In order to be effective and awarded "A status", national human rights institutions must be independent and adequately funded and must have a broad human rights mandate.

Definitions

Traditionally, legislators and judiciary have been extremely wary of being drawn into making any pronouncements as to what may constitute a religion or belief. In more recent years, as the jurisprudence relating to human

---

[32] Established by UN General Assembly resolution 60/251 of 3 April 2006, this procedure aims to review national human rights performance at 4-yearly intervals.
[33] See National Institutions for the Promotion and Protection of Human Rights, UN Doc A/RES/48/134 (20 December 1993).

rights and equality has mushroomed, so the need has grown to at least clarify what cannot fit within any reasonable understanding of such terms.

Freedom of Religion

The freedom to pray and worship in accordance with religious beliefs, whether in private or through participation in public rituals, has long been upheld as one of the most important aspects of a democratic society. This freedom is one that has, however, always been tightly circumscribed by the rights of others not to have their freedoms interfered with.

The Right

This right is stated in many international instruments, including Article 10 of the Charter of Fundamental Rights of the European Union, which was proclaimed on 7 December 2000 and entered into force on 1 December 2009. It is, as has been said:[34]

> one of the most vital elements that go to make up the identity of believers and their conception of life, but it is also a precious asset for atheists, agnostics, sceptics and the unconcerned. The pluralism indissociable from a democratic society, which has been dearly won over the centuries, depends on it.

Article 9 of the ECHR provides for the right to freedom of thought, conscience and religion[35] as follows:

1. Everyone has the right to freedom of thought, conscience and religion; this right includes freedom to change his religion or belief and freedom, either alone or in community with others and in public or private, to manifest his religion or belief, in worship, teaching, practice and observance.

2. Freedom to manifest one's religion or beliefs shall be subject only to such limitations as are prescribed by law and are necessary in a democratic society in the interests of public safety, for the protection

---

[34] *Moscow Branch of the Salvation Army* v. *Russia* [2006] ECHR 7288/01, [57]. See e.g. *Lithgow* v. *United Kingdom*, op. cit.; *Fredin* v. *Sweden*, op. cit.; *Abdulaziz, Cabales and Balkandali* v. *United Kingdom*, op. cit.

[35] Together with the associated ECtHR caselaw, including: *Buscarini and Others* v. *San Marino*, Application No. 24645/94, 1998; *Kokkinakis* v. *Greece*, Application No. 14307/88, 1993; *Leyla Sahin* v. *Turkey*, 2004; *Pichon and Sajous* v. *France*; *Leela Forderkeis E.V. and Others* v. *Germany*, Application No. 58911/00, 2008; *Universelles Leben E.V.* v. *Germany*, Application No. 29745/96, 1996; and *Lautsi* v. *Italy*, 2011.

of public order, health or morals, or for the protection of the rights and freedoms of others.

Article 14 of the same Convention provides:

> The enjoyment of the rights and freedoms set forth in [the] Convention shall be secured without discrimination on any ground such as sex, race, colour, language, religion, political or other opinion, national or social origin, association with a national minority, property, birth or other status.

For the purposes of this Article, a difference in treatment is discriminatory if it does not pursue a legitimate aim or if there is not a relationship of proportionality between the means employed and the aim sought to be realised. In assessing whether and to what extent differences in otherwise similar situations justify a different treatment, the Contracting States enjoy a margin of appreciation.

Article 18 of the ICCPR extends specific protection to religion:

1. Everyone shall have the right to freedom of thought, conscience and religion. This right shall include freedom to have or to adopt a religion or belief of his choice, and freedom, either individually or in community with others and in public or private, to manifest his religion or belief in worship, observance, practice and teaching.
2. No one shall be subject to coercion which would impair his freedom to have or to adopt a religion or belief of his choice.
3. Freedom to manifest one's religion or beliefs may be subject only to such limitations as are prescribed by law and are necessary to protect public safety, order, health, or morals or the fundamental rights and freedoms of others.
4. The States Parties to the present Covenant undertake to have respect for the liberty of parents and, when applicable, legal guardians to ensure the religious and moral education of their children in conformity with their own convictions.

Elaborating upon Article 18 obligations, the UN Human Rights Committee issued "General Comment 22", which defined the right to freedom of religion or belief as:[36]

> protect[ing] theistic, non-theistic and atheistic beliefs, as well as the right not to profess any religion or belief. The terms "belief" and "religion" are

---

[36] UN Human Rights Committee, General Comment No. 22, UN Doc. CCPR/C/21/Rev.1/ Add.4, [8].

to be broadly construed. Article 18 is not limited in its application to traditional religions or to religions and beliefs with institutional characteristics or practices analogous to those of traditional religions.

Importantly, the Committee then went on to explain that the concluding words of Article 18, "worship, observance, practice, and teaching", should be interpreted to "include not only ceremonial acts but also such customs as the observance of dietary regulations, the wearing of distinctive clothing or headcoverings, participation in rituals associated with certain stages of life, and the use of a particular language customarily spoken by a group". Also specifically included is the right to conscientious objection.

Religion and Beliefs

In recent years, the definitions of "religion" and "belief" have become increasingly elastic, and they now extend to include Rastafarians, Zoroastrians and the Bahá'í, as well as to those espousing such philosophical beliefs as vegans, pacifists and environmentalists.[37] Our understanding of what constitutes a "religion" or "belief" has grown to become much more complex and contentious than could possibly have been foreseen only a couple of decades ago.

Religion

While all Conventions and the ECtHR refrain from providing a definition of "religion", the latter now requires any interpretation to be applied objectively, to have reasonable justification[38] and to be non-discriminatory; any differential treatment must comply with strict standards. With the ruling in *Campbell and Cosans* v. *United Kingdom*,[39] it become clear that theistic beliefs were no longer essential to satisfy a legal definition of "religion". The ECtHR then held in favour of complainants who alleged that the system of corporal punishment in Scottish State schools offended their philosophical convictions under Article 2 of Protocol 1 of the ECHR. ECtHR caselaw has since accepted that Jehovah's Witnesses, the Church of Scientology and the Moon sect are protected by Article 9(1) of the Convention, as are pacifists, Druids, vegans and atheists. Article 18 of the UDHR upholds the freedom of a person "to change his religion or belief", although Islamic

---

[37] *Grainger plc* v. *Nicholson* [2010] IRLR 4.

[38] See e.g. *Tsirlis and Kouloumpas* v. *Greece*, op. cit. See also the *Belgian Linguistic Case* (1968)(No 2) 1 EHRR 252.

[39] [1982] 4 EHRR 293. See also *Arrowsmith* v. *United Kingdom* [1978] 3 EHRR 218.

apostacy laws forbid this,[40] while under Article 26 it is asserted that "parents have a prior right to choose the kind of education that shall be given to their children".

Beliefs

The Article 9 right concerns religious beliefs in particular, but also applies more generally to all personal, political, philosophical and moral convictions, although it does not protect every act motivated or inspired by a religion or belief. The veracity of a "belief" is to be determined by having regard to its cogency, seriousness, cohesion and importance to the holder.[41] It extends to ideas and philosophical convictions of all kinds,[42] with the express mention of a person's religious beliefs and their means of comprehending their personal and social life, which could, for example, include pacifism and conscientious objection. This interpretation is also proclaimed in the European Directive on Race, issued in 2000.[43]

"Race" and "Caste"

Very few opportunities, surprisingly, seem to have arisen for the ECtHR to explore issues relating to race, and even fewer to explore issues of caste.

A leading case was *D.H. v. Czech Republic*,[44] which concerned the routine practice whereby Roma children were diverted into "special" schools designated for those with learning difficulties. The ECtHR confirmed that a difference in treatment may take the form of disproportionately prejudicial effects of a general policy or measure which, although couched in neutral terms, discriminates against a racial or ethnic group. The court considered that there may in effect be an "obligation to make reasonable adjustments". To the extent that others excluded by a specific differentiation (in this case, ethnicity) are in all respects identical to those selected, that exclusion constitutes discrimination.[45]

Redfearn v. United Kingdom[46] concerned a driver who had been dismissed when it had come to light that he was a member of the British

---

[40] See e.g. *Lina Joy v. Majilis Ayama Islam Wilayah Persekutuan & 2 Lagi*, Malaysian Federal Court, No. 01-2-2000 (30 May 2007).

[41] See *Campbell and Cosans v. United Kingdom* (1982) Application No. 7511/76, 4 EHRR 293, at para. 36.

[42] See *Knudsen v. Norway*, Application No. 11045/84 (1985).

[43] Both the European Directive on Race and the Employment Framework Council Directive were issued in 2000; they are known jointly as "the Article 13 Directives".

[44] (2007), Application No. 57325/00.

[45] See e.g. *Pla and Puncernau v. Andorra* (2006), Application No. 69498/01, 42 EHRR 25.

[46] [2013] IRLR 51.

National Party. His employer was worried for the safety of the disabled people, mostly Asian, who were being transported, as they feared that the driver's politics might lead to attacks. The comments of the ECtHR, in upholding the claim for unfair dismissal on grounds of unlawful discrimination, that Article 11 gives protection to an individual even in circumstances where his or her views may "offend, shock or disturb" are a reminder that the right of free speech and the principle of proportionality must always be taken into account.

"Manifestation" of Religion or Belief

Article 18 of the the UN Declaration on the Elimination of All Forms of Intolerance and of Discrimination based on Religion or Belief stresses the right to "manifest" one's religion.[47] The ECtHR has ruled that the right includes the freedom to manifest one's religion alone and in private, in community with others, in public and within the circle of those whose faith one shares.[48] However, in exercising that freedom, an applicant "may need to take his specific situation into account".[49]

In Article 9 of the ECHR, a distinction is drawn between the "right of freedom of thought, conscience and religion" and the "freedom to manifest one's religion or beliefs". The latter right is subject to the "rights and freedoms of others". This caveat is recognised by the ICCPR:[50] Article 18(1) establishes the right to so manifest – but Article 18(3) makes this subject to restrictions in specified circumstances. In its previously mentioned "General Comment 22", the UNHRC notes that the State may interfere in the right to manifest a religion or belief, but only if it can show that this was both "prescribed by law" and "necessary to protect public safety, order, health, or morals or the fundamental rights and freedoms of others", and that any restrictions were "directly related and proportionate to the specific need on which they [were] predicated".

The threshold for conduct justifying interference, often the subject of ECtHR rulings, places an onus upon those interfering to justify doing so if they are to avoid an accusation of religious discrimination. As the court ruled in *Kosteski* v. *"The Former Yugoslav Republic of Macedonia"*,[51] while

---

[47] GA Res 36/55, UN GAOR, 36th sess., UN Doc. A/36/684 (1981).
[48] See e.g. *Perry* v. *Latvia* (2007), Application No. 30273/03.
[49] *Kalac* v. *Turkey* [1997] EHRR 552, at para. 27.
[50] See also UN Human Rights Committee, General Comment No. 22, UN Doc. CCPR/C/21/Rev.1/Add.4, [8].
[51] 3 April 2006 ECHR.

Article 9 lists a number of forms which manifestation may take, it does not protect every act motivated or inspired by a religion or belief. In that instance, it was not persuaded that attendance at a Muslim festival was a manifestation of the applicant's beliefs such as warranted protection under Article 9. In recent years, the onus would seem to have become heavier: the belief in question must have attained a certain level of cogency, seriousness, cohesion and importance; and the related manifestation must be intimately linked to the religion or belief. In *Manoussakis* v. *Greece*,[52] the ECtHR ruled that "the right to freedom of religion... excludes any discretion on the part of the State to determine whether religious beliefs or the means used to express such beliefs are legitimate". This approach was underlined in the seminal *Eweida and others* v. *the United Kingdom* when the court stressed that:[53]

> the existence of a sufficiently close and direct nexus between the act and the underlying belief must be determined on the facts of each case. In particular, there is no requirement on the applicant to establish that he or she acted in fulfillment of a duty mandated by the religion in question.

Free Speech and Freedom of Association

Advocacy and dissension are important aspects of the right to free speech and have been upheld by the ECtHR in rulings which include *Handyside* v. *The United Kingdom*,[54] where the court declared that the right:

> is applicable not only to "information" or "ideas" that are favourably received or regarded as inoffensive or as a matter of indifference, but also to those that offend, shock or disturb the State or any sector of the population. Such are the demands of that pluralism, tolerance and broadmindedness without which there is no "democratic society".

It has also issued rulings condemning government bans on public demonstrations by LGBT groups.[55] A notable development came with the decision in *Vejdeland and Others* v. *Sweden*[56] when the ECtHR applied hate speech principles in relation to sexual orientation issues. Additionally, the Human Rights Committee has ruled on related issues, including in

---

[52] (18748/91) (1996) 21 EHRR CD3.   [53] Op. cit., at para. 82.
[54] (5493/72) [1976] ECHR 5.
[55] *Bączkowski and Others* v. *Poland*, Application No. 1543/06 (2007); *Alekseyev* v. *Russia*, Application Nos 4916/07, 25924/08 and 14599/09 (2010); and *Genderdoc-M* v. *Moldova*, Application No. 9106/06 (2012).
[56] Application No. 1813/07 (2012).

Faurisson v. France,[57] when it upheld the criminal prosecution of a "Holocaust denier".[58]

A religious organisation can be the subject of legal proceedings,[59] and has been so in all the common law jurisdictions considered in Part III as a consequence of clergy involvement in historical child abuse. Also, the ECtHR has ruled that if an association's activities constitute widespread intimidation, the association can be lawfully banned[60] – but it was the State closure of the Juma Mosque Congregation that gave it an opportunity to consider the juxtaposition of the rights to freedom of religion and to freedom of association.[61] The closure was on the basis that while the organisation purported to be a non-government organisation delivering community support services, it was in fact engaging in religious activities and functioning as a religious organisation (registration requirements differentiated between the two) when it was prohibited from doing so. In the second case, the court noted a broad principle, with application to associations engaging in religious activities, that:[62]

> citizens should be able to form a legal entity in order to act collectively in a field of mutual interest is one of the most important aspects of the right to freedom of association, without which that right would be deprived of any meaning. The way in which national legislation enshrines this freedom and its practical application by the authorities reveal the state of democracy in the country concerned.

In this instance, however, the technicality that there was no statutory definition of what constituted "religious activity" allowed the court to sidestep any ruling on a possible conflict of rights (see also Chapter 12).

Blasphemy

Blackstone, in dealing with offences against religion, refers to the heinous offence "of blasphemy against the Almighty, by denying his being or

---

[57] Communication No. 550/1993, U.N. Doc. CCPR/C/ 58/D/550/1993(1996).

[58] Note that in 1986, the Human Rights Commission appointed a Special Rapporteur on Religious Intolerance with a mandate focused on the Declaration on the Elimination of All Forms of Intolerance and of Discrimination Based on Religion or Belief, and in 1993, it appointed a Special Rapporteur on the Promotion and Protection of the Right to Freedom of Opinion and Expression (Resolution 1993/45 of 5 March 1993).

[59] *X & Church of Scientology v. Sweden*, Application No. 7805/77 (1979).

[60] *Vona v. Hungary*, Application No. 35943/10 (2013).

[61] See *Juma Mosque Congregation & Ors v. Azerbaijan*, Application No. 15405/04 (2013) and *Islam-Ittihad Association & Ors v. Azerbaijan*, Application No. 5548/05 (2014).

[62] Ibid. at para. 39.

providence; or by contumelious reproaches of our Saviour Christ . . . these are offences punishable at common law by fine and imprisonment, or other infamous corporal punishment: for Christianity is part of the laws of England".[63] Blasphemy attracted severe punishment, including banishment and, in certain circumstances, the death penalty. Although abolished in England and Wales in 2008, the offence remains on the statute books in fifty-nine countries, including some common law jurisdictions.[64] It is now mostly significant in an Islamic context, however, where expressions of irreverence towards Muhammad can have serious consequences: acts of blasphemy have resulted in the deaths of many in Pakistan and in protests, violence and death in Europe, where those judged to have insulted or acted with disrespect towards the prophet Muhammad have been attacked by his followers. Blasphemy, as interpreted by some Muslim communities in contemporary Western societies, is a signature benchmark of religious/cultural difference.

The ICCPR, Arts 18 and 19, which protects the freedom of expression, does so in terms which do not prohibit blasphemy laws.

Proselytism

Although long recognised in law as a legitimate aspect of religious adherence, proselytism is subject to a test of reasonableness and must not be exercised improperly[65] – as will be the case, for example, if it interferes with the right of others to be free from the inappropriate promotion of religion either as a service user or while working.[66] This is reinforced by Article 18(1) of the ICCPR, which provides that no one shall be subject to coercion which would impair the ability to choose a religion and that freedom to manifest one's religion may be subject to domestic legal restrictions such as are "necessary to protect public safety, order, health, or morals or the fundamental rights and freedoms of others". Arguably, Islamic proselytism – or *dawa* – is not ICCPR–compliant, as it goes far beyond information dissemination and persuasion to license indoctrination.[67]

---

[63] See Blackstone, *Commentaries*, bk 4, c. 4, s. iv, at http://avalon.law.yale.edu/18th_century/blackstone_bk4ch14.asp.
[64] See 2011 Pew Research Centre report at www.pewforum.org/2011/08/09/rising-restrictions-on-religion6/.
[65] *Kokkinakis* v. *Greece* [1993] 17 EHRR 397.
[66] *Chondol* v. *Liverpool City Council* [2009] UKEAT 0298/08.
[67] See further Ali, A. H., "The Challenge of Dawa", at www.hoover.org/sites/default/files/research/docs/ali_challengeofdawa_final_web.pdf.

In *Kokkinakis* v. *Greece*, the ECtHR defended the right to proselytise as follows:[68]

> [T]o manifest one's religion ... [is] not only exercisable in community with others, "in public" and within the circle of those whose faith one shares, but can also be asserted "alone" and "in private"; furthermore, it includes in principle the right to try to convince one's neighbour ... through "teaching", failing which ... "freedom to change [one's] religion or belief" ... would be likely to remain a dead-letter.

The court then drew a distinction between "evangelism" and "improper proselytism" when it found that the Greek courts were wrong to convict a Jehovah's Witness for "improper proselytism" following his attempt to bring his neighbour "good news" by entering her house and offering to sell to her some booklets advertising his religion; the court ruled that the Greek anti-proselytism law impermissibly interfered with freedom of religion. There are circumstances in which the proactive dissemination of doctrines and observances might include activities that others find objectionable and which some could experience as discriminatory. In *D.H.* v. *Czech Republic*,[69] the ECtHR considered that the Islamic veil was a "powerful external symbol" capable of having a proselytising effect, at least on very young children. However, as in *Lautsi* v. *Italy*,[70] it would seem that where symbols manifesting religious beliefs are of a passive nature – not such as to constitute indoctrination or misplaced proselytism – then they should be accommodated.

Conscientious Objection

That "everyone shall have the right to freedom of ... conscience" is clearly established in Article 18 of the ICCPR and most often gives rise to issues in the context of health care provision and military service when individuals decline, on religious grounds, to perform a statutory requirement.

In *Pichon and Sajous* v. *France*,[71] the ECtHR gave the following explanation for its ruling that two pharmacists who refused to sell contraceptives were imposing their beliefs on the public: "as long as the sale of contraceptives is legal and occurs on medical prescription nowhere other than in a pharmacy, the applicants cannot give precedence to their religious beliefs and impose them on others as justification for their refusal

[68] *Kokkinakis* v. *Greece* [1993] 17 EHRR 397, at p. 418.
[69] Application No. 42393/98, 2001-V ECtHR 449.
[70] Application No. 30814/06, ECtHR (18 March 2011).
[71] Application No. 49853/99 (2 October 2001).

to sell such products". The action of the pharmacists constituted religious discrimination.

The claims of individual citizens to exemption from compulsory military service in their country's armed forces on religious or political grounds has been brought before the courts over many decades.[72] Not until *Bayatyan v. Armenia*,[73] however, was it determined that such claims could find protection under Article 9. This case concerned a Jehovah's Witness who alleged that his conviction for refusal to serve in the army had violated his right to freedom of thought, conscience and religion. The ECtHR noted that, initially, the position as set out in *Grandrath v. the Federal Republic of Germany*[74] was that Article 4 of the Convention, containing a provision which expressly dealt with the question of compulsory service exacted in the place of military service in the case of conscientious objectors,[75] should be considered the appropriate protective provision. However, there had since been developments in international instruments (e.g. Article 18 of the ICCPR and Article 10 of the Charter of Fundamental Rights), and the court took the view that as the Convention was a living instrument, it should be interpreted in the light of present-day conditions and of the ideas currently prevailing in democratic States. Accordingly, the court considered that opposition to military service, where it is motivated by a serious and insurmountable conflict between the obligation to serve in the army and a person's conscience or their deeply and genuinely held religious or other beliefs, constitutes a conviction or belief of sufficient cogency, seriousness, cohesion and importance to attract the guarantees of Article 9.[76]

Bringing conscientious objection within the ambit of Article 9(1) is important, as, within that provision, freedom of conscience is recognised as an absolute right, in contrast to the conditioned rights of Article 9(2). This decision offers protection not only to Jehovah's Witnesses and Quakers, whose religions clearly prohibit military service, but also to anyone who holds authentic beliefs to the same effect; arguably, it also applies to

---

[72] The UNHRC's decision in *J.P. v. Canada*, Communication No. 446/1991, was the first time, albeit obiter dictum, it accepted that Article 18 of the ICCPR afforded protection to conscientious objectors.

[73] [2011] 234/9/03.

[74] Application No. 2299/64, Commission report of 12 December 1966, Yearbook, vol. 10, at p. 626.

[75] Confirmed in such cases as *X. v. Austria*, Application No. 5591/72 (1973); *X. v. the Federal Republic of Germany*, Application No. 7705/76 (1977); *Conscientious objectors v. Denmark*, Application No. 7565/76 (1977); and *A. v. Switzerland*, Application No. 10640/83 (1984).

[76] *Bayatyan v. Armenia*, op. cit., at para. 110.

conscientious objection in other contexts, such as the delivery of abortion services. It thereby significantly extends the protection of the law in relation to those suffering religious discrimination.

Discrimination

"Discrimination" is an unjustified difference of treatment. The UN Human Rights Committee has defined it as:[77]

> any distinction, exclusion, restriction or preference which is based on any ground such as race, colour, sex, language, religion, political or other opinion, national or social origin, property, birth, or other status, and which has the purpose or effect of nullifying or impairing the recognition, enjoyment or exercise by all persons, on an equal footing, of all rights and freedoms.

Subsequent ECtHR caselaw has explained that this means "treating differently, without an objective and reasonable justification, persons in analogous, or relevantly similar, situations".[78] Under Article 14, a lack of "objective and reasonable justification" is understood as meaning "that it does not pursue a 'legitimate aim'" or that there is no "reasonable proportionality between the means employed and the aim sought to be realised".[79] A legitimate aim is one that has a reasonable social policy objective, is planned to be consistent with the lawful carrying out of that objective and is not itself discriminatory. Proportionality is "the need to balance the interests of society with those of individuals and groups".[80] Discriminatory treatment may, therefore, be justified if it arises in pursuit of a legitimate aim or, as expressed in *Schmidt v. Germany*,[81] where there is a "reasonable relationship of proportionality between the means employed and the aim sought to be realised".

Religious Discrimination

Proportionality is a principle that needs to be borne in mind when examining contemporary instances of religious discrimination. The right not to be discriminated against on religious grounds is one that is prone to becoming entangled with other fundamental rights. In particular, it can

---

[77] See UN Human Rights Committee, "General Comment relating to Discrimination under the International Covenant on Civil and Political Rights", 1989, no. 18, at para. 7.
[78] *Kiyutin v. Russia*, Application No. 2700/10, March 2011.
[79] See *EB v. France* (2008) 47 EHRR 21, at para. 91.
[80] *Huang v. Secretary of State for the Home Department* [2007] UKHL 11.
[81] [1994] 18 EHRR 513. See also *EB v. France*, op. cit., at para. 91.

be impacted by the right to freedom of expression, or by rights related to equality, especially equality on grounds of sexual orientation. However, the legal niceties involved in parsing such rights need to be seen relative to the brutality of numerous attacks by Islamic extremists in Europe[82] (also, of course, in the Middle East and elsewhere), which constitute extreme instances of contemporary religious discrimination.

As already mentioned, Article 2 of the UDHR initially established the right not to be discriminated against. This has since been superseded for all practical purposes by the following provision in Article 14 of the European Convention:

> The enjoyment of the rights and freedoms set forth in this Convention shall be secured without discrimination on any ground such as sex, race, colour, language, religion, political or other opinion, national or social origin, association with a national minority, property, birth or other status.

This broadly prohibits discrimination "on any ground", including religion, but takes effect solely in relation to the enjoyment of the rights and freedoms safeguarded by other Convention provisions.[83] Where a substantive Article of the Convention or its protocols has been relied upon – either on its own or in conjunction with Article 14 – and a separate breach has been found of the substantive Article, it is not generally necessary for the court to consider the case under Article 14 also, although the position is otherwise if a clear inequality of treatment in the enjoyment of the right in question is a fundamental aspect of the case.[84]

Article 14 is supported by: Article 9 of the ECHR (the right to freedom of thought, conscience and religion); Article 1 of the First Protocol (the right to peaceful enjoyment of property); and the ICCPR.[85] Articles 2(1) and 26 of the latter bind every signatory nation in relation to discrimination on the basis of religion, while Article 20(2) provides that "any advocacy of national, racial or religious hatred that constitutes incitement to discrimination, hostility or violence shall be prohibited by law".

---

[82] Among the worst of which were: the 1988 Lockerbie plane bomb (270 dead); the March 2004 train bombings in Madrid (192 dead); and the November 2015 Paris attacks on the Bataclan and other venues (89 dead).

[83] See *Schmidt v. Germany* [1994] EHRR 513, 526, at para. 22.

[84] See *Chassagnou and Others v. France* [GC], Nos. 25088/94, 28331/95 and 28443/95, s.89, ECHR 1999-III and *Dudgeon v. United Kingdom* (Ser. A) No. 45 (1982) ECtHR.

[85] Opened for signature by General Assembly resolution 2200A (XXI) of 16 December 1966 and entered into force on 23 March 1976. As of March 2012, the Covenant had seventy-four signatories and 167 parties.

Article 14 is further reinforced by the Employment Framework Council Directive 2000/78/EC, issued by the Council of the European Union, the purpose of which, as stated in Article 1, is to "lay down a general framework for combating discrimination on the further grounds of religion or belief, disability, age or sexual orientation, as regards employment and occupation". Article 4 declares:

> Member States may provide that a difference of treatment which is based on a characteristic related to any of the grounds referred to in Article 1 shall not constitute discrimination where, by reason of the nature of the particular occupational activities concerned or of the context in which they are carried out, such a characteristic constitutes a genuine and determining occupational requirement, provided that its objective is legitimate and the requirement is proportionate.

Article 4(2) provides that such a difference of treatment, based on a person's religion or belief, is permitted:

> in the case of occupational activities within churches and other public or private organisations the ethos of which is based on religion or belief, a difference of treatment based on a person's religion or belief shall not constitute discrimination where, by reason of the nature of these activities or of the context in which they are carried out, a person's religion or belief constitute a genuine, legitimate and justified occupational requirement, having regard to the organisation's ethos

Also relevant for present purposes is the International Labour Organisation Discrimination (Employment and Occupation) Convention 1958 (ILOC).[86] The ILOC provides, in Article 1.2, an exemption relating to the employment of people by "religious institutions", where discrimination is "required by the tenets and doctrines of the religion, is not arbitrary, is consistently applied" or "is an inherent requirement of a particular job". One of the most important UN documents protecting religious freedom is the UN Declaration on the Elimination of All Forms of Intolerance and of Discrimination based on Religion or Belief, which, in addition to elaborating upon the right to "manifest" one's religion in Article 18,[87] sets out in considerable detail what the international community regards as basic standards for the protection of religious freedom, and which, in Article 3,

---

[86] Adopted by the General Conference of the International Labour Organisation (ILO) on 25 June 1958 and coming into effect on 15 June 1960. As of May 2011, the Convention had been ratified by 169 out of 183 ILO members.

[87] GA Res 36/55, UN GAOR, 36th sess., UN Doc A/36/684 (1981).

cautions that "discrimination between human beings on grounds of religion or belief constitutes an affront to human dignity".

Direct Discrimination

Direct religious discrimination occurs, as explained in in Article 2(2)(a) of Directive 2000/78, when, on account of religion, one person "is treated less favourably than another is, has been or would be treated". The intent is clear, and the fact of direct discrimination is proven by the outcome. The ECtHR has generally adopted a broad understanding of this concept and has assumed discrimination to be present where a measure was inseparably linked to the relevant reason for the difference of treatment. In all cases, the court was concerned with individuals' immutable physical features or personal characteristics – such as gender, age or sexual orientation – rather than with modes of conduct based on a subjective decision or conviction – such as the wearing of religious apparel.

Indirect Discrimination

Discrimination is "indirect" when an apparently neutral practice or condition has a disproportionate and negative effect on one of the groups against whom it is unlawful to discriminate, and when the practice or condition cannot be justified objectively. An indirect difference of treatment based on religion may be objectively justified by a legitimate aim, provided that the measure at issue is appropriate and necessary for achieving that aim.

Some thirty years have passed since the court, in *Bilka-Kaufhaus GmbH v. Weber von Hartz*,[88] laid down this test for indirect discrimination. Subsequently, in *Thlimmenos v. Greece*,[89] the ECtHR considered the effects of indirect discrimination in relation to a Jehovah's Witness who was refused an appointment as a chartered accountant because of a felony. His conviction had arisen from a refusal to wear a military uniform because to do so would have been in breach of his particular religious beliefs. The court held that Article 14 was not limited to cases where a State treats differently persons in analogous situations without providing an objective and reasonable justification, but was "also violated when States without an objective and reasonable justification fail to treat differently persons whose situations are significantly different".[90] For minority religious groups, among others, this was an important decision, as it recognised that the right to non-discrimination also operates to afford protection from legal

---

88 (1986) C-170/84.   89 (2001) 31 EHRR 411.   90 Ibid., at para. 44.

provisions that, although applied equally to all, have an adverse effect and discriminatory consequences for a few.

Exemptions and Exceptions

Equality and discrimination laws exempt religious entities from obligations imposed upon others. Indeed, all common law jurisdictions provide statutory exemptions enabling those of religious belief to behave in ways that would be discriminatory for ordinary citizens.

Exemptions

That religions and associated organisations are entitled to a degree of autonomy is recognised in the UN Declaration on Religious Intolerance, which provides for the right to "train, appoint, elect, or designate by succession appropriate leaders" and the right to "establish and maintain appropriate charitable and humanitarian institutions".[91] The right to appoint clergy and fill other key leadership posts, free from the restrictions of anti-discrimination and equality law, has been extended to permit appointments to commercial entities, hospitals schools, etc. and to restrict access to services, schools, social care facilities owned by religious organisations. The extent to which such an extension is permissible – exempting the selection of ancillary staff such as cleaners, janitors, gardeners, etc. from such legislative provisions – varies somewhat across the common law jurisdictions, but is challenged by secularists and others in all. Exemption privileges in equality legislation, permitting religious organisations to restrict employment opportunities to those who share their religious beliefs, have been condemned by some as statutorily licensing religious discrimination by religious bodies; they argue that there can be little justification in exempting those of religious belief from the penalties associated with religiously discriminatory behaviour, thereby benefitting those who are ostensibly more morally cognisant than others.

Church and State

The Council of Europe, in its Recommendation concerning religion,[92] states: "the Assembly reaffirms that one of Europe's shared values,

---

[91] The UN Declaration on the Elimination of All Forms of Intolerance and of Discrimination Based on Religion or Belief, Article 6(g) and (b), respectively.
[92] Council of Europe, Parliamentary Assembly, State, Religion, Secularity and Human Rights, Recommendation 1804 (2007).

transcending national differences, is the separation of Church and State".[93] It declares that States must require religious leaders to take "an unambiguous stand in favour of the precedence of human rights, as set forth in the ECHR, over any religious principle"[94] and urges that they "remove from legislation, if such is the will of the people, elements likely to be discriminatory from the angle of democratic religious pluralism".[95]

The Church/State Boundary

Article 18 of the UDHR, the precursor to Articles 9 and 14 of the ECHR, was first invoked to limit State action in 1993.

Most of the rights recognised under Article 9 of the ECHR are individual rights that cannot be challenged. However, some may have a collective aspect. The ECtHR has recognised that "religious communities traditionally and universally exist in the form of organised structures and that, where the organisation of the religious community is at issue, Article 9 of the Convention must be interpreted in the light of Article 11, which safeguards associative life against unjustified State interference".[96] The State is thus prevented from intervening in: the decisions of religious communities to admit or exclude members;[97] doctrinal differences within the membership;[98] and the freedom to choose employees according to criteria specific to the religious community.[99]

Protecting Religion from the State

The right to freedom of religion is recognised by Article 9, which is mainly concerned with protecting freedom of religion and belief against State interference, and is reinforced by Article 14, which protects against State discrimination in the enjoyment of any Convention rights on grounds which include religion and belief. It excludes any discretion on the part of the State to determine whether religious beliefs or the means used to express such beliefs are legitimate.[100]

The State must maintain a level playing field when it comes to the status of religious groups. As the ECtHR stated in *Religionsgemeinschaft der*

---

[93] Ibid., at para. 4.   [94] Ibid., at para. 17.   [95] Ibid., at para. 24.2.

[96] *Obst v. Germany* (2010), Application No. 425/03, at para. 44.

[97] *Svyato-Mykhaylivska Parafiya v. Ukraine* (2007), Application No. 77703/01.

[98] *Holy Synod of the Bulgarian Orthodox Church (Metropolitan Inokentiy) and Others*, op. cit.; *Karlsson v. Sweden* (1988), Application No. 12356/86; *Spetz and Others v. Sweden* (1994), Application No. 20402/92; and *Williamson v. the United Kingdom* (1995), Application No. 27008/95.

[99] *Obst v. Germany*, op. cit.   [100] *Hasan and Chaush v. Bulgaria*, op. cit., ss.62 and 78.

Zeugen Jehovas and Others v. *Austria*:[101] "the obligation under Article 9 of the Convention incumbent on the State's authorities to remain neutral in the exercise of their powers in this domain requires therefore that if a State sets up a framework for conferring legal personality on religious groups to which a specific status is linked, all religious groups which so wish must have a fair opportunity to apply for this status and the criteria established must be applied in a non-discriminatory manner". Article 9 cannot be allowed to diminish the role of a faith or a Church with which the population of a specific country has historically and culturally been associated;[102] but also, "new" religious communities cannot be disadvantaged relative to traditional religious organisations. This duty of neutrality and impartiality "is incompatible with any power on the State's part to assess the legitimacy of religious beliefs or the ways in which those beliefs are expressed".[103]

Intervention in Church Disputes

The principle that State neutrality in relation to religion is necessary for "the preservation of pluralism"[104] has been considered in a number of cases.

Hasan and Chaush v. *Bulgaria*[105] concerned a dispute as to the leadership of the Bulgarian Muslim community which had in effect been resolved by the Bulgarian government replacing the incumbent with another candidate who had previously held the post. The court found there had been a failure by the authorities to remain neutral in the exercise of their powers in the administrative registration of religious communities and concluded that the State had interfered with the believers' freedom to manifest their religion within the meaning of Article 9 of the Convention. This case was closely followed by *Metropolitan Church of Bessarabia and Others* v. *Moldova*,[106] which concerned the Moldovan authorities' refusal to recognise the Metropolitan Church of Bessarabia, an Orthodox Christian church, on the ground that it had split from the Metropolitan Church of Moldova, which was recognised by the State. The court took the view that the Moldovan government had failed to discharge its duty of neutrality and impartiality, and that its refusal to recognise the applicant

---

[101] (2008), Application No. 40825/98.
[102] *Members of the Gldani Congregation of Jehovah's Witnesses and Others* v. *Georgia* (2007), Application No. 71156/01.
[103] See *Bayatyan* v. *Armenia* [2011] 234/9/ 03.
[104] See *Metropolitan Church of Bessarabia and Others* v. *Moldova*, op. cit.
[105] Application No. 30985/96 (2000).   [106] Op. cit.

church constituted an interference with the right of that church and the other applicants to freedom of religion, as guaranteed by Article 9. Some time later, in *Jehovah's Witnesses of Moscow* v. *Russia*,[107] the court considered a complaint about the dissolution of the religious community of Jehovah's Witnesses of Moscow, the banning of its activities and the refusal of the Russian authorities to re-register its organisation. The court found that the decision regarding the community's dissolution constituted a violation of Article 9, as this had been an excessively severe and disproportionate sanction. The court also held that there had been a violation of Article 11 of the Convention, read in the light of Article 9, finding that in denying re-registration to the Jehovah's Witnesses of Moscow, the Moscow authorities had not acted in good faith and had neglected their duty of neutrality and impartiality vis-à-vis the applicant community. Most recently, in *Magyar Keresztény Mennonita Egyház and Others* v. *Hungary*,[108] the applicants were various religious communities which had been registered as churches in Hungary and received State funding until the introduction of the Church Act in 2012. Thereafter, only a number of recognised churches continued to receive funding, while all other religious communities lost their status as churches but were free to continue their religious activities as associations. The court considered that the deregistration had not been "necessary in a democratic society" and therefore held that there had been a violation of Article 11, read in the light of Article 9. The Hungarian government had not shown that there were not any other, less drastic solutions available, and it was inconsistent with the State's duty of neutrality in religious matters that religious groups had to apply to Parliament to obtain re-registration as churches.[109]

Similarly, *Jehovah's Witnesses Association and Ors* v. *Turkey*[110] concerned an allegation that the thirty-four groups of Jehovah's Witnesses in Turkey were discriminated against because they were members of a minority religious community and effectively denied any legal place of worship, as these were likely to be closed by the authorities at any time and the worshippers prosecuted. The court found that the State took no account of the needs of small religious communities, even though all they required was a simple meeting room in which to worship, meet and teach their beliefs. This amounted to a direct interference with the applicants'

[107] Application No. 302/02 (2010).
[108] Application Nos 70945/11, 23611/12, 26998/12, 41150/12, 41155/12, 41463/12, 41553/12, 54977/12 and 56581/12 (2014).
[109] See also *Magyar Keresztény Mennonita Egyház and Others* v. *Hungary (Just Satisfaction)* [2016] ECHR 593.
[110] [2016] ECHR 453.

freedom to manifest their religion that was neither proportionate to the legitimate aim pursued nor necessary in a democratic society.[111] The same principle was applied in *Savez crkava "Riječ života" and Others* v. *Croatia*,[112] where the question for the court was whether the difference in State treatment had "objective and reasonable justification"; that is, whether it pursued a "legitimate aim" and whether there was a "reasonable relationship of proportionality" between the means employed and the aim sought to be realised. The court held that, in this instance, State intervention amounted to religious discrimination.

As "the autonomous existence of religious communities is indispensable for pluralism in a democratic society, and is thus an issue at the very heart of the protection which Article 9 affords",[113] the court gave the matter of such autonomy close examination in *Sindicatul "Păstorul cel Bun"* v. *Romania*,[114] which concerned a dispute regarding trade union rights. The applicants, who were Orthodox priests and lay employees of the Romanian Orthodox Church, had formed a trade union to defend their professional interests, but the respondent State authorities had refused to register the union as this was debarred by statute. The Archdiocese had opposed recognition, arguing that the aims set out in the union's constitution were incompatible with the duties accepted by priests by virtue of their ministry and their undertaking towards the archbishop. It asserted that the emergence within the structure of the Church of a new body of this kind would seriously imperil the freedom of religious denominations to organise themselves in accordance with their own traditions, and that the establishment of the trade union would therefore be likely to undermine the Church's traditional hierarchical structure. The court found that it had been reasonable to take the view that a decision to allow the registration of the applicant union would create a real risk to the autonomy of the religious community in question, and it disallowed the appeal.

The State, Religion and Religious Discrimination

As noted, from an early stage the rulings of the ECtHR[115] seemed to establish a requirement that the institutions of the State adopt at least a neutral

---

[111] Ibid., at para. 108.   [112] Application No. 7798/08 (2010).

[113] *Obst v. Germany*, op. cit., at para. 44, citing: *Hasan and Chaush v. Bulgaria*, op. cit., s.62; *Metropolitan Church of Bessarabia and Others*, op. cit.; and *Holy Synod of the Bulgarian Orthodox Church (Metropolitan Inokentiy) and Others v. Bulgaria*, op. cit.

[114] Application No. 2330/09 (2013).

[115] See e.g. *Dahlab v. Switzerland*, App. No. 42393/98, 2001-V Eur. Ct. H.R 449 and *Leyla Sahin v. Turkey*, Application No. 44774/98, 2005-XI Eur. Ct. H.R. 819.

stance in relation to religious matters,[116] in order to ensure the preservation of pluralism and the proper functioning of democracy.[117] When doing so, they would enjoy a wide margin of appreciation.[118]

Balancing Religion and Secularism

Arguably, however, State neutrality often amounted to an inverted form of religious discrimination: religion per se was to be denied its traditional status, with all to be treated equally and be uniformly subordinated to a secularist approach.

It was in *Refah Partisi (The Welfare Party) and Others* v. *Turkey*[119] that the court gave its strongest ruling against any discretionary exercise of State authority in relation to religion. It then declared that "the State's duty of neutrality and impartiality [among beliefs] is incompatible with any power on the State's part to assess the legitimacy of religious beliefs and requires the State to ensure mutual tolerance between opposing groups". In *Savez crkava "Riječ života" and Others* v. *Croatia*,[120] the court noted that "the State had a duty to remain neutral and impartial in exercising its regulatory power in the sphere of religious freedom and in its relations with different religions, denominations and beliefs".[121] More recently, in the context of ongoing discrimination against the Alevis in Turkey, the ECtHR found against the State in *Cumhuriyetçi Eğitim ve Kültür Merkezi Vakfi* v. *Turkey*[122] when it ruled that Alevi places of worship had been discriminated against in the supply of free electricity.

An emphasis on the importance of State impartiality hardened into a more positive secularist approach, as was clearly evident in an education context regarding the introduction of symbols manifesting religious beliefs in the public sphere.[123] This gradually became tempered by a concern to ensure that the established cultural identity of a Member State did not become neutralised by the secularism of its institutions. So, for example, in *Folgerø & Others* v. *Norway*,[124] which concerned an objection to

---

[116] For an analysis of the relationship between religion, the right to religious freedom and democracy, see Boyle, K., "Human Rights, Religion and Democracy: The Refah Party Case", *Essex Human Rights Review*, 2004, vol. 1:1.

[117] *Metropolitan Church of Bessarabia and Others* v. *Moldova*, op. cit., ss.115–116, ECHR 2001-XII

[118] *Cha'are Shalom Ve Tsedek* v. *France* [GC], No. 27417/95, s.84, ECHR 2000-VII.

[119] 13 February 2003 [ECtHR]. Cases nos 41340/98, 41342/98, 41343/98, at para. 91.

[120] (2010), Application No. 7798/08.

[121] Ibid., at para. 88.   [122] [2014] ECHR 1346.

[123] See Habermas, "Religion in the Public Sphere".

[124] Application No. 15472/02, ECtHR, [GC] (29 June 2007).

the compulsory teaching in State schools of religious knowledge that concentrated on Christianity to the detriment of other religions, the Grand Chamber – finding that such an institutional representation of a nation's majority religion did not in itself contravene Article 2 of Protocol No. 1 – ruled as follows:[125]

> [T]he fact that knowledge about Christianity represented a greater part of the Curriculum for primary and lower secondary schools than knowledge about other religions and philosophies cannot, in the court's opinion, of its own be viewed as a departure from the principles of pluralism and objectivity amounting to indoctrination ... In view of the place occupied by Christianity in the national history and tradition of the respondent State, this must be regarded as falling within the respondent State's margin of appreciation in planning and setting the curriculum.

This ruling clearly came down in favour of the right of the State to exercise positive religious discrimination. At much the same time, there was evidence of judicial notice being taken that adherents of traditional religious beliefs are as much entitled to court protection from discrimination as those minority groups wishing to assert their newly established human rights:[126]

> The belief in question is the orthodox Christian belief that the practice of homosexuality is sinful. The manifestation in question is by teaching, practice and observance to maintain the choice not to accept, endorse or encourage homosexuality. Whether the belief is to be accepted or rejected is not the issue. The belief is a long established part of the belief system of the world's major religions. This is not a belief that is unworthy of recognition. I am satisfied that Article 9 [of the European Convention] is engaged in the present case. The extent to which the manifestation of the belief may be limited is a different issue.

However, the evolving nature of the caselaw was evident in *Lautsi* v. *Italy*,[127] which revealed how far the ECtHR had retreated from the secular high ground of earlier rulings (see later).

State Funding of Faith-Based Facilities and Services

Very few cases have been brought before the ECtHR on issues relating to this matter, which is surprising. In relation to faith-based schools, there

---

[125] Ibid., at para. 89.
[126] See *Christian Institute and Others* v. *Office of First Minister and Deputy First Minister*, Neutral Citation No. [2007] NIQB 66, per Weatherup J., at para. 50.
[127] Application No. 30814/06, ECtHR (18 March 2011).

are issues concerning their eligibility for tax exemption and for direct government funding, which cause heated controversy and court cases in many countries. Of those heard by the ECtHR, three concerned France and the tax-exemption entitlement of religious organisations, in respect of which judgments were handed down at the beginning of 2013.[128] All three had been found to be in breach of relevant tax requirements due to their receiving direct donations, which had resulted in a loss of exemption status and the imposition of harsh financial penalties. The three organisations argued that requiring them to pay tax on direct donations infringed their right to manifest and exercise their freedom of religion, contrary to Article 9. The ECtHR upheld their claim, ruling that direct donations were a major source of funding of a religious body and that taxing them might have an impact on its ability to conduct its religious activities. This decision was in keeping with an earlier ruling[129] in which the court had held that the amount of money demanded from the Jehovah's Witnesses by the French tax authorities had constituted an interference with their right to manifest under Article 9, because it had the effect of reducing the vital resources of the Association.

Christian Symbols/Prayers in State Facilities

This is a problematic issue commonly arising in school settings following parental complaints of infringement of their rights under Article 2 of Protocol No. 1. Indeed, it was the presenting issue in the case of *Folgerø & Others* v. *Norway*[130] and had earlier featured in *Valsamis* v. *Greece*,[131] which concerned a complaint from Jehovah's Witness parents that their child, who attended a State school, had been punished for not participating in the National Day celebrations commemorating the outbreak of war between Greece and Italy. As their religious beliefs forbade any association with war commemorations, they alleged a violation of both Article 9 and Article 2 of Protocol No. 1. The court found that it could "discern nothing, either in the purpose of the parade or in the arrangements for it,

---

[128] *Association Cultuelle du Temple Pyramide* v. *France* 50471/07 – HEJUD [2013] ECHR 105 (31 January 2013); *Association des Chevaliers du Lotus D'Or* v. *France* 50615/07 – HEJUD [2013] ECHR 104 (31 January 2013); and *Eglise Evangelique Missionnaire and Salaûn* v. *France* 25502/07 – HEJUD [2013] ECHR 107 (31 January 2013). See www.lawandreligionuk.com/2013/02/06/taxation-and-religious-organisations-three-french-cases-at-the-ecthr/.

[129] *Fédération chrétienne des Témoins de Jéhovah de France* v. *France* [2001] No 53430/99 (6 November 2001).

[130] Application No. 15472/02, ECtHR [GC] (29 June 2007).

[131] (1996) Reports of Judgments and Decisions 1996-VI.

which could offend the applicants' pacifist convictions... such commemorations of national events serve, in their way, both pacifist objectives and the public interest".[132] The court held that neither set of provisions had been breached.

The issue is also one which occasionally surfaces in the context of an official requirement to swear an oath before undertaking certain responsibilities. So, in *Buscarini and Others* v. *San Marino* [GC],[133] some Members of Parliament, as a prerequisite to taking up their duties, had to swear an oath on the Bible. The court held that there had been a violation of Article 9 because requiring them to take an oath was tantamount to obliging them to swear allegiance to a particular religion. Article 9 was found to be similarly violated in *Dimitras and Others* v. *Greece*[134] by an obligation imposed on the applicants, as witnesses in a number of sets of judicial proceedings, to disclose their religious convictions in order to avoid having to take an oath on the Bible.

ECtHR Caselaw

As the ECtHR has been engaged in an evolving examination of religion-related matters for some decades, the judgments emanating from that source provide a particularly rich archive of material, documenting the culturally conditioned instances of religious discrimination emerging from all forty-seven Member States of the Council of Europe. Themes are extracted from this material to focus the examination conducted in Part III.

Religious Conduct, Symbols, Icons, Apparel, etc.

Everyday personal routines – the clothing or symbols worn, the food eaten, what is drunk or not, the holidays taken, etc. – have a high visibility and can draw public attention to private religious affiliation. Such expressions of religious adherence cross-cut many social settings, including employment, education, media and service provision, and often give rise to contention. This was well illustrated in *Lautsi* v. *Italy*[135] by the presence of a crucifix in every classroom of a school in which a parent wished for a secularist education for her child (see later).

---

[132] Ibid., at para. 31.   [133] Application No. 24645/94, s.34, ECHR 1999-I.
[134] (2010), Application Nos 42837/06, 3237/07, 3269/07, 35793/07 and 6099/08.
[135] Application No. 30814/06 (2011).

Ethnicity/Religion-Specific Customs

The heavy onus placed upon those interfering in a manifestation of religious belief to justify that interference was evident in *Cha'are Shalom ve Tsedek* v. *France*.[136] This case concerned a Jewish liturgical association's complaint about the French authorities' refusal to grant it the approval necessary for access to slaughterhouses that performed ritual slaughter in accordance with the ultra-orthodox religious prescriptions of its members, for whom meat is not kosher unless it is "glatt". It also alleged a violation of Article 14 (prohibition of discrimination) of the Convention, in that only the Jewish Consistorial Association of Paris (Association Consistoriale Israélite de Paris, ACIP), to which the large majority of Jews in France belong, had received the approval in question. In the court's opinion, while observing dietary rules can be considered a direct expression of beliefs in practice – in the sense of Article 9 – there would have been an interference with the applicant association's right to freedom to manifest its religion only if the illegality of performing ritual slaughter had made it impossible for ultra-orthodox Jews to eat the meat of animals slaughtered in accordance with the religious prescriptions they considered applicable. But, since it had not been established that Jews belonging to the applicant association could not obtain "glatt" meat, or that the applicant association could not supply them with it by reaching an agreement with the ACIP in order to be able to engage in ritual slaughter under cover of the approval granted to the ACIP, the court considered that the refusal of approval did not constitute an interference with the applicant association's right to the freedom to manifest its religion. While the interference was found to be justified in that case, it was not in *Jakobski* v. *Poland*,[137] where the court ruled that it was unlawful for prison authorities to deny a Buddhist prisoner a vegetarian diet even though such a diet was not strictly required by Buddhism; it was sufficient and not unreasonable that the prisoner believed it necessary to manifest his beliefs in that way. Arguably, the threshold of conduct required to justify interference would seem to have changed in recent years and now places a heavier onus upon those engaging in such conduct to justify their actions.

Religious Apparel

Issues relating to private religious belief often take the form of religion-specific clothing worn by a person who wishes to publicly demonstrate

---

[136] Application No. 27417/95 (2000).
[137] [2010] 30 BHRC 417. See also *Bayatyan* v. *Armenia* [2011] 23459/03.

the nature and sincerity of their religious or irreligious convictions. The critical aspect is the degree of visibility given to personal convictions in the clothing worn relative to overall appearance. Interference with such practices has been examined by the ECtHR under the heading of "indirect" rather than "direct" religious discrimination.

This was the case in *Ahmet Arslan and others* v. *Turkey*,[138] where the court found that the State had not established a satisfactory reason for imposing a prohibition on the wearing of religious clothing in public spaces, and had failed to demonstrate that the restriction was necessary in a democratic society. The clothing in question did not conceal the face, and the prohibition was "expressly based on the religious connotation of the clothing in question".[139] Where the plaintiff is a civil servant, the court is prepared to give greater weight to the right of the State as employer to give effect to its secularist policy by prohibiting the wearing of such clothing in the workplace. In *Kurtulmus* v. *Turkey*,[140] for example, it found that in a democratic society, the State was entitled to restrict the wearing of Islamic headscarves if the practice clashed with the aim of protecting the rights and freedoms of others. By choosing to become a civil servant, the plaintiff teacher could be deemed to have accepted the State's policy. In the similar case of *Dahlab* v. *Switzerland*,[141] the court noted that a teacher wearing a headscarf might have a proselytising effect, and took into account the fact that it was sanctioned by principles in the Qur'an which were hard to square with the principle of gender equality. It considered that it was difficult to reconcile the wearing of an Islamic headscarf with the message of tolerance, respect for others and, above all, equality and non-discrimination that all teachers in a democratic society must convey to their pupils.

There have been innumerable cases, including the previously mentioned *Eweida* case,[142] concerning the wearing of the Islamic face-covering niqab in court and the wearing of religious apparel in schools, the workplace and public places, which have been considered – somewhat inconsistently – by both the ECtHR and the Human Rights Committee. In *Dogru* v. *France*[143] and *Kervanci* v. *France*,[144] for example, the ECtHR upheld the expulsion of two girls from schools where they had refused to remove their Islamic headscarves, ruling that such State action was not a violation of

---

[138] Application No. 41135/98 (2010).   [139] Ibid., at paras 136 and 151.
[140] Application No. 65500/01 (2006).   [141] Application No. 42393/98 (2001).
[142] Op. cit.   [143] Application No. 27058/05 (2008).
[144] Application No. 31645/04 (2010).

the private right to manifest one's religion under Article 9. Similarly, in *Leyla Sahin* v. *Turkey*,[145] a university rule barring students who refused to remove their head coverings from attending classes or exams was held not to violate such rights. The powerful significance of religion-specific symbols was also at issue in *S.A.S.* v. *France*,[146] where the ECtHR examined the French "burqa ban", which rested on the proposition that wearing clothing which concealed the face in public is incompatible with the "ground rules of social communication". In upholding the right of the State to introduce such a law, the court noted that: "the respondent State is seeking to protect a principle of interaction between individuals, which in its view is essential for the expression not only of pluralism, but also of tolerance and broadmindedness without which there is no democratic society". The ECtHR acknowledged that the blanket ban was broad, carried the possibility of criminal sanctions, primarily affected Muslim women and could result in the isolation and restriction of autonomy of women who choose to wear a veil over their faces,[147] but it accepted the State's submission that the law pursued two legitimate aims: public safety[148] and respect for the minimum set of values of an open and democratic society. As regards the second, it noted that in a democratic society with diverse religious beliefs, "it may be necessary to place limitations on freedom to manifest one's religion or beliefs in order to reconcile the interests of the various groups and ensure that everyone's beliefs are respected".[149] In a ruling that may well have wider ramifications, the ECtHR found that while a blanket ban on face coverings was not necessary for the promotion of public safety:[150]

> It indeed falls within the powers of the State to secure the conditions whereby individuals can live together in their diversity. Moreover, the court is able to accept that a State may find it essential to give particular weight in this connection to the interaction between individuals and may consider this to be adversely affected by the fact that some conceal their faces in public places.

[145] Application No. 44774/98 (2005).   [146] Application No. 43835/11 (2014).
[147] Ibid., at paras 145–146.
[148] See also *Phull* v. *France*, Application No. 35753/03 (2008), which upheld the right of airport security officials to require the removal of a turban, in sharp contrast to *Ranjit Singh* v. *France*, Communication No. 1876/2009, where the Human Rights Committee found a requirement to remove a turban for an identification photo violated the right to freedom of religion under the ICCPR; and *El Morsli* v. *France*, Application No. 15585/06 (2008), which concerned the right to deny entry to the French consulate on refusal to remove a veil in front of a man for an identity check.
[149] *S.A.S.* v. *France*, op. cit., at para. 26.   [150] Ibid., at paras 141–142.

The decision has been criticised by Human Rights Watch, as this type of ban disproportionately affects Muslim women and violates their rights to be free from discrimination on the basis of gender and religion, and by Amnesty International, on the grounds that it "represents a profound retreat for the right to freedom of expression and religion and sends a message that women are not free to express their religious beliefs in public". It is also at variance with decisions taken on similar issues by the Human Rights Committee. For example, in *Raihon Hudoyberganova v. Uzbekistan*,[151] the Committee found that the expulsion of a student for refusing to remove her hijab, in the absence of justification from the State, violated her right to be free from "coercion which would impair [her] freedom to have or to adopt a religion or belief of [her] choice" as protected by Article 18(2) of the ICCPR. It would seem that, in this context, the threshold of "public safety" and "the values of an open and democratic society" is higher for the HRC than for the ECtHR, resulting in a heavier onus being placed on the State to produce evidence that the religious apparel poses a real threat to safety and/or imposes a serious burden on the rights of others.

Interestingly, a third European legal forum has recently also ruled on the wearing of religious apparel in the workplace. The EC Court of Justice, in *Samira Achbita & Anor v. G4S Secure Solutions NV*[152] and in *Bougnaoui v. Micropole SA*,[153] considered whether a private employer was permitted to prohibit a female Muslim employee from wearing a headscarf in the workplace and to dismiss her if she refused to remove it. The hearings, conducted by different Advocates General, reached different conclusions: rejecting and affirming the appeals, respectively. The ruling of Advocate General Kokott in *Achbita* is the more interesting, because of the reasoning in what was a lengthy judgment. She began by noting that "the legal issues surrounding the Islamic headscarf are symbolic of the more fundamental question of how much difference and diversity an open

---

[151] Communication No. 931/2000. See also *Bikramjit Singh v. France*, Communication No. 1852/2008, where the Human Rights Committee found that plaintiff's expulsion from school for refusing to remove his religious head covering violated his rights under the Covenant; and *Rahime Kayhan v. Turkey*, Communication No. 8/2005, where CEDAW considered a complaint from a teacher that the required removal of her headscarf violated her right to work under Article 11 of the Convention on the Elimination of All Forms of Discrimination against Women.

[152] [2016] EUECJ C-157/15 (31 May 2016).

[153] [2016] EUECJ C-188/15 EU:C:2016:553 (13 July 2016).

and pluralistic European society must tolerate within its borders and, conversely, how much assimilation it is permitted to require from certain minorities".[154] She warned that "in the specific case of a headscarf ban, we should not rush into making the sweeping assertion that such a measure makes it unduly difficult for Muslim women to integrate into work and society".[155] That said, however:[156]

> The wearing by male or female employees of visible signs of their religious beliefs, such as, for example, the Islamic headscarf, in the workplace may be prejudicial to the rights and freedoms of others in two principal respects: on the one hand, it may have an impact on the freedoms not only of their colleagues but also of the undertaking's customers (particularly from the point of view of the negative freedom of religion); on the other hand, the employer's freedom to conduct a business may be adversely affected.

The reasoning adopted by the Advocate General, although not binding on the ECJ and national courts, will be important in all EC countries and influential elsewhere:

1. The fact that a female employee of Muslim faith is prohibited from wearing an Islamic headscarf at work does not constitute direct discrimination based on religion within the meaning of Article 2(2)(a) of Directive 2000/78/EC if that ban is founded on a general company rule prohibiting visible political, philosophical and religious symbols in the workplace and not on stereotypes or prejudice against one or more particular religions or against religious beliefs in general. That ban may, however, constitute indirect discrimination based on religion under Article 2(2)(b) of that directive.
2. Such discrimination may be justified in order to enforce a policy of religious and ideological neutrality pursued by the employer in the company concerned, in so far as the principle of proportionality is observed in that regard.

In that connection, the following factors in particular must be taken into account:

- the size and conspicuousness of the religious symbol;
- the nature of the employee's activity;
- the context in which she has to perform that activity; and
- the national identity of the Member State concerned.

---

[154] Ibid., at para. 3.　　　[155] Ibid., at para. 124.　　　[156] Ibid., at para. 132.

The decision – that company rules banning the wearing of visible religious, political or philosophical symbols do not constitute direct discrimination on the grounds of religion or belief – would seem to be in contradiction to that delivered by the ECtHR in *Eweida*. Recently, the ECJ revisited the French ban in *Bougnaoui* and *ADDH*,[157] but it seems unlikely that these cases will be resolved before the end of 2017.

Family-Related Issues

As declared in the International Covenant on Economic, Social and Cultural Rights: "the widest possible protection and assistance should be accorded to the family, which is the natural and fundamental group unit of society".[158] This is where many of the most contentious morality-driven issues originate.

Sexuality

Homosexuality, explicitly prohibited by some religions, was for most of the twentieth century also a criminal offence in many developed common law nations and elsewhere. This, for example, was the case in Northern Ireland, where repeal of the relevant legislation – the Offences Against the Person Act 1861 – was resisted by a majority of the population. In *Dudgeon v. The United Kingdom*,[159] the ECtHR heard submissions that the prevailing religious culture of that jurisdiction was such that removing the criminal sanction "would be seriously damaging to the moral fabric of society". While pointedly taking into account the particular cultural and religious mores, the court was unable to find a "pressing social need" to make such acts criminal offences and, applying the proportionality principle, considered that any such justification for retaining the law in force was outweighed by its detrimental effects. This decision was taken despite a minority argument suggesting that imposing such a change, resisted by the majority as offensive to their religion and culture, would constitute a form of religious discrimination – which, of course, could be countered by a reciprocal claim from the minority that perpetuating the status quo would be similarly discriminating.

Following on from a widespread de-criminalising of homosexual relations, the legal sanctioning of gay marriages was a logical next step in an environment increasingly conditioned by considerations of equality

---

[157] [2016] CJEU C-188/15.   [158] Article 10, para. 2.
[159] Application No. 7525/76 (1981).

and human rights. In *Schalk and Kopf* v. *Austria*,[160] for example, while the ECtHR found that it could not force States to make marriage available for same-sex couples, it noted that the right to marry is granted to "men and women", and includes the right to found a family, which could be interpreted as granting the right to two men or two women, because, as the court observed, all other Convention rights are granted to "everyone". The court stated that it would no longer consider that the right to marry enshrined in Article 12 must in all circumstances be limited to marriage between two persons of the opposite sex.[161]

Conception, Abortion, IVF and Related Issues

A host of legal issues relating in general terms to the concept of "life" have exercised the ECtHR for many years, but it has been the availability of legal processes for accessing abortion and contraceptives that has most persistently challenged the established religious mores of many jurisdictions. Christianity and Islam, in keeping with probably most other religions, place a high premium on parenting, but, as the ECtHR stated in *Sijakova* v. *The Former Yugoslav Republic of Macedonia*,[162] neither the right to marry and to found a family, nor the right to private and family life, nor any other right guaranteed by the Convention implies a right to procreation.

The "principle of sanctity of life"[163] finds explicit protection under a number of international instruments, including the UDHR, the ECHR, the ICCPR and the Preamble of the 1989 Convention on the Rights of the Child. However, given the rich and varied duration of the European religious cultural heritage, it is unsurprising that abortion, in particular, has proven to be highly contentious, with the ECtHR struggling to balance "on the one hand, the need to ensure protection of the foetus and, on the other hand, the woman's interests".[164] It has avoided going so far as to suggest that there exists such a thing as a right to abortion[165] (although the Article 8 right to private life does extend to respect for decisions to become a parent or not[166]), but, once a State does allow it in some circumstances, then

---

[160] Application No. 30141/04, Council of Europe: European Court of Human Rights, 24 June 2010.
[161] Ibid., at para. 61.   [162] Application No. 67914/01 (2003).
[163] *Reeve* v. *The United Kingdom*, Application No. 24844/94 (2002).
[164] See *Boso* v. *Italy*, Application No. 50490/99, Eur. Ct. H.R. 846 (2002).
[165] *P. & S.* v. *Poland*, Application No. 57375/08 (2012), at para. 99.
[166] *Evans* v. *the United Kingdom*, Application No. 6339/05, s.71, ECHR 2007-IV.

the court has repeatedly stressed that the State is under a positive obligation to create a procedural framework informing and enabling a pregnant
woman to effectively exercise her right of access to such a service.[167]

In contrast to its approach towards the cultural significance of homosexuality in *Dudgeon*, the ECtHR has been much more cautious in relation
to abortion. It has repeatedly ruled that a State is entitled to rely upon a
significant margin of appreciation when balancing the rights of a mother
against its duty to protect the unborn,[168] and in doing so may take into
account the interests of society in relation to the protection of morals,[169]
and those of institutions based on ethical or religious beliefs.[170] When,
in 2008, the Parliamentary Assembly of the Council of Europe adopted a
Resolution[171] on accessing abortion services, it restricted itself to merely
"invit[ing] the Member States of the Council of Europe to decriminalise
abortion within reasonable gestational limits, if they have not already done
so". In 2011, the same body adopted Resolution 1829 and Recommendation 1979, which conceded that abortion has negative effects on society,
and therefore must be limited and, where it is legal, must be regulated.
Contention has now spread from the initial focus on the "right" to access
abortion to issues such as abortion for minors, eugenic abortion, gender-
specific abortion, the interests of fathers and grandparents and the rights
and duties of the professionals involved.

The use of reproductive technology has often given rise to court cases.
One such was *S. H. and others* v. *Austria*,[172] which concerned the Austrian
ban on using sperm and ova donations for IVF treatment. In confirming
the ban and overturning its 2010 decision, the court restored the concepts
of "natural procreation" and "natural family" as the basic foundations for
the parenting model known to the law and affirmed that techniques for
artificial procreation would continue to be developed within that model.
In so ruling, the court laid to rest the fears of religious adherents, and others, that science rather than biology would govern future artificial procreation by facilitating *à la carte* IVF, with "life" being engendered by means

---

[167] See e.g. *A., B. & C.* v. *Ireland*, Application No. 25579/05 (2010); *Tysiąc* v. *Poland*, Application No. 5410/03 (2007); and *Vo* v. *France*, Application No. 53924/00 (2005).
[168] See *Vo* v. *France*, op. cit.
[169] See *Open Door & Dublin Well Woman* v. *Ireland*, Application No. 14234/88 (1992), at para.
63 and *A., B. & C.* v. *Ireland*, op. cit., at paras 222 and 227.
[170] See *Rommelfanger* v. *FRG*, Application No. 12242/86 (1989).
[171] The Assembly adopted on 16 April 2008 Resolution No. 1607, entitled "Access to Safe and
Legal Abortion in Europe".
[172] Application No. 57813/00 (2011).

of test-tube selection. It confirmed that the central rule – *mater semper certa est* (the mother is always certain) – would remain the governing principle, and thereby hoped to avoid the possibility of multiple parents claiming legal rights or responsibilities in respect of a child born by means of IVF.

Assisted Suicide

While there is no right to procreate, nor to have an abortion, the Strasbourg court has stated in clear terms that Article 8.1 encompasses the right to choose to die. In *Haas v. Switzerland*,[173] which concerned the right of an individual to avail themselves of the services of Dignitas in Switzerland, the court found: "that an individual's right to decide by what means and at what point his or her life will end, provided he or she is capable of freely reaching a decision on this question and acting in consequence, is one of the aspects of the right to private life within the meaning of Article 8 of the Convention".[174] This ruling pointedly stops short of conceding that such an individual has any entitlement to medical assistance when exercising this right. The UNHRC is currently preparing an updated General Comment on the right to life, following a day of discussion of the matter at its 114th session in July 2015.[175]

Employment-Related Issues

For those able to choose their occupation – perhaps a majority of the population in developed Western nations – employment has come to define their social role, and as such to shape their sense of identity. It can be a measure of self worth. Because of its social significance, the courts have been alert to the possibility of its being compromised by religion in the workplace. As explained in *Achbita*:[176]

> While an employee cannot "leave" his sex, skin colour, ethnicity, sexual orientation, age or disability "at the door" upon entering his employer's premises, he may be expected to moderate the exercise of his religion in the workplace, be this in relation to religious practices, religiously motivated behaviour or (as in the present case) his clothing.

---

[173] Application No. 31322/07 (2011).

[174] Ibid., at para. 51. See also *Koch v. Germany* (2013) 56 EHRR 6, at paras 46 and 51 and *Gross v. Switzerland* (2014) 58 EHRR 7, at para. 60.

[175] See "General Comment No. 36 – Article 6: Right to Life" at www.ohchr.org/EN/HRBodies/CCPR/Pages/GC36-Article6Righttolife.aspx.

[176] Op. cit., at para. 116.

If employment is threatened by religious discrimination, the cost to the individuals concerned will be severe, but the workforce and wider society also pay a price. The EU Directive – the Framework Equality Directive 2000/78/EC – gives direct protection against discrimination based on religion or belief in employment. In particular, Article 21 of the Charter of Fundamental Rights, which is given specific expression in that Directive, is intended to ease the disadvantages of cultural minorities and facilitate their access to employment.

Hiring/Firing Staff

Religious Organisations Exemption privileges favouring religious organisations can allow employment contracts to be religion-specific. These have not, however, prevented the firing of staff hired on those terms. This was demonstrated in *Obst* v. *Germany*[177] when the applicant, the European Director of the Public Relations Department of the Mormon Church, was dismissed without notice for adultery, which was a formal breach of one of the clauses of his employment contract. The ECtHR then agreed with the Employment Appeal Tribunal (EAT) that because of the importance of adultery in the eyes of the Mormon Church, and the important position that the applicant occupied in that Church, heightened duties of loyalty were placed upon him. It noted that "the special nature of the occupational requirements imposed on the applicant derives from the fact that they were established by an employer whose ethos is based on religion or belief".[178] In the very similar case of *Schüth* v. *Germany*,[179] a judgment delivered on the same date, in which the applicant, who was an organist and choirmaster at a Catholic church, was dismissed with notice on grounds of adultery, the ECtHR came to a different conclusion. It noted that that the EAT had not examined the proximity between the applicant's activity and the Church's proclamatory mission but had simply relied upon the Church's view that his functions as organist and choirmaster were so closely connected to the mission that the parish church could not continue to employ him without losing all credibility, and that it was barely conceivable for the general public that he and the Dean could carry on performing the liturgy together. The court considered that such a decision to dismiss could not be subjected,

---

[177] Application No. 425/03 (2010).
[178] Ibid., at para. 51, citing Article 4 of Council Directive 2000/78/EC and *Lombardi Vallauri* v. *Italy*, Application No. 39128/05 (2009).
[179] Application No. 1620/03 (2010).

on the basis of the employer's right of autonomy, only to a limited judicial scrutiny. Instead, regard must be had to the nature of the post in question and to a proper balancing of the interests involved in accordance with the principle of proportionality.

Secular Organisations   There is an acceptance that employers, whose ethos is based on religion or belief, have a right to impose related occupational requirements upon employees.[180] This is balanced to a degree by the right of employees to bring personal religious beliefs into the workplace, provided this does not infringe the sensitivities of others nor negatively impact upon the working environment. Moreover, individuals have a responsibility to choose occupations which do not fundamentally conflict with their beliefs and to accept that, once employed, their religious beliefs are not grounds for refusal to undertake the duties of a post. In *Kottinenen v. Finland*,[181] for example, the ECtHR upheld an employer's right to dismiss a Seventh-Day Adventist who had refused to continue working after sunset on Fridays as required by his contract.

Accommodating Religious Beliefs in the Workplace

A restriction on the manifestation of a religion or belief in the workplace needs to be justified even in a case where the employee voluntarily accepts an employment or role which does not accommodate the practice in question or where there are other means open to the individual to practice or observe his or her religion – as, for instance, by resigning from the employment or taking a new position.

In *Kosteski v. The Former Yugoslav Republic of Macedonia*,[182] the ECtHR did not find it unreasonable that an employer might regard absence without permission or apparent justification – to attend a Muslim festival – as a disciplinary matter. In *Francesco Sessa v. Italy*,[183] the complaint of a Jewish lawyer that the refusal to adjourn his case to a date which did not coincide with the Jewish holidays of Yom Kippur and Sukkot was an interference with his right to manifest his religion was dismissed. The court considered that interference in the exercise of an employee's religious commitments, prescribed by law, was justified on grounds of the protection of the rights and freedoms of others – and in particular the public's right to the proper administration of justice. This majority decision, which does not sit very

---

[180] *Lombardi Vallauri v. Italy*, Application No. 39128/05 (2009).
[181] (1996) 87 DR 68. See also *Stedman v. United Kingdom* (1997) 23 EHRR CD 168.
[182] Application No. 55170/00 (2006).   [183] Application No. 28790/08 (2012).

well alongside earlier rulings,[184] and from which it can perhaps be distinguished, would seem to reflect a view that the restrictions imposed on the applicant were a consequence of his contractual obligations and therefore had little or nothing to do with the freedom of religion.[185] Again, in *Eweida and others* v. *the United Kingdom*,[186] the ECtHR considered the appropriateness of restricting two employees from using a religious symbol – a crucifix on a necklace – while at work. In the case of the first, an airline employee, the court found a violation of the applicant's right to manifest her religion, because such use was discreet and there was no evidence that it had breached the rights of others, for example by negatively impacting the company's image. In the case of the second, a nurse employee, it held that the requirement to remove the necklace was justified for health and safety reasons.

Proselytism in the Workplace

Proselytism in itself is perfectly legal. The tension between the rights to disseminate personal religious beliefs, to protect private family life from the intrusive views of others and to freedom of speech can, however, give rise to difficulties – much depends on cultural context. In Turkey, for example, where an imperfect democratic State struggles – ostensibly – to maintain a balance between secularism and Islam, Christian proselytism can present a greater threat to social stability than it would elsewhere; or, perhaps, it just provides a convenient opportunity for local government and media to appease a vociferous Islamic constituency.[187]

In *Larissis and Others* v. *Greece*,[188] airforce officers were disciplined for seeking to convert a number of people to their faith, including three airmen who were their subordinates. On appeal, the ECtHR did not find that the disciplinary measures were disproportionate or that there had been a violation of Article 9 as it was necessary for the State to protect junior airmen from being put under undue pressure by senior personnel. However, it did find a violation of Article 9 with regard to the measures taken against two of the applicants for the proselytising of civilians, as they were not subject to pressure and constraints as were the airmen. In *Dahlab*

---

[184] See e.g. *Jakobski* v. *Poland* (2010) 30 BHRC 417 and *Gatis Kovalkovs* v. *Latvia*, Application No. 35021/05 (2012).

[185] In keeping with, for example, *Stedman* v. *United Kingdom*, op. cit. and *Konttinnen* v. *Finland*, op. cit.

[186] Op. cit.   [187] See *Bremner* v. *Turkey* [2015] ECHR 877.

[188] Application Nos 23372/94, 26377/94 and 26378/94.

v. *Switzerland* (dec.),[189] the ECtHR acknowledged that wearing religious clothing or symbols may be proselytising in intention and/or effect.

Education-Related Issues

Educational facilities are of particular significance in relation to religious discrimination. These value-sensitive settings can allow a State religion to be preferenced – particularly in State schools, where education is compulsory – and information dissemination to be biased or used selectively for proselytising purposes. In addition to the institutional effect, the role model that teachers provide for their pupils can also be extremely influential in colouring the latter's religious beliefs.

Government Funding and Religious Education

In *Kjeldsen, Busk Madsen and Pedersen* v. *Denmark*,[190] concerning sex education lessons organised in Danish State schools, which were alleged to be offensive to the religious sentiments of some parents, the ECtHR warned that "the State is forbidden to pursue an aim of indoctrination that might be considered as not respecting parents' religious and philosophical convictions". An infringement of the beliefs of parents, contrary to Protocol 1 Article 2, was also at issue in *Campbell and Cosans* v. *UK*,[191] in which the plaintiffs successfully challenged the existence of corporal punishment in State schools, on the basis that it was contrary to their philosophical beliefs. The ECtHR then held that the obligation to respect religious and philosophical convictions in schools is not confined to educational content but extends to how education is carried out. More recently, in *Lautsi* v. *Italy*,[192] it was the alleged more subtle indoctrination via religious icons in Italian State schools that caused contention. This long-running, landmark case began in 2001, when Ms Lautsi objected that her two children, then aged eleven and thirteen and attending a state secondary school in Italy, were exposed to crucifixes displayed in every classroom. Arguing that such a practice was contrary to the principle of secularism by which she wished to bring up her children, she requested that the crucifixes be removed. Following a succession of failed national court hearings, the plaintiff appealed to the European Court, claiming that this practice

---

[189] Application No. 42393/98, ECHR 2001-V.
[190] (1979–80) 1 EHRR 711. See also *Hasan and Eylem Zengin* v. *Turkey* (2008) 46 EHRR 44, [2007] ECHR 787.
[191] [1982] 4 EHRR 293.   [192] Application No. 30814/06 (2011).

violated her right to educate her children in accordance with her philosophical convictions, as protected by Article 2 of Protocol No. 1, as well
as her and her children's right to freedom of conscience, guaranteed by
Article 9 of the Convention. In 2009, a Chamber of the Court unanimously upheld the applicant's claim,[193] ruling that the presence of crucifixes in State schools could not be reconciled with "the educational pluralism which is essential for the preservation of 'democratic society'", and
that the compulsory display of this symbol, especially in classrooms, was
"incompatible with the State's duty to respect neutrality in the exercise of
public authority"[194] and violated Article 2 of Protocol No. 1 taken together
with Article 9.[195] In January 2010, the case was referred to the Grand
Chamber in an appeal backed by the governments of Slovakia, Lithua-
nia and Poland. The outcome emphasised that Article 2 of Protocol No. 1
did not prohibit a State from including any matters touching on religion
in a school's curriculum; rather, the aim of the provision was to safeguard
pluralism in education and to prevent indoctrination by the State.[196] It
stressed that the State's duty to respect parents' religious and philosophical convictions was also relevant to the organisation of the school environment. Finding that the crucifix was primarily a religious symbol, the
Grand Chamber held that it was nevertheless impossible to conclude that
its presence in classrooms was capable of influencing school children. The
applicant's subjective perception in that regard – although recognised by
the Grand Chamber as being understandable – was not in itself sufficient
to establish a breach of Article 2 of Protocol No. 1. Crucially, the Grand
Chamber ruled that the presence of crucifixes in classrooms was a matter
falling within the margin of appreciation of the respondent State, which
was justified by the need to "take into account the fact that Europe is
marked by a great diversity between the States of which it is composed,
particularly in the sphere of cultural and historical development",[197] and
that the contracting States' decisions in such matters, including the place
they accord to religion, should in principle be respected. It held that "a crucifix on a wall is an essentially passive symbol" that cannot be regarded
as having an effect on pupils comparable to that of didactic speech or
the requirement to participate in religious activities, and therefore cannot constitute indoctrination.[198] The Grand Chamber concluded that Italy
had acted within its margin of appreciation in deciding how to "respect"
the rights of parents under Article 2 of Protocol No. 1, that it had not

---

[193] Ibid.   [194] Ibid., at para. 56.   [195] Ibid., at para. 59.
[196] Ibid., at para. 66.   [197] Ibid., at para. 68.   [198] Ibid., at para. 72.

violated that provision and, further, that no separate issue arose under Article 9 of the Convention.[199] This important decision would seem to recognise a State right to passively allow positive religious discrimination in State institutions and facilities in relation to icons or symbols that represent the State's cultural heritage.

Faith Schools

The right of a parent to determine the religious education of their child is recognised in an array of international provisions, but explicitly in Article 2 of Protocol No. 1. Article 18 of the ICCPR similarly specifies that States Parties to the Covenant must undertake to respect the right of parents and legal guardians to ensure the religious and moral education of their children is in conformity with their own convictions. Furthermore, Article 14(3) of the Charter of Fundamental Rights of the European Union also guarantees parents the right "to ensure the education and teaching of their children in conformity with their religious, philosophical and pedagogical convictions ... in accordance with the national laws governing the exercise of such freedom and right". In religiously divided societies, such a strong legal mandate can do much to institutionalise and ensure the perpetuation of existing religious discrimination.

Religious Discrimination and Educational Content

The role of the State with regard to education and teaching is to ensure that information or knowledge included in the curriculum is conveyed in an objective, critical and pluralistic manner, but without censoring or embellishing to allow for particular religious or secular viewpoints. Otherwise, it is obliged to grant children full exemption from lessons in accordance with their parents' religious or philosophical convictions. As expressed in the previously mentioned *Kjeldsen, Busk Madsen and Pedersen* v. *Denmark*:[200]

> In fact, it seems very difficult for many subjects taught at school not to have, to a greater or lesser extent, some philosophical complexion or implications. The same is true of religious affinities if one remembers the existence of religions forming a very broad dogmatic and moral entity which has or may have answers to every question of a philosophical, cosmological or moral nature.

Religious discrimination was among the issues raised in the case of *Mansur Yalçın & Ors* v. *Turkey*[201] by Alevi parents of children at secondary school, who alleged that they were the direct "victims" of a violation of

---

[199] Ibid., at paras 76–77.   [200] Op. cit., at para. 53.   [201] Op. cit.

their rights under Articles 9 and 14 of the ECHR. While stressing that religious education was not contrary to the Convention, provided pupils were not forced to participate in a particular form of worship or exposed to religious indoctrination,[202] the ECtHR was concerned about the mandatory nature of the course content on the Islamic religion. It found that because the syllabus in question gave more importance to Sunni Islam over various minority interpretations and over other religions and philosophies, this could amount to a breach of the principles of pluralism and objectivity; and given the particularities of Alevism over the Sunni understanding of Islam, the applicants could legitimately consider that the methods of teaching the subject were likely to result in a conflict of allegiance between the school and their children's own values.[203] The mandatory nature of the course could not avoid facing students with such conflicts and did not, therefore, meet the criteria of objectivity and pluralism in respecting religious or philosophical convictions.[204] The subsequent introduction of a law extending compulsory Islamic religious education throughout Turkey to all school grades, exempting Armenian and Orthodox schools, can only exacerbate the religious discrimination experienced by the Alevis[205] and all others not exempted.

Medicine-Related Issues

Progress in science has pushed back the frontiers of medical knowledge and increased the range and complexity of benign interventions now possible in human affairs. Pharmaceutical developments can assist fertilisation, contain disease and prolong or terminate life. Gene editing can sculpt genetic material to eliminate faults, increase effectiveness or improve design. These and other advances have application across many different fields, from paediatrics to agriculture, from immunology to fishing, and bring in their wake commercial issues of supply, distribution and costs, legal issues relating to intellectual property (IP) and patents, and, of course, profound ethical issues.

Medical Intervention and Religious Beliefs

Invasive medical treatment can give rise to religious issues. Most obviously, Jehovah's Witnesses encounter difficulties when a blood transfusion is required, but surrogacy and IVF are also among the medical treatments

---

[202] Ibid., at para. 64.   [203] Ibid., at para. 71.
[204] Ibid., at para. 75, citing *Hasan and Eylem Zengin* v. *Turkey* (2008) 46 EHRR 44, [2007] ECHR 787.
[205] See also *Sinan Işık* v. *Turkey*, Application No. 21924/05 (2010).

they regard as prohibited on religious grounds. When parents refuse to permit medical treatment for their child if this involves the use of blood products, which occurs quite frequently, then arguably they are practising a form of religious discrimination. This self-imposed prohibition has been used by Russian State authorities to single out communities of Jehovah's Witnesses for surveillance and harassment. The ECtHR has considered three applications filed against Russia by Jehovah's Witnesses, finding in each case that there had been violations of the Convention.

Treatment issues and religion also intersect in relation to matters such as palliative care and euthanasia.

Genetic Engineering and Patents, etc.

Biotechnology has unquestionably increased the capacity of the human race to feed itself and promises to eradicate malaria and other enduring afflictions. However, the genetic engineering of resources required by humans evokes a different response from that triggered by the genetic editing of human material. In particular, the transfer of genetic tissue from one species to another can be viewed by adherents across a range of religions as a heretical secular trespass into the realm of the sacred. Although many countries now have domestic legislation that allows therapeutic research and production processes in respect of the cloning of stem cells, issues relating to "life" – e.g. research involving human embryos and related patents – still generate contention, as religious beliefs clash with science on matters associated with "creation", the "origin of species" and plagues.

The complexity, competitiveness and innovative nature of work in this field is such that patent design can be of the "boiler-plate" variety: intended to cover most possibilities while revealing as little as possible. For such reasons, patent applications in respect of technological developments in the manipulation of human genetic material cause controversy, as was recently the case in relation to stem cell research. This is generally legal in Europe, under an EU Biotech Directive,[206] subject to a caveat in Article 6 specifically forbidding patenting the "uses of human embryos for industrial or commercial purposes". The caveat was explored in *Netherlands* v. *European Parliament and Council*[207] when it was recognised that crucial to the application of Article 6(1) was the question: At what point does an embryo gain full moral status as a human – from conception or later? There was no consensus regarding the degree of rights conferred on

---

[206] See Directive 98/44/EC, the Legal Protection of Biotechnological Inventions, 1998.
[207] ECJ, Case C-377/98 (2011).

the embryo relative to the duration of its existence. The court revisited this issue in *Oliver Brüstle* v. *Greenpeace e. V*,[208] which concerned the plaintiff's patent for cells produced from human embryonic stem cells for use in the treatment of neurological diseases, and prompted the ECJ to examine the definition of a human embryo and the legal protection available in respect of biotechnological inventions. In keeping with religious principles, particularly but not exclusively Catholicism, the court found that the concept of "human embryo" begins at the moment a human ovum is fertilised and that this definition can be applied to a "non-fertilized human ovum into which the cell nucleus from a mature human cell has been transplanted and a non-fertilized human ovum whose division and further development have been stimulated by parthenogenesis".[209] Ultimately, the court, in a watershed judgment, ruled that an invention is non-patentable if any of the necessary steps regarding its implementation result in the destruction of human embryos, or if the invention is used in the destruction of future embryos. This decision, binding on all forty-seven Member States, gives precedence to religious precepts over scientific research and either presupposes a common cultural acceptance of those precepts or seeks to put such a foundation in place – either would seem a considerable stretch. It may cause some European geneticists to perceive themselves, in a sense, as victims of religious discrimination in relation to their US counterparts, whose equivalent commercial patenting applications are not constrained on such grounds.

Service-Provision Issues

Regardless of whether the provider is operating in the public or private domain, religious discrimination can and does arise across every aspect of the service sector, from bed and breakfasts to bakeries, hospitals, education and housing. The latter can become a tipping point for religious/cultural confrontation, as it did in Northern Ireland in 1968, when blatant religious discrimination in the allocation of public housing triggered a civil rights march and subsequent violence.[210] It can be distinguished from individual manifestations of religion or belief in the workplace, as illustrated by the wearing of crucifixes on a necklace, in that

---

[208] ECJ, Case C-34/10 (2011).   [209] Ibid., at para. 36.
[210] In May 1968, No. 9 Kinnard Park, Caledon, was allocated to a 19-year-old single Protestant girl, employed by the prospective unionist candidate for West Belfast, in preference to 269 other applicants, mainly Catholic families, on the housing waiting list.

it is more structural in effect, such as in the refusal to deliver services to a class of persons.[211]

Service Provision by Religious Organisations

The actions of Ms Ladele and Mr McFarlane in refusing to carry out certain duties they perceived as condoning homosexuality were not unlike those of the Catholic adoption agencies in various countries that have chosen to shut down their adoption services rather than make them available to gay couples. Independent religious service providers – including many charitable institutions, such as the YMCA – can avail themselves of statutory exemption privileges that excuse them from many actions that, if undertaken by other entities, would constitute religious discrimination. If, however, they are funded and contracted to deliver public services on behalf of a government body, they then lose their exemption privileges and are obliged to act in a non-discriminatory manner. Many education, health and social care services are provided on the latter basis – notwithstanding the resulting compromised beliefs of the providers.

Provision of Public Services

Services provided by public-sector employees (e.g. in schools and in health and social care facilities), as well as those provided by agencies funded and contracted to do so on behalf of governments, are required to be wholly compliant with all human rights, equality and non-discrimination legislation.

In some circumstances, it can be difficult to disentangle the strands involved and be certain that the dynamic is not in fact one of reverse discrimination. Take *Eweida and others*,[212] for example, where both Ms Ladele and Mr McFarlane were appealing against their employers' disciplinary action for their refusal to carry out their duties. Their argument that the employers acted in a discriminatory fashion by failing to accommodate fundamental principles of the appellants' religion in their work roles was ultimately not accepted by the ECtHR, which relied on the principle of proportionality – rather than contractual obligations and the freedom of employees to seek alternative employment – to uphold the employers' decision. In part, this was a ruling that justified the actions of employers on the grounds that they were seeking to avoid sexual orientation discrimination in the provision of a public service. However, it could be argued that the employers failed to make simple adjustments to

---

[211] See, generally, *Eweida and others v. the United Kingdom*, op. cit.   [212] Ibid.

working arrangements and instead forced both Ms Ladele and Mr McFarlane to choose between employment and violating their conscience. As the latter is an unqualified fundamental freedom, which they were free to exercise, the employer's actions could be construed as unjustifiable discrimination. On the other hand, of course, the plaintiffs could be seen as the ones engaging in direct religious discrimination, as they pointedly refused, on religious grounds, to provide one class of persons with a service that they were otherwise happy to provide to all other classes.

Private Goods and Service Provision

For many contemporary developed jurisdictions, much the same range of commercial services seems to provide settings for allegations of religious discrimination: bed and breakfast accommodation, hotels and social function venues, outdoor pursuit centres, etc.

Broadcasting Services

There are few rights longer and more firmly established by common law – and therefore implanted in all jurisdictions currently being considered – than the freedoms of speech and of the press.[213] Further, as the ECtHR has frequently emphasised, the freedom of expression constitutes one of the essential foundations of a democratic society, but, as Article 10(2) expressly recognises, the exercise of that freedom carries with it duties and responsibilities which, in the context of religious beliefs, include the general requirement to ensure the peaceful enjoyment of the rights guaranteed under Article 9 to the holders of such beliefs. This requirement includes a duty to avoid any expression that is, in regard to objects of veneration, gratuitously offensive to others and profane.[214] In relation to expressing views by means of radio and TV broadcasting, it is clear that any restriction on disseminating information necessarily interferes with the right to receive and impart it.[215] It is less clear, however, as to where the threshold for interference lies – where the balance is to be struck between Articles 9 and 10.

In *Otto–Preminger–Institut* v. *Austria*,[216] it was maintained that those who hold religious beliefs must tolerate and accept their denial by others, including the latter's propagation of doctrines hostile to their own. Even

---

[213] See e.g. Blackstone, *Commentaries*, bk 4, pp. 151–152.

[214] *Otto-Preminger-Institut* v. *Austria*, Series A No. 295-A (20 September 1994), at paras 46, 47 and 49.

[215] *Öztürk* v. *Turkey* [GC], No. 22479/93, s.49, ECHR 1999-VI.   [216] Op. cit.

an expression which could be considered offensive, shocking or disturbing to the religious sensitivities of others will find protection under Article 10. The court then found, as a matter of fact, however, that the views expressed were in this instance so offensive as to constitute a malicious violation of the spirit of tolerance. In a ruling not without relevance for the controversy that has more recently come to surround the *Charlie Hebdo* satirical cartoons, the court held that there was an obligation to avoid, as far as possible, expressions that were gratuitously offensive.[217] Similarly, in *Wingrove v. The United Kingdom*,[218] which concerned a soft-porn video purportedly depicting the erotic fantasies of St Teresa, entitled "Visions of Ecstasy", the ECtHR considered the ban imposed by the regulatory authority as justified in a democratic society and therefore compliant with Article 10(2) of the Convention. In both cases, the court indicated that a greater margin of appreciation was to be accorded to the State in matters of morals and religion. However, there is a balance to be struck. As the court pointed out in *Murphy v. Ireland*:[219] "the concepts of pluralism, tolerance and broad-mindedness on which any democratic society is based mean that Article 10 does not, as such, envisage that an individual is to be protected from exposure to a religious view simply because it is not his or her own".[220]

Conclusion

Given the impact of 2015/16 events, it seems appropriate to look to the European experience as the starting point for a much wider examination of contemporary religious discrimination. As this and the previous chapters have shown, there is much to be learned from the history of that phenomenon in those countries and as filtered through the ECtHR in recent years. The caselaw patterns and trends outlined in this chapter suggest that profiling the Part III jurisdictions in accordance with the following indices would offer a sound basis for gathering the information necessary for comparative analysis: the Church/State relationship; religious icons, apparel, etc.; the family; and issues relating to "life", employment, medicine and service provision. The many key judgments of the ECtHR in these subject areas provide useful benchmarks for probing jurisdictional similarities and differences in the law relating to religious discrimination.

---

[217] Ibid., at paras 46–50.   [218] 19/1995/525/611 (25 November 1996).
[219] Application No. 44179/98 [2004] 38 EHRR 212.   [220] Ibid., at para. 72.

PART III

Contemporary Religious Discrimination in Common Law Jurisdictions: The Judicial Rulings

5

England and Wales

Introduction

"The religious landscape in this country has been transformed in the last few decades", states the 2015 report of the Commission on Religion and Belief in British Public Life,[1] a claim that finds support in statistics published by the British Social Attitudes Survey[2] for the same year, which show that approximately half the UK population had no religion (a trend that has increased from 31 per cent in 1983 and 43 per cent in 2004) and less than 42 per cent self-identified as Christian. In particular, the proportion of the population belonging to the "established" Church of England stood at just 17 per cent (falling from 21 per cent in 2012 and 29 per cent in 2004). Of those subscribing to a religious belief: most were Christians, with Anglicanism being the most widely practiced and declared religion; Islam, Hinduism and Sikhism were numerically the next most popular; while the Jewish population, which fifty years ago was the largest non-Christian community, has slipped to fifth. Other faiths – including Bahá'ís, Buddhists, Jains, Rastafarians, Zoroastrians and Druids – together with humanists and pagans, also contribute to the increasingly diverse mix of believers and non-believers that now make up modern British society.

These trends are well established, and their implications inescapable: secularism in this jurisdiction is becoming steadily more dominant; the population proportionately less Christian; and multi-culturalism is a firmly embedded characteristic.[3] Consequently, "twenty-first century ethno-religious issues and identities here in the UK and globally are reshaping society in ways inconceivable just a few decades ago", with "resulting uncertainties about national identity, cohesion and

---

[1] See Commission on Religion and Belief in British Public Life, Living with Difference, at p. 6.
[2] See www.bsa.natcen.ac.uk/latest-report/british-social-attitudes-32/key-findings/introduction.aspx.
[3] See Woodhead, L., who suggests that the picture is complicated by pockets of deep faith, at https://kenanmalik.wordpress.com/2013/08/15/religion-is-not-what-it-used-to-be.

community".[4] Thus, among other things, "it will become increasingly difficult for government to justify things like discrimination on the basis of religion in schools, compulsory collective worship and the presence of an established or national church in England".[5]

This, the first of the jurisdiction-specific chapters, begins with a brief overview of public policy, to the extent that it impacts upon religious discrimination. This leads into an outline of the legal framework of the courts and the law, with attention to the meaning of key definitional terms. The next section considers the occurrence and significance of religious discrimination in the Church/State relationship. Then we reach the heart of the chapter – an examination of contemporary religious discrimination caselaw as it has featured in the context of: custom, icons and apparel; the family, including matters of sexuality; employment; education and faith schools; medicine; and service provision.

Public Policy: An Overview

From the Reformation, discrimination favouring Protestantism – specifically Anglicanism – and penalising all other religions – especially Catholicism – was a characteristic of the law that shaped the cultural roots of religion in this jurisdiction. Religious discrimination, sanctioned by the State, was unremitting against those who questioned the orthodox beliefs of the Church, and was often accompanied by the most severe punishments then known to the law, some of which remained on the statute books until relatively recently.

Religion and the Constitution

Although lacking a formal constitution, this jurisdiction has in place a body of laws and negotiated agreements – most notably embodied in Magna Carta[6] – that have acquired over time the status of constitutional arrangements.

---

[4] See Commission on Religion and Belief in British Public Life, *Living with Difference*, at pp. 6–7.

[5] See Copson, A., for the British Humanist Association, at https://humanism.org.uk/2015/06/01/new-british-social-attitudes-survey-shows-continued-decline-for-christianity-in-britain/.

[6] Signed in June 1215 between King John and the barons of mediaeval England, the Magna Carta is considered to be the foundation stone of parliamentary democracy in England.

The Constitution

Statutes such as the Bill of Rights 1689 and the Act of Settlement 1701, together with the singular legal standing granted to the Church of England, virtually embedded an acceptance of religious discrimination into the constitutional framework. They made a fundamental contribution to shaping the constitutional arrangements and to the evolving cultural context; indeed, they had something of a similar influence throughout the British Empire. Both addressed pressing contemporary political and monarchical issues, but in so doing they also firmly established the precedence of Protestantism. The Act of Settlement went further by specifically and solely discriminating against Catholicism. For three centuries, this Act stood as a constitutional benchmark for religious discrimination until the relevant provisions were eventually amended – excepting the prohibition on a Catholic ascending to the throne – throughout the Commonwealth in 2015.

The Church of England, as the "established church", has prevailed over all other religions under constitutional arrangements which provide for the reigning monarch to be both its Supreme Governor and Head of State.[7] It also enjoys a stronger relationship with government: all twenty-six Anglican bishops (the Lords Spiritual) sit as of right in the House of Lords on the government benches;[8] a right exclusive to that religion, and one that confers an entitlement to contribute to the shaping of government policy.

Religious Discrimination and the Constitution

As mentioned, the singular constitutional standing of the Church of England constitutes a form of religious discrimination, as no other religion is permitted any such legal or political status. This overt legal preferencing is reflected in a long series of cases concerning conditions attached to bequests, stretching well into the last half of the twentieth century,[9] in which the right of English testators to exercise direct religious

---

[7] Under the Act of Union 1707, Article 2, the monarch is required to belong to the Church of England.

[8] The Bishopric of Manchester Act of 1847 limited the number of places for Lords Spiritual to twenty-six.

[9] Including: *Hodgson v. Halford* [1977] EWCA Civ 11, [1978] 1 All ER 1047; *In re Allen* [1953] 1 Ch. 810; and *Re Tuck's Settlement Trusts, Public Trustee v. Tuck* [1977] EWCA Civ 11, [1978] 1 All ER 1047. Also note the Marriage Act 1753, which, because it denied recognition to the marriages of Quakers and Jews, created a gap that was bridged by community-based religious tribunals. Such tribunals oversaw, for example, Jewish and Muslim marriages (Beit Din and Shari'a tribunals) and divorces. (The author acknowledges advice from Maleiha Malik on this matter; note to author, 14 March 2017.)

discrimination when disposing of their estates was upheld in the courts. The established judicial view was that such conditions were not void for being in breach of public policy.

Public Policy

As Bingham LJ noted: "British law not only tolerated but imposed disabilities on Roman Catholics, Dissenters and Jews not rationally based on their religious beliefs, and disabilities on women not rationally connected with any aspect of their gender".[10] Such discrimination has a long history in this jurisdiction, where feudalism gradually translated into the class system, while gender inequality remained underpinned by many laws – including those governing marriage, patriarchy, primogeniture and suffrage – into the early decades of the twentieth century. Discrimination remains institutionalised in a system of governance that has at its head a monarch, a "House of lords" and an "established" Church. The latter is of particular significance for present purposes because, for 800 years, Lambeth Palace in London has signified the political leverage of the Church as a counterweight to the government of the day, exercising an influence on current morality issues, a role assisted by the fact that the three most prominent leaders of that Church sit as members of the Privy Council to advise the sovereign on such issues.

Background

In 1976, when considering the validity of a clause requiring the forfeiture of a child's inheritance if they should "be or become a Roman Catholic",[11] the House of Lords acknowledged that "the law of England was now set against discrimination on a number of grounds including religious grounds". Nonetheless, Lord Wilberforce, noting the judicially entrenched principle of a testator's freedom of disposition, warned against the dangers of licensing unwarranted intrusions into the exercise of parental rights. These views were endorsed by his colleague, Lord Simon, who added:[12]

> Turning to the question of public policy, it is true that it is widely thought nowadays that it is wrong for a government to treat some of its citizens less favourably than others because of differences in their religious beliefs; but it does not follow from that that it is against public policy for an adherent of one religion to distinguish in disposing of his property between adherents of his faith and those of another.

[10] Bingham, T., *The Rule of Law*, London, Allen Lane, 2010 at p. 57.
[11] *Blathwayt v. Lord Cawley* [1976] AC 397, [1975] 3 All ER 625 (HL).
[12] Ibid., at paras 429–430.

Religious Discrimination and Contemporary Public Policy

As Weller summarises: "the emphasis over the past decade in England and Wales has shifted legal attention from freedom of religion or belief in itself to addressing anti-discrimination through a wider equalities agenda."[13]

State Agencies for Religious Matters

While there is no specific government agency dealing specifically with religious matters, this jurisdiction does have a Government Equalities Office, created in 2007 and transferred to the Dept of Education in 2014. It currently leads the Discrimination Law Review.

Domestic Policy

In the first year of this century, an important survey noted that "the majority of Muslim organisations reported that their members experienced unfair treatment in every aspect of education, employment, housing, law and order, and in all the local government services".[14] Public policy initiatives designed to address the evidence of widespread social inequity were severely jolted by the Islamist terrorist attack on civilians in London on 7 July 2005, which left fifty-two dead and many hundreds injured. This event registered the fact that this jurisdiction was now engaged in a new era of religious discrimination. As a consequence, there followed the introduction of domestic security and anti-terrorism legislation, surveillance and accelerated deportation measures, a review of multi-cultural policies and a new policy emphasis on preventing radicalisation and building a closer rapprochement between local government and Muslim communities. This approach balanced a strategy to prevent radicalisation[15] with specific counter-terrorism legislation.[16]

Government support for ecumenical initiatives with the potential to counter religious discrimination has led to grant-aiding of the 230 groups that now constitute the Inter Faith Network, among other things. A joint policy for government and religious groups was outlined in *Face to Face*

---

[13] See Weller et al., Religion or Belief, at p. 42.

[14] Home Office Research, Development and Statistics Directorate, "Religious Discrimination in England and Wales" (Research Study 220), London, Home Office, 2001, pp. vii–viii; see further www.religionlaw.co.uk/reportad.pdf.

[15] The "Prevent Strategy"; see further www.gov.uk/government/publications/counter-terrorism-strategy-contest.

[16] For example, the Protection of Freedoms Act 2012 and the Terrorism Prevention and Investigations Measures Act 2011.

and Side by Side: A Framework for Partnership in Our Multi-Faith Society.[17] During 2008–11, funding was dispersed under a new Faiths in Action Fund in support of local activities, including inter-religious work. In 2012, the government published *Creating the Conditions for Integration*[18] and provided major funding for the Church Urban Fund, its Near Neighbours programme and the Together in Service programme. More recently, the All Party Parliamentary Group on Faith and Society, together with FaithAction, developed a Faith Covenant, which offers "a set of principles that guide engagement, aiming to remove some of the mistrust that exists and to promote open, practical working on all levels". As of October 2015, five local authorities in England had adopted the covenant.

Foreign Policy

The 7/7 atrocity in 2005, together with increasing disquiet at events unfolding in the Middle East, led to a government commitment to join in a collaborative international strategy to degrade ISIS forces in their putative caliphate and to counter their terrorist campaign in Western countries.

Public policy relating to immigration, anti-terrorism and asylum in this jurisdiction has also had to adjust to comply with international convention requirements. In *A(FC)* v. *Secretary of State for the Home Department*,[19] for example, Bingham LJ found that UK anti-terrorism legislation discriminated on grounds of nationality and immigration status. Also, in *R* v. *Immigration Officer at Prague Airport, ex parte European Roma Rights Centre*,[20] Steyn LJ expressly ruled that the immigration service operation put in place at Prague airport, which led to closer scrutiny of Roma people seeking to enter the UK than of non-Roma, was discriminatory.

Contemporary Law Governing Religious Discrimination

As noted by Toulson LJ:[21]

> Religion and English law meet today at various points . . . Individuals have a right to freedom of thought, conscience and religion under article 9 of the European Convention. They enjoy the right not to be discriminated against on grounds of religion or belief under EU Council Directive 2000/78/EC and under domestic equality legislation

---

[17] Department for Communities and Local Government (2008).
[18] Department for Communities and Local Government (2012).
[19] [2004] UKHL 56.   [20] [2003] EWCA Civ 666.
[21] See *R (on the application of Hodkin and another)* v. *Registrar General of Births, Deaths and Marriages* [2013] UKSC 77, per Toulson LJ at paras 32–33.

The International Framework

As outlined in Chapter 4, the main components of this framework are Articles 9 and 14 of the ECHR, as applied in conjunction with: the ICCPR, which the government ratified in 1976, with certain reservations and declarations; the International Convention on the Elimination of Race Discrimination (ICERD), to which the UK is a signatory nation; and CEDAW, with its Optional Protocol. The EC series of Directives is also relevant, particularly the Employment Equality Directive 2000/78/EC (the "framework" Directive), which was given effect in England and Wales by the Employment Equality (Religion or Belief) Regulations 2003, and the EU Charter of Rights and Freedoms.

International Reports

The 2012 Universal Periodic Review, which considered a composite report on the four UK nations, made no specific reference to issues of religious discrimination but noted its concern with some associated areas, including poor implementation of laws prohibiting FGM, human trafficking, indefinite detention of migrants and asylum seekers and the need to promote multi-culturalism. Also noteworthy is the 2016 report of the UN Committee on the Rights of the Child, which called for an end to compulsory school worship (paras 34 and 35).

The Domestic Framework

Essentially, the current equality and human rights law emanates from the governing principles outlined in the United Nations Declaration of Human Rights, as enlarged in the same European Convention, and subsequently established in both the Human Rights Act 1998 and the Employment Equality (Religion or Belief) Regulations 2003.

The Equality Act 2010

The 2010 Act,[22] which consolidates 116 pieces of legislation, together with the Human Rights Act 1998, provides the basic structure of the current anti-discrimination framework for the UK. The former prohibits unfair treatment on any of nine "protected grounds", which include religion or belief, whether occurring in the workplace, when providing goods, facilities and services, when exercising public functions, in the disposal and

[22] c. 15.

management of premises, or in education and by associations (such as private clubs), and whether the discrimination is direct, indirect or takes the form of harassment or victimisation. Schedule 9, paragraph 2 (giving effect to Article 4 of the previously mentioned Framework Equality Directive 2000/78/EC) deals with employment "for the purposes of an organised religion"[23] and provides that if certain criteria are met, it will not be unlawful to apply to employees or applicants any of the following:

- a requirement to be of a particular sex; a requirement not to be a transsexual person;
- a requirement not to be married or a civil partner; a requirement not to be married to, or the civil partner of, a person who has a living former spouse or civil partner;
- a requirement relating to circumstances in which a marriage or civil partnership came to an end; or
- a requirement related to sexual orientation.

Religion is treated the same as any other "protected characteristic", a fact which causes considerable disquiet among religious adherents, who claim that legislators, by adopting such a reductionist approach, have wholly failed to take into account religion's inherent transcendental quality. There is also some uncertainty regarding the relationship between Article 14 of the Convention, which requires non-discrimination in the enjoyment of Convention rights, and the protection against direct and indirect discrimination under the Equality Act 2010: the latter would seem to impose a narrower and more strict interpretation of conduct constituting discrimination than is required by the former. The Act offers protection for individuals; indeed, it was the view of the Court of Appeal in *Mba v. London Borough of Merton*[24] that group disadvantage was not covered under the Equality Act.[25]

This legislation also introduced a general public sector equality duty (PSED), which applies to specified "public authorities"[26] and to private organisations carrying out "public functions".[27] Part 2 of the Act makes provision for the "advancement of equality", and s.149 requires public authorities, or private bodies carrying out public functions, when dealing with those who are the subject of a protected characteristic, to: eliminate

---

[23] See also Equality Act 2010, Sch. 12, para. 5 (Designation of Institutions with a Religious Ethos) (England and Wales) Order 2010, SI 2010/1915.

[24] [2013] EWCA Civ 1562.

[25] See *Chatwal v. Wandsworth Borough Council* [2011] UKEAT 0487/10/0607, where it was noted that there are no settled criteria for what constitutes a "group".

[26] Equality Act 2010, Sch. 19.   [27] Equality Act 2010, s.149(2).

discrimination, harassment, victimisation and any other conduct that is prohibited by the Act; advance equality of opportunity between persons who share a relevant characteristic and persons who do not share it; and foster good relations between such persons. In addition, the Act gives effect to the Employment Equality Directive 2000/78/EC, which protects against direct and indirect discrimination, harassment and victimisation perpetrated on the grounds of religion or belief.

The Human Rights Act 1998

The ECHR was applied in this jurisdiction by the Human Rights Act 1998. Article 9 of the Convention, applied by ss.9 and 13 of the 1998 Act, provides for freedom of thought, conscience and religion, including the right: to change religion or belief; to exercise religion or belief publicly or privately, alone or with others; and to exercise religion or belief in worship, teaching, practice and observance; it also provides for the right to have no religion and to have non-religious beliefs protected. This is a qualified right, and as such the freedom to manifest a religion or belief can be limited, or subject to "interference", so long as that limitation: is prescribed by law; is necessary and proportionate; and pursues a legitimate aim (viz. the interests of public safety, the protection of public order, health or morals or the protection of the rights and freedoms of others). It does not provide a free-standing right to initiate religious discrimination proceedings. It is further limited by being restricted to public authorities or those acting on behalf of a public body. The Act allows the provision of services or "benefits" to a certain section of society if such actions are a proportionate means of achieving a legitimate aim, such as improving health or the protection of children. It is also a group right.

Article 14 of the Convention, applied by s.14 of the 1998 Act, broadly prohibits discrimination "on any ground", including religion. Section 13 of the 1998 Act adds:

> If a court's determination of any question arising under this Act might affect the exercise by a religious organisation (itself or its members collectively) of the Convention right to freedom of thought, conscience and religion, it must have particular regard to the importance of that right.

The Employment Equality (Religion or Belief) Regulations 2003

Following the introduction of the 1998 Act, further domestic provision took the form of the Employment Equality (Religion or Belief) Regulations, introduced on 2 December 2003, which made it unlawful for employers to discriminate on the grounds of religion or belief and enacted in UK law the religion or belief provisions of the Framework Equal Treatment Directive (2000/78/EC). These were subsequently consolidated in the Equality Act 2010, Sched. 2.

Other Legislation

The Crime and Disorder Act 1998, as amended,[28] created specific offences of racially and religiously aggravated crime based on the offences of wounding, assault, damage, harassment, threatening or abusive behaviour and stalking. Those convicted of "religiously aggravated offences" (where there is evidence of religious hostility in connection with a crime) face higher maximum penalties.

The Racial and Religious Hatred Act 2006 prohibits "incitement to religious hatred"[29] but does not define religion or what constitutes a religious belief. The Public Order Act 1986, as amended by the 2006 Act, created new offences: s.29B(i) provided that "a person who uses threatening words or behaviour, or displays any written material which is threatening, is guilty of an offence if he intends thereby to stir up religious hatred", subject to the caveat in s.29J that this does not prohibit or restrict discussion, criticism or expressions of antipathy, dislike, ridicule, insult or abuse of particular religions, beliefs or practices of adherents, or proselytising.

The Charities Act 2011 is relevant to religious discrimination – not only because it accommodates a non-theistic interpretation of "religion" which discounts the traditional significance of tenets and doctrines and includes "belief systems", but because, in s.3(1), it encodes the promotion of religious or racial harmony as a specific charitable purpose.[30] Government initiatives such as the Hate Crime Action Plan and anti-terrorism legislation have also had an impact: specifically, the Counter-Terrorism Act 2008 and the Counter-Terrorism and Security Act 2015.

Courts and Tribunals

The framework of courts and tribunals established to address issues of alleged religious discrimination, like the content of the law itself, is an amalgam of European and domestic components.

---

[28] By the Anti-Terrorism, Crime and Security Act 2001 and the Protection of Freedoms Act 2012.

[29] See also *Abrahams v. Cavey* [1968] 1 QB 479, at pp. 481–482.

[30] The Charities Act 2006, s.2(2)(h) first gave statutory recognition to the promotion of religious or racial harmony or equality and diversity as a charitable purpose.

International

For England and Wales, EU membership brought with it a requirement that they accept the superior jurisdiction of the ECtHR and the ECJ. This will cease in time, as the UK withdraws its membership. The persuasive capacity of future European court rulings remains to be seen, but the established accountability to other international committees will continue.

The European Court of Human Rights (ECtHR)   The ECtHR hears complaints alleging that any one of the forty-seven Member States has violated rights enshrined in the Convention and its protocols. In making its determinations, the court is guided by principles such as "proportionality" and "compatibility with democracy".[31] Its decisions are reached in the light of "a margin of appreciation", which permits States a degree of latitude in their interpretation of human rights obligations[32] (see further Chapter 4).

Other Fora   The ECJ, the Human Rights Committee and various other committees established by their respective international conventions in order to monitor implementation may also be relevant (see further Chapter 4).

Domestic

Issues are mainly resolved by regulators, but many are adjudicated in the county court and High Court, and some go on appeal to the Appeal Court and possibly to the Supreme Court (formerly the House of Lords).

The Equality and Human Rights Commission (EHRC)   Established by the Equality Act 2006, this body consolidates the functions of its predecessors (the Equal Opportunities Commission, the Commission for Racial Equality and the Disability Rights Commission) and acts as the regulator in respect of matters – such as religious discrimination – arising under the Equality Act 2010, including enforcement of the PSED. To date, the ERHC has published three important reports on the law relating to religion and belief.[33]

---

[31] See *Refah Partisi* v. *Turkey*, op. cit., where the ECtHR ruled that Shari'a law is not consistent with democracy and therefore that the Turkish government was justified in banning a political party seeking to introduce such law.

[32] See e.g. *Lithgow* v. *United Kingdom*, op. cit.; *Fredin* v. *Sweden*, op. cit.; and *Abdulaziz, Cabales and Balkandali* v. *United Kingdom*, op. cit.

[33] See, most recently, "Religion or Belief: Is the Law Working?" (December 2016).

The Employment Appeal Tribunal (EAT)   This body hears appeals against decisions made by the Employment Tribunal. A further right of appeal may lie to the High Court.

The Employment Tribunal   Allegations of discriminatory practices in the workplace are heard by this Tribunal, the decisions of which have effect throughout Great Britain, but not in Northern Ireland.

Other   There are also some religious tribunals, the rulings of which can affect the lives of many but may be at variance with the principles applied in the official court system; the Church of England, for example, has always had its own internal consistory courts for settling disputes affecting members. For centuries, the Beth Din network of private tribunals has sought to resolve civil disputes arising among Jews, while Shari'a law is attracting a growing constituency as a resource for resolving issues arising in an Islamic cultural context; both offer mediation on marital disputes, family matters and finance.[34] The Islamic Shari'a Council, established in the 1980s, has at least sixteen Islamic tribunals operating in the country, dealing with several hundred cases of marriage and divorce per month. The role of religious minority tribunals can be controversial, due to the tension between their religion-specific governing principles and the provisions of British statute law: the rights of women, for example, can be jeopardised.[35]

Freedom of Religion and Beliefs: The Principle and the Law

The right to freedom of thought, conscience and religion is guaranteed under international law by Article 18 of the UDHR (ECHR, Art 9) in conjunction with Article 18 of the ICCPR, and under domestic law by the Human Rights Act 1998, s.9.

Definitions

The law relating to "religion" or "belief" and to "religious discrimination" suffers considerably from definitional deficit: international and domestic

---

[34] Douglas, G., Doe, N., Gilliat-Ray, S. et al., "Social Cohesion and Civil Law: Marriage, Divorce and Religious Courts", Cardiff, Cardiff University, 2011, at www.law.cf.ac.uk/clr/Social%20Cohesion%20and%20Civil%20Law%20Full%20Report.pdf.

[35] See Bano, S., *Muslim Women and Shariah Councils: Transcending the Boundaries of Community and Law*, Basingstoke, Palgrave Macmillan, 2012.

legislators have neither defined such terms nor agreed parameters for their interpretation; however, although the judiciary has yet to subscribe to a finite set of definitions, the caselaw reveals its efforts to do so.

"Religion"

The contemporary understanding of what is meant by "religion" now extends to accommodate non-theistic and philosophical beliefs. In the Equality Act, it is broadly defined to include: any religion; any religious or philosophical belief; a lack of religion; and a lack of belief.

The landmark ruling in R *(on the application of Hodkin and another) v. Registrar General of Births, Deaths and Marriages*[36] is of crucial importance. The Supreme Court unanimously decided that a Scientologist chapel was "a place of meeting for religious worship" (as referred to in s.2 of the Places of Worship Registration Act 1855) because the term "has to be interpreted in accordance with contemporary understanding of religion and not by reference to the culture of 1855".[37] As explained by Toulson LJ:[38]

> religion should not be confined to religions which recognise a supreme deity. First and foremost, to do so would be a form of religious discrimination unacceptable in today's society. It would exclude Buddhism, along with other faiths such as Jainism, Taoism, Theosophy and part of Hinduism.

Acknowledging that "there has never been a universal legal definition of religion in English law",[39] he then offered the following guidance:[40]

> I would describe religion in summary as a spiritual or non-secular belief system, held by a group of adherents, which claims to explain mankind's place in the universe and relationship with the infinite, and to teach its adherents how they are to live their lives in conformity with the spiritual understanding associated with the belief system. By spiritual or non-secular I mean a belief system which goes beyond that which can be perceived by the senses or ascertained by the application of science. I prefer not to use the word "supernatural" to express this element because it is a loaded word which can carry a variety of connotations. Such a belief system may or may not involve belief in a supreme being, but it does involve a belief that there is more to be understood about mankind's nature and relationship to the universe than can be gained from the senses or from science.

[36] [2013] UKSC 77. [37] Ibid., per Toulson LJ, at para. 34.
[38] Ibid. at para. 51. [39] Ibid. at para. 34. [40] Ibid. at para. 57.

Accordingly, belief in a "Supreme Being", the practice of worship and adherence to a specific body of doctrines, tenets, etc. are no longer essential to the definition of "religion". Druids are now included (although the Jedi[41] are not) among the range of recognised religions in this jurisdiction, and, in 2013, the Employment Tribunal extended recognition to the beliefs of the Wiccas.[42]

"Beliefs"

Beliefs must amount to more than just mere opinions or deeply held feelings: they must involve a holding of spiritual or philosophical convictions which have an identifiable formal content. In *Campbell and Cosans* v. *United Kingdom*,[43] the ECtHR affirmed the validity of beliefs grounded in cultural values when it ruled in favour of complainants who alleged that the system of corporal punishment in Scottish State schools offended their philosophical convictions under Article 2 of Protocol 1 of the ECHR. Some twenty years later, in the similar case of *Willamson*,[44] Walker LJ asserted that "pacifism, vegetarianism and total abstinence from alcohol are uncontroversial examples of beliefs which would fall within Article 9 (of course pacifism or any comparable belief may be based on religious convictions, equally it may be based on ethical convictions which are not religious but humanist . . .)".[45] As Nicholls LJ explained:[46]

> Article 9 embraces freedom of thought, conscience and religion. The atheist, the agnostic, and the sceptic are as much entitled to freedom to hold and manifest their beliefs as the theist. These beliefs are placed on an equal footing for the purpose of this guaranteed freedom.

In the same year, however, membership of the British National Party was found not to be a religion or belief,[47] while a non-belief in Christianity was deemed to be a "similar philosophical belief" for the purposes of the definition.[48] A decade later, in *United Grand Lodge of England* v. *Commissioners of HM Revenue and Customs*,[49] the "canons" of the Freemasons were dismissed as they were not "adopted to give effect to the belief". The latter ruling was subsequently reinforced by an EAT

---

[41] They have also been denied religious status in New Zealand, but have acquired it in some jurisdictions, such as Texas and Canada.
[42] *Holland* v. *Angel Supermarket Ltd and another* [2013] Employment Tribunal 3301005–2013.
[43] [1982] 4 EHRR 293.
[44] *R (Williamson)* v. *Secretary of State for Education and Employment*, op. cit.
[45] Ibid., at para. 55.   [46] Ibid., at para. 24.   [47] *Baggs* v. *Fudge* ET 1400114/05.
[48] *Nicholson* v. *The Aspire Trust* ET 2601009/04 (4865/142) March 2005.
[49] [2014] UKFTT 164.

decision,[50] which found that Freemasonry was not a protected belief for the purposes of employment law because, although members were required to have a religious belief, it didn't matter what that belief was so long as it included a belief in a "Supreme Being" and was compatible with the three "Grand Principles" of Freemasonry: brotherly love, relief of those in distress and truth. Freemasonry did not, itself, offer a core belief or set of beliefs.

In *McClintock* v. *Department of Constitutional Affairs*,[51] Elias P reiterated the established view of the ECtHR that "the test for determining whether views can properly be considered to fall into the category of a philosophical belief is whether they have sufficient cogency, seriousness, cohesion and importance and are worthy of respect in a democratic society".[52] In *Grainger* v. *Nicholson*,[53] the EAT declared that the appellant's strongly held philosophical belief about climate change and the alleged morality thereof was capable of constituting a philosophical belief within the meaning of the Employment Equality (Religion or Belief) Regulations 2003, which made provision for such a belief to have a similar weight and significance as a religious belief in the context of human rights jurisprudence.[54] On appeal, Burton J and Nicholls LJ were clear that determining what constituted a "belief" required a threshold test, comprising certain requirements implicit in Article 9 of the European Convention, and comparable guarantees in other human rights instruments. Burton J suggested the following criteria:[55]

(i) The belief must be genuinely held.

(ii) It must be a belief and not, as in *McClintock*, an opinion or viewpoint based on the present state of information available.

(iii) It must be a belief as to a weighty and substantial aspect of human life and behaviour.

(iv) It must attain a certain level of cogency, seriousness, cohesion and importance.

(v) It must be worthy of respect in a democratic society, be not incompatible with human dignity and not conflict with the fundamental rights of others (paragraph 36 of *Campbell* and paragraph 23 of *Williamson*).

---

[50] See *Conway* v. *Secretary of State for the Home Department* [2015] ET 2205162/2013.
[51] [2008] IRLR 29.   [52] Ibid., at para. 41.
[53] [2009] UKEAT 0219 09 0311 (EAT).
[54] Paragraph 2(1) of the 2003 Regulations states that "'belief' means any religious or philosophical belief".
[55] [2010] IRLR 4 (EAT) at para. 24.

The court duly found that "the claimant has settled views about climate change, and acts upon those views in the way in which he leads his life...his belief goes beyond mere opinion".[56] Within a year, other tribunals had applied this test to extend recognition to a range of belief systems, each with their own cultural constituency, such as anti-fox hunting[57] and a belief in the higher purpose of public service broadcasting.[58] Even a lack of consistency will not prove fatal provided the beliefs (humanist) are sincerely held.[59] Whereas, in the past, a person could be construed as having a religious belief by the mere fact of their belonging to a church which carried an implied commitment to its doctrines, now it is the demonstrable sincerity of an individual's beliefs that is the crucial legal determinant.[60] However, due regard must be given to the judicial warning regarding the inherent contradictions and dangers for legal objectivity in attaching undue weight to subjectively perceived "truths".[61]

Courts and regulators have thus not only moved away from examining institutional structures and referencing doctrines and tenets, which were the customary indicators for defining an "organised religion", but have also shifted their focus from religion as an institution to the authenticity of an individual's subjective interpretation and experience of it.[62] The views expressed by Nicholls LJ in *Williamson*[63] were echoed by the EAT in *Eweida*[64] ("it is not necessary for a belief to be shared by others in order for it to be a religious belief"[65]), by Bingham LJ in *Begum*[66] and by the comment of Baroness Hale for the Court of Appeal in *Gha*[67] ("it matters not for present purposes whether it is a universal, orthodox or unusual belief"). Moreover, "all beliefs are equally protected",[68] including a belief

---

[56] *Grainger v. Nicholson*, op. cit., at para. 13.

[57] See *Hashman v. Milton Park (Dorset) Ltd (t/a Orchard Park)* ET/3105555/09.

[58] See *Maistry v. BBC* ET/1313142/10.

[59] *Streatfield v. London Philharmonic Orchestra* [2012] ET 2390772/2011.

[60] See *Christian Institute and Others v. Office of First Minister and Deputy First Minister*, Neutral Citation no. [2007] NIQB 66, per Wetherup J, at para. 48.

[61] *McFarlane v. Relate Avon Ltd* [2010] EWCA Civ 880, [2010] IRLR 872, per Laws LJ, at paras 23–24.

[62] See *Saggers v. British Railways Board* [1977] IRLR 266 for an early ruling to that effect. See further Edge, "Determining Religion in English Courts".

[63] [2005] UKHL 15, [2005] 2 AC 246 (HL), at para. 75. An approach very much in keeping with the views expressed by Lord Greene MR in *Re Samuel* [1942] 1 Ch 1, CA at p. 17.

[64] *Eweida v. British Airways* [2008] UKEAT 0123, 08, 2011 (EAT).   [65] Ibid., at para. 29.

[66] *R (On the application of Begum (by her litigation friend, Rahman)) v. Headteacher and Governors of Denbigh High School* [2006] UKHL 15 (HL), at para. 18.

[67] *Ghai, R (on the application of) v. Newcastle City Council & Ors* [2010] EWCA Civ 59.

[68] *GMB v. Henderson* EAT 73/14/DM (13 March 2015), at para. 62.

in "democratic socialism".[69] All of this lends weight to Trigg's comment that "freedom of religion has been attenuated into freedom of 'religion or belief', and all too often it seems to become freedom of conscience".[70]

"Race" and "Caste"

Under the Race Relations Act 1976, some religious groups were classified as ethnic groups. In s.3A, "harassment" is defined as when, on grounds of race or ethnic or national origins, a person engages in unwanted conduct that has the purpose or effect of violating another person's dignity or creating an intimidating, hostile, degrading, humiliating or offensive environment for that person.[71] The 2010 Act, s.9, continues the definition of "race" to include colour, nationality and ethnic or national origins;[72] this has since been extended, by the Enterprise and Regulatory Reform Act 2013, to accommodate "caste" as a sub-category of race and thereby ensure compliance with the ICERD. Indirect discrimination can occur when a rule or procedure with a general application has a disproportionate impact upon the religious practices associated with an ethnic group.

Chandhok and another v. *Tirkey*[73] concluded proceedings[74] concerning Tirkey, a member of the Adivasi caste (inherited and immutable), known as the "servant caste", who, over a four-and-a-half-year period: worked an eighteen-hour day, seven days a week; slept on a foam mattress on the floor; was prevented from bringing her Bible to the UK and going to church; had her passport confiscated by Mr and Mrs C; was not allowed to call her family; and was given second-hand clothing. In determining that the Chandhoks were guilty of discrimination, albeit rooted in a particular cultural/religious context, this ruling suggests that for all practical purposes the fact that "caste" is not currently included among the specified protected characteristics listed in in the 2010 Act makes little difference, as caste discrimination can constitute unlawful race discrimination. This may open the door to other claimants in this jurisdiction who suffer caste-associated discrimination imported from countries where such practices are sanctioned by their religion and culture.

---

[69] Ibid., and also *Olivier* v. *Department for Work and Pensions* ET/1701407/2013.
[70] Trigg, *Equality, Freedom and Religion*, at p. 134.
[71] An amendment intended to implement the terms of EU Council Directive 2000/43/EC (the Race Directive).
[72] See *Moxam* v. *Visible Changes Ltd and anor* [2011] UKEAT/0267/11, and, further, EHRC research reports 91, "Caste in Britain: Socio-legal Review", 2014 and 92, "Caste in Britain: Experts' Seminar and Stakeholders' Workshop", 2014.
[73] [2015] IRLR 195. [74] See ET/3400174/13 and [2014] UKEAT O190.

Manifesting Religion or Belief and Free Speech

The right of an individual to express their religion is qualified by Article 9(2), which requires the manifestation of religion or belief to be subject to such limitations as are "prescribed by law and are necessary in a democratic society in the interests of public safety, for the protection of public order, health or morals, or the protection of the rights and freedoms of others". It also requires a clear link between conduct and belief, although in *Eweida* the ECtHR would seem to have established that the conduct need not be mandated by the belief: it is sufficient that the manifestation is a sincere reflection of an adherent's commitment.[75] As the EHRC has explained:[76]

> Manifestations of a religion or belief could include treating certain days as days for worship or rest; following a certain dress code; following a particular diet; or carrying out or avoiding certain practices. There is not always a clear line between holding a religion or belief and the manifestation of that religion or belief. Placing limitations on a person's right to manifest their religion or belief may amount to unlawful discrimination; this would usually amount to indirect discrimination.

The important caveat that the right to manifest religion or belief is, to some degree, subject to the obligation on the person concerned to take responsibility for knowingly placing themselves in a position where their principles might be compromised was alluded to by Weatherup J in *Christian Institute*, when he remarked that "in exercising his freedom to manifest his religion, an applicant may need to take his specific situation into account".[77] This rationale would seem to have been in play in *Cherfi*,[78] *Chaplin*[79] and *Playfoot*[80] – where, in each case, the claimant had knowingly placed themselves in a position which could potentially compromise their beliefs – but has been blunted somewhat by the ECtHR ruling in *Eweida* that "the better approach would be to weigh that possibility in the overall balance when considering whether or not the restriction was proportionate".[81]

---

[75] *Eweida and others v. the United Kingdom*, op. cit., at para. 84. However, note EHRC Code 2011, para. 2.61, which indicates that there is no clear dividing line between holding and manifesting a religious belief.

[76] See EHRC Code 2011, para. 2.61.   [77] Citing *Kalac v. Turkey*, op. cit., at para. 27.

[78] *Cherfi v. G4S Security Services Ltd* [2011] UKEAT 0379 10 2405 (24 May 2011).

[79] *Chaplin v. Royal Devon & Exeter Hospital NHS Foundation Trust* [2010] ET 1702886/2009. See also *X v. UK*, No. 7992/77, 14 DR 234 (1978).

[80] *Playfoot (a minor), R (on the application of) v. Millais School* [2007] EWHC 1698.

[81] *Eweida and others v. the United Kingdom*, op. cit., at para. 83. The author acknowledges advice from Frank Cranmer on this matter (email comments 27 January 2017).

Free Speech and Freedom of Association

A manifestation of religion or belief is not permissible if it's likely to cause alarm or distress, as with posters stating "Islam Out of Britain"[82] or as when a Christian preacher displayed signs reading "Stop Immorality", "Stop Homosexuality" and "Stop Lesbianism".[83] However, an exercise of free speech, such as publication of *The Satanic Verses*,[84] is permissible even if it incites lethal religious hatred outside the jurisdiction. More recently, charges against a preacher who had berated Islam in a sermon on the Internet were dismissed on the grounds that such conduct was not so grossly offensive that it forfeited the protection given to the freedoms of speech and religion under the ECHR.[85] While there is an argument that prohibiting incitement to religious hatred, through the Racial and Religious Hatred Act 2009, is open to abuse as offering a means to censor genuine debate, this is countered by some with the view that not outlawing such behavior might permit the reckless insulting of the religious and incite lethal responses.

The right of individuals to meet, or form associations, for the purposes of worship, religious teaching or any other religion-related reasons is long established. Difficulties arise when the activities of any such association conflict with equality or non-discrimination laws.[86]

Blasphemy

The Criminal Justice and Immigration Act 2008 abolished the common law offences of blasphemy and blasphemous libel.

Conscientious Objection

Cases concerning professional participation in abortion procedures are, as Lady Dorian pointed out, "a matter on which many people have strong moral and religious convictions, and the right of conscientious objection is given out of respect for those convictions and not for any other reason".[87] In addition to that particular context, the only two other areas in which

---

[82] *Norwood* v. *DPP* [2003] EWHC 1564.   [83] *Hammond* v. *DPP* [2004] EWHC 69 (Admin).
[84] Rushdie, S., *The Satanic Verses*, New York, St Martin's Press, 2002 [1988]. See also the more recent controversy relating to Corso, S., *The Jewel of Medina*, New York, Beaufort Books, 2008.
[85] *DPP* v. *McConnell* [2016] NIMag 1.
[86] See e.g. *Catholic Care (Diocese of Leeds)* v. *The Charity Commission for England and Wales* [2011] EqLR 597.
[87] *Doogan & Anor* v. *NHS Greater Glasgow & Clyde Health Board* [2013] ScotCS CSIH 36, at para. 38.

the law of this jurisdiction recognises a right to object on grounds of conscience are as regards IVF treatment and military service in times of conscription.

Proselytism

Proselytising, or "spreading the word", is pursued in an overtly discriminatory manner – extolling the merits of one religion to the detriment of
all others – and has always been an activity readily recognised as being
for the public benefit and assured of charitable status.[88] In *Redmond-
Bate* v. *DPP*,[89] the provocative views of three fundamentalist Christian
preachers, which had generated a heated response from a crowd and
threatened to "disturb the peace", were found to be permissible. As Sedley
LJ commented:

> Free speech includes not only the inoffensive but the irritating, the con-
> tentious, the eccentric, the heretical, the unwelcome and the provocative
> provided it does not tend to provoke violence. Freedom only to speak inof-
> fensively is not worth having

Discrimination

The ECtHR has defined discrimination as "treating differently, without
objective and reasonable justification, persons in analogous, or relevantly
similar, situations",[90] but it is also necessary to be mindful of the advice of
Steyn LJ that "discrimination cases are generally fact-sensitive, and their
proper determination is always vital in our pluralistic society".[91]

Religious Discrimination

Where conduct can be shown to have been clearly motivated by the fact
that the recipient was of a particular religion or held specific beliefs then,
ipso facto, the perpetrator will have deliberately intended an affront to
the religion or beliefs of that person. Where that affront amounts to religious discrimination or harassment,[92] the conduct "speaks for itself" and
no other inference is plausible.[93]

---

[88] *Commissioners for Special Purposes of the Income Tax Act* v. *Pemsel* [1891] AC 531
(H.L.).
[89] [2000] HRLR 249.   [90] See *Kiyutin* v. *Russia*, Application No. 2700/10 (March 2011).
[91] *Anyanwu* v. *South Bank Student Union* [2001] ICR 391 HL, at para. 24.
[92] *Martin* v. *Devonshires* [2011] ICR 352.
[93] *Richmond Pharmaceuticals* v. *Dhaliwal* [2009] ICR 724, per Underhill J, at para. 16.

Type The Equality Act 2010, in keeping with the Employment Equality Directive 2000/78/EC, identifies four types of religious discrimination: direct, indirect, harassment and victimisation. The first takes the form of unequal treatment, whereby some are directly treated less favourably than others because of their religious beliefs.[94] The second incidentally disadvantages a certain religious group, as when a service provider's provision, criterion or practice imposes restrictions that affect their ability to access services available to others.[95] The third results from "whistleblower" circumstances involving a complaint about religious discrimination. The fourth is behaviour that may range from physical attack, to verbal abuse, to causing discomfort because of a religious or racial difference.

Exemptions and Exceptions

The Equality Act 2010, Schedule 9, provides exemptions and exceptions from generally applicable non-discrimination duties. These are variable in nature and differ in application depending on the "protected characteristic" to which the discrimination relates. This inconsistency could be circumvented by an alternative model based on the theory of religious autonomy, a concept recognised by human rights law.[96]

The "Religious" Exemption

The Equality Act 2010, para. 2 of Schedule 9, permits a body representing an "organised religion" to impose explicitly discriminatory restrictions on employment opportunities in relation to gender, marital status and sexual orientation.[97] However, there is uncertainty as to: where the line may be drawn between an "organised religion" and a religious organisation; whether protections are available on the grounds of religion, sex or race; and what are the different types of post that may or may not be entitled to protection.

---

[94] See e.g. *Showboat Entertainment Centre Ltd* v. *Owens* [1984] IRLR 7 (EAT) and *Weathersfield Ltd* v. *Sargent* [1999] IRLR 94 (CA).

[95] See e.g. *Eweida* v. *British Airways*, op. cit., at para. 6. See also *Azmi* v. *Kirkless M.C.* [2007] ICR 1154

[96] See, for example, *Hasan and Chaush* v. *Bulgaria*, op. cit.; *Svyato-Mykhaylivska Parafiya* v. *Ukraine*, op. cit.; and *Sindicatul "Pastorul cel Bun"* v. *Romania*, Application No. 3220/09.

[97] See the Equality Act 2010, Sched. 9. See also the School Standards Framework Act 1998, s.60, which provides that foundation or voluntary schools with a religious character can give preference in employment, remuneration and promotion to teachers whose beliefs are in accordance with the tenets of that religion.

Para. 3 of Schedule 9 – giving effect to Employment Equality Directive 2000/78/EC, Article 4 and 4(2) – states that an employer with an ethos based on religion or belief is permitted to discriminate on the grounds of religion or belief[98] if it is an occupational requirement for the particular post, is genuine and determining and, having regard to that ethos, and to the nature or context of the work, the application of the requirement is a proportionate means of achieving a legitimate aim. Because of the narrowing effect of the "determining" requirement, this exemption has been virtually restricted to employing religious organisations.[99] So, for example, in *Muhammed v. The Leprosy Mission International,*[100] a small Christian charity was allowed to refuse applications from non-Christians, because Christianity permeated the organisation (see later). Despite this judicial confirmation of its narrowness, in November 2009 the European Commission issued a Reasoned Opinion to the UK expressing its view that the exceptions to the principle of non-discrimination on the basis of sexual orientation for religious employers were broader than that permitted by the directive.[101]

Schedule 23, para. 2 of the same Act allows "organisations relating to a religion or belief" – but without a commercial sole or main purpose (unlike in the USA, following the *Hobby Lobby* ruling) – to discriminate on the grounds of religion, belief or sexual orientation in the way they operate. Their purpose must be to: practice, advance or teach, or enable adherents to receive a benefit from or engage in an activity within "the framework of that religion or belief"; or to foster or maintain good relations between persons of different religions or beliefs. Such organisations may exercise religious discrimination when determining membership of the organisation, participation in its activities, use of its premises or "the provision of goods, facilities or services in the course of activities undertaken by the organisation". Such a restriction may be imposed either because of the purposes of the organisation or to avoid causing offence on grounds of its religion or belief to adherents. However, it must be exercised reasonably.

---

[98] See further Sandberg, R. and Doe, N., "Religious Exemptions in Discrimination Law", *Cambridge Law Journal*, 2007, vol. 66:2.

[99] See *R (on the application of Amicus) v. Secretary of State for Trade and Industry* [2004] IRLR 430 QBD [2004] EWHC 860 (Admin).

[100] ET 2303459/0989 (16 December 2009).

[101] See reasoned opinion to the UK, 2009, at europa.eu/rapid/press-release_IP-09-1778_en .htm?locale=en.

Additionally, the sexual orientation provisions of the Equality Act 2010 allow a religious organisation to restrict provision of a service to persons of one sex or to separate services for persons of each sex – but only if this is necessary to comply with the doctrines of the religion, or if it is for the purpose of avoiding conflict with the strongly held religious convictions of a significant number of the religion's followers.[102] An organisation cannot lawfully discriminate in the provision of goods and services on the grounds of sexual orientation where such provision is undertaken on behalf of a public body.

The "Charity" Exemption

Specific exemptions for charities from the laws governing religious discrimination – previously to be found in Regulation 18[103] – are now more restricted than formerly, and consigned to s.193 of the Equality Act 2010. These allow a charity to limit its benefits to people who share a "protected characteristic" – such as a religion or belief. They may do so in circumstances where either the restriction is justified as a means of furthering the charity's aim to tackle a particular disadvantage borne by people with such a characteristic or the charity is seeking to achieve some other legitimate aim in a fair, balanced and reasonable ("proportionate") way. Numerous carve-outs are specified, such as one exempting those who provide single-sex services,[104] if it can be demonstrated that this is a proportionate means of achieving a legitimate aim under s.193(2)(a) or a way of preventing or compensating for disadvantage under s.193(2)(b).

The Charities Act 2006, s.2(2)(h) made a positive contribution to countering religious discrimination by introducing the charitable purpose of promoting religious harmony (now s.3(1) of the 2011 Act). In general, the 2011 Act narrows the range of religious organisations that may qualify for exemption privileges, as it removed the previous legal presumption that such an organisation *de facto* satisfied the public-benefit test and was entitled to charitable status. Instead, it now requires all entities to demonstrate they satisfy the test as a pre-condition for registration. Tax-exemption entitlement is a matter of not inconsiderable interest to the established Church, as owner of most of the nation's architectural heritage, a significant proportion of its inner-city property and 100 000 acres of its farmland and as recipient of most of its citizens' Gift Aid donations.

---

[102] Equality Act 2010, Sched. 23, S. 2 (7) and s.2(9).
[103] The Sexual Orientation Regulations 2007, Regulation 18 was issued under powers provided by the Equality Act 2006.
[104] See e.g. the Equality Act 2010, ss.114 and 120.

Section 193 also exempts any charity which, prior to 18 May 2005, made acceptance of a particular religion or belief a condition of membership with an entitlement to the benefit, service or facility provided by that charity, and has since continued to impose that condition, from being in contravention of the Act. Certain schools and associations also benefit from exemptions. This exemption is important as, in 2014, there were 32 735 faith-based charities, representing nearly one in five of all registered charities.

The tension between beliefs and equality can be acute for religious charities. This is especially true as regards the right to equal treatment of members of groups protected under the Act, particularly those identified by their sexual orientation.

The "Positive Action" Provisions

Introduced by the Equality Act 2010, s.158, these provide specific opportunities for intervention in circumstances that would otherwise constitute unlawful discrimination.[105] Positive action is permitted if it is a proportionate means of addressing the disadvantages of a group with shared protected characteristics[106] and if it serves to encourage a more proportionate take-up in activities or services by members of such a protected group. It may come into play where a group identified by one or more of the protected characteristics (e.g. Muslim women, Afro-Caribbean schoolboys) is perceived to be socially or economically disadvantaged, or to be subject to systemic discrimination.[107] Positive action is only lawful if the statutory criteria are met: it must be "reasonably thought" that one of the conditions applies, such as disadvantage or disproportionately low participation. It permits, for example, targeted bursaries and scholarships where the potential recipients share a particular religious faith or belief.

Religious Discrimination: Church and State

Political, judicial and academic commentators repeatedly assert that neither religion in general nor the Church of England in particular has any influence upon contemporary affairs of State: "We live in this country in a democratic and pluralistic society, in a secular state and not a

---

[105] See also the Employment Equality Directive 2000/78/EC, Art. 2(2)(b).

[106] The "protected characteristics" being age, disability, gender reassignment, marriage and civil partnership, pregnancy and maternity, race, religion or belief, sex and sexual orientation.

[107] See R (Kaur and Shah) v. Ealing LBC [2008] EWHC 2062 (Admin).

theocracy"[108] and "We are secular judges serving a multi-cultural community of many faiths".[109] Nevertheless, residual traces of the common ties that for centuries bound Church and State in this jurisdiction continue to be very evident, and some are very secular.

The Church/State Boundary

This is the only common law jurisdiction presently being considered that has an established Church. Anglican canon law has been assimilated into national law, which gives it, and Protestantism more broadly, a favoured legal status relative to all other religions. Moreover, specific constitutional arrangements have long granted an exclusive role to the Church of England.

Protecting Religion from the State

The principle that the law must treat all religions equally has been established since at least *Re Pinion (deceased)*,[110] when it was held that "the court cannot discriminate between religions". This point was reiterated more recently by Laws LJ in *McFarlane*; when continuing his peroration against religious preferencing, he advised that:[111]

> We do not live in a society where all the people share uniform religious beliefs. The precepts of any one religion – any belief system – cannot, by force of their religious origins, sound any louder in the general law than the precepts of any other. If they did, those out in the cold would be less than citizens; and our constitution would be on the way to a theocracy

Nonetheless, as already outlined, the Church of England has been singled out among the religions of this jurisdiction as having a distinct and superior status, and one which formally binds it to the State. The fact that – under the Marriage (Same Sex Couples) Act 2012–13, accompanied by amendments to the Equalities Act 2010 – it is relieved of any duty to conduct gay marriages (as was the Church in Wales) is, on the face of it, problematic.[112] The associated anomalies cannot be justified without recourse to cultural context rationalisations.

---

[108] *R (Eunice Johns and Owen Johns) and Derby City Council and Equality and Human Rights Commission* (2011) EWHC 375 (Admin), at para. 36.

[109] Ibid., at para. 39.   [110] [1965] Ch. 85. See also *Nelan v. Downes* (1917) 23 CLR 546.

[111] *McFarlane v. Relate Avon Ltd* [2010] EWCA Civ 880, [2010] IRLR 872, at para. 24.

[112] The Church of England will be able of its own accord, under the Church of England Assembly (Powers) Act 1919, to bring legislation before Parliament to rescind its exemptions and "opt in".

The Church has been compromised, albeit willingly, in relation to the equality principle, as the law now operates in a discriminatory fashion: functioning to the clear detriment of the Church's same-sex couples who wish to be married within its precincts and thereby discriminating against such couples relative to those of other religions, and indeed against those of its clergy who would wish to perform the service offered by their counterparts; and relieving one specific religious organisation of an obligation imposed on other similar organisations and, by doing so, discriminating against all others wishing for similar exemption. As there can be no doubt that for some other religions within this jurisdiction, the issue of gay marriage is every bit as difficult as it is for the Church of England, the only justification for singling out the latter as statutorily exempted from the equality measures introduced by the 2014 Act lies in its status as the "established" Church. This, with all the implied weight of tradition and cultural affinity, would seem to require that special legislative recognition be given to the wishes of its representatives. Notwithstanding the assurances given by Laws LJ, the following comment offered by Bielefeldt seems apt: "it seems difficult, if not impossible, to conceive of an official 'State religion' that in practice does not have adverse effects on religious minorities, thus discriminating against their members".[113]

Intervention in Church Disputes

"A secular judge must be wary of straying across the well-recognised divide between Church and State" warned the court in *Johns & Anor, R (on the application of)* v. *Derby City Council & Anor*.[114] The principle that, in a democracy, the judiciary, like the State, should not intervene in the affairs of the Church is well established, although perhaps less well understood.

In *Wachmann*,[115] the judiciary adopted the traditional approach when it drew the line at examining Jewish doctrines: it "would never be prepared to rule on questions of Jewish law" and "must inevitably be wary of entering so self-evidently sensitive an area, straying across the well recognised divide between Church and State". More recently, however, Neuberger LJ explored this area in some detail in *Shergill* v. *Khaira*.[116] He explained

---

[113] See Bielefeldt, "Report of the Special Rapporteur".
[114] [2011] EWHC 375 (Admin), at p. 41.
[115] *R (Wachmann)* v. *Chief Rabbi of the United Hebrew Congregations of Great Britain and the Commonwealth* [1992] 2 All ER 249, at pp. 255–256. See also *R (E)* v. *The Governing Body of JFS* [2008] EWHC 1535 (QB).
[116] Op. cit., at paras 45–59.

that while the court does not adjudicate on the truth of religious beliefs or on the validity of particular rites, it will, in response to an application to enforce private rights and obligations which depend on religious issues, determine such of those issues as are capable of objective ascertainment to the extent necessary to resolve the presenting dispute. As he put it: "the court addresses questions of religious belief and practice where its jurisdiction is invoked either to enforce the contractual rights of members of a community against other members or its governing body or to ensure that property held on trust is used for the purposes of the trust". Consequently, as regards the present dispute, he warned that unless the parties were able to resolve their differences, "the court may have to adjudicate upon matters of religious doctrine and practice in order to determine who are the trustees entitled to administer the trusts".[117]

The State, Religion and Religious Discrimination

Despite appearances – as suggested, most obviously, by the constitutional position of the Church of England and its influence in the House of Lords and upon education and social care provision, etc. – in practice, the institutions of the State seem to take care to keep all religions and religious organisations at arm's length from executive policy and decision-making.

Balancing Religion and Secularism

Munby J, in *X* v. *X*,[118] succinctly explained this balancing act as follows: "although historically this country is part of the Christian west, and although it has an established church which is Christian, I sit as a secular judge serving a multi-cultural community". The balance to be struck was made clear in *McFarlane* v. *Relate Avon Ltd*,[119] a religious discrimination case, when Lord Carey, the former Archbishop of Canterbury, sought to intervene by making suggestions as to the desired composition of the court (suggestions deemed by Laws LJ to be "deeply inimical to the public interest"[120]) and the need to address what he perceived to be an alleged "lack of sensitivity to religious belief"[121] by the judiciary when dealing with such cases. In response, Laws LJ drew attention to two principles generally considered to be central to liberal democracy: that the State should remain neutral in relation to religion; and that public policy should be rigorously secular. He pointed out that:[122]

---

[117] Ibid., at para. 59.   [118] [2002] 1 FLR 508, at para. 12.   [119] Op. cit.
[120] Ibid., at para. 26.   [121] Ibid., at para. 20.   [122] Ibid., at para. 22.

> In a free constitution such as ours there is an important distinction to be drawn between the law's protection of the right to hold and express a belief and the law's protection of that belief's substance or content. The common law and ECHR Article 9 offer vigorous protection of the Christian's right (and every other person's right) to hold and express his or her beliefs. And so they should. By contrast they do not, and should not, offer any protection whatever of the substance or content of those beliefs on the ground only that they are based on religious precepts. These are twin conditions of a free society.

He added: "the conferment of any legal protection or preference upon a particular substantive moral position on the ground only that it is espoused by the adherents of a particular faith, however long its tradition, however rich its culture, is deeply unprincipled".[123] Nonetheless, such an implicit assumption may, perhaps, help to explain why the Church of England recently felt it necessary to publish a long, considered policy proclamation that it had come to view fracking as "a morally acceptable practice".[124]

State Funding of Faith-Based Facilities and Services

According to the Dept of Education, there are 6814 faith-based schools, constituting 34 per cent of the maintained sector, of which about 67 per cent are Church of England and 29 per cent are Catholic.[125] Most often, they receive government grants of up to 90 per cent of capital costs of the buildings and 100 per cent of running costs (including teachers' salaries). Inevitably, the majority of State funding for faith schools goes to the Church of England, as does that for chaplaincy services.

In *National Union of Teachers* v. *Governing Body of St Mary's Church of England (Aided) Junior School*,[126] the Court of Appeal found that the Church of England school was in the State system and that the governors were a body charged by the State with the running of the school and were exercising their functions with a view to securing provision by the school of the national curriculum. In these circumstances, the governors were to be regarded as an emanation of the State for the purposes of the doctrine of direct effect.[127]

---

[123] Ibid., at para. 23.

[124] See Church Commissioners, "Shale Gas and Fracking", Church of England, December 2016.

[125] See further at www.education.gov.uk/aboutdfe/foi/disclosuresaboutschools/a0065446/maintained-faith-schools.

[126] [1997] 3 CMLR 630.

[127] See *Cali & Figli SrL* v. *SEPG* [1997] ECR I-1547, [1997] 5 CMLR 484, at para. 23.

Until 2002, the only chaplains employed by the Prison Service were Christian chaplains. Since then, it has also provided prisoners with Jewish and Muslim chaplains. In *Naeem v. the Secretary of State for Justice*,[128] the claimant, a Muslim chaplain employed since 2004, failed in his claims that his lack of career advancement was due to race discrimination and discrimination on grounds of religion or belief. Although the pay disparity between Christian and Muslim chaplains was such as to substantiate indirect discrimination on the grounds of religion or belief (and race), the claims failed because the employer had been able to establish "justification".[129]

Christian Symbols/Prayers in State Facilities

In February 2012, the High Court in *NSS v. Bideford Town Council*[130] ruled against the council, declaring that it was unconstitutional to continue with the long-standing practice of holding prayers at the beginning of their meetings. Prayer, Ouseley J ruled, is a private matter that has no place in the formal proceedings of a legal assembly. This judgment attracted the comment from Britain's first Muslim cabinet minister "that a militant secularisation is taking hold of our societies . . . "[131] In response to the ruling, the government promptly introduced amending legislation with the effect that councils wanting to continue holding formal prayers may now do so. Three years later, the Commission on Religion and Belief in British Public Life advised that "the legal requirement for schools to hold acts of collective worship should be repealed".[132] These skirmishes indicate that the continuation of settled and familiar Christian rituals in State facilities is under constant challenge from secularists.

Religious Discrimination: Contemporary Caselaw

The following thematic exploration of the caselaw considers, in turn, each of the everyday settings in which the vast majority of all incidents of religious discrimination occur.

---

[128] UKEAT/0215/13/RN, 2014.
[129] See also [2015] EWCA Civ 1264. This was subsequently appealed to the Supreme Court: see www.supremecourt.uk/cases/uksc-2016-0005.html.
[130] [2012] EWHC 175 (Admin).
[131] See Baroness Warsi, then minister without portfolio and chair of the Conservative Party, who used the term in response to the ruling of Ouseley J.
[132] Commission on Religion and Belief in British Public Life, *Living with Difference*, at p. 8.

Religious Conduct, Symbols, Icons, Apparel, etc.

Religious/cultural identity is often represented in symbolic form. It can be a powerful manifestation of religious affiliation, whether exhibited by institutions of the State or by an individual. Equally, it can be perceived as intimidating by those of other religions or of none.

Ethnicity/Religion-Specific Customs

In *Ghai*,[133] the Court of Appeal considered a request from Ghai, a Hindu, that the Council make available some land outside the city precincts to allow the practice of open-air cremation, as his religion required that cremation take place by traditional fire, in direct sunlight and away from man-made structures. The court held that Mr Ghai's wishes as to how, after his death, his remains were to be cremated should be accommodated. Of particular significance is the fact that the Master of the Rolls, following the approach taken earlier by Baroness Hale in *Williamson*,[134] emphasised the importance of the individual's belief: "What we are concerned with in this case is, of course, what Mr Ghai's belief involves when it comes to cremation, and it matters not for present purposes whether it is a universal, orthodox or unusual belief for a Hindu".[135] This accords with the views expressed earlier by Elias P in *Eweida*:[136]

> it is not necessary for a belief to be shared by others in order for it to be a religious belief, nor need a specific belief be a mandatory requirement of an established religion for it to qualify as a religious belief. A person could, for example, be part of the mainstream Christian religion but hold additional beliefs which are not widely shared by other Christians, or indeed shared at all by anyone.

In relation to the tension between animal welfare and the freedom of religion, it is important to note that the slaughter of animals without pre-stunning, to satisfy the demands of Halaal consumers, is a permitted exception to Article 9 of the ECHR – despite the provisions of Directive 93/104/EC on animal welfare.

---

[133] *Ghai, R (on the application of)* v. *Newcastle City Council & Ors*, op. cit.
[134] *R (Williamson)* v. *Secretary of State for Education and Employment*, op. cit.
[135] *Ghai, R (on the application of)* v. *Newcastle City Council & Ors*, op. cit., at para. 19.
[136] *Eweida* v. *British Airways*, op. cit., at para. 29. See also *Kelly and Others* v. *Unison* (2010, Case No 2203854/08, ET.

Religious Apparel

This jurisdiction has a reputation for being quite relaxed about the public display of private religious affiliation: there has never been any legal prohibition on adults wearing turbans or other headwear denoting religious affiliation in their places of employment. When problems do arise, there is an onus on the wearer to show a sincere conviction that the particular item is a necessary and appropriate manifestation of their belief. Any imposed restriction, in terms of uniform and dress codes, requires good reason – such as health and safety requirements.

In *Begum*,[137] for example, the House of Lords considered the wish of a schoolgirl to wear the jilbab in keeping with the professed religious beliefs of herself and family, despite the prohibition on doing so in the school dress code. The court heard evidence that the wearing of the jilbab was not considered necessary by a considerable proportion of those who shared the plaintiff's religious beliefs, but nonetheless upheld her right to consider it to be so. Lord Bingham of Cornhill added that "it was not the less a religious belief because her belief may have changed, as it probably did, or because it was a belief shared by a small minority of people".[138] Nonetheless, there had been no interference with her right to manifest her belief in practice or observance. In choosing to attend Denbeigh High School, Ms Begum found limitations imposed on the manifestation of her religious belief, but was otherwise uninhibited in that regard. However, if a rule is ostensibly neutral but has a disproportionate effect on an ethnic minority then it must be justified. This was evident in *R (Watkins-Singh) v. Aberdale Girls' High School*,[139] where the school ban on wearing jewellery was held to impose a particular constraint on Sikh pupils. That there are limits to judicial tolerance of dress as a manifestation of belief was apparent at London's Blackfriars Crown Court when Murphy J, commenting that "the niqab has become the elephant in the courtroom", ruled that a Muslim woman defendant should remove her niqab when giving evidence.

A pre-condition for any manifestation must be, as in *Begum*, that it relates meaningfully to the belief which is sincerely held. In *Playfoot (a minor), R (on the application of) v. Millais School*,[140] for example, the court found that an item of jewelry (a "purity ring") was "representative of a

---

[137] *R (On the application of Begum (by her litigation friend, Rahman)) v. Headteacher and Governors of Denbigh High School*, op. cit.
[138] Ibid., at para. 18.   [139] [2008] EWHC 1865, [2008] 3 FCR 203.
[140] [2007] EWHC 1698.

moral stance and not a necessary symbol of Christian faith". In contrast, the court in *Azmi*[141] upheld the earlier Employment Tribunal finding that the beliefs of the claimant – a classroom-based bilingual support worker – concerning the veil were "genuine and held by a sizeable minority of Muslim women".[142] It found that the restriction on wearing the niqab was a neutral rule which put the claimant at a disadvantage, but was justified as it was a proportionate measure given the interests of the children in having the best possible education. The school had examined the effects of teaching with the niqab in place and had evidence to show that, in those circumstances, the indirect discrimination was justified. But in *Noah v. Sarah Desrosiers (trading as Wedge)*,[143] a Muslim applying for a hairdressing position was held to have suffered indirect discrimination when her employer warned that she would be required to remove her hijab while at work if appointed. The Employment Tribunal found that there was an onus on the employer to produce evidence that the wearing of the headscarf would have an adverse effect on the business. In the absence of any such evidence, the requirement was found not to be justified. Some years later, in the not dissimilar case of *Begum v. Barley Lane Montessori Day Nursery*,[144] a Muslim claimed that she had suffered religious discrimination at a job interview when she was told that she would not be permitted to wear a jilbab of appropriate length and therefore had been unable to accept the post. The EAT concluded that the prospective employer was justified in considering that the particular length of the jilbab might constitute a tripping hazard to staff or to the children in their care: no requirement had been placed on the claimant not to wear a jilbab, only that her particular jilbab should not constitute a tripping hazard. This approach was not indirectly discriminatory to Muslim women: it applied equally to staff of all religions, and if it did put some Muslim women at a particular disadvantage, any indirect discrimination was justified as being a proportionate means of achieving a legitimate aim, i.e. protecting the health and safety of staff and children.

It was *Eweida v. British Airways*[145] that most clearly marked a turning point. This case concerned Ms Eweida, a committed Christian working for British Airways (BA) in a customer service area, who wanted to display a small cross around her neck in contravention of BA policy that no jewellery was to be visible. She claimed that BA's refusal to allow this was indirect discrimination, as a general policy was applied to all visible

---

[141] *Azmi v. Kirkless M.C.*, op. cit.   [142] Ibid., at para. 101.   [143] ET 2201867/2007.
[144] UKEAT/0309/13/RN, 2015.   [145] Op. cit.

jewellery (although exceptions were allowed for apparel that could not be worn discretely, such as a hijab, a turban and a skullcap worn by other members of staff). This was rejected by the Employment Tribunal, and again on appeal to EAT and the Court of Appeal. However, on appeal to the ECtHR,[146] it was held that BA had breached Ms Eweida's human rights, in particular her right to freedom of thought, conscience and religion. Noting that religious freedom "is primarily a matter of individual thought and conscience", the court took the view that her desire to wear a cross openly was a sincere manifestation of her religious beliefs and that "there was no evidence that the wearing of other, previously authorised, items of religious clothing, such as turbans and hijabs, by other employees, had any negative impact on British Airways' brand or image".[147]

The importance of the latter caveat was demonstrated in *Chaplin* v. *Royal Devon & Exeter Hospital NHS Foundation Trust*,[148] which concerned a nurse who refused on religious grounds to stop wearing a crucifix with her uniform in contravention of the Trust's health and safety policy. The ECtHR upheld the earlier ruling that the nurse had not been subjected to direct or indirect discrimination. It differentiated the ruling from *Eweida* by reference to the proportionality principle: the health and safety dimension tipped the balance against Ms Chaplin, who, unlike Ms Eweida, was in a position where her wish to manifest her religious belief might well adversely impact upon the interests of others.

These cases indicate that justification for imposing restrictions on the wearing of clothing, jewellery or other accessories as a manifestation of religion or belief will require supporting evidence that in the particular circumstances – environmental, business or professional – the manifestation has a disproportionate impact on others.

Family-Related Issues

This jurisdiction has long accepted the ECtHR definition of "family" as not restricted to one based on marriage but as including unmarried couples and non-marital children, and more recently has been equally accepting of the definitional extension to accommodate homosexual relationships.[149] Any intervention in family affairs must be in accordance with the

---

[146] *Eweida and others* v. *the United Kingdom*, op. cit.   [147] Ibid., at para. 94.
[148] [2010] ET 1702886/2009.
[149] See e.g. *Smith and Grady* v. *United Kingdom* (2000) 29 EHRR 548 and *Goodwin* v. *United Kingdom* (2002) 35 EHRR 447.

obligation under Article 8 of the ECHR to respect the private and family life of its members.

Sexuality

Since 1967, consensual private sexual relations between those of the same gender have been de-criminalised.[150] Civil partnerships have been legally available since 2004, and gay marriages since the introduction of the Marriage (Same Sex Couples) Act 2013. Legislative intent in confronting sex-related taboos to broaden the legal definition of marriage has moved a long way from the the Table of Kindred and Affinity and the Deceased Wife's Sister's Marriage Act 1907.[151]

The system of Islamic beliefs – which is centred upon a model marital family unit, ascribes gender roles and sexual orientation and directs severe punishments for any breach of the related rules – is fundamentally challenged by the new legislation. In the "honour" crimes that accompany this model, the victims are almost always Muslim women. There were 11 000 such cases recorded in this jurisdiction between 2010 and 2014, including forced marriages, desertion of abusive husbands, FGM, abductions, beatings and murders. The persistence of FGM, although not exclusive to Muslims, is a particularly worrying phenomenon. A total of 5702 cases were recorded for 2015, the first year of mandatory reporting by health officials, and there has yet to be a successful prosecution for a practice that is well known and has been legally prohibited for decades. It is difficult, also, not to make a link between Muslim religion/culture and the sexual abuse of non-Muslim women. As the independent inquiry "Child Sexual Exploitation in Rotherham"[152] revealed, disparity in cultural mores was a factor that allowed gangs of Asian men to abuse some 1400 young girls over a sixteen-year period: local authority staff were averse to "identifying the ethnic origins of perpetrators for fear of being thought racist; others remembered clear direction from their managers not to do so". Religious discrimination conflated with ethnicity was again in play: the perpetrators were Muslim males; Muslim girls were not victims; and those in authority were inhibited from intervening for fear of being accused of religious/racial discrimination.

---

[150] For context, they have been legal in Ireland since 1993, in Australia since 1972–91 (different states in succession) and in India since 2009.

[151] The author thanks Frank Cramner for pointing this out (note to author, 8 April 2017).

[152] See www.rotherham.gov.uk/downloads/file/1407/independent_inquiry_cse_in_ rotherham.

The new cultural context also presents challenges for the established Church. The 2013 Act, accompanied by amendments to the Equalities Act 2010, has relieved the Church of England of any duty to conduct gay marriages. It is thereby statutorily handicapped relative to other religions, its functional capacity diminished by the State, and it is required to operate in a discriminatory fashion to the detriment of Anglican same-sex couples.[153] There is also, of course, the fact that the permission not to officiate at same-sex marriages is restricted exclusively to the Church of England: all other religious institutions, wishing for similar exemption, may well protest that this provision makes them victims in a form of religious discrimination.

Conception, Abortion, IVF and Related Issues

The extent to which maternity is now a chosen option has increased. Pregnancy may be achieved by artificial insemination (see later), avoided through the use of improved contraceptives or terminated by abortion, while surrogacy has rendered the choice to parent a gender-free option – available to single persons and same-sex couples – doing much to broaden the diversity of contemporary family forms, intensify religious disquiet and attract (sublimated or otherwise) a level of religious discrimination.

Abortion, in particular, has long been a watershed issue for religious adherents. The current bitter face-off between pro-choice and pro-life camps bears testimony to the accuracy of Diplock LJ's comment nearly forty years ago that "the legalisation of abortion, at any rate in circumstances in which the termination of the pregnancy is not essential in order to save the mother's life, [is] a subject on which strong moral and religious convictions are held".[154] The attendant legal issues rarely come before the courts – because the governing Abortion Act 1967 (revised 1990) is quite permissive in scope[155] – but recently surfaced in *Greater Glasgow Health Board* v. *Doogan and Wood*,[156] which concerned two Catholic

---

[153] Note that in *O'Donoghue and others* v. *UK* [2010] ECHR Application No. 34848/07, the ECtHR had already identified government exemption of Church of England marriages from legislative provisions with a general application – the Asylum and Immigration (Treatment of Claimants, etc.) Act 2004 – as being in breach of the Article 14 guarantee of freedom from discrimination and, as such, as constituting religious discrimination.

[154] *Royal College of Nursing of the United Kingdom* v. *Department of Health and Social Security* [1981] AC 800 at 824G-H.

[155] But not so permissive in Northern Ireland, where the Abortion Act 1967 does not apply and abortion is legally permitted only if a woman's life is in danger, or if there is a permanent risk to her mental or physical health.

[156] [2014] UKSC 68.

midwives who had refused, on religious grounds, to work as required by their employing hospital in its abortion clinic: a refusal not accepted by their managers. As it turned out, the court did not need to consider the possible issue of religious discrimination as it was sufficient to resolve the case, upholding the plaintiff's right to direct the involvement of midwives in abortion procedures, by relying on a narrow interpretation of what constituted "participation" for the purpose of the conscientious objection provisions of s.4 of the Abortion Act 1967, with the caveat that "it may be reasonable to expect an employer to accommodate an employee's objections".

For Muslims, the qur'anic injunction that "their mothers are only those who conceived them and gave birth to them (*waladna hum*)"[157] denies the distinction between genetic and gestational mothers, which can result in family and community rejection on religious grounds of anyone participating, whether as donor or recipient, in such procedures.

Assisted Suicide

Suicide as a criminal offence was abolished by the Suicide Act 1961, but the offence of assisting someone to commit suicide was continued under s.2(1) of the same Act. Although any legally and mentally competent person is entitled to refuse food and water or to reject any invasive treatment, and medical practitioners must comply with their wishes, euthanasia – or medically assisted death – has nonetheless remained illegal.

The religious dimension to this issue was noted by Hoffmann LJ in *Bland*:[158] "those who adhere to religious faiths which believe in the sanctity of all God's creation and in particular that human life was created in the image of God himself will have no difficulty with the concept of the intrinsic value of human life". This view was later echoed by Steyn LJ in *Pretty* v. *DPP*:[159]

> There is a conviction that human life is sacred and that the corollary is that euthanasia and assisted suicide are always wrong. This view is supported by the Roman Catholic Church, Islam and other religions.

However, as the latter then went on to say, "there are many millions who do not hold these beliefs . . . the personal autonomy of individuals is predominant". The logic of this argument seemed to prevail in the recent, extensive and thoroughly considered judgment of *Nicklinson & Anor R*

---

[157] See the Qur'an, *ayah* in *Surah al-Mujadalah* (58: 2).   [158] Op. cit., at p. 826C-E.
[159] *R (Pretty)* v. *Director of Public Prosecutions* [2002] 1 AC 800, at para. 54.

(on the application of) (Rev 1),[160] which found: that s.2(1) of the Abortion Act 1961 could not be aligned with s.3(1) of the Human Rights Act 1998 in such a way as to remove the culpability of those who assist others to commit suicide; and that the law was incompatible with Article 8 of the ECHR, which, in the light of *Haas* v. *Switzerland*,[161] must be regarded as recognising a positive legal *right* to commit suicide. Acknowledging that its hands were tied by the existing fifty-year-old legislation, the Supreme Court referred the matter for remedial action to Parliament. Again, given the tenor of these judicial comments, it is hard to avoid recognising that religious beliefs – and discrimination on the basis of those beliefs – would seem to have played a part in allowing the law to continue to obstruct the principle that the personal autonomy of the individual is predominant.

Employment-Related Issues

The absolute right to religious freedom and the qualified right of an employee or employer to manifest any such religion or belief in the work-place are matters governed by Article 9 of the European Convention and by the Equality Act 2010. Section 15(4) of the latter requires related issues to be resolved by taking into account the Code of Practice on Employment 2011, paras 2.50–2.61. As already mentioned, the Framework Equality Directive 2000/78/EC is also important (see further Chapter 4).

Hiring/Firing Staff

Religious Organisations   Religious organisations in this jurisdiction do not have *carte blanche* for operating a "closed-shop" employment policy exclusively favouring persons of a designated religion or belief. This was clearly illustrated in *Hinder & Sheridan* v. *Prospects for People with Learning Disabilities*,[162] which concerned Prospects, a Christian organisation that provided housing and day-care for people with learning disabilities. It introduced a policy based on its Christian ethos whereby it would recruit only practising Christians for the vast majority of roles (except cooking, cleaning, gardening, maintenance), as those in post might have to lead prayers or give spiritual guidance,[163] and told existing non-Christian

---

[160] [2014] UKSC 38, on appeal from [2013] EWCA Civ 961.
[161] Op. cit., at para. 51; see also *Koch* v. *Germany*, op. cit., at paras 46 and 51 and *Gross* v. *Switzerland*, op. cit., at para. 60.
[162] [2008] ET 2902090/2006 & 2901366/2008.
[163] Thereby ostensibly complying with the "genuine occupational requirement" of the Employment Equality (Religion or Belief) Regulations 2003.

employees that they were no longer eligible for promotion. The Tribunal found that it was insufficient to assume that, as a matter of principle, every job in a Christian organisation should be done by Christians. In order to comply with the provisions of the 2003 Regulations, it was necessary to carry out a job evaluation for every post. In a decision that sent a clear message to faith-based organisations regarding blanket policies which discriminate on this protected characteristic, the Tribunal held that Prospects had unlawfully discriminated against one of its managers by requiring him to only employ Christians and not to promote its existing non-Christian employees. In *Reaney* v. *Hereford Diocesan Board of Finance*,[164] the plaintiff acknowledged on his application form for a job as a youth worker with the diocese that he had been in a same-sex relationship until recently. An interview panel decided that he was the best candidate, but his appointment was vetoed by the Bishop of Hereford, even though Reaney had undertaken to remain celibate for the time he was employed. The Tribunal noted that the job was to represent the diocese in youth work and therefore could be said to be closely bound up with the Bishop as the Head of the Diocese, and that it did fall within that small number of posts outside of the clergy that are for the purposes of organised religion. Requiring Reaney to be celibate could be said to be in compliance with the doctrines of the religion, or to avoid conflicting with the strongly held religious convictions of a significant number of the religion's followers. Given, however, that Reaney met the requirement (celibacy), it was not reasonable to refuse to employ him.

Where being of a particular gender, race, religion or sexual orientation is a genuine occupational requirement, then an employer is legislatively permitted to discriminate by expressly restricting staff recruitment accordingly.[165] This exception to the prohibition on discrimination has applicability to employment in a religious organisation, most obviously demonstrated in the appointment or otherwise of female bishops and non-celibate gay clergy, but was also explored in *McNab* v. *Glasgow City Council*,[166] which concerned an atheist maths teacher in a Roman Catholic High School who had never been promoted, had failed in his head of department application and had applied for a post of Acting Principal

---

[164] ET/1602844/2006.
[165] See: the Framework Directive EC (2000/78), Article 4(2); the Equality Act 2010, Sched 9(2); and the Employment Equality (Religion or Belief) Regulations 2003, Regulation 7(3).
[166] UKEATS/0037/06/MT, [2007] IRLR 476. See also *Mayuuf* v. *The Governing Body of Bishop Challoner Catholic Collegiate School* ET 3202398/04 (December 2005).

Teacher of Pastoral Care but not been interviewed. Both the Tribunal and the EAT concluded that a Catholic teacher would have been interviewed for the job and that, considering the nature and context of the post, non-Catholics such as Mr McNab who had acted as pastoral care teachers should also be entitled to an interview. Therefore, being a Catholic could not be a "genuine and determining" occupational requirement for the post. The EAT upheld the Tribunal's finding that there was no genuine occupational requirement and that the plaintiff had suffered direct discrimination under the Employment Equality (Religion or Belief) Regulations 2003. In *Muhammad v. The Leprosy Mission International*,[167] the Muslim plaintiff had applied for the position of finance administrator in an organisation that required an applicant incumbent to be "a practising Christian committed to the objectives and the values" of the organisation. After failing to obtain the post, Mr Muhammed claimed discrimination on the ground of religion, but the Tribunal found that being a practising Christian was a genuine occupational requirement and held the requirement objectively justified, as employing a non-Christian would have a very significant adverse affect on the maintenance of the respondent's ethos.

Secular Organisations The importance of employers having in place a clearly stated formal staffing policy when their organisation is located in a multi-cultural environment has been evident in some cases. In both *Bodi v. Teletext Ltd*[168] and *Shah v. Harish Finance Ltd*,[169] for example, the complainants were Muslims. The first had not been shortlisted for a job: none of the shortlisted candidates were Asian, and no Asian Duty Editor had been appointed by the company in ten years, which the Tribunal found "surprising", as the catchment area, Greater London, was multi-racial. The second was employed in a workshop where the owners and most of the workers were Hindus but was dismissed following alleged abuse and mistreatment by his colleagues. In both cases, the Tribunal examined the racial and religious make-up of the workforces, took into account the absence of any equal-opportunities policy and found that the complainants had suffered, among other things, religious discrimination.

The principle that acceptance of the contractual terms of employment nullifies any subsequent grounds for refusing to undertake duties for reasons of religious belief was initially applied almost routinely in many cases. In *Esson v. London Transport Executive*,[170] the appeal of a Seventh-Day

[167] Op. cit. [168] ET 3300497/05 (4961/85) (Nov 2005).
[169] ET 3302110/2004 (4887/26) (July 2005). [170] [1975] IRLR 48.

Adventist, dismissed after trying to take Saturdays off for religious reasons, was rejected, with the court ruling that it was his duty to reconcile the "insurmountable conflict" between his religious beliefs and his contractual obligations. In *Ahmad* v. *Inner London Education Authority*,[171] the Court of Appeal held that the right to freedom of thought, conscience and religion established by Article 9 of the European Convention did not entitle an employee to be absent from work for the purpose of religious worship in breach of contract. This decision was subsequently upheld by the ECtHR,[172] which reiterated that Article 9(1) rights must necessarily be subject to Article 9(2) limitations: the court held that freedom of religion "may, as regards the modality of a particular religious manifestation, be influenced by the situation of the person claiming that freedom".[173] Again, in *Stedman* v. *UK*,[174] a dismissal for refusal to work on a Sunday was held not to constitute a breach of the right to freedom of religion: the employee's freedom to resign in effect guaranteed her Convention rights.

However, in recent years, the issues involved have required closer examination. In *Ladele* v. *London Borough of Islington*,[175] which was similar to and followed shortly after the previously mentioned *McClintock* case, the Court of Appeal considered the dismissal of Ms Ladele, a Christian marriage registrar, who refused to be involved in registering same-sex "civil partnerships" in accordance with newly introduced statutory procedures. The court took the view that the registration process was a public service, that it had significant human rights implications for the community and that administering the process formed part of Ms Ladele's contractual duties. It noted: "the effect on Ms Ladele of implementing the policy did not impinge on her religious beliefs: she remained free to hold those beliefs, and free to worship as she wished".[176] It concluded that:[177]

---

[171] [1978] QB 36, CA. A decision seemingly followed in *Safouane & Bouterfas* v. *Joseph Ltd and Hannah* [1996] Case No. 12506/95/LS & 12569/95, when the appeal of two Muslims dismissed for praying during breaks was rejected. However, both seem at variance with *JH Walker Ltd* v. *Hussain* [1996] IRLR 11 EAT, where it was decided that actions taken by an employer causing detriment to Muslims as a class, such as refusal to allow time off for religious holidays, might be held to constitute indirect racial discrimination against those from an ethnic or national origin that is predominantly Muslim.

[172] (1982) 4 E.H.R.R. 126.   [173] Ibid., at p. 11.

[174] *Stedman* v. *United Kingdom*, op. cit., following *Ahmad* v. *UK* (1981) 4 EHRR 126. See also *Cherfi* v. *G4S Security Services Ltd*, op. cit. and *MBA* v. *London Borough of Merton*, op. cit.

[175] [2009] EWCA (Civ) 1357 (15 December 2009).

[176] Ibid., per Lord Neuberger at para. 51.

[177] Ibid., the Master of the Rolls (with whom Dyson and Smith LJJ agreed) at para. 52.

Ms Ladele was employed in a public job and was working for a public authority; she was being required to perform a purely secular task, which was being treated as part of her job; Ms Ladele's refusal to perform that task involved discriminating against gay people in the course of that job; ... Ms Ladele's objection was based on her view of marriage, which was not a core part of her religion; and Islington's requirement in no way prevented her from worshipping as she wished.

Similarly, in *McFarlane* v. *Relate Avon Ltd*,[178] which concerned a charity that provided relationship support, including counselling, Mr M, a relationship counsellor, had been dismissed when he indicated to his employer that he did not approve of same-sex relationships on biblical grounds and did not wish to be involved in counselling same-sex couples. The court, following the approach it had earlier adopted in *Ladele*,[179] ruled that Mr M had not suffered religious discrimination. Both decisions were subsequently upheld on appeal to the ECtHR. Again, in *McClintock* v. *Department of Constitutional Affairs*,[180] which concerned the request of a JP member of a statutory panel that he be excused from officiating in cases where he might have to decide whether same-sex partners should adopt children, and who resigned when his request was refused, the EAT found that McClintock had not been disadvantaged because of any religious belief he held and that, even if he had been, such discrimination would have been justified.

These cases indicate that religious beliefs will not justify a refusal to perform contractual duties, even when these emerge post-contract, if this disproportionately affects the rights of others. As Lady Hale acknowledged in *Greater Glasgow Health Board* v. *Doogan and Wood*:[181] "refusing for religious reasons to perform some of the duties of a job is likely[182] to be held to be a manifestation of a religious belief", although "there would remain difficult questions of whether the restrictions placed by the employers upon the exercise of that right were a proportionate means of pursuing a legitimate aim ... and the Equality Act 2010 requires that any employer refrain from direct or unjustified indirect discrimination against his employees on the ground of their religion or belief".[183]

---

[178] Op. cit. See also *R (on the application of Johns)* v. *Derby City Council* (2011) EWHC 375 (Admin), [2011] 1 FLR 2094.
[179] Op. cit.   [180] Op. cit.   [181] Op. cit.
[182] Citing *Eweida and others* v. *the United Kingdom*, op. cit.
[183] *Greater Glasgow Health Board* v. *Doogan and Wood*, op. cit., at paras 23–24.

Matters become more complicated when the beliefs in question are specific to a small minority. For example, *James* v. *MSC Cruises Limited*[184] concerned a Seventh-Day Adventist who was not prepared to work from sunset on Friday until sunset on Saturday, but who failed to mention this during her job interview. She then claimed religious discrimination when the job offer was withdrawn following that disclosure. The Tribunal found that MSC had a "real business need" for Saturday working and balanced that against the significance of the disadvantage caused to the complainant. It concluded that the business needs outweighed the discriminatory effects on the complainant and so dismissed her claim. However, in *Holland* v. *Angel Supermarket Ltd and another*,[185] the Tribunal upheld the appeal of a Wiccan who claimed that she was mocked and later dismissed after switching her shifts to celebrate All Hallows' Eve.

Accommodating Religious Beliefs in the Workplace

In this jurisdiction, the difficulties involved in making allowances for an individual's need to manifest their religious affiliation, within a regime that generally operates to the exclusion of such practices, often lead to allegations of indirect discrimination: when religious individuals are placed at a disadvantage compared to others, this needs to be justified; reasons may relate to the business needs of the employer or service users. The problem has been evident since at least *X* v. *UK*,[186] when it was held that the practice of wearing a turban did not absolve Sikh motorcyclists from the obligation, on health and safety grounds, to wear crash helmets. It was evident more recently in *Mohmed* v. *West Coast Trains Ltd*,[187] which concerned a Muslim customer services assistant who complained that his dismissal was due to his beard, the length of which he regarded as a religious requirement. However, the Tribunal found that in fact the dispute regarding the beard had been resolved as he had voluntarily shortened it from 8 inches to 4, and this had been acceptable to his employers. The EAT concluded that "the Tribunal was thus entitled to find that there was no difference in treatment, let alone less favourable treatment, when comparing the claimant's case with that of a non-Muslim employee. In other words, the beard issue had nothing to do with the claimant's religion and, having been resolved, had no bearing on the dismissal."

---

[184] No. 2203173/05 (April 2006).
[185] Op. cit. See also *Khaira & Ors* v. *Shergill & Ors* [2014] UKSC 33.
[186] No. 7992/77, 14 DR 234 (1978).
[187] No. 2201814/04 (October 2004) and UKEAT/0682/05/DA (August 2006).

As already mentioned, the *Eweida* case established that no clear dividing line existed between holding and manifesting a religious belief: in that instance, not untypically, there was a balance to be struck between the conduct of a religious adherent and the impact of that conduct upon others and upon the requirements of their terms of employment. Recently, the courts have shown a sympathetic understanding of the detrimental effects on working relationships caused by those who foist their religious views on colleagues who object to such an imposition. In *Mr H Monaghan v. Leicester Young Men's Christian Association*,[188] the Tribunal considered an instruction from the complainant's manager that he should not seek to convert those using the YMCA's services to Christianity. The Tribunal upheld the manager's action. Given the Christian ethos of the organisation, this was a strong decision that strengthens the "neutrality of the working environment" principle. In *Drew v. Walsall Healthcare NHS Trust*,[189] the EAT upheld the dismissal of a consultant paediatrician whose teamwork was heavily influenced by his faith; his actions included circulating a prayer – which he described as a personal inspiration – and religious references in his professional communications. In both *Chondol v. Liverpool CC*[190] and *Grace v. Places for Children*,[191] the EAT had upheld the firing of staff – who were committed Christians – not because of their beliefs, but because they had chosen to manifest them in ways that adversely impacted upon others and were inappropriate in terms of their respective employment responsibilities (delivering a social work service on behalf of a public authority and managing a nursery). Similarly, in *Apelogun-Gabriels v. London Borough of Lambeth*,[192] which concerned an employee who complained of religious discrimination because of his dismissal for distributing "homophobic material" to co-workers during prayer meetings he had organised for Christian staff (the material consisted of verses from the Bible which were critical of same-sex sexual activity and which some staff found offensive), the Tribunal confirmed that the material was offensive and held that any indirect discrimination involved in his dismissal was justified. In *Haye v. London Borough of Lewisham*,[193] a Christian administrative assistant was dismissed after posting similar views about LGBT practices on the Lesbian and Gay Christian Movement's website, and again the employer's action was found to be justified, albeit on the grounds of the assistant having misused her employer's

---

[188] (2004), ET Case No. 1901830/04.   [189] UKEAT/0378/12/SM, 2013.
[190] Op. cit.   [191] UKEAT/02/17/13/GE.
[192] (2006), ET Case No. 2301976/05.   [193] (2010), ET Case No. 2301852/09.

email facility. Employment in this jurisdiction involves working in a multi-cultural environment, which must accommodate a diversity of religions and belief.

However, the right to freedom of speech requires that room be made for "give and take" in the workplace. In *Smith* v. *Trafford Housing Trust*,[194] Briggs J considered whether an employer was entitled to discipline an employee, a Christian manager, for posting on Facebook his view that holding civil partnership ceremonies in churches was "an equality too far". Expressing his opinion that the posting was not, "viewed objectively, judgmental, disrespectful or liable to cause upset or offence", Briggs J accepted that the complainant could have considered this as homophobic and have been offended but "her interpretation was not in my view objectively reasonable".[195] The judge advised that:[196]

> The frank but lawful expression of religious or political views may frequently cause a degree of upset, and even offence, to those with deeply held contrary views, even where none is intended by the speaker. This is a necessary price to be paid for freedom of speech.

Similarly, "a reasonable person" would be expected to understand that religiously offensive language used by an irritable employer under the stress of tight publishing deadlines was thoughtless but did not constitute religious discrimination.[197] This, as Underhill J explained in *Dhaliwal*,[198] with a weary reasonableness that could be applied to many similar situations, is because "dignity is not necessarily violated by things said or done which are trivial or transitory, particularly if it should have been clear that any offence was unintended ... it is also important not to encourage a culture of hypersensitivity or the imposition of legal liability in respect of every unfortunate phrase".[199] The sensible person, however, does not express negative views towards LGBT people in conversation with colleagues, and in such circumstances, as the Employment Tribunal recently determined, disciplinary action by an employer will not amount to harassment.[200]

---

[194] [2012] EWHC 3221.   [195] Ibid., at para. 85.
[196] Ibid., at para. 82.   [197] Appeal No. UKEATPA/1305/12/BA.
[198] *Richmond Pharmaceuticals* v. *Dhaliwal*, op. cit. One cannot help wondering if the same view would have been taken had the derisory expletive referred to Muhammad and been directed towards a Muslim employee. See also *Land Registry* v. *Grant* [2011] ICR 1390.
[199] *Dhaliwal*, op. cit., at para. 22.
[200] *Mbuyi* v. *Newpark Childcare* [2015] Case No. 3300656/2014 and *Wasteney* v. *East London NHS Foundation Trust* [2015] Case No. 3200658/2014.

The importance of the proportionality principle was evident in *Thompson v. Luke Delaney George Stobbart Ltd*,[201] which concerned a Jehovah's Witness who had been refused permission for time off work on Sundays. Her discrimination claim was upheld: the refusal was not proportionate because there were other employees who could have covered the Sunday shift without difficulty. In contrast, a plaintiff of the same religion with the same complaint failed in *Patrick v. IH Sterile Services Ltd*[202] to establish religious discrimination. The Tribunal considered that the employer could justify interference with the plaintiff's right to manifest his religious beliefs as its contractual obligation to provide sterile laboratory services to its customers on Sundays was a legitimate aim, and sharing out the obligation to work on Sundays equally across the workforce was a proportionate means of achieving it. Similarly, in *Cherfi v. G4S Security Services Ltd*,[203] the refusal of a security guard's request that his working hours be adjusted to facilitate attendance at a mosque for prayer on Fridays was found to be justified and his indirect discrimination claim was unsuccessful. The employer required a certain number of security staff to be on site during operating hours, and so his request was turned down. The employer offered a number of alternative options but these were refused.

Education-Related Issues

Schooling, in this jurisdiction, has experienced a considerable shift away from standardised local authority control in recent years. This has been accompanied by a significant growth in the number of independent schools opting for a religion-specific ethos.

Government Funding and Religious Education

National education is governed by the Schools Standards and Framework Act 1998, as amended by the Education and Inspections Act 2006 and subject to the provisions of the Equality Act 2010. The provisions of the 1998 Act distinguish between voluntary aided and voluntary controlled schools, community schools, foundation schools and academies. This distinction is based on funding arrangements and responsibility for employing staff. In voluntary controlled or foundation schools with a religious character, religion can be taken into account in appointing the head teacher, and up to a fifth of the teaching staff can be "selected for their

---

[201] [2011] NIFET 00007 11FET (15 December 2011).   [202] ET 3300983/11.
[203] [2011] UKEAT 0379_10_2405 (24 May 2011).

fitness and competence" to give religious education in accordance with the tenets of the faith of the school. Voluntary aided schools can impose religious requirements on all teaching staff.

No church or religious organisation receives direct funding from the government. Faith schools, however, which now constitute a third of all schools, receive financial support of up to 90 per cent of capital costs and 100 per cent of running costs, including salaries. In addition, several hundred independent schools of a religious nature receive no State support but must meet government quality standards, which now include a focus on promoting the concept of fundamental British values within the framework of spiritual, moral, social and cultural development.

Faith Schools

Although two-thirds of schools in England remain secular, there has been a recent and rapid spread of faith schools. Nearly all the approximately 7000 faith schools are associated with Christian denominations – mainly Church of England – although there are Jewish, Islamic, Sikh and one Hindu school. Controversy arose in 2006 regarding more than 100 Islamic schools when an Office of Standards in Education (Ofsted) evaluation showed many were "little more than places where the Qur'an was recited". As of October 2009, reports from the Mosques and Imams National Advisory Board (MINAB) indicated there were approximately 2000 official madrassas.

As a general rule, voluntary aided and voluntary controlled schools are faith schools, foundation schools and academies may or may not be faith-based, and community schools are rarely faith-based. As regards academies, which are rapidly growing in number, government policy has been that academy faith schools should allow 50 per cent of school places to be reserved for children of the relevant faith and 50 per cent to be allocated without reference to faith. However, in 2016, the government declared a policy change that would remove the 50 per cent cap on the proportion of religion-specific pupils new faith schools may recruit, thereby, arguably, intensifying the ghettoisation of education.

As might be expected, the Equality Act permits exceptions to the prohibition on discrimination on grounds of religion or belief in faith schools.[204] Government-funded faith-based schools permit an extensive range of discriminatory practices: preferential treatment in terms of funding; permission to discriminate in pupil admissions and staffing; a

---

[204] Equality Act 2010, Sch. 11, pt 2.

teaching curriculum skewed in favour of religious belief; and a corresponding alignment of social values in regard to issues such as gay marriage, abortion, etc.; although they are not entitled to State-subsidised transport.[205]

The Commission on Religion and Belief in British Public Life, in its 2015 report, recommended that faith schools "should take measures to reduce selection of pupils and staff on grounds of religion".[206] It has warned:[207]

> In England successive governments have claimed in recent years that faith schools and free schools create and promote social inclusion which leads to cohesion and integration. However, in our view it is not clear that segregation of young people into faith schools has promoted greater cohesion or that it has not in fact been socially divisive and led rather to greater misunderstanding and tension. Selection by religion segregates children not only according to religious heritage but also, frequently and in effect, by ethnicity and socio-economic background. This undermines equality of opportunity and incentivises parents to be insincere about their religious affiliation and practice ... Bodies responsible for school admissions should take measures to reduce selection on grounds of religion in state-funded schools.

It would, indeed, seem anomalous that faith schools, initially established in a spirit of altruism to assist poor children overcome the effects of deprivation, should have become a State-subsidised religiously discriminating vehicle for filtering out such children and assisting instead those of middle-class parents with social aspirations.[208]

Religious Discrimination and Educational Content

The law requires that religious education is provided for all children between the ages of 3 and 19 in publicly maintained schools and that it should reflect the predominant place of Christianity, while taking into account the teachings and practices of other principal religious groups in the country. Syllabi must be non-denominational. All parents have the legal right to request that their children do not participate in religious education. Daily collective prayer or worship of "a wholly or

---

[205] *Diocese of Menevia & Others* v. *City & County of Swansea Council* [2015] EWHC 1436 (Admin).

[206] Commission on Religion and Belief in British Public Life, *Living with Difference*, at p. 8.

[207] Ibid., at p. 33.

[208] See further the Casey Review at www.gov.uk/government/uploads/system/uploads/attachment_data/file/574565/The_Casey_Review.pdf.

mainly... Christian character" is practised in schools in England and Wales. The Standing Advisory Councils for Religious Education (SACREs) are required to advise local authorities responsible for education on matters connected with religious education and religious worship. The Commission on Religion and Belief in British Public Life comments that:

> The arguments in favour of retaining compulsory Christian worship in UK schools are no longer convincing... religious practices should not be required in publicly funded schools, but also they should not be prohibited... If the curriculum is objective, fair and balanced, and does not contain elements of confessional instruction or indoctrination, then this teaching should be required in all schools and there is no reason for a legal right to withdraw from learning about religion and belief... governments across the UK should repeal requirements for schools to hold acts of collective worship or religious observance... recognise the negative practical consequences of selection by religion in schools, and that most religious schools can further their aims without selecting on grounds of religion in their admissions and employment practices; require bodies responsible for school admissions and the employment of staff to take measures to reduce such selection.[209]

Education Facilities and Religious Discrimination

A long-standing English case on such matters is *Mandla (Sewa Singh) and another* v. *Dowell Lee and others*,[210] which concerned a Sikh boy, Gurinder Singh, who was denied admittance to a private school because he refused to comply with the school uniform requirement to cut his hair and remove his turban: a turban being emblematic of communal identity, he could not remove it without sacrificing that identity. The House of Lords held that it was unlawful indirect discrimination for a headmaster of an independent school to insist on a uniform requirement of short hair and caps for boys, thereby excluding Sikhs who wear turbans with long hair; a ruling echoed in *R (Watkins-Singh)*.[211]

An important reminder that religious discrimination law is also available to protect atheists from discrimination by religious organisations was demonstrated in *Glasgow City Council* v. *McNab*.[212] The EAT then upheld a Tribunal's decision that an atheist teacher employed by a Catholic school maintained by the council had suffered direct discrimination under the

---

[209] Commission on Religion and Belief in British Public Life, *Living with Difference*, at pp. 34–37.
[210] Op. cit.   [211] *R (Watkins-Singh)* v. *Aberdale Girls' High School*, op. cit.
[212] UKEATS/0037/06/MT, [2007] IRLR 476.

Employment Equality (Religion or Belief) Regulations 2003 when he was refused an interview for the post of Principal Teacher of Pastoral Care. The Tribunal had been entitled to conclude that the post was not on the list of those for which the Roman Catholic Church required a teacher to be a Catholic.

The seminal case of *R (E) v. Governing Body of JFS*[213] is now the most important in this field. It concerned the rules of admission to a Jewish school that had, for fifty-two years, required a child – in accordance with Orthodox Jewish doctrine – to have a mother who was born Jewish. The issue for the court was whether the school could claim an exemption against a charge of racial discrimination on the grounds of its religious commitments. The High Court ruled that a school that accepts State funding must not discriminate in its admission policy on the basis of ethnicity. Subsequently, the UK Supreme Court, in a majority ruling, found that what in the High Court had been characterised as religious grounds were in fact racial grounds, notwithstanding their theological motivation, and no faith school could be excused from the prohibition on race discrimination. The observations of Mance LJ, on the underlying policy of the prohibition on racial discrimination in the Act, are interesting:[214]

> the policy is that individuals should be treated as individuals and not assumed to be like other members of a group.[215] To treat individual applicants to a school less favourably than others, because of the happenstance of their respective ancestries, is not to treat them as individuals, but as members in a group defined in a manner unrelated to their individual attributes ... To treat as determinative the view of others which an applicant may not share that a child is not Jewish by reason of his ancestry is to give effect not to the individuality of the interests of the applicant, but to the viewpoint religiously and deeply held though it be, of the school applying the less favourable treatment. That does not seem to me either consistent with the scheme or appropriate in the context of legislation designed to protect individuals from discrimination.

Arguably, this judgment at least strongly implies that, in addition to the confirmed racial discrimination, to deny access to a faith school on the basis of an applicant not being – or perhaps not being – an adherent of that faith amounts also to religious discrimination. Malik adds that the

---

ruling "demonstrates that current definitions of race and religion are insufficiently inclusive of non-Christian religious traditions".[216] Most recently, in (R) The British Humanist Association v. LB of Richmond upon Thames,[217] the court considered and dismissed a claim that the opening of new Catholic primary and secondary schools would mean operating admissions policies focused predominantly on children who are Catholic, rather than being more widely available to children resident in the area.

Medicine-Related Issues

As already noted, recent years have seen a range of improved medical interventions: from conception to assisted euthanasia (even if not yet lawful), medical breakthrough has greatly increased the probability, quality and length of life. Additionally, genetic modification and editing is constantly extending the boundaries of benign science to permit adjustments to matters previously left to nature, and is thereby stretching the received wisdom derived from orthodox religious beliefs.

Medical Intervention and Religious Beliefs

More than a century has passed since R v. Senior,[218] when a member of the Peculiar People sect was convicted of the manslaughter of his baby by neglect as he had refused to provide the child with medical aid or medicine, believing that to do so would show insufficient faith in God and the power of prayer. In the meantime, a considerable weight of caselaw has accumulated in this jurisdiction testifying to the principle that there can be no justification for the withholding of lifesaving treatment from someone without a legal capacity for decision-making. Most often, these cases concern Jehovah's Witnesses and blood products.[219]

Genetic Engineering and Patents, etc.

In this jurisdiction, the introduction of IVF treatment, as governed by the Human Fertilisation and Embryology Act 1990 (as amended in 2008), signaled that even wholly beneficial medical intervention in matters customarily left to nature would incite controversy:[220]

---

[216] Maleiha Malik (note to author, 14 March 2017).
[217] [2012] EWHC 3622 (Admin).   [218] [1899] 1 QB 283.
[219] See e.g. Birmingham Children's NHS Trust v. B & C [2014] EWHC 531 (Fam); Re S (A Minor) (Medical Treatment) [1993] 1 FLR 376; and Re R (A Minor) (Blood Transfusion) [1993] 2 FCR 544.
[220] Regina v. Secretary of State for Health (Respondent) ex parte Quintavalle (on behalf of Pro-Life Alliance) (Appellant) [2003] UKHL 13, per Bingham LJ at para. 12.

There were those who considered the creation of embryos, and thus of life, *in vitro* to be either sacrilegious or ethically repugnant and wished to ban such activities altogether. There were others who considered that these new techniques, by offering means of enabling the infertile to have children and increasing knowledge of congenital disease, had the potential to improve the human condition, and this view also did not lack religious and moral arguments to support it.

Since the 1990 legislation, science has made possible the creation of an embryo without the need for fertilisation by using cell nuclear replacement in unfertilised eggs, resulting in "cloned embryos" (Dolly the sheep being an early product of such cloning), and Parliament had introduced the Human Fertilisation and Embryology (Research Purposes) Regulations 2001 and, subsequently, the Human Tissue Act 2004. Since 2016, science has moved on to embryo augmentation (mixing genetic material to correct an embryo deficit), permitting "three-parent" babies. Licensed research can only take place on embryos created *in vitro* (developed from eggs fertilised outside the body). Most embryos used in UK stem cell research were initially created for use in fertility treatment, but never used. These "surplus" IVF embryos, if donated with the full consent of the parents, can be used for research.

Whether the law should permit the patenting of inventions which directly use human embryonic stem (hES) cells, or which have used them in their development, would therefore attract controversy anyway, but this is exacerbated by those who base their arguments on religious grounds. An important case in this jurisdiction was *Eli Lilly*,[221] which upheld the validity of a patent for an aspect of gene sequencing. This ruling is likely to open the door for more extensive research, and will therefore further alarm those who, for religious reasons, believe that human genes should not be patentable.

Service-Provision Issues

A Joseph Rowntree research report published at the beginning of this century declared that "religious and cultural identity was very important to many people from minority ethnic communities but it was rarely responded to by mainstream service providers".[222] Since then, the ECHR and the Equality Act 2010 have changed the legal landscape; the law in

[221] *Eli Lilly* v. *Human Genome Sciences* (HGS) [2011] UKSC 51, on appeal from [2010] EWCA Civ 33.

[222] The Joseph Rowntree Foundation, "Ethnic Diversity, Neighbourhoods and Housing", 2000.

this jurisdiction goes further than the Convention, as it protects against discrimination in the supply of goods and services, including accommodation, as well as in employment, occupation and vocational training. It is to be noted that under s.29(8) of that Act, harassment on grounds of religion or belief is only prohibited in relation to employment, not in relation to the provision of goods and services.

Service Provision by Religious Organisations

While religious organisations may avail themselves of their statutory exemption to the general prohibition on inequality and religious discrimination, the law is clear that when engaged in public service provision, they will be considered to be acting in a discriminatory and unlawful fashion should they refuse to provide services to a potential service user, alter the terms on which a service is provided, terminate the provision of the service or subject the service user to any other detriment, on the grounds of religion.[223]

Allegations of religious discrimination, restricting access to services, formed the basis for rulings by judicial and regulatory authorities in relation to the policy of the Catholic Care adoption agency. The agency's argument that it was outside the tenets of the Roman Catholic Church to provide adoption services to same-sex cohabiting couples or civil partners and, in fact, that it provided adoption services only to married couples, was rejected by the regulatory authority. On appeal to the High Court, Briggs J remitted the case back to the regulatory authority and directed that the issues be reconsidered in the light of certain principles he set out in his judgment,[224] which essentially stressed that the services could be restricted on the basis of sexual orientation only if the restriction amounted to a proportionate means of achieving a legitimate aim. Noting that the intended beneficiaries of Catholic Care's adoption service were children in need of adoption, rather than prospective adoptive parents, the authority concluded that this test was not satisfied, reasoning that religious conviction was insufficient to justify the discrimination by the charity because of the public nature of its activities. This decision was then appealed to the First-tier Tribunal (Charity),[225] where it was dismissed following the Tribunal's finding that the charity had failed to meet the statutory test imposed by s.193 of the Equality Act 2010, requiring it to

---

[223] Equality Act 2010, s.29.
[224] *Catholic Care (Diocese of Leeds)* v. *The Charity Commission for England and Wales*, op. cit.
[225] Ibid.

demonstrate that the less favourable treatment it proposed to offer same-sex couples would constitute a proportionate means of achieving its legitimate aim of providing suitable adoptive parents for a significant number of "hard to place" children.[226]

Provision of Public Services

Some of the difficulties inherent in mixing religious beliefs with public service provision were illustrated in *R (on the application of Johns) v. Derby City Council*.[227] The case concerned members of the Pentecostal Church, which has strong religious views against homosexuality, who had been rejected as foster carers by Derbyshire County Council. Their claims that their beliefs were not a legitimate fostering concern, that these beliefs would not impede them from offering a foster care service and that their rejection constituted religious discrimination by the council were dismissed by the court. Munby LJ, following the decisions in *Ladele* and *McFarlane*, reasoned that the rejection was due to their stance on sexual orientation, not because of their religious belief, and that the Council was entitled – indeed, required – to ensure that its public service provision was compliant with equality and non-discrimination legislation. There was no indirect discrimination, because the Christian couple was being treated the same as would anyone without religious beliefs but with the same objections to homosexuality. As the court explained: "if the defendant's treatment is the result of the claimants' expressed antipathy, objection to, or disapproval of homosexuality and same-sex relationships, it is clear... that it would not be because of their religious belief".[228]

An anti-discrimination initiative by the All Party Parliamentary Group on Faith and Society should be noted. This has seen the launch of a Faith Covenant, which includes a pledge by local authorities "to welcome the involvement of faith groups in the delivery of services and social action on an equal basis with other groups" and one by faith-based organisations to serve equally all local residents seeking to access the public services they offer, "without proselytising, irrespective of their religion, gender, marital status, race, ethnic origin, age, sexual orientation, mental capability, long term condition or disability". As of October 2015, five local authorities – all in England – had adopted the Covenant.

---

[226] See also *St Margaret's Children and Family Care Society* v. OSCR [2014] SCAP App 02/13, which found in favour of the Society on very similar facts (as noted by Frank Cranmer by email on 27 January 2017).
[227] Op. cit.   [228] Ibid., at para. 99.

Private Goods and Service Provision

The Supreme Court in *Bull v. Hall and Preddy*[229] confirmed that it was unlawful discrimination for Christian hotel owners to refuse a double-bedded room to a same-sex couple and dismissed their argument that they should not be compelled to run their business in a way which conflicts with their deeply held religious beliefs. Lady Hale emphasised that the decision did not amount to replacing legal oppression of one community (homosexual couples) with legal oppression of another (Christians and others who share the appellants' beliefs about marriage), as the law equally prohibits a hotel keeper from refusing a particular room to a couple because they are heterosexual or because they have certain religious beliefs.[230] It was considered that very weighty reasons would be required to justify discrimination on grounds of sexual orientation.[231] Among a number of similar cases, the judgment in *Black and Morgan v. Wilkinson*[232] held that a same-sex couple requesting a double bedroom, who were neither married nor in a civil partnership, had been unlawfully discriminated against on the grounds of their sexual orientation in breach of regulation 4 of the Equality Act (Sexual Orientation) Regulations 2007. As the court noted: "the application of the regulations to the defendant's bed and breakfast establishment does not prevent her from holding her religious beliefs".

Where the service provider is expected not only to provide a service but, in doing so, to express support for a position with which they disagree, it might be argued that the right to freedom of expression should be weighed alongside the other interests to mean that some form of exception becomes warranted. A case in which such issues arose was *Gareth Lee v. Ashers Baking Company Ltd, McArthur and McArthur*,[233] when the court ruled that it was unlawful direct discrimination on grounds of sexual orientation for a bakery owned by two Christians to refuse to bake a cake which had printed on it a picture of Bert and Ernie from Sesame Street and the caption "Support Gay Marriage". Morgan LCJ for the Court of Appeal, in upholding the earlier ruling, explained why making such an exception was not an option:[234]

> To prohibit the provision of a message on a cake supportive of gay marriage on the basis of religious belief is to permit direct discrimination. If

---

[229] [2013] UKSC 73. See also the similar case *Black and Morgan v. Wilkinson* [2013] EWCA Civ 820, [2013] 1 WLR 2490.

[230] Ibid., at para. 34.　　[231] Ibid., at para. 53.　　[232] Op. cit.

[233] Neutral Citation No. [2015] NICty 2. See also a US decision to the same effect (Chapter 7).

[234] *Gareth Lee v. Colin McArthur, Karen McArthur and Ashers Baking Co Ltd*, Neutral Citation No. [2016] NICA 39, per Morgan LCJ at para. 64.

businesses were free to choose what services to provide to the gay community on the basis of religious belief the potential for arbitrary abuse would
be substantial.

Further:[235]

> Anyone who applies a religious aspect or a political aspect to the provision
> of services may be caught by equality legislation, not because the legislation
> treats their religious belief or political opinion less favourably but because
> that person seeks to distinguish, on a basis that is prohibited, between those
> who will receive their service and those who will not. The answer is not to
> have the legislation changed and thereby remove the equality protection
> concerned. The answer is for the supplier of services to cease distinguish-
> ing, on prohibited grounds, between those who may or may not receive the
> service.

Broadcasting Services

The transmission of religious beliefs – reaching out to "the faithful" or
preaching "the word of God" – through radio or TV broadcasts can be a
potent form of manifesting religion and a powerful proselytising tool.
If, in that process, a work is published that offends the sensitivities of
an individual or group, this will not impose a positive obligation on the
State to introduce legislation criminalising blasphemy, nor, where blasphemy laws are exist, will there be any duty on public authorities to bring
proceedings.[236] In *Sunday Times* v. *the United Kingdom (no. 1)*[237] and
Handyside v. *the United Kingdom*,[238] the ECtHR considered that the protection of Article 10 extended to the broadcasting of religious advertisements that "offend, shock or disturb". Most recently, a 60-second advertisement based on the Lord's Prayer, due to be shown immediately before
Star Wars: The Force Awakens, was banned by the cinemas in which it was
to play on the grounds that it was likely to cause offence. This elicited the
following admonition from the EHRC:[239]

> Freedom to hold a religion and freedom to express ideas are essential
> British values … There is no right not to be offended in the UK; what is
> offensive is very subjective and lies in the eye of the beholder.

---

[235] Ibid., at para. 100.
[236] *Choudhury* v. *United Kingdom*, Application No. 00017439/90 (1991).
[237] Series A no. 30 (judgment of 26 April 1979).
[238] Series A no. 24 (judgment of 7 December 1976).
[239] See further Pocklington, D., *"That* Cinema Advert", *Law & Religion UK*, 24 November
2015, at www.lawandreligionuk.com/2015/11/24/that-cinema-advert/.

Conclusion

For many centuries, it had been axiomatic that to be British was to be Christian. However, as year after year the evidence mounts that British society is becoming more secular and multi-cultural, it is clear that this assumption is no longer tenable. Moreover, and despite the fading shadow of the "established" Church, the levelling effect of equality and anti-discrimination legislation is pushing all religions and beliefs, all pagans and atheists, to share the same platform, on which they can be assured of equal treatment from government and of being equally unable to influence it. The growing body of human rights jurisprudence is also exerting its own pressure upon those with and those without belief: rights such as those of free speech and freedom of conscience, cultural and sexual identity are shrinking the public space traditionally influenced – if not governed – by religion; while developments in the world of science, particularly genetics, are constantly supplying new verities to displace the old.

Religious discrimination is becoming more elusive, as it hides behind political righteousness and social concern. In the UK, which confronted religious discrimination in its thirty-year sectarian manifestation in Northern Ireland and in its most undisguised and virulent form in the 2005 and 2017 atrocities in London and Manchester, the range and volume of caselaw presented in this chapter demonstrates the assiduousness with which such discrimination is now recognised and addressed by many different judicial and regulatory bodies, all applying Convention principles. The results reveal that religious discrimination is often fused with sexuality issues, but beyond that there is little firm ground. Some see a tendency for sexual orientation equality to be prioritised over religion or belief equality; others view human rights as losing out to the levelling effect of an equality ethos. Some are adamant that a secularist ideology is corroding and diminishing a proud Christian culture; others protest that opt-out clauses unfairly preference religion and religious organisations over their secular counterparts.

6

Ireland

Introduction

Ireland, still a staunchly Christian country, is becoming progressively less so. The 2011 Census revealed that 90.64 per cent of the population claimed to be Christian, of which 84.2 per cent self-identified as Roman Catholic and 2.8 per cent as Church of Ireland. It shows that while the number of Catholics has risen slightly, Protestant religions overall are in decline: Orthodox and Pentecostalism, Evangelical and Methodism all show a fall. Non-Christians, however, are firmly on the increase. The 50 000 Muslims (a rise of 51 per cent since 2006) now constitute the third largest religious group in Ireland, while those identifying as having no religion have grown from 83 500 in 2006 to 269 800 in 2011, an increase of 47 per cent. It is against this backdrop that this chapter examines the law as it relates to religious discrimination.

Beginning with a brief historical overview of religious discrimination and the crucial role of the Constitution, the chapter considers the extent to which this has shaped Ireland's main public policy themes. It then outlines the current legal framework governing religion and religious discrimination, before focusing on the key legal principle of freedom of religion and its related definitional concepts, and exploring how these are given effect in both the Irish Constitution and the ECHR. There then follows a section which assesses the Church/State relationship as a prelude to a detailed examination of contemporary Irish caselaw relating to religious discrimination in the areas of: symbols, icons, apparel, etc.; the family and associated matters; employment; education; medicine; and service provision.

Public Policy: An Overview

In the formative years after Ireland achieved independence, it could be argued that government policy demonstrated such a strong preference for supporting Catholicism that this was the "established" religion in all but name: the State/Church relationship verged on the theocratic, such was the degree of mutual support embodied in the Constitution and reflected in the thrust of the nation's public policy; abortion, contraception and divorce were among the no-go policy areas cordoned off by Church veto.

Religion and the Constitution

For many generations, the national experience of religion in Ireland revolved around the dominance of the Roman Catholic Church.[1] The affirmation given to Roman Catholicism as a hallmark of the nation's cultural identity was embedded in constitutional and legislative provisions. While Article 44 prohibited any State establishment or endowment of religion,[2] or any State discrimination on the basis of religious belief, it nonetheless gave clear precedence to theism, to Christianity and to Catholicism, in that order.

The Constitution

In 1937, Bunreacht na hÉireann, the Irish Constitution, was enacted by plebiscite following a vote by Parliament – the Oireachtas. Article 44.1.2, reflecting Irish social mores until the 1960s, gave a degree of primacy to Catholicism, as was broadly acknowledged by O'Higgins CJ in *Norris v. Attorney General*;[3] although there was some judicial opinion to the effect that this provision did not confer any special privileges on the Roman Catholic religion or on Roman Catholics.[4] Article 44.1.3 also extended State recognition to:

> the Church of Ireland, the Presbyterian Church in Ireland, the Methodist Church in Ireland, the religious Society of Friends in Ireland, as well as the Jewish Congregations and the other religious denominations existing in Ireland at the date of the coming into operation of this Constitution.

Essentially, however, as Senator Bacik commented in 2009, "the Constitution still embodies what has been called 'a pro-religion ethos' apparent in Article 44.1 and the Preamble, committing the courts to a set of

---

[1] Bunreacht na hÉireann, Article 44.1. 2: "The State recognises the special position of the Holy Catholic Apostolic and Roman Church as the guardian of the Faith professed by the great majority of the citizens". Deleted by the Fifth Amendment of the Constitution Act 1972.

[2] The Irish Church Act 1869 dis-established the Church of Ireland.

[3] [1984] IR 36.

[4] See *In re Tilson, Infants* [1951] IR 1, per Black J at p. 36 and *Campaign to Separate Church and State Ltd v. Minister for Education* [1998] 2 ILRM 81, per Barrington J.

constitutional propositions that no liberal democracy should countenance. The theocratic ideology underlying the text is no longer appropriate or sustainable in modern Ireland".[5]

Religious Discrimination and the Constitution

There can be little doubt that the Constitution, by specifying certain religions and not others, intended and achieved a conferring of preferential status on those mentioned. While the Fifth Amendment of the Constitution Act 1972 deleted both provisions, as they had come to be viewed as dated and discriminatory, the Preamble still begins with "in the name of the Most Holy Trinity", while Article 6 provides that "All powers of government, legislative, executive and judicial, derive, under God, from the people". Article 44 continues to make special reference to the Christian nature of the State. It pledges the State to uphold its duty to pay "the homage... due to Almighty God", and religious values are commended as being of central importance to Irish society. This is balanced to some degree by the assurance given in Article 44.2.1 that freedom of conscience and the free profession and practice of religion are guaranteed to every citizen, subject to public order and morality, and by the directive in Article 44.3 that the State must not impose any disabilities or make any discrimination on the ground of religious profession, belief or status. Nevertheless, it remains the case that there is no express reference to faiths that do not profess belief in a god, nor to polytheistic religions, nor to beliefs of a wider philosophical nature, such as humanism. The continued leaning towards a theistic rather than a secular State can also be seen in the enduring constitutional and statutory ban on blasphemy.[6] By implicitly favouring Christianity, with an overlay of Roman Catholicism, the Constitution is open to the challenge that it indirectly adversely discriminates against all other religions, beliefs and non-beliefs. It has to be acknowledged that an alternative view can be found in the judgment given by Barrington J in the Supreme Court case of *Corway* v. *Independent Newspapers (Ireland) Ltd.*[7] When considering the standing of the Muslim, Hindu and Jewish religions under Article 44 of the Constitution, he commented that it:

> is an express recognition of the separate co-existence of the religious denominations, named and unnamed. It does not prefer one to the other

---

[5] Bacik, I., "Is Ireland Really a Republic?", *Irish Journal of Public Policy*, 2009, vol. 1:1, at http:// publish.ucc.ie/ijpp/2009/01/bacik/08/en.

[6] See Article 40.6.1 of Bunreacht na hÉireann and the Defamation Act.

[7] [1999] 4 IR 484, at p. 502. See also *Quinn's Supermarket Ltd* v. *Attorney General* [1972] IR 1 per Walsh J, at p. 24

and it does not confer any privilege or impose any disability or diminution of status upon any religious denomination, and it does not permit the State to do so.

The courts in Ireland, following the precedents established by their English counterparts, similarly endorsed the religious discriminatory preferences of testators. For example, in *Duggan* v. *Kelly*,[8] a condition against marrying a Papist was upheld, and so, in *Re McKenna*,[9] was a condition against marrying a Roman Catholic, while, in *Re Knox*,[10] the court upheld a condition restricting marriage to a Protestant wife with Protestant parents. Only when the right to make such a conditional testamentary disposition was trumped by what was considered to be a greater duty, such as the educational obligation of parents under Article 42 of the Constitution, did the courts rule religiously discriminatory dispositions invalid.[11]

Public Policy

Successive Irish governments traditionally demonstrated a strong preference for supporting Catholicism and its associated values, organisations and varied emanations. One measure of this policy can be seen in the nature and scale of legislative omission. The continued shelf-life of much of the Offences Against the Persons Act 1861, for example, speaks volumes in terms of those areas of family law and sexuality-related matters where legislators have feared to tread.[12]

Background

By the end of the twentieth century, Ireland was slowly transforming from a mono-cultural white Catholic society, coalesced around the Church and with the highest level of regular church attendance in Europe, to a much more multi-cultural and multi-faith society. In the early years of the twenty-first century, this process accelerated with the publication of two crucial reports – the Ryan Report[13] of the Commission to Inquire into Child Abuse in orphanages and schools and the Murphy Report[14] regarding sexual abuse in the archdiocese of Dublin – both detailing

---

[8] (1847) 10 Ir. Eq. R. 295.   [9] [1947] IR 277.   [10] (1889) 23 L.R. Ir. 542 (Ch.).
[11] See *Burke* v. *Burke* [1951] IR 216 and *Re Blake, deceased* [1955] IR 89.
[12] Although, as Gerard Whyte points out, some fifty-six sections have now been repealed (note to author, 16 February 2017).
[13] See further www.dcya.gov.ie/viewdoc.asp?fn=/documents/Child_Welfare_Protection/RyanImplementation.htm.
[14] See further www.justice.ie/en/JELR/Pages/PB09000504.

many decades of child abuse perpetrated by Catholic clergy. The powerful impact of these disclosures led to a fall in popular support for the Catholic Church and permitted a more distinctive shaping of public policy as government began to feel itself less constrained by its customary deference to Church influence.

Religious Discrimination and Contemporary Public Policy

The conservative pull of established religious institutions and their all-pervading ethos may be a factor contributing to the lack of any government drive to formulate a policy to address the needs of contemporary Irish multi-culturalism. For example, despite the fact that Islam is the fastest growing religion in Ireland, there has yet to be a national study on the implications arising, and there has been no analysis as to whether the phenomenon of Islamophobia, experienced in countries with a similar pattern of immigration, is becoming an issue for this society.

State Agencies for Religious Matters

There is no government agency with specific responsibility for religious matters. However, several State agencies, including the Irish Human Rights and Equality Commission (IHREC) and the Garda's Racial and Intercultural Office, enforce equality legislation and work on behalf of minority religious groups.

Domestic Policy

The long absence of government initiatives in respect of matters that would challenge the authority of the Catholic Church is particularly evident in the continued lack of a modern legal framework for contraception and abortion services. Throughout the second half of the twentieth century and into the second decade of the twenty-first – notwithstanding the deaths of pregnant women and teenage girls, reports of boards of inquiry, referendums and legislative tweaks –sad journeys to the UK have persisted, as there is still no straightforward legal procedure facilitating access to domestic abortion services. This is due in part to the fact that the major hospitals and clinics are controlled by religious bodies – mainly Catholic, although some are Protestant.

Education is the other public service largely subject to the control of religious bodies. In particular, the national primary school system has remained almost exclusively governed by the Catholic Church since the founding of the State.[15] This necessarily results in the education of most Irish children being delivered through a particular religious ethos, whether or not this is compatible with that practised in their family home. As Irish society becomes steadily more multi-cultural, so does the religiously discriminating basis of its education system become correspondingly less appropriate. Government initiatives to moderate this state of affairs have repeatedly failed. Most recently, in 2011, the government established the Forum of Patronage and Pluralism in the Primary Sector, conducted by an independent advisory group, but this has yet to produce a plan for acceptable change.[16]

Foreign Policy

Ireland has a long and well-established reputation for providing overseas aid. Traditionally, this has been linked with missionary work, with establishing hospitals and general health care and with building and staffing schools. As this was very largely undertaken as outreach work on behalf of the Catholic Church, the "missions" were accompanied by a strong proselytism component. To the extent that Irish missionaries were emissaries of the Catholic Church and supported by government, they may perhaps be fairly viewed as the product of a Church/State public policy to export aid and assistance on a religiously discriminating basis to underdeveloped countries.

Unlike many other Western developed nations, Ireland's policy of neutrality has kept it out of active participation with "the allies" in their wars in Islamic countries: it not only declined to send troops to the Iraq wars, but there was strong resistance to the use of its airport at Shannon for the purpose of US-led "extraordinary rendition". Ireland is currently a non-combatant nation for the purposes of the ongoing war against a militant Islam.

Contemporary Law Governing Religious Discrimination

The legal framework governing religious discrimination in Ireland is provided by: the European Convention, Article 10 of the EU Charter of Fundamental Rights, provisions in other Conventions and EU Directives;

[15] Although, as Eoin Daly points out, primary school education is "*controlled* by Protestant as well as Catholic churches depending on demographics, and the State is constitutionally obliged to give equal funding to various faiths based on demand . . . the State set the curriculum" (note to author, 26 March 2017).

[16] See: Government of Ireland, "Government for National Recovery 2011–2016", 6 March 2011, as cited in Vasquez del Aguila, E. and Cantillon, S., "Discrimination on the Ground of Religion or Belief in Ireland", *Social Justice Series*, 2012, vol. 12:4, pp. 65–87, at p. 71.

decisions of the ECtHR and of the ECJ as it interprets the Directives and rights under the EU Treaty; the Constitution, particularly Article 44.2.3, which prohibits the State from imposing any disabilities or making any discrimination on the ground of religious profession, belief or status; the Irish human rights and equality legislation; and certain domestic regulatory and judicial bodies.

The International Framework

The main constituent parts of this framework are as in England and Wales (see further Chapter 5). Essentially, they comprise: Articles 9 and 14 of the ECHR, as applied in conjunction with International conventions;[17] certain EU Directives;[18] and decisions of the ECtHR and of the ECJ as they interpret Directives and rights under the EU Treaty.

The Convention guarantees religious freedom and prohibits discrimination on religious grounds. It requires that any interpretation of "religion" be applied objectively, have reasonable justification[19] and be non-discriminatory; any differential treatment must comply with strict standards. Article 14 of the Convention, as supported by Article 9 (the right to freedom of thought, conscience and religion) and by Article 1 of the First Protocol (the right to peaceful enjoyment of property), now has a direct bearing upon Irish domestic law. Moreover, express provision is made by Article 29.4.6 of the Constitution for EU law to prevail over Irish domestic law where the two are in conflict, but only to the extent that such EU law is "necessitated" by Ireland's membership. In making its determinations, the ECtHR allows States a wide margin of appreciation when it comes to placing limitations on the manifestation of one's religion and belief. In deciding whether there has there been a limitation or interference on the exercise of an applicant's religion, the infringement must be (a) prescribed by law and (b) necessary in a democratic society for a permissible purpose, i.e. directed to a legitimate purpose and proportionate in scope and effect.

---

[17] In particular: the International Covenant on Civil and Political Rights (ICCPR); the UN Convention on the Elimination of all forms of Discrimination Against Women (CEDAW), with its Optional Protocol; and the International Convention on the Elimination of Race Discrimination (ICERD).

[18] See, in particular, the Equal Pay Directive (75/117/EEC), the Equal Treatment Directive (76/207/EEC) and the General Framework Directive (2000/78/EC).

[19] See e.g. *Tsirlis and Kouloumpas v. Greece*, op. cit. See also the *Belgian Linguistic Case*, op. cit., where the ECtHR held that there must be an objective and reasonable justification for differential treatment and that this will only exist where there is a "legitimate aim" for the action and where the action taken is "proportionate" to that aim.

International Reports

The UN has repeatedly criticised Ireland's record on human rights and government inaction on several fronts, many of which are linked to religious values – specifically Catholicism – and to that extent can be fairly seen as an oblique form of religious discrimination: the treatment of survivors of the Magdalene laundries; the absence of safe and lawful abortion; gender parity; and the rights of transgender people. It has also called upon Ireland to give formal recognition to Travellers as an ethnic group.

In July 2014, following its fourth "universal periodic review" of Ireland's compliance with the ICCPR, the report of the UN's Human Rights Committee called for two referendums to be held: on abortion and on the place of women in society. It reported that both the new abortion legislation and the Constitution must be revised to ensure women who are pregnant as a result of rape or incest, or who have a diagnosis of fatal foetal anomaly, have access to abortion if they so choose, and it called for access to abortion where a woman's health is at risk. It reiterated its "previous concern regarding the highly restrictive circumstances under which women can lawfully have an abortion owing to article 40.3.3 of the Constitution and its strict interpretation by the State party".

The Committee also considered Article 41.2, which declares that "by her life within the home a woman gives to the State a support without which the common good cannot be achieved" and guarantees to protect mothers from having to work outside the home "to the neglect of [their] duties within the home". It recommended that "the State party should take concrete steps ... to facilitate the amendment of Article 41.2 of the Constitution to render it gender neutral and further encourage greater participation of women in both public and private sectors".

The Committee raised concerns about domestic and sexual violence against women and the institutional abuse of women and children, and called for corporal punishment to be banned "in all settings". It referred to "the lack of prompt, independent, thorough and effective investigations into all allegations of abuse, mistreatment or neglect of women and children in the Magdalene Laundries, children's institutions, and mother-and-baby homes".

The Domestic Framework

The Constitution sets the overarching parameters for the law relating to discrimination in general, while the provisions of the Equality Acts and other employment and gender-parity legislation have a more direct bearing upon specific aspects of discrimination.

The Constitution

Articles 40–44 of the Constitution specifically provide protection for fundamental rights, including freedom of religion and belief. Article 40.1 states:

> All citizens shall, as human persons, be held equal before the law. This shall not be held to mean that the State shall not in its enactments have due regard to differences of capacity, physical and moral, and of social function.

The limitations of this constitutional equality assurance were recognised in the comment offered by Henchy J in *Dillane v. Ireland*:[20]

> When the State . . . makes a discrimination in favour of, or against, a person or category of persons, on the express or implied grounds of a difference of social function the courts will not condemn such discrimination as being in breach of Article 40.1 if it is not arbitrary, capricious, or otherwise not reasonably capable, when objectively viewed in the light of the social function involved, of supporting the selection or classification complained of.

Shortly afterwards, O'Higgins CJ acknowledged that the preferential State treatment of religion could be seen as being among such limitations. In *Norris v. Attorney General*,[21] he declared that, as he understood it, the Irish people had proclaimed in the Preamble to the Constitution a "deeply religious conviction and faith and an intention to adopt a Constitution consistent with that conviction and faith and with Christian beliefs". Notwithstanding the declaration in Article 44.2.3 that the State shall not discriminate on religious grounds, a considerable body of caselaw accruing before and after the O'Higgins pronouncement testifies to such preferential treatment.

The European Convention on Human Rights Act 2003[22]

This legislation partially incorporates the European Convention, together with several of its Protocols, into domestic law. Irish courts are consequently instructed: in s.2, that "in interpreting and applying any statutory provision or rule of law, a court shall, in so far as is possible, subject to the rules of law relating to such interpretation and application, do so in a manner compatible with the State's obligations under the Convention provisions";[23] and in s.4, that "judicial notice" be taken of the Convention

---

[20] [1980] ILRM 167.   [21] Op. cit., at p. 64.
[22] (Commencement) Order 2003 (SI No. 483 of 2003).
[23] See *Foy v. An t-Ard Chlaraitheoir & Others* [2007] IEHC 470, where a declaration of incompatibility was made concerning the lack of legal recognition for transgender people under Irish law.

provisions and of judgments of the ECtHR or any decision of the Committee of Ministers established under the Statute of the Council of Europe on any question in respect of which it has jurisdiction; they must also, when interpreting and applying the Convention provisions, take due account of the principles laid down in such judgments or decisions. Under s.5, a court may make a "declaration of incompatibility" where it finds that legislation or a rule of law is incompatible with the State's obligations under the ECHR, in which case the matter must be referred to Parliament.

The Workplace Relations Act 2015

This legislation governs the rights and responsibilities of employers and employees. It provided a new adjudication process to settle disputes in the workplace by consolidating the various functions of the Labour Relations Commission, the Employment Appeals Tribunal (EAT), the National Employment Rights Authority and the Labour Court into a single body – the Workplace Relations Commission – which commenced in October 2015. There is a right of appeal to the Labour Court, with a further appeal, on a point of law only, to the High Court.

The Employment Equality Acts 1998–2015

This legislation came into effect in 1998 and has since been amended by the Equality Act 2004 (exemption for religious bodies is provided in both this and in the Equal Status Act, s.7), the Civil Partnership Act 2010 and other statutes. It provides protection for workers against discrimination, harassment and sexual harassment in the workplace. It promotes equality in the workplace and bans discrimination across nine different grounds: gender; civil status; family status; sexual orientation; religion; age; race; disability; and membership of the Traveller Community.

The Equal Status Acts 2000–2015

This legislation came into effect on 25 October 2000 and includes the Equal Status Act 2000, the Equality Act 2004, the Equal Status (Amendment) Act 2012 and the Equality (Miscellaneous Provisions) Act 2015. These statutory provisions prohibit discrimination in employment, housing assistance, vocational training, advertising, collective agreements, the provision of goods and services and other opportunities to which the public generally has access on any of the previous nine grounds.

The Equality Act 2004

This legislation abolished the age limits of 18 and 65 which were in the 1998 Act; now, there are no upper or lower age thresholds. Section 8 broadened the definition of "harassment" in the 1998 Act to include harassment more generally.

Other Legislation

Other relevant statutes include: the Pensions Act 1990–2008; the Unfair Dismissals Act 1977–2007; the Social Welfare (Miscellaneous Provisions) Act 2004, which prohibits discrimination in the provision of occupational pensions; and the Prohibition of Incitement to Hatred Act 1989, which outlaws hate speech, including incitement to hatred based on *inter alia* sexual orientation. Of considerable importance, too, is the currently pending Equal Status (Admission to School) Bill 2016 (see later).

Courts and Tribunals

The framework of judicial and regulatory bodies is much the same in this jurisdiction as in England and Wales (see further Chapter 5).

International

Ireland, unlike England and Wales, is to continue its EU membership for the foreseeable future, and will therefore continue to accept the superior appellate jurisdiction of the ECJ and the ECtHR and remain accountable to various international committees for progressing the implementation of convention provisions.

The European Court of Human Rights (ECtHR)   The ECtHR, which was established in 1959 and replaced the European Commission of Human Rights in 1998, hears complaints alleging that one of the forty-seven Member States has violated rights enshrined in the Convention and its protocols. Under s.4 of the European Convention on Human Rights Act 2003, "judicial notice" is required to be taken of ECtHR judgments. In making its determinations, the court is guided by principles such as "proportionality" and "compatibility with democracy".[24] Its decisions are reached in the light of "a margin of appreciation", which permits States a

---

[24] See *Refah Partisi* v. *Turkey*, op. cit., where the ECtHR ruled that Shar'ia law is not consistent with democracy and therefore that the Turkish government was justified in banning a political party seeking to introduce such law.

degree of latitude in their interpretation of human rights obligations[25] (see further Chapter 4).

Other Fora   The bearing of European and other international fora on Irish affairs is much the same as in England and Wales. For present purposes, the ECJ, the Human Rights Committee and various other committees established by their respective international conventions to monitor implementation, will have intermittent relevance (see further Chapter 4).

Domestic

As elsewhere, in practice most matters of alleged religious discrimination are addressed by the national regulator for human rights and equality, although the High court also plays a well-established role, as will the new Court of Appeal, and occasionally matters with a constitutional dimension will be determined by the Supreme Court.

The Irish Human Rights and Equality Commission (IHREC)   On 1 November 2014, the Equality Authority (established in 1999) and the Irish Human Rights and Commission (established in 2000) merged to become the IHREC, which assumed responsibility for regulating matters arising under the Employment Equality and Equal Status legislation and under the Human Rights Commission Act 2000.

The Workplace Relations Commission (WRC)   Established under the Workplace Relations Act 2015, the Commission replaces the EAT and consolidates the functions of many other bodies, including the Labour Relations Commission, Rights Commissioner Service, Equality Tribunal and the National Employment Rights Authority.

The Labour Court   Equality claims may be heard by the Labour Court on appeal from the WRC.

Other   As in England and Wales, religion-specific mediation forums play a role in seeking to resolve private personal and family issues.

---

[25] See e.g. *Lithgow* v. *United Kingdom*, op. cit.; *Fredin* v. *Sweden*, op. cit.; *Abdulaziz, Cabales and Balkandali* v. *United Kingdom*, op. cit.
    See further Legg, A., *The Margin of Appreciation in International Human Rights Law*, Oxford University Press, Oxford, 2012.

Freedom of Religion and Beliefs: The Principle and the Law

The right to freedom of thought, conscience and religion is guaranteed under international law by Article 18 of the UDHR (ECHR, Article 9) in conjunction with the EU Charter of Fundamental Rights and Article 18 of the ICCPR, and under domestic law primarily by the Constitution and the European Convention on Human Rights Act 2003.

The Constitution

Article 44.1 of the Constitution declares:

> the State acknowledges that the homage of public worship is due to Almighty God. It shall hold His Name in reverence, and shall respect and honour religion.

This provision is reinforced by: Article 44.2.1, which guarantees a citizen's freedom of religious conscience, practice and worship, "subject to public order and morality"; Article 44.2.2, which declares that the State may not "endow" any religion; and Article 44.2.3, which provides that "the State shall not ... make any discrimination on the ground of religious belief, profession or status". As Hogan J commented:[26]

> Article 44.2.1 protects not only the traditional and popular religions and religious denominations – such as, for example, Roman Catholicism, the Church of Ireland and the Presbyterian Church – but perhaps just as importantly, it provides a vital safeguard for minority religions and religious denominations whose tenets are regarded by many as unconventional.

Article 14 of the Convention, as supported by Article 9, by Article 1 of the First Protocol and by various Directives, together with various domestic statutory provisions, may also come into play. Consequently, it might be reasonable to assume, in the words of McKechnie J in *Foy* v. *An t-Ard Chlaraitheoir & Others*,[27] that:

> Everyone as a member of society has the right to human dignity, and with individual personalities, has the right to develop his being as he sees fit; subject only to the most minimal of State interference being essential for the convergence of the common good. Together with human freedom, a person, subject to the acquired rights of others, should be free to shape his personality in the way best suited to his person and to his life.

---

[26] See *Temple Street* v. *D. & Anor* [2011] IEHC 1, per Hogan J at para. 27. [27] Op. cit.

However, it is clear from the relatively limited jurisprudence on the constitutional guarantee of freedom of religion that, in practice, the rights of individuals and of organisations will often have to give way to the protection of religious interests: the exemption privileges available to those of religious belief will trump the constitutional guarantees of others – although, undoubtedly, the Oireachtas has a legislative capacity to balance the freedom of religion against other freedoms/rights (e.g. in relation to school admissions), and in light of the decision in *Tuohy* v. *Courtney*[28] the courts would probably take a very deferential attitude to any such legislation.[29]

Definitions

The traditional definition of "religion" has dominated relevant Irish caselaw. The continued leaning towards a theistic rather than a secular State can be seen in the enduring constitutional and statutory ban on blasphemy[30] – itself at variance with ECHR principles of equality.

"Religion"

The view that a legal definition of religion could be satisfied by a system of belief not involving faith in a god has never been unequivocally affirmed by the judiciary, and the legislators have clearly chosen not to avail themselves of the opportunity to break with tradition by extending recognition to either non-theistic faiths or philosophical beliefs. The effect of judicial consideration of constitutional guarantees has been to retain a traditional emphasis on theism, if balanced with respect for other beliefs. As Barrington J put it:[31]

> The effect of these various guarantees is that the State acknowledges that the homage of public worship is due to Almighty God. It promises to hold his name in reverence and to respect and honour religion. At the same time it guarantees freedom of conscience, the free profession and practice of religion and equality before the law to all citizens be they Roman Catholics, Protestants, Jews, Muslims, agnostics or atheists.

Worship must have at least some of the following characteristics: submission to the object worshipped, veneration of that object, praise,

---

[28] [1994] 3 IR 1.

[29] The author acknowledges advice from Gerard Whyte on this matter (note to author, 17 February 2017).

[30] See Article 40.6.1 of Bunreacht na hÉireann and the Defamation Act 2009.

[31] See *Corway* v. *Independent Newspapers (Ireland) Ltd*, op. cit.

thanksgiving, prayer or intercession. The necessity for doctrinal evidence to substantiate an ostensible religious practice was demonstrated recently in *McNally & Anor* v. *Ireland & Ors*,[32] which concerned the distribution and sale of mass cards contrary to s.99 of the Charities Act 2009.[33] As MacMenamin J noted, "the purchase of mass cards is a Roman Catholic practice, governed by canon law and the regulation of that faith".[34]

Article 14 of the Convention, as supported by Article 9 (the right to freedom of thought, conscience and religion) and by Article 1 of the First Protocol (the right to peaceful enjoyment of property), requires the government and other public bodies to give parity of recognition to Christian and non-Christian religions. This approach finds constitutional support, as Hogan J noted in *Temple Street*.[35] However, given the fact that the Constitution leans heavily towards Christianity – particularly Roman Catholicism – there remains some doubt as to the reality of that equality, and considerably more regarding parity between those of religious belief and those without.

A distinctive characteristic of religion in this jurisdiction has been and remains an emphasis on the importance of private piety. This has been evident in gifts to closed contemplative religious orders, as opposed to those actively engaged in good works in the community,[36] and stands in sharp contrast to comparable practice in England and Wales. In *Maguire* v. *Attorney General*,[37] Gavan Duffy J gave a reasoned rejection of the relevance of equivalent English caselaw:

> Perpetual adoration is an expression well known to members of the Catholic Church. It is a form of devotion to the Blessed Sacrament whereby in some suitable church or chapel arrangements are made, necessarily by a community for an unbroken succession of persons to be present in private prayer and in contemplation before the Blessed Sacrament exposed to the full view of the worshippers ... The adoration of the Blessed

---

[32] [2009] IEHC 573.

[33] Ibid. Judicial notice was taken of the scale of this business: the plaintiff's sales amounted to €250 000 for 2008, the Irish market being estimated at approximately €4 million. This is a practice traditionally known as "simony", defined in the Oxford English Dictionary (2nd edn) as the buying and selling of benefices, ecclesiastical preferments or other spiritual things.

[34] Ibid., at para. 8.   [35] *Temple Street* v. *D. & Anor*, op. cit.

[36] See e.g. *Cocks* v. *Manners* (1871) LR 12 Eq 574.

[37] [1943] IR 238. See also *re Howley* [1940] IR 109, where Gavan Duffy J stated:

> The assumption that the Irish public find no edification in cloistered lives, devoted purely to spiritual ends, postulates a close assimilation of the Irish outlook to the English, not obviously warranted by the traditions and mores of the Irish people.

> Sacrament might be considered an extension of the ceremony and sacrifice of the Mass ... The existence of a convent devoted to Perpetual Adoration was unquestionably a source of edification and of spiritual and moral benefit to all Catholics.

Referring to such a convent as a "spiritual powerhouse", he commented that:

> it is a shock to one's sense of propriety and a grave discredit to the law that there should, in this Catholic country, be any doubt about the validity of a trust to expend money in founding a convent for the perpetual adoration of the Blessed Sacrament.

He concluded that a purpose could satisfy the definition of "religious" in Irish law even if it was wholly secluded from the public and entirely devoted to private piety.

"Beliefs"

There is no specific provision in any Irish statute for recognition of "religion" as encompassing philosophical beliefs. Article 44.2.1 of the Constitution, however, under the heading "Religion", does provide that "freedom of conscience and the free profession and practice of religion are subject to public order and morality, guaranteed to every citizen". Attempts to broaden recognition to include recognition for humanism, for example, have failed. The interpretation of "religion" remains close to the definition in *Bowman v. Secular Society Ltd*,[38] where it was held to mean a faith in a higher power, to the exclusion of ethical principles or rationalism. However, while Irish statutory law retains the traditional requirement of a belief in god, the caselaw explicitly extends the constitutional guarantee of freedom of religion beyond monotheistic Christian religions.

"Race" and "Caste"

The 2012 report of the Equality Tribunal records that among all the referrals to it, "race continued to be the most frequently cited single ground".[39] It is to be noted that membership of the Traveller community is a prohibited ground of discrimination under the equality code, and the legislation provides a definition of "Traveller community". In July 2014, following its fourth "universal periodic review" of Ireland's compliance with the ICCPR, a report of the UN's Human Rights Committee called upon

---

[38] Op. cit.
[39] See further www.workplacerelations.ie/en/Publications_Forms/Archived_Publications/ Equality_Tribunal_Annual_Report_2012.pdf.

the State to "take concrete steps to recognise" the ethnicity of Travellers and to address their housing needs. Concerns were also raised about such other matters as accommodating asylum seekers, the lack of non-denominational schools, the lack of appropriate assistance given to victims of human trafficking and prison conditions.

Manifesting Religion or Belief and Free Speech

Article 44 of the Constitution declares "the free practice and profession of religion ... subject to public order and morality" is to be "guaranteed to every citizen". As in other jurisdictions, this "free practice" clause is conditional upon its exercise being compliant with other rights – particularly free speech and freedom of association – and has been scrutinised in the Irish courts.[40] In the long run, however, it may be that the issue of what constitutes "religion" and thereby entitles an adherent to the free practice of their beliefs – subject to the rights of others – will become particularly contentious in this jurisdiction.

Free Speech and Freedom of Association

The Constitution, Article 40.6.1, protects the right to free speech. However, it is qualified by the caveat that this may not be used to undermine "public order or morality or the authority of the State". The same provision also guarantees the right to form an association, but makes its exercise subject to legislative requirements protecting public order and morality.[41]

Blasphemy

Article 40.6.1 explicitly criminalises the publication of "blasphemous, seditious, or indecent matter". A year after the offence of blasphemy was removed from statute law in England and Wales, it was placed on the Irish statute books by provisions declaring that a person will be guilty of an offence if:

> he or she publishes or utters matter that is grossly abusive or insulting in relation to matters held sacred by any religion, thereby causing outrage among a substantial number of the adherents of that religion, and

> (b) he or she intends, by the publication or utterance of the matter concerned, to cause such outrage.

---

[40] See e.g. *Quinn's Supermarket* v. *Attorney General*, op. cit. and *Campaign to Separate Church and State Ltd* v. *Minister for Education* [1998] 3 IR 321.
[41] See e.g. *Equality Authority* v. *Portmarnock Golf Club* [2009] IESC 73.

Notably, however, the offence has been removed from its traditional Christian cultural context and extended to encompass any defamation of religion.

Conscientious Objection

Article 44.2.1 of the Constitution affords citizens the right to freely express their conscience, as well as the profession and practice of their religion, subject to public order and morality. Any restriction on this right would have to be proportionate under the Constitution, meaning that the restriction would have to be rational, intrude as little as possible and be proportionate to the aim it sought to achieve.[42] As noted in *AM* v. *Refugee Appeals Tribunal*,[43] the provision has for the most part dealt with freedom of conscience in the religious context.[44] In that case, the court held that s.2 of the Refugee Act 1996 was to be interpreted in accordance with the right to freedom of conscience under Article 40.3 of the Constitution, and required that international protection should be accorded to a full conscientious objector who has a well-founded fear of persecution.

Proselytism

The experience of proselytism in Ireland is largely a function of its colonial history, with England pursuing a forceful policy of inducing the conversion of its Catholic neighbours to Protestantism – a policy which, in Ireland, is irredeemably associated with the mid-nineteenth century famine. More recently, the Irish contribution to Catholic missionary work in Africa and elsewhere has been very considerable, and in that context, proselytism was undoubtedly vigorously pursued.

In *Murphy* v. *Ireland*,[45] the ECtHR upheld the State's restriction of a radio advertisement on a local independent commercial radio station that promoted the screening of a film in praise of the Christian faith. The prohibited religious advertisement in fact neither opposed nor denied the religious claims of other groups (see later).

---

[42] See *Heaney* v. *Ireland* [1994] 3 IR 531.

[43] [2014] IEHC 388. The author thanks Gerry Whyte for bringing this case to his attention (note to author, 17 February 2017).

[44] Citing *McGee* v. *Attorney General* [1974] IR 284 per Fitzgerald CJ, pp. 291–292 and Walsh J, p. 303, as well as Henchy J at p. 326. It is difficult to contemplate a "freedom of conscience" excluding conscientious objection, which is in itself an obvious exercise of conscience rooted in religious or other moral or philosophical convictions.

[45] Op. cit.

Discrimination

The constitutional fusion of State institutions, citizenship and Catholicism constituting the religious ethos in which the independent Republic of Ireland was launched to a considerable extent continues to provide the context for dealing with contemporary issues of religious discrimination. This legacy is largely responsible for the conflation of issues of sexuality and religion which now seems to characterise many of the cases that result in Ireland appearing before the ECtHR.

Religious Discrimination

The basic principles governing religious discrimination are laid down in the Constitution, particularly Article 44.2.3, which prohibits the State from imposing any disabilities or making any discrimination on the ground of religious profession, belief or status. A suggestion that the Constitution implied preferential treatment for Christian religions was refuted by Walsh J in *Quinn's Supermarket* v. *Attorney General*,[46] and subsequently by Barrington J in the Supreme Court case of *Corway* v. *Independent Newspapers (Ireland) Ltd.*[47] However, there can be little doubt that religious considerations have played a prominent part in the legislature's historical reluctance to address matters such as abortion, surrogacy, gay marriage and other LGBT issues – at least, until the 2015 referendum on same-sex marriage.

Currently, the Equal Status Act 2000 (2000–15) provides that "discrimination" can be taken to occur: when (a) a person is treated less favourably than another person is, has been or would be treated in a comparable situation on any of the nine specified grounds which (i) exists, (ii) existed but no longer exists, (iii) may exist in the future, or (iv) is imputed to the person concerned; (b) a person who is associated with another person (i) is treated, by virtue of that association, less favourably than a person who is not so associated is, has been or would be treated in a comparable situation, and (ii) similar treatment of that other person on any of the discriminatory grounds would constitute discrimination. As between any two persons, the discriminatory grounds under s.6(2)(e) include "that one has a different religious belief from the other, or that one has a religious belief and the other has not".

---

[46] Op. cit.   [47] Op. cit., at p. 502.

Type

The Equality Act 2004, s.85A, in keeping with the Employment Equality Directive 2000/78/EC, states that in addition to "direct" discrimination, there is also indirect victimisation and harassment or sexual harassment.

Exemptions and Exceptions

There is clearly a tension between the assurance of Article 40.1 that "all citizens shall, as human persons, be held equal before the law" and the exemption permitted by statutory and Convention provisions from the operation of that law available to those citizens of religious belief. In practice, the rights of individuals and of organisations will often have to give way to the protection of religious interests: the exemption privileges available to those of religious belief will trump the constitutionally guaranteed rights of others.

The "Religious" Exemption

Certain institutions are exempted from the requirements of the Employment Equality Acts 1998–2011. Under s.37(1), a religious, medical or educational institution established for a religious purpose may discriminate where it is reasonable to do so in order to maintain the "religious ethos" of the institution or it is reasonably necessary to avoid undermining that ethos.[48] The problem is, there is no definition of "ethos": while the legislative intent would seem to be to extend definitional parameters beyond "religion", it remains uncertain as to where they end and what can be safely excluded. It is reasonably certain that a religious preference may be legitimately exercised in respect of employees or job applicants, including reserving quotas of places available in certain teaching and nursing institutions, and will include disciplinary action against employees who breach the established standards and traditions of a religious institution.[49]

In *Quinn's Supermarket Ltd* v. *Attorney General*[50] and in *re Article 26 and the Employment Equality Bill 1996*,[51] the Supreme Court confirmed that a religious action may be exempt from general laws if a failure to provide an exemption would restrict or prevent the free profession and practice of religion. It is clear, however, that not every "distinction

---

[48] Note, s.37 was amended in 2015. The author acknowledges the advice of Eoin Daly on this matter (note to author, 26 March 2017).

[49] Note the Equality (Miscellaneous Provisions) Act 2015, s.11.

[50] Op. cit.   [51] [1997] 2 IR 321, at p. 358.

necessary to achieve this overriding objective will be valid".[52] In the latter case, the Supreme Court ruled that it is constitutionally permissible to discriminate on grounds of religious profession, belief or status if this is necessary to "give life and reality" to the constitutional guarantee of freedom of religion.[53]

The "Charity" Exemption

Religious organisations in Ireland, unlike in England and Wales, are legally presumed to satisfy the public-benefit test and therefore automatically qualify for charitable status. Under s.2 of the Charities Act 2009, the definition of "charitable organisation" extends to include religious organisations or communities, which are granted particular tax and other privileges on the basis of their religious status; the exemption from registration under s.48(6) applies to an "education body", which will mainly be religious. Exemption is also evident in the freedom that permits many religious bodies to establish member-only outreach charities: for example, Jah-Jireh homes are charitable facilities established and run wholly and solely to give accommodation and care to members of the community of Jehovah's Witnesses. As a very large proportion of all charitable entities in this jurisdiction – gifts, donations, bequests, educational and health service facilities, and many other organisations – have religious status, this could be construed as constituting a State policy of positive discrimination in favour of religion.

The "Positive Action" Exception

The Employment Equality Act 1998, ss.24(1) and 33, together with the Equality Act 2004, ss.15 and 22, provides for positive action.

The decision in *Quinn's Supermarket* was unequivocally based upon a perceived need to extend "positive discrimination" to the interests of a religious minority. The plaintiff's argument – that special exemption for Jewish kosher butchers from the Sunday trading laws was discriminatory against non-Jewish shop keepers – was rejected, although the exemption was struck down on the basis that it went further than was necessary to protect religious freedom. Again, in *re Article 26 and the*

---

[52] See Casey, J., *Constitutional Law in Ireland*, 3rd edn, London, Thomson & Maxwell, 2000, at p. 698.

[53] The 1996 Bill was declared unconstitutional on other grounds, but s.37(1) of the 1998 Act, its replacement, virtually replicates it. See also *Greally v. Minister for Education (No 2)* [1999] 1 IR 1, [1999] 2 ILRM 296.

Employment Equality Bill 1996,[54] s.12 of the Bill provided that the prohibition on religious discrimination would not apply to the selection of nurses or primary teachers for employment in any "religious, educational or medical institution which is under the direction or control of a body established for religious purposes". Such institutions were permitted to give "favourable treatment" on grounds of religion to employees, and to prospective employees in terms of recruitment, if it was necessary "to uphold the religious ethos of the institution".[55] This was termed "positive discrimination" by counsel for the Attorney General, but must now be read subject to s.11 of the 2015 Act.

Religious Discrimination: Church and State

Church and State in Ireland have had a long and close relationship. Religion, specifically Roman Catholicism, has provided a basis for social cohesion: before independence, it united by far the majority of the population, differentiating them from the ruling Protestant ascendancy, and offering a platform for stoical resistance to colonialism; afterwards, it imbued and united rulers and ruled in a common allegiance to build a national civic polity.[56]

The Church/State Boundary

While the Constitution declares that the State may not "endow" any religion (Article 44.2.2), nor discriminate on religious grounds (Article 44.2.3), it also asserts the Christian values of the State – derived specifically from Catholic teachings – in the Preamble and in various Articles.[57] This legacy of an earlier era, when Ireland had the highest rate of church attendance in Europe, continues to pervade much of the law and institutions of the State. Indeed, this is apparent from remarks made relatively recently by the then head of the Irish government:[58]

> There are those who would argue that religious belief should be confined to the private domain, as a matter of purely personal choice and practice... That is not my position, nor that of my Government. Neither is it

---

[54] Opt. cit.   [55] Ibid., at p. 351.

[56] Eoin Daly adds: "It is worth noting Catholic domination stems in large part from the partition of the country which was sectarian in intent and effect" (note to author, 26 March 2017).

[57] In *Norris* v. *Attorney General*, op. cit.

[58] See address by Taoiseach Berti Ahern (04 February 2008), at www.taoiseach.gov.ie/eng/index.asp?locID=582&docID=3747.

one of privileging religion and religious organisations . . . The State must acknowledge and recognise the spiritual dimension of its citizens. It must see as legitimate . . . the importance of their religious faith for so many of our citizens.

This candid acknowledgment that the symbiotic Church/State relationship in Ireland has not yet been wholly consigned to history has been reinforced by the reflections of a former President, who refers to "the dubious relationship between the State and the Catholic Church, the constitutional prohibition on divorce, the ban on the use of contraception, the criminalisation of homosexuality".[59] It is evident also in: the control of large parts of the public sector – primarily schools and hospitals – by the Catholic Church; the recent enactment of a provision declaring that "the publication or utterance of blasphemous, seditious, or indecent matter" is a criminal offence;[60] the lack of information and advice available to women concerning abortion; and an enduring culture that permits inequality of rights and status for women in the workplace and in the family.[61]

Protecting Religion from the State

As Whyte has pointed out,[62] the constitutional constraints in Article 44 – prohibiting State endowment of religion and State discrimination on grounds of religious profession, belief or status – have been considered in a series of cases. The earlier cases were concerned with religious practices[63] and the decisions of ecclesiastical authorities,[64] but, more recently, they have embraced the promotion of social conditions which are conducive to – although not strictly necessary for – the fostering of religious beliefs.[65] The record also provides evidence of judicial diligence in policing the Church/State interface in order to restrain cross-contamination.

---

[59] See Robinson, M., *Everybody Matters: A Memoir*, London, Hodder and Stoughton, 2012.
[60] See the Defamation Act 2009, introduced in response to the finding in *Corway v. Independent Newspapers (Ireland) Ltd*, op. cit., that there was no coherent definition of this offence.
[61] Daly, E., *Religion, Law and the Irish State*, Dublin, Clarus Press, 2012.
[62] See Whyte, G., "Religion and Education – the Irish Constitution", paper presented at the TCD/IHRC conference on Religion and Education: A Human Rights Perspective, Dublin, 27 November 2010.
[63] *Quinn's Supermarket Ltd v. Attorney General*, op. cit.
[64] *McGrath and Ó Ruairc v. Trustees of Maynooth College* [1979] ILRM 166.
[65] See: *re Article 26 and the Employment Equality Bill 1996*, op. cit.; *Greally v. Minister for Education (No 2)*, op. cit.; and *Campaign to Separate Church and State Ltd v. Minister for Education* [1998] 2 ILRM 81.

Intervention in Church Disputes

The courts follow case precedents by not inquiring into the inherent validity of a particular religion or examining the relative merits of different
religions. The broad governing principle remains as initially expressed by
Walker LC in the Irish case of *O'Hanlon* v. *Logue*:[66]

> the Court does not enter into an inquiry as to the truth or soundness of any
> religious doctrine, provided it be not contrary to morals or contain nothing
> contrary to law.

Again, in *McGrath and Ó Ruairc* v. *Trustees of Maynooth College*,[67] which
concerned two former priests who had been dismissed from their teaching posts for breaching the Catholic standards of the seminary, who
claimed they had been wrongfully dismissed and had suffered religious
discrimination. Ruling in favour of the respondent, Henchy J explained
that the court had no power to intervene in the appointment procedures
of religious dominations, which were protected by Article 44.2.3 of the
Constitution:[68]

> far from eschewing the internal disabilities and discriminations which flow
> from the tenets of a particular religion, the State must on occasion recog-
> nise and buttress them. For such disabilities and discrimination . . . are part
> of the texture and essence of the particular religion

This approach was later confirmed by Barrington J, who commented,
when considering the standing of the Muslim, Hindu and Jewish religions
under Article 44 of the Constitution, that it:[69]

> is an express recognition of the separate co-existence of the religious
> denominations, named and unnamed. It does not prefer one to the other
> and it does not confer any privilege or impose any disability or diminution
> of status upon any religious denomination, and it does not permit the State
> to do so.

Given the scale of social infrastructure governed by the Catholic Church,
the corresponding extent of constitutional protection afforded it might be
viewed as considerably disadvantageous to its secular counterparts.

---

[66] [1906] IR 247.   [67] Op. cit., per Henchy J at p. 187.

[68] As Gerard Whyte points out: "this reasoning was subsequently relied on by MacMenamin
J in the High Court in *McNally* v. *Ireland* [2009] IEHC 573". (Note to author, 17.02.17).

[69] See e.g. *re Article 26 and the Employment Equality Bill 1996*, op. cit., at p. 359. See also
Corway v. *Independent Newspapers (Ireland) Ltd*, op. cit.

The State, Religion and Religious Discrimination

It would be difficult to overestimate the damage inflicted by the previously mentioned Ryan and Murphy reports – detailing decades of systemic child abuse perpetrated by and within religious organisations – on what for many generations had been the established authority of the Catholic Church on a relatively underpopulated island bound by strong family and clan linkages. Some indication of the powerful impact these disclosures had upon the Church/State relationship can be gauged from the response of the then head of government to reports that the Church was endeavouring to dissimulate the significance of findings made in the Cloyne child abuse report:[70]

> Because for the first time in Ireland, a report into child sexual-abuse exposes an attempt by the Holy See, to frustrate an Inquiry in a sovereign, democratic republic, as little as three years ago, not three decades ago ... the Cloyne Report excavates the dysfunction, disconnection, elitism, the narcissism that dominate the culture of the Vatican to this day. The rape and torture of children were downplayed or "managed" to uphold instead, the primacy of the institution, its power, standing and reputation ... this is not Rome ... this is the Republic of Ireland 2011. A Republic of laws of rights and responsibilities of proper civic order where the delinquency and arrogance of a particular version of a particular kind of morality will no longer be tolerated or ignored

The overtly discriminating patronage traditionally exercised at all levels by the clergy and accepted by adherents has now been at least severely diluted, if not largely dissipated, along with the trust necessary to maintain the clergy's status in the community.

Balancing Religion and Secularism

Ireland is now ostensibly a secular State. The national census results published in December 2012 showed a fourfold increase in the number of people who said they had no religion, or were either atheist or agnostic, between 1991 and 2011. It is a State, however, in which many institutions, such as hospitals and residential care facilities, and most notably schools, have retained their capacity for religious permeability.

The UN Human Rights Committee advised in 2014 that Ireland was breaching the fundamental human rights of atheists and members of

---

[70] Enda Kenny, Dail Motion, 20 July 2011. As quoted in Vasquez del Aguila and Cantillon, "Discimination on the Ground of Religion", at p. 71. See further www.rte.ie/news/2011/0720/cloyne1.html.

minority faiths – including freedom of conscience, equality before the law and freedom from discrimination – in contravention of the ICCPR. The United Nations Committee on Economic, Social and Cultural Rights has similarly expressed concerns regarding: the failure of the Irish State to protect the human rights of atheists and secularists in the Irish Education system; discrimination against women under the right to health; and blasphemy laws.

State Funding of Faith-Based Facilities and Services

The government commitment to supporting the work of religious organisations in Ireland, by means that include direct funding, has never been in question. In practice, this policy has been directed almost exclusively towards assisting Roman Catholic organisations, most usually in their role as service providers in health care and education. Many hospitals have been built, and continue to be managed by, Catholic bodies, and the permeation of religious belief has on occasion resulted in medical treatment being made available subject to religious doctrine: abortion and contraception being the two areas where religious sanctions have generated most social controversy.[71] The long-established government practice of funding the mainly Catholic (but partially Protestant)-controlled service provision in some hospitals and most schools (see later) is set to continue for the foreseeable future.

In *Campaign to Separate Church and State*,[72] a challenge to the constitutionality of the State funding of school chaplains was launched by an organisation opposed to State involvement with religion, arguing that this use of funding discriminated against those of non-Christian beliefs and secularists, and that the funds would be better directed towards improving non-religious education services. The court found that parents had the right to have religious education provided in the schools which their children attended, and were not obliged to settle merely for religious "instruction". The role of the chaplain helped to provide this extra dimension to the religious education of children and therefore:[73]

> the State by paying the salaries of chaplains in community schools is having regard to the rights of parents vis-a-vis the religious formation of their

---

[71] The government announcement, in April 2017, of its intention to vest ownership of the new national maternity hospital in the Sisters of Charity provoked much controversy. See www.thesun.ie/news/900916/new-national-maternity-hospital-must-obey-the-church-claims-bishop/.

[72] *Campaign to Separate Church and State Ltd v. Minister for Education* [1998] 3 IR 321.

[73] Ibid., at pp. 241–242.

children and enabling them to exercise their constitutionally recognised rights

and:[74]

> the present system is merely a manifestation, under modern conditions, of principles which are recognised and approved by Articles 44 and 42 of the Constitution.

Barrington J concluded his judgment in the Supreme Court by adding two caveats to his decision. First, the system of salaried chaplains had to be available to all community schools of whatever denomination on an equal basis, in accordance with their needs, and, second, it was constitutionally impermissible for a chaplain to instruct a child in a religion other than its own without the knowledge and consent of its parents (see later).

Christian Symbols/Prayers in State Facilities

The Constitution requires the President, judges and members of the Council of State to swear a religious oath before taking office (Articles 12, 31 and 34). Among other religious references, the Preamble refers to all authority coming from the Holy Trinity and to obligations owed to our divine Lord Jesus Christ. While not mentioning Catholicism, such references might nevertheless be perceived as discriminating in favour of religion – specifically, Christianity – to those who adhere to neither. The practice of commencing daily parliamentary business with a prayer calling upon "Christ our Lord" for guidance is likely to be similarly perceived.

Religious Discrimination: Contemporary Caselaw

Given its compact population and relatively homogenous religious culture, it is unsurprising that Ireland has not generated very much caselaw in relation to religious discrimination: the low level of religious diversity is such that minorities perhaps see litigation as a high-risk strategy likely to lead to further exposure and less community acceptance, while the size and cohesion of the main religious/cultural group possibly allows it to accommodate rather than litigate when difficulties arise.

Religious Conduct, Symbols, Icons, Apparel, etc.

In the previously mentioned *Campaign to Separate Church and State*,[75] the court considered, among other matters, the presence of Catholic icons

---

[74] [1998] 2 ILRM 81, at p. 101.   [75] Ibid.

and artwork in classrooms. Barrington J then ruled that publicly funded schools are not obliged "to change the general atmosphere of its school merely to accommodate a child of a different religious persuasion". The branding of Catholicism in public institutions is, however, surprisingly extensive. As noted by Vasquez del Aguila and Cantillon:[76]

> In terms of religious symbols in public institutions, the majority of schools and training schools for teachers, and public hospitals display Catholic images, pictures of the Pope, crucifixes, and other Catholic iconography without restriction. Religious signs and symbols are widespread across the country almost as "cultural habits", such as the ring of the "Angelus" bell at noon and six p.m. every day on the RTE, the biggest media broadcaster that is also a State-founded company. Clerical presence in everyday life has simply been taken for granted as part of the national identity. The identity of the school is usually conveyed by the name of the school with religious names after saints. Christian festivities are also celebrated across all these schools. It is common also to find altars in classrooms, grace before meals, prayers at the start and end of the day, visits to churches and visits from clergy, which creates the religious "climate" in the school

Such is the saturation level and duration of such iconography, testifying to a history of religious/cultural homogeneity no longer representative of contemporary Irish society, that it cannot be perceived as anything other than religiously discriminating by those of other religions or of none.

Religious Apparel

Issues relating to religion-specific clothing worn by employees have generated cases in this as in other jurisdictions. In particular, the continuing, if occasional, presence of nuns in schools, hospitals, social care facilities, etc., while reassuring to many, is probably experienced as at least incongruous by non-Catholics. The variable spectrum of female Islamic clothing (from hijab to chador and burqa) has not given rise to much controversy. However, in *Tavoraite*,[77] the firm belief of the plaintiff that whereas previously her religious belief did not mandate wearing the hijab, it now did, led to problems in her workplace regarding the effect of the hijab on her capacity to perform her duties. This matter was ultimately settled out of court (see later).

---

[76] Vasquez del Aguila and Cantillon, "Discrimination on the Ground of Religion", at p. 72, citing Coen, M., "Religious Ethos and Employment Equality: A Comparative Irish Perspective", *Legal Studies*, 2008, vol. 28:3, pp. 452–474.

[77] *Tavoraite* v. *Dunnes Stores* (unreported, Employment Appeals Tribunal, Dublin, 13 November 2012).

Family-Related Issues

Article 41.1.1 of the Constitution "recognises the Family as the natural primary and fundamental unit group of Society, and as a moral institution possessing inalienable and imprescriptible rights, antecedent and superior to all positive law", and guarantees its protection by the State, while Article 41.3 avows that "the State pledges itself to guard with special care the institution of marriage, on which the Family is founded, and to protect it against attack". The inescapable corollary is that non-marital families, one-parent families and others are relatively disadvantaged in the eyes of the Constitution. A whole nexus of issues concerning the respective rights of parent and child, as compounded by the marital statuses of those concerned, revolves around this constitutional presumption favouring the marital family.

Given that, in Ireland, the non-marital family has always attracted less protection in law than the family based on marriage,[78] there is a probability that the protection afforded human rights in this jurisdiction may be structurally flawed, being inherently discriminatory in its prejudicial treatment of non-marital parents and children (and also in its treatment of family units led by single parents or by same-sex couples) relative to members of a marital family. There can be little room for doubt that this circumstance arises directly from the ethics and moral values of Catholicism that underpin and permeate the Constitution: the extent to which the law relating to the family (and to associated medical and health issues) is non-ECHR-compliant is arguably a measure of an intrinsic bias favouring such values; it is also, therefore, a measure of religiously based discrimination against practices found to be non-compliant with the outworkings of those values.

Sexuality

In Ireland, the conflation of religion and sexuality found early expression in the law relating to homosexuality: consensual sexual relations between those of the same sex, in private,[79] were only de-criminalised in 1993;[80] same-sex couples acquired formal legal recognition of their

---

[78] See e.g. *The State (Nicolaou) v. An Bord Uchtála* [1966] IR 567. The then Mr Justice Walsh of the Supreme Court stated that: "the family referred to in [Article 41 was] the family which is founded on the institution of marriage". See also *G v. An Bord Uchtála* [1980] IR 32 and *WO'R v. EH (Guardianship)* [1996] 2 IR 248.

[79] *Norris v. Attorney General*, op. cit.

[80] Compared with e.g. 1967 in the UK and from 1972 onwards in various Australian states.

status in 2010;[81] and provision for same-sex marriage was eventually signed into law in August 2015 by the President of Ireland as the Thirty-fourth Amendment of the Constitution of Ireland.[82] It can also be seen in the stereotypical constraints imposed upon women. As Buckley has pointed out,[83] the fact that the role and status of women has also been compromised is unsurprising in a country where Catholicism had such a powerful constraining effect for so long on sex and gender issues: only in 1973 was the ban removed on married women working in the civil service; before that date, they were not allowed to sit on juries,[84] and single mothers were not entitled to social assistance; contraceptives only became available to everyone in 1984; a limited form of divorce was introduced in 1986; and not until 1991 did it became illegal for a man to rape his wife. Article 40.1 of the Constitution, which allows the State to have "due regard to the differences of capacity, physical and moral, and of social function" between men and women, has probably been a contributory factor in maintaining constraints upon women in Irish society: constraints now reinforced by the Criminal Justice (Sexual Offences) Act 2017, which, in criminalising prostitution, represents a continuation of the conservative morality in Irish law that has so often worked to the disadvantage of its female citizens, particularly when sex is involved.

In modern Ireland, the balancing of a traditional culturally prescribed identity – in which Catholicism plays a central role – against the identity needs of emerging or minority groups in what is an increasingly multicultural society inevitably throws up problems. In that context, the case of *Foy* v. *An t-Ard Chlaraitheoir & Others*[85] was of considerable significance, as it revealed some interesting tensions. In what was the nation's first declaration of incompatibility between domestic legislative provisions and human rights requirements, McKechnie J ruled that Irish law was deficient and in breach of such rights, as it failed to provide legal recognition for transgender people. His comments have a broad application to identity issues per se:

> Everyone as a member of society has the right to human dignity, and with individual personalities, has the right to develop his being as he sees fit; subject only to the most minimal of State interference being essential for

---

[81] *Zappone and Gilligan* v. *Revenue Commissioners* [2006] IEHC 404, [208] 2 IR 417.
[82] Following an overwhelming majority favouring gay marriage in the May 2015 national referendum.
[83] See further Buckley, S-A., at http://nuigalway.academia.edu/SarahAnneBuckley/
[84] See *de Burca and Anderson* v. *Attorney General* [1976] IR 38.   [85] Op. cit.

the convergence of the common good. Together with human freedom, a person, subject to the acquired rights of others, should be free to shape his personality in the way best suited to his person and to his life.

The Gender Recognition Act 2015 now provides legal recognition for the acquired gender of transgender persons and should extend the ambit of legal prohibition from discrimination on sexual grounds. The Children and Family Relationships Bill 2015 has also been signed into law, amending (among other statutes) the Adoption Act 2010, which will undoubtedly lead to a clash between traditional culturally prescribed values and ECHR and equality values.

Conception, Abortion, IVF and Related Issues

This jurisdiction has a long history of controversy surrounding legal access to contraception[86] and abortion.

In *Open Door and Dublin Well Woman v. Ireland*,[87] the ECtHR upheld the claim of both plaintiff organisations that women had the right to receive information relating to birth control, as protected by Article 10. In recent years, religiously discriminatory practices in relation to the availability of abortion – which has long been prohibited by both the Offences Against the Person Act 1861 and Article 40.3.3 of the Constitution – have been the subject of considerable national[88] and international controversy. In *A, B and C v. Ireland*,[89] the ECtHR considered the rights of a Lithuanian resident of Ireland who was denied access to abortion (see later). The court held that a broad margin of appreciation should be accorded to Ireland because of the "acute sensitivity of the moral and ethical issues raised by the question of abortion or as to the importance of the public interest at stake".[90] Interestingly, this was challenged in the dissenting opinion of six judges, who considered that such reasoning justified exactly the

---

[86] See *McGee v. The Attorney General*, op. cit. and Henchy J's comment regarding "the right of a married woman to use contraceptives, which is something which at present is declared to be morally wrong according to the official teaching of the Church to which about 95% of the citizens belong" in *Norris v. Attorney General*, op. cit., at p. 72.

[87] Application No. 14234/88, [1992] ECHR 68.

[88] See *Attorney General v. X* [1992] IESC 1, [1992] 1 IR 1, which established the right of Irish women to an abortion if their life was at risk because of pregnancy, including the risk of suicide. The tragic death of Savita Halappanavar at the University Hospital in Galway in 2012 was attributed to a professional decision to deny her an abortion because Ireland was a Catholic country.

[89] [2010] ECtHR (GC) (No. 25579/05) (16 December 2010).   [90] Ibid.

opposite approach: the existence of a consensus on abortion among Member States should instead be used to narrow the width of the margin of appreciation enjoyed by Ireland. They pointed out that it was "the first time that the court has disregarded the existence of a European consensus on the basis of 'profound moral views'". They argued that the fact that these "moral views . . . can override the European consensus, which tends in a completely different direction, is a real and dangerous new departure in the court's caselaw". Such an interpretation of the margin of appreciation was viewed as presenting a potentially serious obstacle for the judiciary in any future adjudication on moral and sensitive matters. Nonetheless, it was held that it was for the Irish government to consider in what circumstances there is a "real and substantial risk to the life of the mother" and to provide for an "accessible and effective procedure" by which a pregnant woman can establish whether or not she fulfills the conditions for a lawful abortion according to Article 40.3.3 of the Constitution, i.e. whether the risk to her life is real and makes the abortion necessary. Consequently, the government introduced the Protection of Life During Pregnancy Act 2013. This legislation provides for the termination of pregnancy in cases where there is a risk of loss of life from physical illness in an emergency or a risk of suicide. It does not provide directly for the termination of pregnancy as a result of rape or incest, and it continues the long-standing discriminatory impact on Irish women relative to those in England and elsewhere in Europe.

Subsequent developments have not served to facilitate legal access to abortion services. The 2012 insertion of Article 42A (the Children's Rights Amendment) into the Constitution, with its specific reference to "all children", has been judicially interpreted as intended to extend protection to the unborn, and as a consequence to give the unborn a right to family life.[91] The comments of delegates to the Committee of Ministers, during its 6 December 2012 meeting, remain pertinent: they invited Ireland to answer the issue of the "general prohibition of abortion in criminal law", as it constitutes "a significant chilling factor for women and doctors because of the risk of criminal conviction and imprisonment".

Surrogacy services are also problematic. There is, as yet, no specific legislation governing surrogacy:[92] while not illegal, surrogacy agreements are

---

[91] See *IRM* v. *MJELR* (HC), 29 July 2016. See also *In re E* [2008] IEHC 68. Eoin Daly adds: "these are isolated first-instance judgments, controversial and not yet confirmed by the Supreme Court" (note to author, 26 March 2017).

[92] See www.citizensinformation.ie/en/birth_family_relationships/adoption_and_fostering/ surrogacy.html.

unenforceable;[93] consequently, it is estimated that there are now several hundred children living in Ireland born to surrogate mothers whose legal status is uncertain and whose human rights are seriously compromised[94] – a state of affairs which, the Supreme Court has pointed out, "makes statutory law reform in this area more than urgent".[95]

Assisted Suicide

The freedom to end your own life, with or without the assistance of a third party, is probably a lead item on the agenda of contemporary moral imperative issues in most developed nations. In Ireland, while the Criminal Law (Suicide) Act 1993, s.1, de-criminalises suicide, s.2 makes it an offence punishable by fourteen years' imprisonment for anyone to aid, abet, counsel or procure the suicide or attempted suicide of another. This places Irish law among the most strict in Europe: in the Netherlands, Belgium and Luxembourg, active, direct euthanasia is legal; in France, the law acknowledges a right to die; and in Sweden, Austrian, Germany and Norway, as well as in Ireland,[96] passive euthanasia is permitted under certain conditions.

"It is important to emphasise that the Court can never sanction steps to terminate life." This declaration, made by Hamilton CJ,[97] was reaffirmed by the Supreme Court ruling in *Fleming v. Ireland & ors*,[98] confirming an earlier decision of the High Court.[99] The court determined that the right to life in Article 40.3.2 of the Constitution "does not import a right to die", ending any further judicial equivocation, and leaving it to the Oireachtas to address the matter – should it choose to do so – by introducing new legislation "within the boundaries of what was constitutionally permissible".[100] In so concluding, the court quoted the following passage from the judgment of Henchy J in *Norris*:[101]

> Having regard to the purposive Christian ethos of the Constitution, particularly as set out in the preamble ("to promote the common good, with due

---

[93] See the Report of the Commission on Assisted Human Reproduction, Dublin, 2005, which recommends that a child born through surrogacy should be presumed to be that of the commissioning couple. See also *M.R. & Anor v. An tArd Chlaraitheoir* [2013] IEHC 91.

[94] See www.aclsolicitors.ie/news-events/current-news/legal-status-of-surrogacy-in-ireland/.

[95] *M.R. and D.R. (suing by their father and next friend O.R.) & ors v An t-Ard-Chláraitheoir & ors* [2014] IESC 60 (7 November 2014), per Hardiman J.

[96] See *Fitzpatrick v. FK* [2009] 2 IR 7, per Laffoy J.

[97] *In Re a Ward of Court (withholding medical treatment) (No. 2)* [1995] 2 ILRM 401, per Hamilton CJ at p. 120.

[98] [2013] IESC 19.   [99] [2013] IEHC 2.   [100] Op. cit., at para. 108.

[101] *Norris v. Attorney General*, op. cit., per Henchy J at pp. 71–72.

observance of Prudence, Justice and Charity, so that the dignity and freedom of the individual may be assured, true social order attained, the unity
of our country restored, and concord established with other nations"), to
the denomination of the State as "sovereign, independent, democratic" in
Article 5, and to the recognition, expressly or by necessary implication,
of particular personal rights, such recognition being frequently hedged in
by overriding requirements such as "public order and morality" or "the
authority of the State" or "the exigencies of the common good", there is
necessarily given to the citizen, within the required social, political and
moral framework, such a range of personal freedoms or immunities as are
necessary to ensure his dignity and freedom as an individual in the type
of society envisaged. The essence of those rights is that they inhere in the
individual personality of the citizen in his capacity as a vital human component of the social, political and moral order posited by the Constitution.

As Denham CJ said of the constitutional protection of the right to life, this
cannot logically include a right to terminate that life or to have it terminated, as "in the social order contemplated by the Constitution, and the
values reflected in it, that would be the antithesis of the right rather than
the logical consequence of it".[102] Given "the purposive Christian ethos of
the Constitution", it is hard to see how statute law can be changed to grant
a right to die, or to assist someone to do so, within constitutional boundaries. The corollary is that those who do not subscribe to that ethos may
well be justified in feeling that they are being discriminated against on religious grounds when they are denied recognition of a right now acknowledged by the ECtHR.[103]

Employment-Related Issues

Issues relating to employment are largely governed by provisions in the
Constitution, the Workplace Relations Act 2015, the Employment Equality Acts 1998–2015 as amended by the Equality Act 2004 and various
EU Directives.[104] Their cumulative effect is to point up the advisability
of employers having in place policies that address discrimination, including on the grounds of religion, and programmes for their implementation,
including staff training.

Hiring/Firing Staff

Religious Organisations Given that by far the majority of all schools
in Ireland, and many hospitals, are denominational, the right to

---

[102] [2013] IESC 19, at para. 113.   [103] *Haas v. Switzerland*, op. cit., at para. 51.
[104] Mainly, the General Framework (Council Directive 2000/78/EC), but also the Equal Pay
Directive (75/117/EEC) and the Equal Treatment Directive (76/207/EEC).

discriminate on religious grounds when employing staff – under s.37(1) of the Employment Equality Act 1998 – is of considerable significance. This right has been judicially endorsed, for example, by the Supreme Court in *Re Article 26 and the Employment Equality Bill 1996*,[105] when it was asked to rule on the constitutionality of ss.12 and 37(1) of the Bill, which exempted from the statutory ban on religious discrimination in employment any "religious, educational or medical institution which is under the direction or control of a body established for religious purposes or whose objectives include the provision of services in an environment which promotes certain religious values". Such institutions were permitted to give "favourable treatment" on grounds of religion to employees, and to prospective employees in terms of recruitment, if it was necessary "to uphold the religious ethos of the institution".[106] Indeed, s.12, which provided that the prohibition on religious discrimination would not apply to the selection of nurses or primary teachers for these institutions, was termed "positive discrimination" by counsel for the Attorney General. It upheld both provisions on the basis that it is constitutionally permissible to discriminate on grounds of religious profession, belief or status if this is necessary to "give life and reality" to the constitutional guarantee of freedom of religion.[107] Two years later, in *Greally* v. *Minister for Education (No 2)*,[108] Geoghegan J upheld the constitutionality of a recruitment system for secondary school teachers that gave priority to the employment of teachers who had experience teaching in Catholic schools. This was held to be justified in light of the constitutional right of parents to have their children educated in denominational schools. Again, in *O'Shiel* v. *Minister for Education*,[109] Laffoy J held that the requirement that publicly funded schools only employ teachers with qualifications generally recognised by the State, and that such schools employ teachers with qualifications that enable them to teach Irish to a reasonable standard, is a valid condition having regard to the Constitution; the broadening of the religious ethos of State schools to also include preferential recognition for the Irish language is interesting.

The much criticised s.37 of the 1998 Act has now been amended by the Equality (Miscellaneous Provisions) Act 2015, s.11. However, as it further entrenches the central importance of "religious ethos", it remains to be seen what difference the amendment will make to staff recruitment by

---

[105] Op. cit.   [106] Ibid., at p. 351.
[107] The 1996 Bill was declared unconstitutional on other grounds, but s.37(1) of the 1998 Act – its replacement – virtually replicates its predecessor.
[108] Op. cit.   [109] [1999] 2 IR 321, [1999] 2 ILRM 241.

religious organisations and what added protection it provides to staff in post at such organisations who belong to the LGBT community or who are divorcees, single parents or persons of another religion or of none.

An interesting case is *Mulloy* v. *Minister for Education*,[110] which concerned a member of a religious order who, on his return from teaching in Africa, failed to gain increments for his service there on a par with similarly placed lay teachers. He succeeded in his claim that he was discriminated against on the grounds of his religious status. The Supreme Court held that the term "status" in Article 44.2.3 related to the position or rank of a person in terms of religion in respect to others – either of the same religion, of another religion or of no religion. The decision not only (as expected) upheld the right of an employee of a religious organisation not to be disadvantaged on account of their religion relative to their non-religious counterparts but also shows that Article 44.2.3 provides implied constitutional protection for persons of no religious faith.

If a plaintiff has knowingly placed themselves in a position in which contractual obligations will impair their freedom to manifest personal religious beliefs, then they may not have any rightful cause for complaint if their position in fact becomes so compromised. An inverted version of this problem was brought before the court in *Flynn* v. *Power*,[111] which concerned an unmarried teacher working in a convent school who was dismissed after becoming pregnant by her married partner. Costello J held that as she had been openly having a relationship with a married person, the dismissal was reasonable in order to prevent the undermining of the religious ethos of the school: her lifestyle was openly in conflict with the values the school sought to promote.

Secular Organisations   This is an area in which the caselaw is inconsistent. Recently, in *Tavoraite* v. *Dunnes Stores*,[112] the EAT in Cork heard an unfair dismissal case concerning a conflict between an employee's religious belief and the dress standards of the employing agency. The Muslim employee had her employment terminated after two years of warnings that, while at work, she was required to conform to the company's dress code and desist from wearing a hijab, despite her protests that this was necessitated by her religious beliefs. The Tribunal hearing ended when the plaintiff reached a settlement with the company. While it is not possible to guess the outcome of this case, relevant factors to be taken into account would have included: the fact that the plaintiff converted to Islam

---

[110] [1975] IR 88.   [111] [1985] ILRM 336.   [112] Op. cit.

after some years of employment in that post; her firm belief that her religion now required her to wear the hijab; the effect of the hijab on her capacity to perform her duties (including health and safety considerations); and the extent to which other staff were permitted to wear similar religious/culture-specific apparel in addition to or instead of the company uniform (Sikh turbans, etc.).

Conflating religion and culture, the 2010 case of Michelle McKeever, a member of the Church of Ireland, illustrates the symbiotic relationship of State and Catholicism in the national school system. A Catholic school, which had offered Ms McKeever a permanent teaching post, withdrew the offer following a post-interview phone call in which she was questioned about holding a certificate in religious studies – a compulsory requirement of the Irish Catholic Bishops' Conference for teachers working in Catholic-managed primary schools. The Equality Tribunal found that she had suffered direct religious discrimination because of her membership of the Church of Ireland, and awarded her maximum compensation. Curiously, s.37.1 of the Employment Equality Act, which allows schools to discriminate if necessary to maintain their religious ethos, was not relied upon by the defendants; presumably because it had not been included in a transparent manner in the pre-interview selection criteria and the discrimination occurred after completion of the selection process. The case is important, as it sounds a warning to all employers that any post-interview attempt to withdraw an offer of appointment due to new information will be liable to a similar legal sanction if that information leads to a person's rights – e.g. as a member of the LGBT community – being breached on any of the nine designated grounds.

Accommodating Religious Beliefs in the Workplace

While this is an employers' duty, the obligation is one that is also shared among employees: there is an acceptance that a degree of give-and-take, compatible with efficient working arrangements, is permissible, subject to a reasonableness test.

The complainant in *Cristian Zamfir v. Lorien Enterprises Limited*,[113] a Romanian Orthodox Christian, was employed in a restaurant where he worked largely with Muslim staff and complained about discrimination on the grounds of race. He had initially worked as a kitchen porter, then as a commis chef or pizza chef, but unlike the Muslim staff he was made to clean the toilets. His complaint, relating to allegations of discrimination

---

[113] Case No. DEC-E2016–063.

on both race and religion, was found to be unjustified as there was no evidence to suggest that he was being singled out for toilet-cleaning duties. Although derogatory language was used by staff in the kitchen, this was not such as would constitute harassment.

Education-Related Issues

In Ireland, religion and education are clearly very closely linked. The link is governed by legislative provisions that, in theory, should obviate any religious discrimination problems. The Education Act 1998 obliges every person concerned with the implementation of the Act: "to give practical effect to the constitutional rights of children";[114] "to promote equality of access to and participation in education"; and to promote "the means whereby pupils may benefit from education".[115] This is endorsed by the provisions of the Equal Status Acts 2000–2015, which provide that an educational establishment shall not discriminate in relation to: (a) the admission or the terms of conditions of admission of a person as a student to the establishment or (c) any other term or condition of participation in the establishment by a student.[116] However, unlike in the UK, a very large proportion of the buildings and teachers making up the educational system were and continue to be provided by religious bodies, and all teacher training colleges are denominational. So, although the system is State-funded, it is in practice controlled by religious bodies – almost exclusively Roman Catholic – which have consistently ensured that the system maintains a specific religious ethos.[117] This can give rise to discriminatory issues for those belonging to minority religions or to none. It has been said that "our school system is fundamentally sectarian".[118]

Government Funding and Religious Education

Article 44.2 of the Constitution declares that "State aid for schools shall not discriminate between schools under the management of different religious denominations". However, although this Article did not arise for consideration in *Crowley* v. *Ireland*,[119] that decision clearly established

---

[114] Education Act 1998, s.6(a).   [115] Ibid., s.6(c).
[116] The Equal Status Acts 2000–2008, s.7(2).
[117] Relying on s.15(2)(b) of the Education Act 1998, which obliges Boards of Management to uphold the Characteristic Spirit (ethos) of their Patron.
[118] Bacik, "Is Ireland Really a Republic?"
[119] [1980] IR 102. The author acknowledges the advice of Gerard Whyte on this matter (note to author, 17 February 2017).

that the State could support denominationally controlled education in discharging its obligation to provide for free primary education. The issue of the very considerable Catholic influence upon the State education system came before the courts again in *Campaign to Separate Church and State*,[120] when both Barrington and Keane JJ invoked Article 44.2.4 in support of the proposition that the public funding of denominational schools did not constitute an endowment of religion. According to Keane J:[121]

> [Article 44.2.4] makes it clear beyond argument, not merely that the State is entitled to provide aid to schools under the management of different religious denominations, but that such schools may also include religious instruction as a subject in their curricula. It is subject to two qualifications; first, the legislation must not discriminate between schools under the management of different religious denominations and, secondly, it must respect the right of a child not to attend religious instruction in a school in receipt of public funds.

Elaborating on the latter point, Barrington J said that the Constitution distinguished between religious "education" and religious "instruction", and that the right of a child not to attend religious instruction at a publicly funded school did not protect that child from being influenced, to some degree, by the religious ethos of the school.

The Equal Status Act 2000, s.7(3)(c), now allows schools – including those in receipt of public funding – to discriminate in admissions on the grounds of religion where the objective is to provide education in an environment which promotes certain religious values. However, s.3(1) of the 2003 Act places a statutory duty on "organs of the State" to "perform [their] functions in a manner compatible with the State's obligations under the Convention provisions", unless there is a law stating that this is not required. There is thus a presumption that public bodies will respect the requirements of the ECHR. Arguably, this gives rise to a significant problem in the field of education. As already stated, the government retains responsibility for school funding and for curriculum development (excepting religious instruction) and staffing. Despite the views of Barrington J, while government funding does not constitute "endowment", it may suggest a level of involvement that, taken in conjunction with other factors, could indicate a controlling relationship. Given the extent of that control, in a relationship where the ownership of most schools rests

---

[120] *Campaign to Separate Church and State Ltd* v. *Minister for Education* [1998] 3 IR 321, [1998] 2 ILRM 81.

[121] Ibid., at pp. 360 and 84.

with the Catholic Church, as does the management and delivery of educational services, it is at least arguable that the role of the Church in the national education system for children in Ireland can be construed as that of a public body. This is important because, if that is the case, then, while functioning as such, that organisation cannot avail itself of the statutory exemption provided for religious bodies, and full Convention compliance will be required.[122]

One aspect of the problems associated with the State funding of schools is evident in the long-standing grievance felt by the small and scattered Protestant community. To be assured that their children will receive an education within an appropriate religious ethos, many Protestant parents – unlike their Catholic neighbours – must send them to boarding schools. Compared to their UK counterparts, such schools are most often not elitist. In fact, a large proportion of their annual intake is from quite poor families, who, until 1966, had to rely on their local church and on charities to pay the fees. The government "block funding" available to parents since that date continues in place, but government cuts to the ancillary grant enabling such schools to pay for non-teaching staff such as secretaries and caretakers, implemented in 2015, threaten their future.

Faith Schools

In Ireland, State education is faith-based: some 97 per cent of primary schools and perhaps 50 per cent of secondary schools are State-funded, but managed by religious organisations; 90 per cent of all primary schools are controlled by the Catholic Church;[123] some 110 secondary schools, representing approximately 58 000 students (or one in six of all second level students) and 4000 teachers and administrative staff, are members of CEIST, which is committed to embedding Catholic values in education. The assertion of Barrington J in *Campaign to Separate Church and State*[124] that "the Constitution contemplated that if a school was in receipt of public funds any child, no matter what his religion, would be entitled to attend it"[125] has not always reflected reality, and indeed was turned on its head by the unequivocal provision under the previously mentioned Equal Status Acts

---

[122] Note, however, the success of "Educate Together", a charity founded in 1984 to promote multi-denominational schools. As of 2016, it was the patron of eighty-one national schools.

[123] *Campaign to Separate Church and State Ltd* v. *Minister for Education* [1998] 3 IR 321, [1998] 2 ILRM 81, which clearly established that the State could support denominationally controlled education in discharging its obligation to provide for free primary education.

[124] Ibid.   [125] Ibid., at p. 356.

2000–2012, ss.7(3)(c) and 7(2), which enables a school to refuse admittance to a pupil who is not of its denomination where it can prove that "the refusal is essential to maintain the ethos of the school". The government's plan to address this issue suffered a setback in August 2016 when it announced a further 12-month delay to the already much delayed Equal Status (Admission to School) Bill 2016. This legislation amends s.7 of the Equal Status Act 2000 to provide:

> (c) where the establishment is a school supported by public funds providing primary or post-primary education to students and the objective of the school is to provide education in an environment which promotes certain religious values –
>
> 1. (i) it admits persons of a particular religious denomination in preference to others, if it is proved that such a policy is essential in order to ensure reasonable access to education for children of that denomination within its catchment area in accordance with the conscience and lawful preference of their parents, or
> 2. (ii) it refuses to admit as a student a person who is not of that denomination, if it is proved that the refusal is essential to maintain the ethos of the school,";
>
> (3A) In determining for the purposes of subsection (3) (c) whether an admission policy referred to in sub-paragraph (i) or a refusal referred to in sub-paragraph (ii) is essential for the purposes referred to, due regard shall be had to –
>
> 1. (a) the constitutional right of any child to attend a school receiving public money without attending religious instruction at that school, and
> 2. (b) the concomitant obligation that every such school must be so organised as to enable that right effectually to be enjoyed.

Religious Discrimination and Educational Content

In *Campaign to Separate Church and State*,[126] the court considered the right of a child not to receive religious instruction: that such a child was suffering discrimination by being burdened with instruction that was detrimental to their needs as a non-believer or believer in another religion. Both Barrington and Keane JJ were of the view that Article 44.2.4 imposed a duty upon any school receiving government funding to provide alternative arrangements for such a child. This was reinforced in the 2016 report issued by the United Nations Committee on the Rights of the Child, which recommended that Ireland "ensure accessible options for

---

[126] Ibid.

children to opt-out of religious classes and access appropriate alternatives to such classes, in accordance with the needs of children of minority faith or non-faith backgrounds". It also expressed its concern that "children are not [currently] ensured the right to effectively opt-out of religious classes and access appropriate alternatives to such classes". However, it remains the case that, in practice, the State has not to date funded the supervision of any such children, with arrangements for those who are opted out having been designated a parental responsibility; this is particularly difficult for parents of non-Catholic children in the second and sixth forms of primary school when their classes are preparing for "first communion" and "confirmation". The 2016 Bill promises to resolve this matter.

Education Facilities and Religious Discrimination

Accessing the education services provided by a national educational system controlled by religious bodies can be problematic for those who do not share the beliefs of such bodies. This was graphically demonstrated in early 2007, when a number of children of Nigerian origin failed to access any local schools in an area of north Co. Dublin because they did not hold Catholic baptismal certificates.[127] Access was also an issue in 2007 for the four Irish Protestant schools initiating proceedings seeking a declaration that their constitutional rights had been breached by a Department of Education employment scheme which would require them to accept teachers of other denominations, redeployed from schools that had closed, who might not subscribe to their Protestant ethos. This, they alleged, would constitute unwarranted State interference with the rights of Protestant parents and their children to access education that was in accordance with their religious ethos.[128]

The fact that access is a systemic and ongoing problem became obvious when, in February 2016, the United Nations Committee on the Rights of the Child issued a report which urged Ireland to "expeditiously undertake concrete measures to significantly increase the availability of

---

[127] See: "Is Your Child Catholic Enough to Get a Place at School?", *The Irish Times*, 1 May 2007; "New Catholic School Policy Could Produce Unintended 'Apartheid'", *The Irish Times*, 8 September 2007; "Faith before Fairness", *The Irish Times*, 8 September 2007; and "Ireland Forced to Open Immigrant School", *The Guardian*, 25 September 2007. See also Daly, E. and Hickey, T. "Religious Freedom and the Right to Discriminate in the School Admissions Context: A Neo-Republican Critique", *Legal Studies*, 2011, vol. 31:4, pp. 615–643.

[128] The High Court case was settled in 2008 on terms that were not disclosed.

non-denominational or multidenominational schools and to amend the existing legislative framework to eliminate discrimination in school admissions, including the Equal Status Act". The report concluded that "schools are continuing to practice discriminatory admissions policies on the basis of the child's religion", and the Committee said it remained "concerned at the very small number of non-denominational schools".

Medicine-Related Issues

While advances in medicine have had a hugely beneficial impact upon the range of treatment options in this jurisdiction, as in others, they have occurred here against a social backdrop where the traditional values of Catholicism tend to outweigh those of secularists in the hospitals, clinics and social care settings where relevant services are dispensed. Indeed, such public health facilities are often owned and controlled by religious bodies: the nation's two largest hospitals, St Vincent's and the Mater, both in Dublin, are owned and governed by the Catholic Church.

Medical Intervention and Religious Beliefs

As already mentioned, in this jurisdiction there have been and continue to be problems in the tension between improved medical treatment options in "family planning" and their availability when filtered through gateways that are religiously influenced or controlled.

The troubling cases of Jehovah's Witnesses and their approach to blood products have become as familiar to the judiciary in Ireland as to its counterparts elsewhere. Much the same approach has been adopted to their discriminatory accessing of lifesaving medical treatment on religious grounds: adults are entitled to make informed decisions not to avail themselves of blood transfusions, but cannot veto the availability of that treatment option for their children. In *Temple Street v. D. & Anor*,[129] when a blood transfusion was urgently required for a three-month-old baby but was refused by his Jehovah's Witness parents on grounds of their religious belief, the court had little difficulty in overruling the parental veto as disproportionate.

In recent years, religiously discriminatory practices in a health care context have been the subject of considerable national and international controversy. In *A, B and C v. Ireland*,[130] the ECtHR held that the Article 8

[129] Op. cit.   [130] Op. cit.

rights of a Lithuanian national resident in Ireland, suffering from a rare form of cancer, had been violated since:

> the criminal provisions of the [Offences Against the Person Act 1861] ... would constitute a significant chilling factor for both women and doctors in the medical consultation process, regardless of whether or not prosecutions have in fact been pursued under that Act. Both the third applicant and any doctor ran a risk of a serious criminal conviction and imprisonment in the event that a decision taken in medical consultation, that the woman was entitled to an abortion in Ireland given the risk to her life, was later found not to accord with Article 40.3.3 of the Constitution.

This case proved to be a sad precursor to the 2012 tragedy of an Indian woman who died in an Irish hospital after being told by a midwife who was treating her that she could not have an abortion because Ireland was "a Catholic country". As a direct consequence, the Irish government introduced the Protection of Life During Pregnancy Bill in May 2013 to make abortion available – but only on a limited basis.

Genetic Engineering and Patents, etc.

As a core belief of Catholicism is that life begins at the moment of fertilisation and that the embryo should be regarded with the same moral status as that of the newborn child, research involving embryos – as with contraception and abortion – was always going to be contentious in this jurisdiction. The patenting of inventions which directly use hES cells, or which have used them in their development, was initially considered to be constitutionally prohibited. At present – following the High Court ruling in *M.R. v. T.R.*,[131] subsequently confirmed by the Supreme Court,[132] that embryos held in cryopreservation and created outside the womb are not protected under the Constitution – the situation is uncertain. Bills have since been drafted to prevent or otherwise regulate the use of embryos for research, including the Human Tissues Bill 2008, but have never become law. In 2009, the Irish Medical Council banned medical practitioners from creating embryos specifically for research.

Service-Provision Issues

In Ireland, where so much public sector provision is delivered by religious organisations and where porous sector boundaries facilitate the permeation of Catholicism throughout the social infrastructure, discriminatory

---

[131] [2006] IEHC 359 (15 November 2006).   [132] *M.R. v. T.R.* [2009] IESC 82.

practices could in theory occur anywhere, but in fact very few allegations would seem to reach court or regulator. This may be due to Ireland's relatively high level of religious/cultural homogeneity. The record of cases determined by regulatory bodies shows that by far the majority concern allegations of racial rather than religious discrimination, although it is possible that in some instances the former might be hiding the latter – and, indeed, more generally, the latter may be hiding behind sexual-orientation and other LGBT issues.

Service Provision by Religious Organisations

Historically, Irish religious organisations have a proud record of contributing to social infrastructure – in education, hospitals, clinics and general health and social care – both in Ireland and across the world. The Christian Brothers, for example, from their origins in Waterford in 1802, are now renowned in all the countries presently under study for establishing, and teaching in, their many schools. This record has been overshadowed by recent revelations of abuse.

In Ireland, the mid-decades of the twentieth century was an era when the State shamefully colluded with the Church to isolate single mothers as a threat to the institutions of marriage and the family, to public morality as prescribed by Catholicism and more generally to the integrity of civic values jointly upheld by Church and State.[133] An "illegitimate" child was treated by the State as *sui juris* (outside the law) and by the Church as "lost to God": an invidious religiously discriminating formula which, with the backing of those twin pillars of authority, was culturally embedded by way of law and sermon upon citizens and congregations. The resulting immense suffering caused to untold numbers of unmarried mothers and their children included a proliferation of private nursing homes in which very many babies died, to be buried in unmarked graves,[134] and from which many others were spirited away to new homes overseas.[135] This State-sanctioned form of religious discrimination also gave rise to the notorious "Magdalene laundries" scandal. Religious institutions, ostensibly providing laundry facilities for the public and a care service for single

---

[133] In 1967, some 96.9 per cent of non-marital births resulted in adoption.

[134] See *The Irish Post*, and reports that the bodies of some 800 babies and infants were found in a burial pit at one mother and baby home in Tuam, at www.irishpost.co.uk/news/philomena-journalist-lands-new-bbc-series-irelands-lost-babies

[135] See Milotte, M., *Banished Babies: The Secret History of Ireland's Baby Export Business*, Dublin, New Island Press, 2014.

mothers (many of whose babies were taken for adoption[136]), in fact perpetrated abuse, oppression and discrimination on some 30 000 women over several decades.[137] It was also an era when the care and training services supposedly provided by religious organisations in residential institutions such as Letterfrack (where an estimated 147 boys died) were in practice often thinly disguised programmes of cruelty and systemic child abuse.[138] By the early years of the twenty-first century, Ireland was coming to terms with the shock of these and similar revelations and beginning to review the cultural role of religion and religious organisations, which had been so accepted and respected for many generations.

Contemporary religious organisations rely on their exemption to the statutory prohibition on discriminatory practice to lawfully discriminate in certain circumstances on the basis of religion, belief or sexual orientation. This necessarily impacts upon provision in education, hospital and hospice care and in general social care, but, for whatever reason, there is a dearth of caselaw on discrimination inflicted by or upon religious organisations. One recent idiosyncratic instance, indicative perhaps of a more general truth, was the first appointment – not just in Ireland but in all of the British Isles – of an Anglican female bishop (for the diocese of Meath and Kildare). The appointment highlights the absence of any comparable initiative within the main religious organisation in Ireland, and suggests a stoical acceptance of the status quo – with its religiously discriminating ethos – as it relates to the possible appointment of female and gay clergy.

Provision of Public Services

A (perhaps innate) deference towards the traditional religious ethos pervades some public service institutions and is evident in the constraints on user choice. Where it shows itself in the resistance of staff in some hospitals – operating under the control of religious bodies but funded by

---

[136] In February 2014, a report by the UN Committee on the Rights of the Child urged the Vatican to conduct an investigation into the Magdalene laundries, the last of which closed in 1996.

[137] See the 2013 Oscar-nominated film *Philomena*, about an Irish mother forced to give up her son for adoption. Ms Philomena Lee, a teenager in 1952, was consigned to the care of Catholic nuns after she became pregnant, and, like many thousands of other young Irish women, had her baby removed and adopted.

[138] See e.g. Report of the Commission to Inquire into Child Abuse (the Ryan Report), 2009, at www.dcya.gov.ie/documents/publications/Implementation_Plan_from_Ryan_Commission_Report.pdf.

the State – to performing abortions or being involved in IVF and other family-planning procedures, the following warning issued by CEDAW is pertinent:[139]

> It is discriminatory for a State party to refuse to legally provide for the performance of certain reproductive health services for women. For instance, if health service providers refuse to perform such services based on conscientious objection, measures should be introduced to ensure that women are referred to alternative health providers.

One public service that is likely to suffer some turmoil in the immediate future, as a consequence of a clash between the traditional religious ethos and contemporary legal principles of equality and non-discrimination, is adoption. Although adoption is a national public service delivered by the Health Service Executive (HSE) and regulated by the Adoption Board, it has traditionally been dominated by religious organisations, several of which continue to provide services through their registered (religion-specific) adoption agencies. Following the publication of the Adoption (Amendment) Bill 2016 in May of that year, same-sex couples in Ireland have been enabled for the first time to jointly adopt children and step-children. This is likely to trigger the same problems for Irish Catholic adoption agencies as it has for their counterparts in the UK, the USA and elsewhere.

Broadcasting Services

Manifestations of religious belief can take the form of radio or TV broadcasts. Perhaps the most obvious and enduring example of this is the daily two-minute broadcast of "the angelus" by RTÉ, the national radio and television company: this State-sponsored, nationwide, perpetual reminder of the country's Catholic ethos is open to interpretation as institutionalised religious discrimination.

Murphy v. *Ireland*[140] is an interesting case concerning a pastor attached to the Irish Faith Centre, a Bible-based Christian ministry, who wished to transmit an advertisement for his ministry on an independent commercial radio station. This was stopped by the national regulator on the grounds that the planned transmission would be in breach of the public-interest requirement protected by s.10(3) of the Radio and Television Act 1988, a ruling confirmed by both the High Court and the Supreme Court.

---

[139] CEDAW General Recommendation 24 on Women and Health, 1999, at para. 11.
[140] Op. cit.

Subsequently, before the ECtHR, the government defended its position on the basis that:[141]

> religious division had characterised Irish history, a history which included proselytising and the creation of legal and social systems to undermine one religion. That historical context, the current manifestation of religious division in Northern Ireland together with the fact that the vast majority of the Irish population adhered to a religion (indeed, to one dominant religion) entitled the State in 1960 and again in 1988 to apprehend unusual sensitivity to religious issues in contemporary Irish society on the part of adherents of both dominant and minority religions. Given this potentially incendiary situation, the State was entitled to act with caution in conditioning the circumstances in which religious material, and in particular religious advertising, would be made available in the broadcast media.

The ECtHR, ruling in favour of the government, reiterated its established view "that even expressions which could be considered offensive, shocking or disturbing to the religious sensitivities of others fall within the scope of the protection of Article 10, the question for the court being whether any restriction imposed on that expression complies with the provisions of that Article".[142] However, the court:

> considers it reasonable for the State to consider it likely that even a limited freedom to advertise would benefit a dominant religion more than those religions with significantly less adherents and resources. Such a result would jar with the objective of promoting neutrality in broadcasting and, in particular, of ensuring a "level playing field" for all religions in the medium considered to have the most powerful impact.

Given the margin of appreciation accorded to the State in such matters, the ECtHR took the view that the State had demonstrated that relevant and sufficient reasons existed to justify the interference with the applicant's freedom of expression within the meaning of Article 10 of the Convention. Subsequently, the relevant Irish legislation was amended: s.41(4) of the Broadcasting Act 2009 provides that a broadcaster shall not broadcast an advertisement addressing the merits or otherwise of adhering to any religious faith or belief or of becoming a member of any religion or religious organisation.

---

[141] Ibid., at para. 38.   [142] Ibid., at para. 61.

Conclusion

The observation that "religion is still inextricably interwoven with the whole fabric of life in Ireland",[143] while certainly less accurate than when it was made in the last quarter of the twentieth century, retains enough truth to distinguish that nation from its neighbours. The discriminatory leanings of the Constitution towards religion – Christianity in general, and Catholicism in particular – as traditionally defined has permeated and shaped Irish culture. Although this now seems increasingly like a legacy of a rapidly receding era, it continues to colour the nature and application of much Irish law, and is most apparent where religious values conflate with sex and gender issues.

Although this jurisdiction has in place a modern legal framework governing matters of equality and non-discrimination, its established culture, centred around the Catholic religion, together with the continuing overshadowing affect of the Constitution, conspires to perpetuate a level of discrimination prejudicial to those of other religions or of none. Until the current process of piecemeal constitutional amendment succeeds in bringing its provisions into closer alignment with those of the ECHR, there will continue to be areas of social life in which the law fails to provide all Irish citizens with equal protection from religious discrimination.

[143] See Brady, J. C., *Religion and the Law of Charities in Ireland*, Belfast, Northern Ireland Legal Quarterly, 1975, at p. xiii.

7

The United States of America

Introduction

This, the world's third most populous country, with a population estimated at 325 million in 2016, of whom by far the majority are religious, has experienced considerable change in the religious profile of its citizens in recent years. According to the Pew Research Centre,[1] between 2007 and 2014: the Christian proportion of the population slipped from 78.4 to 70.6 per cent, due largely to a decline in the numbers of Catholics and mainline Protestants; while non-Christians rose from 4.7 to 5.9 per cent; and non-believers increased from 16.1 to 22.8 per cent, or from roughly 36 million to 56 million. An interesting finding is the proportion of religious adherents who have changed religions: a total of 34 per cent of adults have a religious identity different from the one in which they were raised; and a quarter of those raised as Christians have ceased their adherence. Also interesting is Prothero's observation, in 2008, that "forty percent of Americans call themselves born-again Christians".[2]

Against that background, this chapter explores contemporary religious discrimination in the USA. Beginning with a brief overview of public policy and the Constitution, it outlines the legal framework relating to religion and religious discrimination, before examining the key principles of freedom of religion, related definitional concepts and the law relating to the manifestation of religion and beliefs. The central importance of the Church/State relationship is assessed as a prelude to a detailed examination of contemporary caselaw relating to religious discrimination in the areas of: symbols, icons, apparel, etc.; the family and associated matters; employment; education; medicine; and service provision.

---

[1] Pew Research Centre, "America's Changing Religious Landscape", at www.pewforum.org/2015/05/12/americas-changing-religious-landscape/.

[2] Prothero, S., *Religious Literacy*, New York, Harper One, 2008 at p. 31.

Public Policy: An Overview

Well before the USA gained independence, religion played a prominent role in shaping its social mores. Since independence, federal public policy as it relates to religion and religious discrimination has been governed by the checks and balances built into the Constitution.

Religion and the Constitution

The Declaration of Rights was proclaimed in Virginia in 1776. The section on religion was crafted by James Madison, who, inspired by the French Revolution, repudiated the institutionalised role of religion in England and set the USA on its own singular path.

The Constitution

The rights and freedoms embedded in the Constitution have formed the legal context for shaping US public policy, a major strand of which has always focused on discrimination – particularly religious, racial and gender – gradually expanding to address the range of incidences of inequality now known to law.

Religious Discrimination and the Constitution

As in all common law jurisdictions, the formative legal foundations of the USA are set in the same mould shaped by a shared Christian heritage.

The First Amendment of the Bill of Rights,[3] adopted in 1791, declares that "Congress shall make no law respecting an establishment of religion, or prohibiting the free exercise thereof". These two clauses – the Establishment Clause and the Free Exercise Clause[4] – are crucial for present purposes. Also relevant are the Speech Clause of the First Amendment and the Fourteenth Amendment, which declares that the states may not "deprive any person of life, liberty, or property, without due process of law" – the courts have held that the protections of the Fourteenth Amendment are fundamental, and therefore extend to the states' due processes of law and provide constitutional protection against religious discrimination.[5]

---

[3] The first ten amendments to the Constitution make up the Bill of Rights.
[4] *The Employment Division (Department of Human Resources of Oregon)* v. *Smith*, 494 US 872 (1990), per Scalia J.
[5] See e.g. *Bolling* v. *Sharpe*, 347 US 497 (1954).

As in other common law jurisdictions, testamentary dispositions subject to a religiously discriminatory condition have long been found to be valid. In *Shapira* v. *Union National Bank*,[6] for example, a father left his money to Israel, his wife and their three sons, subject to the latter being married to Jewish girls or marrying Jewish girls within seven years of their father's demise. The court found that it was dutybound to honour his intentions. Similarly, in *re the Estate of Max Feinberg*,[7] the Illinois Supreme Court upheld a condition in the will of a deceased Chicago dentist which prohibited marriage outside the Jewish faith with the effect of disinheriting his four grandchildren.

Public Policy

US independence brought with it a public policy determined to break with the "established" religion that had underpinned the British Empire and fuelled a history of religious persecution.

Background

It was no coincidence that the "first freedom" listed in the First Amendment was the pledge to uphold religious liberty.[8] This proclamation was intended to assure citizens that, unlike in the European countries from which they and their families had migrated, in the USA all faiths and none would be equally respected and religious discrimination would not be tolerated. The entitlement to hold and profess personal beliefs, free from State interference, has since been treated in law and policy as a right of citizenship.

Religious Discrimination and Contemporary Public Policy

Successive governments have struggled to implement policies intended to balance the constitutional duty to uphold the freedom of religion and prohibit religious discrimination with the need to support the public benefit contribution of religious organisations and the obligation to maintain a relationship of neutrality and non-discrimination with them while doing so. In recent decades, this has played out against a background dominated

---

[6] 39 Ohio Misc. 28, 315 N.E.2d 825 (1974).   [7] (2009) 235 Ill. 2d 256.

[8] Fred Gedicks comments: "Actually, I think it *was* a coincidence … What became the 1st Amendment was actually the 3rd Article of Amendment, after a proposed amendment to the Preamble and another about when Congress could raise its salaries. This was the consequence of Madison's original plan to insert the amendments into the text of the Constitution, rather than gathering them at the end" (note to author, 19 April 2017).

by foreign wars in Muslim countries and by culture wars in the homeland; responding to religiously driven fundamentalism has become a significant public policy theme.

State Agencies for Religious Matters

The USA has an established federal policy and agency infrastructure designed to maintain open relationships between government and religious bodies, while the Civil Rights Division of the Department of Justice has specific responsibility for enforcing federal statutes that prohibit religious discrimination in education, employment, housing, public accommodations and access to public facilities.

In January 2001, President George W. Bush established the White House Office of Faith-Based and Community Initiatives.[9] Later, executive orders created centres for the Office within the Departments of Justice, Labor, Health and Human Services, Housing and Urban Development, Education and Agriculture, as well as at the USAID. Many states have since created Offices of Faith-Based and Community Initiatives and have passed legislation or enacted administrative policy changes to give effect to faith-based initiatives. Critics have argued that this represents a violation of the Establishment Clause. The same administration also launched the Charitable Choice initiative; intended to replace public welfare benefit entitlement with non-profit and privatised service provision, it provided direct government funding to religious organisations to facilitate their provision of social services.[10] Implemented primarily through a variety of executive orders issued by President Clinton, Charitable Choice was made part of the Children's Health Act of 2003 by President George W. Bush. Most recently, the Obama administration announced an expansion of government funding for "faith-based initiatives".[11]

In July 2013, the White House issued a National Strategy on Religious Leader and Faith Community Engagement, with objectives that included advancing pluralism and human rights, particularly the protection of religious freedom. At the same time, it established the Office of Religion and Global Affairs to advise the Secretary of State on policy matters as they relate to religion. That Office now accommodates the Office of

---

[9] This was rechristened by the Obama administration as the White House Office of Faith-based and Neighborhood Partnerships.

[10] See Executive Order No. 13 279, 67 Fed. Reg. 77141 (12 December 2002).

[11] President Obama's White House Office of Faith-based and Neighborhood Partnerships developed a comprehensive partnership guide, "Partnerships for the Common Good".

International Religious Freedom, established to promote religious freedom as a core objective of US foreign policy, and is headed by an Ambassador-at-Large for International Religious Freedom.

Domestic Policy

While State neutrality towards religion now forms the backdrop to contemporary domestic policy, it would be naïve to overlook the lengthy history of sporadic terrorist attacks conducted by religiously inspired ideological groups[12] or lone extremists,[13] the experience of dealing with nilihistic religious communities[14] or the impact of the 9/11 atrocity in 2001 on that policy, or their combined influence in shaping contemporary homeland security measures. Fundamentalism, often directed with lethal consequences against those whose conduct is seen as "sinful", has been a feature of US society for some time.

The principal domestic security measure taken by the US government following the 9/11 terrorist attacks was the USA Patriot Act 2001. This comprehensive statute substantially revised dozens of existing laws to allow the security agencies to take invasive measures, including giving them powers of search and surveillance, detention and seizure of property. The Detainee Treatment Act 2005 denied those detained without trial by the military in Guantanamo Bay access to the federal justice system, thereby allowing the continued inhuman treatment of several hundred detainees.[15] Given that foreign policy since 9/11 has been dominated by security concerns centred on Muslim countries, it is unsurprising that many Muslims within the USA perceived the new domestic counter-terrorist measures as being applied in a religiously discriminating fashion, largely directed towards them; this perception was reinforced by the early 2017 ban on anyone with nationality or dual nationality in respect of seven named Muslim countries from entering the USA.

---

[12] See, for example, the "Covenant, The Sword, and the Arm of the Lord", the "Aryan Nations", the "Jewish Defence League" and the "Army of God", which launched a series of bombings against abortion clinics, an LGBT night club, etc. in the 1990s.

[13] See the many lethal lone gunman attacks on abortion clinics, LGBT night clubs and religious centres, such as: the assault by Timothy McVeigh, a Christian nationalist, on the Oklahoma City federal building in 1995; the Wisconsin Sikh temple attack in 2012; the Boston Marathon bombing in 2013; the San Bernadino attack in 2015; and the Orlando night club attack in 2016.

[14] For example: the mass suicides of "Heaven's Gate" in California in 1997 and the "People's Temple" in Guyana in 1978; and the Branch Davidians and the "Waco siege" in 1993.

[15] Notwithstanding the USSC decision in *Boumediene* v. *Bush* 553 US 723 (2008) that detainees at Guantanamo Bay have a constitutional right to habeas corpus.

Foreign Policy

Clearly, the 9/11 terrorist attacks on the World Trade Center and the Pentagon must be viewed within a religious discrimination frame of reference. The strike against these most iconic structures by al Qaeda Muslim extremists – with links to the Taliban in Afghanistan and Wahhabism in Saudi Arabia – seemed intended to demonstrate the rising power of Muslim fundamentalism, to rally others to that cause and to point to what was seen as representing the biggest threat to their religion and culture. Undoubtedly, provoking the ensuing conflict as a means of reinforcing solidarity among their followers and sharpening religious/cultural differences with Western society was also a factor.

The Agency for International Development (USAID),[16] the world's largest humanitarian agency, makes a significant contribution to alleviating human suffering, but this assistance is made conditional upon recipients of federal funds being in agreement with government policy.[17] As US international policy has for at least the past fifteen years been dominated by its counter-insurgency strategy in Iraq, Afghanistan and many other Muslim countries, the citizens of these countries have long felt themselves to be doubly disadvantaged relative to others in need. Currently, the Global Counterterrorism Forum platform, with thirty founding members, led by the USA, promotes a strategic, long-term approach to dealing with international terrorism by mobilising resources to address related issues.

Contemporary Law Governing Religious Discrimination

The overarching provisions of the Constitution, particularly its Bill of Rights, provide a framework for the law relating to religious discrimination, and any issues arising are regulated through the courts and Commissions, with ultimate recourse to the United States Supreme Court (USSC).

The International Framework

The USA was a leading nation in ensuring the adoption of the UDHR, and in recent decades it has become a signatory nation to most of the ten core international human rights instruments, some with optional protocols. In 2010, it declared its support for the United Nations Declaration on the

---

[16] See www.usaid.gov/documents/1870/usaid-policy-framework-2011-2015.
[17] See *Agency for International Development et al. v. Alliance for Open Society International, Inc. et al.*, 570 US (2013).

Rights of Indigenous Peoples. It has also signed and ratified ICERD and has signed but not ratified CEDAW, the Convention on the Rights of the Child and the International Convention on Economic, Social, and Cultural Rights.

The International Covenant on Civil and Political Rights (ICCPR)

The USA has signed and ratified the ICCPR, thereby undertaking to provide protection against religious discrimination through Articles 2(1) and 26 and to review its progress through the mandatory Universal Periodic Review procedure.

International Reports

In 2015, at the second Universal Periodic Review, concerns were expressed regarding the increasing restrictions on women's right to abortion in some states,[18] and there were direct challenges regarding the abortion restrictions that the USA periodically imposes on the disbursement of its foreign aid. The UNHRC has expressed concern regarding the lack of free prior and informed consent of Indigenous People when decisions are taken in relation to issues such as sacred sites and mineral extraction on their lands.[19]

The Domestic Framework

Protection is afforded domestically, on a federal basis, mainly through the Constitution: by the Free Exercise Clause of the First Amendment and by the Equal Protection and Due Process Clauses of the Fourteenth Amendment.

The Religious Land Use and Institutionalised Persons Act 2000

This statute includes a section protecting individuals, houses of worship and other religious institutions from discrimination in zoning and landmarking laws and a section protecting the religious rights of persons confined to institutions, such as prisoners. It amended the 1993 Act by redefining an exercise of religion as any exercise "whether or not compelled by, or central to, a system of religious belief", which is to be "construed in favor of a broad protection of religious exercise, to the maximum extent permitted by the terms of this chapter and the Constitution".

---

[18] See www.wired.com/2014/03/united-nations-human-rights-committee-considers-report-united-states/.

[19] Ibid.

This was upheld by the USSC in *Gonzales* v. *O Centro Espirita Beneficente Uniao do Vegetal*,[20] which emphasised that in establishing the existence of a "compelling interest" that would justify interfering with an exercise of religion, the burden of proof always rested on the government, and that if, as in this case, the evidence were in equipoise, the court must rule against the government.

The International Religious Freedom Act 1998

This requires the State Department to focus its international intervention on the humanitarian objectives of denouncing persecution and saving victims.

The Religious Freedom Restoration Act 1993 (RFRA)

The RFRA, a legislative response to the USSC ruling in *Employment Division* v. *Smith*,[21] prohibits federal government from applying its laws in a way that substantially burdens a person's religious conduct, and requires all federal laws to satisfy a "compelling interest test" in circumstances where the protection of national security or of human life is at risk.[22] The prohibition applies "even if the burden results from a rule of general applicability", except when the compelling interest test can be satisfied by demonstrating "that application of the burden to the person (1) is in furtherance of a compelling government interest; and (2) is the least restrictive means of furthering that compelling governmental interest".[23]

The Civil Rights Act 1964: Title VII

This federal legislation prohibits employers with fifteen or more employees from discriminating against employees or prospective employees on specified grounds, including religion, and also requires employers to "reasonably accommodate" the religious practices of employees, provided that this does not cause the employer "undue hardship". As the USSC has pointed out:[24]

> Title VII does not demand mere neutrality with regard to religious practices – that they be treated no worse than other practices. Rather, it gives them favored treatment, affirmatively obligating employers not "to fail or refuse to hire or discharge any individual ... because of such individual's

---

[20] 546 US 418 (2006).   [21] Op. cit.

[22] The non-applicability of the RFRA to state laws was confirmed in *City of Boerne* v. *Flores*, 521 US 507 (1997).

[23] Reference 42 US Code 2000bb, s.3(a) and (b).

[24] *Equal Employment Opportunity Commission (EEOC)* v. *Abercrombie & Fitch Stores Inc.*, 575 US (2015), per Scalia J at p. 7.

"religious observance and practice" ... Title VII requires otherwise-neutral policies to give way to the need for an accommodation.

Further, in *Trans World Airlines, Inc.* v. *Hardison*,[25] the USSC interpreted Title VII to require employer accommodation only if the cost of doing so was *de minimis*.

Other Legislation

The US Commission on International Religious Freedom and the Ambassador for that Commission, both of which were established by the International Religious Freedom Act 1998, have been influential. There are also a number of federal statutes (and much state-specific legislation), some quite dated, that address matters of equality and diversity. In 2013, the Islamic Society of North America – the largest Muslim organisation in the USA – declared its approval of the Employment Non-Discrimination Act (ENDA), adding its name to an interfaith coalition.

Courts and Tribunals

In the USA, issues of alleged religious discrimination are exclusively domestic matters that are very largely heard and resolved in federal and state courts and administrative proceedings, with recourse on appeal to the USSC.

International

Religious discrimination cases in the USA are not amenable to an appeal process outside the country.

Domestic

The USSC is vested with ultimate appellate jurisdiction over all US courts. Through the course of its very many rulings on religious matters, this court has defined the key concepts and formulated and applied the principles that have become central to the law relating to religion and religious discrimination. Each state has its own judicial and regulatory system.

The Equal Employment Opportunity Commission (EEOC)   This federal agency administers and enforces civil rights laws, and as such is the regulatory body for matters arising under Title VII of the Civil Rights Act

----

[25]   432 US 63 (1977).

1964. It determines all complaints of discrimination based on religion, and other statutorily prescribed indices of inequality. Many states have equivalent agencies with a right of appeal to the courts (which adjudicate on points of law) and, ultimately, to the USSC.

Freedom of Religion and Beliefs: The Principle and the Law

Gedicks has asserted that "freedom of religion in the United States is less a liberty right than an equality right",[26] and this would seem to be borne out by the weight of caselaw which addresses the manifestation of belief as one of a flux of what can be competing rights – most often to do with privacy, gender and sexual orientation.

Definitions

While it has been said that "the theistic theme has always been well to the fore in definitions of religion in American cases",[27] nonetheless the courts in the USA moved away from reliance upon a belief in one "Supreme Being" as the defining characteristic of "religion" earlier than their UK counterparts.

"Religion"

An exclusively theistic approach was rejected in 1961 by Black J in *Torcaso* v. *Watkins*[28] when the USSC struck down a Maryland law requiring officials to declare a belief in God in order to hold office in that state and referred to a list of what could be termed "religions" – including "Buddhism, Taoism, Ethical Culture, Secular Humanism and others". In *Fellowship of Humanity* v. *County of Alameda*,[29] the court identified four characteristics of religion: "a belief not necessarily referring to supernatural power, a cult involving a gregarious association openly expressing the belief, a system of moral practice resulting from adherence to the belief, and an organization within the cult designed to observe the tenets of the belief".

---

[26] See Gedicks, F. M., "The Permissible Scope of Legal Limitations on the Freedom of Religion or Belief in the United States", *Emory International Law Review*, 2005, vol. 19, at p. 1187. See also Kurland, P., *Religion and the Law: Of Church and State and the Supreme Court*, Chicago, IL, University of Chicago Press, 1961.

[27] Picarda, H., *The Law and Practice Relating to Charities*, 3rd edn, London, Butterworths, 1999, at p. 73.

[28] 367 US 488 (1961).   [29] 153 Cal. App. 2d 673 (1957).

"Beliefs"

The shift from reliance upon the traditional theistic definition was furthered by: *United States* v. *Seeger*,[30] in which the court defined a "religious belief" as one that included "a sincere and meaningful belief which occupies in the life of its possessor a place parallel to that filled by the God of those admittedly qualifying for the exemption"; *Welsh* v. *United States*,[31] when the USSC held that the definition of "religion" is not dependent on belief in a "Supreme Being"; and *Wooley* v. *Maynard*,[32] when "belief" was held to include mere written or verbal affirmations or other manifestations of what one does (or does not) believe. In *United States* v. *Meyers*,[33] as Shah points out, the court found that religious organisations generally exhibit: ultimate ideas, metaphysical beliefs, a moral or ethical system, comprehensiveness of beliefs and the accoutrements of religion.[34] Although they were clear that "religious beliefs need not be acceptable, logical, consistent, or comprehensible to others in order to merit First Amendment protection",[35] there were limits to what the courts were prepared to accept as constituting "religion" or "belief". In *Brown* v. *Pena*,[36] the court summarily rejected a plaintiff's religious discrimination claim based upon his "personal religious creed" that Kozy Kitten People/Cat Food contributed significantly to his state of well being, and thus to his overall work performance, by increasing his energy; this was dismissed as a mere personal preference. It then cited three factors to determine whether a belief is religious:[37] (1) whether the belief is based on a theory of "man's nature or his place in the Universe"; (2) which is not merely a personal preference but has an institutional quality about it; and (3) which is sincere. Unique personal moral preferences cannot be characterised as religious beliefs. Neither, as was demonstrated in *Cloutier* v. *Costco Wholesale Corp.*,[38] can body piercings; it was then argued, unsuccessfully, that these were a manifestation of beliefs required by the "Church of Body

---

[30] 380 US 163, 186 (1965).   [31] 398 US 333 (1970).

[32] 430 US 705, 713 (1977). See also *Malnak* v. *Yogi* (1979), 592 F (2d) 197.

[33] 906 F. Supp. 1494, 1501 (D. Wyo. 1995).

[34] Shah, A., "The Impact of *Gonzales* v. *O Centro Espirita Beneficente Uniao do Vegetal*, 546 US 418 (2006)", at www.lawandreligion.com/sites/law-religion/files/Impact-of-Gonzales-Shah.pdf, p. 25.

[35] *Thomas* v. *Review Bd of Indiana Employment Security Div.*, 450 US 707 (1981) at p. 714.

[36] 441 F. Supp. 1382 (D.C. Fla. 1997), aff'd, 589 F.2d 1113 (5th Cir. 1979).

[37] See *Brown* v. *Dade Christian Schools, Inc.*, 556 F.2d 310, 324 (5th Cir. 1977) (dissent).

[38] 390 F. 3d 126 (1st Cir. 2004).

Modification". In *Peterson* v. *Wilmur Communications, Inc.*,[39] the plaintiff's white supremacist belief system, called "Creativity", was deemed to be a religion within the meaning of Title VII because it "functions as religion in [his] life". However, in *Swartzentruber* v. *Gunite Corp.*,[40] it was held that membership in the Ku Klux Klan (KKK) did not qualify as religious belief; the employee had suffered harassment not because of his religious beliefs but because of his self-identification as a member of the KKK, which is "political and social in nature".[41]

The liberties and rights latent in the First Amendment – specifically those practices and privileges associated with manifesting "beliefs" – were the subject of USSC scrutiny in *Employment Division* v. *Smith*.[42] In this case, Native Americans dismissed from their jobs for the illegal use of peyote (which they claimed was an important aspect of a ceremony associated with their religion) found they were unable to claim unemployment benefits and sought to have their conviction overturned on grounds that essentially rested on alleged religious discrimination. As already mentioned, the decision to uphold the conviction established the principle that government could impose legal restrictions upon religious freedom provided the law was neutral and applied to all persons equally. This led to the introduction of the RFRA and, subsequently, to the ruling in the analogous case of *Gonzales*,[43] which upheld a law prohibiting the importation of a sacramental tea (an hallucinogenic) used for similar purposes. An important aspect of that judgment (see later) was the judicial acknowledgement that the "RFRA requires the government to demonstrate that the compelling interest test is satisfied through application of the challenged law to the person . . . the particular claimant whose sincere exercise of religion is being substantially burdened".[44] This denotes an emphasis upon the particular person's burden, not the burden on society; but it must still satisfy the test in *Brown* v. *Pena* by demonstrating the veracity of a claimed sincere belief. This both greatly complicates the law relating to religion and (necessarily) religious discrimination, and also brings it into closer alignment with the corresponding interpretation currently prevailing in the UK and in the ECtHR. Nonetheless, it will be of little assistance to a defendant who seeks to shield their illegal actions by protests that they believed these to

---

[39] 205 F. Supp. 2d 1014 (E.D. Wis. 2002).
[40] 99 F. Supp. 2d 976 (N.D. Ind. 2000).
[41] See *Slater* v. *King Soopers, Inc.*, 809 F. Supp. 809 (D. Colo. 1992).   [42] Op. cit.
[43] *Gonzales* v. *O Centro Espirita Beneficente Uniao do Vegetal*, op. cit.
[44] Ibid., at pp. 419–420.

be a permissible means of giving effect to their religious beliefs – as in *S.D. v. M.J.R.*,[45] where a Muslim husband was convicted of sexually assaulting his wife despite a plea that his beliefs negated the wilful intent necessary for him to have committed a crime.

"Race", "Caste" and Indigenous People

The histories of the ignominious treatment of Indigenous People in the USA, Canada and Australia are not dissimilar: abuse and containment on reservations; a policy of enforced assimilation involving the use of boarding schools; and the outlawing of language and culture. Again, in keeping with their counterparts in Australia and Canada, a history of persecution followed by exploitation and then neglect has left Native Americans often impoverished, with scant recognition given in law to their beliefs and customs, and with a greatly weakened sense of cultural identity. Not until the Freedom of Religion Act 1978 was State-enforced religious discrimination – the threat of imprisonment for practising religious rituals – finally removed; although, arguably (see later), it continues to be manifested in court cases regarding matters such as the ceremonial use of eagle feathers and peyote.

Manifesting Religion or Belief and Free Speech

Permissible constraints on constitutional guarantees of freedom of action, particularly as regards the freedoms of religion, speech and association – and their inter-relationship – have generated centuries of caselaw and a vast body of academic work, which cannot be done justice here. Nor does space permit an analysis of the extent to which home-grown Islamic violence – such as the 2016 attack on servicemen and women by a Muslim US soldier[46] – can be legitimately interpreted as a manifestation of religious discrimination.

The religious clauses of the First Amendment confer both a freedom to believe and a freedom to act, the former being absolute, the latter not.[47] The distinction has been the subject of much litigation, starting

---

[45] 415 N.J. Super. 417, 427–29, 431 (N.J. Super. Ct. App. Div. 2010).

[46] On 5 November 2009, thirteen people were killed and more than thirty injured in a mass shooting at Fort Hood in Texas by a US Army major claiming allegiance to Islamic militants.

[47] See further Pepper, S., "Reynolds, Yoder, and Beyond: Alternatives for the Free Exercise Clause", *Utah Law Review*, 1981, vol. 309.

with *Reynolds* v. *United States*,[48] when the USSC, in a landmark decision, refused to grant an appeal against a conviction for polygamy because to do so would "make the professed doctrines of religious belief superior to the law of the land, and in effect . . . permit every citizen to become a law unto himself".[49] In *Heffron* v. *International Society for Krishna Consciousness*,[50] manifesting beliefs took the form of distributing pamphlets at a fair in defiance of a state ordinance prohibiting such behaviour, as it would interfere with the orderly movement and control of crowds. The ordinance was upheld: even if the plaintiff's peripatetic solicitation was part of a church ritual, it did not entitle church members to solicitation rights in a public forum superior to those of members of other religious groups that raise money but do not purport to ritualise the process. The judiciary adopted much the same approach towards the illegal use of peyote[51] and illegal hunting of eagles by Native Americans:[52] recognising such activities as authentic manifestations of religion or belief, but upholding the right of state governments to prohibit them as part of uniform laws of general application.

Following the introduction of the RFRA and the "compelling reason" of the "highest order" test, the USSC developed a more affirmative approach towards defending manifestations of sincerely held beliefs.[53] Twenty years after *Heffron*, in *Watchtower Bible and Tract Society of New York* v. *Village of Stratton*,[54] the court considered town ordinances which made it a misdemeanor to engage in door-to-door advocacy without first registering with town officials and receiving a permit. Jehovah's Witnesses argued that these ordinances violated their First Amendment right to canvass door-to-door as part of their religious belief that they should share the Gospel with others. The USSC agreed and stated that the ordinances were "offensive, not only to the values protected by the First Amendment, but to the very

---

[48] 98 US (8 Otto.) 145 (1878).

[49] (1879) 98 US 145, at p. 167; 25 Law Ed 244, at p. 250.

[50] 452 US 640 (1981). See also *Int'l Society for Krishna Consciousness Inc* v. *Lee*, 505 US 672 (1992).

[51] *Myke Freeman* v. *State of Florida*, Department of Highway Safety and Motor Vehicles Case No. 2002CA2828 (9th Cir.).

[52] *US* v. *Friday*, 2006 WL 3592952 (D. Wyo. Oct. 13, 2006).

[53] See Currier, P., "*Freeman* v. *State of Florida*: Compelling State Interests and the Free Exercise of Religion in Post September 11th Courts", *Catholic University Law Review*, Spring 2004, vol. 53.

[54] 122 S. Ct. 2080 (2002).

notion of a free society".[55] Again, in *Gonzales*,[56] the USSC ruled that the government – in prohibiting the importation of a sacramental tea required for manifesting the beliefs of a Brazilian church – had failed to meet the burden imposed by the 1993 Act and demonstrate that its intervention served a compelling government interest; therefore, the prohibition was invalid.

Free Speech and Freedom of Association

Constitutionally framed in the First Amendment[57] by clauses guaranteeing the free exercise of religion and of free speech, the law governing constraints upon the dissemination of religious views[58] has been the subject of continuous judicial probing in the USA,[59] particularly in respect of religious speech by Jehovah's Witnesses.[60] The USSC has ruled that laws which compel public disclosure of information that could attract threats or harassment would breach the free speech clause of the First Amendment,[61] and such constraints have been extended to include the expression of views judged to be obscene or sexually offensive.

As the USSC declared in *Roberts* v. *United States Jaycees*:[62] "implicit in the right to engage in activities protected by the First Amendment" is "a corresponding right to associate with others in pursuit of a wide variety of political, social, economic, educational, religious, and cultural ends", but this does not permit exclusion on the basis of criteria unrelated to an association's purpose – e.g. on the basis of gender. As subsequently clarified in *Hurley* v. *Irish American Gay, Lesbian and Bisexual Group of Boston*,[63] this rule does permit the exclusion of those whose membership would seriously compromise an association's purpose (see later).

---

[55] Ibid., at p. 2087.

[56] *Gonzales* v. *O Centro Espirita Beneficente Uniao do Vegetal*, op. cit.

[57] See the Virginia Statute of Religious Freedom 1777, drafted by Thomas Jefferson, guaranteeing freedom of religion to all, endorsed by the USSC in *Reynolds* v. *United States*, op. cit.

[58] See the "clear and present danger" cases.

[59] See e.g. *Good News Club* v. *Milford Central School*, 533 US 98 (2001); *Rosenberger* v. *Rector and Visitors of Univ. of Va.*, 515 US 819 (1995); *Capital Square Review and Advisory Bd* v. *Pinette*, 515 US 753 (1995); *Lamb's Chapel* v. *Center Moriches Union Free Sch. Dist.*, 508 US 384 (1993); *Bd of Educ.* v. *Mergens*, 496 US 226 (1990); and *Widmar* v. *Vincent*, 454 US 263 (1981).

[60] See e.g. *Marsh* v. *Alabama*, 326 US 501 (1946); *W. Va. State Bd Educ.* v. *Barnette*, 319 US 624 (1943); *Martin* v. *City of Struthers*, 319 US 141 (1943); *Cox* v. *New Hampshire*, 312 US 569 (1941); and *Cantwell* v. *Connecticut*, 310 US 296, 309–310 (1940).

[61] *Brown* v. *Socialist Workers Party*, 459 US 87 (1982)   [62] 468 US 609 (1984).

[63] 515 US 557 (1995). See further *Boy Scouts of America* v. *Dale*, 530 US 640 (2000).

Blasphemy

Nationally, blasphemy laws in the USA have been deemed unconstitutional, but they remain on the statute books in some states. In *Joseph Burstyn, Inc.* v. *Wilson*,[64] the USSC held that:

> the State has no legitimate interest in protecting any or all religions from views distasteful to them ... It is not the business of government in our nation to suppress real or imagined attacks upon a particular religious doctrine

No one has been jailed in the USA for blasphemy since 1838.

Conscientious Objection

The history of the law relating to the treatment of US citizens who, on religious grounds, refuse to bear arms on behalf of their country probably begins in the early nineteenth century, when many states exempted Quakers and other religious objectors from military service by statute. During World War I, imprisonment and harsh punishment was meted out to Hutterites, Mennonites and others who refused to serve. By World War II, this approach had been moderated to one of mandatory public service work in camps. In *Gillette* v. *United States*,[65] the USSC broadened the definition of "conscientious objector" to include any person with "no particular sectarian affiliation or theological position ... who has deeply held beliefs that cause them to oppose participation in war in any form".

Proselytism

Proselytism finds stronger recognition in the USA than elsewhere due to the protection offered by the First Amendment – although this will be breached if federal funds are used for that purpose.[66] Otherwise, any impairment of the right to distribute pamphlets – religious or otherwise, and even anonymously – is contrary to the First Amendment's Free Speech Clause, as was recognised in *McIntyre* v. *Ohio Elections Comm'n*.[67] Where, however, as in *Heffron* v. *International Society for Krishna Consciousness*,[68] such distribution would interfere with the State's legitimate interest in ensuring public health and safety, then a state ordinance preventing this so as to allow for control of crowds at a fair will be upheld. When the

---

[64] 343 US 495 (1952). [65] 401 US 437 (1971), per Marshall J.
[66] See *Hein* v. *Freedom From Religion Foundation*, 551 US 587 (2007).
[67] 514 US 334 (1995).
[68] Op. cit. See also *Int'l Society for Krishna Consciousness Inc* v. *Lee*, op. cit.

proselytism becomes harassment, as in *Ng* v. *Jacobs Engineering Group*,[69] the normal civil liberties of others will be upheld. In that case, an evangelical Christian, whose religious beliefs compelled her to share those beliefs with her co-workers in order to save them, persisted in using company equipment and facilities for religious proselytising. When eventually fired, she filed a claim for religious discrimination based on her employer's failure to accommodate her religious beliefs and practices. The court found in favour of the employer: it considered that the company could potentially be liable for religious harassment claims by the plaintiff's co-workers if she were allowed to continue her proselytising; and it held that Ms. Ng's proselytising violated the company's policies on anti-harassment and e-mail use.

Discrimination

The law relating to discrimination in the USA has been well tested in the context of racial and gender inequality. At least as regards the latter, this country has arguably shown the way in shaping the key principles that now govern the ever-growing body of jurisprudence in the common law jurisdictions.

Religious Discrimination

Religious discrimination occurs when someone is denied "the equal protection of the laws, equality of status under the law, equal treatment in the administration of justice, and equality of opportunity and access to employment, education, housing, public services and facilities, and public accommodation because of their exercise of their right to religious freedom".[70]

Type Unlike in UK law – with its focus on the distinction between direct and indirect religious discrimination – in the USA, the focus tends to be site-based and in separate blocks of legislation. The Civil Rights Division of the Department of Justice divides the range of relevant laws as follows:[71]

- laws barring discrimination based on religion in employment, public education, housing, credit, and access to public facilities and public accommodations;

---

[69] Super. Ct. No. BC320996, filed 16 October 2006.
[70] US Commission on Civil Rights, 1979: Religious Discrimination: A Neglected Issue; A Consultation Sponsored by the United States Commission on Civil Rights, Washington, DC, 9–10 April 1979.
[71] See www.justice.gov/crt/spec_topics/religiousdiscrimination/.

- the Religious Land Use and Institutionalized Persons Act, which bars zoning authorities from discriminating against houses of worship and religious schools; and
- laws protecting the religious rights of institutionalised persons; and criminal statutes such as the Church Arson Prevention Act making it a federal crime to attack persons or institutions based on their religion, or otherwise interfere with religious exercise.

Exemptions and Exceptions

Government must grant exemptions to religious entities from legislative constraints governing equality and non-discrimination wherever appropriate.

The "Religious" Exemption

The "exemption doctrine" emerged in the 1960s to provide special protection for religion under the Free Exercise Clause, as this seemed a permissible way of balancing the special disabilities imposed on religious activity under the Establishment Clause. It empowered courts to excuse individuals from complying with a law if they could show that the law unduly burdened their sincere religious practices, unless the government could show that mandating uniform obedience to the law was required by a compelling interest that could not be protected in any less-intrusive manner.[72] In practice, the court rejected most exemption claims.[73]

In 1987, the USSC, in *Corp. of Presiding Bishop of Church of Jesus Christ of Latter-Day Saints* v. *Amos*,[74] upheld the constitutionality of a law permitting religious organisations to exercise a religious preference when making employment decisions. An exemption was held to apply only to those organisations whose "purpose and character are primarily religious". This often refers to the tax-exemption status of such organisations, perhaps particularly with reference to property tax.[75] By the 1980s, it had seemed that the exemption was being narrowly interpreted: religious entities were not as a matter of course able to claim immunity from state laws intended to have universal application.[76] This was underlined by

---

[72] See Greene, A., "The Political Balance of the Religion Clauses", *Yale Law Journal*, 1993, vol. 102, pp. 1611–1644.

[73] See e.g. *Thomas* v. *Colins*, 323 US 65 S.Ct. 315. 89 L.Ed. 430.

[74] 483 US 327, 329, 339 (1987).

[75] See e.g. *Provena Covenant Medical Centre* v. *Department of Revenue*, Docket No. 107328 (Ill. 18 March 2010).

[76] For example, in *Alamo Foundation* v. *Secretary of Labor*, 471 US 290 (1985). See also *United States* v. *Lee*, 455 US 252 (1982).

the USSC, in *Employment Division* v. *Smith*,[77] when it ruled that religion could not be used to shield professed religious adherents from the consequences of engaging in a prohibited activity. Following the introduction of the RFRA in 1993, the USSC developed a more affirmative approach to the exemption in rulings which emphasised that the burden of proof continued to rest firmly upon federal government to satisfy the "compelling interest" test established in *Sherbert* v. *Verner*[78] (see later) if it was to justify any law that interfered with religious organisations. The *Smith* decision, however, has not been wholly legislatively overturned: it remains the case that religion does not give a blanket indemnity from the requirements of neutral laws of general applicability – there remains an onus on the entity claiming exemption to show evidence both of religious status and of the extent to which the entity functionally gives effect to it – but the RFRA and associated caselaw have undoubtedly imposed severe restrictions upon its scope. The decision in *Gonzalez*[79] introduced further complications by ruling that in calculating whether a compelling interest is justified, the government should take into account the sincere belief of those likely to be affected: their subjective perception of what constituted a religious belief was to be the benchmark, which would vary from case to case.[80] The RFRA, it has been said, "forces courts into the awkward position of assessing the sincerity of a group's religious beliefs and then carving out exceptions to federal statutes in order to accommodate these beliefs".[81] In addition, the exemption has been further restricted to protect only those activities of a religious organisation which are religious in nature.[82]

However, in *Burwell* v. *Hobby Lobby*[83] (see later), the USSC greatly extended the potential scope of the religious exemption by ruling that commercial entities, if "closely held" (i.e. with few shareholders whose shares are not traded on public markets), were equally eligible. It then acknowledged "worries about forcing the federal courts to apply the RFRA to a host of claims made by litigants seeking a religious exemption from generally applicable laws . . . (citing the ruling in *Smith*)", but nevertheless asserted "Congress, in enacting RFRA, took the position that 'the compelling interest test as set forth in prior Federal court rulings is a workable test for striking sensible balances between religious liberty and competing

---

[77] Op. cit.   [78] 374 US 398 (1963).   [79] 546 US 418 (2006).
[80] See *Multi Denominational Ministry of Cannabis and Rastafari, Inc.* v. *Gonzales*, 474 F. Supp. 2d 1133 (N.D. Cal. 2007).
[81] Ibid., at 1145.
[82] *Redhead* v. *Conference of Seventh-Day Adventists*, 440 F. Supp. 2d 211 (EDNY 2006).
[83] 573 US 134 S.Ct. 2751 (2014).

prior governmental interests'... The wisdom of Congress's judgment on this matter is not our concern".[84] In so widening the scope of the religious exemption, the USSC has, arguably, correspondingly increased the potential for it to be used to religiously discriminate against the interests of others: there are many commercial entities, such as the Hobby Lobby organisation, whose employees do not share their employers' religious views and stand to be disadvantaged by the constraints the latter are now licensed to impose.[85] As noted by Ginsberg J in her dissenting opinion: "the decision gives commercial companies an opt-out from any law, except tax laws, considered to be incompatible with their sincerely held religious beliefs".[86] It is a decision that, by extending the religious exemption to include hybrid organisations – neither religious nor charitable, but mainstream commercial entities that happen to be owned by those with religious beliefs – sets the USA on a different course to that followed in other common law jurisdictions.

Churches were exempted from the requirement in the Health and Human Services Act 2012 that companies providing health insurance for their employees must include coverage for sterilisation procedures and birth-control medication. However, religious entities delivering public services, such as Catholic hospitals, universities, schools, agencies, etc., were required to allow their employees to freely choose whether or not to avail themselves of such coverage.

The "Charity" Exemption

Based on an interpretation of freedom of religion in the First Amendment, churches generally are presumed to be charitable and are tax-exempt.[87] Many religious congregations and thousands of churches are not required by law to register with the IRS, and choose not to do so.

The "Positive Action" Exception

In *Zelman* v. *Simmons-Harris*,[88] the USSC examined the school voucher scheme, whereby public money is made available to pay for tuition at private schools, including religious schools. It found that the programme

---

[84] Ibid., at p. 54.

[85] Fred Gedicks adds: "It is a point of contention whether its reasoning could be extended to widely held publically traded corporations" (note to author, 19 April 2017).

[86] *Burwell* v. *Hobby Lobby*, op. cit., at pp. 60–61.

[87] See IRS Publication 1828, "Tax Guide for Churches & Religious Organizations", at www .irs.gov/pub/irs-pdf/p1828.pdf.

[88] 536 US 639 (2002).

did not violate the Establishment Clause of the First Amendment, mainly because it was enacted for a secular rather than a religious purpose. The point of allowing parents to use public money to send their children to private schools was to enable parents in poor areas with failing public schools to get a better education for their children. The fact that, in practice, most used their vouchers to transfer to religious schools was incidental: they were entitled to make that choice; it did not mean that government was funneling public dollars to religious institutions. The court found it important that whether any particular secular or religious private school received voucher funds depended on the decision of the individual student and his or her parents or guardians, and not on the government. However, it is hard to avoid concluding that despite the fact that State funding of religious schools is technically unconstitutional, voucher schemes to the same effect are permissible.

Religious Discrimination: Church and State

The framing of the American Constitution and its Bill of Rights sought to ensure, among other things, that federal powers would not interfere with the independence of law-abiding individuals, communities and associational activity.

The Church/State Boundary

The combined effect of "the Establishment Clause"[89] and "the Free Exercise Clause"[90] in the First Amendment was, as declared in *Everson* v. *Board of Education*,[91] to erect "a wall of separation between Church and State. That wall must be kept high and impregnable." The first clause operates to prevent any attempt by Congress to permit the collection of taxes or provision of public money to support any specific religion. The second prohibits Congress from interfering with the manner in which any person chooses to worship.

Protecting Religion from the State

The Establishment Clause "stands at least for the proposition that when government activities touch on the religious sphere, they must be secular

[89] See *Everson* v. *Board of Education of Ewing Township*, 330 US 1 (1947): it cannot "set up a church" or "adopt . . . teach or practice religion" (at pp. 15–16).
[90] See e.g. *Sch. Dist. of Abington Twp., Pa.* v. *Schempp*, 374 US 203, 305 (1963).
[91] Op. cit.

in purpose, evenhanded in operation, and neutral in primary impact".[92] It is deemed violated by government if an action by the latter has the purpose or effect of "endorsing" religion: i.e. favouring religion per se, relative to secularism, or favouring one religion over another. As the USSC explained, such a violation occurred when a Christmas nativity scene was displayed on the staircase of a courthouse: the prohibition against governmental endorsement of religion "preclude[s] government from conveying or attempting to convey a message that religion or a particular religious belief is favoured or preferred".[93] This is a theme that Souter J returned to in *Kiryas Joel*,[94] when he advised that "government should not prefer one religion to another, or religion to irreligion".

The initial landmark cases in this context have been *Reynolds*[95] and *Everson*,[96] in both of which the USSC essentially ruled that government tax revenues could be raised by neutral laws of general application – against the wishes of citizens – and used in support of religion.[97] In *Everson*, the court upheld a reimbursement programme set up to offset the travel expenses incurred by parents whose children attended either public secular schools or Catholic schools; the latter were what gave rise to the litigation, as a complainant alleged that the programme thereby breached the Establishment Clause. The court found that as the programme was a public service benefitting all families – religious and non-religious – equally, it was constitutionally compliant.

In the process of interpreting the Establishment Clause, the USSC has wrestled with guiding principles. The most enduring – and enduringly contentious[98] – of these has been the "Lemon test", formulated by Burger CJ in *Lemon v. Kurtzman*.[99] This concerned the practice of authorities in Rhode Island and Pennsylvania of supplementing the salaries of teachers in religiously based private schools for teaching secular subjects; a practice found to violate the Clause. The test has three parts: first, the statute must have a secular legislative purpose; second, its principal or primary effect must be one that neither advances nor inhibits religion; finally,

---

[92] *Gillette v. United States*, op. cit., per Marshall J.

[93] *County of Allegheny v. American Civil Liberties Union (Greater Pittsburgh Chapter)*, 492 US 573 (1989).

[94] *Kiryas Joel Village School District v. Grumet*, 512 US 687 (1994).

[95] *Reynolds v. United States*, op. cit.

[96] *Everson v. Board of Education of Ewing Township*, op. cit.

[97] See also *Larson v. Valente*, 456 US 228 and *Kiryas Joel Village School District v. Grumet*, op. cit., both of which involved religious discrimination.

[98] See e.g. *Lynch v. Donnelly*, 465 US 668, 679 (1984).   [99] 403 US 602 (1971).

the statute must not foster "an excessive government entanglement with religion". Most recently, the ruling in *Awad* v. *Ziriax*[100] is very much on point. This concerned an attempt to pass legislation in Oklahoma – supported by 70 per cent of voters – to prohibit the use of Shari'a law in state courts, an initiative challenged by a Muslim citizen who asserted that the proposed proscription of Shari'a law interfered with his right to practise his religion. The Tenth Circuit, although upholding the decision of the court of first instance, did so on a different rationale, grounded on the Establishment Clause: by singling out Shari'a law, the statute had breached this Clause, as it had explicitly discriminated between religions and against Muslims. Additionally, the government had failed to satisfy the "compelling interest" test, as it had not identified an actual pressing problem to which the statute proposed an appropriate solution, let alone one in compliance with the minimal intervention rule.

The Free Exercise Clause governs the freedom to manifest religious beliefs (see earlier), and, as declared in *Kedroff*,[101] religious organisations have "power to decide for themselves, free from State interference, matters of church government as well as those of faith and doctrine". Again, *Reynolds* set an early benchmark for assessing the circumstances constituting a breach. This case concerned George Reynolds, a Mormon residing in Utah, who challenged his 1878 polygamy conviction under federal law by arguing that as this marital practice was sanctioned by his religion, the law constituted religious discrimination against Mormons. In rejecting his argument, the USSC applied a distinction between religious belief and religious conduct: while the right to religious belief was absolute, the government had a responsibility to curb religious conduct that conflicted with the broader interests of the community.[102] Nearly a century later, in *Sherbert*,[103] the USSC resolved a dispute concerning a Seventh-Day Adventist denied welfare benefits following her sacking for refusal to work on Saturdays due to religious beliefs, by formulating and narrowly construing a "compelling interest test" for any law licensing State intervention in religious practice. Such a law would be valid only if: it imposed an actual burden on the exercise of the religion in question; there was a "compelling interest" justifying the particular infringement complained of; and there was no reasonable alternative that would achieve State objectives while causing a lesser degree of infringement. This test, as already

---

[100] 670 F 3d 111 (2012).
[101] *Kedroff* v. *St Nicholas Cathedral*, 344 US 94, 116, 73 S.Ct. 143, 97 L.Ed. 120 (1952).
[102] See further Pepper, "Reynolds, Yoder, and Beyond".   [103] *Sherbert* v. *Verner*, op. cit.

mentioned, was severely constrained by the *Smith*[104] ruling that "the right of free exercise ... does not relieve an individual of the obligation to comply with a valid and neutral law of general applicability on the ground that the law proscribes (or prescribes) conduct that his religion prescribes (or proscribes)".[105] The constraints were eased in 1993 by the introduction of the RFRA, which reinforced the protection available to religious organisations from State interference in their affairs.[106] In *Church of Lukumi Babalu Aye, Inc. v. City of Hialeah*,[107] the court was concerned with city ordinances forbidding animal slaughter, except kosher slaughter, within city limits. It found that the ordinances were discriminatory,[108] as they intended to prevent adherents of Santeria from conducting animal sacrifices in accordance with the rites of their religion, and explained: "although a law targeting religious beliefs is never permissible, if the object of the law is to infringe upon or restrict practices because of their religious motivation, the law is not neutral".[109] As the USSC later revealed in *Gonzalez*,[110] the RFRA did more than reinforce the protection then available: it had the capacity to invalidate federal legislation enacted for the health and safety of all American citizens, if it should incidentally infringe some practices of a tiny minority of religious adherents.

Nevertheless, it remains the case that proof must be adduced to show that legislation does in fact unduly burden any such practice. This was demonstrated in *US v. Winddancer*,[111] where the defendant, charged with six separate counts relating to having eagle feathers in violation of federal statutes, claimed he was a Native American and that the government was infringing his religious beliefs. While federal law allows Native Americans an exemption for their religious practices in keeping eagle feathers, the defendant was not part of a recognised Native American tribe and therefore was unable to show that the law burdened his practice of religion. At much the same time, and on much the same issue, the court in *US*

---

[104] *Employment Division v. Smith*, op. cit.   [105] Ibid., at p. 879

[106] See, for example, *Navajo Nation v. US Forest Serv.*, 479 F.3d 1024 (9th Cir. 2007); *Gonzales v. O Centro Espirita Beneficente Uniao do Vegetal*, op. cit.; *Cutter v. Wilkinson*, 544 US 709 (2005); *Tenn. v. Lane*, 541 US 509 (2004); *Kimel v. Fla Bd of Regents*, 528 US 62 (2000); *City of Boerne v. Flores*, op. cit.; and *Swanner v. Anchorage Equal Rights Comm'n*, 513 US 979 (1994).

[107] 508 US (1993).

[108] Fred Gedicks explains that these ordinances are "commonly referred to as a *religious gerrymander* because the patter of application and exemption left only Santeria sacrifices subject to prohibition" (note to author, 19 April 2017).

[109] *Church of Lukumi Babalu Aye, Inc. v. City of Hialeah*, op. cit., at p. 533.

[110] *Gonzales v. O Centro Espirita Beneficente Uniao do Vegetal*, op. cit.

[111] 435 F. Supp. 2d 687 (M.D. Tenn. 2006).

v. *Tawahongva*[112] dismissed the claim of a Native American, charged with possessing golden eagles, that he was entitled to RFRA protection because he did not have standing to bring such a claim. Interestingly, in the more recent case of *Salazar* v. *Buono*,[113] an appeal against a judicial ruling – permitting a large Latin cross at a military monument – was upheld. Concluding a protracted process of litigation, the USSC then upheld the initial proposal that the cross and the land upon which it was erected should be transferred by statute from public to private ownership. This resolution of a fraught issue was viewed by many as compromised because: all options considered seemed to discriminate in favour of a government-assisted solution to protect Christian interests; it entailed a good deal of judicial equivocation as to how government intervention could minimise its accepted necessary infringement of the parties' free-exercise rights; and, arguably, it was not wholly successful in avoiding an entanglement in establishment issues (see later).

Intervention in Church Disputes

A considerable body of caselaw attests to the fact that in the USA, it is impermissible for government to intervene in Church property disputes[114] or to contradict a Church's determination of who can act as its minister:[115] the Free Exercise Clause protects a religious group's right to shape its own faith and mission through its appointments. However, as Gedicks points out, "the courts may decide these cases if they can do so on the basis of religiously neutral, secular principles of law".[116]

As regards church property disputes, the court noted in *Jones* v. *Wolf*[117] that "the First Amendment severely circumscribes the role that civil courts may play in resolving church property disputes . . . it prohibits civil courts from resolving [such] disputes on the basis of religious doctrine and practice". This ruling was in marked contrast to the approach adopted by the English courts, which, instead of regarding such matters as Church business to be resolved by the Church authorities, instead treated them as straightforward property disputes and adjudicated in favour of the faction it found to represent the "true standard of faith".[118]

---

[112] 456 F. Supp. 2d 1120 (D. Ariz. 2006).   [113] 130 S Ct 1803 (2010).

[114] See, for example, *Watson* v. *Jones*, 80 US (13 Wall.) 679 (1871) and *Presbyterian Church* v. *Mary Elizabeth Blue Hull Memorial Presbyterian Church*, 393 US 440, 441, 449–450 (1968).

[115] See, for example, *Watson* v. *Jones*, op. cit.; *Kedroff* v. *St Nicholas Cathedral*, op. cit.; and *Serbian Eastern Orthodox Diocese for United States and Canada* v. *Milivojevich*, 426 US 696.

[116] Note to author, 19 April 2017.   [117] 443 US 595, 602 (1979).

[118] See Corbin, C. M., "The Irony of Hosanna-Tabor Evangelical Lutheran Church and School v. EEOC", *Northwestern University Law Review*, 2015, vol. 106:2, at p. 956.

The existence of a "ministerial exception", grounded in the First Amendment, was established by Title VII of the Civil Rights Act of 1964 and other employment discrimination laws, and by cases such as *Elvig v. Calvin Presbyterian Church*,[119] which confirmed that appointments of ministers and clergy are exclusively matters for determination by religious organisations – thus, the Catholic Church may deny ordination to women – and are completely immune from Title VII challenge. In *Rayburn*,[120] the court found that "if the employee's primary duties consist of teaching, spreading the faith, church governance, supervision of a religious order, or supervision or participation in religious ritual and worship, he or she should be considered 'clergy'".[121] More recently, in *Hosanna-Tabor*,[122] the USSC considered whether the Lutheran Church could avail itself of the exemption in response to an unfair dismissal claim by an employee teacher at one of its religious elementary school who had taught the full secular curriculum, but who also taught daily religion classes, was a commissioned minister and regularly led students in prayer and worship. The court found that the teacher had functioned as a minister – in part because her employers had held her out as a minister with a role distinct from that of its lay teachers, and in part because she held herself to be a minister by accepting the formal call to religious service required for her position – and concluded that her status as such outweighed the secular aspects of her job. Roberts CJ explained that the purpose of the exemption privilege is not limited to hiring and firing decisions made for religious reasons, adding, "we cannot accept the remarkable view that the Religion Clauses have nothing to say about a religious organization's freedom to select its own ministers". The USSC reaffirmed that the Establishment and Free Exercise Clauses bar suits brought on behalf of ministers against their churches claiming termination in violation of employment discrimination laws. It distinguished its *ratio decidendi* from that in *Smith* as follows:[123]

> *Smith* involved government regulation of only outward physical acts. The present case, in contrast, concerns government interference with an internal church decision that affects the faith and mission of the church itself.

Consequently, there is a probability that future legislation will inadvertently cause an increase in religious discrimination. As has been argued,

---

[119] 397 F.3d 790, 790 (9th Cir. 2005).
[120] *Rayburn v. Gen. Conference of Seventh-Day Adventists*, 772 F.2d 1164, 1166 (4th Cir. 1985).
[121] Ibid., at 1169.
[122] *Hosanna-Tabor Evangelical Lutheran Church v. EEOC*, 565 US (2012).
[123] Ibid., at p. 697.

"the combination of *Smith* and *Hosanna-Tabor* means that religious individuals have absolutely no protection from neutral laws of general applicability, even if the laws bar them from participating in a sacrament (the *Smith* rule), while religious institutions may be protected absolutely, even if their acts have no religious basis (the ministerial exception approved by *Hosanna-Tabor*)".[124] However, Gedicks adds: "*Hosanna-Tabor* applies only to ministers ... while churches have been aggressive trying to classify employees as 'ministers', the courts have not given them carte blanche on this".[125]

By way of comment, it seems only fair to note that whether an issue presents as a Church property dispute or a religious organisation's employment dispute, a preliminary task is to determine if the parties can be defined as coming within the religious parameters required by the exemption privilege. This must necessitate some enquiry into the religious status of the organisation and of the parties involved. To that extent, at least, an adjudicating court or other body has to intervene in Church matters – to establish the "religiosity" of both organisation and parties and to analyse the functional roles of those concerned – notwithstanding First Amendment constraints.

The State, Religion and Religious Discrimination

The Christian cultural heritage in this jurisdiction, as in other common law jurisdictions, is undeniable, remains dominant and provides the background against which the requirements of a modern pluralistic society must be asserted.

Balancing Religion and Secularism

"The Establishment Clause prohibits government from abandoning secular purposes in order to put an imprimatur on one religion, or on religion as such, or to favour the adherents of any sect or religious organization."[126] Instead, the State is required to hold a position of neutrality: favouring neither religion nor atheism; ensuring that it does not lend its resources or authority to preference adherents of any particular religion or those of none; and choosing to proceed on the basis of furthering an accommodation of diversity. This, perhaps, may be read subject to Jackson J's caveat

---

[124] Corbin, "The Irony of Hosanna-Tabor", at p. 955.
[125] Note to author, 19 April 2017.
[126] *Gillette* v. *United States*, 401 US 437,450, 91 S.Ct. 828, 836, 28 L.Ed.2d 168 (1971).

"that for good or for ill, nearly everything in our culture worth transmitting, everything which gives meaning to life, is saturated with religious influences".[127]

State Funding of Faith-Based Facilities and Services

As the Aspen Institute has noted, "religiously affiliated colleges and universities, social service agencies, hospitals, and other institutions have been central actors in government-financed human service activities almost from the founding of the republic".[128] However, care is needed to ensure that such government support does not inadvertently give rise to religious discrimination by preferencing one religion relative to another or any religious organisation to the detriment of a secular counterpart.

The aversion to "established" religion in the USA is reflected in a history crammed with legislative and judicial evidence of a determination to keep matters of Church and State separate. The State cannot provide facilities for religious use without giving prohibited support to an institution of religion.[129] This has been particularly evident in the context of government funding of schools, causing the courts to strike down many such funding arrangements.[130] In recent years, the courts have moved towards interpreting the Establishment Clause as permitting funding, but only in a manner that maintains a position of "neutrality".[131] As O'Scannlain J stated in *Spencer* v. *World Vision, Inc.*,[132] the Establishment Clause commands "neutrality among religious groups". This would seem to justify, for example, the government grants that currently provide two-thirds of the funding for Catholic Charities USA and 75 per cent of the funding for the Jewish Board of Family and Children Services, for the non-discriminatory

---

[127] *McCollum* v. *Board of Education*, 333 US 203 (1948), per Justice Jackson at pp. 235–236.

[128] Aspen Institute, *Religious Organizations and Government*, 2001, at p. 5; see further www .aspeninstitute.org/sites/default/files/content/docs/RELIGION.PDF.

[129] *Tilton* v. *Richardson*, 403 US 672 (1971).

[130] See, for example, *Meek* v. *Pittenger*, 421 US 349 (1975), government loans to religious schools; *Wolman* v. *Walter*, 433 US 229 (1977), government loans for services away from the religious school campus; *Illinois ex rel. McCollum* v. *Board of Education of School District*, op. cit., disallowing the use of public buildings for optional religious instruction; *Bowen* v. *Kendrick*, 487 US 589 (1989), disallowing the use of public buildings for optional religious instruction; and *Rosenberger* v. *Rector and Visitors of Univ. of Va.*, op. cit., requiring that equal funding be granted to evangelical Christian groups.

[131] The IRS treatment of churches and religious organizations has been judicially scrutinised to ensure compatibility with the "neutrality principle": see *Walz* v. *Tax Commissioner*, 397 US 664 (1970) and *Committee for Public Education* v. *Nyquist*, 413 US 756 (1973).

[132] 619 F.3d 1109 (9th Cir. 2010). See also *Epperson* v. *Arkansas*, 393 US 97, 103–104 (1968).

provision of contracted services. Nonetheless, such government funding continues to generate contention.

In *Young* v. *Shawnee Mission Med. Ctr.*,[133] the court determined that a religious hospital did not lose its Title VII exemption simply because it received thousands of dollars in federal Medicare payments, because such payments did not "transform [the hospital] into a federally funded institution". In assessing whether or not the State is acting properly when funding faith-based bodies, facilities and services, O'Connor J employed "the Lemon test" in *Mitchell* v. *Helms*,[134] and concluded that religious organisations should monitor and "compartmentalize" government funding received in the form of aid for education programmes (see later). Where the aid is used for secular educational functions, there will be no problem. If, however, the aid flows into the entirety of an educational activity and some "religious indoctrination [is] taking place therein", then that indoctrination "would be directly attributable to the government".[135]

Contention is noticeably acute in relation to programmes whose participants lack true freedom of choice (children and prisoners, in particular[136]), because these can in practice allow government funds to flow along channels that discriminate between recipients and non-recipients on religious grounds. In 2006, the InnerChange Freedom Initiative (IFI), an intensely religious rehabilitation programme delivered under the auspices of the Prison Fellowship Ministries, which required an enrolled prisoner to constantly satisfy an evangelical Christian programme, was found to be "pervasively sectarian".[137] The following year, the civil rights group Freedom from Religion Foundation filed a lawsuit challenging the legality of the White House Office of Faith-Based and Community Initiatives, alleging that any such preferencing of religious organisations breached the Establishment Clause. The resulting decision of the Supreme Court in *Hein* v. *Freedom From Religion Foundation*[138]

---

[133] No. 88-2321-S, 1988 US Dist. LEXIS 12248 (D. Kan. Oct. 21, 1988).

[134] 530 US 793, 120 S Ct 2530 (2000).

[135] See also *Grand Rapids School District* v. *Ball*, 473 US 373, 398–400 (1985).

[136] In recent years, several judges have concluded that children and teenagers, like prisoners, have too few options and too little power to make the voluntary choices the USSC requires when public money flows to programmes involving religious instruction or indoctrination. See *Teen Ranch* v. *UDOW*, 389 F. Supp. 2d 827 (W.D. Mich. 2005) and *Freedom From Religion Foundation* v. *Towey*, No. 04-C-381-S, 2005 US Dist. LEXIS 39444 (W.D. Wis. 11 January 2005).

[137] *Americans United For Separation of Church and State* v. *Prison Fellowship Ministries*, 432 F. Supp. 2d 862 (S.D. Iowa 2006).

[138] Op. cit.

ruled that taxpayers do not have the necessary *locus standi* to challenge the constitutionality of expenditures by the executive branch of the government – a decision that in effect gave the green light to further executive funding of faith-based initiatives.

Christian Symbols/Prayers in State Facilities

While the Christian heritage of the USA is proclaimed on its coinage – "In God we trust" – and in the Pledge of Allegiance – "one nation under God" – it has long been the case that the swearing of an oath or any other type of religious test is prohibited as a requirement for accepting a public post. The USSC affirmed this in *Torcaso* v. *Watkins*,[139] when it unanimously held that Maryland's requirement for a person holding public office to state a belief in God violated the First and Fourteenth Amendments.[140] It had earlier ruled that the same principle applies to prayers or other religious ceremonies in State schools.[141] The importance attached to the need for the State to stay at arm's length from the scholastic environment has been demonstrated in decades of *School Prayer* cases, which established that any memorial service sponsored or organised by a school and involving a prayer would compromise the neutrality of the public education system.[142]

Religious Discrimination: Contemporary Caselaw

Striking the right balance between the interests of the State, different religions and secularists is particularly challenging, in the USA as in all other jurisdictions presently being studied, when this involves: clashes between freedom of religion and other fundamental rights; new forms of belief and ancient ethnic customs competing for recognition with Christianity in contemporary consumerist society; and an increasingly vociferous secularist lobby. All offer myriad opportunities for religious discrimination or permutations thereof.

Religious Conduct, Symbols, Icons, Apparel, etc.

The State may interfere with a manifestation of religious belief by persons with heartfelt attachments to religious customs, costumes, symbols

---

[139] Op. cit.   [140] *Elk Grove Unified School District* v. *Newdow*, 542 US 1 (2004).
[141] *McCollum* v. *Board of Education*, op. cit.
[142] See: *Santa Fe Indep. Sch. Dist.* v. *Doe*, 530 US 290 (2000); *Lee* v. *Weisman*, 505 US 577 (1992); *Wallace* v. *Jaffree*, 472 US 38 (1985); *Sch. Dist. of Abington Twp., Pa.* v. *Schempp*, op. cit.; and *Engel* v. *Vitale*, 370 US 421 (1962).

and rituals only when it has "compelling reason" of the "highest order".
In *Cutter* v. *Wilkinson*,[143] a case involving five Ohio prison inmates with
quite different belief affiliations (two Norse pagans, a Wiccan witch, a
Satanist and an evangelical Christian), the plaintiffs collectively and successfully claimed that their access to ceremonial items and opportunities
for group worship was mandated under the Religious Land Use and Institutionalised Persons Act 2000. More recently, the USSC refused to order
the removal of a 7-foot-tall crucifix, which had stood as a war memorial for seventy years on a dominant rock on federal land in the Mojave
desert,[144] as requested by a plaintiff who claimed to be "deeply offended
by the display of a Latin Cross on government-owned property". Although
the court ultimately ruled in favour of a government statute that ensured
the retention of the commemorative cross by transferring ownership of it
and the land on which it stood to a private party, the powerful dissenting
judgment of Stevens J, joined by Ginsburg and Sotomayor JJ, indicates just
how uncertain and divided the court was:

> it is undisputed that the "[L]atin cross is the preeminent symbol of Chris-
> tianity. It is exclusively a Christian symbol, and not a symbol of any other
> religion." We have recognized the significance of the Latin cross as a sec-
> tarian symbol, and no participant in this litigation denies that the cross
> bears that social meaning. Making a plain, unadorned Latin cross a war
> memorial does not make the cross secular. It makes the war memorial
> sectarian.

Ethnicity/Religion-Specific Customs

The RFRA states that the "government shall not substantially burden a
person's exercise of religion even if the burden results from a rule of
general applicability".[145] It may do so "only if it demonstrates that application of the burden... is in furtherance of a compelling governmental
interest and... is the least restrictive means of furthering that compelling
governmental interest".[146] Such an interest may not be present, as demonstrated in *Lukumi*[147] when the right of Santeria adherents to practise ritual animal sacrifice was upheld. Kennedy J then explained that "religious
beliefs need not be acceptable, logical, consistent or comprehensible to
others in order to merit First Amendment protection".[148]

---

[143] Op. cit.   [144] *Salazar* v. *Buono*, op. cit.   [145] 42 USC, s.2000bb-1(a).
[146] 42 USC, s.2000bb-1(b).
[147] *Church of Lukumi Babalu Aye, Inc.* v. *City of Hialeah*, op. cit.   [148] Ibid., at p. 545.

This test is well established.[149] For example, the USSC has ruled that certain customs, based on religious beliefs, are not compliant with national laws: the use of peyote by Native Americans for religious reasons was a justifiable ground for the State of Oregon to refuse unemployment benefits;[150] and the claim by an Amish employer that he was exempt from paying taxes as this violated his freedom of conscience was held to breach the social security system that must be uniformly applicable to all.[151] When followers of a particular sect choose to place themselves in a position – such as commercial activity – where their religious beliefs clash with established government regulations, they thereby accept the limits that are binding on others in that activity. Even where there is no overt commercial component – as in the previously mentioned "eagle cases", where Native Americans have claimed an entitlement, on grounds of religious belief, to hunt, keep or take the feathers of eagles in contravention of neutral laws of general application – the test requires proof either that the legislation does unduly burden any such practice or that, nonetheless, the government's interest is sufficiently compelling to justify the restriction imposed. So, in *US v. Friday*,[152] where the defendant was charged with taking one bald eagle without asking permission from the Secretary of the Interior, he claimed that as a Native American he was exempt from the charges and that, even if the Bureau of Native Americans did not recognize him as such, the charges should still be dismissed as his actions were protected by the RFRA. The court, having analysed the RFRA claim and citing *Gonzales*, ruled in favour of the defendant, specifically noting that:[153]

> The Government may be able to meet [the compelling interest burden], as the Tenth Circuit considered the protection of bald eagles to be [a compelling interest]. Nonetheless, the RFRA test is not satisfied by generalized assertions.

The same principle grounded the ruling of Ambro J that Eruv Association members had no intrinsic right to add attachments to telephone poles on borough property and that the borough, if it wished, could enact a general, neutral ordinance against all attachments to utility poles that could be enforced against the *eruv*.[154] However, in that instance the borough

---

[149] *Gonzales v. O Centro Espirita Beneficente Uniao do Vegetal*, 126 S Ct 1211, 163 L.Ed.2d 1017 (2006).
[150] *Myke Freeman v. State of Florida*, op. cit.   [151] *United States v. Lee*, 455 US 252 (1982).
[152] Op. cit.   [153] Ibid., at pp. 1–2.
[154] *Tenafly Eruv Association v. Borough of Tenafly* (309 F.3d 144). An *eruv* is an urban area enclosed by a wire boundary which symbolically extends the private domain of Jewish

had not enacted a genuinely general or neutral ordinance, as it permitted a wide variety of attachments to utility poles for non-religious purposes, including posting signs and other items; therefore, it could not selectively exclude attachments for religious purposes. Such cases, dating back to *Reynolds*,[155] are often referenced to demonstrate that religious beliefs cannot trump secular US law and that religious discrimination, in its many and varied forms, will be caught by constitutional and legislative filters along with all other forms of discrimination.

Religious Apparel

While the weight of caselaw affirms that wearing religious apparel is not of itself sufficient to breach the Establishment Clause,[156] there is a good deal of state legislation that explicitly prohibits teachers from doing so in classrooms, the linking of private religious belief to the authority of a public service representative being viewed as compromising for the neutral status of a state school. *United States* v. *Board of Educ. Sch. Dist. Phil.*,[157] for example, was not untypical of a number of cases[158] concerning the wearing of religious apparel, usually by Muslim female teachers, in public schools, contrary to a statute directive that "no teacher in any public school shall wear in said school or while engaged in the performance of his duty as such teacher any dress, mark, emblem or insignia indicating the fact that such teacher is a member or adherent of any religious order, sect or denomination".[159] This case concerned a Muslim teacher who worked as a substitute and full-time teacher in the Philadelphia School District and, pursuant to her beliefs, wore a hijab while teaching. Having been refused the opportunity to teach in a succession of state schools because of her religious clothing, she initiated proceedings alleging religious discrimination. The court, finding that the statute explicitly discriminated against certain practices precisely because they were religious, followed the

---

households into public areas, permitting activities within it that are normally forbidden in public on the Sabbath.

[155] *Reynolds* v. *United States*, op. cit.

[156] See further the US Equal Employment Opportunity Commission (EEOC), "Religious Garb and Grooming in the Workplace: Rights and Responsibilities", at www.eeoc.gov/eeoc/publications/qa_religious_garb_grooming.cfm.

[157] 911, F.2d 882 (3rd Cir. 1990).

[158] See e.g. *Bhatia* v. *Chevron USA Inc.*, 734 F.2d 1382,1384 (9th Cir.1984) and *EEOC* v. *Sambo's*, 530 F. Supp. 86, 89–90 (N.D.Ga.1981).

[159] Section 4(a) of what is commonly referred to as Pennsylvania's Garb Statute 1895. But note the decision of the Supreme Court of Pennsylvania in *Hysong* v. *Gallitzin*, 164 Pa. 629, 30 A. 482 (1894), which held that there was no barrier to garbed Catholic nuns and priests teaching in public schools.

rationale developed in the earlier and very similar case of *Cooper* v. *Eugene School District No. 4J*,[160] in which the plaintiff was a Sikh teacher who wore white clothes and a white turban and whose teaching certificate was revoked when she continued doing so despite repeated warnings. In that case, the findings of the Oregon SC – that "a rule against such religious dress is permissible to avoid the appearance of sectarian influence, favoritism, or official approval in the public school"[161] – were accepted by the USSC, which dismissed the appeal. Consequently, the court adopted the *Cooper* proposition that such statutes permissibly advance a compelling interest in maintaining the appearance of religious neutrality in the public school classroom and do not breach Title VII. Ackerman J stressed the importance of "preventing subtle inculcation of the message that religion is preferred over nonreligion (irrespective of whether that message is intentional or inadvertent) by forbidding one to teach in public schools while clothed in religious raiment keeps public-school classrooms swathed in constitutional neutrality".[162]

Teaching in public schools while clothed in religious raiment may be forbidden, but being taught while so attired is not: this distinction owes something to the absence of any public representative role on the part of the child, and also to the bearing of established caselaw precedents upholding children's right to freedom of expression.[163] *Hearn and United States* v. *Muskogee Public School District*[164] concerned a Muslim girl who was suspended twice from school for wearing a hijab as required by her faith. The court ruled that she was entitled to do so: the school authorities, by singling her out because of her Islamic faith, had intentionally discriminated against her, and the court quoted from the ruling in *Lukumi* that "at a minimum, the protections of the Free Exercise Clause pertain if the law at issue discriminates against some or all religious beliefs".[165]

The same issue is transferable to other settings,[166] as illustrated by the sequence of cases concerning the policy of clothing retailer Abercrombie & Fitch to ban the wearing of the hijab by its Muslim staff and job

---

[160] 301 Or. 358, 723 P.2d 298 (1986).   [161] Ibid., at 723 P.2d at p. 308.

[162] *United States* v. *Board of Educ. Sch. Dist. Phil.*, op. cit., at para. 90.

[163] See, for example, *Tinker* v. *Des Moines Indep. Cmty. Sch. Dist.*, 393 US 503, 506 (1969), pupils wearing black armbands to signify disapproval of Vietnam war; *Chalifoux*, 976 F. Supp. 659 (1997), high school students wearing white rosary beads to signify their Catholicism; and *Alabama and Coushatta Tribes* v. *Big Sandy Schools District et al.*, 817 F. Supp. 1319 (1993), Native American school children with long hair to signify tribal identity.

[164] 020, No. Civ. 03 598-S (E.D. Ok., 2003).

[165] *Church of Lukumi Babalu Aye, Inc.* v. *City of Hialeah*, op. cit., at p. 532.

[166] See e.g. *United States* v. *New York Metropolitan Transit Authority*, No. CV-04 4237 (2004) and *Axson-Flynn* 356 F.3d 1277 (10th Cir. 2004).

applicants. In the absence of any evidence that permitting Muslim employees to wear their hijabs placed an undue hardship on the employers, the latter were found to be guilty of religious discrimination.[167] The USSC made the important point that "Title VII gives favored treatment to religious practices, rather than demanding that religious practices be treated no worse than other practices".[168]

Family-Related Issues

The fundamental freedoms of religion, liberty and personal autonomy provide a constitutional nexus that generates family-related issues centred on matters of individual belief. Abortion, gay marriage and assisted death are among the many topics produced by these tensions which have grown to form the present moral minefield for those with and those without religious belief.

Sexuality

LGBT issues have proven to be very socially divisive in the USA. When this is compounded by Islamic fundamentalism, as would seem to have been the case in the Orlando gay nightclub massacre,[169] it reveals just how potent sexual issues can be in triggering dangerous cultural polarisation. However, even if contentious, not all cultural/sex-related issues are litigated: despite FGM being illegal since 1996, many thousands of young girls are known to suffer this practice every year and there have yet to be any prosecutions.[170]

Marriage, the social institution that traditionally brought sexuality and religious belief into legal alignment, was naturally profoundly challenged by its extension to accommodate same-sex relationships, which indeed did not gain nationwide legal acceptance until the 2015 ruling in *Obergefell* v. *Hodges*.[171] In fact, however, multi-culturalism introduced religion-based complications to this institution many years ago. The basic definition of "marriage" was first tested by the polygamous practices of the Mormons,

---

[167] *Equal Employment Opportunity Commission (EEOC)* v. *Abercrombie & Fitch Stores Inc.*, op. cit.

[168] Ibid., at pp. 2–7.

[169] The June 2016 attack on Pulse – a gay nightclub in Orlando, FL – which left forty-nine dead and fifty-three wounded was perpetrated by a Muslim who proclaimed allegiance to ISIS.

[170] See www.newsweek.com/fgm-rates-have-doubled-us-2004-304773.

[171] 576 US (2015).

then by the prescribed roles and duties of the parties as laid down in religious law for Muslims (*shari'a*) and Jews (*ketubah*). Currently, the difficulty in aligning religiously defined divorce proceedings – particularly the Islamic *mahr* agreements[172] and the Jewish *get* – with statutory requirements can trigger allegations of religious discrimination from both those who believe their cultural traditions are being disrespected by being subordinated to statutory law and those disadvantaged as a consequence of their enforced adherence to those traditions.

While it would be simplistic to suggest that sexuality issues necessarily align with religious belief, it would be naïve to deny that they often do. The closer the alignment, the more likely the issue is to fall into the "religious exemption" frame of reference, which will entail an examination of the beliefs involved. The looser the alignment, the more complex the difficulties, particularly where the entity concerned does not openly profess any particular set of beliefs. For example, *Boy Scouts of America* v. *Dale*[173] concerned the Scouts, an independent ecumenical association, with a moral code derived from the teachings of its principal sponsors – mainly the Catholic, Methodist and Mormon Churches – and consequently infused with a traditional sexual morality. Thus, references in the Scout code and membership oath to terms such as "morally straight" and "clean" implicitly mean traditional heterosexual relationships, compliance with which could be understood as constituting a criterion for membership and a significant rationale for the existence of the association. When the USSC ruled that the organisation was constitutionally exempt from a law prohibiting discrimination against homosexuals, it was acknowledging that any association was entitled to set its terms of membership and include or exclude accordingly: the freedom of association guaranteed by the First Amendment (within the freedoms of speech and of assembly) and the Fourteenth protected the organisation from accepting the forced inclusion of Dale, an LGBT activist, whose presence would be likely to infringe its freedom of expression by significantly compromising its capacity to give effect to its purpose for associating. Rehnquist CJ cited in support the earlier decision in *Hurley*,[174] when the USSC concluded that a St Patrick's Day parade organised by a private association should not be compelled

---

[172] See Sizemore, C.A., "Enforcing Islamic *Mahr* Agreements: The American Judge's Interpretational Dilemma", at www.georgemasonlawreview.org/wp-content/uploads/2014/06/18-4-SIZEMORE.pdf.

[173] Op. cit.

[174] *Hurley* v. *Irish-AmericanGay, Lesbian and Bisexual Group of Boston*, op. cit.

to accept an LGBT group, which would be likely to represent a message it deemed to be at variance with its associative purpose. Both decisions are limited by the distinctive nature of the organisations involved – expressive associations – whose raison d'être is to represent a particular set of ideas. Both are therefore held to be distinguished from earlier decisions, particularly the USSC rulings in *Jaycees*[175] and *Rotary*[176] requiring male-only organisations to admit women. Nonetheless, the distinction is difficult to understand on any basis other than the greater importance then attached to discrimination by gender relative to that by sexual orientation: if overriding a group's associational rights is justifiable only by a compelling State interest then, while it was formerly judged necessary to ensure that an association complied with what were viewed as the more fundamental classes of discrimination, this approach has now been moderated as the prohibited spectrum of classes has lengthened and the weighting given to constitutional protections increased. In effect, there may now be a hierarchy in law, in which civil liberties trumps religious discrimination.

Conception, Abortion, IVF and Related Issues

The 1973 decision in *Roe* v. *Wade* was a foundation stone for legal abortion in the USA, for women's rights and for women's future in the workplace and, it could be argued, it allowed a new definition of women's social role which until then had been largely religiously defined. Since *Roe* v. *Wade* the pro-life/pro-choice litigation has at least twice given the USSC the opportunity to reflect on the Fourteenth Amendment principle – which declares, "nor shall any State deprive any person of life, liberty, or property, without due process of law" – and observe that "if the right of privacy means anything, it is the right of the individual, married or single, to be free from unwarranted governmental intrusion into matters so fundamentally affecting a person as the decision whether to bear or beget a child".[177] So, when ruling in favour of the plaintiff in *Planned Parenthood* v. *Casey*,[178] the USSC struck down the spousal notice requirement, finding that for many women this breach of their right to privacy would impose a substantial obstacle in their path to having an abortion, and upheld the constitutional right to avail oneself of that procedure; a principle that was

---

[175] *Roberts* v. *United States Jaycees*, op. cit.
[176] *Board of Directors of Rotary International* v. *Rotary Club of Duarte*, 481 US 537, 544 (1987).
[177] *Eisenstadt* v. *Baird*, 405 US 438 (1972) per Justice Brennan and reiterated in *Planned Parenthood* v. *Casey* 505 US 833 (1992).
[178] Ibid.

later a central rationale in striking down the Texas sodomy laws.[179] In *Rust* v. *Sullivan*,[180] however, the USSC upheld Title X of the federal Public Health Service Act, which authorised federal grants to health care organisations offering family planning services but prohibited the funds from being "used in programs where abortion is a method of family planning". It ruled that this prohibition did not violate the First Amendment: the court found that the grant recipients were not thereby banned from engaging in abortion advocacy, as they were free to engage in programmes that were independent from those that were federally funded.

The decades of pro-life/pro-choice confrontations, and the profound divisions in religious and secular principles that they and associated culture-war issues represent, may be a contributory factor in explaining why the USA – unlike the UK – has been so cautious in legalising assisted-reproduction procedures.

Assisted Suicide

In 2016, Colorado became only the sixth state to allow terminally ill patients to legally end their lives with medical assistance. The caselaw leading to this point had been protracted and cautious with respect to USSC rulings: in *Curzon*,[181] in 1990, that while there is no constitutional right to suicide, there is a fundamental right to refuse medical treatment; in *Glucksberg*,[182] in 1997, that the Due Process Clause gives a terminally ill individual the right to commit suicide, but not a right to medical assistance in doing so; and in *Gonzales*,[183] in 2006, that Oregon's Death With Dignity Act, or "right to die law", was constitutional and that physician-assisted suicide had a "legitimate medical purpose" – which paved the way for five other states to enact similar provisions. In regard to this and other family-related issues, including those already discussed, a religious dimension is most often present and is likely to trigger protests of religious discrimination from those disadvantaged by impeded access to related services.

Employment-Related Issues

While a raft of federal anti-discrimination legislation exists, in practice it is the exemption provided under ss.702 and 703 of the Title VII

---

[179] *Lawrence* v. *Texas*, 539 US 558 (2003).   [180] 500 US 173 (1991).
[181] *Curzon* v. *Director, Missouri Dept of Health*, 497 US 261 (1990).
[182] *Washington* v. *Glucksberg*, 521 US 702 (1997).
[183] *Gonzales* v. *Oregon*, 546 US 243 (2006).

exemption, as regulated by the EEOC, that generates most litigation. As noted by Burger CJ in *Griggs* v. *Duke Power*[184] – where promotion opportunities were found to be biased in favour of white employees – "it proscribes not only overt discrimination but also practices that are fair in form but discriminatory in operation".[185] Title VII expressly forbids employers with fifteen or more employees to discriminate on the grounds of race, colour, sex, religion or national origin.[186] Discrimination is interpreted to include harassment, segregation and a failure to provide reasonable accommodation – including allowing for the wearing of religious apparel, prayer and flexibility with regard to observance of religious ceremonies – in the workplace. Employers may not make any employment decisions based on such grounds, including hiring, firing, promoting, demoting and determining assignments and workloads. Exceptions are provided under s.703(e), in respect of employment or training situations where any such grounds constitute a bona fide occupational requirement (BFOR) for the post, and under s.702(a), in respect of a religious organisation employing persons to give effect to their religious activities. For Title VII purposes, Congress defined "religion" as "includ[ing] all aspects of religious observance and practice, as well as belief".[187] Employment law was further complicated in 2010 when Congress passed the Affordable Care Act.

Hiring/Firing Staff

Religious Organisations   The Free Exercise Clause of the First Amendment permits religious organisations to discriminate when hiring and firing staff, on the basis of their religion, contrary to the Title VII prohibition, and in addition to both the "ministerial exception" and the bona fide occupational requirement (BFOR). This is also permitted by the Establishment Clause, as was confirmed in *Corp. of Presiding Bishop of Church of Jesus Christ of Latter-Day Saints* v. *Amos*[188] when the USSC upheld the constitutionality of a law permitting religious organisations to exercise a religious preference when making employment decisions. The right to discriminate is not restricted to jobs that are wholly religious in nature, but also includes those that are only "connected" with the activities of a religion. While the law does not define "religious organisation", it is clear that

---

[184] 401 US 424, 91 S Ct 849 (1971).   [185] Ibid., at 431.
[186] In 1972, Congress added an exemption, codified in s.702 of the Act, to the prohibition against religion-based discrimination for "religious corporation[s], association[s], educational institution[s], or societ[ies]".
[187] 42 USC, s.2000e(j).   [188] Op. cit.

in addition to churches, mosques and other such institutions, the term also includes a "religious corporation, association, educational institution, or society" and any other entity the purpose and character of which is primarily religious.

The decision in *Dodge v. Salvation Army*[189] provides authority for the view that a religious organisation loses its protected right to discriminate in the hiring or firing of staff if the latter are engaged in government-funded service provision. The court then ruled that a Salvation Army Domestic Violence Shelter was wrong to terminate the employment of a counsellor because of her religious beliefs. As the employing religious corporation was in receipt of substantial government funding, it was not entitled to rely on the exemption normally available to such bodies from laws prohibiting religious discrimination. Instead, it was appropriate for the court to apply the "Lemon test", and, in doing so, it was found that the termination constituted a violation of the second prong – government activity and funding had essentially advanced religion. It was a ruling that raised a crucial issue, particularly in the context of the so-called "faith-based funding": should religious groups be required to choose between an entitlement to discriminate and eligibility for government funding?

The hiring/firing practices of religious organisations are illustrated in the volume of cases generated by school staffing issues. In general, the courts have held that religious schools must comply with Title VII and the Equal Pay Act, even though their doctrines tend to provide for an in-built gender disparity,[190] but it is often issues that combine sex, gender and an organisation's ethos that lead to disputed firings. In *Dayton*,[191] a pregnant teacher in a born-again Christian school was told she could not return to school because of her employers' belief that mothers should stay home with their preschool children. When she threatened litigation, the school fired her for violating the mandatory internal dispute resolution provision in her contract, arguing that Christians should not sue other Christians. Similarly, in *Redhead*,[192] a teacher at a Seventh-Day Adventist school and adherent of that religion was dismissed because, by being pregnant and unmarried, she was considered to be exhibiting "immoral or unsatisfactory personal conduct inconsistent with the principles of the

---

[89] Op. cit.

[90] See, for example, *EEOC v. Tree of Life Christian Schs*, 751 F. Supp. 700, 716–717 (S.D. Ohio 1990); *EEOC v. Fremont Christian Sch.*, 781 F.2d 1362, 1364 (9th Cir. 1986); and *Tony & Susan Alamo Found. v. Sec'y of Labor*, 471 US 290, 303–306 (1985).

[91] *Ohio Civil Rights Commission v. Dayton Christian Schools*, 477 US 619 (1986).

[92] *Redhead v. Conference of Seventh-Day Adventists*, op. cit.

Seventh-day Adventist Church". The school stated its employment agreement with the woman was based on following the guidelines of the Church, which included possible termination if an employee was found to fornicate outside of marriage. The plaintiff filed a Title VII action against the school, which responded by arguing that Title VII did not apply to it, citing the RFRA. The court found that the ministerial exception was irrelevant, as the plaintiff's teaching duties were primarily secular. It reasoned that her discrimination lawsuit was permissible so long as it did not cause excessive government entanglement with religion, and as her status was a a teacher rather than clergy, the court determined that it would not. The previously mentioned case of *Hosanna-Tabor*[193] is also important, because its effect has been to extend the protection of the "ministerial exception" parameters available to religious organisations when they employ teacher to staff their schools.

Secular Organisations The obligation not to allow religious considerations to restrict employment opportunities can come into play at an early stage, as was demonstrated in a series of rulings upholding applicants' claims of unlawful discrimination. For example, in *EEOC* v. *Cover gys Corp.*,[194] an applicant mentioned during the course of his job interview that he would be unavailable for work on the Jewish sabbath and, allegedly, was then advised that the interview was terminated. Similarly, in *EEOC v. Voss Elec. Co. D/B/A Voss Lighting*,[195] despite being considered qualified for the position, an applicant was denied employment on the basis of his religious beliefs.

When claiming unlawful dismissal on the grounds of religious discrimination, the operative time for holding religious beliefs is when the alleged discrimination took place. So, in *EEOC* v. *IBP, Inc.*,[196] the fact that after being fired an employee discontinued his beliefs was beside the point: the court held that he observed the Sabbath while employed by the defendant and had lost his job as a result of his religious practices. Moreover, the discriminatory behaviour need not be attributable to the actual employer; other decision-makers may be culpable. In *Bernstein* v. *Sephora*,[197] for example, statements of antipathy towards Jews made in temporal proximity to a promotion decision – such as "[we must] work together to get rid of that JAP bitch" and "[s]he and her princess ways ha[ve] to go" were held to constitute direct proof of discrimination.

---

[193] *Hosanna-Tabor Evangelical Lutheran Church* v. *EEOC*, op. cit.   [194] (E.D. Mo. 2011).
[195] Civil Case No. 4:12-cv-00330-JED-FHM (2013).   [196] 824 F. Supp. 147 (C.D. Ill. 1993).
[197] Div. of DFS Group, 182 F. Supp. 2d 1214 (S.D. Fla. 2002).

The courts have affirmed the existence of religious discrimination in circumstances where an employee, who does not share the same religious beliefs as their employer, is fired and there is evidence that the religious difference has been at least a contributory factor in the termination. In *Campos* v. *City of Blue Springs*,[198] for example, there was sufficient evidence to demonstrate religious discrimination where an employee who followed the tenets of Native American spirituality was denied compensation for additional work, taken off counselling assignments, denied leave to meet with her dissertation professor and ultimately forced to quit because her supervisor wanted someone in the job who shared the supervisor's religious beliefs. The grounds, however, do have to be genuinely religious. In *Seshadri* v. *Kasraian*,[199] the court ruled that an employee bringing a religious discrimination claim need not belong to an established church but cannot avoid an inquiry being made into whether he or she actually has a religion. The court found it unnecessary, in *Storey* v. *Burns Int'l Sec. Servs*,[200] to enquire as to whether being a "Confederate Southern-American" constituted a religious belief, when it affirmed the right of an employer to dismiss an employee who had refused to remove Confederate flag stickers from his lunch box and pickup truck. This followed an earlier ruling that there was no authority to determine whether such an entity was a valid religion.[201]

The USSC, in the landmark case of *Burwell* v. *Hobby Lobby*,[202] considered the claim that government had a compelling interest in providing the insurance coverage necessary to protect the health of female employees – specifically, whether, under the RFRA, the religious beliefs of an employer of a secular commercial company could prevail over the "contraceptive mandate": a regulation adopted by the US Dept of Health and Human Services under the Affordable Care Act requiring employers to financially provide for certain contraceptives. It found that "closely held"[203] for-profit corporations were entitled to rely on their established religious beliefs to avoid being compelled to provide contraception under their health care plans, as the statutory contraceptive mandate did not show

---

[198] 289 F.3d 546 (8th Cir. 2002). See also *Backus* v. *Mena Newspapers, Inc.*, 224 F. Supp. 2d 1228 (W.D. Ark. 2002).

[199] 130 F.3d 798 (7th Cir. 1997).   [200] 390 F.3d 760 (3d Cir. 2004).

[201] *Chaplin* v. *Du Pont Advance Fiber Sys.*, 293 F. Supp. 2d 622 (E.D. Va. 2003).

[202] Op. cit.

[203] "Closely held" corporations, as defined by the IRS, are estimated to constitute approximately 90 per cent of US corporations and employ approximately 52 per cent of the US workforce.

how this was "the least restrictive means of furthering (the State's) compelling interest".[204] The court concluded by addressing "the possibility that discrimination in hiring, for example on the basis of race, might be cloaked as religious practice to escape legal sanction" but considered that the decision "provides no such shield".[205] Arguably, however, it may provide a shield for companies owned by those whose religious beliefs may in future be manifested in constraints on employees' rights and liberties, e.g. family-planning services, same-sex relationships or even access to blood transfusions.

Accommodating Religious Beliefs in the Workplace

Under Title VII, employers have a duty to accommodate the religious beliefs of their employees. As in Canada, the duty is subject to this not imposing undue hardship on the employer, and in fact most Title VII religion cases have turned on this caveat.[206] In practice, the duty differs somewhat between the two countries, because the reasonableness test, used to determine whether or not an accommodation should be made, is applied more routinely in the USA – normally, a simple request should be sufficient – and gives rise to an expectation that the employer will offer an accommodation that is reasonable, not the one that it is the most reasonable, nor the one that is the employee's first preference.[207]

The early and important case of *Trans World Airlines* v. *Hardison*[208] concerned an employee who was dismissed following a protracted dispute between management and the unions regarding his inability to work Saturdays on religious grounds. He claimed that his dismissal constituted religious discrimination, in violation of s.703(a)(1) of Title VII, which, in conjunction with the 1967 EEOC guidelines, required an employer, short of "undue hardship", to make "reasonable accommodations" regarding the religious needs of employees. Ultimately, the court ruled in favour of TWA on the basis that, in the circumstances, requiring the employer to bear more than a *de minimis* cost in order to give the respondent Saturdays off would be an undue hardship, as it would then have to bear the considerable costs arising from other employees requesting similar rights. The legislative intent was to eliminate discrimination in employment, and

---

204   *Burwell* v. *Hobby Lobby*, op. cit., at p. 46.   205   Ibid., at p. 52.
206   See e.g. *Trans World Airlines* v. *Hardison*, op. cit.; *Protos* v. *Volkswagen*, 797 F.2d 129 (3rd Cir.), 479 US 972, 107 S.Ct. 474, 93 L.Ed.2d 418 (1986); *Bhatia* v. *Chevron USA Inc.*, op. cit.; and *EEOC* v. *Sambo's*, op. cit.
207   *Ansonia Board of Educ.* v. *Philbrook*, 479 US 60, 107 S.Ct. 367, 93 L.Ed.2d 305 (1986).
208   Op. cit.

this could not be construed to require an employer to discriminate against some employees in order to enable others to observe their Sabbath.

An employee's belief or practice can be "religious" even if the employee is affiliated with a religious group that does not espouse or recognize that belief or practice, or if few – or no – other people adhere to it. Title VII's protection also extends to those who are discriminated against or need accommodation because they profess no religious beliefs. An exception to this rule exists if an individual's religion is a BFOR, as when it is an essential part of their job description. The law applies to federal, state and local employers. The ruling in *United States* v. *Lee*[209] adds that an employer cannot deprive employees of a statutory right because of religious beliefs, noting that "mandatory participation is indispensable to the fiscal vitality of the social security system" and that the "tax system could not function if denominations were allowed to challenge the tax system because tax payments were spent in a manner that violates their religious beliefs".

However, a necessary prerequisite is that the sincerity of professed beliefs must be established as a matter of fact. So, in *EEOC* v. *Ilona of Hungary, Inc.*,[210] the court upheld an earlier decision that a former employee sincerely believed she should refrain from work on Yom Kippur even though she did not observe every Jewish holiday. The requirement to assess the sincerity of a professed belief does not permit an employer to objectively assess its accuracy. Nonetheless, as was noted in *Burns* v. *Warwick Valley Cent. Sch. Dist.*,[211] it is permissible to inquire into the religious basis of a request for accommodation in order to assess whether the belief is sincerely held. In *Hussein* v. *Waldorf-Astoria*,[212] the claim that a beard was necessitated by Islamic beliefs might well have found a sympathetic hearing if there had been evidence of the plaintiff having an interest in religious beliefs or in growing a beard during his previous fourteen years of employment. In *EEOC* v. *Chemsico, Inc.*,[213] where questions existed as to whether an employee who did not follow all of the teachings of her Church and had stopped attending church services had a sincere religious belief that precluded her from working on the Sabbath, the jury nevertheless concluded that the belief was sincere because she continued to engage in Bible study and had consistently refused to work on the Sabbath. On the other hand, *Eatman* v. *United Parcel Serv.*[214] concerned an employee

---

[209] Op. cit.   [210] 108 F.3d 1569 (7th Cir. 1997) (en banc).
[211] 166 F. Supp. 2d 881 (SDNY 2001).   [212] 134 F. Supp. 2d 591 (SDNY 2001).
[213] 216 F. Supp. 2d 940 (E.D. Miss. 2002).   [214] 194 F. Supp. 2d 256 (SDNY 2002).

who sincerely considered his dreadlocks to be a testament or outward expression of his commitment to Protestantism and the principles of Nubianisn. The court found that this was not a requirement of his beliefs but a matter of personal choice and held that his employer's policy of requiring its drivers with unconventional hairstyles, including dreadlocks, to wear hats did not constitute religious discrimination. In *Bailey* v. *Associated Press*,[215] it was found that an employer did not violate Title VII by denying a request for time off on Sundays from an employee who had not before made such a request during the fourteen years of his employment, did not inform the employer that the request was made for religious reasons and testified that he did not attend religious services on Sundays and was subject to no religious prohibition against working on Sundays. Similarly, while in principle an employer would be expected to respect a Seventh-Day Adventist's objection to union membership, where there is evidence that such an employee has often acted in a manner inconsistent with the associated religious beliefs (by being divorced, taking an oath before a notary upon becoming a public employee, working five days a week instead of the six required by their faith) then they may forfeit any claim to the protection of accommodation.[216] However, in *Sherbert* v. *Verner*,[217] the court upheld a claim by a person denied State unemployment benefits because he refused to work on Saturdays due to his religious beliefs.

Education-Related Issues

Title IV of the Civil Rights Act 1964 prohibits discrimination based on religion in public primary and secondary schools, as well as public colleges and universities.

Government Funding and Religious Education

The need to police the use of government funds intended for educational purposes, ensuring a distinction is maintained between their religious and secular application, was stressed in *Mitchell* v. *Helms*.[218] This case concerned the scope of the Establishment Clause when evaluating a

---

[215] 2003 WL 22232967 (SDNY 29 September 2003).
[216] *EEOC* v. *Union Independiete De La Autoridad De Acueductos y Alcantarillados De Puerto Rico*, 279 F.3d 49 (1st Cir. 2002).
[217] Op. cit.   [218] Op. cit.

programme of governmental assistance entailing direct aid to organisations, including religious organisations. Guided by the analysis used in *Agostini v. Felton*,[219] O'Connor J employed the "Lemon test" in the following process of analysis. First, does the programme of aid have a secular purpose? Second, does it have the primary effect of advancing religion?: Is the aid actually diverted to religious indoctrination?; Does the programme define the eligibility of participating organisations without regard to religion?; and Does the programme create excessive administrative entanglement? She noted that the educational aid in question was to supplement rather than supplant monies from private sources, that the nature of the aid was such that it could not reach the coffers of a religious school and that the aid's use was statutorily restricted to "secular, neutral, and non-ideological" purposes. She noted also that the aid consisted of materials and equipment rather than cash, and that the materials were loaned to the religious schools, with the government retaining ownership. O'Connor J went on to reject a rule of unconstitutionality where the character of aid is capable of diversion to religious indoctrination. The effect of this decision was to overrule the two 1970s cases and to hold that the government may provide instructional equipment to parochial schools.[220] This approach is in keeping with rulings that have upheld the use of federal funds for construction work at a religious hospital[221] and required that equal funding be granted to evangelical Christian groups.[222]

The decisions in both *Bowen v. Kendrick*[223] and *Mitchell v. Helms*[224] reveal a strong judicial awareness of circumstances in which government funding could result in an assigning of functional responsibility from a service delivery religious organisation to its government funder in accordance with the agent/principal rule. In particular, the comments by O'Connor J stand as a general warning to all educational facilities in receipt of government funding.

---

[219] 521 US 203 (1997). This landmark decision, reversing *Aguilar v. Felton* (1985), found that it was not a violation of the Establishment Clause for a State-sponsored education initiative to allow public school teachers to instruct at religious schools, so long as the material was secular and neutral in nature and no "excessive entanglement" between government and religion was apparent.

[220] See further Esbeck, C. H., "The Establishment Clause as a Structural Restraint on Governmental Power", *Iowa Law Review*, 1998, vol. 84, pp. 1–113.

[221] *Bradfield v. Roberts*, 15 US 291 (1899).

[222] *Rosenberger v. Rector and Visitors of Univ. of Va.*, op. cit.

[223] 487 US 589, 623 (1988).   [224] Op. cit.

Faith Schools

The USSC has often upheld the principle that parents have the fundamental right to direct the education and upbringing of their children.[225] For example, in applying the previously mentioned "compelling interest" of the "highest order" test, the USSC held that this was not satisfied where Amish parents were penalised for refusing to send their children to high school when they had "deep religious convictions" for not doing so.[226] An interesting case in this context is the USSC ruling in *Kiryas Joel*,[227] which found that a local government administrative decision to create a school district with boundaries aligned with those of a religious community of Hasidic Jews, thereby explicitly designating those schools "faith schools", was unconstitutional, and warned against "the forced separation that occurs when the government draws explicit political boundaries on the basis of peoples' faith". The dissenting judgment of Scalia J, seemingly grounded on multi-culturalism, clearly has some importance for this book:

> On what basis does Justice Souter conclude that it is the theological distinctiveness rather than the cultural distinctiveness that was the basis for New York State's decision? The normal assumption would be that it was the latter, since it was not theology but dress, language, and cultural alienation that posed the educational problem for the children.

He argued that treating the residents as a culture rather than a religion would be in keeping with State policy in relation to other groups such as Native Americans, and similarly:

> the creation of a special, one-culture school district for the benefit of those children would pose no problem. The neutrality demanded by the Religion Clauses requires the same indulgence towards cultural characteristics that are accompanied by religious belief.

Religious Discrimination and Educational Content

As has been said, the Establishment Clause prohibits public schools from "conveying a message that religion or a particular religious belief

---

[225] See, for example, *Pierce* v. *Society of Sisters*, 268 US 510 (1925); *Farrington* v. *Tokushige*, 273 US 284 (1927); *Lehr* v. *Robertson*, 463 US 248, 257–258 (1983); *Hodgson* v. *Minnesota*, 497 US 417 (1990); and *Troxel* v. *Granville*, 530 US 57 (2000).

[226] *Wisconsin* v. *Yoder*, 406 US 205 (1972).

[227] *Kiryas Joel Village School District* v. *Grumet*, op. cit.

is preferred".[228] There is a considerable body of caselaw upholding the policy of insulating public schools from religious influence: *Edwards* v. *Aguillard*,[229] invalidating mandatory teaching of creationism; *Stone* v. *Graham*,[230] invalidating mandatory display of the Ten Commandments; *Epperson* v. *Arkansas*,[231] invalidating prohibition on teaching evolution; *McCollum* v. *Board of Education*,[232] prohibiting in-class sectarian religious instruction; and *Bd of Educ. of Kiryas Joel Village School District* v. *Grumet*,[233] where it was noted that "the Religion Clauses do not require the government to be oblivious to impositions that legitimate exercises of State power may place on religious belief and practice". Other State educational supports struck down by the judiciary on the grounds of facilitating impermissible religious influence include: government loans to religious schools of maps, photos, films, projectors, recorders and lab equipment, as well as services for counselling, remedial and accelerated teaching and psychological, speech and hearing therapy;[234] the use of public school personnel to provide guidance, remedial and therapeutic speech and hearing services away from the religious school campus;[235] the use of public buildings for optional religious instruction;[236] and the loan of instructional materials to religious schools and transportation for field trips by religious school students.[237] Recently, the courts have addressed more subtle attempts to cross that line, such as: ordering the removal of stickers placed on science books stating that "evolution is a theory, not a fact";[238] and ruling that an "Intelligent Design Policy" requiring teachers to inform students of the "gaps/problems in Darwin's Theory" and to introduce "other theories of evolution including, but not limited to, intelligent design" violated the First Amendment.[239] Alongside these have been USSC rulings to the effect that impartial teaching about religion "when presented objectively as part of a secular program of education" is not to be discouraged and warning that the public school system must not be used to preach the "religion of secularism".[240]

---

[228] *Board of Education of the Westside Community Schools* v. *Mergens*, US 110 S Ct 2356, 2372–73, 110 L.Ed.2d 191 (1990) per Rehnquist, CJ.
[229] 482 US 578 (1987).   [230] 449 US 39 (1980).   [231] 393 US 97 (1968).   [232] Op. cit.
[233] 512 US 687, 705 (1994).   [234] *Meek* v. *Pittenger*, op. cit.
[235] *Wolman* v. *Walter*, op. cit.
[236] *Illinois ex rel. McCollum* v. *Board of Education of School District*, op. cit.
[237] *Bowen* v. *Kendrick*, op. cit.
[238] *Selman* v. *Cobb County School District*, 449 F.3d 1320 (11th Cir. 2006).
[239] *Kitzmiller* v. *Dover Area School District*, 400 F. Supp. 2d 707 (2005).
[240] *Sch. Dist. of Abington Twp., Pa.* v. *Schempp*, op. cit., per Justice Clark.

Education Facilities and Religious Discrimination

The principle that the public-service duty of the State to ensure provision for the education of children is outweighed by the fundamental right of parents to freedom of religion has been established since at least *Wisconsin v. Yoder*,[241] when the USSC ruled that Amish parents could not be compelled to send their children to high school, thereby setting a legal precedent for the home schooling of children. The rationale for a parental right to insulate children from an unwanted religious influence in the classroom setting was explained as follows by Brennan J in *Edwards v. Aguillard*:[242]

> families entrust public schools with the education of their children, but condition their trust on the understanding that the classroom will not purposely be used to advance religious views that may conflict with the private beliefs of the student and his or her family. Students in such institutions are impressionable and their attendance is involuntary... The State exerts great authority and coercive power through mandatory attendance requirements, and because of the student's emulation of teachers as role models and the children's susceptibility to peer pressure.

The fact that this approach also applies more generally in the education system was established in *Bob Jones University v. United States*[243] when the USSC found that a religious university with a racially discriminatory admissions policy and other policies relating to religious beliefs against interracial dating and marriage was not protected by the religion clauses of the First Amendment. Justice Burger reasoned that, given their charitable status and income tax privileges, such institutions "must serve a public purpose and not be contrary to established public policy".[244] Where a state university adopts a blanket policy that singles out, and thereby discriminates against, religious speech, then, as in *Widmar v. Vincent*,[245] it may find itself accused of religious discrimination. That case concerned a student religious group at a state university, which, on being advised that the use of university buildings or grounds was prohibited "for purposes of religious worship or religious teaching", responded by alleging that this breached the students' rights to free exercise of religion and freedom of speech. The USSC agreed and upheld the earlier ruling of the Court of Appeals that the prohibition was a content-based discrimination against religious speech,

---

[241] Op. cit.
[242] 482 US 578, 107 S Ct 2573, 96 L.Ed.2d 510 (1987), at p. 584. See also *Grand Rapids School District v. Ball*, 473 US 373, 105 S Ct 3216, 87 L.Ed.2d 267 (1985).
[243] 461 US 574 (1983).   [244] Ibid.   [245] Op. cit.

for which there was no compelling justification.[246] By way of contrast, in *Christian Legal Society* v. *Martinez*,[247] the USSC upheld the right of a College of Law to prohibit the Christian Legal Society (CLS), a student organisation in the college, from restricting membership to those who signed a "statement of faith", which, among other commitments, required members to comply with a ban on heterosexual relations outside marriage. Justice Stevens noted that the argument made by CLS in refusing membership to those who engage in "unrepentant homosexual conduct" could be made by groups that "may exclude or mistreat Jews, blacks, and women". Justice Alito, in his dissenting judgment, expressed the interesting but arguably blinkered view that "it is fundamentally confused to apply a rule against religious discrimination to a religious association".[248] Meanwhile, *Ward* v. *Polite*[249] concerned a student in her final semester of a counselling course at Eastern Michigan University who told her professors that she had no problem counselling individual gay and lesbian clients but could not in good conscience assist them with their same-sex relationships; her subsequent expulsion for violating the school's anti-discrimination policy was upheld.

Medicine-Related Issues

The right to self-determination, and accountability for the consequences thereof, has perhaps always been a central cultural characteristic of life in the USA. In contemporary society, this is wrapped up with an implied and broadly interpreted constitutional "privacy right",[250] which encompasses a doctrine of informed consent that allows and respects decisions – often based on religious beliefs – to refuse to accept or deliver certain medical treatment or to participate in related research projects.

Medical Intervention and Religious Beliefs

The right of an adult to make an informed decision to refuse medical treatment is well established, was reaffirmed by the USSC ruling in *Mills* v. *Rodgers*[251] and has since been reiterated many times by the same court (see earlier). The exercise of that right, a fundamental aspect of personal liberty, is based upon respect for the right of an autonomous adult to live

---

[246] See also *Good News Club* v. *Milford Central School*, op. cit., where the USSC ruled that religious groups must be allowed to use public schools after hours if the same access is granted to other community groups.
[247] 130 S Ct (2010).   [248] Ibid. at 3012.   [249] 667 F.3d 727 (6th Cir. 2012).
[250] See *Griswold* v. *Connecticut*, 381 US 479 (1965).   [251] 457 US 291 (1982).

or die in accordance with their beliefs, subject only to a countervailing compelling interest of the State.[252]

Equally clear is the fact that the right does not extend to sanctioning the use of parental authority, on religious grounds, to either veto medical intervention professionally advised to secure the health of one's children or insist on intervention that is not advised, or is detrimental, to one's children's health. In this as in many other jurisdictions, it has been the religious beliefs and parental vetoes of Jehovah's Witnesses that have most frequently engaged the courts,[253] which continue to be guided by the principle first stated in *Prince v. Massachusetts*:[254]

> Parents may be free to become martyrs themselves. But it does not follow that they are free, in identical circumstances, to make martyrs of their children

The clash of religious beliefs and medical treatment is clearly also an issue for communities such as the Amish and Native Americans, which tend to look more to traditional health remedies than to national immunisation programmes or hospital-based procedures, and also, to an extent, for some fundamentalist Christians, who may be disinclined to accept certain types of treatment. As in other countries, it can similarly become an issue for those health and social care professionals whose religious beliefs prevent them from facilitating certain medical interventions, most usually abortion and related family-planning services. All such circumstances can and do give rise to allegations of religious discrimination as the pressure to conform alienates those whose beliefs do not allow them to do so.

Genetic Engineering and Patents, etc.

Genetic engineering, or genetic modification, is the process of altering the DNA in an organism's genome and has been largely pioneered in the USA. Its development for commercial purposes has resulted in companies such as Monsanto and Dupont holding patents for most of the world's genetically enhanced crops and has the potential to accelerate research into cures for diseases such as cancer, cystic fibrosis and Alzheimer's. For present

---

[252] See e.g. *Georgetown College Inc.*, 377 US 978 (1964) and *Belchertown State Sch. v. Saikewicz*, 370 N.E.2d 417 (1977).

[253] See, for example, *Morrison v. State*, 252 S.W.2d 97 (MO C. of A.1952); *In re Clark*, 185 N.E.2d 128 (OH C. of Corn. Pl., Div. Of Dom. Rel. 1962); *Jehovah's Witnesses v. King County Hospital*, 278 F. Supp. 488 (W.D. Wash. 1967); and *Stamford Hospital v. Vega* (236 Conn. 646) (1996).

[254] (1944) 321 US 158 at 170.

purposes, the relevant issues concern the extent to which religious beliefs have played a role in helping or hindering the development of genetic engineering – and there is no evidence that they have.

Although the science in this country has proceeded largely unchallenged by judicial concerns regarding ethical or religious implications, there have been a few relevant cases. One such was *Diamond* v. *Chakrabarty*,[255] in which the USSC upheld the Court of Customs and Patent Appeals ruling "that the fact that microorganisms are alive is a distinction without legal significance for patent law" and perhaps thereby foreclosed any future judicial examination of the ethics of such patents. Another was *Mayo Collaborative Services* v. *Prometheus Laboratories, Inc.*,[256] in which the USSC emphasised that patent law must not inhibit future discovery by improperly tying up the use of laws of nature and declared that although "laws of nature, natural phenomena, and abstract ideas" are not patentable, "an application of a law of nature . . . to a known structure or process may [deserve] patent protection".[257] A landmark case was *Association for Molecular Pathology* v. *Myriad Genetics, Inc.*,[258] in which the USSC determined that DNA in its natural form cannot be patented in the USA because DNA is a "product of nature". The court decided that as nothing new is created when discovering a gene, there is no IP to protect, so patents cannot be granted; but it did concede that DNA manipulated in a lab is eligible to be patented because DNA sequences altered by humans are not found in nature, which would seem to give the green light to research into genetic editing and cloning. The ruling invalidated more than 4300 patents previously granted in respect of human genes, thereby freeing up a wealth of areas for research and providing opportunities for experiments in commercially viable genetically modified (GM) products.

During the period covered by this caselaw, the saga of the "Harvard mouse" raised ethical concerns among the general public, if not the judiciary. On 12 April 1988, Harvard University acquired the world's first patent for a higher form of life: a mouse specially developed by researchers at the Harvard Medical School through techniques of genetic manipulation. In 2005 and 2009, the relevant patents expired and the ensuing competing commercial interests in acquiring new patents for "oncomouse" experiments brought related moral and legal issues before the court for the first time, in *Myriad Genetics*; interestingly, this was more than a decade after the issue of an "oncomouse" patent had been considered and rejected

---

[255] 447 US 303 (1980).   [256] 566 US (2012).   [257] Ibid., at p. 187.   [258] 569 US (2013).

by the Canadian Supreme Court as constituting an unwarranted incur-
sion into the realm of higher life forms.[259] The equivalent debate in the
USA not only seemingly avoids religious issues relating to the possible
commodification of sentient creatures, but seldom strays beyond considering whether the Thirteenth Amendment, prohibiting the use of a human
for servitude, extends to prohibiting the patenting of animals with some
human genetic component.

Service-Provision Issues

While Titles III and IV of the Civil Rights Act 1964 provide the main statutory protection from discrimination in accessing public services, Title II
prohibits discriminatory practice by any establishment that leases, rents
or sells goods or provides services.[260] Specifically, s.2000a(a) of the Civil
Rights Act 1964 declares that "all persons shall be entitled to the full and
equal enjoyment of the goods, services, facilities, privileges, advantages,
and accommodations of any place of public accommodation ... without
discrimination or segregation on the ground of race, color, religion, or
national origin".

Service Provision by Religious Organisations

In all states where same-sex marriage has been legalised, the relevant legislation imposes no requirement upon religious organisations and their
ministers to provide marriage services (i.e. a celebrant, use of church
premises, etc.). Most such states include exemption clauses for religious
organisations and their ministers (although Massachusetts does not). The
difficulties tend to arise in downstream service provision. While a case
may be made for extending such an exemption to premises and services
provided by a religious organisation (e.g. education and heath care facilities, adoption, etc.), the more removed the activity is from core religious
functions, the harder it is to justify an exemption.

   The withdrawal of adoption and foster-care services, for reasons of discriminatory religious beliefs, has severely impacted child-care provision.
In 2006 in Boston, Catholic Charities failed to gain exemption from Massachusetts' anti-discrimination statute and terminated its adoption work

---

[259] *Harvard College* v. *Canada (Commissioner of Patents)* [2002] 4 SCR 45, 2002 SCC 76.
[260] See e.g. *Heart of Atlanta Motel Inc.* v. *US*, 379 US 241 (1964) and *Katzenbach* v. *McClung*,
    379 US 294 (1964).

rather than continue to place children under the "guardianship of homo-sexuals". Similarly, in Washington, DC in 2010, the same body took the same step when faced with a statutory requirement that government-funded religious entities providing public services do so by including same-sex couples. In the same year, the government declined to renew a contract with the US Conference of Catholic Bishops to provide ser-vices for human-trafficking victims because of Catholic Charities' refusal to refer sexual assault victims for contraception and abortion advice. In 2012, the Illinois Department of Children and Family Services revoked its contract with Catholic Charities after its refusal to provide adoption and foster-care services to same-sex couples, causing the transfer of more than 1000 children to secular agencies. While the religious beliefs, organ-isations and issues are the same as those that brought Catholic Care to court in England, the numbers of children adversely affected in the USA by this form of religious discrimination are far greater.

Spencer v. World Vision, Inc.[261] concerned a Christian humanitarian organisation, heavily funded by the government, which terminated the employment of three staff members because they had ceased attending daily devotions and weekly chapel services held during the workday and because they had denied the deity of Jesus Christ. The staff concerned sued World Vision for unfair dismissal, the latter responded by claim-ing that it was a religious entity and therefore exempt from Title VII, and the protracted court case got underway. Ultimately, the court ruled that even though World Vision was not a traditional house of worship, it was entitled to the institutional religious liberty accommodation – as a "reli-gious corporation", it was exempt from a federal law that bars faith-based discrimination – and a petition for rehearing *en banc* was refused. This important decision, confirming that religious corporations can legally fac-tor religion into hiring and firing decisions, was reinforced three years later by the USSC ruling, in *Burwell v. Hobby Lobby*,[262] which extended the exemption to wholly commercial entities when it upheld the right of the evangelical Christian owners of Hobby Lobby not to provide health insurance cover which included contraception to their female employees. These rulings greatly increase the potential protection available to com-panies engaged in religiously discriminating service provision, although there remains some uncertainty as to whether or not the law allows an organisation to avail itself of the exemption privilege when it is federally contracted to deliver public services.

---

[261] No. 08-35532, 2011 WL 208356 (9th Cir. 25 January 2011).   [262] Op. cit.

Provision of Public Services

Cooke v. Town of Colorado City[263] and its associated cases are a curious hybrid in that they concern the provision of public services by a municipality staffed by members of a particular religion and seemingly managed largely in defence of their religious interests. The plaintiffs successfully challenged housing allocation and utility service provision practices which were biased against them solely because they were not members of the Fundamentalist Church of Jesus Christ of Latter Day Saints. The court proceedings disclosed systemic manipulation of service allocation, on religious grounds, by municipal authorities controlled by members of that religious organisation, intended to disadvantage and discourage all others. This anomalous set of circumstances is reminiscent of the sectarian misuse of municipal powers that characterised society in Northern Ireland and proved to be a precursor to violent civil unrest.

In *Muhammad v. City of N.Y. Dept. of Corrections*,[264] it was held that provision of "generic" worship services by state prison authorities for Protestant, Catholic, Jewish and Muslim inmates but not for Nation of Islam inmates satisfied the compelling interest test, where the prison lacked sufficient officers, space and time to provide additional services while still maintaining internal order, and where it provided the plaintiffs with access to a Nation of Islam clergyman.

Private Goods and Service Provision

Private service providers (owners of hotels, boarding houses, etc.) claiming exemption from equality and religious discrimination provisions on the grounds of personal religious belief give rise to a great deal of controversy throughout the USA. Cases include, as in Northern Ireland, the refusal to bake a cake ordered to celebrate gay marriage.[265] However, as Gedicks points out: "the definition of 'public accommodation' in Title II is quite narrow, restricted to hotels/motels, restaurants, and theaters and other 'places of public amusement'. It does not include most public retail establishments."[266]

The application of religious rights arguments to commercial organisations with legal personality has been given greater prominence by the

---

[263] No. CV 10-08105-PCT-JAT (2012).   [264] 904 F. Supp. 161, 193–195 (SDNY 1995).

[265] See the decision of the Oregon Bureau of Labour and Industries to fine Sweet Cakes by Melissa for such a refusal, in Richardson, V., "Oregon Panel Proposes $135k Hit against Bakers in Gay-Wedding Cake Dispute", *Washington Times*, 24 April 2015.

[266] Note to author, 19 April 2017.

decision of the USSC in *Burwell* v. *Hobby Lobby*.[267] In that high-profile case, a for-profit corporation owned by family members, with a well-documented religious ethos, was found to possess religious rights which could be upheld against obligations to provide particular types of health care to employees.

Broadcasting Services

The First Amendment provides that "Congress shall make no law... abridging the freedom of speech". This freedom is not absolute. While in *Perry Educ. Ass'n* v. *Perry Educators' Ass'n*[268] the court accepted that government can generally impose time, place and manner constraints on its exercise, it added that such restrictions must be content-neutral and narrowly tailored to serve a significant government interest, and must leave open other channels of communication. Unless exercised in a manner that actually or potentially incites hatred or violence, is defamatory or is otherwise in breach of the law, the freedom to express views – however insulting – is constitutionally protected.

In recent years, this has been particularly evident in the tensions between pro-life and pro-choice groups. The courts have been careful to respect the right to peaceful protest – even if abusive and provocative – that remains within the law.[269]

Conclusion

The doctrine of State neutrality with regard to matters of religion and belief broadly sets the policy context for government to address religious discrimination in the USA. The effect of the constitutional prohibition on government using its powers and resources to discriminate for or against religion per se, or in relation to any particular religion, can be seen in the rigour with which the courts scrutinise issues where there is evidence of government entanglement with religion. This is supplemented by equality and non-discrimination legislation, the effect of which has been to constrain the potential of religious discrimination to breach the rights of others. In recent years, the neutrality doctrine has, arguably, been tempered by a growing equality imperative. There may be several aspects to this development.

---

[57] Op. cit.   [268] 460 US 37, 45 (1983).
[59] See *Griffin* v. *Breckenridge*, 403 US 88 and *Bray* v. *Alexandria Women's Health Clinic*, 506 US 263 (1993).

Multi-culturalism and the spiraling "culture wars" in this most litigious of nations are possibly forcing tensions to be expressed in terms of individuals competing rights: as religion and belief become increasingly conflated with cultural difference, political values, sexual orientation and gender inequality, so do complex matters tend to be reduced to more manageable rights issues and thus become more amenable to judicial and regulatory resolution. These competing rights would seem to be becoming a more prominent and permanent challenge for public policy: tensions between fundamental constitutional rights – freedom of speech/expression and freedom of religion – are increasing in frequency and political sensitivity; in particular, the liberty to manifest religious beliefs is becoming steadily more compromised by LGBT-related issues. This trend is compounded by the growing strength of a secularist lobby advocating for religious matters to be treated in accordance with equality principles, and by counter-terrorism concerns – now governing US domestic and international policy – which focus on fanatical religious discrimination as constituting a threat to global and national security.

8

Canada

Introduction

The 2011 National Household Survey reported that 67.3 per cent of Canadian citizens were Christians, a fall of some 10 per cent since the 2001 national census; 38.7 per cent were Catholics and 24 per cent Protestant – mainly United Church or Anglican. The second largest group, at 23.9 per cent, represented those who subscribed to no religion at all; a considerable increase from the 16.5 per cent recorded ten years earlier. Statistics Canada predicts that by 2017, Muslims, Jews, Hindus, Sikhs and Buddhists will make up 10 per cent of Canada's population, up from 6 per cent in the 2001 census. Relative to most other common law jurisdictions, these figures reveal a remarkably religious – and religiously diverse – population, although one in which secularism is steadily gaining ground. Religious discrimination might, therefore, be expected to have a correspondingly higher incidence.

This chapter, like the others in Part III, begins with a brief public policy overview and then outlines the current framework of relevant domestic and international law. It examines definitional terms and concepts relating to "religion" and "beliefs", and their "manifestation", and explores what in law constitutes religious discrimination. It considers the caselaw relating to the Church/State relationship and secularism, before concluding with a focus on contemporary caselaw generated in respect of matters such as family, employment, education, medicine and commerce.

Public Policy: An Overview

The history of colonial settlement in Canada is one in which a religious identity and accompanying bijural system were stamped upon certain provinces – most notably Quebec, being French Catholic, and Ontario, as British Protestant – to the detriment of indigenous communities.[1] The resulting cultural affiliations, legal systems and administrative divisions permitted quite separate provincial governance arrangements to evolve, with weak links between the provinces and between them and the federal government. Framing federal public policy across these very different and relatively independent provinces and territories has proven difficult.

Religion and the Constitution

The preamble to the Canadian Charter of Rights and Freedoms proclaims: "Whereas Canada is founded upon principles that recognize the supremacy of God and the rule of law". In so doing, arguably, it discriminates against all citizens who subscribe to non-theistic or multi-theistic beliefs and against those without any. This interpretation has been judicially challenged – "the reference to the supremacy of God in the preamble to the Canadian Charter cannot lead to an interpretation of freedom of conscience and religion that authorizes the State to consciously profess a theistic faith"[2] – on the basis that it has to be read in the light of the political context of that time, but now "must be given a generous and expansive interpretation".

The Constitution

The Constitution Act 1982, s.52(2), declares the Constitution of Canada to consist of that statute, together with its predecessor, the Constitution Act 1867 (formerly the British North America Act 1867), and all other statutes and orders referred to in the schedule and any amendments.

Religious Discrimination and the Constitution

The Canadian Charter of Rights and Freedoms, part of the Constitution Act 1982, takes priority over other federal or provincial legislation in Canada: s.2 guarantees freedom of conscience and religion; s.15 provides a guarantee of equality. These freedoms are subject "only to such reasonable limits that prescribed by law as can be demonstrably justified in a free and democratic society". However, they are also subject to Clause 33, the "notwithstanding" caveat, which allows the federal or any provincial government to pass laws that breach Charter rights in relation to such matters.

---

[1] The Indian Act 1876, by prohibiting the practise of traditional indigenous ceremomies, can be seen as a denial of Canada's original religious/cultural heritage.

[2] *Mouvement laïque québécois v. Saguenay (City)*, [2015] 2 SCR 3, per McLachlin CJ.

From at least *Laurence v. McQuarrie*[3] – with its forfeiture condition in the event of the beneficiary "embracing the doctrines of the church of Rome" – until the introduction of the Charter of Rights and Freedoms, testamentary conditions in favour of religion had precedence over public policy considerations and went virtually unchallenged by the judiciary. It had seemed that the 1982 Act would inaugurate a new era, but this was not immediately forthcoming. *Canada Trust*,[4] the best known Canadian case on the issue of a religious trust being in breach of public policy, was determined by the Ontario Court of Appeal in 1990, when it ruled that limiting scholarships to white, Protestant, British subjects "is patently at variance with the democratic principles governing our pluralistic society in which equality rights are constitutionally guaranteed and in which the multicultural heritage of Canadians is to be preserved and enhanced".[5] But shortly afterwards, in *Ramsden Estate*,[6] the court found that a testamentary gift to a university for scholarships for Protestant students presented "no ground of public policy which would serve as an impediment to the trust proceeding".[7] On the other hand, Galligan J, in *Fox* v. *Fox Estate*,[8] held that a trustee's use of a power of encroachment to punish the remainder beneficiary for marrying a person not of the Jewish faith was invalid. Most recently, in *Spence v. BMO Trust Company*,[9] the court firmly reiterated its support for testamentary freedom when it upheld the right of a testator to disinherit his adult child on grounds that were overtly discriminatory.

Further, s.93 of the Constitution Act 1867 – as preserved by s.29 of the Charter – explicitly guarantees the rights of denominational schools, and thereby preferences Catholic and Protestant schools. To that extent, the Constitution embeds a degree of religious discrimination.

Public Policy

Pluralism has prevailed as government's preferred mode of nation-building, acknowledging and addressing the needs of different cultural groups, including the Catholic and separatist Québécois; although, arguably, this has been at the price of facilitating the growth of a more cohesive civil society.

---

[3] (1894) 26 N.S.R. 164 at 166.
[4] *Canada Trust Co. v. Ontario Human Rights Commission* (1990) 69 DLR (4th) 321.
[5] Ibid.   [6] (1996) 139 DLR (4th) 746.
[7] Ibid., per MacDonald CJTD at para. 13.   [8] [1996] O.J. No. 375 (Ont. C.A.).
[9] 2016 ONCA 196. The author acknowledges advice from Matt Harrington on this matter (note to author, 6 April 2017).

Background

The challenge of geography, the lack of population homogeneity, the high proportion of first-generation citizens, the separateness of communities – coupled with a tradition of these being strongly self-reliant relative to the removed and non-intrusive government – and the legacy of dominance by institutional religious bodies have all contributed to an overall absence of cultural cohesion and loose governance arrangements.

Anti-Discrimination and Equality

The Charter of Rights and Freedoms explicitly guarantees the freedom of religion and rights of equality. However, unlike the US Constitution, it does not have an anti-establishment clause.

Religious Discrimination and Contemporary Public Policy

Perhaps because of Canada's singular need to ensure equality in its treatment of bijural, bilingual and indigenous communities, the federal government tendency has been to pursue a policy of accommodation. In relation to religious discrimination, the protection afforded by the equality guarantees of s.15 of the Charter, federal legislation and international protocols, as supplemented by a range of statutes at province level, have collectively given effect to this policy.

State Agencies for Religious Matters

The only federal government agency with a specific brief for religion was the Office of Religious Freedom, which was established in 2013 and terminated in 2016. Its objectives were to: protect, and advocate on behalf of, religious minorities under threat; oppose religious hatred and intolerance; and promote Canadian values of pluralism and tolerance abroad.

Domestic Policy

For present purposes, the most relevant domestic public policy is that of State neutrality in relation to religious matters. This has been explained most recently in *Mouvement laïque québécois* as follows:[10]

> The State's duty of religious neutrality results from an evolving interpretation of freedom of conscience and religion. The evolution of Canadian

---

[10] *Mouvement laïque québécois* v. *Saguenay (City)*, op. cit.

society has given rise to a concept of this neutrality according to which the State must not interfere in religion and beliefs. The State must instead remain neutral in this regard, which means that it must neither favour nor hinder any particular belief, and the same holds true for non-belief. The pursuit of the ideal of a free and democratic society requires the State to encourage everyone to participate freely in public life regardless of their beliefs. A neutral public space free from coercion, pressure and judgment on the part of public authorities in matters of spirituality is intended to protect every person's freedom and dignity, and it helps preserve and promote the multicultural nature of Canadian society. The State's duty to protect every person's freedom of conscience and religion means that it may not use its powers in such a way as to promote the participation of certain believers or non-believers in public life to the detriment of others. If the State adheres to a form of religious expression under the guise of cultural or historical reality or heritage, it breaches its duty of neutrality... the State's duty to remain neutral on questions relating to religion cannot be reconciled with a benevolence that would allow it to adhere to a religious belief... In a case in which a complaint of discrimination based on religion concerns a State practice, the alleged breach of the duty of neutrality must be established by proving that the State is professing, adopting or favouring one belief to the exclusion of all others and that the exclusion has resulted in interference with the complainant's freedom of conscience and religion. To conclude that an infringement has occurred, the Tribunal must be satisfied that the complainant's belief is sincere, and must find that the complainant's ability to act in accordance with his or her beliefs has been interfered with in a manner that is more than trivial or insubstantial.

This concept of State neutrality "allows churches and their members to play an important role in the public space where societal debates take place, while the State acts as an essentially neutral intermediary in relations between the various denominations and between those denominations and civil society".[11] Protecting the neutrality of the public space is held to be central to contemporary public policy, as it helps preserve and promote the multi-cultural nature of Canadian society.

While adopting such a policy may place the State in a position to claim that it thereby offers equal recognition to all those who profess adherence to religion or belief or to secularism, it can provide no protection to the State from domestic attacks by religious zealots (nor, of course, from political activists such as the Québécois independence movement). Canada has suffered its share of religiously inspired violence: mostly "lone-wolf"

---

[11] *Congrégation des témoins de Jéhovah de St-Jérôme-Lafontaine v. Lafontaine (Village)*, 2004 SCC 48, [2004] 2 SCR 650, per LeBel J at para. 67.

Islamist attacks causing relatively few casualties, including one in 2014 on Canada's parliament building. It has also been by far the leading common law nation to accept Syrian refugees – necessarily Muslim – during the 2015/16 migrant crisis.

Foreign Policy

An aspect of Canada's foreign policy has been alliance with the USA and other Western powers in the wars in Afghanistan and Iraq, and in the ongoing fight against al Qaeda and ISIS. As a consequence, Canada has in recent years attracted attacks by Islamist terrorists, such as the parliament-building attack.

Contemporary Law Governing Religious Discrimination

Canada has in place a modern domestic platform of human rights and anti-discrimination laws, and it is also a signatory State to most of the international treaties, conventions and protocols with a bearing on such matters.

The International Framework

Canada signed and ratified the UDHR in 1948. For present purposes, it is also relevant to note that it has ratified or acceded to the following: ICERD (1970); the International Covenant on Economic, Social and Cultural Rights (1976); and CEDAW (1981).

The International Covenant on Civil and Political Rights (ICCPR)

Canada ratified the ICCPR in 1976, and subsequently its two Optional Protocols.

International Reports

In 1999, the UN Human Rights Committee condemned Canada – particularly Ontario – for exclusively funding Catholic schools in violation of Article 26 of the ICCPR, and it did so again in 2005 when it published its Concluding Observations regarding Canada's fifth periodic report and observed that Canada had failed to "adopt steps in order to eliminate discrimination on the basis of religion in the funding of schools in Ontario". Canada's human rights record was subject to UN review in July 2015 for the first time since 2005.[12] The Committee then expressed its concern regarding several issues, including the persistence of religiously discriminating grounds for funding and for accessing public schools.

The Domestic Framework

Canada has a federated governance framework, consisting of three territories and ten provinces, each of which maintains an independent administrative system subject to loose regulatory oversight by the national government and various bodies, such as the Canadian Revenue Agency (CRA) and the Supreme Court of Canada (SCC). Of central importance is the Constitution Act 1982, containing the Canadian Charter of Rights and Freedom, which guarantees the freedom of religion. Province-level human rights legislation prohibits, among other things, discrimination on the grounds of race, religion or creed, colour, nationality, ancestry and place of origin.[13]

The Canadian Charter of Rights and Freedoms

The Charter, s.2, declares that everyone has the following "fundamental freedoms: (a) freedom of conscience and religion; and (b) freedom of thought, belief, opinion and expression". Under s.1, this is subject "only to such reasonable limits prescribed by law as can be demonstrably justified in a free and democratic society"; it requires that freedom to be interpreted in accordance with the "preservation and enhancement of the multicultural heritage of Canada" (s.27).[14] Section 15(1) provides a specific guarantee of protection from religious discrimination:

> Every individual is equal before and under the law and has the right to the equal protection and equal benefit of the law without discrimination and, in particular, without discrimination based on race, national or ethnic origin, colour, religion, sex, age or mental or physical disability.

The "Oakes test" for deciding when an infringement of a Charter right is reasonable and justifiable, established by the SCC in *R. v. Oakes*,[15] has

---

[12] See UN International Covenant on Civil and Political Rights, "Concluding Observations on the Sixth Periodic Report of Canada", at http://tbinternet.ohchr.org/_layouts/treaty bodyexternal/SessionDetails1.aspx?SessionID=899&Lang=en#sthash.XzzyC1Bz.dpuf.

[13] The Canadian Multiculturalism Act 1985 and the Canadian Race Relations Foundation Act 1991 have also set benchmarks for legislation at provincial and territorial level.

[14] See e.g. *R. v. S. (R.D.)* (1997), 118 CCC (3d) 353 (SCC), per Cory J at 385.

[15] [1986] 1 SCR 103.

served that purpose for the past thirty years. First, it requires the purpose of the infringing law to be of sufficient importance to warrant overriding a constitutionally protected right or freedom. Second, if that is the case, then there must be a "proportionality test" to establish that the means chosen are reasonable and demonstrably justified: the law must be rationally connected to the objective; the law must impair the right no more than is necessary to accomplish the objective; and the law must not have a disproportionately severe effect on the rights infringed.

As has been noted: "no individuals or religious communities enjoy any less Charter protection than the major and recognizable religions".[16]

The Canadian Bill of Rights 1960

This enshrined only those rights that had existed immediately before it was passed in 1960. It created no new rights and was considered ineffective.

The Canadian Human Rights Act 1985

This consolidated and enlarged the 1960 Bill. Section 3(1) extended the law to ensure equal opportunity for individuals and expressly prohibited discrimination on a federal basis (broadly replicated at province and territory levels) on the grounds of national or ethnic origin, colour, race, religion, age, sex, sexual orientation, marital status, family status, disability or a conviction for which a pardon has been granted or a record suspended.

The International Centre For Human Rights And Democratic Development Act 1985

As stated in the preliminaries, "the purpose of this Act is to extend the laws in Canada that proscribe discrimination".

Other Legislation

The Employment Equity Act 1996 promotes equity in the workplace of the four designated groups: women, Aboriginal peoples, persons with disabilities and members of visible minorities. In addition, the Canadian government has passed into law a set of regulations – the Federal Contractors Program 1986 and the Employment Equity Act 1996 – to address employment opportunities and benefits.

---

[16] *R* v. *Laws* (1998) 41 OR (3d) 499 Ont. CA), per McMurtry CJO at para. 24.

Courts and Tribunals

The jurisdictional division between federal and provincial government naturally affects the courts and regulatory machinery for law relating to religious discrimination: the system of Human Rights Tribunals, with a right of appeal to a court, is replicated in each province and territory.

International

The ICCPR periodic review procedure provides an international peer-monitoring forum for the ongoing review of Canadian progress in addressing human rights concerns, including religious discrimination.

Domestic

The SCC, as final court of appeal, has a federal jurisdiction enabling it to adjudicate and formulate governing principles in cases drawn from all areas of law, including those relating to the freedom of religion and religious discrimination. States and territories each have their own judicial and regulatory systems.

The Canadian Human Rights Commission (CHRC)   An independent body established at federal level, the CHRC was created to administer the Canadian Human Rights Act 1977, and subsequently undertook responsibility for ensuring compliance with the Employment Equity Act 1996.

The Canadian Human Rights Tribunal   Established under the Canadian Human Rights Act 1977, this Tribunal is independent of the CHRC, which refers cases to it for adjudication under the Act.

Freedom of Religion and Beliefs: The Principle and the Law

Religious freedom, as Dickson CJ explained, includes "the right to entertain such religious beliefs as a person chooses, the right to declare religious beliefs openly and without fear of hindrance or reprisal, and the right to manifest religious belief by worship and practice or by teaching and dissemination".[17]

Definitions

From an early stage, the Canadian courts defended a traditional interpretation of "religion", which only in recent years has broadened to accommodate different belief systems.

---

[17] *R. v. Big M Drug Mart* [1985] 1 SCR 295.

"Religion"

In *Fletcher* v. *A.G. Alta*,[18] the SCC offered the following definition:

> [r]eligion, as the subject matter of legislation, wherever the jurisdiction
> may lie, must mean religion in the sense that it is generally understood in
> Canada. It involves matters of faith and worship, and freedom of religion
> involves freedom in connection with the profession and dissemination of
> religious faith and the exercise of worship.

The importance of faith and worship and of having a body of doctrines
was illustrated by the rejection of Christian Science in *Re Cox*[19] because,
in the words of Fitzpatrick CJ, it was "a theory of all things in Heaven
and earth evolved by the Scientists of the Christian Church, rather than a
religion as commonly understood". The 1977 cases *Re Russell*[20] and *Wood
and Whitebread*[21] both determined that theosophy was not a religion. Not
until the ruling by Dickson CJ on behalf of the SCC in *R. v. Big M Drug
Mart*[22] did the courts move away from the orthodox institutional interpretation of "religion" to embrace a wider view based on an individual's
human right to choose their beliefs and how to express them:[23]

> The essence of the concept of freedom of religion is the right to entertain
> such religious beliefs as a person chooses, the rights to declare religious
> beliefs openly and without fear of hindrance or reprisal, and the right to
> manifest religious belief by worship and practice or by teaching and dis-
> semination.

This view was further developed by Iacobucci J in *Syndicat Northcrest v.
Amselem*:[24]

> Defined broadly, religion typically involves a particular and comprehen-
> sive system of faith and worship. Religion also tends to involve the belief
> in a divine, superhuman or controlling power. In essence, religion is about
> freely and deeply held personal convictions or beliefs connected to an indi-
> vidual's spiritual faith and integrally linked to one's self-definition and spir-
> itual fulfillment, the practices of which allow individuals to foster a connec-
> tion with the divine or with the subject or object of that spiritual faith.

In that case, the SCC stated that in determining the existence or otherwise of religious belief, a two-pronged test must be satisfied: it must be

---

[18] [1969] 66 WWR 513, at p. 521.   [19] *In re Cox*, 1953 1 SCR 94.
[20] (1977) 1 ETR 285 (Alta. SCTD).
[21] *Wood and Whitebread v. the Queen in Right of Alberta, Public Trustee of Alberta, The Theo-
sophical Society et al.* (1977) 6 WWR 273 (Alta. S.C.).
[22] Op. cit.   [23] Ibid., at para. 94. See also *R v. Edwards Books and Art Ltd* [1986] 2 SCR 713.
[24] (2004) 2 SCR (Canada) 576, at para. 39.

demonstrated that a person is engaged in a practice or a belief that has a nexus with religion; and the person must be sincere in their belief.

"Beliefs"

The broadening interpretation given to what might constitute the freedom of religion was evident in *Morgentaler*[25] when Wilson J advised that the freedom to hold and exercise beliefs was not restricted to beliefs of a religious nature: "in a free and democratic society 'freedom of conscience and religion' should be broadly construed to extend to conscientiously held beliefs, whether grounded in religion or in a secular morality".[26] This sentiment was endorsed by Dickson J in *Big M* in the same year:[27]

> What unites enunciated freedoms in the American First Amendment, s.2(a) of the Charter and the provisions of other human rights documents in which they are associated is the notion of the centrality of individual conscience and the inappropriateness of governmental intervention to compel or constrain its manifestation.

This "expansive definition of freedom of religion which revolves round the notion of personal choice and individual freedom and autonomy", as acknowledged by Iacobucci J in *Amselem*, has permitted the inclusive recognition of groups such as Falun Gong[28] and Wiccas,[29] and has now become a settled characteristic of the Canadian judicial approach to religion and belief.[30] Essentially, if an individual's asserted religious belief "is in good faith, neither fictitious nor capricious, and . . . is not an artifice",[31] and if they sincerely believe that manifesting that belief by way of a certain practice has spiritual significance or connects them with the divine or spiritual realm, then this will be protected under s.2(a) of the Charter. Moreover, all individuals and religious/belief organisations enjoy equal Charter protection. Further, the reference to "conscience" in that provision, in addition to religion, arguably serves to broaden the scope of protection, extending it to beliefs and convictions unrelated to, or even opposed to, religious precepts. This interpretation is supported by the SCC ruling in *Mouvement laïque québécois* v. *Saguenay (City)*,[32] where it held that for the purposes of Charter protection, the concepts of "belief" and "religion" encompass non-belief, atheism and agnosticism.[33] Meanwhile,

---

[25] See *Morgentaler* v. *R* [1988] 1 SCR 30.   [26] Ibid., at para. 251.

[27] *R.* v. *Big M Drug Mart*, op. cit., at p. 346.

[28] *Huang* v. *1233065 Ontario*, 2011 HRTO 825 (CanLII).

[29] *Re O.P.S.E.U. and Forer* (1985), 52 O.R. (2d) 705 (CA).   [30] Ibid.

[31] *Syndicat Northcrest* v. *Amselem*, op. cit., at para. 52.   [32] Op. cit.

[33] At para. 70. But there are limits: see *Blackmore* v. *The Queen*, 2013 TCC 264 (CanLII).

under s.27, there is a requirement – with direct relevance for this book – that religious freedom be interpreted in relation to Canada's multi-cultural heritage.

"Race", "Caste" and Indigenous People

The rights of Indigenous People are given general recognition in the Charter, s.35(1) and (2), but no specific mention is made of their beliefs or culture. Under-represented in human rights litigation but over-represented as victims, they rarely appear as parties in religious discrimination cases. To that extent, *Kelly*[34] was unusual. It concerned a prisoner who wished to access Aboriginal spiritual services but who instead received visits from a Christian chaplain. His complaint was upheld by the Tribunal, which found that while Christian services were reasonably available, there was no Aboriginal equivalent and no justification for such adverse treatment.

Sahota and Shergill[35] concerned the exclusion of members of the Jat caste from a religious organisation representing the Ravidassi caste. The Tribunal found that the primary purpose of the Sabha was to promote the interests of persons in the Ravidassia community, a group characterised by a common race, religion, ancestry and place of origin. The Sabha were therefore entitled to preference the Ravidassia caste, and this would not necessarily constitute religious discrimination against the complainants.

Manifesting Religion or Belief and Free Speech

It was Dickson J in *Big M*[36] who first stated the cardinal principle that has ever since governed the law relating to manifestations of religion and belief: "the values that underlie our political and philosophic traditions demand that every individual be free to hold and to manifest whatever beliefs and opinions his or her conscience dictates, provided ... only that such manifestations do not injure his or her neighbours or their parallel rights to hold and manifest beliefs and opinions of their own".[37] Subsequently, Iacobucci J explained this balance in the following terms:[38]

---

[34] *Kelly* v. *British Columbia (Public Safety and Solicitor General) (No. 3)*, 2011 BCHRT 18[?] (CanLII).

[35] *Sahota and Shergill* v. *Shri Gur Ravidass Sabha Temple*, 2008 BCHRT 269.

[36] *R.* v. *Big M Drug Mart*, op. cit.

[37] Ibid., at 346; cited in *Syndicat Northcrest* v. *Amselem*, op. cit., at para. 41.

[38] *Syndicat Northcrest* v. *Amselem*, op. cit., at para. 137.

First, there is the freedom to believe and to profess one's beliefs; second, there is the right to manifest one's beliefs, primarily by observing rites, and by sharing one's faith by establishing places of worship and frequenting them. Thus, although private beliefs have a purely personal aspect, the other dimension of the right has genuine social significance and involves a relationship with others.

Adherence to a particular religion or belief does not imply that an adherent is restricted to manifesting their commitment in a preordained manner; it must, however, be more than a peripheral indicator (e.g. the formal reciprocal bow of participants in a judo contest is not a manifestation of the Shinto religion/belief[39]), otherwise the constraints on choice in the manner of manifesting adherence are only those generally pertaining to nuisance, health/safety and the rights of others in public places.[40]

Free Speech and Freedom of Association

In *Ross* v. *Canada*,[41] the subject was a former teacher who in his spare time published books and pamphlets and made public statements reflecting his discriminatory views in relation to Jews.[42] The Human Rights Board of Inquiry concluded that he had contributed to a "poisoned environment" within the school district and recommended that he be transferred to a non-teaching position, which was endorsed by the SCC and also by the UN Human Rights Committee, which agreed that the disciplinary action did not constitute a violation of the freedom of expression as guaranteed by Article 19 (ICCPR).

Freedom of association is guaranteed under s.2(d) of the Charter; this right entitles individuals to establish, belong to, maintain or leave any legal organisation.

Blasphemy

The Criminal Code, s.296(1), declares that anyone who publishes a blasphemous libel is guilty of an indictable offence.

Conscientious Objection

Provisions in the Order of Council 1873 have traditionally exempted certain religious communities, such as Mennonites and Quakers, from military service.

---

[39] *Akiyama* v. *Judo B.C. (No. 2)* (2002), 43 C.H.R.R. D/425, 2002 BCHRT 27.
[40] *R* v. *Laws*, op. cit., at para. 23.   [41] (1996), 25 C.H.R.R. D/175 (SCC).
[42] UN Human Rights Committee, 18 October 2000, Communication No. 736/1997.

Proselytism

In *Zundel* v. *Canada*,[43] which concerned holocaust-denial publications, the SCC considered the limitations imposed on proselytism by s.181 of the Criminal Code. This stated that "[e]very one who willfully publishes a statement, tale or news that he knows is false and causes or is likely to cause injury or mischief to a public interest is guilty of an indictable offence and liable to imprisonment". The court found that s.181 violated s.2(b) of the Canadian Charter of Rights and Freedoms because the restriction on all expressions "likely to cause injury or mischief to a public interest" was too broad and imprisonment for expression was unreasonable. The parameters for proselytism were subsequently amended, and are now set by s.319.(2) of the Code.

In *Friesen* v. *Fisher Bay Seafood*,[44] the Tribunal found that an employee had suffered religious discrimination when sacked because he refused to stop preaching in the workplace, but that his sacking was justified as other employees had a right to work in an environment where they were not subject to religious preaching and the employer did not have a duty to accommodate an employee's beliefs.

Discrimination

The Canadian Human Rights Act specifies eleven grounds in respect of which discriminatory practices are prohibited. In dealing with competing rights claims, the SCC has confirmed that there is no hierarchy of Charter rights: all have equal status; none is more important than any other.[45]

Religious Discrimination

As one of the eleven grounds, religious discrimination attracts considerable litigation in this multi-cultural common law jurisdiction. This was most clearly evident in the previously mentioned *Canada Trust* case,[46] when the court found it was "to expatiate the obvious" that a trust premised on notions of racism and religious superiority was obviously discriminatory and therefore void. As with other allegations[47] of a breach

---

[43] [1992] 2 SCR 731.   [44] (2008), 65 C.H.R.R. D/400, 2009 BCHRT 1.

[45] *Reference re Same-Sex Marriage* [2004] 3 SCR 698; *Dagenais* v. *Canadian Broadcasting Corp.* [1994] 3 SCR 835, at p. 877; *R.* v. *Mills* [1999] 3 SCR 668, at para. 61.

[46] See *Re Canada Trust Co.* v. *Ontario (Human Rights Commission)*; *Re Leonard Foundation Canada Trust Co.* v. *Ontario Human Rights Commission*, op. cit.

[47] See *Spence* v. *BMO Trust Company*, op. cit. See also *Royal Trust Corporation of Canada* v *The University of Western Ontario et al.*, 2016 ONSC 1143. The author acknowledges advice from Matt Harrington on this matter (note to author, 6 April 2017).

of rights, claims of religious discrimination must be evidenced, be objectively verifiable and be proven in accordance with the balance of probabilities test.[48] The comments of Gascon J must also be borne in mind: "I concede that the State's duty of neutrality does not require it to abstain from celebrating and preserving its religious heritage. But that cannot justify the State engaging in a discriminatory practice for religious purposes."[49]

Type The Canadian Human Rights Act lists seven types of discriminatory practice that are prohibited in relation to any of the eleven grounds, including religious discrimination, specified in the Act. The different types are: denying goods, services, facilities or accommodation; providing goods, services, facilities or accommodation in a way that treats someone adversely and differently; refusing to employ or continue to employ someone, or treating them unfairly in the workplace; following policies or practices that deprive people of employment opportunities; paying men and women differently when they are doing work of the same value; retaliating against a person who has filed a complaint with the Commission or against someone who has filed a complaint for them; and harassment.

Exemptions and Exceptions

In keeping with many other common law countries, religious organisations in Canada have long enjoyed special privileges because of their status as such.

The "Religious" Exemption

In addition to the right to discriminate when employing staff in accordance with the bona fide occupational requirements (BFOR)[50] rule, the Constitution Act 1867, s.93(1), protects denominational school privileges from the anti-discrimination strictures of modern human rights law and the Canadian Charter of Rights and Freedoms.

When the Civil Marriage Act[51] was introduced, which extended the meaning of marriage to include same-sex relationships under Canadian federal law and inserted ss.149.1 into the Income Tax Act,[52] it provided that religious organisations would not have their charitable registration revoked solely because they or any of their members exercised freedom of

---

[48] S.L. v. Commission scolaire des Chênes, 2012 SCC 7, at paras 22–24.
[49] Mouvement laïque québécois v. Saguenay (City), op. cit., at para. 116.
[50] See e.g. Canada Trust Co. v. Ontario Human Rights Commission, op. cit., per Tarnopolsky J at para. 98.
[51] SC 2005, c. 33.   [52] RSC 1985 (5th Supp.), c. 1, as amended.

conscience and religion in relation to the meaning of marriage. The SCC had also ruled to similar effect in *Reference re Same-Sex Marriage*.[53] All of this was in keeping with an established acceptance, clearly evident in testamentary dispositions, that religious beliefs conferred a degree of immunity from the otherwise non-differentiating application of the law. As Cambell J pointed out in *Trinity Western University* v. *Nova Scotia Barristers' Society*,[54] the plaintiff university, "like churches and other private institutions, does not have to comply with the equality provisions of the Charter".

The "Charity" Exemption

In *Christian Brothers of Ireland in Canada (Re)*,[55] the Ontario Court of Appeal agreed with the court at first instance that there is no general doctrine of charitable immunity applicable in Canada, and consequently all assets of a charity, whether owned beneficially or held pursuant to a special-purpose charitable trust, were available to satisfy claims by victims of historical child abuse on the winding-up of the religious organisation. The SCC denied leave to appeal.[56] In addition, the CRA grants charitable tax exemption to religious organisations in general and continues the traditional legal presumption that they are for the public benefit.[57]

The "Positive Action" Exception

The equality provision in the Canadian Charter of Rights and Freedoms, s.15(1), is subject to the s.15(2) exception that it "does not preclude any law, program or activity that has as its object the amelioration of conditions of disadvantaged individuals or groups including those that are disadvantaged because of race, national or ethnic origin, colour, religion, sex, age or mental or physical disability".

In the previously mentioned *Canada Trust* case,[58] Justice Tarnopolsky stated that scholarships could be restricted to "women, aboriginal people, the physically or mentally handicapped, or other historically disadvantaged groups", as was applied in *University of Victoria* v. *British Columbia*

---

[53] Op. cit.   [54] 2015 NSSC 25, at para. 10.

[55] 2000 CanLII 5712 (ON CA). See also *Rowland* v. *Vancouver College Ltd* [2000] B.C.J. No 1666 (QL).

[56] [2000] S.C.C.A. No. 277 (QL).

[57] See CRA, "Religious Charities – Exemption", Policy Commentary, CPC – O16, 17 October 2003.

[58] Op. cit. See also *Canadian National Railway Co.* v. *Canada (Human Rights Comm.) and Action travail des femmes* (1987), 8 C.H.R.R. D/4210 (S.C.C.).

(A.G.)[59] to positively discriminate in favour of Roman Catholics. This approach acknowledges that such groups, including those defined by their religion or beliefs, may have distinct needs that are most effectively and efficiently addressed by that form of discrimination. Harrington adds that:[60]

> One of the big qualifications that comes from the cases following *Canada Trust* is that that *Canada Trust* is based on "blatant religious supremacy, racism and sexism". Later courts seem to be restricting Canada *Trust* to its facts. This case, in particular, seems to make that distinction.

Religious Discrimination: Church and State

As Moon has pointed out:[61]

> the requirement that the State show equal respect for different religious groups or belief systems is understood by many to entail the exclusion of religion from public life, the separation of law and religion. Others, however, argue that the privatization of religion does not advance equal citizenship or religious inclusion but instead marginalizes religious individuals or groups and undermines religious pluralism.

The Church/State Boundary

Canada is far from being the only common law jurisdiction in which religion has been constitutionally presumed to refer to Christianity and duly accorded special State recognition; examples range from the reference to the "supremacy of God" in the Charter preamble to the statutory recognition of religious holidays, inscriptions on coinage and the tax exemptions granted to religious institutions. Given that a growing proportion of Canadian citizens are irreligious, or at least non-Christian, such State endorsement of Christianity may seem anachronistic – but no government has sought to change it.

Nonetheless, as the SCC rightly proclaimed in 1955, "in this country, there is no State religion and all denominations enjoy the same degree of freedom of speech and thought".[62] It then ruled that police action in dispersing a peaceful meeting of Jehovah's Witnesses and confiscating religious materials constituted a flagrant violation of the latter's right to "the free exercise and enjoyment of Religious Profession and Worship,

---

[59] [2000] B.C.J. No. 520.   [60] Note to author, 6 April 2017.
[61] Moon, *Law and Religious Pluralism*, at p. 2.
[62] *Chaput* v. *Romain* [1955] SCR 834, per Kerwin CJ, Taschereau and Estey JJ at p. 835.

without discrimination or preference" as guaranteed under s.175 of the Statutes of Canada 1851. Despite that instance of aggressive intervention, the State/Church relationship has long been characterised as one of co-operation, distinctly different from the explicit constitutional separation of the parties in the USA. In particular, the legacy of religion as an established institution and the close relationship between government and Church leaders – with direct funding arrangements – have continued into present times. The doctrine of State neutrality is interpreted in Canada to mean only that the State treats all religions equally, not that an impermeable *cordon sanitaire* is maintained between Church and State. As Justice McLachlin expresses it:[63]

> As a general rule, the State refrains from acting in matters relating to religion. It is limited to setting up a social and legal framework in which beliefs are respected and members of the various denominations are able to associate freely in order to exercise their freedom of worship, which is a fundamental, collective aspect of freedom of religion, and to organize their churches or communities.

Distinguishing the Canadian approach from its US equivalent, Gascon J explains that:[64]

> True neutrality is concerned not with a strict separation of Church and State on questions related to religious thought. The purpose of neutrality is instead to ensure that the State is, and appears to be, open to all points of view regardless of their spiritual basis. Far from requiring separation, true neutrality requires that the State neither favour nor hinder any religion, and that it abstain from taking any position on this subject.

Again, in the latest in the long run of Trinity Western University (TWU) cases:[65]

> State neutrality is essential in a secular, pluralistic society. Canadian society is made up of diverse communities with disparate beliefs that cannot and need not be reconciled. While the State must adopt laws on some matters of social policy with which religious and other communities and individuals may disagree (such as enacting legislation recognizing same-sex marriage), it does so in the context of making room for diverse communities to hold and act on their beliefs.

---

[63] *Congrégation des témoins de Jéhovah de St-Jérôme-Lafontaine v. Lafontaine (Village)* [2004] 2 SCR 650, 2004 SCC 48.

[64] *Mouvement laïque québécois v. Saguenay (City)*, op. cit., at para. 137.

[65] *Trinity Western University v. Law Society of British Columbia*, 2016 BCCA 423, at para. 185.

Protecting Religion from the State

Religious bodies have traditionally been given the freedom to organise as they see fit, largely free from government regulatory requirements, including being able to hire staff on the basis of religious affiliation, and they currently enjoy other exemptions in relation to matters such as sexual orientation and gender parity. Religious communities such as the Hutterites are largely left to regulate their own affairs. Indeed, when Dickson J, in *Big M*, pronounced on the freedom of religion, he did so in terms which emphasised the positive and protective role of the State:[66]

> Freedom in a broad sense embraces both the absence of coercion and constraint, and the right to manifest beliefs and practices. Freedom means that, subject to such limitations as are necessary to protect public safety, order, health, or morals or the fundamental rights and freedoms of others, no one is to be forced to act in a way contrary to his beliefs or his conscience.

In that case, the SCC held that the legislative intent of the federal Lord's Day Act – to make observance of the Christian Sabbath compulsory – was incompatible with the freedom of religion under s.2(a) of the Charter.[67] However, in *R* v. *Edwards Books and Art Ltd*,[68] although the SCC found that legislation prohibiting Sunday shopping had similarly breached the freedom of religion under that section, as it discriminated against certain non-Christian retailers, nonetheless a majority took the view that the purpose of giving people a day of rest was justifiable under s.1 of the Charter, as it it clearly benefitted all workers (particularly those in the retail trade), it was proportionate and it allowed for some exceptions. Most recently, the *Loyola* case[69] is also significant in this context as it is a strong ruling by Canada's highest court affirming the State duty to protect the identity and integrity of religious institutions.

Intervention in Church Disputes

More than a century ago, in the *Guibord* case,[70] it was established that the civil courts of Canada have the jurisdiction to resolve disputes between members of a church and the church organisation. The issue then was whether a Roman Catholic church in Montreal could refuse to bury one of its deceased members because it disapproved of his political views. In determining that it could not refuse, the court confined itself to finding

---

[66] *R* v. *Big M Drug Mart*, op. cit., at para. 95.   [67] Ibid., at para. 39.
[68] Op. cit.   [69] *Loyola High School* v. *Québec (Attorney General)*, 2015 SCC 12.
[70] *Brown* v. *Les Curé et Marguilliers de l'Œuvre et de la Fabrique de la Paroisse de Montréal* (1874), L.R. 6 P.C. 157, [1874] UKPC 70 (PC).

that as a member, the deceased was entitled to be treated in accordance with the internal administrative rules of his church.

Unlike the US courts, which defer to the principle of the free exercise of religion and refrain from engaging in doctrinal argument, in Canada the courts would appear to feel less constrained and will engage in adjudicating on Church matters, including property disputes,[71] without preference for doctrine, but with a forensic respect for trust law and for the right of the Canadian religious organisations to manage their affairs without recourse to doctrinal guidance from elsewhere.

However, while they may have jurisdiction to intervene in Church matters, the courts have become very reluctant to do so. As Iacobucci J explained in *Amselem:*[72]

> It is, of course, axiomatic that courts of law deal with secular matters only. They do not normally concern themselves with matters of religious doctrine or government unless those matters become elements in disputes relating to property or other legal rights.

This view is one that has attracted considerable judicial support since the *Guibord* ruling, with remarks to the effect that "the truth or falsity of religions is not the business of officials or the courts"[73] and that "it is not the role of this court to decide what any particular religion believes",[74] and comments on the general "undesirability of a State-conducted inquiry into an individual's religious beliefs".[75] Most recently, in *Diaferia v. Elliott,*[76] the court drew the line at reviewing decisions taken by members: it had "no intention of getting involved in how the ultimate meeting of the Church members proceeds ... this court must circumscribe the extent to which it becomes involved in the internal affairs of a religious organisation".[77]

The State, Religion and Religious Discrimination

As McLachlin explains:[78]

> a provision of a statute, of regulations or of a by-law will be inoperative if its purpose is religious and therefore cannot be reconciled with the State's

---

[71] *Bentley v. Anglican Synod of the Diocese of New Westminster,* 2009 BCSC 1608 (CanLII).

[72] *Syndicat Northcrest v. Amselem,* op. cit.

[73] See *Church of the New Faith v. Commissioner of Pay-roll Tax* (1983) 154 CLR 120, per Murphy J at p. 150.

[74] See *B. (R.) v. Children's Aid Society of Metropolitan Toronto* [1995] 1 SCR 315, per LaForest J at p. 866.

[75] See *Edwards Books and Art Ltd et al. v. the Queen* (1986) 35 DLR (4th) 1. (SCC), at p. 26.

[76] 2013 ONSC 1363.   [77] Ibid., per Edwards J at p. 22J.

[78] *Mouvement laïque québécois v. Saguenay (City),* op. cit.

duty of neutrality... In a case in which a complaint of discrimination based on religion concerns a State practice, the alleged breach of the duty of neutrality must be established by proving that the State is professing, adopting or favouring one belief to the exclusion of all others and that the exclusion has resulted in interference with the complainant's freedom of conscience and religion.

Balancing Religion and Secularism

As Cambell J noted in *Trinity Western*:[79]

> Canada is a "secular society". The State remains neutral on matters of religion. It does not favour one religion over another. And it does not favour either religion or the absence of it. While the society may be largely secular, in the sense that religion has lost its hold on social mores and individual conduct for many people, the State is not secular in the sense that it promotes the process of secularization. It remains neutral.

Judicial engagement with issues relating to the ordering of public life exclusively on the basis of non-religious practices and values has produced some significant landmark judgments. The first and most notable was the *Big M* case,[80] in which the presenting issue was a clash of interests between commercial and religious bodies. The SCC, however, took the opportunity to examine the balance to be struck between religion and secularism in a modern democratic State.

On Sunday, 30 May 1982, Big M Drug Mart in Calgary was charged with violating the Lord's Day Act by opening for business. Big M was acquitted at trial, the appeal being subsequently dismissed by Alberta Court of Appeal, but nonetheless the case was brought before the SCC to determine whether s.2 of the Charter of Rights and Freedom had a bearing on the matter. The court ruled the Lord's Day Act unconstitutional because laws must have a secular purpose. It left open the possibility for Sunday closing laws based on secular purposes (e.g. "rest days"), but a law based on religious reasons and favoring one denomination over others was deemed unconstitutional. As Dickson CJ then explained:[81]

> In proclaiming the standards of the Christian faith, the Act creates a climate hostile to, and gives the appearance of discrimination against, non-Christian Canadians... The theological content of the legislation remains as a subtle and constant reminder to religious minorities within the country of their differences with, and alienation from, the dominant religious culture.

---

[79] *Trinity Western University* v. *Nova Scotia Barristers' Society*, op. cit., at para. 19. See also Moon, *Law and Religious Pluralism*, at p. 231.
[80] *R* v. *Big M Drug Mart*, op. cit.   [81] Ibid., at p. 354.

This ruling represents an important milestone in the Canadian experience of building a multi-cultural nation in which the rights of religious minorities are assured of equal recognition and protection in law.

Another significant milestone was the *Hutterite* case,[82] which concerned the Alberta government's decision to withdraw an exemption previously available to Hutterites (whose religious beliefs prohibited them from willingly allowing their pictures to be taken) from the requirement that their drivers' licences include photographs: an exemption clearly illustrative of State concern that a neutral law should not adversely discriminate against a religious minority. In rejecting the applicants' claim, McLachlin CJ acknowledged the perspective of religious claimants' rights, but, as she went on to explain, "this perspective must be considered in the context of a multicultural, multi-religious society where the duty of State authorities to legislate for the general good inevitably produces conflict with individual beliefs". In that light, there could be little doubt that the balance between the interests of Hutterites and State would have to be recalibrated:[83]

> Much of the regulation of a modern State could be claimed by various individuals to have a more than trivial impact on a sincerely held religious belief. Giving effect to each of their religious claims could seriously undermine the universality of many regulatory programs, including the attempt to reduce abuse of driver's licences at issue here, to the overall detriment of the community.

Again, in *Amselem*,[84] the SCC ruled that a condominium board had to allow a group of Orthodox Jewish unit-owners to construct succahs on their balconies as part of the Jewish festival of Succot, despite the prohibition in their condominium contract prohibiting tenants from altering property. The property rights of secularists would have to give way to the rights of a minority to publicly celebrate their religion in a religious festival, in the same way that Christians would do at Christmas. This right has since been variously iterated in the human rights legislation of the provinces, and it is there that much related caselaw has been generated.[85] Most recently, in *Loyola High School* v. *Québec (Attorney General)*,[86] the

---

[82] *Alberta* v. *Hutterian Brethren of Wilson Colony*, 2009 SCC 37, [2009] 2 SCR 567.
[83] Ibid., at para. 36.   [84] *Syndicat Northcrest* v. *Amselem*, op. cit.
[85] See e.g. *Rosenberg* v. *Outremont (City)* (2001), File No. 500-05-060659-008. See also *Chamberlain* v. *Surrey School District No. 36*, 2002 SCC 86.
[86] Op. cit.

SCC commented that secularism includes "respect for religious differences" and that "through this form of neutrality, the State affirms and recognizes the religious freedom of individuals and their communities".[87]

State Funding of Faith-Based Facilities and Services

It is widely accepted that any form of State support or preference for the religious beliefs/practices of some over those of others (even when there is no direct coercion) is incompatible with a commitment to religious freedom and equality[88]

This is endorsed by Ryder, who observes: "[t]he entrenchment of freedom of religion in the Canadian Constitution has had the effect of promoting the secularization of the State in the sense that the State must refrain from adopting laws or policies that have the objective or effect of favouring one religion over another". The State, says Ryder, may facilitate or support religious life only if "it does so without discriminating against any particular religious or conscientious belief system": if it is even-handed in its treatment of different groups or belief systems. Indeed, in recent years, the SCC has made it clear that "State sponsorship of one religious tradition" breaches the State's duty of neutrality, and is both discriminatory and destructive of religious freedom;[89] the State has a duty not to "create a preferential public space that favours certain religious groups".[90] However, it remains the case that the Constitution Act 1867, s.93 extends protection to denominational schools and permits partisan State funding (see later). This anomaly was judicially acknowledged in *Adler* v. *Ontario*[91] when Iacobucci J, on behalf of the court majority, ruled that government funding of both Roman Catholic and public schools, but not private religious schools, was entitled to special protection[92] under that constitutional provision.[93]

---

[87] Ibid., at paras 43–44. See further www.carters.ca/pub/seminar/charity/2015/Renderings2015.pdf.
[88] Moon, *Law and Religious Pluralism*, at p. 3.
[89] See, for example, *R.* v. *Big M Drug Mart*, op. cit., at p. 337; *S.L.* v. *Commission scolaire des Chênes* [2012] 1 SCR 235, at para. 17; and *Mouvement laïque québécois* v. *Saguenay (City)*, op. cit., at paras 64 and 80.
[90] *Mouvement laïque québécois* v. *Saguenay (City)*, op. cit., at para. 64.
[91] [1996] SCR 609.
[92] Section 93 of the Constitution Act 1867 was deemed by Iacobucci J to be "immune from Charter scrutiny".
[93] 30 & 31 Victoria, c. 3.

The recent SCC ruling in *Mouvement laïque québécois* v. *Saguenay (City)*[94] confirms judicial preference for the Moon and Ryder approach. The SCC then explained the doctrine of State neutrality as follows:[95]

> If the State adheres to a form of religious expression under the guise of cultural or historical reality or heritage, it breaches its duty of neutrality . . . The legislative objective cannot be to impose or favour, or to express or profess, one belief to the exclusion of all others.

State neutrality should be the rule, but it is not restricted to religion: it is to be applied with equal rigour to other beliefs and to none. While Gascon J then acknowledged that "sponsorship of one religious tradition by the State in breach of its duty of neutrality amounts to discrimination against all other such traditions", he went on to explain that State neutrality "requires that the State neither favour nor hinder any particular belief, and the same holds true for non-belief . . . the State (must) abstain from taking any position and thus avoid adhering to a particular belief . . . it may not use its powers in such a way as to promote the participation of certain believers or non-believers in public life to the detriment of others"; its duty will be breached by any action that "reveal(s) an intention to profess, adopt or favour one belief to the exclusion of all others".[96] Also, "the State . . . does not have a freedom to believe or to manifest a belief; compliance with its duty of neutrality does not entail a reconciliation of rights".[97] Moreover, State neutrality does not constitute preferential treatment of non-believers:[98]

> there is a distinction between unbelief and true neutrality. True neutrality presupposes abstention, but it does not amount to a stand favouring one view over another. No such inference can be drawn from the State's silence.

Nonetheless, the protections of the Constitution Act 1867, s.93 remain in effect.

Christian Symbols/Prayers in State Facilities

The customary recitation of the Lord's Prayer, or a similar Christian blessing, at the commencement of proceedings in public institutions was a cultural characteristic of public life in Canada, as elsewhere in the common law world and beyond. Since 1982, however, a series of cases have mostly

---

[94] Op. cit., at para. 64.
[95] *Mouvement laïque québécois* v. *Saguenay (City)*, op. cit., at paras 78–81.
[96] Ibid., at para. 88.   [97] Ibid., at para. 119.   [98] Ibid., at para. 134.

confirmed that such practices are in breach of the Charter, s.2. *Allen*,[99] interestingly, was an exception, as the plaintiff's claim that the council's practice of opening each meeting with a prayer constituted religious discrimination was rejected by the court.

In a school setting, cases such as *Zylberberg v. Sudbury Board of Education (Director)*[100] and *Russow v. BC (AG)*[101] have established that the compulsory recitation of the Lord's Prayer – to the exclusion of prayers from any other religion – constitutes an impermissible infringement of religious freedom. This approach gained further support from the ruling in *Mouvement laïque québécois v. Saguenay (City)*[102] when the SCC, noting that "the recitation of the prayer at the council's meetings was above all else a use by the council of public powers to manifest and profess one religion to the exclusion of all others", relied upon the doctrine of State neutrality to justify prohibiting Christian blessings in a municipal setting.

Religious Discrimination: Contemporary Caselaw

The religious discrimination thresholds of a society at any point in time can be best ascertained by examining the traffic of related cases through the courts. This section considers such trends and principles as may be discerned from the contemporary flow of such cases.

Religious Conduct, Symbols, Icons, Apparel, etc.

"Religion is a matter of faith intermingled with culture", as McLachlin J noted in the *Hutterite* case.[103] Then, but perhaps more so in *Amselem*, the judiciary wrestled with the weighting to be given to religious/cultural customs relative to neutral public benefit laws of uniform application.

Ethnicity/Religion-Specific Customs

The approach adopted by the SCC in the pre-Charter Indian hunting cases[104] is interesting. These concluded with the dismissal of claims that provincial wildlife protection laws interfered with the freedom of religion

---

[99] *Allen v. Corporation of the County of Renfrew*, 2004 CanLII 13978 (ON SC). See also *Freitag v. Penetanguishene* (1999), 47 O.R. (3d) 301.
[100] (1988), 65 O.R. (2d) 641, 29 O.A.C. 23 (CA)   [101] (1989).   [102] Op. cit.
[103] *Alberta v. Hutterian Brethren of Wilson Colony*, op. cit., at para. 89.
[104] *Kruger and Manuel v. The Queen* (1977), [1978] 1 SCR 104, 75 DLR (3d) 434; *Simon v. The Queen* (1985), [1985] 2 SCR 387, 62 N.R.366; *Arthur Dick v. The Queen* (1985), [1985] 2 SCR 309, 62 N.R. 1, [1986] 1 W.W.R.1; and *Jack and Charlie v. The Queen* (1985), [1985] 2 SCR 332, 62 N.R. 14, [1986] 1 W.W.R.21.

of Indians, for whom hunting formed an integral part of their culture. Notwithstanding the assertion in *Jack and Charlie* that the deer meat-burning ritual represented a traditional core cultural component of the Coastal Salish Indian community – comparable, perhaps, to Christian communion – the court concluded that the wildlife legislation, being of general application, was equally applicable to Indians. This contrasts with the post-Charter SCC rulings in *Hutterite* and *Amselem*, which, it would seem, were resolved by using the proportionality principle to gauge the significance of the custom for the religion/culture concerned against the overall importance of a neutral public benefit law in order to determine whether the latter had such a disproportionate adverse effect on the former as to be in breach of the applicants' freedom of religion. In such cases, an adherent's subjective interpretation of the importance of a custom will need to be supported by hard evidence linking it to the religion/belief.[105]

In *Bruker v. Marcovitz*,[106] the SCC found that a Jewish husband's five-year-long refusal to grant his wife a *get*, thereby preventing her from divorcing him, was contrary to public policy, as "under Canadian law, marriage and divorce are available equally to men and women".[107] The court rejected the husband's defence that he was protected by the right to freedom of religion. Abella J warned that this well-established Jewish principle, confining the granting of a *get* exclusively to the discretion of a husband, was incompatible with Canadian law and that public policy supported the removal of barriers to religious divorce and remarriage.

Religious Apparel

In *Saadi*,[108] the court considered the fraught issue – which presents in many jurisdictions – of a Muslim female employee wearing her hijab. It pointedly overruled the Tribunal, finding that: "[t]he Code guarantees not only a woman's right to wear a religious headdress in the workplace, but also her right to choose the form of religious headdress, subject to any bona fide occupational requirements". Instead, it stated that the issue was: Could the employee have complied with the dress code without compromising her religious beliefs? What was she actually required to wear as part of her religion? Then, consideration could be given to whether the employer's dress code, or the employer's enforcement or interpretation of it, conflicted with what the employee chose to wear. Similarly, the issue

---

[105] See *Whitehouse v. Yukon* (2001), 48 C.H.R.R. D/497 (Y.T.Bd.Adj.).
[106] (2007) 3 SCR.   [107] Ibid., at 3.   [108] *Saadi v. Audmax*, 2009 HRTO 1627.

of wearing the niqab when testifying in court was resolved in *NS*[109] by applying the following guidance: "If the judge concludes that the wearing of the niqab in all of the circumstances would infringe the accused's right to make full answer and defence, the right must prevail over the witness's religious freedoms and the witness must be ordered to remove the niqab".

In *Multani*,[110] the SCC ruled that "a total prohibition against wearing a kirpan (a ceremonial dagger) to school undermines the value of the religious symbol and sends students the message that some religious practices do not merit the same protection as others".[111] The SCC considered that the freedom of a Sikh boy to carry his kirpan outweighed reasons (e.g. alleged safety concerns) to prohibit him from doing so, unlike an earlier Tribunal ruling which held that safety reasons justified a prohibition against wearing it on an aircraft.[112] This exercise in balancing the unintentional adverse effects of a neutral rule on a religious/cultural minority against a general concern to promote the public benefit can be seen in a considerable number and variety of cases.[113] It should not, of course, distract attention from the blunt fact that an item of apparel – such as a turban – which identifies the religion/ethnicity of the wearer is often sufficient to attract discrimination;[114] the policy decision permitting Sikh officers of the RCMP to wear turbans was, therefore, a potent political symbol, neatly conflating religion and culture with nationalism.

Family-Related Issues

The traditional family model has found strong support from the well-established religious institutions – mainly, but by no means exclusively, Christian – in Canada. Consequently, as might be expected, issues have tended to arise most frequently in relation to: homosexuality, same-sex marriages, abortion services and a range of gay,[115] lesbian and transgender[116] matters and the consequences thereof.[117]

---

[109] *R. v. N.S.*, 2010 ONCA 670 (CanLII).

[110] *Multani v. Commission scolaire Marguerite-Bourgeoys* [2006] 1 S.C.R. 256, 2006 SCC 6.

[111] Ibid., at 297.   [112] *Nijjar v. Canada 3000 Airlines Ltd*, 1999 CANLII (CHRT).

[113] See, for example, *Grant v. Canada* [1996] 1 SCR vii, 130 DLR (4th) vii and *Peel Board of Education v. Pandori* (1991) 3 OR (3D) 531 (Div Ct).

[114] *Randhawa v. Tequila Bar & Grill Ltd* 2008 AHRC 3 (CanLII).

[115] See *Egan v. Canada* (1995) 2 SCR 513, where a statutory definition of "spouse" which excluded homosexual partners was deemed to discriminate against a homosexual couple.

[116] See e.g. *Vancouver Rape Relief Society v. Nixon*, 2005 BCCA 601.

[117] See *P. (S.E.) v. P. (D.D.)*, 2005 BCSC 1290, where the British Columbia Supreme Court ruled that the definition of adultery should include affairs between two people of the same gender.

Sexuality

LGBT issues have generated considerable litigation. So, for example
Boisson[118] concerned a letter, written by the appellant to a newspaper, expressing disparaging comments about homosexuals. In overturning the HRC finding of incitement to hatred and upholding the relative importance of freedom of speech, Wilson J ruled that the language
used must disclose a real intention to discriminate or incite others to discriminate. More recently, the same approach was taken by the SCC in
Saskatchewan (Human Rights Commission) v. *Whatcott*,[119] regarding fly-
ers denouncing gays and lesbians, when it emphasised the need to pursue
true hate speech, not just offensive language. Similarly, in *Trinity Western*,[120] the court found no concrete evidence that holding beliefs about
homosexuality would result in actions by its graduates that would be
discriminatory.

Freedom of religion and belief has been locked into the Constitution via
the Charter: s.2(a) specifically prevents the legislature from discriminating
against religious minorities, while s.1 qualifies this with the proviso that
it be exercised subject to such "reasonable limits prescribed by law as can
be demonstrably justified in a free and democratic society". This has provided a context for challenging the right of the legislature to extend the
legal definition of marriage to include same-sex couples. In *Halpern*,[12]
the court concluded that the common law definition of marriage as "the
voluntary union for life of one man and one woman to the exclusion of
all others" infringed the equality rights of same-sex couples under s.15 of
the Charter and rejected the claims of a Christian Church that the new
definition of marriage infringed its freedom of religion, contrary to s.2(a)
and its equality rights as a religious institution. This was followed immediately by *Reference re Same-Sex Marriage*,[122] where the SCC found that
the meaning of marriage is not frozen in time, in accordance with its definition under s.91(26) of the Constitution Act 1867, but must be allowed
to evolve with Canadian society, which currently represents a plurality of
groups. In rejecting the notion that allowing same-sex couples to marry
infringed the religious freedom of those opposed to same-sex marriage

---

[118] *Boisson* v. *Lund*, 2009 ABQB 592.   [119] [2013] 1 SCR 467.

[120] *Trinity Western University* v. *British Columbia College of Teachers* (2001), 39 C.H.R.R
D/357. 2001 SCC 31.

[121] *Halpern* v. *Canada (Attorney General)* [2003] O.J. No. 2268.

[122] Op. cit. See also *R.* v. *Big M Drug Mart*, op. cit., at paras 94–96 and *Gay Alliance Toward
Equality* v. *Vancouver Sun*, 1979 CanLII 225 (SCC), [1979] 2 SCR 435.

the court advised that "the mere recognition... or promotion... of the equality rights of one group cannot, in itself, constitute a violation of the rights of another".[123]

When marriages break down and a non-custodial parent continues to define the religious upbringing of the children, contrary to the wishes of the other parent, then court intervention is often necessary. The courts have explored the respective rights of the parties in a number of cases,[124] including *Young v. Young*,[125] where the non-custodial parent – a Jehovah's Witness – protested that his freedom of religion, including his right to develop his children's religious beliefs, was being obstructed by their mother. The SCC took the view that the welfare of the child was the overriding principle, and therefore the authority of the custodial parent to make decisions over religious activities must be secured in order to protect the children from any harmful stress.

Conception, Abortion, IVF and Related Issues

The difficulties, controversy and extent of litigation generated in regard to abortion can be seen in the many lengthy court battles involving anti-abortion groups,[126] an anti-pornography group,[127] campaigning pro-life groups[128] and abortion clinics,[129] as well as in the uncertain status of the foetus in Canadian law.[130] The long history of *Morgentaler* prosecutions[131] records the changing legal status of abortion clinics in Canada. Abortion is now a wholly legal procedure, and government-funded clinics are widely available throughout most of the country. Similarly, surrogacy, the creation of embryos for assisted-reproduction procedures and the donation of embryos for stem cell research have been legally possible since the Assisted Human Reproduction Act came into effect in 2004.

---

[123] Ibid., at para. 47. See also *Loyola High School* v. *Québec (Attorney General)*, op. cit.
[124] *Hockey* v. *Hockey* (1989) 60 D.L.R. (4th) 765 (Ont. Div. Ct.); *P.(D.)* v. *S.(C.)* [1993] 4 S.C.R. 141; and *Young* v. *Young* [1993] 4 SCR 3.
[125] Op. cit.
[126] E.g., *Human Life International in Canada Inc.* v. *Canada (Minister of National Revenue)*, FCJ No. 365, March 18, 1998 and *Alliance for Life* v. *Canada (MNR)*, 1999 FCJ No. 658 (5 May 1999).
[127] See *Positive Action Against Pornography* v. *MNR* [1988] 1 CTC 232.
[128] See *Interfaith Development Education Association, Burlington* v. *MNR*, 97 DTC 5424.
[129] *Everywoman's Health Centre Society (1988)* v. *Canada (MNR)* [1991] 136 NR 380.
[130] *Tremblay* v. *Daigle* [1989] 2 SCR 530, at p. 533.
[131] Including *R* v. *Morgentaler* [1988] 1 SCR 30 and *R.* v. *Morgentaler*, 1993 CanLII 74 [1993] 3 SCR 463. See also *Borowski* v. *Canada (Attorney General)* [1989] 1 SCR 342 and *Tremblay* v. *Daigle*, op. cit.

More recently, in *C. v. A.*,[132] the HR Tribunal acknowledged that a family medical clinic had accommodated a Christian employee's pro-life beliefs by not requiring her to refer patients for abortions. Abortion referrals were processed by other individuals without compromising patient care.

Assisted Suicide

Suicide was considered a criminal offence in Canada until 1972, and assisting someone to end their life has continued to be treated as such. Recently, however, the SCC has completely transformed the law. While in *Rodriguez v. British Columbia (AG)*,[133] Sopinka J found that the suicide prohibition reflected society's most fundamental values and so could not violate principles of justice as there was no "right to die", this was overturned in the landmark 2015 case of *Carter* v. *Canada*,[134] which gave mentally competent adults, suffering intolerably and enduringly, the right to a medically assisted death. In mid-June 2016, Parliament passed a Bill declaring that "patients suffering from incurable illness whose natural death is 'reasonably foreseeable' are eligible for a medically assisted death". The presence of religious belief tends to be a crucial determinant of views on this subject. In this context, as with same-sex marriage, when religious beliefs prevent a third party charged with responsibility for a facilitative role from undertaking that task, they will be similarly exempted from any legal duty to do so.

Employment-Related Issues

As stated in the 1985 Act, s.7, "It is a discriminatory practice, directly or indirectly: (a) to refuse to employ or continue to employ any individual; or (b) in the course of employment, to differentiate adversely in relation to an employee, on a prohibited ground of discrimination".

Hiring/Firing Staff

Religious Organisations   The statutory right of religious organisations to hire preferentially on the basis of religion, and to fire staff as necessary to preserve their religious character, has been examined in a number of cases.

Many provincial cases have concerned the hiring and firing of teachers and other staff by religious schools. In *Caldwell* v. *St Thomas Aquinas*

---

[132] (2002), 43 C.H.R.R. D/395, 2992 BCHRT 23.   [133] [1993] 3 SCR 519.
[134] 2015 SCC 5.

High School,[135] for example, a teacher alleged that her dismissal from a Catholic school following her marriage to a divorced man constituted discrimination. From the perspective of the Catholic Church, Caldwell had knowingly disobeyed two fundamental marital rules – Catholics must marry in a Catholic church and may not marry divorced people – and had thereby disregarded a BFOR according to which Catholic teachers must model Catholicism to their students by living in strict accordance with Church doctrines. The court ruled in favour of the respondent: Catholic teachers must accept and practise the rulings of the Church both inside and outside the school; this principle was stated explicitly in her contract of employment. This rationale was subsequently echoed in *Schroen* v. *Steinbach Bible College*[136] when the Manitoba Human Rights Commission upheld the right of a Mennonite College to dismiss a secretary who had converted to become a Mormon. She had known that adherence to the Mennonite religious principles would be an aspect of her employment, had willingly placed herself in that position and thus had no just cause for complaint. In *Daly* v. *Ontario (Attorney General)*,[137] the court acknowledged that the aim of Catholic education was not merely the transmission of knowledge and development of skills, but rather the development of the whole person in accordance with the Catholic tradition. Therefore, restricting the recruitment of teachers to those of the Catholic faith was a valid consideration if the aim of the school of creating a community of believers with a distinct sense of the Catholic culture was to be achieved. Likewise in *Caldwell*,[138] the SCC ruled that a Catholic school could terminate the employment of a Catholic teacher who married a divorced man in a civil ceremony in contravention of the tenets of Catholicism. However, the exemption privilege must be exercised reasonably and will not be available in circumstances of peripheral religious significance.[139] These rulings serve to reinforce the principle that religious compliance can be construed as a bona fide component of the terms and conditions of employment within a religious organisation.

---

[35] (1984), 6 C.H.R.R. D/2643. See also *Sahota and Shergill* v. *Shri Gur Ravidass Sabha Temple*, op. cit., which concerned the exclusion of members of a caste from a religious organisation representing a different caste.

[36] (1999), 35 C.H.R.R. D/1 (Man. Bd. Adj.).   [137] 44 O.R. (3d) 349, [1999] O.J. No. 1383.

[38] *Caldwell* v. *Stuart* [1984] 2 SCR 603.

[39] *Hall (Litigation guardian of)* v. *Powers* (2002) 59 O.R. (3d) 423.

Heintz v. *Christian Horizons*,[140] a landmark case, concerned a complaint of discrimination by a support worker employed by Christian Horizons, an evangelical Christian ministry with almost 100 per cent funding from government. Employees were obliged to sign a Statement of Faith and a Lifestyle and Morality Policy, and the complainant, Connie Heintz, resigned after commencing a same-sex relationship as she felt she could no longer honour that commitment, but subsequently commenced proceedings alleging discrimination. Christian Horizons sought to rely on the statutory exemption clause to shield its employment practices from the normal requirements of equality and human rights law, while the Human Rights Commission responded by arguing that because Christian Horizons provided a service to a broader community than Evangelical Christians, and because the general care of its disabled service users did not require religious observance, adherence to the group's religious doctrine and prohibitions against sexual orientation were not a necessary part of the job: the particular constraint imposed on Ms Heintz was unwarranted. Ultimately, the Ontario Divisional Court found for the employers and stated that Christian Horizons and other similar groups could maintain a religious identity even though the people they served were not co-religionists. In an important ruling for all religious organisations in Canada, it declared that there is an entitlement to exemption from the law barring discriminatory hiring if a religious organisation is "primarily engaged in serving the interests of their religious community, where the restriction is reasonable and bona fide because of the nature of the employment".

Secular Organisations   The BFOR, which arises under s.14(a) of the Canadian Human Rights Act, has become a central principle in employment law, and one applied frequently when court or regulator is adjudicating on a discrimination issue. It was perhaps first defined in the *Bhinder* case,[141] when the SCC ruled that a Sikh employee, whose religion obliged him to wear a turban, was not discriminated against when he was required by his employer to wear a hard hat and duly fired when he refused. By a narrow majority, the SCC found that the hard hat requirement had discriminatory effect on members of the Sikh religion but nevertheless it was a BFOR and once that was established the special circumstances of a

---

[140] 2008 HRTO 22, 2010 ONSC 2105 (Div. Ct.).
[141] *Canadian National Railway Co.* v. *Canada (Human Rights Comm.) and Bhinder* (1985), CHRR C/3093 (SCC).

individual should not be taken into account; there was no employer duty to accommodate.

In *Qureshi* v. *G4S Security Services*,[142] an employer was found to have religiously discriminated against an applicant when the recruitment process was terminated on learning of his need for time off for Friday prayers. Again, in *Widdis* v. *Desjardins Group*,[143] the Tribunal found that a Seventh-Day Adventist applicant had suffered religious discrimination during an interview process when, after revealing her unavailability for work on Saturdays, as that was her Sabbath, she was not called for an additional interview. Similarly, three Muslim applicants in *Islam* v. *Big Inc.*[144] were awarded substantial damages when they were found to have suffered significant discrimination on the basis of race, colour, ancestry, place of origin, ethnic origin and creed due to their employer's conduct, which included: attempting to make them taste pork dishes; openly condemning their religious practice of fasting during Ramadan; making reference to their ethnic origin in a derogatory manner; and refusing them time off for religious observances.

Accommodating Religious Beliefs in the Workplace

All Canadian employers have a duty to accommodate their employees and the general public in respect of needs arising under the eleven grounds of discrimination – which include religious discrimination – specified in the Canadian Human Rights Act. In effect, this is an obligation to take steps to eliminate different and negative treatment of individuals, or groups of individuals, based on any such ground. The duty is subject to the "undue hardship" caveat, or reasonableness test, which excuses employers when the necessary adjustments to a policy, practice, by-law or building would cost too much, or create risks to health or safety. While this duty is similar to that applied in the USA, the threshold for determining "reasonableness" is somewhat different: the onus to accommodate rests more heavily on a Canadian employer.

The duty to accommodate was examined thirty years ago by the SCC in *O'Malley*,[145] which concerned a Seventh-Day Adventist employee whose full-time employment had been terminated on her refusal to work Friday evenings and Saturdays, as required by her religion. The court found

---

[142] 2009 HRTO 409 (CanLII).
[143] 2013 HRTO 1367.   [144] 2013 HRTO 2009 (CanLII).
[145] *Ontario (Human Rights Comm.) and O'Malley* v. *Simpson-Sears Ltd* (1985), 7 CHRR D/3102 (SCC).

that it was not necessary to prove that discrimination was intentional to find that a violation of human rights legislation had occurred. An employment rule, neutral on its face and honestly made, can still have discriminatory effects. When that happens, an employer has a duty to take reasonable steps to accommodate the employee, unless accommodation creates an undue hardship for the employer. In this instance, the court held that the employee had been discriminated against because of her religion. This ruling was further developed in *Dairy Pool*[146] when the SCC articulated the principle that an employer must consider whether an employee can be accommodated without undue hardship by showing that no reasonable alternative is possible; Wilson J then acknowledged that staff morale may operate as a factor to be taken into account. This principle was subsequently applied in *Renaud*,[147] when the SCC was faced with a not dissimilar set of facts. The SCC then confirmed that the plaintiff, a school custodian, had suffered religious discrimination from both his employer and his union because – despite knowing that he was a Seventh-Day Adventist – he was nonetheless required to work a Friday shift from 3 pm to 11 pm and, instead of being offered an alternative shift, his employment was terminated when he refused. Although this duty had been set out in his contract of employment, and notwithstanding a finding that it was a bona fide job requirement that a custodian be present in the schools, it was not a bona fide requirement that a custodian in that school should work that particular shift. Specifically rejecting the respondents' argument that the duty to accommodate was a *de minimus* one, the SCC found that the existence of a contractual agreement could be allowed to absolve an employer from their duty to accommodate, although the nature of the agreement should be taken into account when weighing the implications for the workplace and the degree of hardship involved for the parties.[148] Most recently, the individualised nature of the duty was explained in *McGill University Health Centre*[149] as follows:[150]

> The importance of the individualized nature of the accommodation process cannot be minimized. The scope of the duty to accommodate varies

---

[146] *Central Alberta Dairy Pool v. Alberta (Human Rights Comm.)* (1990), 12 CHRR D/41 (SCC).

[147] *Central Okanagan School Dist. No. 23 v. Renaud* (1992), 16 CHRR D/425 (SCC).

[148] See also *Streeter v. HR Technologies* 2009 HRTO 841 (CanLII).

[149] *McGill University Health Centre (Montreal General Hospital) v. Syndicat des employés d' l'Hôpital général de Montréal* 2007 SCC 4, [2007] 1 SCR 161.

[150] Ibid., at para. 22.

according to the characteristics of each enterprise, the specific needs of each employee and the specific circumstances in which the decision is to be made. Throughout the employment relationship, the employer must make an effort to accommodate the employee. However, this does not mean that accommodation is necessarily a one-way street... the court recognized that, when an employer makes a proposal that is reasonable, it is incumbent on the employee to facilitate its implementation. If the accommodation process fails because the employee does not co-operate, his or her complaint may be dismissed.

A variant of the employer duty to accommodate is the obligation to ensure that an employee is not financially disadvantaged as a consequence, relative to those of other religions. In *Chambly*,[151] the SCC found that as the Christian holy days of Christmas and Good Friday were treated as paid holidays, so should Jewish employees be entitled to have Yom Kippur off with pay.

Education-Related Issues

"In a multicultural society, it is not a breach of anyone's freedom of religion to be required to learn (or teach) about the doctrines and ethics of other world religions in a neutral and respectful way."[152] This judicial reminder – that religion and the law relating to it must be contexturalised against the characteristic multi-culturalism of contemporary Canadian society – warns against the dangers of retreating behind traditional partisan religious barricades.

Government Funding and Religious Education

The traditional funding role of government in relation to State schools dates from the Constitution Act 1867, s.93. This provision, being essential to the creation of a united Canada, guaranteed Roman Catholics in Ontario certain rights and privileges: it granted the provinces absolute authority to legislate for education and it protected the rights of denominational schools. The "denominational privileges" then made available are protected under s.29 of the Charter and continue in the constitutional obligation to fund Catholic schools in the provinces of Ontario, Alberta and Saskatchewan.

---

[151] *Chambly (Commission scholaire régionale) v. Bergevin*, [1994] 2 R.C.S. 525.
[152] *Loyola High School v. Québec (Attorney General)*, op. cit., citing *S.L. v. Commission scolaire des Chênes* [2012] 1 SCR 235, per Deschamps J at para. 40.

This archaic anomaly has often given rise to cases alleging religiously biased preferential treatment.[153] In *Reference Re Bill 30*,[154] the SCC found that the right of Catholics to publicly funded high schools was protected by s.93 of the Constitution Act 1867, and that s.29 of the Charter specifically exempted such rights from Charter review. Wilson J endorsed the conclusions reached earlier by a majority in the Court of Appeal that:[155]

> These educational rights, granted specifically to the Protestants in Quebec and the Roman Catholics in Ontario, make it impossible to treat all Canadians equally. The country was founded upon the recognition of special or unequal educational rights for specific religious groups in Ontario and Quebec.

This appraisal was supported by Estey J in the SCC, who added: "It is axiomatic...that if the Charter has any application to Bill 30, this Bill would be found discriminatory and in violation of ss.2(a) and 15 of the Charter of Rights."

In *Adler*,[156] the SCC considered the claim of non-Catholic religious minorities – from the Calvinistic or Reformed Christian tradition and from the Sikh, Hindu, Muslim and Jewish faiths – that the Ontario government had violated their rights under the Charter, s.15 and s.2(a), to equality and freedom of religion by fully funding Catholic religious schools exclusively. The court ruled that the Ontario government had no obligation to fund the religious schools of non-Catholics and reiterated that denominational rights granted to Catholics are immune from Charter challenge. Again, in *Waldman*,[157] the fact that Roman Catholic schools in Ontario were the only non-secular schools receiving full and direct public funding was challenged as being in breach of Article 18(1) of the ICCPR taken in conjunction with Article 2. The plaintiff, a Jewish parent, claimed that he experienced financial hardship in order to provide his children with a Jewish education, a hardship not experienced by Roman Catholic parents and that this constituted religious discrimination, and he sought recompense for the tuition fees he paid to enable his two children to

---

[153] See e.g. *Tiny Township Catholic Separate Schools Trustees* v. *The Queen* (1928) A. C. 363 and *Attorney General of Quebec* v. *Greater Hull School Board* [1984] 2 SCR 575.

[154] [1987] 1 SCR 1148.

[155] *Reference Re an Act to Amend the Education Act* (1986), 53 O.R. (2d) 513, at pp. 575–576

[156] *Adler* v. *Ontario*, op. cit.

[157] *Waldman* v. *Canada*, Comm. No. 694/1996. See also *Tadman et al.* v. *Canada*, Comm. No. 816/1998.

attend a private Hebrew day school. The Committee specifically rejected the State's argument that "the preferential treatment of Roman Catholic schools is nondiscriminatory because of its Constitutional obligation".[158] It was of the view that if the State "chooses to provide public funding to religious schools, it should make this funding available without discrimination". The Committee held that the plaintiff's rights under Article 26 of the Covenant – to equal and effective protection against discrimination – had been breached, and that Articles 18 and 27, read in conjunction with Article 2(1) of the Covenant, had been violated. Consequently, in 1999, the UN Human Rights Committee declared that Ontario's policy of fully funding Roman Catholic schools, while denying full funding to other religious schools, was discriminatory. Prompted more by cost-effectiveness considerations than anything else, Newfoundland, New Brunswick, Nova Scotia and Prince Edward Island have, in recent years, moved towards unified secular school systems and no longer fund faith schools; but these continue to be partially publicly funded (typically 40–60 per cent) in British Columbia, Alberta, Saskatchewan, Manitoba and Quebec, subject to rudimentary regulatory controls.

Faith Schools

This constitutional preferencing of denominational schools has undoubtedly elevated the standing of Canadian faith schools. However, their reputation has suffered severely from their historical association with Indian residential schools, which were mainly emanations of the Catholic and Anglican Churches, funded by the federal government. In a policy of "cultural genocide" consolidated by the Indian Act 1876, some 150 000 Aboriginal children were removed from their homes, communities and culture to residential educational institutions (the first such residential school were established in 1620, the last closed in 1986), triggering what is now recognised as "the beginning of an intergenerational cycle of neglect and abuse".[159]

Under s.2(a) of the Charter, parents are said to have the right to oversee the spiritual welfare of their children, and many do so by enrolling them in faith schools. A religious school enjoys a special exemption under human rights law; it has the power to engage in preferential

[158] Ibid., at para. 10.4.
[159] See Saskatchewan Child Welfare Review Panel, "For the Good of our Children and Youth: A New Vision, a New Direction", http://cwrp.ca/sites/default/files/publications/en/SK_ChildWelfareReview_panelreport.pdf, at p. 18.

employment practices that would otherwise be considered discriminatory. In *Loyola*,[160] the SCC gave some consideration to the significance of faith schools as inter-generational transmitters of beliefs for a community of religious adherents. The court was clear that such schools – in this case, a Catholic private school – needed to be assured of State protection in order to safeguard "the liberty of the members of [their] community who have chosen to give effect to the collective dimension of their religious beliefs by participating in a denominational school".[161] This decision, with clear implications for other religion-specific schools, underpins the accuracy of Campbell J's observation in *Trinity Western*:[162]

> Equality rights have not jumped the queue to now trump religious freedom. That delineation of rights is still a relevant concept. Religious freedom has not been relegated to a judicial nod to the toleration of cultural eccentricities that don't offend the dominant social consensus.

Roman Catholic schools are by definition faith schools, but, rather than forming part of the private sector, they are a wholly incorporated and fully funded component of the public school system. All other faith schools are ineligible for full public funding and are of necessity private schools. There is no province in Canada in which private schools receive funding on an equal basis to public schools: direct funding of private schools ranges from 0 per cent (Newfoundland, New Brunswick, Ontario) to 75 per cent (Alberta).

Religious Discrimination and Educational Content

"Because religion plays an important role in the life of many communities, these views [of the parents and communities represented by the school board] will often be motivated by religious concerns, and cannot be left at the boardroom door." So said McLachlin CJ, in relation to the decision-making process of a public school board, in *Chamberlain*.[163] This was a case in which the SCC considered the refusal of the Surrey School Board to approve three controversial books depicting same-sex parented families – which had been promoted as supplementary learning resources – as teaching aids in the family life education curriculum. The court found that "children cannot learn unless they are exposed to views that differ from those they are taught at home" and held that the board members, by

---

[160] *Loyola High School* v. *Québec (Attorney General)*, op. cit.   [161] Ibid., at para. 62.
[162] *Trinity Western University* v. *Nova Scotia Barristers' Society*, 2015 NSSC 25, at para. 196.
[163] *Chamberlain* v. *Surrey School Board District 36* (2002), 221 D.L.R. (4th) 156 (SCC), at para 19. See also *Hall (Litigation guardian of)* v. *Powers*, op. cit.

refusing to permit the use of such books, were imposing their own religious values and seeking to deny children an important learning opportunity. It suggested that on matters of public policy, religious concerns cannot exclude the concerns of other members of the community, and that there was a principle of public decision-making under which "each group is given as much recognition as it can consistently demand while giving the same recognition to others".[164] Arguably, however, the guidance implied that secularism should be interpreted as atheism, and that this, rather than State neutrality, should govern public service decision-making – to the exclusion of religious principles. Such an interpretation would amount to discriminating against religion, in contravention of the neutrality principle, which would surely be incompatible with Charter requirements.

Loyola High School v. *Québec (Attorney General)*[165] now stands as a landmark case for the competing tensions operating on the religion/equality interface in Canada. It concerned the Quebec government's mandatory core curriculum for high schools, the Program on Ethics and Religious Freedom (ERC). In 2008, the principal of a private Catholic high school in Quebec objected not so much to the ERC – which required schools to teach a range of religious and non-religious ethical systems – as to the accompanying obligation to do so impartially. Approval had been sought and refused to teach the objectives of the ERC from a Catholic rather than a neutral perspective. Ultimately, the SCC unanimously found that the refusal to release Loyola in any way from the requirement of strict neutrality in the teaching of the ERC disproportionately interfered with the religious freedom of the Loyola community. It reasoned that "requiring Loyola's teachers to take a neutral posture even about Catholicism means that State is telling them how to teach the very religion that animates Loyola's identity", which would amount to "requiring a Catholic institution to speak about Catholicism in terms defined by the State rather than by its own understanding of Catholicism".[166] A majority held that it was constitutionally sound to require the Catholic school to teach the ethics of other religions in as neutral a manner as possible. In so ruling, the SCC reinforced the broader message of *S.L.* v. *Commission scolaire des Chênes*[167] when it considered whether the mandatory nature of the ERC course interfered with the freedom of religion of the Catholic parents who requested exemption for their children because the course's content was considered incompatible with their family beliefs. Deschamps J, while

---

[164] Ibid.   [165] Op. cit.   [166] Ibid., at para. 63.   [167] [2012] 1 SCR 235.

endorsing the desirability of religious neutrality as a policy of the State, dismissed the appeal:[168]

> The suggestion that exposing children to a variety of religious facts in itself infringes their religious freedom or that of their parents amounts to a rejection of the multicultural reality of Canadian society and ignores the Quebec government's obligations with regard to public education.

Education Facilities and Religious Discrimination

As mentioned earlier, scholarships are invariably targeted towards a narrowly defined set of prospective beneficiaries, and thus have always been a vehicle for discriminatory selection. The most notable case is *Canada Trust*,[169] concerning a trust established in 1923 for the provision of scholarships which limited its recipients to "a British Subject of the White Race and of the Christian Religion in its Protestant form" and included a statement that the "progress of the World depends in the future, as in the past, on the maintenance of the Christian religion".[170] The court ordered a striking-out of all references to and restrictions regarding race, colour, creed or religion, ethnic origin and sex. Subsequently, in *University of Victoria*,[171] a provincial case, the court upheld a scholarship for practising Roman Catholics, reasoning that a "scholarship or bursary that simply restricts the class of recipients to members of a particular religious faith does not offend public policy".[172]

Teaching has been a particularly sensitive area, in part because a teacher acts as a role model, but also because of the potential for proselytism. Religious discrimination was very evident in *Ross*,[173] when the SCC ruled that the removal of a teacher from the classroom was justifiable on the grounds that his distribution of antisemitic material created a poisoned environment for Jewish students and that school teachers must be held to a higher standard of behaviour. The court stressed that the freedom of religion is "subject to such limitations as are necessary to protect public safety, order, health or morals, or the fundamental rights and freedoms of others". The *Trinity Western*[174] cases are illustrative of the commonly accepted truth, as expressed by Iacobucci and Bastarache JJ on behalf of the majority during the SCC stage of those proceedings, that "the freedom to hold

---

[168] Ibid., at para. 40.   [169] *Canada Trust Co.* v. *Ontario Human Rights Commission,* op. cit.
[170] Ibid., at p. 328.   [171] *University of Victoria* v. *British Columbia (A.G.),* op. cit.
[172] Ibid., per Maczko J at para. 25.
[173] *Ross* v. *New Brunswick School Dist. No. 15* [1996] 1 S.C.R. 825.
[174] *Trinity Western University* v. *British Columbia College of Teachers* (2001), 39 C.H.R.R. D/357, 2001 SCC 31.

beliefs is broader than the freedom to act on them".[175] Those cases concerned a teacher training college, the TWU – an emanation of the Evangelical Free Church of Canada – which chose to manifest its beliefs in a Community Standards Contract stating its evangelical Christian values – including abstinence from sex outside marriage and rejection of homosexual relationships – that all students were required to sign. The British Columbia College of Teachers (BCCT) refused TWU accreditation on the basis that that graduates of this private institution would be inadequately prepared to provide educational services without discrimination in BC's diverse public school classrooms. Ultimately, the SCC, in a majority ruling, held in favour of TWU. It found that the existence of the Community Standards Contract, signed by the students, was insufficient to support the BCCT conclusion that TWU graduates would behave in a discriminatory manner towards future homosexual students and that there was no evidence that this in fact had ever occurred. In short, the court upheld the right of TWU to manifest its religious beliefs through its mandatory contract, even though this constituted an act of religious discrimination against those wishing to access its services who were unwilling to subscribe to contract principles. Subsequently, TWU failed to gain accreditation from the Law Society of Upper Canada for its planned new law school, entry to which would again be via the contract gateway[176] – a decision upheld by the appeal court.[177] However, most recently the Court of Appeal has held that the decision of the Law Society of British Columbia to refuse accreditation to practise law in the province to graduates of a new proposed TWU law school was unlawful.[178] After considering previous decisions of the SCC requiring any interference with religious freedom to be "proportionate" to the relevant conflicting aims and "no more than is necessary" to meet those aims, the Court of Appeal concluded that the right balance had not been struck in this case:[179]

> The balancing of conflicting Charter rights requires a statutory decision-maker to assess the degree of infringement of a decision on a Charter right. While there is no doubt that the Covenant's refusal to accept LGBTQ expressions of sexuality is deeply offensive and hurtful to the LGBTQ community, and we do not in any way wish to minimize that effect, there is no Charter or other legal right to be free from views that offend.

---

[175] Ibid., at paras 36–37.
[176] *Trinity Western University (TWU)* v. *Law Society of BC*, 2015 BCSC 2326.
[177] *Trinity Western University (TWU)* v. *Law Society of Upper Canada*, 2016 ONCA 518.
[178] *Trinity Western University* v. *Law Society of British Columbia*, 2016 BCCA 423.
[179] Ibid., at para. 188.

The court finding that the TWU community had a right to hold and act on its beliefs, and that, in the absence of any evidence of actual harm, this was a legitimate expression of the right to freedom of religion, is one that is likely to resonate with future regulatory and judicial decision-makers.[180]

Medicine-Related Issues

The medicine/religion interface is fraught with moral hazards. As the frontiers of science push forward, matters once viewed as best left "in the hands of the Gods" become amenable to medical intervention. The resulting moral maze – affecting medical practitioners, patients and the treatment options available – is as legally troublesome in Canada as elsewhere.

Medical Intervention and Religious Beliefs

With unfortunate regularity, the relevant issues tend to revolve around Jehovah's Witness parents refusing a blood transfusion for their child, triggering dilemmas for the parties and professionals involved, and ultimately for the court. As in *B. (R.) v. Children's Aid Society of Metropolitan Toronto*,[181] these cases are resolved by giving precedence to the welfare of the child through a court order directing that the infant be given a blood transfusion contrary to parental wishes. The issue may also present in the form of a refusal by a medical practitioner to participate in a treatment procedure on religious grounds. For example, *Moore*[182] concerned a Catholic public service employee who, having objected to abortion and refused to work with a client who sought a termination, was disciplined and eventually fired. The HR Tribunal found that because the employer knew of her religiously based objection, an onus rested on the employer to accommodate the employee by transferring the client to other employees.

Genetic Engineering and Patents, etc.

For those with religious or other beliefs, the private ownership of genetic material and the redesigning of such for commercial purposes is problematic: for some, this constitutes an almost heretical interference in the laws of nature and a trespass into matters ordained by god. Canada has

---

[180] The SCC has granted leave to appeal: the hearing is set for 30 November 2017 (note from Matt Harrington to that effect, 6 April 2017).
[181] (1992) 10 O.R. (3d) 321 Ontario Court of Appeal.
[182] *Moore v. British Columbia (Ministry of Social Services* (1992), 17 C.H.R.R. D/426 (B.C.C.H.R).

led the way in exploring the legal and moral issues that arise in this context.[183]

Harvard College[184] concerned the efforts of the plaintiffs to secure – in many countries, including, in this instance, Canada – exclusive patent rights to a process for creating GM mice (an "oncomouse" genetically modified to make it susceptible to cancer); a process intended to have application in the long term to other animals and to humans. The SCC – unlike its judicial counterparts in many other countries, including the UK, Ireland, the USA and New Zealand – found that higher life forms are not patentable: patents are applicable to inventions, including those for "manufacture", which implies "a non-living mechanistic product or process"[185] – they do not apply to "a conscious, sentient living creature";[186] higher life forms have unique qualities and characteristics that transcend the particular genetic matter of which they are composed;[187] indeed, some interveners – the Canadian Council of Churches and Evangelical Fellowship of Canada – objected to Harvard claiming credit for inventing a form of life.[188] It has been argued that the rationale behind this decision, being based upon a differentiation between higher and lower life forms, is "more properly a matter of religion than a matter of law"[189] – the implication being that a religiously discriminating perception influenced the judiciary.

Following on from this ruling, the SCC, in *Monsanto*,[190] was concerned first to adjudicate upon a dispute between parties regarding patent rights on certain GM seeds and second on the prohibition on patents in respect of matters subject to the laws of nature and the ownership of higher life forms. As the law cannot permit patents to monopolise genes that exist in nature, the Monsanto claim was aimed not at securing rights to the plant itself, but towards the patented genes, the modified cells and the DNA sequencing processes that had come to constitute the GM canola plant. The Monsanto patent could not vest the owner with rights in the plant: it was confined to the genes and cells; once they developed into plant tissue

---

[183] See the Canadian Biotechnology Advisory Committee, "Patenting of Higher Life Forms and Related Issues: Report to the Government of Canada Biotechnology Ministerial Coordinating Committee", 2002.

[184] *Harvard College* v. *Canada (Commissioner of Patents)*, op. cit.

[185] Ibid., at para. 159.   [186] Ibid., at para. 160.

[187] Ibid., at para. 163.   [188] Ibid., at para. 68.

[189] See Burk, D. L., "Reflections in a Darkling Glass: A Comparative Contemplation of the Harvard College Decision Symposium on the Harvard Mouse Decision of the Supreme Court of Canada", *Canadian Business Law Journal*, 2003, vol. 39:2, at p. 221.

[190] *Monsanto* v. *Schmeiser* [2004] 1 SCR 902, 2004 SCC 34.

and became defined as a plant, the patent ceased. The court was plainly aware of the analogous implications for human reproductive research (use of stem cells, cultivation of embryos, etc.), as it noted that "inventions in the field of agriculture may give rise to concerns not raised in other fields – moral concerns about whether it is right to manipulate genes".[191] However it took the view that it fell to Parliament rather than to the judiciary to address such concerns, and confined itself to affirming that Monsanto had patent rights to products and processes, if not to the plant itself. Taken in conjunction with its *Harvard* ruling, this decision warns of a growing need for legislators to bring overall coherence to the laws governing boundaries in the new biotechnologies, including genetic engineering, and to identify principles that may serve to protect research from possible contamination by religiously discriminating value judgments.

Service-Provision Issues

As stated in the 1985 Act, s.6, "it is a discriminatory practice in the provision of goods, services, facilities or accommodation customarily available to the general public: (a) to deny, or to deny access to, any such good, service, facility or accommodation to any individual; or (b) to differentiate adversely in relation to any individual, on a prohibited ground of discrimination". Interestingly, the spectrum of service entitlement is now steadily encroaching on the domain hitherto cordoned off on religious grounds: medically assisted death for the terminally ill has joined same-sex marriages and abortion as among the public services now available in Canada.

Service Provision by Religious Organisations

Historical abuse perpetrated by Canadian religious organisations has damaged their reputation and overshadows their contemporary service provision role. Given that residential schools were implementing an enforced assimilation policy from at least the Indian Act 1876,[192] and continued to do so for the next century, while records of child sexual abuse by Catholic Church clergy date back to Newfoundland in the 1980s and earlier, it has taken the authorities a long time to recognise and address the dark side of service provision by religious organisations.

---

[191] Ibid., at para. 93.
[192] Not until 2008 did Parliament amend the Canadian Human Rights Act to give full human rights protection to those subject to the Indian Act.

More recently, the *Hall*[193] case concerned a Roman Catholic school board which had refused permission for a same-sex couple to attend a school graduation dance on the grounds that homosexuality is incompatible with Roman Catholic teaching. The board held that any State interference with that decision would amount to denying the school its religious freedom. MacKinnon J, noting that "there is an obvious tension between the individual's free expression and equality rights when contrasted against the equality rights and the religious freedom of Catholic schools", and taking into account that "the Board is, in law, a religiously oriented State actor",[194] but side-stepping constitutional issues, ruled in favour of the plaintiff and ordered the school to admit the couple.

Same-sex marriages are contentious in Canada, as elsewhere. Ordained ministers are exempted from any obligation to conduct such marriage ceremonies. In *Knights of Columbus*,[195] a religious discrimination claim was made by a same-sex couple when their rental application for a facility they wished to use to celebrate their marriage was rejected by the Catholic organisation that owned it. The Tribunal concluded that the organisation sincerely believed it had a duty to protect a traditional view of marriage, which excluded same-sex unions, and that rejecting the plaintiff's application was an appropriate manifestation of that belief: renting out the hall for the purpose for which it was required would force the organisation to act against its religious beliefs, and this would violate its rights under s.2(a) of the Charter. Nevertheless, the organisation was fined, as it had failed in its duty of reasonable accommodation as no consideration had been given to the effect its actions would have on the couple and no attempt had been made to meet with them and explain the reasons for their rejection.

Provision of Public Services

As mentioned earlier, public service provision has been particularly exposed to religiously motivated disruption in relation to family-planning matters. The tensions between pro-life and pro-choice groups have generated difficulties, uncertainties and extensive litigation.

Teaching has also proven to be a sensitive area. In the previously mentioned *Ross* case,[196] the SCC ultimately upheld the decision of a Board of Inquiry that the Board of School Trustees had discriminated with respect

---

[193] *Hall* v. *Durham Catholic School Board* [2002] OJ No. 1803.   [194] Ibid., at para. 57.
[195] *Smith and Chymyshyn* v. *Knights of Columbus and others*, 2005 BCHRT 544 (CanLII). See also *Whiteley* v. *Osprey Media Publishing*, 2010 HRTO 2152 (CanLII).
[196] *Ross* v. *New Brunswick School Dist. No. 15*, op. cit.

to a public service because it failed to take appropriate action against a teacher who had distributed antisemitic materials. Most prominent has been the case of *Trinity Western University* v. *British Columbia College of Teachers*,[197] which graphically illustrates the difficulties that can arise when the provision of an education service conflicts with religious principle. As Justices Iacobucci and Bastarache then noted, "for better or worse, tolerance of divergent beliefs is a hallmark of a democratic society".[198]

As in other jurisdictions, the refusal of public officials to undertake statutory duties in respect of same-sex couples has predictably generated court cases, with equally predictable outcomes. So, for example, in *Nichols*,[199] a Saskatchewan court upheld an HR Tribunal ruling that a government-appointed marriage commissioner had discriminated against a same-sex couple by refusing to perform their marriage ceremony.

Private Goods and Service Provision

A not untypical range of commercial services provided the context for several Canadian religious discrimination cases. For example, *Brillinger* v. *Brockie*[200] concerned the competing claims of sexual orientation discrimination and violation of freedom of religion. The Ontario Board of Inquiry found that Brockie, a born-again Christian, had discriminated against Brillinger (and the Canadian Lesbian and Gay Archives) on the prohibited ground of sexual orientation by refusing to provide printing services to homosexuals and homosexual organisations, and it ordered Brockie and his company to provide the same printing services to them as they provided to others. However, on appeal, the Ontario Superior Court of Justice held that the Board's order went further than was necessary and added a condition to the effect that the order should not require Brockie to print material of a nature that could reasonably be considered to be in direct conflict with the core elements of his religious beliefs. A judicial comment on this added caveat has noted that "on the above approach the believer is not required to undertake action that promotes that which the essence of the belief teaches to be wrong".[201]

---

[197] (2001), 39 C.H.R.R. D/357. 2001 SCC 31.   [198] Ibid., at p. 44.
[199] *Nichols* v. *M.J.*, 2009 SKQB 299. See also *Marriage Commissioners Appointed Under The Marriage Act (Re)*, 2011 SKCA 3 (CanLII).
[200] (No. 3) (2000), 37 C.H.R.R. D/15.
[201] See *Christian Institute and Others* v. *Office of First Minister and Deputy First Minister*, Neutral Citation No. [2007] NIQB 66, per Weatherup J at para. 88.

In *Smith and Chymyshyn* v. *Knights of Columbus and others*,[202] the Tribunal found that the respondents' hall did meet the definition of a "service" or "facility" and dismissed the respondents' argument that in the light of their belief system and their own right to freedom of religion they could refuse to rent that hall for the celebration of a gay marriage. In the more recent but not dissimilar case of *Eadie and Thomas* v. *Riverbend Bed and Breakfast and others (No. 2)*,[203] a couple had reserved a room in bed and breakfast accommodation offered by a pair of married Christians in their own home, but when the husband learned that the couple was gay, the booking was cancelled. Again, the Tribunal ruled in favour of the gay couple who had been denied a service.

Broadcasting Services

Dagenais,[204] the leading Canadian case on the conflict between freedom of expression[205] and publication bans on trial information, concerned the proposed transmission of a TV fictional mini-series giving an account of the alleged sexual abuse of young boys by members of the Christian Brothers, who were arraigned for trial and who sought to ban the programme. The SCC advised that a proposed ban must be shown to be necessary, in that it relates to an important objective that cannot be achieved by a reasonably available and effective alternative measure; that it must be as limited as possible; and that there must be proportionality between the salutary and deleterious effects of the ban. Emphasising that the Charter context required a balanced approach, the court warned that:[206]

> Publication bans, however, should not always be seen as a clash between freedom of expression for the media and the right to a fair trial for the accused. The clash model is more suited to the American constitutional context and should be rejected in Canada.

In this instance, the subject matter did not warrant a blanket ban.

In addition to the previously mentioned SCC ruling in *Ross*,[207] there have been a number of provincial cases involving individuals placing advertisements in newspapers protesting about LGBT issues. One such was *Owens*,[208] where the court ruled that although an advertisement connecting Bible verses related to homosexuality with gay marriage was

[202] Op. cit. See also *Whiteley* v. *Osprey Media Publishing*, op. cit.
[203] 2012 BCHRT 247.   [204] *Dagenais* v. *Canadian Broadcasting Corp.*, op. cit.
[205] See *Edmonton Journal* v. *Alberta (Attorney-General)* (1989), 64 D.L.R. (4th) 577 (SCC).
[206] Ibid., at p. 839.   [207] *Ross* v. *New Brunswick School District No. 15*, op. cit.
[208] *Owens* v. *Saskatchewan (Human Rights Commission)*, 2006

"offensive and jarring to many", it did not constitute the offence of religious discrimination. Importantly, however, the court did acknowledg that statements designed to provoke "extreme emotions and strong feel ings of detestation, calumny and vilification" may be deemed hate speech Harrington adds that there are also cases involving government propert and advertising – specifically, advertisements on buses – and raises th question: Can a public transport authority discriminate in what adverts will accept?[209]

Conclusion

As Gascon J noted:[210]

> It must be recognized that the Canadian cultural landscape includes many traditional and heritage practices that are religious in nature. Although it is clear that not all of these cultural expressions are in breach of the State's duty of neutrality, there is also no doubt that the State may not consciously make a profession of faith or act so as to adopt or favour one religious view at the expense of all others.

The Christian cultural legacy is undoubtedly the most formative influenc in that landscape: its manifestation in language, architecture, values an the commonplace areas of social life examined in this chapter has bee deep, pervasive and enduring. Its overall effect can only be guessed at, bu as Gascon J hints, the weight and extent of that cultural expression ha traditionally been associated with the State – even if the duty of neutralit means the latter may no longer favour it.

The challenges of geography, together with Canada's binary coloni experience, continuation of "denominational privileges" under s.29 of th Charter and the patchwork of First Nations, Inuit and Metis commun ties, have, perhaps, proven particularly conducive to growing the pluralit of cultures that are now to be found in that country. The caselaw revea the vibrant, authentic, cultural life of Jews, Hutterites, Sikhs, Muslims an others. It also points to the growing assertiveness of secularism. As th spreading array of different religious organisations and groups of belie ers and non-believers seek recognition (to be registered as tax-exem charities) under the twin governing principles of religious freedom an

---

[209] Note to author, 6 April 2017, citing *American Freedom Defence Initiative* v. *Edmont (City)*, 2016 ABQB 555 and *American Freedom Defence Initiative* v. *Edmonton (City)*, 20 ABQB 555.

[210] *Mouvement laïque québécois* v. *Saguenay (City)*, op. cit., at para. 87.

equality, so the State has resorted to upholding the doctrine of State neutrality to justify distancing itself equally from all of them, stripping religion from public life and thereby positioning itself to deal objectively and impartially with all forms of religious discrimination. There are some who would argue that this process is one in which the State, by lending its authority to strengthening secularism in public life, has in practice made secularism more partisan than neutral, and has correspondingly reduced the significance of religion; and that in so doing, it is in danger of comprehensively devaluing those cultures that formed the foundations of the confederation and neutralising those that have come to constitute modern Canada.

9

Australia

Introduction

Whereas a century ago almost all religious adherents subscribed to either Anglicanism or Catholicism, together with one or two other minority religions, the 2006 national census revealed the religious affiliation of the Australian population to consist of: 27.4 per cent Protestants (18.7 per cent Anglican, 5.7 per cent Uniting Church, 3 per cent Presbyterian and Reformed), 25.8 per cent Catholics, 2.7 per cent Eastern Orthodox, 7.9 per cent other Christians, 2.1 per cent Buddhists, 1.7 per cent Muslims, 2.4 per cent other, 11.3 per cent unspecified and 18.7 per cent no religion. By 2011, the ABS census revealed: Hinduism as the fastest growing religion; Christianity as the most common religion, at 61.1 per cent; and a significant increase in the number reporting "no religion", from 18.7 per cent in 2006 to 22.3 per cent in 2011.[1] The large numbers of immigrants from Asia, particularly from Cambodia and Vietnam, have made Buddhism the third largest religion in Australia.

This chapter, like the others, begins with brief overview of public policy themes and considers the significance of the Constitution. It then outline the current legal framework governing religion and religious discrimination, before focusing on the definitions of "religion", "belief", "discrimination" and related concepts. It examines the Church/State relationship and concludes with a survey of contemporary caselaw relating to religious discrimination in the areas of: symbols, icons, apparel, etc.; the family and associated matters; employment; education; medicine; and service provision.

---

[1] See the Australian Bureau of Statistics (ABS), Census of Population and Housing Dat for 2011, at www.abs.gov.au/websitedbs/censushome.nsf/home/CO-61?opendocument& navpos=620.

Public Policy: An Overview

Over the past few decades, Australia's white Anglo-Saxon orientation has faded, and concern for its Indigenous People has grown, as has its proportion of Asian-born citizens. Some resulting implications for public policy in relation to religion and religious discrimination can perhaps be seen in a loosening of established Church/State relationships as the Christian church hegemony gives way under pressures that include: internal schisms; divisive culture-war issues, such as abortion and gay marriage; a heightened Indigenous cultural profile; increased secularism; and a growing Muslim presence.

Religion and the Constitution

Constitutional provisions impose restrictions on the legislative powers of the Commonwealth that have the effect of "making religion, religious observance and religious tests irrelevant" to the "structure or conduct" of the federal government and appointment to federal office.[2] Otherwise, the Constitution has no direct bearing on religion or religious organisations in Australia.

The Constitution

Taking effect on 1 January 1901, the Constitution marked the formation of the federation of Australia, and thereafter both conferred and limited the legislative capacity of the Commonwealth Parliament. However, neither religion nor human rights are among the "heads of power" available to Parliament for legislative purposes. While this does not prevent Parliament legislating on some aspects of such matters, it can only do so incidentally. The Constitution does not contain a "bill of rights" – in fact, Australia has the singular distinction of being the only modern democratic country without such protection[3] – but it does provide, directly or implicitly, for certain rights and freedoms. For present purposes, the most relevant of these is s.116, which states that:

> The Commonwealth shall not make any law for establishing any religion, or for imposing any religious observance, or for prohibiting the free exercise

See *Harkianakis v. Skalkos* (1997) 42 NSWLR 22, per Dunford J at p. 26.
See further Saunders, C., "The Australian Constitution and Our Rights", *Future Justice*, 2010, pp. 117–135.

of any religion, and no religious test shall be required as a qualification for any office or public trust under the Commonwealth.

However, s.116 applies only to the Commonwealth. Each state and territory has its own constitution, formulated between 1840 and 1859, and only Tasmania's has a similar provision.[4]

Religious Discrimination and the Constitution

The constitutional protection for religion lies in the first three clauses of s.116. In practice, however, this provision has been narrowly interpreted, and indeed, no court has ever ruled a law to be in breach of it. Such are its limitations that it has been found not to be violated by laws authorising the government funding of religious schools, the dissolution of a branch of Jehovah's Witnesses and the forcible removal of Indigenous children from their families.

The principle that a testator has a right to make a bequest subject to an overtly discriminatory religious condition is well established in Australia, as elsewhere in the common law world.[5] So the bequest to sons, conditional upon their wives converting to Protestantism, in *Trustees of Church Property of the Diocese of Newcastle* v. *Ebbeck*,[6] was valid in itself. Indeed, Windeyer J, in making his determination, declared the general validity of testator-imposed religious restraints on marriage.[7]

Public Policy

For present purposes, the elements of public policy that are most relevant are those that relate to the relationship between the State and the institutions of the Christian religion. By the mid-nineteenth century, Christianity in Australia – represented by the Roman Catholic, Anglican, Presbyterian, Methodist, Lutheran and Pentecostal Churches – was well established, as was the porous interface between Church and State, with many instances of prominent persons being members of both.

---

[4] See Tasmanian Constitution Act 1934, s.46, and *Corneloup* v. *Launceston City Council* [2016] FCA 974.

[5] See e.g. *Omari* v. *Omari* [2012] ACTSC 33. See further Butt, P., "Testamentary Conditions in Restraint of Religion", *Sydney Law Review*, 1977, vol. 8, p. 400.

[6] (1960) 104 CLR 394, [1961] ALR 339.

[7] (1960) 104 CLR 394, at para. 5. Neil Foster questions whether s.116 would apply to State Supreme Court decisions on matters of succession (note to author, 20 February 2017).

Background

The presence of a sizeable population of Indigenous People proved no obstacle to the continued growth of the Christian C Christian Churches, as an array of different missions engaged in competitive conversion campaigns. The policies of conversion and assimilation, which continued up until the mid-twentieth century and included the tragically misguided "Stolen Generation" episode, were wholly prejudicial towards traditional religious and cultural practices. The Stolen Generation scandal marked a significant milestone in the tangled relationship between State, Christianity and the Indigenous People. Beginning with the Aboriginals Ordinance 1918 (NT) and officially ending – at least in New South Wales – in 1967, it authorised the removal of some 30 000 aboriginal children from their parents for adoption by white Caucasian families. While it was a federal government policy, enforced directly by official agencies which denied aboriginal access to the courts, implementation depended greatly on the role of Church missions and other religious bodies to arrange the adoption placements.[8] Among the retrospective objections to the Aboriginals Ordinance 1918 was the argument that it breached the right of Indigenous People to the free exercise of religious belief under s.116 of the Constitution, but patently this was not an argument advanced to any avail on their behalf at the relevant time.[9]

Despite the preponderance of non-Christians in the adjacent Pacific Rim nations, the dominance of Christianity in Australia was continued and reinforced as a by-product of the White Australia policy, which restricted immigration to people of European origin and continued from the 1890s to the 1950s, with elements surviving into the 1970s. By the late twentieth century, changes in immigration policy had generated a considerable rebalancing of religious/ethnic affiliations – but by then, the Christian Churches had become an integral part of Australia's social fabric.

A side effect of the substantial and sustained presence of Christian Churches, accompanied by a well-developed outreach capacity, was their ability to achieve a partnership with government on public-benefit

---

See the Human Rights and Equal Opportunity Commission, *Bringing Them Home: A Guide to the Findings and Recommendations of the National Inquiry into the Separation of Aboriginal and Torres Strait Islander Children from their Families*, Australian Government Publishing Service, 1997. On 13 February 2008, Prime Minister Kevin Rudd delivered an official apology on behalf of the Parliament of Australia to those affected by the Stolen Generation policy.
See *Kruger v. Commonwealth*, op. cit., per Gaudron J. Note the provision made in the 2013 Act for an Aboriginal Association.

service provision that is possibly unique in the common law world. From an early stage, government policy has largely been to fund, where it can, the delivery of public-benefit services – such as education – by religious organisations, rather than do so itself; a policy accelerated in the last few decades by privatisation, which, as Beth Gaze points out,[10] has ensured many more services are now contracted out to religious organisations.

This arrangement continues with government funds being channeled through Church organisations, enabling them to run schools, hospitals, social care facilities, etc. It necessarily gives the Christian Churches, relative to all others, an institutional presence and influence – on government and local communities – that may be perceived as overbearing by those of other faiths or of none.

Religious Discrimination and Contemporary Public Policy

Religious discrimination has not been specifically addressed on a nationwide basis by the Australian Constitution, the legislature or government public policy.[11] While discrimination and equality of opportunity are governed generally by statute, to a large extent discrimination in relation to religion has been treated as a subsidiary of discrimination in relation to race, and largely subsumed within a broad public-policy focus on social inclusiveness.[12]

State Agencies for Religious Matters

There are no federal government departments or agencies with a specific brief for religious affairs.

Domestic Policy

The 2002 Bali bombing by Islamic militants, which killed and maimed many Australians, had much the same effect on domestic policy in this jurisdiction as the similar 2005 London atrocity had in the UK. The consequent introduction of the Australian Anti-Terrorism Act 2005 (revised), intended to hamper the activities of any potential terrorists, included measures such as the banning of organisations and the criminalisation of membership in certain associations. As a result, the freedoms of association and expression were thereafter constrained. Increased social

---

[10] Note to author, 22 February 2017.
[11] Section 116 does not specifically address religious discrimination, although individual states have so legislated. See further Foster, N. J., "Religious Freedom in Australia", 201? Asia Pacific JRCLS Conference, 2015, at https://works.bepress.com/neil_foster/94/.
[12] See further Miller, C. and Orchard, L., Australian Public Policy, Bristol, Policy Press, 2016

tensions, evident in the 2005 Cronulla riots,[13] left Muslim and other minority ethnic communities feeling conspicuous and vulnerable.

For present purposes, the role played by the "religious test" of s.116 is a particularly significant theme in Australian domestic policy. As in Canada, the approach is one of State neutrality towards religion, in contrast to the separation of Church and State in the USA. Consequently, a prominent public-policy theme is the focus on differentiating government funding of public service provision by religious organisations from preferential government support for particular religions; a distinction that is not readily made, and which at times requires the "religious test" to be deployed (see later).

Foreign Policy

Being drawn into supporting the USA and its allies in a succession of wars in Afghanistan, Iraq and, to an extent, Syria has compromised Australian relations with its Muslim neighbours in countries such as Indonesia, as well as with its own domestic Muslim communities. Consequently, Australia – like Canada and the UK – is left more exposed to terrorist attacks by Islamic extremists. The evolving socio-economic strands of Australian foreign policy are also to a considerable degree trailing in the wake of US strategic aims. As the latter develops its "pivot" towards Asia – particularly India and Japan – Australia is having to carefully balance its relationships on that continent – particularly with China and Indonesia – against its ties to the USA. The possibility of Australia being seen by its Muslim neighbours as allowing itself to become a bridgehead for US interests in the region may further increase its exposure to Islamic violence.

Contemporary Law Governing Religious Discrimination

Statute law prohibiting religious discrimination in Australia is of surprisingly recent origin; it has been in existence for little more than three decades.

The International Framework

In Australia, "human rights" is statutorily defined at federal level[14] to mean the rights and freedoms recognised or declared by: the International

---

[13] These clashes, involving several thousand youths, occurred between Lebanese immigrants and the white Caucasian settled community in Sydney on the nights of 11 and 12 December 2005.

[14] See the Human Rights (Parliamentary Scrutiny) Act 2011, s.3(1).

Convention on the Elimination of all Forms of Racial Discrimination 1965; the International Covenant on Economic, Social and Cultural Rights 1966; the ICCPR 1966; the Convention on the Elimination of All Forms of Discrimination Against Women 1979; the Convention Against Torture and Other Cruel, Inhuman or Degrading Treatment or Punishment 1984; the Convention on the Rights of the Child 1989; and the Convention on the Rights of Persons with Disabilities 2006. Australia is a party to all of these.

The International Covenant on Civil and Political Rights (ICCPR)

This has been ratified by Australia and, although not assimilated into its domestic law, its provisions and monitoring process are fully binding upon it. The ICCPR is supplemented by General Comment 22 (see also Chapter 4).

International Reports

In 2009, the UNHR Committee reported its concern that "the rights to equality and non-discrimination are not comprehensively protected in Australia in federal law".[15] Concern was also expressed about specific matters – such as the high level of violence against women, the need for greater promotion and protection of the rights of people who are lesbian, gay, bisexual, trans, gender-diverse and intersex (LGBTI) and the use of enforced sterilisation procedures – which, as argued in this book, can be associated with religious beliefs and discrimination.

The Domestic Framework

In 2011, the Human Rights Law Centre noted that Australia has a number of laws that address discrimination. It viewed this piecemeal protection of the right to non-discrimination as deficient, because the laws: are reactive and complaints-based; fail to actively promote equality or address systemic discrimination; do not address all grounds of discrimination or intersectional discrimination; and are ineffective in areas that have been granted permanent exemptions.[16] The federal legislation listed in this section is matched in each state and territory by broadly equivalent statutes.

---

[15] See UNHR Committee, Concluding Observations: Australia (2009), at para. 12.5.

[16] See further www.humanrightsactionplan.org.au/nhrap/focus-area/equality-and-non-discrimination-laws.

The Human Rights (Parliamentary Scrutiny) Act 2011

This took effect on 4 January 2012, and requires all new legislation intro-duced to the Federal Parliament to be assessed for compatibility with human rights. It also established a new parliamentary joint committee on human rights, and a National Action Plan for implementing related com-mitments was launched in 2012. The Act implemented "Australia's Human Rights Framework", but did not create a Charter of Rights.

The Fair Work Act 2009 (Cth)

This protects freedom of association and extends the specific legal protec-tion previously given to religious non-discrimination in the workplace.[17]

The Human Rights and Equal Opportunity Commission Act 1986 (Cth)

This statute established the Human Rights and Equal Opportunity Com-mission, which, in 2008, was renamed the Australian Human Rights Commission (AHRC).

The Racial Discrimination Act 1975 (Cth)

This does not provide any specific protection against discrimination on the basis of religion, although s.10 does establish a general right to equal-ity before the law. If a religious group can also be classified as an "ethnic" group, the racial hatred provisions may then cover direct and indirect dis-crimination and vilification against it or its members. Even if a religious group cannot be classified in that way, the Act may cover discrimination on the basis of religion in certain circumstances, such as indirect race dis-crimination. Its deficiencies are such that, since enactment in 1975, the statute has been modified three times, including in 1995 to prohibit racial vilification. In *Jones* v. *Scully*,[18] the court found that Jews constitute an eth-nic group for the purposes of this statute, and their vilification constitutes racial discrimination.[19]

Other Legislation

At Commonwealth level, anti-discrimination provisions are to be found in a range of legislation, of which some, such as the Fair Work Act 2009 (Cth),

---

[7] Neil Foster points out that the protections in the employment area in relation to discrim-ination on the grounds of religion only apply where the relevant state provides such pro-tection, citing s.351(2)(a) (note to author, 20 February 2017).
[8] [2002] 120 FCR 243. [19] *Jones* v. *Tonen* [2002] FCA 1150.

offers limited protection against discrimination on the basis of religious belief. In November 2012, the government released a draft of its Human Rights and Anti-Discrimination Bill 2012, which was intended to consolidate Commonwealth anti-discrimination law, replacing the existing Acts listed in this section, and which would have included protection against discrimination based on religion. Instead, the Bill was suspended and the government settled for amending the more deficient features of the Sex Discrimination Act.

At states level, there are various laws that prohibit the vilification of persons, singularly or as a group, on the basis of their religion (Queensland, Tasmania and Victoria); while all states except New South Wales and South Australia have legislation that makes "religious belief" a prohibited ground.

Courts and Tribunals

Australia's court and regulatory systems operate with almost complete independence and autonomy.

International

Australia is not subject to any international judicial fora, other than the monitoring role of the Universal Periodic Review procedure.

Domestic

The Commonwealth, states and territories each have their own regulatory and court systems, against the decisions of which a right of appeal lies to the federal High Court of Australia (HCA) – the supreme court and final court of appeal. The federal jurisdiction of the HCA is derived from authority vested in it by the Constitution, s.75 and s.76, and its appellate jurisdiction is defined by s.73. Appeals lie to it from the Federal Court of Australia (FCA), which has jurisdiction to deal with most civil disputes governed by federal law.

The Australian Human Rights Commission (AHRC)   A national independent statutory body with responsibility for investigating matters protected by Australia's anti-discrimination legislation, including discrimination on the grounds of religion, the AHRC has issued important reports on religious belief.[20]

---

[20] See the Australian Human Rights Commission, "Freedom of Religion and Belief", 1998 and "Freedom of Religion and Belief in the 21st Century", March 2011.

The Australian Council of Human Rights Agencies (ACHRA) This body provides a unified voice for all Commonwealth, state and territory anti-discrimination and human rights agencies. The ACHRA issues annual reports, on behalf of the Australian Council of Human Rights, giving an account of progress made towards meeting concerns recorded at the last Universal Periodic Review.

The Human Rights and Equal Opportunity Commission This Commission is the regulating body for such law and practice as is governed by: the Racial Discrimination Act 1975; the Sex Discrimination Act 1984; the Disability Discrimination Act 1992; and the Human Rights and Equal Opportunity Commission Act 1986. The latter gives rise to the Commission's responsibilities in respect of religious discrimination, which are informed by Articles 18, 20 and 26 of the ICCPR 1966 and by the Declaration on the Elimination of All Forms of Intolerance and of Discrimination Based on Religion or Belief 1981.

Freedom of Religion and Beliefs: The Principle and the Law

The "freedom of religion, the paradigm freedom of conscience, is of the essence of a free society", proclaimed Mason ACJ and Brennan J in *Church of the New Faith*, adding that its protection under s.116 extends to those without religious belief and can accommodate all nascent minority religions that may yet emerge.[21] More recently, the judiciary described the "freedom of religious belief and expression" as an "important freedom generally accepted in Australian society".[22] Nonetheless, academics claim that "Australia has only relatively weak constitutional and legal protection of freedom of religion or belief and prohibition of discrimination on the basis of religion or belief".[23]

Definitions

There are no domestic legislative provisions that provide a basis for defining and differentiating forms of religion, beliefs and their associated organisations.

[1] *Church of the New Faith* v. *Commissioner of Pay-roll Tax*, op. cit.
[2] *Evans* v. *New South Wales* (2008) 168 FCR 576, per French, Branson and Stone JJ at p. 596.
[3] Evans, C. M., *Legal Aspects of the Protection of Religious Freedom in Australia*, Annandale, NSW, The Federation Press, 2009, at p. 8.

"Religion"

In *New South Wales Stewards' Co. Ltd* v. *Strathfield Municipal Council*,[2] the court relied on orthodox principles to determine whether a company, which had among its objects the promotion of the true welfare of humankind in Christian or benevolent principles and the teaching of the word of God, was a "religious body" and on that basis entitled to a rating exemption. Noting that "religious body" and "religion" were not defined in the rating statute, the court found that these terms were to be given their popular meaning – which imputed a belief in a "Supreme Being". Forty years later, in *Church of the New Faith* v. *Commissioner of Pay-roll Tax*,[25] when considering whether a particular set of beliefs and practices would constitute a religion, Mason ACJ and Brennan J suggested that:[26]

> for the purposes of law, the criteria of religion are twofold: first, belief in a supernatural Being, Thing or Principle; and second, the acceptance of canons of conduct in order to give effect to that belief

More recently, *OV and OW*[27] was significant from many perspectives including for its exploration of what constitutes a "religion". The Wesley Mission had sought to rely upon the "fundamental Biblical teaching that 'monogamous heterosexual partnership within marriage' is both the 'norm and ideal'", but the New South Wales Administrative Decisions Tribunal (NSWADT) initially found, given the diversity of views across Christendom on this issue, that: "it does not follow, and nor is it asserted, that that belief can properly be described as a doctrine of the Christian religion". Ultimately, the Court of Appeal held that the search for such doctrine and the need to establish its conformity or otherwise with the act or practice of the Mission was "misguided"[28] and referred the issue back to the Tribunal. In reconsidering the matter, the NSWADT took the view that "doctrine" was broad enough to encompass not just formal doctrinal pronouncements such as the Nicene Creed, but effectively whatever was commonly taught or advocated by a body – including moral as well as religious principles – in a contemporary timeframe, rather than as traditionally prescribed.

---

[24] (1944) 15 LGR 139.
[25] [1983] HCA 40, (1983) 154 CLR 120 (27 October 1983), at p. 137.   [26] Ibid., at p. 74.
[27] *OV* v. *QZ (No. 2)* [2008] NSWADT 115; *Member of the Board of the Wesley Mission Council* v. *OV and OW (No. 2)* [2009] NSWADTAP 57; *OV & OW* v. *Members of the Board of the Wesley Mission Council* [2010] NSWCA 155.
[28] *OV and OW*, op. cit., at para. 40.

Subsequently, Hampel J, in *Cobaw Community Health Services Limited v. Christian Youth Camps Limited & Anor*,[29] considered the Equal Opportunity Act 1995, ss.75(2) and 77, which declare that discrimination is not prohibited by a body established for religious purposes, where the conduct conforms with the doctrines of religion or is necessary to avoid injury to the religious sensitivities of the people of the religion; or where it is necessary to comply with genuine religious beliefs or principles. Having heard expert evidence from theologians on the meaning of "doctrines of religion" and the interpretation that should be given to "conforms with the doctrines of the religion", she found that the plenary inspiration (the words of the Bible must be believed and acted upon) is a doctrine of the Christian religion. However, as the evidence showed no reference to marriage, sexual relationships or homosexuality in the creeds or declarations of faith adhered to by members of the Christian Brethren, she held that their beliefs about these matters could not be construed as "doctrines of the religion". The judicial finding included the observation that not everything in the Scriptures amounts to "doctrine": the prevailing cultural beliefs at the time must also be taken into account.[30] The Court of Appeal, endorsing Hampel J's ruling, found that Christian Youth Camps (CYC) had unlawfully discriminated against Cobaw and a group of same-sex-attracted young people on the basis of their sexual orientation. It held that: CYC was not "a body established for religious purposes", and therefore could not rely on the s.75(2) exemption; even if it was such a body, the refusal was not "necessary" to avoid injury to religious sensibilities; nor could CYC rely on the s.77 exemption, as corporations cannot hold religious beliefs and anyway the refusal was not "necessary" to comply with genuine religious beliefs or principles.

Among the implications of these decisions is an awareness that the Australian courts and regulators will focus on any declared doctrines of an organisation claiming to be a religious body. This focus appears more pronounced than in other jurisdictions, because some legislation makes explicit reference to "doctrines". In construing this term, the courts are unlikely to be limited by traditional interpretations. Moreover, not all adherents of a particular religion need to subscribe to its doctrines; it is sufficient that some do. Significant also is the finding that when a legal issue arises, which makes it necessary to ascertain the doctrines of a religion, it will be the formulation of those doctrines at the time the issue arose

---

[29] [2010] VCAT 1613 (8 October 2010).
[30] See also *Ananda Marga Pracaraka Samgha Ltd v. Tomar (No. 6)* [2013] FCA 284.

that is crucial: an approach which, by requiring the doctrine to be con-texturalised within contemporary cultural values and norms, may allow traditional religious dogma to be side-stepped, at least in circumstances where a particular religious group cannot show that it currently wholly or largely subscribes to traditional religious beliefs.

"Beliefs"

In *Church of the New Faith*, the court considered whether the doctrines and beliefs of Scientology could be construed as meeting the definition of "religion". Although unable to agree on what might constitute such a def-inition, there was consensus that it should extend to philosophies which "seek to explain, in terms of a broader reality, the existence of the universe, the meaning of human life and human destiny".[31] The indicia of religion, as discussed by Wilson and Deane JJ, were: that the particular collection of ideas and/or practices involved belief in the supernatural, i.e. a belief that reality extended beyond that which was capable of perception by the senses; that the ideas related to man's nature and place in the universe and his relations to things supernatural; that the ideas were accepted by adher-ents as requiring or encouraging them to observe particular practices hav-ing supernatural significance; and that, however loosely knit and varying in beliefs and practices adherents might be, they constituted an identifiable group or identifiable groups.[32] In unanimously concluding that Scientol-ogy is a religion, the HCA reached the opposite decision to that made in England and Wales on the same set of facts (as also occurred in relation to closed religious orders).[33]

Where, however, the purposes of an organisation are clearly antitheti-cal to religion, the Australian judiciary has adopted the same approach as its British counterparts. The *Freethinkers* case,[34] for example, concerned a society the beliefs of which included that "science provides for life and that materialism can be relied upon in all phases of society". The court consid-ered that as the purpose of the organisation was to work against already established religions or against the idea of religion, the organisation could not be construed as "religious".

---

[31] *Church of the New Faith* v. *Commissioner of Pay-roll Tax* (1983) 1 VR 97, at para. 13.

[32] *Church of the New Faith* v. *Commissioner of Pay-roll Tax* (1983) 154 CLR 120, at para. 18.

[33] For a critique of the decision, see Sadurski, W., "On Legal Definitions of Religion", *Aus-tralian Law Journal*, 1989, vol. 63, pp. 834–843. See also *Nelson* v. *Fish* (1990) 21 FCR 430. Note that in *R (on the application of Hodkin and another)* v. *Registrar General of Births, Deaths and Marriages*, op. cit., the Supreme Court adopted much the same approach.

[34] *Re Jones* [1907] SALR 1990 (Incorporated Body of Freethinkers of Australia).

Despite Latham CJ's assertion, in *Adelaide Co. of Jehovah's Witnesses Inc. v. Commonwealth*,[35] that "it is not an exaggeration to say that each person chooses the content of his own religion" in determining what constitutes a religion or belief, Australian law has not strayed far from its roots. In the *Scientology* case,[36] for example, the initial judgments had rejected the claim that Scientology was a religion, finding instead that it was a philosophy and that the trappings of religion had only been acquired after its establishment in order to give the organisation the semblance of one. While this finding was overturned by the High Court,[37] its rationale for doing so was that Scientology beliefs sufficiently approximated religious beliefs to justify extending recognition to it. However, both Mason Acting CJ and Brennan J were alert to the dangers of overstretching the interpretation of religion to allow for such inclusion and warned that "the mantle of immunity would soon be in tatters if it were wrapped around beliefs, practices and observances of every kind whenever a group of adherents chose to call them a religion".[38]

There are no Australian statutory provisions designed to recognise and accommodate the dreamtime rites – which vary from tribe to tribe in accordance with tribal boundaries, topography and ancestor narratives – that constitute the religious beliefs of Indigenous People. The case for extending such recognition has been well made.[39] Despite the analytical difficulties involved, there can be no doubt that the concepts and beliefs of Indigenous culture offer a sufficiently valid and coherent parallel to Christianity, for example, to warrant equal recognition in law. Indeed, enquiries undertaken to establish whether such beliefs could be so construed were the subject of judicial scrutiny in *ALRM* v. *State of South Australia*.[40] The Supreme Court of South Australia then held that an inquiry into the genuineness of the belief of Ngarrindjiri women, notwithstanding that those beliefs were, under Aboriginal rule, confidential to women, was lawful. Subsequently, in *Kruger* v. *Commonwealth*,[41] Gaudron J leant judicial weight to the parallels between the beliefs of Indigenous People and those

[35] (1943) 67 CLR 116, at 124.

[36] *Church of New Faith* v. *Commissioner of Pay-Roll Tax* (1983) 1 VR 97.

[37] *Church of New Faith* v. *Commissioner of Pay-Roll Tax* (1983) 154 CLR 120.

[38] Ibid., at p. 132.

[39] See e.g. Gallois, W., "On Dreaming Time", in *Time, Religion and History*, London, Pearson Education, 2007.

[40] *Aboriginal Legal Rights Movement Inc.* v. *State of South Australia and Iris Eliza Stevens* (1995) 64 SASR 551.

[41] See (1997) 190 CLR 1.

of more orthodox religious adherents when, in considering whether th
removal of Aboriginal children breached s.116, she stated that "the Abo
riginal people of the Northern Territory, or at least some of them, ha
beliefs or practices which are properly classified as a religion". This wa
endorsed by Toohey J, her colleague on the bench, who seemed to recog
nise also that such beliefs had been met by State-sanctioned religious dis
crimination when he commented that "it may well be that an effect of th
Ordinance was to impair, even prohibit the spiritual beliefs and practice
of the Aboriginal people in the Northern Territory".[42]

"Race", "Caste" and Indigenous People

Construing religious belief as a component of race or ethnicity has give
rise to difficulties. When allegations of discrimination by members o
racial or ethnic groups, such as Jews or Muslims, have been pursued o
religious grounds, this has often proved unsuccessful because, instead o
laws providing protection against religious discrimination, the legal focu
is on the racial/ethnic overlay.[43] For example, *A obo V and A* v. *NSW Dep
of School Education*[44] concerned the complaint of a Jewish father that th
imposition of overtly Christian rituals, ceremonies (e.g. at Christmas an
Easter) and school prayers on the education received by his children i
a public school constituted a form of discrimination that offended the
religion and culture. This was dismissed on the grounds that members o
ethno-religious groups – such as Jews – cannot pursue religious discrim
ination complaints "by the back door". Again, in *Khan* v. *Commissione
Dept of Corrective Services*,[45] when a Muslim prisoner protested that th
failure to provide him with halal meat was discriminatory, the Tribuna
found that in the absence of a "close tie between that faith and his rac
nationality or ethnic origin" there was no case to answer as the prohib
tion against religious discrimination was inoperable, and it dismissed th
matter.[46] Similarly, in *Abdulrahman* v. *Toll Pty Ltd T/As Toll Express*[47] an
in *Trad* v. *Jones and Anor (No. 3)*,[48] the Tribunal determined the allege
discrimination issues on the basis of ethno-religious grounds rather tha

---

[42] Ibid., at p. 86.
[43] See e.g. Bloul, R., "Anti-Discrimination Laws, Islamophobia and Ethnicization of Musli
Identities in Europe and Australia", *Journal of Muslim Minority Affairs*, 2008, vol. 28:1.
[44] [2000] NSWADTAP 14.   [45] [2002] NSWADT 131.
[46] See further Thornton, M. and Luker, T., "The Spectral Ground: Religious Belief Discrin
ination", *Macquarie Law Journal*, 2009, vol. 9, pp. 71–91. The author acknowledges h
reliance on some material presented in this article.
[47] (2006) EOC 93-445.   [48] [2009] NSWADT 318.

as instances of religious discrimination.[49] Gaze makes the important point that "this is because they were NSW cases and religious discrimination is not covered – but in other states and territories it is protected, so these cases may well have been decided differently in other states".[50]

For Indigenous People, recognition of their distinctive ethnicity and culture is particularly important. This has occasionally been acknowledged: "the Nyungah elders are an ethnic group in that they have a shared history, separate cultural tradition, common geographical origin, descent from common ancestors, a common language and a religion different to the general community surrounding them";[51] and "the freedom of certain Ngarrindjeri people to hold and practise their religion" has been argued for.[52] The most relevant provision specific to protection for the beliefs of Indigenous People is Article 12 of the United Nations Declaration on the Rights of Indigenous Peoples, which states:

> Indigenous peoples have the right to manifest, practice, develop and teach their spiritual and religious traditions, customs and ceremonies; the right to maintain, protect, and have access in privacy to their religious and cultural sites; the right to the use and control of their ceremonial objects; and the right to the repatriation of their human remains. States shall seek to enable the access and/or repatriation of ceremonial objects and human remains in their possession through fair, transparent and effective mechanisms developed in conjunction with indigenous peoples concerned.

The importance of their sacred sites to Indigenous People has been judicially recognised, as has the justification for affording protection to lands of religious relevance from acquisition under the s.116 "free exercise clause".[53] In practice, as is evident in the *Cheedy* case,[54] the protection has not always been effective. This case concerned provisions in the Native Title Act 1992 (Cth) allowing mineral extraction on the land of Indigenous People – if necessary, without their consent – even if that land was regarded by them as an important site for spiritual beliefs. The provisions

---

[49] See also *Ekermawi* v. *Harbour Radio Pty Limited & Ekermawi* v. *Nine Network Television Pty Limited (No. 2)* [2010] NSWADT 198.

[50] Note to author, 22 February 2017.

[51] *Wanjurri* v. *Southern Cross Broadcasting (Aus.) Ltd* (2001) EOC 93-147, per Commissioner Innes.

[52] *Aboriginal Legal Rights Movement Inc.* v. *State of South Australia and Iris Eliza Stevens*, op. cit., per Doyle CJ at pp. 552–553.

[53] See *Milirrpum* v. *Nabalco Pty Ltd* (1971) 17 FLR 141 (the Gove Land Rights case) and *Coe* v. *Commonwealth* [1979] HCA 68.

[54] *Cheedy on behalf of the Yindjibarndi People* v. *State of Western Australia* [2010] FCA 690, [2011] FCAFC 100.

were found not to breach s.116 as they did not have the object of prohibit
ing the free exercise of religion. The socio-economic significance – and
indeed, the political ramifications – of recognising the link between the
beliefs of Indigenous People and the land they have traditionally occupied
is far-reaching, and brings a whole new dimension to what, in that partic
ular cultural context, may be construed as "religious discrimination" and
its effects.

Manifesting Religion or Belief and Free Speech

The right to manifest religion or belief is protected by Article 18(1) of
the ICCPR, as ratified by Australia in 1980. Also relevant is the Dec
laration on the Elimination of All Forms of Intolerance and of Dis
crimination Based on Religion or Belief,[55] which elaborates upon the
ICCPR provision. Again, a degree of protection is afforded by the Aus
tralian Constitution. Latham CJ, in *Adelaide Co. of Jehovah's Witnesses Inc*
v. *Commonwealth*,[56] was certain that s.116 protection extended beyond
beliefs to include the manifestation of such beliefs, as were Mason AC
and Brennan J in *Church of the New Faith* v. *Commissioner of Pay-roll Ta*
(Vict).[57]

The right to manifest religious belief is constrained in at least two
respects. First, the action must be appropriately linked to the belief: clearly
not all action taken by a religious person or organisation is necessaril
related to, let alone a manifestation of, their religious beliefs. As Dal Pon
has expressed it:[58]

> Importantly there must be a connection between a person's belief in the
> supernatural and his or her conduct as a result of that belief. Conduct
> such as worship, teaching, propagation or observance is religious only if
> the motivation for engaging in it is religious.

Second, any such action must be proportionate, comply with freedom of
speech standards and be respectful of the rights of others. As Hampel
noted in *Cobaw*,[59] the right to hold a belief is broader than the right to

---

[55] GA Res 36/55, UN GAOR, 36th sess., UN Doc A/36/684 (25 November 1981).
[56] Op. cit., at 124.   [57] (1983) 154 CLR 120, 135.
[58] Dal Pont, G., *Charity Law in Australia and New Zealand*, Melbourne, Oxford Universit
Press, 2000, at p. 149.
[59] Ibid., citing both s.14 of the Charter and Art 18 of the ICCPR. Endorsed by the Victoria
Court of Appeal in *Christian Youth Camps Limited & Ors* v. *Cobaw Community Heal*
Services Limited & Ors [2014] VSCA 75.

act upon it. In particular, she emphasised that the right to freedom of religious belief does not confer a right on members of a religion to impose their beliefs on a secular society.[60] Clearly, while the right to so manifest incorporates a right to cause offence when doing so, this must not be exercised to the point where it becomes vilification.

Free Speech and Freedom of Association

The right to manifest religious belief is constrained by the rights of others; in particular, by the fundamental right of free speech. So, for example, in *Francis v. YWCA Australia*,[61] a complaint against the YWCA for selling and distributing T-shirts bearing the slogan "Mr Abbott, get your rosaries off my ovaries" was dismissed: manifesting the organisation's religious beliefs in that manner was construed as within the confines of free speech and insufficient to incite hatred of Catholics. Similarly, in *Evans v. NSW*,[62] the right to free speech was found to be obstructed by statutory provisions intended to prohibit the "annoying" of Roman Catholics participating in World Youth Day celebrations in 2008. Again, in *Deen v. Lamb*,[63] a pamphlet implying that all Muslims were obliged to disobey the law of Australia was held to be permissible as it was published "in good faith". However, in *Menzies & Ors v. Owen*,[64] the court upheld a charge of publicly vilifying homosexuals and incitement to hatred despite an assertion that this was sourced in "ancient religious text such as the Bible, the Torah or the Koran", while in *Youssef v. Khani*,[65] repeated vile abuse of Islam in a private meeting was construed as religious discrimination. In *Catch the Fire*,[66] a tirade against Muslims was found to be lawful because the relevant legislation did not "prohibit statements concerning the religious beliefs of a person or group of persons simply because they may offend or insult the person or group of persons" (see later). Not dissimilarly, in *Adelaide Preachers*,[67] the HCA upheld the validity of a local by-law that prohibited "preaching, canvassing and haranguing" in a public place without a license from the city, adding that it did not breach any right to free speech under s.116.

Where statements stray beyond being offensive to become "errors of fact, distortions of the truth and inflammatory and provocative language",

---

[60] Citing Laws J in *McFarlane v. Relate Avon Ltd* [2010] EWCA Civ B1.
[61] [2006] VCAT 2456.   [62] [2008] FCAFC 130.   [63] [2001] QADT 20.
[64] [2008] QADT 20, at para. 129.   [65] [2006] TASADT 8.
[66] *Catch the Fire Ministries Inc. v. Islamic Council of Victoria Inc.* [2006] VSCA 284, per Nettle JA at p. 15.
[67] *Attorney-General (SA) v. Corporation of the City of Adelaide* [2013] HCA 3.

as when a blogger named persons whom he claimed were "fair-skinned Aborgines" trading on their self-identified status for personal gain, then this is impermissible.[68] Recently, *Gaynor*[69] concerned an officer in the armed forces who had his commission terminated when he refused to stop publicly expressing offensive views – which he claimed were related to his Catholic religion – on matters such as LGBTI rights and Muslim extremists. While the court found that the plaintiff was entitled to exercise his right to freedom of speech in the way he did, and duly set aside the decision terminating his commission, Buchanan J made the point that he was "satisfied that the applicant acted by choice to make the statements which he did" and did not accept "that even as a matter of conscience, he felt he had no choice but to defy the instructions and orders given to him".[70] Even more recently, in *Sisalem*,[71] a Muslim who claimed that a newspaper article constituted religious intolerance and vilification when it suggested, after the Paris attacks, that Islam needed to undergo fundamental change had his claims dismissed on the grounds that the article could not be shown to have generated the degree of hatred and contempt of Muslims necessary to negate the paper's exercise of its right to free speech.

There is no express right to freedom of association guaranteed by the Australian Constitution, but its importance has been confirmed by the HCA,[72] and its protection is ensured by recourse to international law (the ICCPR and the International Covenant on Economic, Social and Cultural Rights). As in other countries, this right is subject to statutes governing public order and safety.

Blasphemy

Blasphemy continues to be a criminal offence in some states and territories. In 2016, the Australian Capital Territory amended the Discrimination Act 1975 to introduce the offence of "religious vilification" and "offensive behaviour", ostensibly for the protection of Muslims, but with potential application to the criticism of all religions.

Conscientious Objection

Australia was the first country to statutorily recognise the right to refuse military service on the grounds of personal belief. The Defence Act

---

[68]　*Eatock v. Bolt* [2011] FCA 1103.
[69]　*Gaynor v. Chief of Defence Force (No. 3)* [2015] FCA 1370.　　[70]　Ibid., at p. 215.
[71]　*Sisalem v. The Herald & Weekly Times Ltd* [2016] VCAT 1197.
[72]　*Unions NSW v. New South Wales* [2013] HCA 58.

903 granted total exemption from military service to "those who could emonstrate a conscientious objection to bearing arms". However, such ecognition did not prevent the court, in *Krygger* v. *Williams*,[73] from find-ng that a conscientious objector could not object to compulsory military ervice on the ground of religious belief. The then Chief Justice, Sir Samuel iriffith, described such a proposition as "absurd" and added that s.116 nly protected "the doing of acts which are done in the practice of religion. 'o require a man to do a thing which has nothing to do with religion is ot prohibiting him from a free exercise of religion."

In *Judd* v. *McKeown*,[74] the appellant, a committed socialist who as a natter of conscience had refused to vote, was convicted of failing to do o "without a valid and sufficient reason", contrary to the compulsory vot-ng provisions of the Commonwealth Electoral Act 1918 (Cth). However, Higgins J expressed the view, at variance with the *Krygger* decision, that the appellant had had a religious objection to voting then this would ave been protected under s.116.[75] More recently, conscientious objec-ons on religious grounds to paying taxes that could be used to provide or abortions[76] and to revealing the contents of a religious confession were ummarily dismissed.[77]

Proselytism

earing witness to one's faith – and seeking to persuade others, by vari-us peaceful means, as to its merits – is viewed by many religious adher-nts as a duty. It is as permissible under Australian law, as it is in other ommon law countries, and has been defended in the HCA by Kirby [78] So long as it is free from government influence, does not violate the ights of others and is directed at those who are in a position to make an nformed choice – i.e. not children, prison inmates or mentally impaired ersons – then proselytism is a perfectly lawful activity. It is possible, how-ver, that the Commonwealth-funded school chaplains programme, man-ating government-funded, exclusively Christian counselling (which in ractice facilitates proselytising) on a nationwide basis, could be consid-red to breach all three conditions.

(1912) 15 CLR 366.   [74] (1926) 38 CLR 380.
See further Foster, "Religious Freedom in Australia".
Daniels v. *Deputy Commissioner of Taxation* [2007] SASC 431 (unreported, Debelle, Sulan and Vanstone JJ, 7 December 2007).
SDW v. *Church of Jesus Christ of Latter-Day Saints* (2008) 222 FLR 84.
See *NABD of 2002* v. *Minister for Immigration and Multicultural and Indigenous Affairs* [2005] HCA 29, (2005) 216 ALR 1, (2005) 79 ALJR 1142, at p. 121.

In *Catch the Fire*,[79] the Victorian Court of Appeal considered whether the conduct of Catch the Fire Ministries, an evangelical religious organisation, contravened s.8 of the Racial and Religious Tolerance Act 2001 (Vic). The conduct concerned statements made at a seminar in 2002, in a newsletter in 2001 and in an article on the organisation's website in 2001 including the following: that the Qur'an promotes violence and killing that the Qur'an teaches that women are of little value; that Allah is no merciful; and that Muslims practising Jihad are following the Qur'an. The ruling that there had been no incitement to hatred of Muslims because of their faith – as opposed to hatred of the religious beliefs of Muslims – (a distinction the significance of which may not be readily apparent to Muslims) places a high value on the relative importance of freedom of speech but is in keeping with the generous latitude traditionally allowed to proselytising religious entities.[80]

Discrimination

As Neave JA has pointed out:[81]

> Attributing characteristics to people on the basis of their group membership is the essence of racial and religious prejudice and the discrimination which flows from it.

Religious Discrimination

In Australia, neither the Constitution nor any federal legislation specifically address religious discrimination, but the majority of states and territories – Victoria, Queensland, Western Australia, Tasmania, the ACT and the Northern Territory – have introduced legislation that does so. Consequently, the absence of federal legislation prohibiting discrimination on the basis of religion in areas such as employment, accommodation and education forces reliance upon international conventions and protocols Of particular relevance, potentially, would be Article 3 of the Declaration on the Elimination of All Forms of Intolerance and of Discrimination Based on Religion or Belief, which defines religious discrimination as "any distinction, exclusion, restriction or preference based on religion or belief

---

[79] Op. cit.

[80] See further Parkinson, P., "Enforcing Tolerance: Vilification Laws and Religious Freedom in Australia", 2005, at http://sydneyanglicans.net/blogs/indepth/enforcing_tolerance patrick_parkinson.

[81] *Catch the Fire Ministries* v. *Islamic Council of Victoria* (2006) 15 VR 207, at p. 258.

and having as its purpose or as its effect nullification or impairment of the recognition, enjoyment or exercise of human rights and fundamental freedoms on an equal basis". In fact, however, as Gaze comments: "this has no significance at all in Australian law – apart from any role in relation to unenforceable complaints under the AHRC Act 'discrimination' provisions".[82]

Type Although the Human Rights and Equal Opportunity Commission Act 1986 (Cth) does not refer to direct or indirect discrimination, the four Commonwealth anti-discrimination acts do define these terms, and Katz J in *Commonwealth of Australia v. Human Rights and Equal Opportunity Commission and Hamilton*[83] found the distinction to be implied in the s.3 definition of that Act.

Exemptions and Exceptions

Australia, in keeping with all other common law jurisdictions currently being considered, extends religious and charitable privileges to religious organisations. Interestingly, such exemptions have been defended on the basis of the freedom of association. Parkinson expressed concern regarding a "new fundamentalism about 'equality'" and argues that faith-based organisations should have a right to select staff who fit with the values and mission of the organisation, just as political parties, environmental groups and LBGT organisations do. To select on the basis of "mission fit" is not discrimination. Rather, it is essential to the right of freedom of association.[84]

The "Religious" Exemption

The exemptions are addressed primarily in the Sex Discrimination Act 1984 (Cth) and the Fair Work Act 2009 (Cth), but also in all state and territory anti-discrimination statutes. These provide that religious organisations and religious educational institutions are granted an exemption where a discriminatory act or conduct has been required to ensure conformity with the doctrines, tenets or beliefs of a religion, or is necessary to avoid injury to the religious sensitivities of adherents of that religion. It allows such bodies to discriminate: in the provision of accommodation;

[82] Note to author, 22 February 2017.   [83] [2000] FCA 1854.
[84] Parkinson, P., "Traditional Rights and Freedoms – Encroachments by Commonwealth Laws" (ALRC Interim Report 127), Submission 9, 2015.

in the ordination or appointment of priests or ministers of religion, or in the training or education of such persons; in the appointment of persons to perform religious duties or functions, and any other act or practice of a body established for religious purposes; and in relation to the employment of staff and the provision of education and training on the part of educational institutions established for religious purposes – provided that the discrimination is in "good faith". In *Walsh* v. *St Vincent de Paul Society Queensland (No. 2)*,[85] the respondent was found to be a society of lay faithful closely associated with the Catholic Church, rather than a "religious body", and therefore not entitled to avail itself of the religious exemption. The 1984 Act has been amended by the Sex Discrimination Amendment (Sexual Orientation, Gender Identity and Intersex Status) Act 2013, which revises certain exemption privileges traditionally enjoyed by religious organisations, but specifically exempts private schools and hospitals owned by religious organisations from its gender-identity and sexual-orientation provisions.

The religious exemption was clearly central to the lengthy proceedings that constituted the previously discussed *OV and OW* and *Cobaw* cases.[86] The exemption was also central to *Mornington Baptist Church Community Caring Inc.*,[87] when a Baptist Church unsuccessfully sought to avail itself of the exemption privilege to restrict staff selection to those who had "publicly confessed Jesus Christ" and were "walking in daily fellowship with Jesus". Its claim failed because the organisation was unable to show why its religious beliefs required it to so restrict employment in order to fulfill the functional tasks of its community care projects.

In the light of the many international experiences of child abuse by clergy, the exemption privileges accorded to religious bodies have been called into question in Australia, as elsewhere.[88] Indeed, in July 2015, the Royal Commission into Institutional Responses to Child Sexual Abuse noted that the Jehovah's Witnesses (with approximately 70 000 Australian members) had failed to report any of their 1006 alleged offenders over six decades of recorded child abuse.[89]

---

[85] [2008] QADT 32.   [86] Op. cit.   [87] (2006) EOC 93-422 (VCAT).

[88] See Royal Commission, "Institutional Responses to Child Sexual Abuse", 2017, at www.abc.net.au/news/2017-02-06/child-sex-abuse-royal-commission:-data-reveals-catholic-abuse/8243890.

[89] See further www.childabuseroyalcommission.gov.au/media-centre/media-releases/2015-07/public-hearing-into-the-jehovah's-witnesses.

The "Charity" Exemption

The privileges traditionally accorded to religions and religious organisations in Australia have been continued by the Charities Act 2013, which excuses them from the mandatory registration requirement that otherwise applies to all charities. Testators may continue to add religiously discriminating conditions to their bequests. Moreover, charitable status, together with associated exemption priviliges, is more broadly interpreted than in the UK, as Australian charity law does not interpose a public-benefit test as a determinant of entitlement to that status and to accompanying tax privileges. While its extension to "closed" religious orders was established in *Assoc. of Franciscan Order of Friars Minor v. City of Kew*,[90] thereafter confirmed in relation to other religious entities,[91] and is now endorsed by the Charities Act 2013.

Kirby J, however, in his strongly worded dissenting judgment in the HCA decision of *Commissioner of Taxation v. Word Investments Limited*, may have cast a shadow over the future approach to the exemption privileges of religious organisations:[92]

> Charitable and religious institutions contribute to society in various ways. However, such institutions sometimes perform functions that are offensive to the beliefs, values and consciences of other taxpayers. This is especially so in the case of charitable institutions with religious purposes or religious institutions. These institutions can undertake activities that are offensive to many taxpayers who subscribe to different religious beliefs or who have no religious beliefs. Although the Parliament may provide specific exemptions, as a generally applicable principle it is important to spare general taxpayers from the obligation to pay income tax effectively to support or underwrite the activities of religious...organisations with which they disagree.

The "Positive Action" Exception

"Positive action" – or "positive discrimination", "positive measures" or "special measures" – refers to action taken that aims to foster equality by providing targeted support to offset the particular disadvantages suffered by certain specific groups. An anomalous instance of what might be construed as "positive action" was the subject of judicial scrutiny in *Kay v.*

[90] (1967) VR 732.

[91] *Council of the Municipality of Canterbury v. Moslem Alawy Society Ltd* (1987) 162 CLR 145 and *Crowther v. Brophy* [1992] 2 VR 97, 100.

[92] (2008) 236 CLR 204, 248 [110], per Kirby J. See also 249–250 [112]–[116].

South Eastern Sydney Area Health Service,[93] which concerned a fund for the treatment of white babies. The court ultimately upheld the fund as charitable on grounds that included the banal rationale that "the receipt of a fund to benefit white babies would just mean that more of the general funds of the hospital would be available to treat non-white babies so that, in due course, despite the testatrix's intention things will even up".

Religious Discrimination: Church and State

The Preamble to the Australian Constitution acknowledges its Christian roots and the presumed Christianity of Australians – but overlooks the beliefs of those citizens who are Indigenous People, and of those who adhere to multi-theistic religions or to none – in the proclamation that we, the Australian people, are "humbly relying on the blessings of Almighty God".

The Church/State Boundary

The Australian constitution, unlike its US counterpart, does not provide for the firm separation of Church and State, but it does prohibit the establishment of a State church or religion, thereby requiring the State to treat all religions equally. This was acknowledged by McHugh JA in *Canterbury Municipal Council* v. *Moslem Alawy Society Ltd,*[94] who claimed that "the preservation of religious equality has always been a matter of fundamental concern to the people of Australia and finds its place in the Constitution, s.116". It has been evident also in the many instances of synergy between government and Christianity on issues such as gay marriage and abortion. However, there is a school of thought which argues that the preferential treatment of one religion over another is permissible providing it falls short of seeking the establishment of that religion. It must also be recognised that the boundaries between Church and State proved sufficiently porous to permit the appointment of the Anglican Archbishop as Governor-General of Australia in 2001, and, as has been noted:[95]

> There are political parties in Australia that are specifically and openly religious in orientation. There are politicians who more or less openly profess religious faith and acknowledge its impact on their own political

---

[93] [2003] NSWSC 292.   [94] (1985) 1 NSWLR 525.

[95] Aroney, N., "The Constitutional (In)validity of Religious Vilification Laws: Implications for their Interpretation", *Federal Law Review*, 2006, vol. 34:2.

perspectives, deliberations and decision-making. And there are different views about the proper content of religious belief, specifically in terms of its implications for political decision-making.

Protecting Religion from the State

Section 116 offers religion little protection from the State: its prohibition is restricted to an "undue infringement of religious freedom".[96] However, as Jackson J once declared, "the true situation is that if an enactment permitted executive action under it which amounted to a prohibition upon the free exercise of any religion, the enactment to the extent that it permitted such action . . . would be invalid".[97] Another issue concerns the bodies entitled to protection. The St Vincent de Paul Society, for example, has been found not to meet the definition of "religious body" and is therefore outside s.116 protection.[98]

The HCA has held that the only laws invalidated under the Establishment Clause are those which: entrench "a religion as a feature of and identified with the body politic"; "constitute a particular religion or religious body as a State religion or State church"; or require "statutory recognition of a religion as a national institution". Moreover, its constitutional protection applies only to the Commonwealth, not to the states:[99] in theory, the latter are free to establish their own religions, although none has ever done so. The limitations of s.116 are such that, as Justice Sir Ninian Stephen once said, it "cannot readily be viewed as a repository of some broad statement of principle concerning the separation of Church and State, from which may be distilled the detailed consequences of such separation".[100] Indeed, its limitations were evident in *Krygger v. Williams*,[101] when the HCA held that compulsory military training for teenage boys did not prohibit the free exercise of religion, and again in *Adelaide Co. of Jehovah's Witnesses Inc. v. Commonwealth*,[102] when, at the height of World War II, the court struck down wartime regulations and found that the freedom of religion had to give way to national security considerations. This, in turn, caused the Adelaide branch of the Jehovah's Witnesses to be dissolved and its

---

[96] *Jehovah's Witnesses Case* (1943) 67 CLR 116, per Latham CJ at p. 131.

[97] *Minister for Immigration and Ethnic Affairs v. Lebanese Moslem Ass'n* (1987) 71 A.L.R. 578, at p. 584.

[98] *Walsh v. St Vincent de Paul Society Queensland (No. 2)*, op. cit.

[99] See *Grace Bible Church Inc. v. Reedman* (1984) 54 ALR 571, when the Supreme Court of South Australia decided that the s.116 right did not apply to state laws.

[100] *Attorney-General (Vic) (Ex rel Black) v. Commonwealth* (1981) 146 CLR 559.

[101] Op. cit.   [102] Op. cit.

property to be acquired by the government – notwithstanding the irony of Latham CJ's observation at the time that "s.116 is required to protec the religion (or absence of religion) of minorities and, in particular, o unpopular minorities".[103] Further evidence of inadequacy emerged witl the ruling in *Kruger* v. *Commonwealth*,[104] which found that the Aborigi nal Protection Ordinance 1918 (NT), authorising the forcible removal o Indigenous children, even if this did have the effect of terminating thei free exercise of religion, was compliant with s.116 (see earlier).

Intervention in Church Disputes

It is well established that Australian courts are not competent to adjudicat on theological matters. Their inability to assess the validity or invalidity o the doctrines or tenets of any religion, or to differentiate between them was acknowledged by Murphy J in *Church of the New Faith* v. *Commis sioner of Pay-roll Tax*:[105]

> The truth or falsity of religions is not the business of officials or the courts.
> If each purported religion had to show that its doctrines were true, then
> all might fail … It is not within the judicial sphere to determine matters of
> religious doctrine and practice.

This approach was confirmed in the Federal Court, in *Iliafi* v. *The Churc of Jesus Christ of Latter-Day Saints Australia*,[106] when it found that if th respondent's argument concerned the correctness or otherwise of the con tent – of ritual, doctrine or ecclesiastical issues – then the court woul not have jurisdiction. It is perhaps noteworthy that, considering the num ber of inter-church disputes, schisms and consequent property contests i recent years – unlike in the USA – there do not appear to be any relate Australian court judgments.

The State, Religion and Religious Discrimination

There is a particularly strong relationship between government and th traditional Christian religions in Australia. This, together with the wea constitutional safeguards separating Church and State and the absence c a bill of rights, may leave those of other religious beliefs and those of non

---

[103] Neil Foster points out that the regulations were struck down as invalid, but not on s.11 grounds (note to author, 20 February 2017).
[104] [1997] HCA 27, 190 CLR 1, 146 ALR 126.
[105] (1983) 154 CLR 120, per Murphy J at pp. 150–151. [106] [2014] FCAFC 26.

with a perception that they are relatively discriminated against in terms of institutional leverage.

Balancing Religion and Secularism

Given the relatively strong and lasting public-benefit service partnership between government and the Christian religions, it is unsurprising that in practice the government's avowed secularist public policy is quite constrained – as is evident in its funding of religious schools, hospitals, community service providers, etc., and in the unrepealed laws prohibiting blasphemy, both of which are clearly discriminatory.

In *Grace Bible Church Inc. v. Reedman*,[107] the court gave short shrift to the appellant's claim that "there was an inalienable right to religious freedom". Parliament, as White J commented, had "an absolute right to interfere with religious worship and the expression of religious beliefs at any time that it liked"[108] – and indeed, had done so when the nation was at war, as illustrated in the Jehovah's Witnesses cases – but this draconian approach did little to stem the flow of cases dealing with clashes between the rights to religious freedom and to freedom of speech.[109] Nor did the court give much credence to a challenge to the introduction of the goods and services tax (GST) that it would breach the obligation of Muslims not to collect taxes on behalf of government, finding that "the importance of maintaining a sound tax system is of such a high order that the religious belief in withholding GST is not protected by s.116".[110] The weak enforcement available to guarantee the freedom of religion was demonstrated in the previously mentioned *Iliafi* case, which concerned an internal dispute regarding language, when the full Federal Court confirmed that in such circumstances, an individual's freedom of religion was protected by the right to leave the Church; which, it has to be said, is not much of a right.[111]

---

[107] Op. cit.   [108] Ibid. at p. 385.

[109] See, for example, *Fletcher v. Salvation Army Australia (Anti Discrimination)* [2005] VCAT 1523 (1 August 2005); *Bropho v. Human Rights and Equal Opportunity Commission* [2004] FCAFC 16; *Judeh v. Jewish National Fund of Australia Inc* [2003] VCAT 1254; and *John Fairfax Publications Pty Ltd v. Kazak* [2002] NSWADTAP 35.

[110] See *Halliday v. Commonwealth of Australia* [2000] FCA 950, per Sundberg J at p. 20. See also *Daniels v. Deputy Commissioner of Taxation* [2007] SASC 431, where the challenge – on religious grounds – to paying tax was in relation to government funding of abortion services.

[11] Op. cit., at pp. 85–86.

The alleged use of a "religious test"[112] arose in *Church of Scientology Inc.* v. *Woodward*,[113] which concerned advice supposedly given to government ministers by the Australian Security Intelligence Organisation (ASIO) claiming that certain persons employed or seeking employment in the Commonwealth posed a security risk due to their membership of the Church of Scientology. The plaintiff argued that, in effect, this amounted to the application of a "religious test" by the ASIO. The court dismissed the application on a technicality of defective wording. Subsequently, in *Attorney-General (Vic) (Ex rel Black)* v. *Commonwealth*,[114] Stephen J seemed satisfied that the s.116 clause "prohibits the imposition, whether by law or otherwise, of religious tests for the holding of Commonwealth office". In coming to a majority decision – that indirect government funding of religious schools did not breach the "establishment" clause of s.116 – there was consensus among six of the seven judges that s.116 differed from the corresponding US First Amendment clause in that it did not presume to represent a liberty right but was limited to suppressing any initiative by the Commonwealth government to impose a law giving preference to any one religion or church.

State Funding of Faith-Based Facilities and Services

Section 116 of the Constitution does not prohibit the State from encouraging or giving aid to religion, and there is no constitutional obstacle to laws that indirectly assist the religious to further their religious goals. As Barwick CJ once explained, s.116 was "directed to the making of law...not...the administration of a law".[115] This has permitted, for example, the adoption of explicit policies of State aid for denominational schools (during the 1960s) and State funding of chaplaincy services.[116]

The appointment of chaplains to the armed forces requires the prospective appointee to be "a member of a church or faith group approved by the Religious Advisory Committee to the services". This, clearly being a "religious test", has triggered some debate as to whether it could be s.116-compliant and whether non-Christians or atheists are thus unfairly treated. However, considerably more controversy was generated by the

---

[112] See further Beck, L., "The Constitutional Prohibition on Religious Tests", *Melbourne University Law Review*, 2011, vol. 35, at pp. 323–353.

[113] (1979) 154 CLR 79. See also *Sykes* v. *Cleary* (1992) 176 CLR 77.

[114] Op. cit., at p. 605.

[115] *Attorney-General (Vic) (Ex rel Black)* v. *Commonwealth* (1981), op. cit., per Barwick CJ, at pp. 580–581.

[116] *Hoxton Park Residents Action Group Inc.* v. *Liverpool City Council* [2016] NSWCA 157.

National School Chaplaincy Programme. Introduced in 2007, by 2016 it was using some $60 million of federal public funds per annum to provide a school chaplaincy service – "a chaplain is an individual who is recognised through formal ordination, commissioning, recognised religious qualifications or endorsement by a recognised or accepted religious institution"[117] – to nearly 3000 schools across Australia. Debate has focused on the provision of a service that is: religious (no equivalent secular service is available); almost exclusively Christian; delivered by religious organisations in the main to public schools; and paid for by taxpayers, some of whom are atheists, agnostics or belong to non-Christian religions, and many of whom argue that schools should be strictly secular. In *Williams (I)*,[118] the plaintiff challenged the constitutionality of the programme, claiming that he had a right to secure a secular education for his children. The High Court held that while the chaplaincy programme was not in breach of the s.116 religious test, the Commonwealth's funding arrangements were unauthorised by statute and therefore unconstitutional. Within days of the decision, the Commonwealth Parliament passed the Financial Framework Legislation Amendment Act (No. 3) 2012 (Cth), which sought to regularise the funding arrangements and secure the national network of chaplaincy posts, but this was challenged by the plaintiff in *Williams (II)*,[119] and again the court found the funding arrangements to be unconstitutional, although this time on the more fundamental grounds that the statutory provisions purporting to authorise the programme were invalid because they did not fall within any of the Commonwealth's legislative powers. Since then, the programme has been centrally funded by the federal government, to enable all states and territories to place and administer chaplains in public and private schools – the "placing" being contracted to evangelical Christian organisations such as Scripture Union.

Christian Symbols/Prayers in State Facilities

The establishment clause in s.116 of the Constitution states that "no religious test shall be required as a qualification for any office or public trust under the Commonwealth". This has not prevented the parliamentary standing orders from requiring a full recitation of the Lord's Prayer by the

---

[7] As defined in the Project Agreement for the National School Chaplaincy Programme, 2014.

[8] *Williams v. the Commonwealth of Australia* [2012] HCA 23.

[9] *Williams v. Commonwealth of Australia* [2014] HCA 23.

Speaker of the House of Representatives and the President of the Senate a the commencement of each day's business: a practice that is plainly Chris tian, overtly Protestant, arguably disrespectful of the rights of all other reli gious adherents and non-believers, but authorised by the highest authorit in the land.[120] In the one recorded case concerning the taking of an oath a a requirement for public office, this was found to constitute an interferenc with the free exercise of religion.[121]

Religious Discrimination: Contemporary Caselaw

There is no federal statute specifically dealing with religious discrimina tion. In practice, the relevant domestic federal legislative framework con sists of the Fair Work Act 2009 (Cth),[122] the Human Rights and Equa Opportunity Act 1986 (Cth) and the Racial Discrimination Act 197 (Cth). The domestic deficit tends to be buttressed by reference to inter national conventions and protocols, perhaps in particular the UDHR an ICCPR.[123] In practice, it is left to the legislators and judiciary of individ ual states and territories to address and resolve such issues; compared wit other jurisdictions, relatively few cases reach the higher or federal court As already noted, the relevant caselaw is equivocal as to the extent to whic religious and racial discrimination can be conflated, and, as in other juris dictions, religious discrimination often finds expression through prox issues – particularly those relating to sexuality.

Religious Conduct, Symbols, Icons, Apparel, etc.

The distinction between racial and religious discrimination is of particula relevance in relation to disputes regarding ethnic/religious conduct, dres and accoutrements. Unusually, however, there would seem to be a dearth of caselaw relating to such matters: even the protracted 2004 campaig against the building of a mosque in Bendigo county, Victoria, was resolve without any need for judicial involvement.

---

[120] See further Puig, G.V. and Tudor, S., "To the Advancement of Thy Glory?: A Constitu tional and Policy Critique of Parliamentary Prayers", *Public Law Review*, 2009, vol. 20: at p. 56.

[121] *R v. Winneke; Ex parte Gallagher* (1982) 152 CLR 211.

[122] As Ruth Gaze points out: "s.351 of the Fair Work act does include religion as a prohibit basis for adverse action (which includes forms of discrimination) at work" (note to auth 22 February 2017).

[123] As, for example, in *Evans v. NSW* [2008] FCAFC 130 and *Iliafi v. The Church of Jesus Chr of Latter-Day Saints Australia*, op. cit.

Ethnicity/Religion-Specific Customs

Any requirement banning the display of tattoos could amount to a breach of the Racial Discrimination Act 1975 if this occurred in circumstances where a particular tattoo was considered to be representative of ethnic or cultural affiliation, as might well be the case, for example, with persons from the Samoan or Indigenous communities.

Religious Apparel

There is no Australian federal legislation, and virtually none among the states and territories, that addresses matters of religious dress and symbols. As a general rule, there is no restriction on wearing religious apparel in the workplace, school or college unless doing so constitutes a safety hazard or confirmation of personal identity is required. The absence of any caselaw would seem to reflect a broad social acceptance of religion-specific apparel in public places.

Family-Related Issues

Australia has a well-documented history of non-traditional family units, including polygamy (unlawful in that a bigamous/polygamous marriage cannot be entered into in Australia). It is also a country in which there tends to be a significant time lag between established practice – such as single-parent families or same-sex parenting – and the introduction of legislation, particularly federal legislation, to recognise that practice and protect the parties involved.[124]

Sexuality

The Church has always had an interest in ensuring that the State, through its laws, manages sexual matters in accordance with religious beliefs. The restraining influence of religious organisations in relation to the liberalisation of laws governing LGBTI issues has been a feature of Australian society in recent years, the Australian Christian Lobby, the Australian Family Association and the Australian Federation of Islamic Councils being to the fore in opposing such matters. Evidence of this is apparent, for example, in the statutory exemptions from equality and non-discrimination legislation that enable religious organisations and their public-benefit service facilities – schools, hospitals, social care units – to discriminate against the

---

[124] See further Evans, C. and Gaze, B., "Between Religious Freedom and Equality: Complexity and Context", *Harvard International Law Journal*, 2008, vol. 49.

LGBTI community, even when in receipt of government funds (except in respect of aged care provision).

Not until legislation was enacted following the UN decision in *Toonen* v. *Australia*[125] were same-sex relationships finally de-criminalised nation wide. Thereafter, civil unions became possible in Queensland, Tasmania, Victoria, New South Wales and ACT. The legal definition of what might constitute a family unit has since been broadened by legislation such as the Sex Discrimination Amendment (Sexual Orientation, Gender Identity and Intersex Status) Act 2013 (amending the 1984 Act to provide new protections from discrimination on the basis of sexual orientation, gender identity and intersex status).[126] However, although anti-homosexuality laws were gradually repealed across Australia between 1975 and 1997, marriage remains as defined in the Marriage Act 1961, which does not allow for same-sex marriage.[127] Discrimination on the basis of sexual orientation and gender identity is now banned in all states and territories, while federal reforms – resulting in the Same-Sex Relationships (Equal Treatment in Commonwealth Laws-General Law Reform) Act 2008 and the Same-Sex Relationships (Equal Treatment in Commonwealth Laws-Superannuation) Act 2008 – have sought to eliminate discrimination against same-sex couples and their children in relation to matters such as taxation, superannuation, health, social security, aged care and child support, immigration, citizenship and veterans affairs.

That the status of transgender and intersex Australians has also been given legal recognition was demonstrated in *Hanover Welfare Service Ltd (Anti-Discrimination Exemption)*.[128] This concerned the ruling of regulatory authority that a women's shelter was exempted from the relevant anti-discrimination legislation, thereby allowing it to reject male-to-female transgender persons as "women" for the purposes of providing shelter. The life-changing adjustments of a transgender process constitute

---

[125] Communication No. 488/1992, UN Doc CCPR/C/50/D/488/1992.

[126] See further the Australian Human Rights Commission, "Same-Sex: Same Entitlements 2007, at www.humanrights.gov.au/our-work/sexual-orientation-sex-gender-identity publications/same-sex-same-entitlements.

[127] Note that despite the HCA ruling in *The Commonwealth of Australia* v. *The Australian Capital Territory* [2013] HCA 55, confirming that the federal parliament has the power under the Constitution to introduce same-sex marriage, there has yet to be any enabling legislation.

[128] [2007] VCAT 640. Beth Gaze comments: "the Hanover case is controversial and is likely not to be accepted as a valid decision today – the applicaton by Hanover Services was withdrawn by them after discssions with the Victorian EOC about the case, when they realised this was not a good way to resolve the issue" (note to author, 22 February 2017).

a complex physical and emotional journey, often traumatic, which may be pursued for many years, and which an individual may in fact never "complete".[129] Unsurprisingly, therefore, the long-established Australian practice of surgical intervention to "correct" physiological anomalies in small children, often involving their sterilisation, has been much criticised. Such intervention achieves physical gender alignment, but only by reducing a complex psychosocial matter of sexual identity to a simple one of surgically induced gender conformity, with all the eugenic connotations of enforced engineering, and without the consent of the child. The surgery is undertaken on the authorisation of parents who may often be motivated, at least in part, by religious beliefs – if only in the conviction that God made man and woman, so intervention to ensure their child fits within this binary model is giving effect to God's will. In 2013, the Australian Senate published a report which condemned the practice of "normalising" surgeries and made fifteen recommendations, including ending cosmetic genital surgeries on infants and children and providing for legal oversight of individual cases.[130] It's worth noting that in 2016, Australia was the only country in the world requiring court involvement in the medical procedures necessary for transgender children.

Conception, Abortion, IVF and Related Issues

The law relating to abortion varies across the states and territories. It remains criminal in some, while in others, such as Victoria, medical practitioners can refuse to undertake or participate in an abortion procedure if to do so would be against their religious beliefs. In *Fraser* v. *Walker*,[131] a person displaying a poster featuring pictures of aborted foetuses outside an abortion clinic in Melbourne was convicted of "displaying an obscene figure in a public place". Her defence that display of the poster was part of her "right to freedom of conscience and religion", along with other human rights defences, was rejected. The judicial comment that, "assuming the appellant's stance on abortion comes from her religious belief, the display of obscene figures is not part of religion nor can it be said the display is

---

[29] See *NSW Registrar of Births, Deaths and Marriages* v. *Norrie* [2014] HCA 11, where the respondent, having undergone sex-affirmation surgery, was found to be androgynous and entitled to be registered as neither a man nor a woman.

[30] See The Senate: Community Affairs Reference Committee, "Involuntary or Coerced Sterilisation of Intersex People in Australia", October 2013, at www.aph.gov.au/~/media/Committees/Senate/committee/clac_ctte/involuntary_sterilisation/second_report/report.ashx.

[31] [2015] VCC 1911.

done in furtherance of religion"[132] is interesting as it treads the uncertain line that separates the right to manifest personal religious belief from the duty to do so in a manner compliant with the freedom of expression. That line has been complicated by political involvement in determining the legal availability of RU-486 (an abortifacient), and significantly adjusted by the recent introduction of "protest-free zones" in a number of states and territories to exclude anti-abortion activity within 50 metres of a clinic.

The law relating to surrogacy, which generally restricts its availability to heterosexual couples on an altruistic basis, would seem poorly aligned with current practice. Commercial surrogacy is banned nationwide, although surrogacy is legal on an altruistic basis within all Australian jurisdictions except Western Australia (where it is illegal for singles and same-sex couples). As a result, only an estimated 5 per cent of surrogacy arrangements made by Australians occur in Australia. The consequent legal issues regarding parental rights and citizenship for the many children born to surrogates in Asia and the USA and brought back to Australia are complicated and discriminatory.

Assisted Suicide

The Northern Territories became, if briefly, the world's first jurisdiction to legalise euthanasia[133] with the Rights of the Terminally Ill Act 1996, but nevertheless there has never been any enabling federal legislative provision, and since the Euthanasia Laws Act 1997 euthanasia has been illegal[134] in all states and territories.

Employment-Related Issues

The International Labour Organisation (ILO)'s Discrimination (Employment and Occupation) Convention, ratified by Australia in 1973, requires the removal of employment-related discrimination on grounds which include religion. The Workplace Relations Act 1996 (Cth) prohibited the termination of employment on the basis of religion, while its replacement, the Fair Work Act 2009 (Cth), in s.351(1) prohibits any adverse action based on religion, but in s.351(2)(c) exempts employers from prosecution

---

[132] Ibid., at para. 49.
[133] See *Toonen v. Australia*, op. cit. and *Christopher John Wake and Djiniyinni Gondarra v. Northern Territory of Australia and the Honourable Keith John Austin Asche AC, The Administrator of the Northern Territory of Australia* (unreported judgment of the Supreme Court), No. 112 of 1996 (24 July 1996).
[134] See e.g. *R v. Shirley Justins* [2011] NSWSC 568.

in respect of action taken against staff in good faith and on the basis of religious doctrine or in order to avoid injury to the religious suscepti-bilities of adherents. "Discrimination", in the context of employment or occupation, is as defined in the Human Rights and Equal Opportunity Commission Act 1986.

Hiring/Firing Staff

Religious Organisations   Staff selection on the basis of criteria that include an applicant's religious belief does not constitute religious discrim-ination for the purposes of the 1986 Act if: this is necessitated under Part (d) of the definition of "discrimination" in s.3 to ensure compliance with the doctrines, tenets, beliefs or teachings of a particular religion, and is made in good faith and in order to avoid injury to the religious suscepti-bilities of adherents of that religion; or it is necessary to fulfill the inherent requirements of the post.

In *Thompson v. Catholic College Wodonga*,[135] the plaintiff teacher, who had been summarily dismissed on return from maternity leave due to her unmarried status being at variance with the beliefs of her employing organisation, had her unfair dismissal complaint upheld by the EOC. So, also, in *Griffin v. Catholic Education Office*,[136] the complaint of an LGBTI activist teacher who had been refused employment in Catholic schools for the same reason was similarly upheld. However, when an irreligious employee is placed in an invidious position in the form of a new con-tract requiring them to become an active church member of their employ-ing religious organisation, then – with legal recognition now extending to those with no religious belief – such an employee will be entitled to pro-tection against discrimination.[137] Also, state laws (e.g. in Victoria) pro-vide protection against discrimination based not only on religious belief or activity, but also on the absence of such belief or activity.[138]

Australian caselaw, as in other jurisdictions, reveals the legal signifi-cance attached to the closeness of the relationship between the functional duties of a post and the religious beliefs of an employing religious organ-isation. So, in *Ciciulla v. Curwen-Walker*,[139] the complaint of discrimi-nation by an employee who had resigned in response to pressure from

---

[135] (1988) EOC 92–217 (Vic ESCAB).   [136] (1998) EOC 92–928 (HREOC).
[137] See *Dixon v. Anti-Discrimination Commissioner of Queensland* (2004) EOC 93–327 (SCQ).
[138] The author acknowledges advice of Beth Gaze on this matter (note to author, 22 February 2017).
[139] (1998) EOC 92-934 (Vic ADT).

her employer to attend services at their Pentecostal church was upheld because of the lack of any such relationship. This rationale was also evident in *Walsh v. St Vincent de Paul Society Queensland (No. 2)*[140] when the Tribunal rejected the respondent's claim that being a Catholic was a "genuine occupational requirement" for the post of president of that society – particularly given that the respondent knew that the claimant was not a Catholic, welcomed her as a member, saw her elected as president of three of its conferences, saw her inducted as a president of a conference by a priest of the church and allowed her to work without challenge for years as a conference president.

Secular Organisations Staff selection on the basis of criteria that include an applicant's religious belief does not constitute religious discrimination if that belief is necessary to fulfill the inherent requirements of the post, which include not only the duties of the employee but also the circumstances in which the particular employment is to be carried out.[141]

While grounds of religious belief can also play their usual role in the firing of staff, this may be complicated in Australia by a racial/ethnic component. For example, in *T v. Dept of Education (Vic)*[142] and in *Kapoor v. Monash University*,[143] the plaintiff teachers, a Sikh and a Hindu, respectively, were both the subject of ridicule and harassment by their pupils, and ultimately their employment contracts were terminated or not renewed because their employers took the view that their appearance and communication skills undermined their teaching capacity, despite the plaintiffs' protests that their roles in the classroom were conditioned by their religious beliefs. Their claims of religious discrimination were unsuccessful, at least in part, because the Victorian legislation forced the issues to be determined on the basis of the ethnic/racial component.

In *Marett v. Petroleum Refineries (Australia) Pty Ltd*,[144] the claim of religious discrimination by an employee who refused to pay union dues on the grounds of his religious beliefs, resulting in his being ostracised by his co-workers and eventually sacked, was upheld.

---

[140] Op. cit.
[141] See *X v. The Commonwealth* (1999) 167 ALR 529, per Justices Gummow and Hayne, where the discrimination concerned disability rather than religion.
[142] [1997] HREOC 38.   [143] (1999) EOC 92-971 (VCAT).
[144] (1987) EOC 92-206 (VCAT); *Petroleum Refineries (Australia) v. Marett* (1988) EOC 92-237 (SCV).

Accommodating Religious Beliefs in the Workplace

The Fair Work Act 2009, s.351, provides that an employer must not take adverse action against a person who is an employee or prospective employee because of their religion, and, in general, the equal-opportunities and non-discrimination legislation of states and territories imply that employers should make reasonable accommodation for employees' religious practices in the workplace.

In *Ahmad McIntosh v. TAFE Tasmania*,[145] an allegation of religious discrimination, made by a Muslim teacher who had not been provided with a dedicated prayer room nor released from duties on Fridays and on Islamic holy days, was dismissed. So too was a claim in *D'Urso v. Peninsula Support Service Inc.*[146] by an employee who was asked to remove a notice about holding a prayer service during work hours in a secular workplace. In *Abdulrahman*,[147] an Australian Muslim from Lebanon, subject to taunting from his work colleagues on the basis of spurious "terrorist" sympathies, was found to have been unlawfully discriminated against – although on ethno-religious grounds, because the relevant legislation did not provide for religious discrimination; the same was true in *Trad v. Jones and Anor (No. 3)*.[148]

Education-Related Issues

A primary area of concern in the Australian education system relates to the freedom of government-funded religious schools, in an increasingly religiously diverse and secular society, to claim exemption from religious discrimination laws: a privilege that inevitably brings greater benefits to the established Christian religious organisations relative to all others.

Government Funding and Religious Education

The issue of government funding for faith-based schools has generated continuous controversy. In the 1950s, and again in the early 1970s, the government decided to break with its previous policy of abstaining from funding religious schools, especially Catholic schools, prompting opponents to take the issue to the High Court in the landmark case of

---

[145] [2003] TASADT 14.
[146] [2005] VCAT 871 (unreported, Member Davis V-P, 11 May 2005).
[147] *Abdulrahman v. Toll Pty Ltd T/As Toll Express*, op. cit.   [148] Op. cit.

Attorney-General (Vic) (Ex rel Black) v. *Commonwealth.*[149] The plaintiffs, Defence of Government Schools (DOGS), sought a court order declaring that State funding of Church schools amounted to establishing a religion, contrary to s.116. The court rejected the plaintiffs' petition and ruled that s.116 does not prevent the "giving of aid to or encouragement of religion" and therefore cannot prevent the government from providing financial assistance to schools operated by religious organisations on the same basis as other private schools. Such funding was deemed constitutionally compliant because it was intended for educational rather than religious purposes. The ruling permits the preferential treatment of one religion over another providing it falls short of the establishment of religion.

That a failure to satisfy the definition of "religious school" could entail forfeiting an entitlement to government funding was demonstrated in the interesting *Best Practice* case.[150] This concerned a non-denominational school which espoused religious beliefs in general, but none in particular, and for that reason found itself disadvantaged as regards funding arrangements. In justifying the ruling that this did not constitute religious discrimination, Peedom DP cited the Mason CJ and Brennan J dictum in the *Scientology* case to explain that the school approach to religion lacked the crucial component that it be "based upon a supernatural being, thing or principle". This rationale is questionable because: it relies upon a theistic definition of what constitutes a "religion" or "belief"; it ignores an equality interpretation which would give equal status to secularism; and it raises the issue of the presence or absence of a legislative reference to religious belief, which varies across the states and territories. It also, of course, seemingly rests on a "religion test" which, although confined by the fourth clause of s.116 to the Commonwealth, is contrary to that principle. The scope of s.116 was recently examined in *Hoxton Park Residents Action Group Inc.* v. *Liverpool City Council.*[151] This concerned the channeling of Commonwealth funding to the state of NSW (in accordance with s.96 of the Constitution) for the running of the Malek Fahd Islamic School, a school run on Islamic principles. The court held that the federal government did not thereby breach the Constitution by "establishing" a religion: providing funds to a religious school (where such funds are conditioned on objective, secular, educational criteria and are also provided on a

---

[149] Op. cit. Also known as the State Aid or Defence of Government Schools (DOGS) case.
[150] *Best Practice Education Group Ltd T/as Blue Gum School* v. *Dept of Education & Community Services* [2002] ACTDT 1.
[151] Op. cit.

eeds-based and in an even-handed manner to other religious schools
:om different traditions) did not amount to the establishment of a State
:eligion. Section 116 will only be breached by a law which has as its clear
urpose an outcome prohibited by that provision.

Faith Schools

aith schools in Australia, as already noted, are not a distinct category out-
ide the public education system. They are free to require religious affil-
ttion when employing staff and enrolling students; have a discretionary
apacity to require adherence to the tenets and ethos of their respective
:eligious organisations; and can integrate theories such as "creationism"
tto the school curriculum. All of which may disadvantage those pupils –
:r their families – with different values, for example in relation to sex-
al orientation. Such overt government endorsement for faith schools was
:einforced by the rejection of the plaintiff's claim in *Williams* v. *the Com-
tonwealth of Australia*[152] that he had a right to secure a secular education
)r his children.

Religious Discrimination and Educational Content

:lassroom-based religious instruction, usually one hour per week, is pro-
ided in most states and territories, and has been for many years. The
ontent consists of materials approved by the relevant religious organi-
ttion, none of which are subject to approval by the Department of Edu-
ation and Training.[153] The efforts of Safe Schools Coalition Australia to
ttroduce a nationwide programme offering guidance on how to com-
at anti-LGBTI abuse and bullying has generated much controversy, with
:hristian organisations lobbying – sometimes successfully – for the use
f conceptual material relating to gender and sexuality to be prohibited in
rimary schools.

Education Facilities and Religious Discrimination

could, perhaps, be argued that the National School Chaplaincy Pro-
:amme constitutes a State-funded form of religious discrimination
ithin the public school system because the service is restricted to provi-
on by qualified religious personnel who are Christian and are employed
y Christian organisations such as Scripture Union and who provide

---

[2] [2012] HCA 23. See further www.hcourt.gov.au/cases/case-s307/2010.
[3] Beth Gaze adds that "this has now been abolished in Victoria and challenged in NSW"
(note to author, 22 February 2017).

evangelical programmes and activities such as Bible Clubs. Some secularists, adherents of non-Christian religions and others may perceive it as
at best anomalous and at worst intimidating to have such a programme
defined as an in-built constituent part of their children's education. That
the option to withdraw a child from scripture classes may not resolve this
issue was demonstrated in *The State of Victoria, Department of Education
& Early Childhood Development (Anti-Discrimination)*[154] when parents
claimed that such a "singling out" would also give rise to religious discrimination; a claim rejected on the grounds that there was no evidence
of adverse impact upon the children.

Medicine-Related Issues

Effective lobbying by the traditional Christian organisations tends to
restrain government initiatives on medical matters – as it does in other
areas, most notably education – that might impinge upon religious beliefs.

Medical Intervention and Religious Beliefs

Such intervention is commonly required in relation to the vexed issue
of blood transfusions for Jehovah's Witnesses. Australia, in keeping with
many other countries, respects an "advance directive" given by an adult
refusing such intervention,[155] but allows health authorities to apply for
a court order to overrule a parental veto on the provision of treatment
for their child. The Supreme Court (WA) recently ruled that staff at
the Princess Margaret Hospital for Children could give a teenage cancer patient blood transfusions despite parental objection on religious
grounds. Again, in *X v. the Sydney Children's Hospital Network*,[156] when
dismissing an appeal in respect of a parental refusal to permit intense
chemotherapy for a child suffering from Hodgkin's disease because it
would probably lead to a blood transfusion, in contravention of their religious beliefs, Basten J said: "the interest of the State in preserving life is
at its highest with respect to children and young persons who are inherently vulnerable, in varying degrees". This principle was also in play in
2015, when the federal government terminated the long-standing exemption enjoyed by some religious groups – most notably the Christian Scientists – from national child vaccination programmes. In so doing, it
brought to an end a curious instance of religious discrimination. Although

---

[154] [2012] VCAT 1547.   [155] See *Qumsieh v. GAB* (1998) 14 VAR 46.
[156] [2013] NSWCA 320.

ostensibly privileging a particular religious group, the exemption permitted an un-inoculated minority to jeopardize the health of others – an imposition on the whole population, justified as necessary to protect that group's religious belief. As already noted, religious-based contention was also a prominent aspect of the political debate regarding access to the aborion drug RU-486.

Genetic Engineering and Patents, etc.

Whether the law should permit research – or the patenting of inventions – that involves hES cells has been disputed on religious grounds in Australia, as in many other jurisdictions. In 2007, remarks made by an Australian Catholic Cardinal opposing such research were referred to the New South Wales parliamentary privileges committee for allegedly being in "contempt of parliament". The Cardinal was cleared of the charge and described the move as a "clumsy attempt to curb religious freedom and freedom of speech".[157]

Religious and ethical reservations regarding interference with "the stuff of life" for commercial commodification and monopolisation purposes were at the heart of the *Cancer Voices*[158] controversy. This was the first Australian decision on the issue of whether a valid patent may be granted for naturally occurring DNA and RNA that had been isolated and separated from human cells. The case concerned a gene – BRCA1 – which, having been extracted from the human body, was found by the Federal Court to be an "isolated" gene and one to which the biotechnology company Myriad Genetics Inc. was entitled to patent. Cancer Voices, a support group opposed to a commercial company having exclusive research rights, argued unsuccessfully that the isolated gene was a product of nature, not the result of a "manufacturing" process, and therefore could not be a patentable invention. In endorsing its decision, the full Federal Court[159] upheld the earlier finding that a manufacturing process had occurred, resulting in the gene being isolated, which satisfied the Australian patent law requirement that an "artificial state of affairs" must exist. The HCA,[160] however, took a different view, finding that isolating a gene – BRCA1 – did not in itself constitute a manufacturing process; in overturning the earlier decisions, it brought Australian law on this matter into conformity

---

157 See www.catholicculture.org/culture/library/view.cfm?id=7801.
158 *Cancer Voices Australia v. Myriad Genetics Inc.* [2013] FCA 65.
159 *D'Arcy v. Myriad Genetics Inc.* (2014) 313 ALR 627.
160 *D'Arcy v. Myriad Genetics Inc. & Anor* [2015] HCA 35.

with that in the USA,[161] but away from the European approach. While this decision turned squarely on legal technicalities, the underlying issue in Australia, as on other continents, has been, and will continue to be the extent to which the law of patents may permit companies to carve out commercial monopolies in the use of genetic material: should a "product of nature" be available for commercial exploitation? The answer given is open to be determined on religious grounds: the legal systems of a country with a sustained coherent religious culture – e.g. Islam or Catholicism are likely to respond quite differently from those of a more diverse or secular culture, with results that will inevitably have adverse discriminatory consequences – in terms of treatment options – for their citizens.

Service-Provision Issues

In Australia, whether as a cause or an effect of the lack of any federal legislation specifically prohibiting religious discrimination, Christian organisations continue to dominate public-benefit service provision more so than elsewhere in the common law world. Some, by virtue of their size and longevity, have managed to remain true to their roots as local providers while also acquiring a nationwide brief; almost all are engaged in the delivery of social services.

Service Provision by Religious Organisations

The previously mentioned *OV and OW* and *Cobaw*[162] cases both centre on alleged discrimination by religious organisations. The first concerned the right of the Wesley Mission to withhold services by not accepting an application to place a child in the foster care of a same-sex couple, on the grounds that its religious beliefs would be breached if it treated them the same as it did those whose status complied with the core Wesleyan doctrine of "monogamous heterosexual partnership within marriage". Ultimately, the court rejected the allegation of discrimination on finding that the Wesley Mission was able to avail itself of the statutory exemption as, at the relevant time, its doctrines were binding upon the Mission and could be construed as religious (see earlier). In the second case, the issue was whether CYC, a religious charity, could withhold services from people because of their sexual orientation and claim statutory exemption from

---

[161] See *Association for Medical Pathology* v. *Myriad Genetics Inc.* 596 – (2013).
[162] Op. cit. See further www.austlii.edu.au/au/cases/vic/VCAT/2010/1613.html.

what would otherwise be discriminatory practice. Justice Hampel's conclusion, endorsed by the Court of Appeal,[163] was that it was not necessary for the respondents to refuse services in order to comply with their genuine religious beliefs and that in taking that step they had discriminated in breach of the Act. As in the UK, faith-based groups will not be able to avail themselves of the religious exemption in order to refuse services to same-sex adoption applicants. The Catholic Care adoption agency, in keeping with its US counterpart, will withdraw from adoption services if it is required to abide by the new rules (see further Chapters 5 and 7).

This traditionally respected right of religious organisations – to condition service provision in accordance with their religious beliefs – has recently been constrained by the Sex Discrimination Amendment (Sexual Orientation, Gender Identity and Intersex Status) Act 2013. Care homes owned by such organisations are no longer able to exclude people from aged-care services based on their LGBTI or same-sex relationship status. However, in most other respects, their discretionary discriminatory practices remain in place: Catholic hospitals, for example, are free to continue their embargo on conducting vasectomies, tubal ligation and abortions; faith schools maintain their religious access filters and are exempt from gender-identity and sexual-orientation provisions; and family-planning services provided by religious organisations, even if receiving government funding, can continue to provide advice and information that excludes access to contraception or abortion.

Provision of Public Services

The piecemeal effects of disparate state and territory legislation on matters of equality and non-discrimination are particularly apparent in relation to public-service provision and associated anomalous caselaw. For example, while an Orthodox Jew was unsuccessful in alleging that it was discriminatory for the relevant authority to fail to provide him with a house within walking distance of a synagogue, he succeeded in his claim that his refusal of other accommodation should not be deemed "unreasonable" by that authority.[164] Again, while it was accepted that a public school system did not accommodate the religious beliefs of many parents, forcing them into having their children schooled outside that system, the parents were

---

[63] *Christian Youth Camps Limited & Ors* v. *Cobaw Community Health Services Limited & Ors* [2014] VSCA 75.

[64] *Azriel* v. *NSW Land & Housing Corporation* [2006] NSWCA 372. Mr Azriel was an Orthodox Jew who could not drive or travel by public transport on the Sabbath.

successful in their appeal against the refusal of public transport concession cards to fund their additional travel costs.[165]

Private Goods and Service Provision

The previously mentioned 2013 Act prohibited discrimination on the basis of sexual orientation, or gender identity or expression, throughout Australia. Aside from the *Cobaw* case, there do not appear to be any reported judgments – at any rate, none known to this writer – on issues that elsewhere typically relate to the refusal of commercial services – such as accommodation – on religious grounds.[166]

Broadcasting Services

The importance attached to the freedom of expression was emphasised in *Davis* v. *Commonwealth*,[167] but otherwise few opportunities seem to have arisen for the Australian judiciary to examine its significance in a religious context.

In the absence of any cases specifically dealing with public broadcasting and religious discrimination, the *Threewisemonkeys*[168] decision is of relevance as it illustrates a legal conflation of sexual orientation with religious belief, the weak constitutional protection afforded to religion and the related legal constraints on broadcasting. The case concerned a pamphlet, published by a representative of an organisation known as the "Threewisemonkeys", and distributed in the Sandy Bay area of Hobart in 2013. It stated that "homosexuality should not be tolerated" and that "Scripture rejects homosexuality as utterly abominable" and set out alleged statistics on lifespan expectations and causes of death for gay men and lesbians compared to heterosexual men and women. The complainant alleged that publishing and distributing this pamphlet constituted incitement to hatred on the grounds of sexual orientation under the Tasmanian Anti-Discrimination Act 1998, s.19, while the respondent claimed that such conduct was protected by the right to freedom of religion under s.116 of the Constitution. The court found that the latter:[169]

> does not amount to a complete guarantee of protection. In particular, it does not provide individuals with any avenue of legal redress if their perceived right to freedom of religion has been violated. In any event, any

---

[165] *Christian Family Schools Association of Australia* v. *Public Transport Corporation* (1990) EOC, paras 92–300.

[166] Although, see *Burke* v. *Tralaggan* [1986] EOC 92–161, where a Christian couple was held to have unlawfully refused to rent a flat to an unmarried couple.

[167] (1988) 166 CLR 79.

[168] *Williams* v. *"Threewisemonkeys" and Durston* [2015] TASADT.　　[169] Ibid., at para. 50.

"freedom" must be balanced against the rights of others, as is the case with the rights to freedom of speech and freedom of association. Accordingly, the Tribunal finds no basis for the respondent's reliance on a right to freedom of religion by way of response or defence to this complaint.

Somewhat ironically, the respondent's defeat was due to his reliance upon the weak protection afforded by s.116.

Conclusion

In Australia, the law relating to religious discrimination is inadequate: it lacks a federal Bill of Rights and an extensive human rights legislative base; in addition to insufficient constitutional recognition, there is no specific federal statutory prohibition; the conflation with racial discrimination can lead to a muddling of issues; and even the vilification laws are specific to individual states and territories.

10

New Zealand

Introduction

New Zealand has a population of about 4.7 million, of which approx mately 74 per cent identify with European ethnic groups, mostly Briti or Irish (compared with 67.6 per cent in 2006), and 15 per cent identify Māori, constituting the largest non-European ethnic group; these tend be followers of Presbyterianism, the Church of Jesus Christ of Latter-D Saints (Mormons) or Māori Christian groups such as Ratana and Ringat According to 2013 census returns, 48.9 per cent of those answering t religious affiliation question affiliated with a Christian religion (includi Māori Christian), compared with 55.6 per cent in 2006 and 60.6 per ce in 2001. Around 6 per cent of the population affiliated with non-Christi religions, of which Hinduism was the largest group, with Sikhs, Muslir and Buddhists growing rapidly in number. Despite an overall decrea in Christian religions, some Christian denominations increased, with t five largest in 2001 – Anglican, Catholic, Presbyterian (Congregation ar Reformed), Christian not further defined and Methodist – remaining in 2006 and in 2013; although Catholicism has now replaced Anglicanis as the largest. Census statistics indicate that the proportion of the pop lation without any declared religious belief continues to increase: in 201 42 per cent stated that they had no religion, compared with 34.7 per ce in 2006 and 29.6 per cent in 2001.

It is against that background, seemingly showing nearly half the pop lation as having renounced religion, that this chapter considers the curre significance of religious discrimination in New Zealand. Beginning wi a brief public policy overview, it continues along the same path as oth chapters in Part III: outlining the current framework of relevant domes and international law; examining definitional terms and concepts rel ing to "religion" and "beliefs", their "manifestation" and what in law co stitutes religious discrimination; discussing the Church/State relationsh and secularism; and concluding with a focus on contemporary casel generated in respect of matters such as family, employment, education, medicine and commerce.

Public Policy: An Overview

New Zealand acquired a measure of independence in 1840 with the Treaty of Waitangi. The broad umbrella of the Treaty has come to accommodate the common law, statute law, international treaties and conventions, and has set the boundaries for an evolving public policy which increasingly gives greater weight to Māori culture and interests.

Religion and the Constitution

None of the statutes that contribute to a constitutional framework for New Zealand make any provision for "establishing" a specific religion, nor for separating Church and State; indeed, none refers to religion as a matter of any particular consequence.

The Constitution

New Zealand does not have a Constitution as such,[1] although collectively the following make up a body of law with an overarching constitutional effect:[2] the Treaty of Waitangi; the Constitution Act 1986; the Imperial Laws Application Act 1988; the New Zealand Bill of Rights Act 1990 (NZBORA); and the Human Rights Act 1993.

Religious Discrimination and the Constitution

At the signing of the Treaty of Waitangi in 1840, Governor Hobson declared that "the several faiths (beliefs) of England, of the Wesleyans, of Rome, and also Māori custom shall alike be protected". Nonetheless, the Christian heritage and the associated common law regime of its British settlers continued to decisively shape emerging social norms in New Zealand. One such cultural transference concerned the right of testators to exercise religious discrimination when disposing of their estates.

Until the mid-twentieth century, bequests subject to a condition that the prospective beneficiary "be of the Lutheran religion"[3] or be "in the

See www.justice.govt.nz/policy/constitutional-law-and-human-rights/consideration-of-constitutional-issues-1/members-of-the-constitutional-advisory-panel.
See further Ekins, R. and Tomkins, D., *Constitutional Theory for the Constitutional Review*, Auckland, Maxim Institute, 2013.
Re Carleton [1909] 28 NZLR 1066.

Protestant faith"[4] were compatible with public policy in this jurisdiction as elsewhere in the common law world. However, in *Re Lockie*,[5] when con sidering a gift accompanied by a condition that discriminated on ground of religion, Smith J took quite the opposite approach and refused to recog nise it on the grounds that the testator's blatant religious discrimination had irredeemably corrupted any charitable intent. As he explained: "i is better that what appears to be the testator's manifest object should b defeated, unless he has complied with the rule in all its strictness, rathe than that the control of one person's religion by another, by the method o material reward, should be encouraged". This approach was thereafter fol lowed in relation to attached conditions intended to prevent "contractin; marriage outside the Jewish faith".[6] The absence of rulings upholding th right of testators to make testamentary dispositions subject to discrimina tory religious conditions is a noticeable feature of New Zealand caselaw which differentiates it from that of countries such as England, Canada and Ireland.

Public Policy

For the traditionally Anglo-centric government in New Zealand, the pres ence of Māori, with their distinctive culture and spiritual beliefs, togethe with the proximity of the Pacific Islands and the consequent influx of man non-Christian immigrants, has always made social inclusion a public pol icy challenge.

Background

Government policy has been shaped by the principles[7] embodied in th country's founding document, the Treaty of Waitangi,[8] which provided "constitutional" basis for recognising legal rights and for testing govern ment policy in respect of all citizens: Treaty compatibility is now a politica if not a legal imperative for all government policy initiatives.

---

[4] *In Re Gunn* [1912] 32 NZLR 153.   [5] [1945] NZLR 230, at p. 240.

[6] *Re Biggs, Public Trustee* v. *Schneider* [1945] NZLR 303, 307 and *Re Myers, Perpetual Tru Estate and Agency Co. of New Zealand* v. *Myers* [1947] NZLR 828, 834.

[7] See e.g. *New Zealand Māori Council* v. *Attorney-General* [1987] 1 NZLR 641.

[8] Signed at Waitangi on the Bay of Islands on 6 February 1840 by representatives of the Britis Crown and Māori chiefs from North Island, and eventually consolidated by the Treaty Waitangi Act 1975.

Religious Discrimination and Contemporary Public Policy

In *Quilter* v. *Attorney-General*,[9] the Court of Appeal noted that equality is one of the core principles underlying New Zealand's law on discrimination, even though that law contains no express reference to it.

State Agencies for Religious Matters

There are no State departments or agencies with a specific brief for religious matters, but the government does provide support for such work undertaken by other organisations. For example, it supported the Human Rights Commission initiative to develop the Statement on Religious Diversity.

Domestic Policy

For present purposes, perhaps the most recent and significant domestic public policy trend has been what Ahdar refers to as "a steady pattern of dismantling... historic Christian remnants from the public square", accompanied by "a privileging of Maori spirituality".[10] The resurgence of Māori culture and beliefs – evident, of course, in the *haka* rugby ritual – has been affirmed by the State in practices such as inclusive references in national ceremonies, environmental and planning legislation, the performance of *hikitapu* or spiritual cleansing rituals in overseas embassies and the increasing use of *karakia* (prayers) to commence court proceedings and public meetings.

In keeping with other common law jurisdictions, New Zealand's domestic public policy has responded to global terrorist threats with legislation that necessarily impacts upon religious organisations and their members – some more than others. The Terrorism Suppression Act 2002 contains a range of procedures relating to the protection of human rights and the observance of international obligations. These have been bolstered by the Countering Terrorist Fighters Legislation Act 2014, which allows the Security Intelligence Service to carry out surveillance and interception operations in respect of local ISIS supporters. There are misgivings about potential breaches of civil liberties, as the police now have extensive powers to justify intrusion into private homes and business premises.

---

[9] [1998] 1 NZLR 523.
[10] See further Ahdar, R.T., "The Religious Demography of New Zealand", p. 547, at www.iclrs .org/content/blurb/files/New%20Zealand.pdf.

Foreign Policy

When its close trading ties with Britain were largely broken by the latter joining the EEC, New Zealand re-orientated towards Asia. This, together, with the relaxation of immigration laws in the closing years of the twentieth century, led to a rapid growth in the proportion of Asian citizens; many of whom, naturally, are Muslims. As the nation contributed its support to the wars led by the USA in Afghanistan (although not in Iraq), it had to manage the heightened domestic tensions between Muslim and other communities.

Contemporary Law Governing Religious Discrimination

The commitment to human rights in New Zealand began 130 years ago, when it became the first nation to grant women the right to vote in national elections.

The International Framework

New Zealand has ratified a number of international conventions relating to non-discrimination and fundamental rights for all citizens, including minority groups.[11] It is a signatory to the UDHR, and as such is bound by Article 18(1), which states that: everyone has the right to freedom of thought, conscience and religion; this right includes the freedom to change one's religion or belief and the freedom, either alone or in community with others, and in public or in private, to manifest one's religion or belief in teaching, practice, worship and observance. However, not until 2010 did New Zealand decide to support the UN Declaration on the Rights of Indigenous Peoples.[12]

The International Covenant on Civil and Political Rights (ICCPR)

The New Zealand judiciary and regulators place considerable reliance upon Articles 18 and 18(3) and the guidance offered by the Human Rights

---

[11] The International Convention on the Elimination of All Forms of Racial Discrimination; the ICCPR; and the International Covenant on Economic Social and Cultural Rights.

[12] On 13 September 2007, the General Assembly adopted this landmark declaration outlining the rights of the world's estimated 370 million Indigenous People and outlawing discrimination against them: 143 Member States voted in favour, eleven abstained and four - Australia, Canada, New Zealand and the United States - voted against the text.

Committee in General Comment No. 22 (Article 18) when dealing with allegations of religious discrimination.

International Reports

The second New Zealand universal periodic review in 2014 recorded concerns that included: the delay in signing or ratifying certain Conventions; the lack of any overarching protection for human rights; and the disparities experienced by Māori as demonstrated by key social and economic indicators. The Committee on the Elimination of Racial Discrimination (CERD), in the concluding observations of its 2013 report: noted with regret that the Treaty of Waitangi is still not a formal part of domestic law; urged a raising of awareness to combat existing stereotypes and prejudices against certain ethnic and religious groups; and urged a review of the Marine and Coastal Area (Takutai Moana) Act of 2011 to facilitate the rights by Māori communities, and in particular their access to places of cultural and traditional significance.[13]

The Domestic Framework

New Zealand has in place a not untypical platform of domestic equality legislation, including the Human Rights Act 1993, the NZBORA, the Privacy Act 1993 and the Equal Pay Act 1972, and has introduced other legislative and policy frameworks to promote equality.[14]

The Treaty of Waitangi

This founding document provided a broad statement of principles for building a nation state and government. It offers a "constitutional" basis for recognising legal rights and for testing government policy in respect of all citizens, but it "has to be seen as an embryo rather than a fully developed and integrated set of ideas."[15] Articles 2 and 3 provide protection for Māori to observe and practise their religions and beliefs: the former does so by reference, in the Māori version, to *taonga*, i.e. "everything that is held precious"; the latter by providing for Māori to have "the same rights as those of the people of England".

[13] Committee on the Elimination of Racial Discrimination, "Concluding observations of the Committee on the Elimination of Racial Discrimination: New Zealand", 2013, at www2 .ohchr.org/english/bodies/cerd/docs/co/CERD-C-NZL-CO-18-20_en.pdf.

[14] Citizenship Act 1977; Immigration Act 1987; State Sector Act 1988; Ethnic Perspectives in Policy 2003.

[15] *New Zealand Māori Council* v. *Attorney-General*, op. cit., per Cooke P.

The Human Rights Amendment Act 2001

This restructured the Human Rights Commission and introduced additional safeguards against discrimination on grounds such as age, disabilit or sexual orientation in the policies and practices of government agencie:

The Employment Relations Act 2000 (ERA)

This legislation, in conjunction with the Employment Contracts Act 199] provides employees with the right to take allegations of discrimination t the Employment Court.

The Human Rights Act 1993

This statute amalgamated the Race Relations Act 1971 (RRA) and th Human Rights Commission Act 1977. It prohibits discrimination base on religious and ethical belief (defined as lack of a religious belief, whethe in respect of a particular religion or religions or of all religions) in employ ment, in partnerships, in access to places, vehicles and facilities, in th provision of goods and services and in the provision of land, housing an accommodation.

The New Zealand Bill of Rights Act 1990 (NZBORA)

This crucial statute asserts the freedom of religion and prohibits discrim ination: s.13 provides for the "freedom of thought, conscience, and reli gion – everyone has the right to freedom of thought, conscience, reli gion, and belief, including the right to adopt and to hold opinions withou interference"; s.19 declares the right to freedom from discrimination, o the grounds provided in the Human Rights Act 1993; and s.20 asserts th "rights of minorities – a person who belongs to an ethnic, religious, or lir guistic minority in New Zealand shall not be denied the right, in commu nity with other members of that minority, to enjoy the culture, to profes and practice the religion, or use the language, of that minority". Unlik equivalent legislation elsewhere, the 1990 Act is concerned with secur ing the freedom of the individual from arbitrary State intervention;[16] does not specifically include free-standing rights in relation to principle of dignity, personal autonomy or the liberty and security of the person.] applies only to the actions of government and to persons exercising pub lic functions; where such actions are found to infringe the 1990 Act, th courts may issue "indications of inconsistency" requiring the attention (Parliament.

---

[16] *Mendelssohn* v. *Attorney-General* (1999) 2 NZLR 268 (CA), at p. 273.

The Constitution Act 1986

This is New Zealand's primary constitutional legal instrument. It consolidated the institutional and statutory powers necessary to clarify the country's relationship with the UK government and monarchy, provided for more coherent domestic governance and affirmed its (relatively) independent status.

The Race Relations Act 1971 (RRA)

This made incitement to racial disharmony a criminal offence and presaged the setting up of the Office of the Race Relations Commissioner in 1972, which was merged with the Human Rights Commission in 2002. In *King-Ansell* v. *Police*,[17] the Court of Appeal held that religious discrimination was outside the scope of the RRA.

Other Legislation

There is a considerable range of sector-specific legislation with a bearing on equality and non-discrimination, including: the Crimes Act 1961; the Private Schools Conditional Integration Act 1975; the ERA (which repealed the Employment Contracts Act 1991) and the Employment Relations Amendment Bill 2013; and the New Zealand Marriage (Definition of Marriage) Amendment Act 2013.

Courts and Tribunals

The New Zealand legal system is a three-tiered model, closely resembling its British counterpart.

International

Although subject to the CERD and ICCP monitoring processes but, since 2003, no longer amenable to Privy Council appeal procedures, the New Zealand court and regulatory system operates as an independent, unified and self-contained juridical entity, free of external scrutiny.

Domestic

The Supreme Court is the highest court in the land and ultimate court of appeal. It determines issues where leave has been granted in the interests of justice or because the matter is one of general or public importance.[18] The Court of Appeal hears appeals from civil and criminal cases heard in

---

[17] [1979] 2 NZLR 531. [18] The Supreme Court Act 2003, s.13.

the courts below, including appeals on questions of law from the Employment Court, which determines cases relating to employment disputes or challenges to decisions of the Employment Relations Authority. Also relevant are the Māori Land Court and the Māori Appellate Court, which deal with Māori land matters, and the Environment Court, which has a remit for resource management, planning and development.

The Human Rights Commission   Established by the Human Rights Act 1993, the Commission was subsequently restructured by the Human Rights Amendment Act 2001. Its main functions are: to provide advocacy and support for human rights, cultural diversity and equal employment opportunities; to advise on the law and practice relating to the statutory grounds for unlawful discrimination; and to resolve or adjudicate upon any issues arising in the latter context. The lack of much religious discrimination caselaw in this jurisdiction[19] testifies, perhaps, to the effectiveness of the mediation service introduced by the Human Rights Commission in 2002.

The Human Rights Review Tribunal   The Tribunal is an independent judicial body, separate from the Employment Relations Authority and Employment Court. A complaint regarding alleged religious discrimination begins with a dispute resolution attempt; if that fails, then it is referred to the Office of Human Rights Proceedings; after that, it goes to the Human Rights Review Tribunal, which must rule on the complaint and may issue restraining orders, award monetary damages or declare a breach of the Human Rights Act (which is reported to Parliament).

The Employment Relations Authority   The task of interpreting and applying the ERA falls to the Employment Relations Authority, the Employment Court and the New Zealand Court of Appeal.

Freedom of Religion and Beliefs: The Principle and the Law

The Statement on Religious Diversity declares that "the State seeks to treat all faith communities and those who profess no religion equally before the law, and that New Zealand has no official or established religion".[20]

---

[19] The Human Rights Commission annual report for 2010–11 records that the Office of Human Rights Proceedings provided representation in only one case of ethical belief discrimination in services provision.

[20] Human Rights Commission, "Statement on Religious Diversity", 2007, at www.teara.govt .nz/en/document/28196/statement-on-religious-diversity.

Definitions

n New Zealand, it would seem at first sight that the traditional approach ɔ the definition of "religion" continues to hold sway: the twin common ιw requirements of belief in a "Supreme Being" and worship of that Being re evident, accompanied by the customary necessity for tenets, canons r doctrines. Indeed, the activities of organisations registered as being for he purpose of the advancement of religion also appear to be largely of the raditional orthodox variety, mainly concerned with promoting the work f the Church and with education and health care service provision. In ιct, however, the reality is a little different.

"Religion"

'omkins J, in *Centrepoint Community Growth Trust* v. *Commissioner of ιland Revenue*,[21] having declared that he was not aware of any New .ealand authorities on the meaning of "religion", then applied the Mason ιnd Brennan JJ principles as stated in the leading Australian case of *:hurch of the New Faith* v. *Commissioner of Pay-roll Tax*,[22] which required first, belief in a supernatural Being, Thing or Principle and second, the cceptance of canons of conduct in order to give effect to that belief" – ιese to be interpreted broadly and flexibly.[23] The *Centrepoint* case con-erned an incorporated community of like-minded persons who shared ιe common purpose of advancing the spiritual education and humanitar-ιn teachings of Herbert Thomas Potter and "of all the messengers of god". 'he court found that, while some members of the community believed in supernatural being, others held "a belief in the supernatural in the sense f reality beyond that which can be perceived by the senses". Included in ιch beliefs were concepts that related not only to man's relationship to ιan but also to his relationship to the supernatural in the sense of a Being r a reality beyond sensory perception. The court held that in terms of ιeir formal association and beliefs and practices, the members satisfied ιe definition of religion.[24]

Dal Pont makes the point that, given the Pacific Rim cultural con-ext of Australia and New Zealand, the judiciary in this and other cases ιn be seen as interpreting "religion" to give recognition to the fact "that ɔme, mostly Eastern religions are not theistic which thereby releases the ιw from Judeo-Christian notions".[25] This prompted the New Zealand

[1985] 1 NZLR 673.   [22] (1983) 154 CLR 120.   [23] Ibid., at p. 136.
Ibid., citing as a guiding precedent the earlier ruling in *Church of the New Faith* in the HCA.
Dal Pont, *Charity Law in New Zealand and Australia.*

and Australian judiciaries to digress from the traditional formulaic definition of "religion" at an earlier stage than their contemporary English counterparts.[26]

"Beliefs"

A broad view of what constitutes "religion" in New Zealand has allowed the Church of Scientology and the New Zealand Humanist Society to be recognised as religious organisations at a time when they have been denied such status in the UK. As Mason and Brennan JJ acknowledged in *Church of the New Faith*, tenets in themselves are not a determining constituent of religion.[27] However, as they went on to explain, in order to verify that adherents' beliefs and actions together are sufficiently coherent to constitute a religion, the court needs to establish a binding link. This approach was followed in *Mahuta & Ors v. Waikato Regional Council*[28] when the court warned that "perceptions which are not represented by tangible effects do not deserve such weight as to prevail over the proposal and defeat it". Doctrines can provide that link, but in their absence, or when guided only by vague doctrines, the court or regulator will be faced with correspondingly greater verification difficulties.

Judicial and regulatory notice has been taken of Māori beliefs, which involve *taniwha* (spiritual guardian), *tikanga* (custom), *taonga* (treasures) and *whakapapa* (bloodlines), and are manifested in ways that include *karakia* (prayers) and reverence for *waahi tapu* (sacred sites).[29] Legislative protection has been provided in statutes such as the Ngai Tahu Claims Settlement Act 1998.

"Race", "Caste" and the Māori

In *King-Ansell v. Police*,[30] the court recognised that Jews – because of their shared customs, beliefs, traditions and characteristics, derived from a common or presumed common past – had a "historically determined social identity based ... on their belief as to their historical antecedents", and therefore found that Jewish people could be considered as a group with common ethnic origins within the meaning of the RRA.

For Māori, in common with Indigenous People generally, religion and culture are closely interwoven: religious or spiritual beliefs form shared

---

[26] *Church of the New Faith* v. *Commissioner of Pay-roll Tax*, op. cit., at p. 149.

[27] Ibid., at p. 139.   [28] A91/98 (29 July 1998).

[29] See e.g. *Otararua Hapu* v. *Taranaki Regional Council*, A124/98 and *Bleakley* v. *Environmental Risk Management Authority* [2001] 3 NZLR 213.

[30] Op. cit., at pp. 542–543.

reference points for daily life. The elements (land, air and sea), being the domain of spiritual creatures, are viewed as being unavailable for exclusive "ownership" by people or the State.[31] The Resource Management Act 1991 and the Ngai Tahu Claims Settlement Act 1998 endeavour to integrate Treaty of Waitangi principles – by recognising the role of Māori spiritual beliefs in environmental management – in order to safeguard Māori sacred sites and other cultural interests in local government planning decisions.

Manifesting Religion or Belief and Free Speech

The NZBORA, s.15, provides for the right of any person to manifest their religion or beliefs through worship, observance, practice or teaching, either individually or in community, in public or in private. This right is one that under s.5 "may be subject only to such reasonable limits prescribed by law as can be demonstrably justified in a free and democratic society". Its exercise should be accommodated where feasible,[32] but it may required to be "modified in the public interest to take account of the rights of others and of the interests of the whole community".[33] The need for such a caveat had been demonstrated a few years prior to the introduction of the 1990 Act when an advert for a forecourt attendant referred to a "keen Christian girl".[34]

In relation to Māori beliefs, the right to manifest – which is often tied to topographical features – can run into the obstacle articulated by Wild J as a "difficulty in following how beliefs can be regarded as a natural and physical resource, or how they can be sustainably managed".[35] The fact that "taonga embraces the metaphysical and intangible (e.g. beliefs or legends) as much as it does the physical and intangible (e.g. a treasured carving or mere)", as noted in Bleakly,[36] ensures that judicial and regulatory efforts to identify, weigh and appropriately protect the Māori right to manifest their beliefs is often a torturous exercise that gives rise to correspondingly complex difficulties when determining what, in that context, might constitute religious discrimination.

---

[1] Ngāti Apa v. Attorney-General [2003] 3 NZLR 643.

[2] Feau v. Department of Social Welfare (1995) 2 HRNZ 528.

[3] Noort v. MOT [1992] 3 NZLR 260, at p. 283.

[4] See Human Rights Commission v. Eric Sides Motors Co. Ltd (1981) 2 NZAR 447. The author is grateful to Bill Atkins for drawing his attention to this case (email comment, 31 January 2017).

[5] Friends and Community of Ngawha Inc. v. Minister of Corrections [2002] NRMA 401.

[6] Bleakley v. Environmental Risk Management Authority, op. cit.

Although not directly protected by Constitution or statute, the right to manifest religion or beliefs is given recognition in the NZBORA, s.16 which declares that:

> Everyone has the right to freedom of expression, including the right to seek, receive, and impart information and opinions of any kind in any form.

This broadly worded right encompasses free speech, a free press and the sharing of ideas and information, and is reinforced by the prohibition on hate speech under the Human Rights Act 1993, ss.61 and 131. Its exercise is conditional upon the rights of others, and is subject to public health safety and security considerations.

In 2015, much controversy was generated by hateful and religiously dis criminatory speeches from Shaykh Anwar Sahib, which were viewed as anti-Semitic and sexist, including rants that "Jews are using everybody because their protocol is to rule the entire world" and that the "Jews are the enemy of the Muslim community".[37]

The NZBORA, s.17, guarantees that "everyone has the right to freedom of association".

Blasphemy

Any exercise of free speech is conditional upon it not being blasphemous under the Crimes Act, s.123.

Conscientious Objection

Conscientious objection to national conscription was most obviously an issue for law and public policy during both world wars. Under the Military Service Act 1916 during World War I, exemption was very restricted, dis criminating in favour of religions that had already established pacifism as a belief – most notably Quakers and Seventh-Day Adventists. The belief of all others – whether grounded in religion, politics or philosophy – were ineligible for the status of conscientious objector. This led to a proportion ately greater number being detained or imprisoned than in any other com mon law country. In practice, much the same approach was adopted in World War II, although in theory greater latitude was available to exempt those of other religions or those who objected on ethical grounds. Instead of adjudicating on the basis of an individual's beliefs, religious or other wise, the regulatory authorities placed great weight on church member ship and on whether that church had established pacifist beliefs.

---

[37] See www.youtube.com/watch?v=E9zfYD4Dx_Q.

While arising most acutely in times of war, conscientious objection may also become an issue in the context of medical treatment – providing access to contraception, abortion and sterilisation – when public health care staff may wish to be excused from service provision on religious grounds. In that context, specific statutory protection is available for such staff.[38]

Proselytism

Christian missionary activities among the Māori succeeded in converting many to Catholicism or to one of the range of Protestant churches, but did not wholly displace Māori culture, nor their traditional spiritual beliefs and community structure. To some extent, proselytism is now in reverse, as a resurgent pride in cultural identity is motivating some Māori to encourage others to loosen their ties with Christianity. In contemporary New Zealand, however, references to proselytism are most often heard in the context of accusations levelled at the evangelical Christian organisations which make a voluntary contribution to religious education in the nation's primary schools (see later).

Discrimination

Tipping J, in *Quilter v. Attorney-General*,[39] commented that discrimination is discerned in "the difference of treatment in comparable circumstances. For discrimination to occur one person or groups of persons must be treated differently from another person or group of persons." In this jurisdiction – with its Māori presence, and the growing proportion of ethnic and non-Christian communities – racial discrimination is the most frequent cause for complaint. However, as in practice this is often based upon skin colour, ethnic dress or appearance, racism may obscure the extent of discrimination intended to denigrate instead on the basis of religion or belief; and New Zealand has no legislative equivalent to the UK Racial and Religious Hatred Act 2006, which prohibits the inciting of hatred on the grounds of religion. Each case will, of course, turn on its own set of facts.[40]

---

[38] Health Practitioners Competence Assurance Act 2003, s.174; the NZBORA, s.13; and the Contraception, Sterilisation, and Abortion Act 1977, s.48.
[39] Op. cit.
[40] *Orlov v. Ministry of Justice and Attorney-General* [2009] (NZHRRT 28, 14 October 2009).

Religious Discrimination

As defined under the Human Rights Act 1993, s.21(1), discrimination on
the basis of religion is not a conspicuous feature of life in New Zealand:
racial discrimination is much more prevalent.

Type   The customary distinction between direct and indirect discrimination applies in this jurisdiction, as does the caveat favouring "affirmative
action" to counteract structural inequality.

The Bill of Rights Act 1990, s.19(2), states that:

> Measures taken in good faith for the purpose of assisting or advancing per-
> sons or groups of persons disadvantaged because of discrimination that is
> unlawful by virtue of Part II of the Human Rights Act 1993 do not consti-
> tute discrimination.

This and similar provisions in the HRA require, as a pre-condition, that
any such measures are actually needed: the intended recipients must be
disadvantaged relative to others; and they must need, or be reasonably
supposed to need, assistance in order to achieve equality.[41]

Exemptions and Exceptions

Religious organisations, which invariably also have charitable status, are
entitled to tax exemptions and otherwise enjoy privileged exception from
the constraints of a range of equality and non-discrimination legislation.
In New Zealand, as in Australia, the now considerable civic infrastructure of schools, hospitals, social and health care facilities, etc. developed
by such organisations over the centuries is almost exclusively Christian
and tax-exempt.

The "Religious" Exemption

The Human Rights Act 1993, s.28, provides specific "exceptions for purposes of religion". The potential ambit of that discretion is uncertain due to
both the broad legal interpretation now given to "religion" and to Mallon
J's generous interpretation in *Liberty Trust* v. *Charities Commission*[42] of
activities that may be seen as "outworkings" of religious faith. Exemption
is also available under the Marriage Act 1955, s.29, as amended by the

---

[41] See *Amaltal Fishing Co. Ltd* v. *Nelson Polytechnic (No. 2)* (1996) 2 HRNZ 225 and *Avis Rent
    A Car Ltd* v. *Proceedings Commissioner* (1998) 5 HRNZ 501.
[42] HC WN CIV 2010-485-000831 [2 June 2011].

ew Zealand Marriage (Definition of Marriage) Amendment Act 2013, rough the addition of ss.2, to excuse churches from the obligation to olemnise marriages contrary to their religious beliefs; a similar exemp- on exists in relation to religion and conscience in the Contraception, erilisation, and Abortion Act 1977, s.46.

In *Liberty Trust*, Mallon J concluded that: "given the assumption of pub- c benefit, and the court does not intrude into matters of faith except here they are contrary to public policy, it is not for the court to say that aching biblical financial principles is not a public benefit".[43] This deci- on is one that strengthens the position of other religious organisations igaged in secular activities, which may similarly claim that in so doing ey are also pursuing an outworking of their faith. As already mentioned, cemption is provided in the Marriage (Definition of Marriage) Amend- ent Act 2013, s.29(2), which declares that no clergy are "obliged to sol- nnize a marriage if solemnizing that marriage would contravene the reli- ous beliefs of the religious body or the religious beliefs or philosophical · humanitarian convictions of the approved organisation".

The "Charity" Exemption

1e Charities Act 2005 altered neither the traditional presumption that e purpose of advancing religion is charitable nor the assumption that ch a charity is for the public benefit; both of which are heavily freighted ith distinctly Christian caselaw definitions. As Mallon J noted in *Liberty ust*,[44] when dealing with a trust which had as its purpose the advance- ent of religion, "the starting assumption is that it has a public benefit". though it is clear that government activities are required to be compliant ith anti-discrimination standards, including discrimination on grounds sexual orientation, as set out in s.19 of the NZBORA and s.21 of the uman Rights Act 1993,[45] it is less clear whether religious organisations, hen delivering public services on behalf of government, are similarly und by the same provisions.

The ruling in *Hester v. Commissioner of Inland Revenue*[46] established at exemption privileges – in this instance, claimed on both religious d charitable grounds – are subject to constraints. This case, concern- g a superannuation scheme designed to provide for retired clergy and eir families, concluded with a ruling which confirmed in principle that e scheme could be entitled to protection under the 1990 Act if it were

---

[43] Ibid., at p. 102.   [44] Ibid., per Mallon J at para. 125.
[45] See the Human Rights Amendment Act 2001.   [46] [2005] 2 NZLR 172 (CA).

restricted to benefit only those beneficiaries, but as it in fact extended
beyond clergy to include a wide range of Church employees, it was no
tax-exempt.

The "Positive Action" Exception

The Bill of Rights Act 1990, s.19(2), provides for exceptions to the pro
hibition on discrimination in respect of "measures taken in good fait
for the purpose of assisting or advancing persons or groups of person
disadvantaged because of discrimination". This and similar provisions i
the HRA require, as a pre-condition, that any such measures are actuall
needed: the intended recipients must be disadvantaged relative to oth
ers; and they must need, or be reasonably supposed to need, assistance i
order to achieve equality. The Partnership Schools/*Kura Hourua* proje
provides an example of positive action. In June 2013, following the pass
ing of the Education Amendment Bill 2012, the legal framework was cre
ated for a third type of State-funded school, Partnership Schools/*Kur
Hourua*, which are to be accountable to government for raising achieve
ment through a contract to deliver specific outcomes. In return, they wi
have more flexibility to make decisions about how they operate and us
funding.

Religious Discrimination: Church and State

Church and State are not constitutionally separated. Moreover, it remair
the case that the titular Head of State is the British Queen, a status tha
brings with it that of Supreme Governor of the Church of England, whic
must compromise any claim the State may have to be neutral in relatio
to all religions, let alone be wholly secular.

The Church/State Boundary

Doyle v. *Whitehead*[47] is often identified as an early indicator of judici
vigilance to keep separate the interests of Church and State. This ca
concerned the somewhat innocuous issue of Sunday golf. Stout CJ the
invalidated a council by-law prohibiting the playing of golf in Welling
ton on Sundays, because its only purpose was to placate the proprietors
a Presbyterian orphanage located near a golf course. Declaring the mea
sure invalid, as its *only* purpose was to enforce religious doctrine, Stout C

---

[47] [1917] NZLR 308.

explained that "considering that the State is neutral in religion, is secular, and that the State has provided for Sunday observance only so far as prohibiting work in public or in shops, etc., is concerned, and not prohibiting games, it cannot be said that this is a reasonable by-law". A century later, Mabon J, in *Marshall v. National Spiritual Assembly of the Bahá'is of New Zealand Inc.*,[48] referred to the court's duty to adopt an approach "reflecting the separation of Church and State" before reaching its decision. Nonetheless, as in Australia, there is a strong tradition of Church and State working in partnership: for example, there are two registered Christian-associated political parties, and from an early stage the prevailing government policy has been to encourage religious organisations to fill the gaps in public services by providing health and social care facilities for the poor, the ill or those otherwise disadvantaged.

Protecting Religion from the State

The record of State protection for Māori religious beliefs began inauspiciously with the Tohunga Suppression Act 1907, which specifically discriminated against the Māori by criminalising the activities of the *tohunga*: their traditional healers.[49] Since then, matters have improved. In recent years, State authorities have been recognising and giving increasing weight to Māori beliefs, and their prayers – *karakia* – are now frequently recited by Māori in courts and tribunals where their interests are at stake. In 2002, for example, Māori beliefs stopped the construction of a major national highway, which was ultimately rerouted in response to protests from a Māori community that the projected route would disturb the lair of "Karu Tahi", their local *taniwha*. However, there have also been cases which suggest that the Resource Management Act 1991 is ineffective in protecting Māori beliefs from being subordinated to State interests. In the previously mentioned *Mahuta v. Waikato Regional Council*,[50] for example, the court was not convinced by the Māori argument that a treatment plant discharging treated waste water would pollute sacred land. Again, in *Ngawha Geothermal Resource Company Ltd v. Northland Regional Council*,[51] the court, in approving planning permission for a prison, dismissed the Māori claim that to do so would violate their belief that the land concerned was the domain of a revered spirit, with the declaration that "none of us has been persuaded for herself or himself that, to

---

[48] [2003] 2 NZLR 205 at [31]–[34].
[49] 7 Edw. VII No. 13. The Act was not repealed until 1962.
[50] Op. cit., at n. 28.   [51] A117/2006 [2006] NZEnvC 290.

whatever extent *Takauere* may exist as a mythical, spiritual, symbolic o metaphysical being, it would be affected in pathways to the surface or i any way at all by the proposed prison".[52] Clearly, there are difficulties i translating accepted religious discrimination norms into an indigenou context so that appropriate protection can be extended to the topograph ical features that for Māori may function as places of worship in the sam way as churches do for Christians.

Intervention in Church Disputes

As Gresson J noted in *Watch Tower Bible and Tract Society* v. *Mount Roski Borough*,[53] "it is not for a court, in a field in which it can profess no compe tence, to disqualify upon some a priori basis certain beliefs as incapable c being religious in character". This judicial resolve to avoid entanglemen in religious matters was again illustrated in *Liberty Trust*,[54] when Mallo J pointed out that: "it is not for the court to impose its own view as to th religious beliefs that are advanced through the scheme".[55] Most recentl in *Gay and Lesbian Clergy Anti-Discrimination Society Inc.* v. *Bishop c Auckland*,[56] in relation to an assertion by the respondent that the Chris tian doctrine on marriage as traditionally understood was defined as bein between a man and a woman and that sexual relationships could only b approved of within such a marriage, the Tribunal was at pains to stres that:[57]

> the separation of Church and State must be maintained. The Tribunal can-
> not determine what is at heart an ecclesiastical dispute ... the right of reli-
> gious communities to determine and administer their own internal reli-
> gious affairs without interference from the State is referred to as religious
> group autonomy (or "church autonomy", to use the traditional label).

The State, Religion and Religious Discrimination

The Human Rights Commission assertion that New Zealand is a secula State with no State religion, in which religious and democratic structure are separated, is perhaps treating rather lightly the continuing role of th monarchy, the weight of its distinctly Christian colonial heritage and th implicit discriminatory presence both may represent to those of differer cultural origins.

---

[52] Ibid., at p. 439.   [53] [1959] NZLR 1236, at p. 1241.   [54] Op. cit.
[55] Ibid., at para. 125.   [56] [2013] NZHRRT 36.   [57] Ibid., at paras 33 and 42.

Balancing Religion and Secularism

The absence of any equivalent to the established Church in England has from time to time been judicially noted: in *Carrigan* v. *Redwood*, "there is no State Church here";[58] in *Doyle* v. *Whitehead*, "the State is neutral in religion";[59] and in *Mabon* v. *Conference of the Church of New Zealand*, "unlike England and Scotland, New Zealand does not have a national established church".[60] The secularism of State institutions was invoked by Heron J in *Mair* v. *Wanganui District Court*[61] to justify upholding a conviction for contempt of court in respect of a person who, in defiance of a judicial directive, had recited a *karakia* during proceedings. However, the step from that position to one of confidence that New Zealand is a secular State is more difficult.[62]

The public education system, for example, remains somewhat compromised in terms of its exposure to religious influence as permitted under the anachronous provisions of the Education Act 1961. Then, there are the not unusual accompanying vestiges of Christian rule, including the criminality of blasphemous libel under the Crimes Act 1961, s.123.[63]

State Funding of Faith-Based Facilities and Services

The Private Schools Conditional Integration Act 1975 was introduced as a government response to financial difficulties experienced by a large group of Catholic parochial schools; these were designated as "State integrated schools" and incorporated as private schools into the public school system. Although subject to requirements that apply generally to the public education system, they then became government-funded faith-based schools (see later).

Christian Symbols/Prayers in State Facilities

"God Defend New Zealand", the national anthem, proclaims a cultural heritage that proudly asserts the Christianity of the State, which is evident also in the Speaker's prayer that opens parliamentary proceedings in the House of Representatives.

---

[58] [1910] 30 NZLR 244, at p. 253.   [59] Op. cit.
[60] [1998] 3 NZLR 513, at p. 523.   [61] [1996] 1 NZLR 556 (HC).
[62] See Ahdar, R. and Stenhouse, J. (eds), *God and Government: The New Zealand Reality*, Dunedin, Otago University Press, 2000.
[63] *R* v. *Glover* [1922] GLR 185.

Religious Discrimination: Contemporary Caselaw

This, the smallest of the common law jurisdictions currently being studied, and one with a settled Christian culture, network of institutions and overall identity, has not generated a significant volume or range of religious discrimination cases.

Religious Conduct, Symbols, Icons, Apparel, etc.

The increased prominence of Māori culture, and its political adoption to rebrand the national identity, has become a noticeable facet of life in modern New Zealand, and one that has occasionally provoked controversy. In 2001, for example, the Foreign Affairs and Trade Ministry attracted considerable criticism for funding the travel of *kaumatua* (elders) to perform *hikitapu* (spiritual cleansing ceremonies) in its embassies. This is indicative of the increasingly common recognition of Māori beliefs: for example, the use of *karakia* (prayers) to commence court proceedings or public meetings is now quite widespread.

Ethnicity/Religion-Specific Customs

The New Zealand animal welfare code states that all animals commercially processed for human consumption must be stunned prior to slaughter. While this requirement accords with the expectations of the rest of society, it offends the Jewish community, as their kosher laws necessitate slaughter by *shechita* (without stunning). In November 2010, the New Zealand Jewish community reached agreement with the Minister of Agriculture enabling the *shechita* of poultry to continue in New Zealand. Inevitably, the order issued by the High Court in Wellington giving effect to that agreement was perceived by some as discriminating in favour of religion.

The NZBORA, s.15, was specifically extended under s.20 to provide protection for the cultural practices of minorities. In *Haupini* v. *SRCC Holdings Ltd*,[64] a company which required a Māori employee to cover her tattoo was found not to be racially discriminatory as fellow Māori employees were not asked to cover their tattoos and in her case the request was linked to a particular client function. Interestingly, the Tribunal noted that the outcome might have been different if the claim had been based on culture. Such cultural manifestations are generally becoming more common as New Zealand workplaces introduce elements of *tikanga Māori*, such as policies that allow for *karakia* and *waiata*.

[64] [2011] NZHRRT 20.

Religious Apparel

Many of the few religious discrimination complaints noted by the Human Rights Commission in its annual reports concern matters of dress and appearance that are religion- or culture-specific. While there is no statutory provision explicitly addressing such matters, there is an expectation that in settings such as the workplace or classroom the wearing of a headscarf, turban or other form of religious clothing will be accommodated – subject to health and safety concerns.

An issue which has given rise to contention in New Zealand, as elsewhere, is the wearing of the burqa when giving evidence in court proceedings: should the right to so manifest religious beliefs outweigh the justice requirement to be satisfied as to the veracity of a witness's testimony? In 2004, for example, a district court in Auckland was called upon to resolve an issue raised by lawyers for the defence who objected to two Muslim women wearing the burqa while giving evidence as Crown witnesses. The judge called for submissions on the matter and ultimately decided in January 2005 on a compromise: to require the burqas to be removed, but allow screens to be used to ensure that only the judge, counsel and female court staff were able to observe the faces of the witnesses.[65] More recently, in 2010, a Sikh businessman who was refused service at a golf-club bar because he was wearing a turban received a written apology. Also that year, the Cosmopolitan Club voted to maintain its policy forbidding the wearing of headwear on its premises. At the club's annual meeting, a majority of members voted to maintain the ban, which includes turbans. Whether the social disadvantages that ensue from wearing such apparel are a consequence of racism, as opposed to religious discrimination, is clearly a distinction of little meaning to those so denigrated.

Family-Related Issues

New Zealand's reputation for demonstrating leadership in legally adjusting traditional family roles, which began 130 years ago when it granted women the right to vote, has continued with initiatives such as the legalisation of abortion in 1977, the de-criminalisation of homosexuality in 1985 and the legalisation of same-sex marriage in 2013.

Sexuality

Following a succession of cases in which the judiciary wrestled with new definitions of "family" and with the problems entailed in transposing

---

[65] See e.g. *Police v. Abdul Razamjoo* [2005] DCR 408.

familiar concepts into a reconfigured and more challenging social an
legal landscape,[66] the Court of Appeal in *Quilter*[67] considered same-se
marriage and held that the Marriage Act 1955 was incompatible with th
anti-discrimination standards set out in s.19 of the 1990 Act and s.21 o
the 1993 Act. Consequently, on April 17, 2013, Parliament passed the Mar
riage (Definition of Marriage) Amendment Act 2013, enabling gay, bisex
ual, lesbian, transsexual and intersex marriages to be legalised.[68]

While sexual orientation and religious discrimination are quite dis
tinct and separate matters, and are legally processed as such, there are cir
cumstances in which they are in fact conflated. When issues arise whicl
require the complainant to initiate legal or regulatory proceedings unde
one heading, the extent of intersection with the other may pass unac
knowledged or not be taken fully into account. For example, *Hemmingsto*
v. *Swan t/a Barker's Groom Room*[69] concerned the unfair dismissal of
transgender woman who worked as a hairdresser. The Tribunal foun
that the employer had approached the situation with a pre-determine
view that the employee's decision to transition did not suit the busines
At much the same time, in the USA, in not dissimilar circumstances, th
court held that an employer was guilty of religious discrimination as th
unfair dismissal of his transgender employee was attributable primarily t
his religious beliefs. The cases may not be as similar as they appear, an
the statutory framing may differ, but attitudes drawn from religious belief
are often associated with such issues.

Conception, Abortion, IVF and Related Issues

Abortion on demand is illegal in New Zealand.[70] Its availability is gov
erned by the Crimes Act 1961, regulated by the Abortion Supervisor
Committee, and each procedure requires approval from two consultant
on specified grounds; 98.2 per cent of all abortions are in fact authorise
on the basis of the pregnant woman's mental health (see later). IVF is als
available, under the Human Assisted Reproductive Technology Act.

---

[66] See, for example, *VP* v. *PM* (1998) 16 FRNZ 61 (lesbian mother retains custody of tw
children); *Re An Application by T* [1998] NZFLR 769 (second-parent adoption by lesbia
mother of partner's child through donor insemination refused); *A* v. *R* [1999] NZFLR 24
(non-biological mother in *Re An Application by T* held liable for child support paymen
as a step-parent); and *Re application of AMM and KJO to adopt a child* [2010] NZFLR 62
("spouse" includes *de facto* heterosexual partners).

[67] *Quilter* v. *Attorney-General*, op. cit.

[68] Note also, the Human Rights Commission, "To Be Who I Am: Report of the Inquiry int
Discrimination Experienced by Transgender People", January 2008.

[69] [2016] NZERA Auckland.

[70] See *Auckland Medical Aid Trust* v. *Commissioner of Inland Revenue* [1979] 1 NZLR 382.

Assisted Suicide

Controversy regarding this difficult issue was triggered by *Seales* v. *Attorney-General*,[71] which concerned the plaintiff's efforts to secure a declaration to the effect that either: her doctor would not be liable for culpable homicide under the Crimes Act 1961 if she "administered aid in dying", nor for aiding and abetting suicide if she "facilitated aid in dying" (as in UK legislation of the same year); or that the provisions of the Crimes Act that prohibited her doctor from administering or facilitating aid to end her life were inconsistent with her rights under the 1990 Act. Collins J took the view that, notwithstanding the right of physicians to withdraw life support for patients in extreme vegetative states,[72] any action taken by a physician to assist a terminally ill person to take his or her own life upon their request would constitute a serious criminal offence.[73] The Human Rights Commission, in its subsequent review of the law,[74] suggested that: "the right not to be arbitrarily deprived of life does not directly translate into an absolute prohibition on parliament implementing a legislative framework that would permit terminally ill people to obtain assistance to end their lives".[75] It recommended that Parliament might consider reviewing the law, bearing in mind the internationally recognised principle of respect for an individual's inherent dignity, autonomy and freedom to make one's own choices.

While it would be simplistic and misleading to assert that the current prohibition on physician-assisted death is an indicator of religious discrimination, it would perhaps be fair to link the prohibition with the sanctity-of-life principle, a central doctrine of Christianity, a religion that continues to permeate so much of New Zealand's family law.

Employment-Related Issues

In New Zealand, most discrimination occurs in an employment context.[76] The Human Rights Act 1993, s.21, prohibits discrimination in employment on grounds that include ethnic belief, religious belief,

---

[71] [2015] NZHC 828.

[72] *Auckland Area Health Board* v. *Attorney-General* [1993] 1 NZLR 253.

[73] Specifically, under the Crimes Act 1961, s.160 (culpable homicide) and s.179(b) (aiding and abetting suicide).

[74] Human Rights Commission, "Submission to the Health Select Committee in Relation to its Investigation into End of Life Matters", 2016, at www.hrc.co.nz/files/6614/5464/6095/ Submission_to_the_Health_Select_Committee_in_Relation_to_its_Investigation_into_ end_of_life_matters.pdf.

[75] Ibid., at para. 23.

[76] See New Zealand General Social Survey (NZGSS) data at http://stats.govt.nz.

sex (including childbirth and pregnancy) and sexual orientation: where discrimination is alleged, the onus rests on the employer to show justification on grounds of "exception"[77] or "good reason";[78] under s.97, a "genuine occupational qualification (GOQ)" would constitute justification, but only if the employer can show a functional link between the GOQ and the job requirements.[79] This is reinforced by s.22(1)(c), which stipulates that it is unlawful for an employer to terminate the employment of an employee by reason of the employee's religious beliefs (in circumstances in which the employment of other employees employed on work of that description would not be terminated). Curiously, s.27(2) allows for discrimination "based on sex, religious or ethical belief, disability, age, political opinion, or sexual orientation where the position is one of domestic employment in a private household". The Holidays Act 2003 stresses the requirement for "good faith" and the legal obligations of employers and employees when considering the provision of holiday and other leave entitlements. The ERA and the Employment Relations Amendment Bill 2013 are also relevant, while the Statement on Religious Diversity in New Zealand[80] recommends that "reasonable steps should be taken in educational and work environments and in the delivery of public services to recognise and accommodate diverse religious beliefs and practices".

Hiring/Firing Staff

Religious Organisations   The Human Rights Act 1993, s.28(2), which provides religious organisations with a general exemption from the prohibition against discrimination in relation to employment, allows Churches to discriminate on grounds of sex (including sexual orientation) with respect to the appointment of clergy. This exemption gave rise to an issue heard by the Human Rights Tribunal in *Gay and Lesbian Clergy Anti-Discrimination Society Inc.* v. *Bishop of Auckland*,[81] which concerned a gay man who alleged he had been barred from training to become an Anglican priest because he was in an "active" homosexual relationship. To become a priest in the Anglican Church, an applicant must be either single and celibate or in a heterosexual marriage, which the court found to be a valid requirement notwithstanding the introduction of the Marriage

---

[77] Human Rights Act 1993, s.92F(2). See *Claymore Management Ltd* v. *Anderson* [2003] 2 NZLR 537.
[78] Human Rights Act 1993, s.65.   [79] *Claymore Management Ltd* v. *Anderson*, op. cit.
[80] Human Right Commission, "Statement on Religious Diversity in New Zealand", 2007, 2009.
[81] Op. cit. See www.justice.govt.nz/tribunals/human-rights/.

(Definition of Marriage) Amendment Act 2013. It further found that s.39(1) provided an exemption for the Church (and all organised religions) in its ordaining of ministers, but did not allow sexual orientation (unlike sex and religious belief) to be a ground of discrimination for a qualifying body (i.e. the Anglican Church). Placing decisive weight on the doctrines of the Anglican Church and the importance of clearly separating the remit of Church and State, and on ensuring that the court did not trespass into either, the plaintiff's claim of indirect discrimination was dismissed.

The Human Rights Commission has drawn attention to persistent contention over the employment of clergy and religious officers. It has noted, for example, that where an appointment to the post of religious officer is refused because of the applicant's gender or sexual orientation, this is discrimination and constitutes a breach of the applicant's human rights. In 2003, the Commission sought the opinion of four experts on the question of the employment of gay and lesbian clergy. A key question was whether clergy are in fact "employed" as such. Three of the experts concurred with the view expressed in *Mabon*[82] that "a minister is not an employee of the church" and that the prohibition on appointments does not therefore generally apply. The 1998 case determined that for the purposes of the Employment Contracts Act, and in relation to the situation prevailing in the Methodist Church, the relationship between clergy and the Church is not an employment relationship. Accordingly, the question as to whether the discrimination exception provision for Churches in the HRA is applicable did not arise. The alternative view was that, under the HRA, as opposed to the Employment Contracts Act, clergy are in an employment relationship with their Church authorities, which is why the s.28 exemption (allowing discrimination to be lawful) exists. All the opinions thus lead, by differing reasoning, to the same conclusion: that the HRA allows Churches to discriminate on grounds of sex (including sexual orientation) with respect to the appointment of clergy to parish positions – but not of lay people doing e.g. pastoral work. Hospital chaplains are employees, but are usually employed by hospitals or district health boards.[83]

Secular Organisations   The importance of the right to freedom of religion – including the right to manifest one's religion or belief in worship, observance, practice and teaching – and the accompanying duty of

---

[82] *Mabon v. Conference of the Methodist Church of New Zealand* [1998] NZCA 244.
[83] The author acknowledges advice from Bill Atkins on this matter (email comment, 31 January 2017).

employers to accommodate an employee in the exercise of that right were considered in two cases in 2014.

In *Nakarawa* v. *AFFCO New Zealand Ltd*,[84] the religious beliefs of a casual employee prevented him from working between sunset on Friday and sunset on Saturday. When he explained this to his employer, Auckland Farmers Freezing Company (AFFCO), he was advised that his unwillingness to work on Saturdays did not meet the needs of the company, told that he should go home and offered no further shifts. In the resulting hearing before the HRR Tribunal, AFFCO's actions were found to breach s.22(1)(c) of the Human Rights Act 1993, which makes it unlawful for an employer to terminate employment by reason of an employee's religious beliefs. Similarly, *Meulenbroek* v. *Vision Antenna Systems Ltd*[85] concerned an employee who had rejoined the Seventh-Day Adventist Church and, in keeping with his religious beliefs, but contrary to his contract requirements, declined to work on Saturdays and was duly dismissed. Again, the employer's actions were found to breach s.22(1)(c).

More recently, *Satnam Singh* v. *Shane Singh and Scorpion Liquor*[86] illustrates how cases prosecuted on the basis of racism can hide a significant element of religious discrimination. The plaintiff was an Indian national and a Sikh who, on arrival in New Zealand, obtained employment at Scorpion Liquor, where he worked for three months. During this time, he was subjected to serious racial harassment by his manager, who ridiculed his Sikh appearance. In an effort to placate his manager and stop the racist abuse, the plaintiff trimmed both his hair and beard and began to wear a small turban concealed by a cap. This led to his father largely disowning him for bringing dishonour to the family by compromising his "Sikhness". Further assaults followed, and the plaintiff was forced to leave following the manager punching him in the head. Ultimately, the Tribunal firmly concluded in the plaintiff's favour, but solely on the basis of racial harassment, and the manager was required to pay a considerable sum in damages. It may well be that a conflation of ethnicity and religion, leading to such cases being prosecuted and recorded on the basis of racism, results in religious discrimination being significantly underestimated in New Zealand.

Accommodating Religious Beliefs in the Workplace

The Human Rights Act 1993, s.28(3), requires employers to accommodate the religious or ethical belief practices of an employee as long as any

---

[84] [2014] NZHRRT 9.   [85] [2014] NZHRRT 51.   [86] [2015] NZHRRT 8.

adjustment required "does not unreasonably disrupt the employer's activities".[87] As noted in *Nakarawa*:

> The term "unreasonably disrupt the employer's activities" is a relative term and cannot be given a hard and fast meaning. Each case will necessarily depend on its own facts and circumstances and it will come down to a determination of "reasonableness" under the unique circumstances of the particular employer-employee relationship.

This must be read in conjunction with s.35, which requires consideration of reasonable alternatives rather than imposing a strict duty to accommodate. The term "reasonable accommodation", like "reasonable measures", signifies that the law is to be applied with some flexibility: there is an expectation that employers will be prepared to make some adjustments to the terms and conditions of employment in order to accommodate the religious beliefs of staff; and that those with such beliefs will accept that working arrangements may impose a degree of inconvenience.[88] This has to be balanced against health and safety considerations in the work environment.

The ruling in *Nakarawa*, followed in *Meulenbroek*, is particularly important because the Tribunal then emphasised that the HRA requires employers to accommodate the religious practices of employees – so long as any adjustment of the employer's activities is not unreasonably disruptive – and laid down the following guidance:[89]

- an employer's obligations under the HRA are engaged once the employer has actual or constructive notice of the religious practice;
- employers must proactively protect religious practices;
- employers must make a significant, serious and sincere effort to accommodate the employee's religious practices and, in turn, offer a real and acceptable solution; and

in determining what amounts to "unreasonable disruption", an evaluative analysis of the reasonableness or proportionality of the employer's response is required.

---

[87] This requires an evaluative analysis of the reasonableness or proportionality of the employer's response: see *Smith* v. *Air New Zealand Ltd* [2011] 2 NZLR 171, at para. 161.

[88] "Reasonable accommodation" resonates strongly with the "permissive accommodations test" in the USA, which asks what religious accommodations are allowed – but not required (see e.g. *Corp. of Presiding Bishop of Church of Jesus Christ of Latter-Day Saints* v. *Amos*, op. cit.).

[89] *Meulenbroek* v. *Vision Antenna Systems Ltd*, op. cit., per Haines QC at para. 74.

The Tribunal held that AFFCO made "no attempt whatever" to accom modate the employee's religious practices, nor did it attempt to enter int discussion or dialogue with the employee over the issue. In *Meulenbroek* the key issue for the Tribunal was whether Vision had established that th adjustment of its business activities required to accommodate the com plainant would be unreasonably disruptive. It found insufficient evidenc to substantiate such a defence, and noted that "it is clear that staff an contractors were ... of the view that religious beliefs should not get in th way of work. But this is precisely the point of s.28(3) of the HRA."[90] I determining that Vision had breached s.22 of the Human Rights Act,[91] the Tribunal condemned the employer's closing submission that it wa "incumbent on the employee to facilitate implementation" as "based o: a fundamental misunderstanding of the principle involved and of the cas law. The right not to be discriminated against is not a right which operate on some days of the year but not on others."[92]

Education-Related Issues

The national education system was established by the Education Ac 1877, s.84(2), which declared that "teaching shall be entirely of a secula character".

Government Funding and Religious Education

In 2005, government funding to the 239 Catholic schools and seventy-fiv other denomination-specific schools was provided subject to condition such as that they teach the national curriculum, employ State-registere teachers and charge no tuition fees. Such schools retain their religiou ethos, but must also enrol children of other faiths, although the propoi tion of annual school intake reserved for that purpose is unknown.[93] Th correlation between government funding and school status is not absolut although all schools in the public system are government-funded, man also solicit supplementary voluntary contributions from parents; althoug all those that remain outside that system as private schools (catering fc

---

[90] Ibid., at para. 157.

[91] Citing Canadian caselaw in support, particularly *Central Okanagan School District No. :* v. *Renaud* [1992] 2 SCR 970.

[92] *Meulenbroek* v. *Vision Antenna Systems Ltd*, op. cit., at para. 144.

[93] However, note the Private Schools Conditional Integration Amendment Act 1977, ss.3 an 4, which provides powers to "preserve and safeguard the special character of the educatic provided by the school".

only 3.4 per cent of all pupils) rely on fee-paying pupil intake, they also receive some 30–40 per cent of their funding from government.

Faith Schools

The Human Rights Act 1993, s.58(1), provides for educational establishments to be maintained wholly or principally for students of one religious belief, while s.22(2) specifically allows appointments under the Private Schools Conditional Integration Act 1975 to be limited to one sex or to be made in accordance with the religious beliefs of the school. A number of religion-specific private schools – mainly Anglican, but also Presbyterian and some Catholic – have retained their independence by continuing to rely on a fee-paying student intake rather than solely on government funding. This arrangement is particularly contentious: rather than subsidise elective religious discrimination, it is argued that the State should encourage such faith schools to be wholly funded by their respective religious communities. The *Kura Kaupapa* Māori primary schools, government-owned and funded, cater specifically for pupils whose parents wish them to be educated in accordance with Māori culture and values.

Religious Discrimination and Educational Content

The governing legislation, the Education Act 1964, was introduced at a time when the prevailing culture was overwhelmingly white Christian and decidedly Eurocentric. Fundamental population changes in the intervening half-century have brought great diversity to the nation's classrooms, and the resulting tensions between the provisions of the 1964 Act and the Bill of Rights Act 1990 have led to a regular stream of complaints to the Human Rights Commission from non-Christian or secular parents, although they would not seem to have generated any caselaw.

The Education Act 1964, s.77, in keeping with the principle established a century earlier, specifies that teaching in primary schools "shall be entirely of a secular character". However, s.78 permits religious "instruction" and "observances" within defined conditions.[94] If parents require religious instruction for their child, this is generally made available in state schools by voluntary instructors outside of normal teaching hours. If they wish to avoid religious instruction, parents are permitted to exclude their child from a particular class on religious or cultural grounds. Technically, s.78 authorises State schools to provide religious instruction, and it is

---

See Mooney Cotter, A.-M., *Heaven Forbid: An International Legal Analysis of Religious Discrimination*, Farnham, Ashgate, 2009, at p. 79.

difficult for a child to be "opted-out" without being stigmatised; similar difficulties apply to the KidsKlub lunchtime sessions (run in accordance with Scripture Union principles) and the Bible in Schools programme, both of which feature in many primary schools. The Bill of Rights Act, ss.13, 15 and 19, provides, respectively, for the right to freedom of thought, conscience, religion and belief, the right to manifest such and the right to be free from religious discrimination; in short, schools may not discriminate, nor permit discrimination, on the grounds of religious belief or the lack of it. The manifestation of religion may take the form of wearing a religion-specific item, such as a headscarf, kirpan or crucifix.

In practice, Christian values and principles are woven as much into New Zealand education as into its music, art, politics and other cultural manifestations. A 2015 independent academic examination of the content of certain teaching materials (*Launch 1*, *Launch 1: Teacher Book*, *Life Choices* and *Life Choices: Teacher's Manual*) found that they were unsuitable for the religiously diverse environment of contemporary New Zealand.[95] The report referred to an explanation in the *Teacher Book* that the purpose of the course was to learn the "foundational truths of the Christian faith" ("that there is a God, that God loves and cares for them ... that they are able to talk to God" and that "Jesus is God's son"). The aims included making students aware that "their lives can be changed through meeting Jesus". Teachers were encouraged "to pray with the students", and prayers were suggested to end each session. In *Launch 1*, biblical stories were utilised to provide lessons for everyday life and for central religious practices, including the group recitation of the "Words of Wisdom", such as Proverbs 3:6 ("Remember the Lord in everything you do and he will show you the right way to live"). Teachers were encouraged to reinforce particular messages, such as that students should "please and obey God" and "think about God in everything they do". In *Life Choices*, the use of the Bible was viewed as uncritical and as promoting an uncritical reading of scripture as text. In short, the teaching material was deemed unsuitable as being "at odds with the diverse religious demography of our country where nationally a minority are Christian and an even smaller minority are conservative evangelical Christians". It is difficult not to interpret this academic assessment as implying that the surveyed educational material reflects a discriminatory approach by the State, favouring Christianity to

---

[95] See Morris, P., "Review of Christian Education Commission Teaching Materials 2015, at http://religiouseducation.co.nz/wp-content/uploads/2015/08/PAUL-MORRIS-REVIEWS-2-CEC-SYLLABUSES.pdf.

ie detriment of those of other beliefs and of none, in the public school
/stem.

Education Facilities and Religious Discrimination

here are three main types of schools in New Zealand, providing edu-
ition at primary and secondary levels: State (public) schools (catering
ir approximately 85 per cent of all students); State-integrated, mainly
atholic schools (12 per cent); and private or independent schools.[96]
1āori language and culture is available in many schools, in educational
istitutions such as *kohanga reo, kura kaupapa* and *wananga*, and in Māori
nmersion schools. Tertiary education is mainly available through the
)untry's eight universities and polytechnics.

There has been some academic protest that a traditionally Anglo-
:ntric appearance and atmosphere continue to pervade the public school
`stem in New Zealand – most pronounced in places like Christchurch –
hich is prejudicial to non-Christians and secularists. The difficulties
1countered – particularly by Muslim immigrants, who find the school
gime conflicting with their religious/cultural requirements regarding
`ayers, dress, mosque attendance, gender separation, etc. – have been
:ll documented.[97] Unfortunately, steps taken to redress this difficulty
.n also give rise to controversy. This was the case in 2003, when Hagley
ollege, a Christchurch secondary school and perhaps the oldest in the
)untry, with a significant minority of Muslim students, became the first
hool to provide a government-funded purpose-built mosque for student
;e and to impose no restrictions on Muslim dress. Arguably, instead of
is being seen as government-funded religious discrimination in favour
Muslims, it could equally be viewed as "affirmative action" to facilitate
e equal access of a minority group to the public education system.

Medicine-Related Issues

edical issues with religious connotations would seem to have rarely
ached the New Zealand courts.

Medical Intervention and Religious Beliefs

ie NZBORA, ss.10 and 11, recognises the right of a mentally compe-
nt person to make an informed decision to refuse treatment, but where

See New Zealand Ministry of Education, 'Roll by Education Regional & Authority', 2015.
See e.g. Humpage, L., "A 'Culturally Unsafe' Space? The Somali Experience of Christchurch
Secondary Schools", *New Zealand Geographer*, 2009, vol. 65:1, pp. 73–82.

such consent is not available and others seek to substitute their decisio
on behalf of someone needing treatment, and to do so on the basis of the
religious beliefs, then the court may well become involved. Such were th
circumstances in *Re J (An Infant): B and B* v. *Director-General of Socia*
Welfare,[98] which concerned a three-year-old boy whose need for a bloo
transfusion – opposed by his Jehovah's Witness parents – led to a cou
application for a wardship order and permission to override the parent:
veto. Justifying the granting of both applications, the Court of Appe:
commented that "the parents' right to practice their religion cannot exten
to imperil the life or health of the child".[99] Even where children of an ag
of discernment choose to agree with their parents' religious views an
reject treatment, the court may similarly intervene.[100] Consequently, the:
is some uncertainty as to when a young person in New Zealand may giv
or refuse consent – on religious grounds – to medical intervention suc
as invasive treatment, access to contraceptives, etc. The corollary is th
a corresponding uncertainty prevails regarding the age at which a your
person may be refused access – on religious grounds – to contraceptive
abortion, etc. without that refusal constituting religious discrimination.

Genetic Engineering and Patents, etc.

The Resource Management Act 1991 provides for the devolution of
decision-making regarding managing the environmental effects of huma
activity on land, water and air.[101] It requires local authorities to consu
local *tangata whenua*, through *iwi* authorities, and have regard to the
views when preparing a policy statement or plan. In theory, this shou
place real power in the hands of Māori – in those communities whe
they constitute a significant presence – to influence if not determine issu
relating to such matters. However, the associated caselaw suggests that :
practice Māori beliefs, once considered, can be discounted.

For Māori, *taonga* is to be found in the integrity of species ar
bloodlines: the world, or *whenua* as it was known to their spirits ar
ancestors and embodied in legend, should be respected; the particul
wairua or spirit of all living things must be protected. Such beliefs we
weighed by the judiciary in *Bleakley* v. *Environmental Risk Manageme*

---

[98] [1996] 2 NZLR 134.   [99] Ibid., at p. 146.
[100] See *Auckland Healthcare Services Ltd* v. *Liu*, High Court, Auckland, 11.7.1996, M812/
and *Auckland Healthcare Services Ltd* v. *T* [1996] NZFLR 670.
[101] *Meridian Energy Ltd* v. *Southland District Council* [2014] NZHC 3178 (2014) 18 ELRM
473.

Authority,[102] where the High Court recognised that the Treaty of Waitangi imposed a duty on the Crown to actively protect *taonga*, which "embraces the metaphysical and intangible (e.g. beliefs or legends) as much as it does the physical and intangible (e.g. a treasured carving or mere)". The case concerned the right of a government research facility to genetically modify certain Fresian cows so as to allow milk production to include a human protein – a proposition which met with vigorous opposition from Māori, and others, who objected to any such mixing of human and animal genetic material. In particular, the Ngati Wairere Māori community claimed that any alteration of *whakapapa* (genealogy) by mixing the genetic make-up of species would be deeply offensive and contrary to their *tikanga* (custom); these were intangible *taonga*, any interference with which would constitute a breach of the Treaty of Waitangi. The court concluded that the relevant local authority was entitled to take the view that the only way to protect such *taonga* would be to refuse approval for the proposed project, but, in the particular circumstances of this case, it was also entitled to regard the duty to protect as outweighed by broader considerations. The court upheld the earlier decision to grant approval notwithstanding Māori objections. Subsequently, in *Federated Farmers*,[103] Peters J confirmed that the 1991 Act provided authority for local regional councils to make decisions regarding the use and control of GM organisms. Thus it would seem that although the law provides authority for local decision-making in respect of the use of GM material and requires Māori beliefs to be taken into account when such decisions are made, in practice the process is ineffective in ensuring that those beliefs have any influence in determining the outcome. This may indicate that, in reality, the impact of genetic engineering on Māori beliefs – as given effect by the Resource Management Act 1991 – is discriminatory, as it can override the *whenua* and *wairua* components of those beliefs.

Service-Provision Issues

The Human Rights Act 1993, s.44, prohibits discrimination in the provision of goods and services, but there is little caselaw evidence of associated legal issues.

---

[2] Op. cit.
[3] *Federated Farmers of New Zealand* v. *Northland Regional Council* [2015] NZEnvC 89 and *Federated Farmers of New Zealand Incorporated* v. *Northland Regional Council* [2016] NZHC 2036.

Service Provision by Religious Organisations

The Marriage (Definition of Marriage) Amendment Act 2013 is problem atic in terms of guaranteeing gay couples access to a marriage service While it is clear that a religious organisation is now enabled to conduc such a marriage ceremony, it remains somewhat uncertain as to what hap pens if clergy refuse to officiate and/or a couple is denied the use of thei chosen church. In New Zealand, as in many other common law countries this is fraught with religious discrimination issues.

The 2013 Act also gives rise to adoption issues, as same-sex marriec couples will now be eligible to apply jointly to adopt a child. This wil present traditional faith-based adoption charities with the same forcec choice as faced by their counterparts in the USA and UK. Catholic Socia Services in Christchurch and the Latter Day Saints Social Services, fo example, are restricted by their religious beliefs in the range of service they can offer. Specifically, although both engage in ancillary adoptioi work, their discriminatory beliefs exclude the possibility of contractin with same-sex prospective adopters, and they are therefore excluded fron registration and regulation by government as adoption agencies.

Provision of Public Services

Abortion is a controlled public service in New Zealand, the availabilit of which is likely to be affected by the recent Supreme Court decisioi in *Right to Life New Zealand Inc.* v. *Abortion Supervisory Committee.*[10] This confirmed that the Abortion Advisory Committee had the power t enquire as to how the consultants involved in such procedures approache their decision-making and could revoke their appointments if it foun that the consultants' views were incompatible with the tenor of the Ac Consequently, should the Committee discover that a consultant's reli gious beliefs, or lack of such, have influenced their approach to the cir cumstances in which abortion should be made available, this could hav direct implications for their career prospects. As with registrars officiat ing at gay marriages, there is a probability that some consultants will hav views – of a religious or atheist nature – that may be incompatible witl their continuing their public-service functions without leaving themselve vulnerable to the challenge that a decision taken constitutes religiou discrimination.

[104] [2012] NZSC 68.

Private Goods and Service Provision

Department of Labour v. *Books and Toys (Wanaka) Ltd*[105] concerned the proprietor of a bookshop in the tourist resort of Wanaka who, by opening for business on Easter Sunday, breached trading legislation requiring shops to be closed on Good Friday, Easter Sunday, Christmas Day and ANZAC Day morning. Although pleading guilty, the defendant argued that the statutory ban constituted an unreasonable limitation on his right of religious freedom under ss.13 and 15 of the NZBORA. The court sidestepped this issue and, while recording a conviction, relied on the anomalous nature of the law's zoning parameters to resolve the matter.

Broadcasting Services

As in the other common law jurisdictions presently considered, there is a legal tension in New Zealand between the rights not to suffer religious discrimination and to freedom of expression; rights embodied in the NZBORA, ss.19 and 14, respectively. The newly introduced Harmful Digital Communications Act 2015 is intended to curb the more excessive abuses of free speech in media broadcasting.

In a broadcasting context, allegations of religious discrimination are often made in reference to the purportedly religiously offensive content of commercial advertising. Among the many such cases heard by the Broadcasting Standards Authority was that of "the dancing butchers".[106] This concerned a protest from representatives of the Hare Krishna community that a television commercial featuring a group of butchers dancing, singing and chanting along a street, in a mock imitation of Hare Krishna chants, constituted an abuse of their religious beliefs – particularly as they are vegetarian. While that complaint was upheld on appeal, a more recent one from a Presbyterian pastor about the exclamation, "For Christ's sake!", in a similar television commercial was dismissed as it was found not to be blasphemous and did not merit State censure. Generally, the regulatory authorities take the view that socially provocative and sometimes confrontational advertisements, presented as humorous and satirical, should be allowable within a tolerant and open society such as New Zealand.

---

5   [2005] 7 HRNZ 931.
6   *New Zealand Beef and Lamb Marketing Bureau* 03/20 (ASCB, 11 March 2003); Appeal 03/10 (ASCAB, 28 October 2003).

Conclusion

There is a dearth of religious discrimination caselaw in New Zealand. Compared with other jurisdictions, there would seem to be neither the volume, nor the landmark rulings by superior courts, on issues that fall wholly within the definition of this offence: in particular, there is no ongoing judicial narrative regarding the balance to be struck between the interests of Church and State, and little in the way of secularist challenges to the continued status and leverage of religious organisations. Possibly, this reflects a less litigious, more easy-going approach to religion, illustrated perhaps, in the 2001 census recording of 53 000 Jedi followers: an approach that may owe something to the fact that the citizens of a small, isolated island nation, with its culturally diverse population, will have learned to be mutually dependent and to adopt a neighbourly give-and-take attitude. It may also be due to social norms and the framing of laws which focus on racial discrimination and classify offences accordingly. Against that trend, the increased importance attached to Māori spirituality is worthy of note: formal public meetings that might once have opened with a Christian prayer may now do so with a *mihi* or *karakia* – an indication of religious discrimination being displaced by parity of esteem.

PART IV

Religion and Discrimination: An Overview

11

Themes of Jurisdictional Commonality
and Difference

Introduction

The progenitor common law jurisdiction was the source for an institutional infrastructure, mode of governance and a legal system – all equally permeated by Christianity – that enabled the growth of civil society in the nations examined in Part III. As time passed, certain jurisdictional differences emerged, but they continue to share sufficient structural characteristics to permit a thematic comparative analysis of their contemporary dealings with matters such as religious discrimination.

It may at first seem that the jurisdiction of England and Wales has changed the least. After all, constitutionally it retains the binary Church/State institutional arrangement that was in place when it first embarked on empire-building, and it continues to allow the Church of England to be preferred in ways that adherents of other religions and of none would perceive as discriminatory. However, decades of compliance with EC treaties, conventions, protocols, etc. and with ECtHR rulings have done much to reshape the law in England and Wales. Mostly, the binding effect of those rulings, together with the experience of having decisions of its domestic courts overturned by the ECtHR, have contributed to forming the principles now applied to resolve issues of religious discrimination. Quite probably, the experience of absorbing a steady flow of migrant workers availing themselves of the EC open-borders policy, and in so doing exposing its judiciary and regulatory tribunals to a variety of discrimination cases, have added to that effect.

The US legal system, however, has undoubtedly experienced the greatest volume and breadth of relevant caselaw. The effect of the First Amendment in sharpening the separation of Church and State has, most likely, been responsible not only for driving a fast flow of cases through the courts, but also for pushing many of them up to the USSC. This, in turn, has resulted in caselaw principles being formulated at the highest level. Something like the same dynamics are apparent in the neighbouring federated jurisdiction, Canada, where the SCC has also played a leading role in forging governing principles. There, the religious discrimination jurisprudence reflects the constitutional compromises in-built in this bijural jurisdiction, particularly as regards the explicit preferencing of Catholic schools.

The Antipodean jurisdictions share the characteristic of having a low throughput of discrimination cases with an emphasis on racial rather than religious discrimination. In both, the proportion of such caselaw that relates to their respective communities of Indigenous People is surprisingly small – although Māori culture, customs and spiritual beliefs have a higher status relative to their Australian counterparts. On the other side of the world, the empire-builder's closest neighbour has a quite different caselaw profile. The Irish Constitution preferences the Catholic religion, and this preferencing carries through to the public education, health and social care infrastructure, which effectively means that a large part of the national public-service sector is singularly dominated by the Catholic Church. Unsurprisingly, this is reflected in the related caselaw, which typically features secularist challenges to the alleged discriminatory practices of facilities in that sector.

This chapter reflects on the varying jurisdictional characteristics of the material processed in Part III. Beginning with an overview of the legal frameworks as they relate to religious discrimination issues, it considers some of the more important jurisdictional differences and their implications. It then examines the Church/State relationship, giving particular attention to varying jurisdictional interpretations of the State-neutrality doctrine. This leads into the substantive part of the chapter, which focuses on a jurisdictional differentiation of the law and judicial rulings relating to religious discrimination issues in the context of: symbols, icons apparel, etc.; family matters; employment; education; medicine; and service provision.

Religion and Religious Discrimination: Legal Frameworks

All jurisdictions studied retain a conspicuous (in places, dominant) Christian infrastructure – reflected in their institutions, language, music, art, symbols and ritual – which could be seen as representing a culturally based form of discrimination against all non-Christians. The legal frameworks have grown out of that distinctive cultural setting and remain very much in keeping with it.

Policy, Courts and Legislation

In response to general developments in human rights law, the policies, judicial processes and legislation relating to religious discrimination have advanced considerably in recent years.

Policy

The introduction of equality and anti-discrimination legislation in all six jurisdictions in recent decades has necessarily been accompanied by a government policy that requires a correspondingly impartial, even-handed approach to all religions and beliefs and to secularism. That policy has naturally been recalibrated in recent times to address the threat from Islamist terrorists – more so in the USA and the UK, which have both experienced significant domestic attacks on civilians, and less so in Ireland, which has not, and which has consistently maintained its neutrality in relation to US-led wars in Islamic countries. The policy has included some experimentation with government agencies established to bridge the gap between organised religions and government, but only in the USA has this initiative firmly and extensively bedded down. It has attracted protest, which may well be justified, that such agencies are not merely impartial conduits to facilitate mutual communication but positively set out to promote and direct government support for religion.

Adjustment has also been prompted by the 2015/17 influx of refugees and migrants – mostly Muslims – from war-devastated countries into all developed Western nations. The latter's domestic and foreign policies would now seem to be emphasising a new "nation state" awareness; this is evident in the self-protection measures adopted to police borders, scrutinise minority groups (particularly Muslims) and co-ordinate international surveillance of terrorist suspects (again, mainly Muslims).

This more inward-looking approach has triggered a widespread questioning of multi-culturalism as the policy of choice for building social cohesion (see further Chapter 12).

Courts and Regulators

The main weight of responsibility for settling claims of religious discrimination falls to the regulators – mainly employment tribunals – in all jurisdictions, but the role played by the courts is crucial, and some jurisdictional differences are important. Judicial decisions in the courts of England and Wales and of Ireland may be appealed to the ECtHR, and its rulings have a mandatory – if not enforceable – effect on those juris-dictions, as do the full programme of EC conventions, protocols and other instruments. This supra-national source of authority provides the judiciary in both jurisdictions with the guidance of binding precedents derived from a constant flow of caselaw drawn from many different cul-tural settings, the volume and range of which is without parallel in other common law countries, while simultaneously holding them to account for decisions that breach human rights law as expressed in evolving ECtHR rulings. In comparison, the North American jurisdictions rely heavily on the guiding principles developed and adjusted by their respective Supreme Courts. Consequently, in relation to the much more closed domestic judi-cial and regulatory systems of all other jurisdictions, the spread of UK caselaw, in particular, seems more varied and prone to change.

Legislation: Domestic and International

In most jurisdictions studied, the law relating to religious discrimination was subject to the overarching provisions of a Constitution, the religious provisions of which were generally quite dated, and consequently out of sync with the religious characteristics of contemporary society. The slip-page was most apparent in relation to the references to religion, which usually presupposed a theistic – if not an explicitly Christian – religion, made little allowance for other (very varied) belief systems and made even less for the relative growth in importance of secularism.

All jurisdictions studied are variably bound by a set of UN human rights conventions, protocols, etc., which provide an important supra-national layer of standards for identifying any shortfall in law and practice. In par-ticular, it is noticeable how frequently the Antipodean judiciary and reg-ulators reference the ICCPR and, to a lesser extent, the Declaration on the Elimination of All Forms of Intolerance and of Discrimination Based on Religion or Belief in their *ratio decidendi*. One reason for this might be that equivalent domestic legislative provisions are quite dated and fail to squarely address religious discrimination. The international monitoring processes, pursued under the auspices of the ICCPR and ICERD and with the guidance of Rapporteurs, etc., are proving to be effective mechanisms for generating inter-jurisdiction transparency and mutual accountability in relation to national deficits in religious discrimination law and practice. The "name and shame" effect of international reports does seem to trigger appropriate government responses, although not in all cases, and not very promptly.

Definitions and Religious Manifestation

Recent years have seen the judiciary move with considerable jurisdictional consistency from being constrained by a traditional definition of "religion", with its reliance upon a "Supreme Being", doctrines or tenets and worship, to an approach which accommodates a wide range of beliefs or philosophies and allows for their subjective interpretation. This broadening of interpretation has been accompanied by a corresponding increase in the number and range of organisations entitled to exemption privileges. Arguably, however, such practice developments have outgrown the formal structures, often embedded in constitutional provisions, that initially framed the Church/State relationship, and these now need re-alignment to redress the discriminatory weighting favouring religion over secularism and Christianity over all other religions and belief systems, and to take account of the particular inequities faced by Indigenous People. In Australia and New Zealand, discrimination law also needs to be adjusted from its current emphasis on race to allow for a more specific focus on religion.

Definitions

The traditional religions, with their theological underpinnings of theistic belief, doctrines, worship, etc., continue to dominate in all jurisdictions. Ireland, in particular, remains constitutionally bound by a theistic interpretation of religion, with an emphasis on Christianity, accompanied by doctrinal evidence and practices of prayer and worship. Australia, New Zealand and Canada, although accepting a non-theistic definition, tend to look to doctrines for substantiating evidence; the former has led the way in requiring traditional canons or principles – e.g. relating to heterosexual marriage – to be interpreted in accordance with contemporary social mores. In all three, the customs and beliefs of Indigenous People receive less attention and weight than is given to adherents of institutional religions. The USA is home to both the largest number of fundamentalist Christians, who are resolutely theistic and rely on biblical sources for religious definitions, and a burgeoning spectrum of beliefs which, with little in common other than a reach for the transcendant, require supporting evidence of cogency, seriousness, cohesion and importance if they are to acquire parity of legal status with religion. England and Wales, the progenitor Christian common law jurisdiction, has the singular distinction of having become the one that is most rapidly ceasing to be Christian; albeit,

the only one with an in-built "constitutional" endorsement of traditiona
Christian beliefs, as defined by its "established" Anglican Church.

This imbalance between contemporary diversity of beliefs and tradi
tional religious legal frameworks may well be perceived, and possibl
experienced, by those of non-Christian beliefs and of none as discrimi
natory. Moreover, this book has argued that in addition to religious dis
crimination, as it is currently defined in law, there is a need to take accoun
of matters which to a greater or lesser extent function as its proxy exten
sions. While conceding that it is not necessary to be religiously orientate
to take up a position for or against issues such as abortion or gay marriage
it is contended that very many who take up such positions are indeed s
motivated. The sublimation of religion, its values and its adherents int
everyday occupations and facilities has produced the shadowland of th
"culture wars", in which religious discrimination is deflected into moralit
issues, thereby permitting a more discrete confrontation – but one whic
is nonetheless very largely representative of religious and anti-religiou
viewpoints.

Manifestation

The manifesting of religious beliefs is also treated by judiciary and reg
ulators with a consistently liberal approach. Greatest latitude is availab
in the USA, where the constitutional anti-establishment and free-exercis
clauses stand as unique bulwarks against government intervention in cit
izens' freedom of religion unless there is a "compelling reason" of th
"highest order", as supplemented by the right to freedom of expressior
The latter also operates to limit the imposition of expressed beliefs o
those – secularists or others – who object; a limitation that generates th
most litigation in the USA, little in New Zealand and the least in Irelanc
In all jurisdictions, there is now a focus on the interface between thes
two rights: the circumstances in which the right to freedom of expres
sion can restrain the right to manifest religious beliefs is becoming a
interesting testing ground for conflicting liberal rights in all contemporar
democracies.

The judicial interpretation of religion/beliefs and the legal constrain
on manifestation set the context for what constitutes "religious discrim
ination"; clearly, the parameters are wider than previously, as they hav
had to expand to accommodate "beliefs", subjective perception and als
if inadequately, the traditional cultures of Indigenous Peoples. This ne
breadth of interpretation has in the main been addressed by internation
conventions and their respective monitoring mechanisms. The casela

naturally has the greatest volume and range in the UK, Canada and the USA, while in Australia and New Zealand the focus is somewhat obscured by a legislative emphasis on and overlap with racial discrimination.

Exemptions

All jurisdictions studied had in place much the same exemption privileges for religious organisations. All were also dealing with the outcomes of investigations revealing details of extensive and systemic child abuse perpetrated by or within such organisations. All are consequently now experiencing heated controversy regarding the continued justification for exempting religious organisations – both from taxation and from human rights legislation.

The Religious Exemption

The exemption enjoyed by religious organisations is intended to facilitate the maintenance of their traditional core functions (ceremonies of communal prayer and worship, etc.), but in practice the protection afforded to emanations of those organisations (e.g. schools, hospitals, etc.) is also greatly valued, and it is this that often causes contention (for contention regarding service provision, see later). Exemption privileges apply in particular to staffing: appointments, terms and conditions of employment, termination and the types of services they can or cannot deliver.

The principle of exemption is most vigorously challenged in those jurisdictions where the secularist lobby is strongest, viz in the UK and the USA. In Ireland, where it has been weakest but the extent of religious penetration of social infrastructure is greatest, there is now growing protest by secularists and others regarding the proportion of public service facilities that are owned (and usually controlled) by religious organisations, viz almost all primary schools and some major hospitals. The challenge in all is the same: that privileging religious organisations because of their status as such is a form of religious discrimination.

Moreover, in any such organisation, the more attenuated the functional role of staff in relation to its core religious doctrine, the greater the difficulty in sustaining a claim that the role represents a manifestation of religious belief and the greater the risk that the organisation is perceived as unfairly exploiting religious status to gain advantage. Arguably, there is a line to be drawn between the outworkings of religious faith that, being ancillary and incidental in nature, can be seen to manifest an organisation's religious beliefs and those that are related only tenuously, if at all, to such beliefs. In the latter case, the activities may come to be viewed as a reverse form of religious discrimination. In the USA, the social impact of the exemption privilege has been potentially greatly enlarged by the *Hobby Lobby* ruling, which, if adopted in other jurisdictions, will radically strengthen the marketing leverage of those religious organisations with commercial outlets.

Further, there is the problem of religious or belief organisations that accommodate practices which are not human rights-compliant. In all jurisdictions, such organisations are now exempted from certain key requirements of equality legislation, in particular from those relating to matters of gender and sexuality. However, where any such religion or belief imposes negative constraints upon its adherents – e.g. on the role of women, on non-heterosexual relationships, on divorce – and encourages the rejection of those of alternative beliefs or of none, then, even if exemption on the grounds of religious status can in law be justified, the organisation concerned is patently in breach of basic equality precepts, i not benefitting the public and is not conducive to promoting an inclusive civil society.

There is also, arguably, a question mark hanging over the continued necessity for proselytism to be regarded as a core religious function. As the legal interpretation of "religion" and the metastasis of "belief systems" lead to a proliferation of organisations entitled to persuade others to join them, doubt increases as to whether this is a public-benefit activity and whether, as such, it should entitle the organisation to exemption privileges and taxpayer subvention.

The Charity Exemption

Religious organisations invariably have charitable status, and all common law jurisdictions currently being considered have recently undertaken charity law reform. The varying reform outcomes are likely to alter the rough jurisdictional parity that has prevailed for centuries regarding that status. The changes to the public-benefit test, to the statutory range of charitable purposes and to national charity regulatory bodies have yet to be worked through, but they will all have implications for how different jurisdictions determine entitlement to charitable status and its associated exemption privileges – from tax and from equality and non discrimination legislation. There is now considerable jurisdictional uncertainty as to matters such as: the type of religious outworkings and the differing responsibilities of staff that may qualify for exemption; and the

ailability of exemption entitlement to religious organisations engaged in
ublic-service provision.

Given that uncertainty, coupled with the above mentioned evidence of
ternational child abuse perpetrated by clergy, the legal presumption that
ligious organisations and their varied emanations are all equally for the
ublic benefit and thus automatically entitled to exemption from stan-
ard civic responsibilities, is open to question. As the definition of "reli-
on" is broadened, causing the threshold for charitable status to be corre-
ondingly lowered, the alignment between the beliefs of an organisation,
e public-benefit test and exemption privileges may need to be revised.
rguably, the displacement of the tax burden, to be shouldered instead
y ordinary citizens – many of whom are non-religious – constitutes an
omalous structural inequity that could be construed in terms of reli-
ous discrimination.

Church and State

he need for a balanced working relationship between these two pillars of
ciety has featured in the maturation of all modern democracies. While
ntemporary rhetoric has it that their separation is now indispensable
r the proper functioning of society,[1] there is little evidence that this is
ppening, or indeed that it is wholly desirable. Even in the USA, there is
uch equivocation as to the necessity for an absolute separation of Church
d State.

State Neutrality

suring a level playing field for all religions, beliefs and non-beliefs –
cluding the emerging, the peripheral and the transitory, alongside the
aditional institutional religions – is a challenge, but if the national policy
to promote pluralism then the more marginal the beliefs, the greater the
ed for protection.[2] The doctrine of State neutrality is arguably an imper-
ct response to this challenge. It seems least realisable in Ireland, where
atholicism remains constitutionally and politically (if no longer socially)
trenched, and in England and Wales, which continues its Church/State

ee e.g. the Council of Europe, Parliamentary Assembly, "State, Religion, Secularity and
Human Rights", Recommendation 1804, 2007, at para. 4.
uch a strategy for supporting a policy of pluralism has been endorsed by the ECtHR; see
.g. *Metropolitan Church of Bessarabia and Others* v. *Moldova*, op. cit.

ties with the "established" Anglican Church. In the USA, where th
doctrine is most strongly asserted, but where evangelicalism has alway
been a strong social and political force and where secularism is now assert
ing itself, it is interpreted permissively: State support is allowed, and ma
well be unavoidable; it merely requires government to eschew partisa
advocacy and be even-handed in its dealings with religious matters, rel
gious organisations and secularists.

There are, of course, in-built problems with any such purportedly ever
handed approach. A major one is that those of faith would claim tha
it wholly misses the point: religious matters are qualitatively different;
reductionist, level-playing-field approach fails to take into account th
transcendental raison d'être of religion. In effect, a policy of State net
trality is viewed as a policy of discrimination against religion.[3] So, fc
example, when government takes a policy initiative in respect of a moral
imperative issue – abortion, gay marriage, etc. – the differing impact
has upon religious and secularist organisations can be anything but net
tral. Elective abortion, in particular, has been a hugely important politic
issue for decades, and one that is not confined to the USA. Whatever gov
ernment initiative is taken, including doing nothing, will directly affe
such organisations in different ways; but, in particular, it will impact upo
those whose religious beliefs require respect for the "sacredness" of li
from the moment of conception. State neutrality in dealing with the cor
temporary and ever-extending agenda of moral imperatives would see
to be an unattainable aspiration.

State/Religion Relationships

An important jurisdictional difference in the law relating to the State
religion relationship flows from the varying acceptance of and complian
with supra-national sources of authority embodied in international co
ventions, or from the existence or otherwise of any overarching domest
constitutional provision or arrangement. Most obviously, this can be see
in the guarantee of freedom of religion in the First Amendment to the U
Constitution and in the Canadian Charter of Rights and Freedoms, ar
to a lesser degree in s.116 of the Australian Constitution. Both Irelar
and England and Wales have constitutional provisions or arrangements
explicit and implicit, respectively – favouring a specific religion, which
practice would seem to have the legal effect of relatively disadvantagir
all other religions, as well as secularists. In New Zealand, the Treaty

---

[3] See further Ahdar and Leigh, Religious Freedom in the Liberal State, at p. 116.

Waitangi gives the beliefs of the Māori a level of recognition unequalled by constitutional provisions relating to the beliefs of Indigenous People elsewhere. Such an established source of governing authority can do much to facilitate or obstruct a contemporary working relationship between the State and religious organisations.

Public-benefit service provision agreements between the State and religious organisations have brought their own challenges to State neutrality. These long-standing – if variously managed – arrangements, which are common to all six jurisdictions, have cemented relationships between government and the service-delivery emanations of the large institutional religions, to the virtual exclusion of others. Their effect has been to bind the religions concerned in a dependent relationship to government, future contracts being determined by government satisfaction with past performance. This contractual – if not colonising – relationship is not only compromising for those so contracted, as any dissension they may have with government policy is necessarily muted, but it also leaves little room for other religious organisations and new belief systems to effectively compete in what has become a government-controlled market.

Government funding of faith schools in particular, and faith-based social facilities in general, invariably gives rise to controversy in the context of any State neutrality policy, and is distinctly anomalous unless all schools/facilities are equally supported. There are, of course, definitional problems. For example, is a madrassa that concentrates largely on recitations from the Qur'an a faith school? What about denominational schools that function as part of a national public school system? Should religious 'instruction' as opposed to "education" be permissible in the primary schools of such a system? Is it appropriate that the education of children should attract exemption privileges for religious organisation providers? The establishment of government agencies with a specific brief for religion – most notably in the USA – and the sponsoring of national programmes for supporting religious organisations – such as the Charitable Choice initiative, also in that country – may well be perceived as government tipping the scales in favour of religion to the detriment of secularists.

Finally, recent anti-terrorism policies and legislation reflect a common jurisdictional wariness in relation to religion generally, and Islam more specifically. In England and Wales, for example, the "Prevent" strategy, intended to counter radicalisation, may have done more to defeat that intent, as many Muslims were outraged at what they saw as a government-directed programme that singled out and stigmatised their religion.

Protecting Religion from the State

In making the case for State neutrality, Moon explains that:[4]

> By expressing no preference, the State ensures that it preserves a neutral public space that is free of discrimination and in which true freedom to believe or not to believe is enjoyed by everyone equally, given that everyone is valued equally.

Should the State express a preference, it by no means follows that the result necessarily assists the favoured religion. By preferencing religion or a religion, the State creates a hierarchy which identifies that preference as superior, declares an expectation that its public benefit contribution will be greatest and becomes complicit in institutionalising a form of religious discrimination that, in exempting its adherents from tax and equality responsibilities, risks tarnishing their citizenship.

Unquestionably, if the State is entangled with a particular religion – as in Ireland and England and Wales – or even with Christianity more generally – as in all six jurisdictions, to a varying degree – then to that extent it diminishes the relative value of all others: particularly the interests of secularists. However, arguably, this is justified. After all, there is no avoiding the fact that in all instances, for several centuries – and longer in the case of England and Wales – Christianity was imprinted upon and infused within the culture of each jurisdiction; it and its associated artefacts now represent the developmental stages – a memory trail – that explain how each came to acquire its present identity. For the State to assume a neutral role would entail it abandoning ownership and a duty of care for its own particular cultural heritage. State neutrality is thus a questionable option if it actually reinforces a diminution in the role of a faith or Church with which its citizens have historically and culturally been associated. Moreover, equality principles require that "new" or minority religious communities should not be disadvantaged relative to traditional religious organisations, which in turn suggests that the State must assume an affirmative-action role, providing targetted support to selected religion and belief systems sufficient to strengthen their position.

It is possible that, in an era of increasing secularism, the protection of religion is actually impaired by State neutrality, as by standing aside the State is effectively clearing the way for secularism to steadily occupy the "public space". On the other hand, the formal public interaction between

---

[4] Moon, R., "Freedom of Religion Under the Canadian Charter of Rights: the Limits of State Neutrality", *University of British Columbia Law Review*, 2012, vol. 45:2, at p. 497.

State and religion is only part of the picture. Despite census returns, emptying churches, etc., it is at least possible that contemporary reports on the demise of religion – and accompanying speculation regarding the varying effects of State support, regulation or neutrality – are a bit premature. Religious adherence may simply have become more private: a retreat away from being associated with organised religion, as from orthodox politics, may be underway; religious belief, becoming more a matter of private piety, with less need for an infrastructure, and less investment in public institutions or in social issues of the day, may be correspondingly less amenable to State protection or any other form of intervention.

Secularism and a Discriminatory State

Nonetheless, judging from official reports, a striking feature of religion in all jurisdictions studied is that – at least in terms of declared adherents – the established trends show it to be shrinking and irreversibly losing ground to secularism. This would seem to be generating reciprocal allegations of religious discrimination – each side accusing the other of exercising undue influence in the "public square" – and driving the rise of state neutrality as a prudent government policy for managing, ostensibly in a transparent and impartial way, its relationship with religious and secularist organisations. However, despite the loud government rhetoric in support of neutrality, the evidence would suggest that there are difficulties translating this policy into practice.

State Funding

The tradition of Church/State partnership in public-benefit service provision, variously developed in all six jurisdictions, ensured that at least the religious organisations involved would be State-funded. Constitutional barriers, reinforced by the neutrality doctrine, may have been recently effective in substituting contract funding for direct government financial support of religious organisations and their emanations, but this has not prevented ongoing selective government funding in certain areas. In particular, it is the discriminatory funding of schools that most often reveals a failure to exercise neutrality. In the USA, the neutrality policy is pursued most assiduously, but in Ireland, Canada, New Zealand and Australia, it has considerably less traction. In England and Wales, government funding flows mainly to schools linked to the "established" Church, some of which are elite establishments that levy high fees but which also benefit from tax exemption, as they have charitable status. Tax exemptions favour the

emanations of organised traditional religions in all jurisdictions: the benefits thus accrued by religiously affiliated colleges and universities, socia
care facilities, hospitals and other entities enable them to retain their institutional infrastructure and markets; this denies opportunities to minority
and newly emerging religious groups; and it gives such religious service
providers a government-subsidised edge over any secularist competitors.

Christian Symbols/Prayers in State Facilities

State display of allegiance to the Christian faith is ubiquitous in all six jurisdictions: on coinage, in constitutions, oaths and parliamentary prayers, in
official holidays at Christmas and Easter, etc. It is also prevalent in many
if not most government buildings and schools in Ireland, Australia, New
Zealand and England and Wales, sometimes in the form of prayers or crucifixes. Only in the USA, and to a lesser extent in Canada, is the doctrine o
State neutrality applied to curb public displays of State affiliation to Christianity. For secularists, as for all other non-Christians, such overt testimony to the Christianity of the State is difficult to square with professed
State neutrality.

Caselaw: Indices of Jurisdictional Commonality and Difference

The caselaw, examined in Part III, illustrates the difficulties in protecting
the rights of minorities from constraints imposed by a majority within a
Christian culture established and maintained for centuries by that majority. Sifting the material reveals that the areas of jurisdictional commonality
in addressing issues of religious discrimination far outweigh the differences. One point of difference, which seems significant, is the tendency
in Australia and New Zealand for discrimination to be legislatively recog
nised and judicially processed predominately in racial terms. It may be
that this prioritisation is causing the true incidence of religious discrimination to be underestimated.

Symbols, Icons, Apparel, Customs, etc.

The "nailing of colours to the mast" is a blunt and powerful declaration
of identity, an assertion of a stand being made, a line being drawn in the
sand. The use of symbols such as a crucifix, a burqa, a nun's wimple or a
prayer mat laid out in the workplace constitutes such a declaration. However, the form of manifestation must bear a meaningful relationship to the
person's beliefs, and the beliefs must be sincerely held. It will not constitute

public display of religious affiliation, for example, if such a symbol is mere ornamental accoutrement or something that reflects personal or ɔcio-political preferences.

Symbols, Ethnic/Religious Customs, etc.

he rule in the USA that only a compelling reason will justify State ιterference in a religious custom is generally applied in other jurisdic- ɔns, too. Interference will be justified if the custom disproportionately ιfringes the rights of others; a caveat that often arises in the context of ws of universal application (e.g. Sikhs and crash helmets). The issue is of ɑrticular interest when crystalised in the form of a religious/ethnic right hich squarely conflicts with jurisdictional law. The religious significance ˙ traditional practices – including, for example, the Jewish *get* (divorce ɑly at the husband's discretion) and the Islamic *mahr* (price payable to wife on divorce) – may well breach the contemporary equality principle ˙ central importance to modern common law host societies, but, within ιeir respective cultural contexts, there is considerable pressure and will- ιgness for these rules to be respected. They can contribute so much to ιe social coherence of a minority group that repressing them could have ɘgative repercussions for pluralism in those societies.

Also of interest is the variable jurisdictional approach to the public ϰpression of Indigenous customs. Considering that they all pre-date by ɪr the essentially white Christian culture that was superimposed upon ιeir lands and communities, and given the equality legislation now in ace, it is notable that – judging from the dearth of caselaw – relatively :tle legal recognition or weight is given to them. Only in New Zealand ɔ such customs attract positive government encouragement, to the point here they are incorporated into formal national ceremonies and general ɹblic life. Increasingly, by making room for the inclusion of Māori cus- ·m in expressions of national corporate identity, the government in New ɛaland is carving out a precedent that will prove challenging for other risdictions.

Apparel

hoosing to wear clothing or accessories as a manifestation of religion · belief does not usually give rise to legal problems in the jurisdictions ɔnsidered, unless there are health and safety considerations or infringe- ɘnts of the rights of others. Where issues arise, they are often to do with hether the apparel is in fact representative of the associated beliefs. In ιgland and Wales, that question is resolved in the affirmative on the basis

of the subjective understanding of the person concerned. A general excep
tion is the wearing of a burqa, niqab or any face covering when giving evi
dence in court. A particular exception is the wearing of religion-specifi
apparel by teachers in US classrooms, which is forbidden on the basis o
the overriding separation of Church and State rule that requires govern
ment institutions to maintain religious neutrality, and also because of th
weight given to the principle that children are susceptible to the prose
lytising effect of authority figures representing a specific religion.

Family-Related Issues

Cultural assumptions are perhaps most evident in relation to family law
Very often, the issues that surface are ones of religious discrimination
by proxy, which vary in interpretation and in the heat generated accord
ing to their religious/cultural context. This, of course, is hardly surpris
ing in jurisdictions weighed down by their shared Christian heritage, in
which family law in particular has been governed for centuries by reli
gious principles counterpointed by concepts of "sin": lineage was depen
dent upon the legitimate status of the traditional marital family unit (het
erosexual, monogamous spouses for life, together with the children o
their marriage), with the corollary that all other forms of union and their
progeny were illegitimate. All the jurisdictions studied, except Ireland
which remains bound by its singular constitutional constraints, have since
adjusted their legal definition of "family" from the traditional model to
one which depends simply on whether or not the members of a house
hold are linked – as a matter of fact, rather than legal status – by close
familial ties.

Sexuality

If anything, issues arising at the intersection of sexual orientation and reli
gious belief are now more numerous and varied than ever.

In all the jurisdictions studied, excepting some states in the USA, th
legislation necessary to redefine marriage has been introduced, primar
ily to accommodate same-sex couples. Gay marriage, needless to say, i
anathema to those of traditional Christian or Islamic beliefs. For Muslim
citizens, the contemporary cultural context presents particular challenges
The Islamic concept of marriage and family life, if pursued in literal com
pliance with qur'anic guidance, can in many important respects be non
human rights-compliant: for example, as regards the prescriptive rule
governing the role of women and the duties of a wife. "Honour beatings

and other punishments can be fairly interpreted as religious discrimination by proxy, i.e. they are distorted projections of religious values; absent the religious factor and they would probably not be perpetrated.

Conception, Abortion, IVF and Related Issues

Parenting – and becoming a parent, or not – has grown more complicated in recent years. Consequently, it is increasingly challenging for those whose traditional religious beliefs conflate with sex, sexual orientation and reproduction. While this linkage can give rise to similar jurisdictional issues – in relation, for example, to contraceptives, abortion, IVF, surrogacy and transgender matters – it is nowhere more problematic than in Ireland. The long-running pro-life and pro-choice confrontation in the USA, echoed in Canada and Australia, and to a lesser extent in other jurisdictions, functions in part as a cornerstone of the culture wars.

An emerging variant in this minefield of sex, religion and reproduction is mitochondrial replacement therapy (three-person IVF), a technology with potential to edit out degenerative genetic conditions. This would seem to have triggered controversy regarding the possibility that it could be a slippery slope leading to "designer babies". To a considerable extent, the associated eugenic arguments play out along the lines of traditional religious beliefs versus secularism and would seem to be obstructing the introduction in the USA of the facilitating legislation now available in some European countries – even though formal EU approval has yet to be granted.

Assisted Suicide

Opinions on this extremely contentious moral issue tend to divide for or against in accordance with the absence or presence of religious belief, respectively.

While Canada and some states in the USA have legislated to legalise medically assisted death in certain circumstances, Australia, New Zealand, Ireland and England and Wales have not done so. As regards the latter two jurisdictions, it will be interesting to see how long they can continue to take that position in the light of the recent ECtHR ruling[5] which must be regarded as recognising a positive legal *right* to commit suicide. However, as with abortion in Ireland, it is one thing to have a right established in law but quite another to have public-service processes that provide the assistance necessary to give effect to it.

---

[5] *Haas v. Switzerland*, op. cit., at para. 51.

Employment-Related Issues

Employment is hugely important for individuals and for society. Accordingly, religious discrimination by employers in relation to their employees is prohibited. They are obliged to make every effort to accommodate an employee's religion or beliefs.

Hiring/Firing Staff

Religious Organisations   All jurisdictions provide legislative exemptions to equality and anti-discrimination laws, permitting religious organisations to discriminate when hiring and firing staff on the basis of religion, but this right is restricted: it is generally not available if the organisation is contracted to provide public services; it is usually confined to staff engaged in core religious functions (although less so in the USA), rather than in a peripheral role; and it does not permit a "closed-shop" employment policy. The right extends to include exemptions to statutory prohibitions on discriminating on the basis of gender, sexuality and sexual orientation. The clash between the principles embodied in the equality and non-discrimination legislation and those represented by the religious exemption is likely to become an interesting social policy issue in the years ahead: partly because taxpayers, whether secularists or not, may well protest that they are in effect subsidising the inequality perpetrated by tax-exempt religious organisations; but also because many members of such organisations will want the same equality of opportunity as that availed of by ordinary citizens – some ministers, for example, may wish to officiate at gay marriage ceremonies, etc.

A frequent and hotly contested aspect of the exemption privilege, common to all jurisdictions, is the firing of staff when their conduct is judged to have breached the ethos of the employing religious organisation. Particularly in a religious school, the tension between the employer's traditional beliefs and the contemporary lifestyle of staff can result in a direct clash. In Ireland, where large parts of the education sector are owned, staffed and otherwise permeated by religious organisations, such clashes are now an occupational hazard, particularly for female staff.

Secular Organisations   Employment law is generally centred around ensuring fairness in the terms and conditions set by employers, the functionality of the workplace and the rights and duties of individual workers. It also, however, makes room for religion. For example, staff selection on the basis of criteria that include an applicant's religious belief does not constitute religious discrimination if that belief is necessary – a genuine occupational requirement – to fulfill the inherent duties of the post.

A common jurisdictional issue occurs when a public-service employee is sacked for refusing, on the grounds of personal religious belief, to perform a task that is essential to their terms of employment. Such cases serve to illustrate the greater weighting given to direct rather than indirect discrimination: an employer may have indirectly discriminated against a plaintiff by requiring the latter to perform duties that offended their religious beliefs; but this is outweighed by the fact that the refusal would have constituted direct discrimination against those entitled to services.

The *Burwell* v. *Hobby Lobby*[6] ruling deserves special mention because it clearly has implications for the very many employees of commercial companies in the USA that are not religious organisations but are owned by those whose religious beliefs will now allow them to claim the same exemptions when it comes to religiously discriminating practice in the hiring and firing of staff and the imposition of other constraints considered necessary to protect the owners' beliefs. Should the *ratio decidendi* be followed by the judiciary in other jurisdictions, the impact upon the role of religion in the employer/employee relationship will be transformative.

Accommodating Religious Beliefs in the Workplace

The law, which has always required a certain amount of give and take between employer and employee, has in recent years, and in all jurisdictions, generally coalesced around the principle that accommodation should be made where to do so is reasonable and proportionate. This duty to accommodate has been held to include: wearing religion-specific clothing, subject to health and safety requirements; provision of prayer breaks and prayer rooms; being excused from work on religiously significant days; and not being required to do tasks perceived as being in breach of one's religious beliefs. Failure to make appropriate arrangements to accommodate any such request, without adequate reason, could result in an employer being accused of religious discrimination. In effect, the test applied is whether "reasonable adjustments" can be made, subject always to the terms and conditions of employment, to any detrimental effect on others and to the requirements of an efficient workplace. In the USA and Canada, the law specifically employs an "undue hardship" test to establish whether an employer could have made the necessary accommodation

---

[6] Op. cit.

without incurring a disproportionate cost or disruption to policies and practice in the workplace.

One such example of disruption occurs when an employee embarks on proselytising activities. If this occurs in circumstances of a power relationship, where the proselytiser has undue influence over those whom they they are seeking to persuade, then it becomes an illegitimate exercise of authority, which may also constitute religious discrimination. In most situations, and in all jurisdictions, the rights and freedoms of others are held to include the right to protection from such proselytising.

Education-Related Issues

Education and religion have a particularly fraught relationship: because of their crucial role in the trans-generational transference of cultural values, schools and their approach to religious matters are hotspots of contention. While history reveals a record of abuse in Australia and North America, perpetrated against Indigenous children compulsorily removed to residential schools established by religious orders, the lack of any modern caselaw relating to the rights of Indigenous children is noticeable. In Ireland, residential schools run by religious orders were also the setting for historical child abuse.

All national education systems studied involved a mix of public and private provision, the latter containing a varying proportion of schools and colleges provided by religious organisations, by far the majority of which were Christian. Nonetheless, public education in the developed common law nations is generally held to be secular – at least in primary schools – unless clearly registered and regulated as provided under the auspices of a specific religion. Heated debate over alleged government complicity in religious discrimination regarding the funding and accessing of education facilities controlled by religious organisations is common to all.

Government Funding, Religious Education and Faith Schools

The role of religious organisations in the school systems of these jurisdictions is problematic: State funding for denominationally controlled education is a shared, if varying, characteristic; and the facilities concerned are privileged in their exemption from equality and anti-discrimination law in appointing staff and in their capacity to filter pupil intake and educational material in order to preserve their religious ethos. These facilities, being entitled to charitable status, also benefit from tax exemptions giving rise to the argument that such practice constitutes State-subsidised discrimination against present and prospective pupils on the grounds of their parents' religious affiliation.

The issue presents in its starkest form in Ireland, where the government-funded education system is very largely controlled by the Catholic Church, and the growing non-Catholic proportion of the population experiences difficulty in accessing "mixed" or non-denominational education. In England and Wales, a not dissimilar set of circumstances – although on a much reduced scale – applies in relation to the education provision of the "established" Church. The Canadian education system is constitutionally compromised by "denominational privileges" ensuring continued government funding of Catholic schools in the provinces of Ontario, Alberta and Saskatchewan. In the USA, judicial scrutiny of government funding and support for schools to ensure that such arrangements accord with the constitutional requirement for matters of Church and State to be separated has a long and complex history; it seems reasonably clear that such State aid is not prohibited but cannot be used in support of any religious beliefs. The Australian approach currently permits State funding of school provision by religious organisations, on a differential basis at government discretion, provided this falls short of "establishing" a religion. In New Zealand, by far the majority of all denominational schools are incorporated within the government-funded public school system and are required to teach the national curriculum, employ State-registered teachers and facilitate access by pupils of other religions or none, but are entitled to preserve their religious ethos.

State-funded faith schools, a prominent characteristic in the landscape of educational facilities in all jurisdictions, are currently increasing in number and range – although most are Christian – and are usually accommodated within the national public school system. They are allowed to impose discriminatory restrictions on staff employment, admissions, curriculum content and on school worship. They represent, as intended, a separating out of particular religious groupings from all others and from secularists; those so distanced may perceive this as being discriminated against on religious grounds.

Religious Discrimination, Educational Facilities and Content

What, if anything, should be taught about religion in the public education system, particularly in primary schools, is an issue that generates much controversy in all jurisdictions. Leaving aside the transparent approach of faith schools, which select staff and pupils on a religious basis and ensure that educational content reflects their particular religious ethos,

the differing jurisdictional arrangements in public schools seem to be a
follows.

In England and Wales, the official position is that: daily prayer o
religious worship is compulsory; religion is taught and lessons reflec
the dominant Christian culture, although other religions are taken int
account; and there is a parental right to request that one's child be excuse
such lessons. Irish schools require that priority be given to religiou
instruction, rather than religious education, and in practice this mean
teaching the doctrines of Catholicism; the parental right to "opt out" one
children from such teaching is not at present administratively feasible
The principle of separating Church and State in the USA results in car
being taken to ensure that while religion is taught, it is done so impar
tially, with arrangements for religious teaching – as opposed to teachin
about religion – offered outside school hours; children can be "opted out
at parental discretion. The position is similar in Canada, where the State
neutrality principle is employed to permit teaching that reflects both reli
gious and secularist morality, except where this conflicts with the consti
tutional protection available to Catholic schools in places like Quebec. I
Australia and New Zealand, religious instruction is a permitted in-clas
activity: teaching material is tailored by relevant religious organisation
and has been criticised for its evangelical Christian leanings; opportunitie
for pupil opt-out are provided.

Necessarily, educating schoolchildren involves exposing them to a mi
of philosophy, religion and beliefs. The incorporation of humanist, cre
ationist or secular material in classroom teaching is often an area of con
tention, but is generally held to be defensible if delivered in an impartia
non-polemical manner.

The issue of balancing principles of equality and non-discriminatio
against the right of education facilities to erect a religious threshold t
determine access and to tailor educational content in alignment with
specific set of religious values is, again, one which attracts dissensior
The approach taken to access in England and Wales is one of goverr
ment tying funding to the capping of pupil admissions and of the judi
ciary holding that it amounts to religious discrimination for faith schoo
to refuse admission, without good reason, to pupils of another faith or c
none. Accessing the Irish educational system – whether as pupil, teacher c
trainee teacher – for those whose beliefs, or the lack of such, do not matc
those of the relevant religious organisation is far from straightforward, an
it is probable that religious discrimination is routinely practised by man
Catholic schools in relation to pupil intake. In the USA, the right not to b

exposed to unwanted religious beliefs, or the constraints emanating from them, is well established, and applies not just to the school system but to third-level education as well: barring access to a university – or the use of its buildings – on religious grounds is construed as religious discrimination. In Canada, leaving aside the previously noted constitutional protection available to Catholic schools in certain provinces, the long-running series of Trinity Western cases[7] testifies to the difficulties presented by the use of a religious threshold test as a determinant of access to a programme of accredited education. It would seem that where such a restriction is deemed not to be disproportionate and does not unduly infringe the rights of others then the right to freedom of religion, as entrenched in the Charter, will protect an educational facility that chooses to erect such a threshold in order to protect its particular religious beliefs. A significant part of the Australian and New Zealand education systems consists of religion-specific facilities, which retain the right to restrict access on the basis of religious beliefs, and this is underpinned, at least in Australia, by a judicial ruling[8] that there is no such thing as a right to secular education.

Medicine-Related Issues

The pace of development in medicine has profoundly impacted the realm of matters traditionally governed by religious belief. The law in all jurisdictions has had some difficulty in keeping up, perhaps particularly in the area of gene manipulation.

Medical Intervention and Religious Beliefs

Because many medical developments intersect boundaries traditionally set by morality and religious belief, they can feed into and disrupt matters previously accepted as governed by religious principles, such as procreation and suicide. They can attract a form of religious discrimination, as attested to by the sometimes lethal attacks on abortion clinics and by other proxy religious confrontations that contribute to the culture wars.

For those of traditional religious beliefs, there are serious issues in inviting medical intervention to assist or terminate parenting options: contraception, elective abortion, IVF and surrogacy are among the main procedures which fundamentalist Christians, Muslims and others consider to be incompatible with their beliefs. Similarly, at the other end of life,

---

[7] See *Trinity Western University* v. *Law Society of British Columbia*, 2016 BCCA 423.
[8] *Williams* v. *the Commonwealth of Australia* [2012] HCA 23.

assisted suicide is equally problematic on the same grounds for the same religious groups. These issues result in religiously prohibited intervention affecting those hospitals, health centres and residential homes owned by religious organisations and those medical staff whose beliefs conflict with their employers' service-provision requirements. As might be expected, this gives rise to the greatest contention in jurisdictions – such as Ireland and the USA – where traditional religious beliefs are most prominent, and where secularists have correspondingly more opportunities to feel they are being discriminated against.

Parental attempts to deprive their sick children of medical intervention on religious grounds have been challenged in the courts of all jurisdictions for many decades. The rationale for blocking access to life-saving treatment on behalf of those not in a position to make informed decisions would seem to be an inverted form of religious discrimination.

Genetic Engineering and Patents, etc.

The legitimacy of medical intervention and research into the "stuff of life" is often challenged. Any species adjustment, however slight, and whether in respect of plants, humans or other animals, even if wholly ameliorative runs up against religious beliefs – particularly evident in the creationism school of Christianity – that matters are as God intended; to some, evolution can also be theistically attributed. For Islam, the genetic integrity of the bloodline is important, and interference with it is to be resisted.

The science of eugenics has a troubled history, mainly due to its association with the Nazis and their particularly evil discriminatory practices. Its contemporary application in relation to improving the characteristics of farm animals and crops and combating disease, through selection and controlled reproduction processes, is a good deal more positive. Genetic modification, or the process of altering the DNA in an organism's genome, which has significantly improved crop quality and yields, has generated controversy in England and Wales since at least the turn of the century, partly due to concerns regarding the possible long-term implications of genetic mutations for the food chain. However, it is genetic editing that is now firmly on the horizon as a matter of pressing ethical controversy. This technique has seen cross-species experimentation, whereby human organs are grown in animals, such as pigs, for transplant to human recipients, with accompanying protest from those who predict irreversible "species blurring". It has recently attracted media interest in England and Wales, and elsewhere, in relation to the mixing of genetic material to create "three-parent" babies. This innovation has generated considerable alarm

nong religious groups, such as Muslims and evangelical Christians, but
so more generally, as fear takes hold that medicine might perhaps be at
ae beginnings of a slippery slope that leads to a eugenic programme for
liting out "undesirable" aspects of human genes in order to improve the
pecies.

Patenting which threatens to contravene any "laws of nature", encroach
o an uncertain degree) upon natural phenomenon or lock up in private
wnership processes which have hitherto been accepted as available to
everyone is generally legally prohibited. In that context, the use of hES
alls in research or the patenting of inventions which have relied upon
ach research has proven controversial.

Service-Provision Issues

Although the services sector is extensive, including both government-
nded public-benefit provision and commercial outlets, it has not gen-
ated a significant volume or range of caselaw.

Service Provision by Religious Organisations

all jurisdictions considered in Part III, service provision by religious
rganisations provided the setting for sustained child abuse. As perpe-
ated within religious residential facilities, and more generally by clergy,
e historical abuse stands as a warning of the harm that can ensue from
aving unregulated the service provision of organisations legally pre-
med to be for the public benefit.

Religious organisations are increasingly contracted by government to
liver services in education, housing and health and social care. While
ey are universally entitled to exemption privileges from equality and
n-discrimination law, they are not permitted to disadvantage service
ers on religious grounds when acting on behalf of government. The
nsion between religious belief and public service has been evident in
e jurisdictional difficulties relating to the provision of services such as
loption and residential care.

Provision of Public Services

rvice provision by government bodies, or by those contracted to provide
their behalf, is legally required to be non-discriminatory on the basis
a recipient's religion, belief or lack of same. In many jurisdictions, the
ues brought before court or regulator have involved a conflation of sex-
lity, or sexual orientation, with religious beliefs: the services in question

tending to be adoption, officiation at gay marriages and family planning refusal of service, usually by the provider, but occasionally by the prospective recipient, is then on the grounds of religious belief/sexual orientation The outcome of alleged discrimination proceedings brought by a public official, following their sacking after declining to perform a key aspect of their duties on religious grounds, is invariably a decision upholding the sacking on finding that the official was the one who had been guilty of religious discrimination.

Private Goods and Services Provision

Sexual-orientation issues – often religious discrimination by proxy – are prone to arise in a service-provision context. They tend to involve bed and breakfast accommodation and other small family businesses, and to conclude with a ruling that to refuse to provide a service open to all on the basis of the sexual orientation of the customer is discriminatory.

Broadcasting Services

The vexed issue of how to balance the right of freedom of expression with the right not to suffer religious discrimination often arises in the context of conduct, by a person or organisation, intended to manifest particular religious beliefs. This occurs not infrequently in the form of a broadcast of a proselytising nature on radio or television, and generally the courts lean in favour of supporting the freedom of speech; although, as in Ireland, much depends on the prevailing socio-political sensitivities.

Conclusion

While all jurisdictions have retained much the same infrastructure template inherited from their shared colonial experience, with characteristic institutions similarly imbued with a Christian ethos, each has developed its own particular stance towards religion and religious discrimination. All, however, are also struggling to cope with the increasing range of entities that may now qualify as a "religion" or "belief". As that status brings with it an entitlement to certain exemptions, including from statutory equality and non-discrimination provisions, the secularist challenge as to why society should subsidise the inequitable and tax-exempt activities of some of its citizens is getting louder.

The broadening legal interpretations, together with a steady growth in secularism, have also increased the range of circumstances in which religious manifestation may be constrained by the rights of others. In order to ensure a level playing field between those with and those without religious beliefs, and to protect the former from exposure to religious discrimination, the State has generally moved towards adopting a stance of neutrality in its public policy towards religion, belief and secularism. This strongly suggested a multi-culturalist approach as the preferred means for fostering civil society. However, from 2015/16, in response to the combined pressures of the migrant crisis and ISIS, governments in the jurisdictions being considered have generally reviewed their reliance upon multi-culturalism and now instead look more towards pluralism, with a leaning towards nationalism and an emphasis on strengthening borders while reviving and protecting their cultural heritages.

12

Contexting Religion, Culture and Discrimination

Introduction

Culture wars and religious discrimination are joined at the hip. While both are far removed from ideological fundamentalism, as currently represented by the fanaticism of ISIS and formerly by not dissimilar elements in our twentieth-century legacy, they do share a disquieting amount of common ground, and as they have a propensity to play off each other the linkage should not be ignored. These links would seem to be about what are viewed as "moral imperatives": how they are manifested and the response to them.

This concluding chapter takes into account Part III material as it reflects on the likely implications of thematic trends for religious discrimination in a common law cultural context. Beginning with the impact of equality and other human rights provisions, it then considers the relative merits of multi-culturalism and pluralism, before providing a review of the culture wars and their significance and concluding with a final consideration of fundamentalism and its significance for the future.

Equality, Fundamental Human Rights and Religion

As Van Bueren explains: "it is the universality of human rights, as fundamental to our sense of being human, which distinguishes human rights law from other areas of law".[1] Indeed, to many it may seem that by establishing transcendent norms this growing body of rights has become so fundamentally important that it is rapidly attaining the status of a new religion. Having eaten into the space formerly reserved for religious beliefs a new global superstructure of moral verities is being built and progressively refined while Western society stoically views the displacement of

---

[1] See *The Human Dignity Trust* v. *Charity Commission for England and Wales* [2014] UKFTT 2013/0013/B (GRC), at para. 94.

institutional religion as inevitable, a consequence of its tarnished public role being slowly rebranded as private piety. The ascendant trajectory of human rights, aided by the irreversible insights of modern science and an increasingly assertive secularist lobby, is bringing into sharper focus areas of potential rights conflict. For present purposes, this is most apparent as regards the intersection of freedom of religion with rights of equality, speech and association; rights which may be exercised by the religious, by those of other beliefs and by those of none, provided they remain within the law. The Part III jurisdictional study suggests that their exercise, and the interplay between them, is likely to become increasingly important but also increasingly problematic in the years ahead.

Human Rights and Religion

The overall integrative effect of human rights legislation is offset by a tendency for a rights-driven approach to fragment social cohesion. This supra-national source of authority is not without its problems for nation states.

Freedom of Religion

The reach of this fundamental right (see Chapter 4) has broadened greatly, or alarmingly, since its inception. The extension from protecting a pillar of society – represented by traditional institutional religions and their respective congregations – to an attenuated refinement that embraces the protection of beliefs, as subjectively interpreted, threatens to overwhelm its function as initially conceived. By way of contrast, the murderous attacks by ISIS, purportedly in the name of religion, would seem to represent a regression to mediaeval times. They have triggered overt security measures in all the jurisdictions being considered, which, aside from anything else, impose constraints upon their citizens' freedom of religion; some synagogues, for example, now have an armed police presence.

The Part III caselaw graphically illustrates the scope of current legal difficulties. There are the obvious problems of definition, boundaries and relativism. Among the most challenging of these is how to reconcile traditional religious beliefs and doctrines with contemporary values and social mores. In that respect, the indications of a judicial willingness to interpret the former in accordance with the latter – marriage, for example, as being not necessarily exclusively hetrosexual[2] – provides an answer of sorts, but

---

[2] *OV & OW* v. *Members of the Board of the Wesley Mission Council* [2010] NSWCA 155.

sets a precedent that is problematic for those who wish to abide by traditional religious doctrine. Difficulties also accompany the judicial weight now placed upon determining the veracity of a belief. When this is sincerely held, however interpreted and however transient, and if it can be confirmed as "authentic", then the automatic entitlement of any such religion or belief to the privileges and protections that traditionally accompany such status will undoubtedly attract secularist protest. There are also problems in relation to apostasy: this being prohibited by some religions, notably Islam. The tension between apostacy and the freedom of religion is likely to prove challenging for the law in all Part III jurisdictions, given that such a high proportion of religious adherents now exercise their right to change religion.

Freedom of religion is of particular importance when it permits a person or organisation to do something otherwise prohibited – most obviously, in the exemption provisions that allow religious organisations to hire, fire and filter service access in circumstances not permitted to others – or when it provides the grounds for individuals to claim conscientious objection to serving in the armed forces or to undertaking official duties (e.g. medical staff and abortion procedures). However, there is uncertainty as to the required proximity – between organisational function and the religious doctrine – to qualify for an entitlement to exemption.[3] Problems also exist where laws of uniform application unduly burden those of religious beliefs (e.g. Sikhs and motorbike crash helmets). Problematic, too, is the extent to which an adherent may freely choose the means of manifesting their religion – some need to do so by wearing a symbol of their personal belief (a kirpan, crucifix or burqa) in public – whether or not this is a requirement of their religion and regardless of whether any fellow adherent considers this to be necessary; consistency in applying the law in relation to matters which turn on a subjective interpretation is notoriously difficult. Then, there is the difficulty of religion-specific facilities: the freedom of religion includes a parental right to ensure that one's child is taught in accordance with the parent's religion: a right which justifies faith schools, but which must be balanced against a right to be free from proselytism and indoctrination. Most challenging is the situation where there is a clash between theological norms or religious practice and domestic law. There are clear instances where Shari'a and Jewish law – mostly in relation to marriage, divorce and other family matters – are sharply at variance with national legislation, which gives rise to

---

[3] *Greater Glasgow Health Board v. Doogan & Anor* [2014] UKSC 68.

uestions regarding whether the freedom of religion necessitates treating
ll beliefs as equally valid and equally deserving of respect under national
w. An ancillary but fundamental issue concerns the judicial right to
robe theological matters in order to be in a position to adjudicate on
ιe bearing of religious freedom upon a manifestation of belief: exploring
hether or not the beliefs have been correctly interpreted or whether the
ιanifestation is appropriate.

The corollary to this freedom is that it also establishes a right to be free
om religion: a right not to have to risk being placed in a position which
ιight permit religious discrimination. This is best safeguarded constitu-
onally by provisions separating Church and State, and least well by pro-
ιsions that permit an "established" religion or that single out one as incor-
orating the values and ethos that should guide government and citizen.
would include a right not to participate in Christian prayers at the open-
ιg of meetings on State premises, to join in religious celebrations, to swear
ι oath of office, etc. It extends to a right not to participate in classroom-
ιsed religious instruction, and for that opt-out to be managed in a non-
igmatising manner.

Equality

ιat all citizens are held to be free and equal before the law is a cen-
al principle of the liberal democracy that characterises the common law
ιrisdictions considered in this book. Arguably, however, equality law,
ith its levelling and reductionist effect, has turned the morality focus
f contemporary social policy away from the traditional big public issues
ιch as poverty, disease and the depletion of natural resources, not just
ιwards an increased recognition of the rights of minorities, but espe-
ally towards competing private entitlements in developed Western soci-
ies (see later). There is a concern that such a rights-orientated approach,
ιgether with the objective rationalising of the new morality, threatens to
istract from the need to address entrenched global issues and to dilute or
ιdge the significance of cultural heritage, in which religion is so intri-
ιtely entwined. The distraction may include an inability to appreciate
ιe dark side of social inequality (particularly its persistence in non-
ιmocratic countries), a blindness to the depth and extent of estrange-
ιent that lies behind the current confrontation with ISIS and a reluc-
ince to accept the motivating factors that push so many migrants towards
Iestern society.

The common law jurisdictions currently being considered have all put
ι place much the same legislative platform to ensure the provision of

equal opportunities for citizens regardless of factors such as gender, age, disability, race, religion or belief, sexual orientation, equal pay and fair employment, etc. They have also enacted affirmative-action provisions which are problematic in that they do not sit easily alongside equality prin ciples: targeted resources or quota systems unavoidably preference one group at the expense of all others, triggering consequent protests of stig matising and discrimination. In any event, the existence of such a platform requires more than proofing general social legislation against such prin ciples. If minority groups (which have suffered many generations of pro found disadvantage), immigrant ethnic groups and small newly formed faith groups are to achieve parity of opportunity with the traditional institutional religious organisations then proactive State intervention will be needed. There is also a need for analysis to establish whether prox motives are in play that disguise inequality in the treatment of others.

The hierarchically structured Christian religions, emulating their host societies, currently seem more inclined to add to the social fragmentation through schisms than to model equality in their organisations. Equality in matters of gender and sexual orientation, as well as in matters of employ ment and service access, is proving to be seriously problematic for reli gious organisations. This, together with the proliferation of new religions faiths and forms of belief – all being entitled to equality of treatment with the traditional religions – suggests that equality in a domestic religious context may need a more nuanced approach from the State. Arguably, veto by religious entities on matters of equality that are binding on the rest of society must somehow be conditional upon this being demonstrably compliant with the best interests of that society; particularly if tax exemp tion and/or government funding are involved. It also suggests that a strat egy may be needed to provide new forms of intervention in an internal tional context if Western society is to avoid the consequences of inequality elsewhere.

Freedom of Speech

The twenty-first century has, so far, seen no more poignant challenge to the importance of free speech for democracy in Western society than the cruel attack perpetrated by Saïd and Chérif Kouachi on the staff of the *Charlie Hebdo* magazine in Paris.[4] Freedom of the press, an aspect of free dom of speech, is clearly a fundamental hallmark of any democratic State

---

[4] On 7 January 2015, two Islamic gunmen attacked the Paris office of the satirical magazine *Charlie Hebdo*, killing eight staff and others.

and deserves State protection. It must be exercised openly and transparently – subject to the customary constraints of honesty, fair comment and defamation. Among other things, the emotional impact of the Islamist attack brought home the difficulties involved in balancing free speech with the respect due to religious sensitivities in the culturally diverse, highly expressive and potentially volatile Western societies.[5] Some of these difficulties are also very apparent in the common law jurisdictions, as evidenced in the Part III caselaw relating to the religion/free speech interface.

One such area, associated with the *Charlie Hebdo* trauma, concerns the right to express opinions including the rejection of religion. While there is no right not to be insulted or offended by such rejection, there is every right not to be vilified or to suffer hatred as a consequence of the manner in which it is expressed. The law relating to profanity, sacrilege and blasphemy may have been largely consigned to history, but intimidation and harassment are still offences. Much depends on the intent of those relying on their right to freedom of speech when they express views antagonistic to those manifesting their religious beliefs. Although all Part III jurisdictions have laws explicitly prohibiting religious hatred, these bring their own difficulties, as citizens complain that they have a general "chilling" effect on legitimate protest and are often used by State authorities in a discriminatory fashion to censor genuine debate and pre-empt protest marches.

Another area of difficulty concerns proselytism. While issues often surface in relation to unwanted evangelising overtures from those who believe their religion requires them to "spread the word", they are likely to arise more frequently in the future as more Muslims seek to exercise their duty to practise *dawa*, which goes well beyond persuasion. Related issues are also evident in the clashes between adherents of traditional religious values and advocates on behalf of matters such as access to abortion services and LGBT rights. Proselytism generates particular contention in an educational context, especially in a primary school setting, but also in other hierarchical contexts such as the professions, where an authoritative role model can exercise undue influence on subordinates.

In practice, the mode of dissemination can be highly significant: publication in a local community newspaper is qualitatively and quantitatively

---

[5] Note the introduction in Ireland in 2009, firmly against the trend in other common law jurisdictions, of a law prohibiting blasphemy in relation to any religion. An initiative which had seemed decidedly anachronistic at the time may now, following the *Charlie Hebdo* massacre, deserve reassessment.

different from publication through global media, where the probability of reaching and offending someone is much greater. As with so much else, broadcasting information via the Internet speeds up dissemination, and with it the likelihood of precipitating a conflict of views on a real-time basis; the lack of regulatory intervention leaves a heavy onus on those transmitting potentially inflammatory material to exercise responsible self-censorship or be accountable for the consequences.

Freedom of expression – the right to advocate and dissent – is crucial to the citizen's relationship with government, underpinning rights of assembly and association and providing a foundation for all forms of political activity; any interference with it requires a high level of justification. There can be no absolutes in relation to either the "freedom" or the "rights" involved. While there is much to be said for the view concisely expressed by Walker LJ that "in matters of human rights the court should not show liberal tolerance only to tolerant liberals",[6] this is subject to limits; thresholds of tolerance vary according to context. Gratuitously offensive expressions of antagonism towards religion or the religious – whether by satire or other means – may be within the bounds of the law, but they give rise to the suspicion that those responsible are possibly as blinkered, stereotyped and doctrinaire in their views as those being antagonised.

Freedom of Association

The ability of citizens to form a legal entity in order to act collectively in a field of mutual interest has judicially been declared to be "one of the most important aspects of the right to freedom of association, without which that right would be deprived of any meaning".[7] It constitutes a hallmark of democracy,[8] and has been recognised as such by the legislatures of democratic states for centuries, and now the constitutions of most countries contain articles protecting the freedoms of association and assembly.[9] As the Part III caselaw illustrates, this right is increasingly availed of by those

---

[6] R (*Williamson & Ors*) v. *Secretary of State for Education and Employment & Ors* [2005] UKHL 15, per Lord Walker of *Gestingthorpe* at para. 57.

[7] *Sidiropoulos and Others* v. *Greece* (26695/95) 27 EHRR (1998), at para. 40.

[8] The ICCPR and UDHR both guarantee freedom of association internationally, as do the Helsinki Accords of the Organisation (former Conference) on Security and Cooperation in Europe (OSCE). See also the Freedom of Association and Protection of the Right to Organise Convention, 1948 (No. 87) and the Right to Organise and Collective Bargaining Convention 1949 (No. 98).

[9] See, for example, Canada, and the Canadian Charter of Rights and Freedoms, where the freedom of association has become an entrenched right; see also the First Amendment to the US Constitution.

eeking recognition for groups upholding newly formulated religions or
beliefs, or whose links to a long-established one have been severed by theological schism. As the number and variety of organisations claiming religious status has multiplied, so has the freedom of association grown in
significance – but not without indications of complexities that are likely
to prove challenging.

While it is beyond question that associations are vested with legal rights
and can acquire corporate status, the rights of a religious association may
at times conflict with equality rights. Such an association, in the jurisdictions being considered, is entitled to be established in order to further
whatever set of beliefs it espouses, within the law: to determine its place
of worship and the type and frequency of ceremonies; and to choose its
own organisational structure and staff itself in accordance with equality
exemption privileges. However, as already noted, in order to avail itself
of these privileges, it must first prove the veracity, authenticity and sincerity with which its beliefs are held if it is to legally qualify for religious
status. The ephemeral nature of some beliefs means that not all associations will be able to do so. For those that do qualify, there is the further
hurdle of demonstrating that hiring and firing decisions are either compatible with equality provisions or may be exempted from them; in the
latter case, this will require evidence that the duties of a post are contiguous with the association's core beliefs or necessary to preserve its religious ethos. Further, those so qualifying and deciding to set up a commercial outlet will want to avail themselves of the religious tax-exemption
privileges, but these are also, usually, contingent upon the strict rules
governing charity and profits.[10] The jurisdictional caselaw reveals considerable inconsistency in this area, and as service delivery emanations
founded by religious organisations continue to proliferate, so also will the
uncertainties.

The freedom to associate is accompanied by a right to dis-associate: by
definition, a group is entitled to exclude those it perceives as not sharing its rationale for associating – the terms of reference for affiliating
being intended to affirm common interests and to be exclusionary of others. When such a conflict is transparent, as when applicants encounter
the argument that their membership would breach an association's core
terms of reference – e.g. on the basis of it being established specifically for stamp-collectors, etc. – it is amenable to reasonably straightforward legal resolution. When an applicant encounters resistance based

---

[10] Rules now challenged by the decision in *Burwell* v. *Hobby Lobby*, op. cit.

upon a characteristic prohibited under equality and non-discrimination legislation – gender, race disability, etc. – then, again, this can be legally and promptly resolved. Likewise, most usually, when a religious organisation relies upon its exemption rights to refuse applicants to key functional roles or posts, this is quick and easy to resolve. Outside those circumstances, resolution is a good deal less straightforward.

Where an association's status as a religious organisation is somewhat uncertain, and it seeks to rely on exemption privileges to refuse membership on grounds prohibited under equality provisions, this can be problematic. The Part III caselaw, particularly relating to the USA, has many examples where organisations which are either not wholly independent (e.g. university associations) or not primarily religious (e.g. Boy Scouts associations) have sought to rely on the religious exemption to reject members of the LGBT community. Uncertainty also surrounds issues where there is possible proxy motivation on the part of the association or applicant.

There is a sense in which the solidarity necessary for civil society has been weakened by the number and sometimes conflicting nature of new associational forms that have sprung up to assert the separate identities of minority groups. The social coherence that initially accompanied a fundamental human rights approach to structural social disadvantage is now endangered by the splintering effect of minority groups (e.g. gay, transsexual, faith-based) asserting their separate rights and distracting from the collective interests of historically disadvantaged communities (e.g. poor, diseased, racially distinct). While both sets of rights are clearly legitimate, the traction more readily achieved in the former would seem to be detracting from a sustained investment of effort in the latter. It is a sad irony that some of the more basic principles underpinning the Human Rights Convention – equality, non-discrimination – which were initially deployed to gain justifiable recognition for and improvements in the circumstances of a profoundly disadvantaged group would now seem to be licensing incremental social fragmentation. To that extent, the freedom of association has a downside and has served to amplify the problems associated with multi-culturalism.

Cultural Context and Religious Discrimination

Religious discrimination in the Part III jurisdictions, as evidenced in the related caselaw, is very much conditioned by the culture imprinted on each through their shared experience as constituent components of the British

Empire. Two particular indicators of how deeply ingrained that is can be seen in the continuing dominance of Christianity, which colours so much of their public life, and the shallowness of concessions made to any other culture – in particular to those of their own Indigenous Peoples, which, with the limited exception of the Māori in New Zealand, have largely been allowed to remain marginalised.

Multi-Culturalism

Pride in difference has become a prominent characteristic of Western society in recent decades, and multi-culturalism has been the policy of choice for managing it. This policy can be seen as a deliberate strategy for moving beyond the pre-World War II nation-state model, each with its signature dominant culture which distanced it from others and fostered mutually alienating nationalism. Dating probably from the 1970s, when Canada proclaimed it as its chosen method for managing its singular patchwork of communities, including a particularly high proportion of first-generation immigrants, multi-culturalism was subsequently adopted by Australia and many European countries, including England and Wales. Until the second decade of the twenty-first century, it was widely extolled as being an equitable means of keeping in balance a nation's cultural heritage alongside that of the others sheltering within its borders.

While it can be said that it is based on cherishing cultural diversity, beyond that the policy of multi-culturalism is open to wide interpretation. Generally, it places a priority on the importance of respecting and preserving cultural identity: all cultures, including that of the host nation, are to be valued and regarded as of equal status; this is reinforced by equality legislation that requires differences in persons or groups to be accommodated and treated equitably within the range of modern social-service facilities; and it is further reinforced by the doctrine of State neutrality, which requires government to take steps to ensure equal treatment for all religions and secularists. This can be challenging in countries – such as the developed common law jurisdictions – which have long been stamped by a dominant culture. In Ireland and England and Wales, perhaps exceptionally among those jurisdictions, multi-culturalism will require considerable effort if it is to prevail over the domestic deeply ingrained and pervasive religious culture. As a corollary, those jurisdictions with an embedded but socially bunkered population of Indigenous People have similarly experienced considerable difficulty in their so far unsuccessful efforts to assist them to achieve parity of status with other mainstream cultures.

In all common law jurisdictions, where society is heavily freighted with the trappings of Christianity, State intervention has been needed: to reduce that presence and engineer proportionality relative to other religious entities; to shrink other areas where old vested interests have become accustomed to a sphere of influence, thereby accommodating new minority groups; and to initiate affirmative action so as to raise the profile of such groups, assert that of Indigenous People and ensure effective representation for their interests. Essentially, multi-culturalism was considered likely to promote a healthy vitality in society – a richness of cultural diversity – where the authentic identity of all cultures would be equally assured of State support. Cultural differentiation would lead towards cultural affirmation rather than to discrimination.

This was a policy well suited to the common law categorisation approach in which proceedings required potential plaintiffs to fit their claim to a recognised cause of action (see further Chapter 1). Both the policy and common law proceedings gave recognition to those persons and groups who affiliated to a designated status: the access route to State resources or legal redress required identification with an already established entity. Both also permitted the creation of new entities – legal cause of action or cultural groups – if justified by analogy and contiguous with those established. The emphasis on categorisation, with its accompanying necessity for differentiation – a "niche partitioning"[11] – has arguably had significant consequences. First, it may be responsible for the present piecemeal approach that has evolved to govern the way the law relates to religious discrimination: a tendency for it to focus on parts rather than the whole, centring on hate speech, vilification or intimidation, on racial or religious aspects of what might be more holistically conceived as a cultural issue. Second, the assumption that cultural heterogeneity, as a principle of liberalism, should be sufficient in itself – that a nation's traditional culture should be treated on a par with all others within its borders – has in practice proved fatal for multi-culturalism.

Multi-Culturalism: The Practice

The assertion of different cultural identities can lead – and has done so in many of the jurisdictions being considered – to a self-imposed

---

[11] An ecological term referring to the ability of different species to co-exist within the same territory by deliberately emphasising a differentiation in their use of resources. See e.g. Griffin, J. N. and Silliman, B. R., "Resource Partitioning and Why it Matters", *Nature Education Knowledge*, 2011, vol. 3:10.

cultural ghettoisation which allows ethnic groups to remain in independent communities that need not make many concessions to wider society. This separateness is often fuelled by benign government intervention that subsidises faith-based schools and facilities, thereby encouraging a social fragmentation in which culturally distinct communities compete for recognition, status and resources. A side effect of subsidies is to reinforce differences: targeted grants induce prospective recipient groups to emphasise their distinctive cultural or ethnic identity in order to gain government recognition; religious groups may have to present themselves as cultural groups, thereby triggering a cycle which becomes self-fulfilling. It also induces new migrant groups to join the list of those already being nurtured in an ongoing State dependency relationship. In the long run, the cumulative effect may well be to fuel competition among minority groups, exacerbate greater awareness of cultural separateness and incentivise the spin-off of splinter entities, each claiming subsidised autonomy. For decades in the UK, Canada and elsewhere, the policy of celebrating cultural differences translated into a corresponding differentiation in housing allocation, welfare benefits and community support initiatives (see further Chapter 5). Targeted State support did more than reinforce separateness: it disabled minority groups from participating in mainstream society.

The prolonged duration of this policy resulted in jurisdictions developing an unforeseen social complexity. They became layered with a mix of quite separate cultures – many with ethnic identities imported intact from their countries of origin, existing alongside minority groups with identities acquired as a consequence of welfare rights labelling (as disabled, elderly, youths, etc.) and in some cases co-existing with Indigenous People, their differences and separateness reinforced by government funding policies. The more such separate identities were reinforced, and the more communal civic space fragmented to accommodate expressions of difference, the less integrated were the citizens and more inchoate was the state of civil society. By facilitating Freud's "narcissism of the small difference",[12] multi-culturalism unwittingly rewarded those who could group themselves into identifiably distinct cultural communities and distance themselves from all others; and by fostering a mutually alienating "us and them" awareness, it helped turn differentiation into discrimination.

The combined impact of ISIS and the migrant crisis brought to a head an awareness that multi-culturalism was failing as a policy for promoting

---

[12] See Freud, *Civilization, Society and Religion*. See also Chapter 1.

an inclusive civil society. The evidence had been accumulating for some time: in parts of urban England – such as Bradford, Leeds, Rotherham and Stoke – ghettoes had formed where ethnic groups sheltered in internal exile not unlike their counterparts in the Parisian *banlieues*; similarly, if more starkly, the Indigenous People of Canada, the USA and Australia had long been left to lead Third World lives in First World countries; all were marginalised citizens, bound by their own distinct ties of religion and race, leading parallel ways of life, each quite separate from the others and from mainstream culture.[13] The shock of domestic attacks by Islamic "home-grown" terrorists on their fellow citizens was exacerbated by the sudden influx of migrants whose natural wish to be resettled in communities established by their fellow countrymen could only reinforce existing social divisions. The scale of the migrant crisis swamped the housing and other national welfare resources of host countries, but proved to be only the first – and among the least – of the ensuing problems. Usually, the necessary mutual readjustments can be managed, migrants absorbed and multi-culturalism facilitated when the numbers, range and flow of ethnic minorities are not excessive. Unfortunately, in the 2015/16 crisis, they were. The declared preference for multi-culturalism, particularly in European societies – which had consolidated their national cultural heritage over many centuries – wilted when confronted by the number and ethnic/religious origins of waves of homeless refugees. Simultaneously, but not coincidentally, the migrant crisis unfolded against the backdrop of the challenge presented by Islamic militants to Western security, morality and lifestyle. The consequence of these twin events was a marked policy shift away from celebrating diversity and cultural difference towards fostering social integration and promoting support for a common national identity. For most of the jurisdictions studied, the politically driven switch from multi-culturalism to pluralism, from State neutrality to State protectionism, was a prominent feature of the 2016/17 populist surge.

Pluralism

Pluralism rests on the assumption that it is for the greater good if as broad a mix of social groups as possible are enabled to interact equally, subject

---

[13] See e.g. the Commission on Integration & Cohesion, 2007 at http://tedcantle.co.uk/publications/018&20interim&20statement&20Commission&20on&20Integration&20an&20Cohesion.pdf.

nly to the presumption that all will respect and show primary loyalty to ne State – its laws, institutions and culture – a caveat that distinguishes it om multi-culturalism (see also Chapter 3).

Pluralism: The Policy

luralism, like multi-culturalism, implies a duty on the State to facilitate nd promote opportunities for minorities, ethnic groups, etc. to partici- ate alongside and engage with the established culture and its related bod- s and interests in the public arena. This entails making room available for ne interests of emerging groups, both structurally and psychologically: roviding a more level playing field and evidence of welcome, and indeed nploying many of the same culturally affirming strategies as in multi- alturalism. However, in so doing, it must also protect the primacy of the ational culture.

The Part III caselaw would seem to indicate that where domestic leg- lation is subject to an overarching authority – a national Constitution nd/or binding international Conventions – in which legal principles pro- ding for the separation of Church and State, prohibiting the establish- g of a religion and guaranteeing its freedom are firmly entrenched, then policy of pluralism is more likely to attract judicial enforcement. This most clearly the case in the USA, where the First Amendment provi- ons are quite explicit in that regard, if somewhat belied by several gener- ions of institutionalised racial discrimination. While the modern "melt- g pot" effect of pluralism in action has been identified as creating a ealthy and vibrant mix of cultures, it must be added that such an out- ome is also due to the comparatively much weaker welfare support sys- m. New migrants, like their fellow citizens, must find employment and ek out everyday resources if they are to survive: relying on State welfare annelled through government agencies is not an option; participation the community is necessary. This is less likely to be the case in Ireland ld England and Wales, which are "constitutionally" compromised in the tent to which they can fully commit to a policy that requires a long- ominant religious ethos to shrink and allows a pluralism of alternative dtures to be positively encouraged.

Pluralism: The Practice

s already noted, a policy aimed at achieving median parity runs into diffi- lties when faced with embedded extremes: the cultures associated with

both Christianity and Indigenous People proved resistant, for opposin
reasons, to government equalising strategies.

Assimilation is the greatest fear for many new immigrants arriving wit
strong religious/ethnic ties: the fear that they, and/or their children, wi
be wholly absorbed into Western culture and lifestyle; that jettisonir
generations of family and community values and practices may be tl
price they have to pay for migration. For immigrants, therefore, plura
ism presents more of a threat than multi-culturalism, particularly whe
the values of an immigrant culture are required to give way to tho:
embodied in the laws of the host nation. The Part III caselaw reflec
such culture clashes when they occur in relation to overt matters such :
religion-specific apparel and customs or religious practices in emplo
ment, education, etc. – but not the culture clashes that occur in relation
more covert family matters, such as misogyny, FGM, "honour beating
divorce and arranged child marriages. To that extent, the premise that th
book could undertake a comparative jurisdictional analysis of the natu
and incidence of contemporary religious discrimination by monitorir
the traffic of related cases was flawed. It could not take into account tl
difficulties that never reached the courts: either because, although stat
torily proscribed (e.g. FGM), they were not pursued due to associat
"cultural sensitivities", or because, being matters associated with the cu
ture wars (peaceful anti-abortion protests), they operate below the stat
tory radar. It could, however, draw attention to the strata of religio
related – if currently non-juridical – areas of contention, the existence
which has been revealed by a generally sharpened awareness of the si
nificance of cultural context triggered by contemporary political even
The book indicates that religion, belief and discrimination can no long
be viewed in simple stereotypical terms. Religious discrimination wou
seem to be a pervasive social phenomenon, overt and sublimated, leth
and benign, that may be borne or imposed by those of religious persu
sion (whether individuals, organisations, communities or nations) a
those of none. Its systemic nature suggests a more coherent and cultu
ally cognisant response is urgently required on many fronts, including tl
juridical.

Pluralism in practice differs from multi-culturalism in that opting
remain in a minority cultural bunker and ignore, as far as possible, tl
constraints of the host culture is less feasible. A pluralism policy sugges
not just the development of language skills, etc. but also that the needs
immigrants – e.g. an abused wife who wants a divorce, a same-sex co
ple that wishes to marry – should be accommodated within the laws a

attitudes that represent the values of the host culture.[14] Practices such as *talaq* divorce, *nikah* marriage and FGM would then be less likely to be overlooked. It would nonetheless remain the case, as judicially noted, that "the role of authorities in such circumstances is not to remove the cause of tension by eliminating pluralism, but to ensure that the competing groups tolerate each other".[15]

Cultural Context, Religion and Policy

The preservation and promotion of cultural identity, an important principle protected by international human rights conventions,[16] must be taken into account in any national policy for managing diversity. Because religion has a significant function in reinforcing the autonomy and integrity of a group's cultural identity, its role needs to be carefully addressed and balanced, with consideration given to the interests of secularists, if any such policy is to avoid accusations of being discriminatorily biased for or against religion.

Identity and Religion

The need to be recognised and acclaimed as possessing an authentic, distinctive and precious identity – most obvious in the current fixation with "celebrity" – is a feature not only of modern lifestyles but also in the context of religion and culture.

The schisms that continue to fragment the traditional and hitherto monolithic institutional religions, the proliferation of new faiths and belief systems and the fact that such a high proportion of the religious now adhere to a religion different from the one they were born into all testify to this being an era of uncertainty and divisiveness in religion. This would seem to be indicative of a need to identify with a more particular set of beliefs: one customised to fit with lifestyle choices and conducive to a loose multi-cultural society. However, it may be that the confrontation provoked by the tyranny of ISIS will motivate greater mutual respect among religious groups and facilitate social cohesion by inducing disparate religious and cultural entities to set aside their differences, adopt pluralism and work together to rebuild a collective sense of national identity: with

See e.g. Laycock, D., Picarello, A. R. and Wilson, F. (eds), *Same Sex Marriage and Religious Liberty: Emerging Conflicts*, Lanham, MD, Rowman & Littlefield, 2008.
Serif v. *Greece*, Application No. 38178/97 (1999), at para. 53.
See The International Covenant on Economic, Social and Cultural Rights.

British Muslims, for example, becoming and being accepted as wholly British.

Culture and Identity

Despite the presence of a considerable population of Indigenous People in four of the six Part III jurisdictions, and despite spiritual beliefs being crucial to their sense of identity, only a very small proportion of the cases concerned their interests, and only a very few of these touched on the significance they attach to the beliefs integral to their cultural identity. The cases generally tend to be peripheral to their interests, often narrowly concentrated on race, negatively affirming and frequently contingent on an alleged infringement of the interests of the wider population (e.g. eagle feathers and other tribal customs in the USA, hunting deer in Canada, tattoos in New Zealand, etc.). For such people, the identity issues are profound: much more so than the caselaw would suggest; there is a shared awareness of a need to reclaim an identity long submerged by the weight, and often the oppression, of a more powerful culture. The suppression of indigenous culture, or the more recent casual indifference to it, has been greatly compounded by the prolonged proselytising of religious organisations, which resulted in perhaps the majority of such populations acquiring an overlying identity of Christian converts. To a lesser extent, other groups, such as black or Asian Americans, feminists, "the disabled" and of course, "the poor", have also had to settle for an imposed identity – socially constructed objectification that reduces a complex identity to one-dimensional characteristic of difference.

When "identity" issues arose in relation to citizens' religiosity more generally (e.g. crucifixes in England, burqas, etc.), they did so in greater volume, but also more substantively (religious exemptions, faith schools etc.). In the multi-culturalist jurisdiction of Canada, where identity issues (long-standing in relation to the First Nations) have threatened – recently if briefly, in the case of the Québécois – to trigger social unrest not dissimilar to that in Northern Ireland, the challenges of working through the conflicts resulting from a loosely constructed national identity resting on a patchwork of distinctly different cultures is very evident in the caselaw.[17] In contrast, the pluralistic approach is prominent in the USA where *Kiryas Joel*[18] reveals the USSC pointedly considering and rejecting a possible resolution of an issue that would have allowed a State initiative

---

[17] See the *Trinity Western* line of cases and *Mouvement laïque québécois v. Saguenay (City)* op. cit.
[18] *Kiryas Joel Village School District v. Grumet*, op. cit.

o align the boundaries of a school district with those of a Jewish community, as to do so would have been to confer a separate religious identity
upon a State administrative region, breaching the principle of State neu-
rality – notwithstanding Scalia J's credible dissenting judgment that such
an alignment would be conferring a cultural rather than a religious iden-
ity and would be in keeping with similar recognition accorded to Native
Americans, the Amish and other minority groups.

Policy, Religion and Discrimination

Any policy of cultural differentiation, amplified by the tax and religious
exemption privileges to which all religious organisations and their service-
delivery emanations are equally entitled, tends to incentivise and reward
those able to disassociate themselves from other such organisations. Further, the principle of State neutrality, by requiring government to stand
aside from the traditional national culture, including its religion, essentially abandons all religions and beliefs to the marketplace. This encourages the use of religion as a "badge of difference", generating competition
and social divisiveness.

Any sense in which religion can be interpreted as facilitating social
cohesion tends to disappear when it manifests itself in a facility perceived
as excluding others. The caselaw reveals that where a facility is wholly secular, but operates a service which offends the beliefs of religious people,
the effect can be divisive for that community (e.g. the presence of an abortion clinic, a registry office offering marriage services for same-sex couples or an adoption agency that will place children with such couples).
Similarly divisive is the presence of a facility which represents beliefs not
shared by the community within which it is located (e.g. a "closed" convent, a mosque, a halal butcher's shop, a faith-based school with compulsory religious/cultural attire requirements, or any one of a number of such
religion-specific facilities). Some such facilities may also be overtly discriminatory, providing services and facilities to which access and employment opportunities are restricted by religion. Does this matter?

Taylor warns against "needlessly limiting the religious freedom of
immigrant minorities, on the strength of our historical institutional
arrangements" as this risks "sending a message to those same minorities
that they by no means enjoy equal status with the long-established mainstream".[19] However, if we accept that religion is culturally contexturalised

See Taylor, C., "Why We Need a Radical Redefinition of Secularism", in Mendieta, E. and
Vanantwerpen, J. (eds), *The Power of Religion in the Public Sphere*, New York, Columbia
University Press, 2011, at p. 48.

then we must face up to its role in the present cultural dissonance between host countries and immigrant communities; needless to say, this can be particularly abrasive in relation to the often more misogynist values of religious immigrants from the Middle East, Afghanistan and north Africa. The current migrant crisis is occurring against a domestic background of increasing religious fundamentalism, which, although most readily associated with Islam, is also very apparent in the many and varied strains of evangelism recently metastasised from Christianity. This unhappy conjunction of religious fundamentalism and large-scale migration is shifting policy in the developed Western nations away from both pluralism and multi-culturalism towards managing social polarisation with a special emphasis on curbing religious discrimination.

The Culture Wars

The culture wars and religious discrimination are indeed joined at the hip, a Christian hip. Probably first recognised as a sociological phenomenon in the USA in the early 1990s,[20] the culture wars were then, and in subsequent debates,[21] rightly seen as a source of growing social and political polarisation. As suggested in Chapter 2, the dividing line in this clash of values can be seen as one of Christian morality that initially focused on issues such as gun control, the death penalty, abortion and homosexuality. While not necessarily a confrontation between Christians and secularists and while the issues were not necessarily religious, this was nevertheless largely the case. However, some change may be underway. The caselaw in Part III provides evidence suggesting that while culture-war issues are proliferating, the traditional aspects of an underpinning Christian morality may be becoming more susceptible to judicial challenge.

Morality and Christianity

Christian principles established the core moral imperatives – dealing with matters such as marriage, sexuality and sin – that came to inform the law relating to the family in the jurisdictions being considered (see further

---

[20] See Hunter, J. D., *Culture Wars: The Struggle to Define America*, New York, Basic Books 1991.

[21] See, for example, Abramowitz, A. I., *The Polarized Public*, London, Pearson Education 2012; Fiorina, M., *Culture War? The Myth of a Polarized America*, 3rd edn, London, Pearson Education, 2010; and Dahl, R. A., *How Democratic is the American Constitution?*, 2nd edn New Haven, CT, Yale University Press, 2001.

Chapter 2). From that central reference point, the imperatives would seem to have been contiguously extended by analogy – to accommodate matters relating more broadly to "life" – in keeping with the ebb and flow of advances in science, the collapse of confidence in social institutions and a retreat into conservative values.

Morality and the Changing Social Role of Religion

While its doctrines remain relatively immutable, the social role of religion at any point in time within a particular country will be shaped by contextural factors, including leadership, local circumstances, the impact of politics and other extraneous events. Studies have shown how religious communities in the USA have adjusted their approach to issues such as abortion, sexual orientation and the genetic modification of crops over a period of years in response to cultural conditioning as these matters gain broad social acceptance. As the law gradually expands to accommodate matters previously left to conscience and religion, removing them from policy debate and possible religious veto, so people of faith and people without conform to the new order. There is a time lag, but the religious and their associated organisations tend to eventually follow the path established by the wider community. As has been said, "culture is more powerful than religion in determining a person's moral code . . . it shapes how Christians define their beliefs . . . religion exists within a society not outside of it".[22]

However, in democratic States, the law, morality and religion will never be neatly in sync. Unlike their theocratic counterparts, the judiciaries in all Part III jurisdictions have to juggle situations: where statute law has declared the rules to be applied in relation to morality/religion (e.g. in employment, education, etc.); where there is a time lag between an emerging moral imperative (e.g. gay marriage, assisted suicide, etc.) and its statutory recognition; and where the law has not intervened (e.g. artificial life, intra-species research, etc.). In the first category, religious discrimination is clearly labelled, and it may also be subliminally present in the other two, but the culture wars engulf all three. This juggling act has to be performed against a background where the institutional role of traditional religions is shrinking, leaving a public space to be filled not just by an increasingly

---

See Smith, M. A., *Secular Faith: How Culture has Trumped Religion in American Politics*, Chicago, IL, University of Chicago Press, 2015, at p. 211, citing Durkheim, E., *The Elementary Forms of Religious Life*, New York, Oxford University Press, 2001 [1912].

robust secularism but also by a fluctuating assortment of belief system and by fundamentalism.

Moral Imperatives, the Culture Wars and Religious Discrimination

There is a sense in which the culture wars pick up where religious discrimination leaves off: the latter is a statutorily defined offence warranting State intervention and sanctions; the former, more nuanced and sublimated but omnipresent, surfaces from time to time to cohere around and crystallise moral standpoint. Both, however, would seem to straddle much the same religious/morality faultline: one which features a set of distinctive moral imperatives. The consequent legal issues, arising in all jurisdictions, are perhaps those to be expected in countries where the national identity has long been formed by immersion in a Christian ethos.

Moral Imperatives: Sex-Related

Sexuality issues are, of course, the defining battleground for the current phase of the culture wars; and they may, perhaps, have been so from the outset. The list of sex-related issues generating taboos and moral opprobrium over the years is long (e.g. prostitution, single mothers, homosexuality), but currently is mainly focused on gay marriage, other LGBT issues and transgender matters. Sexual relationships, defined for centuries as heterosexual – for all legal, cultural and religious purposes – are no longer so confined, and this has engendered a nexus of issues, of which gay marriage has become the leading moral imperative. While gay marriage causes angst and protest among many conservative Christians, this pales in comparison to the virulent reaction it provokes among some of their Muslim counterparts, as demonstrated in incidents such as the Orlando gay night club massacre[23] (see further Chapter 7).

Moral Imperatives: "Life"-Related

Moral imperatives relating to "life", particularly its beginning and end, are central to both the culture wars and religious discrimination. The fact that rights to abortion, contraceptives, IVF, etc. are statutorily confirmed (less so in Ireland) demarcates them from any equivocation: they are firmly established civil rights. The law is less clear in relation to rights to surrogacy, embryo augmentation and medically assisted death. An ancillary

---

[23] The June 2016 attack in Orlando, Florida was perpetrated by a Muslim who proclaimed allegiance to ISIS.

area, of more direct relevance to the culture wars, is that relating to mod-
ifications to "life" through genetic editing, etc. This amorphous area of
morality generally does not generate justiciable issues unless or until a
patent application is lodged in court, when, as in the "oncomouse" saga, it
can become morally contentious.

Morality Issues and the Culture Wars

Morality issues, being culturally determined, lie along a spectrum which
is prone to change from one society to another and within a single society across time (e.g. patriarchy, slavery, and suffrage). The spectrum can
include issues such as homosexuality that transcend religious boundaries and may unite, for example, traditional Christians and Muslims
against secularists. The dividing line, generating reciprocal discrimination, is unmistakably one formed by traditional religious values. These
embed an intuitive sense of morality which tends to pre-set the approach
adopted to existing and emerging social issues, thereby signposting the
culture-war battlegrounds. However, the bare fact that there is a spectrum,
and that it has proved able to accommodate dissension and a fluctuating
cast of imperatives, is sufficient to dispense with the dire warning issued
half a century ago by Devlin LJ that:[24]

> Societies disintegrate from within more frequently than they are broken up
> by external pressures. There is disintegration when no common morality
> is observed and history shows that the loosening of moral bonds is often
> the first stage of disintegration

The reason morality issues are now socially divisive is to a degree a
consequence of the rise in numbers of citizens who are not just non-
Christian but are firmly irreligious. Probably, also, it simply reflects the
diversity of modern democratic common law societies and the accompanying encouragement for independence and personal responsibility:
a move away from collective, prescribed Christian values towards more
issue-related morality and more flexible social roles, with greater attention being given to "identity", due in no small part to decades of cultivation of multi-culturalism and to the current best efforts of the "selfie"
generation to escape from the mass-categorising effect of global brands.
The contemporary emphasis on identity is of particular interest because

---

[24] See Devlin, P., *The Enforcement of Morals*, Oxford, Oxford University Press, 1965, at
p. 13. This view was opposed by Hart, who responded that "there is no evidence that the
preservation of a society requires the enforcement of its morality 'as such'" (Hart, H. L. A.,
Law, Liberty and Morality, Oxford, Oxford University Press, 1963, at p. 82).

it is now so susceptible to being shaped by sexual orientation – which for some remains firmly a morality issue.

Adherents of the traditional religions – primarily evangelical Christians and, to an extent, Muslims – bring the associated morality to bear on culture-war issues and tend to be resolutely implacable in their opposition to matters judged non-compliant. In contrast, others – particularly, but not exclusively, secularists – adopt a utilitarian approach to the matter at issue, although they tend to be implacable towards those who would deny open access to services deemed ethically, rather than religiously, compromised.

Contemporary Moral Imperatives and Religious Discrimination by Proxy

A theory pursued throughout this book is that culture-war issues often function as a proxy form of religious discrimination – not always, and more so at some times than at others.[25]

Currently, in the jurisdictions considered, there is much contention over an ever-extending spectrum of moral imperatives, all clearly recognisable as pressing social issues, and variously contributing to the culture wars. One end of that spectrum – consisting of issues such as abortion, euthanasia and gay marriage – is closely related to the Christian morality underpinning the law governing religious discrimination; the other – represented by issues such as gun control and women combatants in the armed forces – is only tenuously related; but a considerable number of issues in the middle – including prostitution, genetic editing, embryo research, gene patenting, IVF, transgender matters and many others – often seem to trigger, although not for everyone, the same religious/moral dilemma: one derived by contiguous extension from its roots in Christian morality. Contestants on both sides of most of these issues may at times engage in activity that meets the statutory definition of religious discrimination, whether direct or indirect, and State affirmative action could be initiated to offset its consequences. On the other hand, their activity may not wholly meet that definition – and may take the form of reverse, inverted or projected discrimination – but still be attributable to the same Christian morality. Instead of triggering a discriminatory expression of rejection that is overtly religious, the morality issue will attract a more

---

[25] The following interesting alternative view is posited by Frank Cranmer: "It may, of course, be that in some societies, religion functions as a proxy form of cultural discrimination. Ireland, maybe? Israel, maybe? And, increasingly, Russia" (note to author, 8 April 2017).

veiled response – as, perhaps, in a rejection of homosexuality on health grounds. As Western societies become more sophisticated, and morality more nuanced, so the range of issues and the means of expressing resistance to them become correspondingly subtler. It would therefore be a mistake to attempt to measure the incidence of religious discrimination solely in terms of its statutory definition, the volume of court cases and related judicial rulings: a true estimate must also take into account its proxy extension in the culture wars.

Waiting for the Barbarians

The common law nations considered in the preceding chapters are all now riven by disputes between those who share conservative religious beliefs and those who do not, on much the same agenda of morality issues. As these issues grow in number, so too does their ability to generate religious discrimination, intensify the culture wars and further the fragmentation of civil society.[26] This climate of internal moral dissension pales in comparison to the external threat presented by Islamic extremism. The barbarity of the ISIS onslaught, accompanied by the migrant crisis, prompted the nations concerned to reflect – in keeping with the Cavafy parable[27] – on the value they attach to their cultural heritage. In a reflex reaction to the combined pressure from both sources, governments and citizens across Europe rallied to revive and protect their national cultures and to review the policy and principles of multi-culturalism.

Fundamentalism

For some decades now, the irreconcilability of traditional religious beliefs with contemporary values and lifestyle choices would seem to have driven a wave of didactic moralism, polarising views and politicising the role of religion within many developed nations and between them and other, largely Islamic, nations. This tendency towards "fundamentalism" – apparent in Islam, Judaism and Christianity – is increasingly practised by minorities in the developed nations of the West, if not as lethally as in the Middle East and parts of Africa, and is serving as intended to

---

[26] See e.g. Calabrese, A., "The Promise of Civil Society", *Journal of Media & Cultural Studies*, 2004, vol. 18:3, pp. 317–329.

[27] See Mendelsohn, *Waiting for the Barbarians*, at pp. x–xi; see further Chapter 2.

accentuate religious differences. While the depredations of ISIS now provide more than sufficient evidence of a new wave of religious intolerance, there have also been other indicators. Sectarianism, once thought to have been consigned to history, has shown every sign of undergoing a revival: anti-Semitism, that most invidious benchmark of religious discrimination, has become more common.[28] A steady ramping up of confrontation, grounded on an agenda of moral imperatives, now provides extensive battlefields for those of traditional religious beliefs to confront all others in the culture wars and in wars of a more deadly nature.

Domestic

Paradoxically, the lurch to fundamentalism is occurring in the context of an overall shrinking of religion, at least in the developed common law nations, hastened along by fears associated with the migrant crisis and by the very real effects of murderous Islamic violence directed against innocent civilians. Islamophobia, a real and growing concern in all such nations, which have witnessed some brutal attacks upon Muslims, is accompanied by more Muslim women wearing burqas and by what seems to be an increase in the desecration of Jewish graveyards and synagogues.

Revivalism at the hard end – as ever more evangelical entities are spun off from the institutional religions – is greatly complicating the world of religious discrimination. The internecine theological disputes result not only in further schisms and confrontations over status, ownership of church property and the loyalty of adherents, but also in yet more religious discrimination. Each new faction seeks to consolidate its identity by attacking the beliefs and/or leadership of its erstwhile "mother church" as a means of distancing itself and rallying adherents, and by seeking registration as a religious organisation with an entitlement to tax and equality exemption privileges. As religious discrimination becomes more internalised, so religion itself is put in danger of being seen as more discriminating than discriminated against.

However, if the Cavafy parable carries any weight, one possible outcome is that Western societies might become more cohesive. Being chastened by destructive confrontations with the tyranny of ISIS, and fearful for the future, those divided by religion and its proxy manifestation in the culture wars may be incentivised to develop mutual respect and

---

[28] See e.g. Henley, J., "Antisemitism on Rise across Europe "In Worst Times Since the Nazis"", *The Guardian*, 7 August 2014, at www.theguardian.com/society/2014/aug/07/antisemitism-rise-europe-worst-since-nazis.

work towards greater co-operation. Another possibility is a steady drift towards a "nation state" in mentality and fact – as evidenced by a growing insularity, a heightened sense of identity, increasing alienation and volatile "us and them" tension. At present, this would seem to be the most likely outcome, as several countries have followed the Australian example[29] by introducing tighter border controls, mandatory lessons for immigrants in the language and customs of their host nation and a new emphasis on national socio-economic priorities at the expense of international trade agreements. By 2017, the USA was also imposing strict border controls; although, interestingly, Canada – the leading exponent of multiculturalism – was not.[30] Governments generally adopted measures which asserted and protected, as the primary and governing reference point, the traditional cultural values of a host "nation state".

International

The threat posed by ISIS, while direct and devastating to those in the immediate vicinity, at present shows little sign of impacting greatly on Western society – although, while being steadily degraded in its heartland, it has demonstrated a capacity to metastasise and spread, which means that militant Islam will, in some form, continue to present a level of threat for the foreseeable future; the dangers of another 9/11 in the USA or elsewhere cannot be discounted. Moreover, as the Syria debacle overspills and draws in other fundamentalists, there is always a risk that regional instability will prove uncontainable and precipitate a wider conflict. The general trend of firmer national borders, increased engagement of international armed forces in the Middle East and heightened tensions between global powers is unmistakeable. The religious dimension to these dynamics – evident in the nexus of relationships that coalesce around either Israel, Iran or Saudi Arabia – are clearly dangerous and may yet elevate religious discrimination to a level not seen since the Crusades.

As things stand, however, the risks are less to do with ISIS or its successor as an external aggressor and more about the general climate of anxiety and mistrust generated by the dynamics now in play. While all common law jurisdictions included in this study, with the possible exception

---

In 2017, Australia further tightened its immigration policy by abolishing the "457 visa", which permitted entry for temporary workers, on the grounds that this was necessary in order to safeguard Australian jobs for Australian citizens.

Between November 2015 and January 2017, some 40 000 Syrian migrants settled in Canada. See www.cic.gc.ca/english/refugees/welcome/.

of Ireland, have good reason to guard against "lone-wolf" Islamist attacks launched within their borders, it is the effects of a fear of such attacks that are likely to cause most long-term damage.

The Chilling of Civil Society

By 2016/17, frustration with the seeming inability of governments to fore see, manage or cope with the consequences of a sequence of significant national and international disasters had for some time been fuelling a ris ing level of civilian resentment. Amplified by media coverage and accel erated by the Internet, the exposure of government failures was creating a widespread level of unease and apprehension across Western society.

Disenchantment with Government

Judt, in 2010, warned that "something is profoundly wrong with the way we live today"[31] and pointed to the government practice of farming out public-benefit services – e.g. transport, hospitals, mail, schools, residen tial care for the elderly, prisons, etc. – to private business providers as being at least symptomatic of that problem. He argued that "shifting the owner ship onto businessmen allows the State to relinquish moral obligations".[32] While government was, perhaps, gaining fiscally, it was losing the respec of its citizens.

In addition to shedding responsibility for public-benefit services, gov ernment was conspicuously failing in its most basic duty to protect the homeland. The catalogue of failure in this respect was considerable including: environmental – "mad cow disease", avian flu, global warm ing and ivory poaching; financial – the cavalier rapacity that caused poorly regulated financial sector to collapse, precipitating a global eco nomic recession and leaving extraordinary levels of national debt; family the intercontinental systemic abuse of children by clergy; and security continuing institutionalised police racism and the fifteen years of war in a many Muslim countries. The hope generated by the "Arab Spring"[33] had been displaced by a resigned acceptance of the ensuing chaos and destruc tion as authoritarian regimes fought to assert control over populations that had been encouraged by Western governments to seek regime change a a path to democracy. This was duly followed by the same government

---

[31] See Judt, *Ill Fares the Land*, at p. 1.   [32] Ibid., at p. 114.

[33] A reference to the 2011 wave of populist uprisings that began in Tunisia and spread t Egypt, Yemen, Bahrain, Libya and Syria.

resuming and extending their bombing of Muslim countries, launching an extended bombardment on the densely populated city of Mosul, and by the intractable, interminable and televised tragedy of Syria. Frustration with the ineffectuality of government intervention overseas became more acute when failed domestic intervention exposed civilians to intermittent random slaughter by Islamist extremists, who mostly turned out to be fellow citizens. The consequent intensification of security measures – including the presence on city streets of troops and armed police, many masked – became an accepted aspect of life in Western society. In due course, the migrant crisis and the accompanying evidence of an inability to effectively secure national borders led to serious general disenchantment with politics and with liberal democrat politicians. A populist surge, triggered by the same disenchantment that five years earlier had swept north Africa, seemed poised to seek political change closer to home.

Fundamentalism and an Uncivil Society[34]

Citizenship and civil society are necessarily complementary: one helps define the other. Sharing space is not the same as sharing responsibilities – citizenship and civil society require a level of commitment to common social values. Arguably, a retreat into religious fundamentalism, apart from being a denial of citizenship responsibilities, wholly conflicts with the consensus on broadly shared values and an agreed balancing of interests which would seem essential for civil society.

Citizenship requires respect for a society's cultural heritage, current cultural ethos and adherence to the social norms affirmed and represented by government policy, laws and conduct. To that extent, adherence to religious beliefs which mandate practices that conflict with citizenship requirements conflicts also with those for civil society: it feeds a cultural dissonance that obstructs the essential civic virtues of trust and co-operation.[35] Some of the more fundamental beliefs of Islam present difficulties for those within the Part III jurisdictions wishing to square the status of Muslim and citizen. For migrants whose cultural identity derives from traditional patriarchal tribes, where certain "cultural practices discriminatory to women have been shrouded in religious belief" and "undemocratic regimes have denied human rights to their citizens",[36] the transition to Western citizen is a challenge both for them and for

---

[4] For an overview of academic work on this concept see, Glasius, M., "Uncivil Society", at www.academia.edu/4164816/Uncivil_society.

[5] See Judt, *Ill Fares the Land*.   [36] Ali, *Gender and Human Rights in Islam*, at p. 5.

society. Specifically, the discriminatory treatment authorised by the Qur'an – in relation, for example, to women, homosexuals, sex-offenders and those considered infidels, heretics or apostates – if manifested in practice would present a considerable obstacle to such citizenship.

The extremism and barbaric violence currently manifested by militant Muslims is clearly most at variance with any concept of civil society, even though perpetrated by a small minority and largely in countries outside the scope of this study. This should not detract from an acknowledgment that fundamentalism among Christians, and indeed among secularists, tends to induce xenophobic attitudes and adds to the current social fractiousness.

Conclusion

Kant, in his *Idea for a Universal History with a Cosmopolitan Purpose*,[37] argues that "the greatest problem for the human species, the solution to which nature compels him to seek, is that of attaining a civil society which can administer justice universally". If, as seems likely, the gradual construction of a human rights framework as a supra-national source of authority offers the most promising means of achieving this, then the eruption of Islamic militancy and the response of Western societies to this serves as a reminder that there is some way to go. Religious discrimination in its most extreme form has graphically demonstrated the capacity of the human species to be its own worst enemy when it comes to building the civil society that – maybe – would give it the security of universal justice

---

[37] See Rorty, A. O. and Schmidt, J. (eds), *Kant's Idea for a Universal History with a Cosmopolitan Aim: A Critical Guide*, Cambridge, Cambridge University Press, 2009.

~

Conclusion

he progenitor common law jurisdiction would seem to be steadily shed-
ing the Christianity it once so proudly championed and transplanted
roughout its empire. There are indications that the post-colonial juris-
ictions are now following suit, at a varying pace and subject to qual-
cations in respect of some growth in evangelicalism. The decline in
hristianity is accompanied by a numerically slight but proportionately
gnificant increase in adherents of Islam and some growth in other
inority religions and beliefs. In all, the stoical acceptance of religion's
minishing importance has been shaken by the virulence of the recent
IS onslaught: the realisation that it has attracted the active support of
any fellow citizens; the resulting danger to the general public in every-
ay urban settings, particularly in relation to what may be construed as
ligious targets; and mostly the scale and triumphalism of its many mur-
erous acts of religious discrimination.

Clearly, there are implications not just for the future of Christianity –
deed, for religion – but also as regards government response to the ISIS
nenomenon and to everything it represents. There are questions as to
hat will fill the vacuum created by what seems to be the slow but inex-
able demise of Christianity: will secularism steadily acquire equivalent
gitimation and accede to the social role and leverage that religion once
ercised; will it, too, develop a fundamentalist wing? What will be the
npact on a culture which seemed so inextricably fused with Christian-
? Will these changes – the move away from a reasonably coherent,
ligiously flavoured culture to national accommodation of a spread of
ligions, beliefs and non-beliefs – lead to more, and more varied, oppor-
nities for religious discrimination? Will this in turn push government on
om an equivocating commitment to State neutrality to assert a positive
licing role, regulating for the public benefit, in respect of religious mat-
rs? If Christianity continues to lose its public, institutional character and
comes more a matter of private piety, will the consequent lack of potency
use religious discrimination to be diverted, diluted and sublimated into

an expanding pool of culture wars? How will this post-millennial transition in the West be affected by the unleashing of Islamic mediaeval fundamentalism in the East; in particular, how will it affect the growing population of Western Muslims? Will the current flare up of populism and
pluralism lead to a collective circling of the wagons and a revival c
national cultural identity? Are Western developed nations now stuck i:
a "waiting for the barbarians"[1] phase?

This book opened with a consideration of matters concerning "identity" and "alienation" as precursors of religious discrimination. Durin
the course of writing, the twin phenomena of the migrant crisis and ISIS
both essentially Muslim in nature, and both, in large part, products of sustained warfare by the USA and its allies against Muslim countries – hav
grown to upstage what was to have been no more than a routine academi
research project limited to a comparative analysis of religious discrimina
tion as evidenced in the patterning of jurisdictional caselaw. Overtake
by events, the book has had to be recalibrated to take into account along
side that analysis the significance of ISIS as an unavoidable measure c
the nature and impact of contemporary religious discrimination. As bot
the migrant crisis and ISIS are unmistakably entangled with matters c
identity and alienation, it seems appropriate to conclude by revisiting th
themes outlined at the outset, considering them in conjunction with thes
phenomena and reflecting on some implications for the cultural contex
of religious discrimination in the twenty-first century.

Religion and the Politics of Identity

A theme in the considerable body of academic work on "the politics (
identity"[2] concerns the striving to acquire recognition and status, not s
that an entity may join with others in a community of equals, but rather s
that it may establish its own uniqueness, assert its difference and be fre
and able to stand its own ground, apart from all others. Religion or beli-
can have that effect – as reinforced by religious discrimination, the cu
ture wars and associated ideology or fanaticism. Pluralism may offer th
best policy option for counteracting competitive religiosity, but probab

---

[1] See Mendelsohn, *Waiting for the Barbarians*.
[2] See e.g. Barzilai, G., *Communities and Law: Politics and Cultures of Legal Identities*, A
Arbor, MI, University of Michigan Press, 2003 and Campbell, D., *Writing Security. Unit
States Foreign Policy and the Politics of Identity*, Minneapolis, MN, University of Minnesc
Press, 1998.

only if accompanied by regulatory mechanisms that police and mediate to prevent insularity and polarisation and protect the public interest.

Liberal Democracy: Identity and Alienation

All the Part III jurisdictions share much the same media-dominated lifestyle that typifies modern Western society. It is one of relative wealth, opportunity, personal rights and freedom of choice. For those from more repressed cultures, escaping circumstances of poverty and fear, it may also appear sexualised and permissive. Even without exposure to protracted war, migrants would naturally gravitate towards Western society. The effects of some fifteen years' deployment of high-tech weaponry by these jurisdictions in a range of impoverished Muslim countries, destroying much socio-economic infrastructure, have added greatly to their difficulties and served to push waves of migrants towards safety and opportunity in the West. A logical consequence of the direction, duration and devastation of the allies' war effort can be seen in the numbers and ethnicity of the migrants: never before have so many Muslims sought refuge in Western society within so short a period.

The lifestyle excesses that affect the margins of society in all Part III jurisdictions are anathema to those who adhere to traditional religious beliefs and may well be responsible for the retreat of some Christians into evangelical or fundamentalist bunkers. Similarly, they are likely to be a factor in distancing many Muslims (and others) from mainstream Western culture: dissuading them from fully subscribing to policies of pluralism or multi-culturalism; inducing them instead to cohere in communities around their local imams and madrassas; causing them to look outwards for support – financial and cultural/theological – to ethnic-specific countries, rather than inwards to local government sources; in short, leading them to identify with their religion rather than with the culture of their host nation. The arrival of many more – often direct from patriarchical tribal cultures – exacerbates that distancing.

Arguably, the underlying issue here is more about morality than religion. A widening gap is appearing between those who would champion liberal democracy because they see it as facilitating the freedom of lifestyle choice, subject to the rights of others, and those who object to the excesses licensed by that political model and react by attacking it and/or retreating into religious fundamentalism. This perception would seem to underpin the culture wars as much as religious discrimination, and at a more visceral level it may also be a driving force for Islamic militants. As illustrated by the attacks on tourists on beaches in Tunisia, on a holiday charter flight from Egypt, at airports and in nightclubs, and by that on the free press in Paris, the aggression is often pointedly aimed at targets repre senting the contemporary Western lifestyle: on the identifying hallmarks of liberalism. In response, governments in the developed Western nations are: defiantly extolling the merits of liberalism while also drumming up solidarity by tightening border controls, increasing the visibility of secu rity forces and facilitating public demonstrations where patriotism is rou tinely expressed through flag-waving and the singing of national anthems; expanding their war efforts in Muslim countries; and adopting an increas ingly wary attitude towards Muslim immigrants, towards any overt public displays of Islamic culture and towards related family values that are per ceived as somewhat patriarchical and misogynist.

Morality and Religiosity

It may seem axiomatic that morality and religion are synonymous – from the subjective perspective of an adherent of any particular religion – but objectively, the morality can be seen to vary across religions, and within the same religion across time and cultural context – as it does among the irreligious. It is, therefore, important that social policy in the Part III juris dictions should know and take into account the different morality codes currently represented in their modern multi-cultural societies. If a drift towards alienation is to be forestalled, and with it the risks of radicali sation, it may be best to ensure a more respectful and welcoming public space – in employment, education, etc. – for all whose lawful beliefs are at variance with the mainstream. This suggests that an objective assess ment is required to ascertain whether current difficulties in Western soci ety regarding religious discrimination and the culture wars – leaving aside the ideology represented by Islamic militants – are more about morality than religion.

A useful start could be made with an analysis of the ways in which the Christian heritage continues to shape social norms in the Part III juris dictions – to identify and weigh its presence in laws, institutions and pro cesses – in order to obtain a clearer understanding of its visible and sub liminal affect on others. There may be a need to develop a language to "read" the religiosity in contemporary Western society, to translate the cultures of immigrants and Indigenous People in religious terms and to understand the culture wars accordingly. By so doing, it might be possible to map areas of moral congruity and customise public space to optimise social cohesion – subject to the principles of pluralism, equality and freedom of expression – and subject also to such restraints on the latter as may be necessary to deter conduct that is gratuitously offensive. Arguably, not until we have such a language can we hope to identify the varied positive and negative impacts of religion-based contributions to society and appreciate the consequences for the latter of government intervention[3] – or non-intervention.[4] With that understanding, however, we could then consider the feasibility of formulating a social policy, under the protective human rights umbrella, that would best facilitate the functioning of a coherent civil society. Without such a language, it will remain difficult to anticipate the many different circumstances and levels in which religious discrimination may come into play. Should it prove possible to learn from the religion-related dynamics that now threaten our domestic and international safety, and thus move forward, then the challenge in the concluding lines of the Cavafy parable may come to seem prescient:[5]

And now what's to become of us without barbarians.
Those people were a solution of a sort.

[3] The current tensions in Russia between Jehovah's Witnesses and the government come to mind.
[4] As, for example, in the ambivalent government approach to tensions between Hindus and Muslims in India and between Shia and Sunni Muslims in Iraq.
[5] See Mendelsohn, D., "Waiting for the Barbarians", in *C.P. Cavafy Poems*, New York, Alfred A. Knopf, 2014 at p. 149.

INDEX